SWEDEN

FINLAND (SW)

Stockholm

ESTONIA (SW)

LIVONIA

COURLAND

BRANDENBURG-PRUSSIA

SWEDISH POMERANIA

Danzig

EAST PRUSSIA

LITH.

NB'G
Berlin

VISTULA

SAXONY

Breslau

SILESIA

Prague

BOHEMIA

MORAVIA

AUSTRIA

Vienna

HAPSBURG AUSTRIA

Cracow

GALICIA

Lemberg

Warsaw

POLAND

Kiev

RUSSIA

THE

UNITED PROVINCES
INDEP. 1648

SPANISH NETHERLANDS

Bremen

Amsterdam
Utrecht

Münster

Cologne

THE

EMPIRE

Bruges
FLANDRES
ARTOIS
Antwerp

Brussels

Aix-

RHINE

Mainz

Amiens

FRANCE

Reims

Verdun

Nancy

Toul

100 MILES

KINGDOM OF HUNGARY

Budapest

TRANS-SYLVANIA

DNIESTER

MOLDAVIA

YEDISAN

BESS-ARABIA

CRIMEA

SLAVONIA

DANUBE

Belgrade

BOSNIA

SERBIA

O T T O M A N

WALLACHIA

Bucharest

DANUBE

DOBRUJA

BLACK SEA

BULGARIA

Constantinople

PAPAL STATES

ITALY

Rome

ADRIATIC SEA

MONTE-NEGRO

RUMELIA

E M P I R E

ALBANIA

Naples

KINGDOM OF THE TWO SICILIES

GREECE

IONIAN ISLANDS (VEN.)

AEGEAN SEA

Smyrna

SICILY

RHODES

SEA

CRETE (VEN.)

Modern Europe
1660-1945

MODERN EUROPE

EUROPE

1660-1945

Roger L. Williams

ANTIOCH COLLEGE

ST MARTIN'S PRESS · NEW YORK

To *J.S.I.* and *J.F.F.*

For he lives twice who can at once employ
The present well, and e'en the past enjoy.

—POPE

Library of Congress Catalog Card Number 64-18440
Designer: Mina Baylis
Art Editor: Gabriele Wunderlich
Manufactured in the United States of America

Preface

THIS VOLUME has been designed with two uses in mind: To be used as a textbook for the second half of a course in European Civilization, or to stand alone as a text for a course in Modern History from 1660 to 1945. An Introduction is provided for those students whose study begins in 1660, briefly reviewing the chief political, scientific, and artistic currents of the earlier seventeenth century. Like most other texts, this one has been given a political format; but within that format cultural and intellectual history has been emphasized, often at the expense of social and economic history. This reflects the author's belief that, in the history of any civilization, it is proper to examine primarily the quality of that civilization and ultimately to judge its success in taming, cultivating, and organizing the savage man.

It is probably easier for most students to approach the study of history topically rather than chronologically, especially when the chronological structure becomes the excuse for presenting an array of uninterpreted facts. The trouble is that events do not occur topically. To present them as such defies reality and defeats a second purpose in examining the history of a civilization, namely, to teach the student to think historically. Instructors will vary greatly when it comes to organizing historical materials for class-room presentation, even when they are using a common text; but every student assigned this text should recognize at the outset that each chapter covers a define chronological period, and most of them discuss the various aspects of life which occurred contemporaneously.

Despite this use of chronological format, no attempt has been made to be encyclopedic nor has there been any reluctance to interpret. The mere selection of materials to be included reveals on aspect of the author's interpretation, and the imprint of his mind will be found throughout the book. Not any instructor will agree with all the author's interpretations, and where there are disagreements, the groundwork is laid for a more exciting examination of the facts. Moreover, because the text is not encyclopedic, because it is intended as an introduction and not an end in itself, suggestions for further reading are included and those to be found in paperback editions especially noted.

Textbooks would never be written if their authors were required to work exclusively from primary sources. Necessarily I have had recourse to a myriad of excellent monographs and interpretations, too numerous to be usefully cited here, but for which I must express my gratitude. I am indebted to individuals, also, who have encouraged and criticized this undertaking, first to the former President of Antioch College, Samuel B. Gould, who spurred me beyond my reluctance to begin. Then to those long-suffering souls who read and criticized various chapters: Dean W. Boyd Alexander of Antioch, historians Irwin Abrams and Mrs. Milton A. Goldberg; and the late Gwilym E. Owen whose unfailing kindness was demonstrated during my studies in the history of science. Finally, to those students whose judgment and taste I used as a barometer, notably John Garrett, John W. Levenson, and John F. Friedmann. I wish also to express my gratitude to Theodore R. Miller, whose original ideas are so ably reflected in the maps in this book.

ROGER L. WILLIAMS

Yellow Springs, Ohio
July, 1963

Contents

1 THE APOGEE OF ABSOLUTISM: 1660-1689
[*5*]

2 EUROPE AT WAR: 1689-1715
[*43*]

3 THE ENLIGHTENMENT AND THE OLD REGIME IN THE EIGHTEENTH CENTURY
[79]

4 EMPIRES, AT HOME AND ABROAD 1733-1763
[120]

5 DESPOTISM AND SENTIMENTALITY: THE LATER EIGHTEENTH CENTURY
[156]

LIST OF PLATES

LIST OF MAPS

[Maps planned and executed by Theodore R. Miller]

Modern Europe

1660-1945

Introduction

In America, it was common until recently to begin a course in Modern European history with the date 1492, a date signifying that the Atlantic, rather than the Mediterranean, was the focal sea for European civilization. In Britain, the usual choice was 1485, the date of the founding of the Tudor dynasty. Both dates placed the Reformation on the modern, rather than on the medieval, side of the watershed, in keeping with the traditional view in Protestant countries that the Reformation had been a progressive development congenial to the spirit of the Renaissance. Today, it is more generally believed that the period of the Reformation, roughly 1517 to 1660, was an era of mixed medieval and modern characteristics, and that, if anything, the medieval tended to dominate.

One generalizes about such characteristics only at great peril of distortion and exaggeration; but somewhere during a study of the seventeenth century, one becomes aware that the principal ideals and values of the leaders of the European world had shifted, and that this shift was reflected in new political, social, and economic institutions. Perhaps the key word is *secularization,* notably the secularization of values which was already apparent in the late medieval period and against which the Reformation was a protest. But the Reformation did not succeed in restoring an ideal Christian society—that is, Christendom. Instead, it unwittingly contributed to the continuing disintegration of that universal entity, usually along national lines. The religious wars of the sixteenth and early seventeenth centuries,

1

while obviously involving religious issues, also proved to be the opportunity for the strengthening of secular power. From that time on, and for better or for worse, religious authority found itself increasingly subject to secular authority; and, for that reason chiefly, we suddenly sense in our study of history that we have reached an atmosphere which we recognize as modern. One of the most distinguished students of the seventeenth century has put it this way:

> Somewhere about the middle of the seventeenth century European life was so completely transformed in many of its aspects that we commonly think of this as one of the great watersheds of modern history, comparable with the Renaissance or the Reformation or the French Revolution. For this transition, indeed, we have no single name that we can write with capital letters, but we recognize a change of atmosphere between the earlier part of the century and the later, a change accompanied by storms.[1]

ｆ It has generally been held that the seventeenth century was an age of deepening absolutism—and not merely in the political realm. The quest for order, while perhaps most apparent in politics, affected intellectual and cultural life as well; and the absolute state and absolute truths were often seen as the key to perfect orderｆ The quest is not so strange if we recall the chaotic fighting which had gone on in the name of religion since Luther's time and the intellectual uncertainty which increasingly beset Europeans from the time of Copernicus. To put a stop to chaos and to redefine man's relationship to the rest of the universe were immense challenges, and the European intellectuals responded so magnificently that we still title the seventeenth century "The Age of Genius."

When the student plunges in at 1660, it should be with the knowledge that the date roughly coincides with pivotal events in many countries. The Puritan experiment in England, for example, had just collapsed, producing a restoration of the House of Stuart. In France, Cardinal Mazarin died in 1661, opening the way for the personal reign of Louis XIV. The reign of Czar Alexis (*1645–1676*) gave Russia firm central government, in contrast with the early years of the seventeenth century, and established policies and institutions to be characteristic of Russia well into the nineteenth century. In 1648, the Dutch had achieved their independence from Spain, really an aspect of that great and controversial conflict, the Thirty Years War (1618–1648), whose outcome had been a blow to the predominance of the House

---

1. Sir George Clark, *The Seventeenth Century,* 2nd ed. (New York, Oxford University Press, 1947), p. ix.

of Hapsburg. In fact, if the student is to get some insight into the structure of international politics as of 1660, he would do well to examine the bases of Hapsburg preponderance beginning in the sixteenth century with the Holy Roman Emperor Charles V, whose immense inheritance of territories upset the balance of power on the Continent and gave a decided advantage to the Catholic powers during the Reformation era. Such a situation naturally affected the foreign and domestic policies of the other states of Europe, not merely in the sixteenth century, but through much of the seventeenth. During the Thirty Years War, the French found various instruments to deal with Hapsburg supremacy, instruments which Louis XIV was to expand and exploit after 1660.

It would also be useful, by way of review or introduction, to compare the development of the House of Commons in England with that of the various continental estates. England never had true estates, for the House of Commons represented more than one class; and, given the destruction of the feudal nobility in the War of the Roses and the subsequent creation of a "tame" and suspect nobility by the Tudors, the House of Commons began its rise at the expense of the Lords. Given its diversity of representation, the Commons, in the seventeenth century, could lay claim to represent the nation, not a class, in the campaign to check royal absolutism—an advantage no continental estates or parliament had.

Many of the European powers had claims overseas by the seventeenth century, the beginning of colonial empires which would contribute to the spread of European civilization beyond the confines of Europe. In order to limit the scope of the text, however, the author has deemed it necessary to consider these significant outposts of Europe only insofar as colonial affairs were an extension of European matters. No attempt has been made to include colonial history. Thus, for example, the American Revolution is presented here as a British problem and is seen within the context of a British constitutional crisis. This same intention to keep a European focus means that, in the later chapters of the text, the westernizing movements in non-European countries are not covered.

The text does, however, include cultural and intellectual history, topics often avoided during a student's secondary education, not only because they complicate our problem of seeing the past, but also because they raise some of the most difficult problems of interpretation the historian encounters. The scientific revolution, a major matter in the seventeenth century, is one such problem, and the student is urged at the outset to examine his own prejudices and prior notions as he tackles this subject anew. The devel-

opment of modern, as distinguished from medieval, science coincided with
the Renaissance and the Reformation, periods of great questioning about
the values and ideals of western man. To be historical, one cannot exclude
the ideas of the scientific revolution from that milieu of questioning and
simply treat them as "pure science." Our treatment of the scientific revolution is designed to help the student see why the revolution came when it did,
and why its spirit was congenial to the other main currents of the seventeenth century. The more one delves into the topic, the more a review
knowledge of Aristotelianism and Scholasticism will become essential. At
that point, the student will see a new facet of the secularization of ideals
which has already been tabbed above as the key to understanding modernity.

The first paragraphs of the text deal with the most notable philosophers
of absolutism in the seventeenth century—Hobbes, Bossuet, and Filmer.
Here the author is not merely concerned with presenting the facts of their
political systems but tries to show the connection between political and
religious matters in the seventeenth century, an integrational technique
which he will continue to follow throughout the text when dealing with
intellectual history. A similar technique has been applied to cultural history,
the first instance of which appears in the first chapter in the discussion of
the baroque, which is presented as both an art form and a spirit—a *Zeit-
geist*. The point here is that any art form, including the baroque, is more
than a technique or a style: the art itself has a spirit which reflects the main
currents of its era. In the case of the baroque, one can show that it was
related to the general quest for order so characteristic of the seventeenth
century.

A student taking a course in history will eventually become aware that
a variety of interpretations exists about most events, and this may lead him
to Henry Ford's conclusion that "history is bunk." But such a conclusion
is too easy and gets us nowhere. We may try to ignore the past, but the
penalty for succeeding would be meaningless, chaotic existence. For we
know what we are doing and where we are going only if what we do is seen
in relation to where we have been and why changes have occurred. Like it
or not, we are condemned to struggle with the changing nature of historical
"facts," which we may come to regard as opinions; and we shall learn that
our historical judgments are really tentative. Thus we acquire humility
while learning about the nature of man in his universe.

✎ 1 ✎

The Apogee of Absolutism
1660–1689

A BRIEF GLANCE at the headings in this chapter will reveal that a variety of topics has been included. What is not immediately apparent is that a common thread pervades the chapter—namely, the various aspects of absolutism which reached their peak in the late seventeenth century. Hence, one finds here both the chief philosophers of absolutism in England and France and the actual experiments with political absolutism in each country. A discussion of the arts in general and the baroque in particular follows; it will reveal that, while the baroque art forms differed in various parts of Europe, they were inspired by a common urge: the quest for unity and order which was often the excuse for political absolutism. The same can be said of the scientific revolution: while the ideas and discoveries which revolutionized astronomy and mechanics are important in themselves, the student will be struck by the scientists' search for new definitions and truths, usually expressed absolutely in the form of laws. In the latter part of the chapter we turn to eastern Europe, first, to see the rise of the Russian autocracy with the absolutist institutions which were to serve that monarchy well into the nineteenth century; secondly, to review the revival of absolutist Turkey and her last great attempt to conquer Europe.

THE PHILOSOPHERS OF ABSOLUTISM

The fate of Charles I suggested the inexpediency of arbitrary rule in England, but his two sons read the lesson differently. Charles II (*1660–*

1685) shrewdly intrigued for absolute power behind the facade of a frivolous court. James II (*1685-1688*), at the age of fifty-three, had little time and grabbed for absolute power. Perhaps they were encouraged by the enthusiastic popular demonstrations upon Charles' entry into London after the Protectorate. The success of the absolute monarch Louis XIV (*1643-1715*) in France called for emulation; and, finally, there were philosophers of absolutism in the seventeenth century.

Thomas Hobbes (1588-1679), alarmed by the disorders of the English Civil War, published his *Leviathan,* with its formula for public order, in 1651. He saw nature as anarchy; one fought continually to defend life and property. Thus, man in nature was "solitary, poor, nasty, brutish and short-lived" with "a perpetual and restless desire for power after power." Despite Hobbes' pessimism, he pointed out that men have reason and, thus, seek peace and order. Accordingly, they establish a common power for protection, the Leviathan, a government by consent, and emerge from nature. Hence the theory of the social contract.

Hobbes was indifferent to the form of sovereign power. He asked only that the powerful Leviathan be obeyed unquestioningly: to overthrow a government by consent would be to destroy society. Order he felt to be more important than individual rights; even a tyrannical Leviathan is preferable to the state of nature. His theory justifies the all-powerful state, where power is an end in itself.

Nevertheless, the royalists of the seventeenth century were not enthusiastic for Hobbes. He did not, after all, specifically favor a royal despot, and the Leviathan could have been a military dictator like Oliver Cromwell. Worse for an age which was sincerely Christian, Hobbes was a materialist ("The universe is material and what is not material is not real"), and his materialism made him an atheist. A materialist will insist that all human reality can be explained in bodily terms. Hobbes argued that our conceptions derive from impressions made upon our sense organs by external objects: that knowledge comes from sensations. Such knowledge causes our appetites and fears and leads to our actions. Hobbes saw life as little more than a struggle for material survival, and we may raise the question of whether there could be any individual rights in a philosophy which took his narrow view of God, man, and society.

In the seventeenth century, royalists listened more intently to Sir Robert Filmer (d. 1653) and to Bishop Jacques Bénigne Bossuet (1627-1704) than to Hobbes. Sir Robert's book, *Patriacha, or A Defense of the Natural Power of Kings Against the Unnatural Liberty of the People,* published in

1680, was written almost forty years earlier, and its ideas were known during the Restoration. He sought to explode the social-contract theory by pointing out that there was no documentary evidence of such a contract. His political authority was the Old Testament, where he saw God confer monarchical power upon Adam in the Garden of Eden, from whence it had descended through Noah to Charles I. He expounded government by divine sanction, not by popular consent.

The theory of divine right was more effectively formulated in France by Bishop Bossuet in *Political Ideas Derived from the Very Words of Holy Scripture*. Neither a religious fanatic nor a self-seeking courtier, Bossuet represented seventeenth-century piety and the quest for order. Seeing government divinely ordained to make society possible and monarchy as not only the most ancient and usual form of government but the most natural, he thought of the King as the "father" of his people, responsible only to God. "Greater reason is given to a king than to anyone else, the king is an earthly image of God's majesty, and it is wrong, therefore, to look upon him as a mere man. The king is a public person and in him the whole nation is embodied." Thus, an attack upon the King would be both sacrilege and treason.

THE FRANCE OF LOUIS XIV

No one has ever played the role of God's image on earth more convincingly than Louis XIV (*1643–1715*), who was deeply admired by other monarchs. He sincerely believed in his divine right, and he was pious. His own birth, since he was a late child, aided the notion that he was God-given; and the formality and splendor of his daily life were designed to impress his supremacy on all. The greatest nobles' serving as mere valets at the King's rising every morning signified that royal power had finally triumphed over the feudal nobility. Here is the Duc de Saint-Simon, an embittered memorialist, describing the invariable beginning of the King's day:

At eight o'clock the chief *valet de chambre* on duty, who alone had slept in the royal chamber, having dressed, awoke him [the King]. The chief physician, the chief surgeon, and his [the King's] nurse, as long as she lived, entered at the same time. She went to kiss him, the others rubbing him and often changing his shirt, as he was subject to perspiration. At quarter past the grand chamberlain was called, or in his absence the first gentleman of the *chambre d'année,* along with those who had the right of *grandes entrées.* One of these two opened the bed curtain, which had been reclosed, and presented the holy water from the base at the head of the bed. These gentlemen remained only a moment, which was the time to speak to the King if they had something to say to him or to ask him, in which case the others stood aside. . . . The one who had opened the bed curtain and presented the holy water then presented the prayerbook, following which all passed into the Council Chamber. The short prayers said, the King called; they re-entered. The same officer gave him his dressing gown, and a few moments later, the *secondes entrées* came into the room. As soon as everyone of distinction was present, the rest were admitted, in time to see the King putting on his shoes; he did nearly everything for himself with skill and grace. He was seen to shave himself every other day. He wore a little short wig, and never, even when in bed, was he seen without it. Often he spoke about hunting, and sometimes a word to someone. No dressing table for him; only a mirror was held before him.

As soon as he was dressed, he prayed to God at the bedside, where all the clergy knelt, the cardinals without cushions; the laity remained standing, and the captain of the guards came to the balustrade during the prayer, after which the King passed into the cabinet. Here he found a numerous crowd, for it included all those charged with offices. He gave each one instructions for the day, so that everyone knew in a few minutes what was to be done.[1]

The King's formality bordered on the silly; yet his dignity and sincerity inspired awe, and he had a way of making people feel at ease. If he was conscious of the greatness of his position and person, he was open to advice—at least during the early decades of his reign. Later this balance deserted him: overwhelmed by his own glory, he became extravagant, waged useless wars, and was intolerant of advice, which produced little but financial ruin and popular discontent. Louis XIV ultimately demonstrated that the extremism inherent in autocracy leads to chaos rather than to order.

The centralization of the French monarchy had been under way long before Louis XIV. The alliance of "town and crown" against the nobility was of medieval origin, and, except for the military leaders, the great servants of Louis XIV were of bourgeois origin. Under Louis XIII, Cardinal Richelieu had begun to discipline the nobility, and though the latter were temporarily able to threaten royal power after the Cardinal's death by the revolution known as the Fronde, the royal authority triumphed. Thus, the nobles were virtual prisoners at the court of Louis XIV, deliberately separated from their provincial roots and unable to challenge His Majesty. The King took pride in his large and distinguished court, treating his disarmed enemies with a kindness that has become fabled. Richelieu had sent

1. Louis, Duc de Saint-Simon, *Mémoires sur le règne de Louis XIV et la régence* (Paris, 1911), Vol. III, pp. 139-140. My translation.

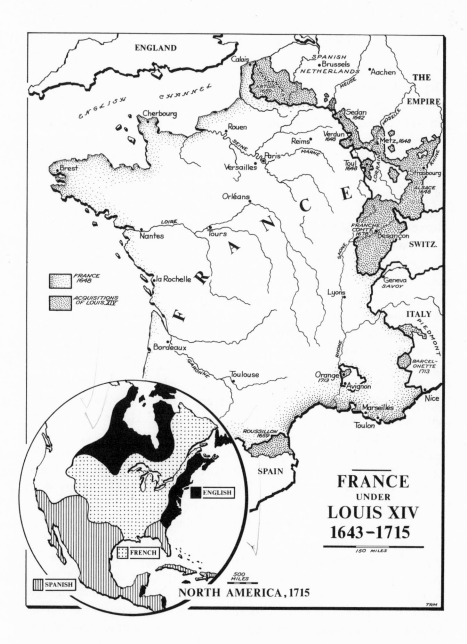

FRANCE
1648

ACQUISITIONS
OF LOUIS XIV

ENGLAND

SPANISH
NETHERLANDS

Calais
Brussels
Aachen

THE

EMPIRE

Cherbourg

ARTOIS
1659

MEUSE

Sedan
1642

Rouen

SEINE

Verdun
1648

MOSELLE

Metz, 1648

Brest

Versailles
Paris

MARNE

Toul
1648

Strasbourg

LORRAINE

RHINE

ALSACE
1648

Orléans

FRANCE

E

LOIRE

Nantes

Tours

SAÔNE

FRANCHE
COMTÉ
1678

SWITZ.

Besançon

la Rochelle

F
R
A
N
C
E

Geneva
SAVOY

Lyons

ITALY

PIEDMONT

Bordeaux

GARONNE

BARCEL-
ONETTE
1713

Toulouse

RHONE

Orange
1713

Avignon

Nice

Marseilles

Toulon

ROUSSILLON
1659

SPAIN

ENGLISH

FRANCE
UNDER
LOUIS XIV
1643–1715

150 MILES

FRENCH

500
MILES

NORTH AMERICA, 1715

SPANISH

TRM

officials called intendants into the provinces as royal inspectors-general;
Louis XIV made them the supreme agents of royal power in the provinces
where they resided, overseeing the local nobility with immense executive,
legislative, and judicial authority. The Provincial Estates (legislatures)
became ceremonial for all practical purposes. Like the intendants, the min-

isters (or secretaries of state) were mostly bourgeois, hostile to the aristocracy, and responsible to the King alone. The first generation of the King's
ministers, inherited from Cardinal Mazarin's administration in 1661, was
superior to the second. As the autocracy deepened, docility was more
valued than ability.

Before Louis XIV, France had become impoverished in becoming
formidable internationally, notably in the Thirty Years War. The history
of the later French monarchy often seems a succession of financial crises
tackled by ministers who were uninterested in economics and untrained in
finance. But in 1661 the King found in Jean Baptiste Colbert (1619–1683)
a statesman who saw that a strong national economy was necessary for a
strong monarchy. Colbert was an ardent protagonist of the economic
philosophy called "mercantilism," the theory that every nation must be
self-sufficient economically. The outward sign of economic well-being was
the accumulation of gold in the treasury. To ensure the inflow of gold, the
state must regulate and protect industry and commerce with an eye to
economic expansion and a favorable balance of trade. Colbert, like other
mercantilists, promoted colonization because colonies produced raw materials unavailable in the mother country and could serve as a market for
goods manufactured in the mother country. There was always the hope
that gold would be discovered. As in England and Holland, joint stock
companies were granted monopolies to develop colonial regions, but comparatively the French companies never prospered. As French industries
lagged, Colbert encouraged foreign artisans to settle in France, and to him
France owed her later supremacy in luxury goods. After Colbert died,
France lost some of her most able artisans; but the King's wars were more
responsible for economic decline than was their emigration.

Colbert wanted to build an orderly, rational system of royal finance that
would be free from administrative corruption. He hated the unproductive
people, especially the idle courtiers and the clergy; a reformed tax system
would have eliminated the exemptions from taxation which they enjoyed.
But Louis XIV was unequal to reform, and Colbert had to content himself
with lesser improvements. He tried to make tax collection efficient, and he
introduced a royal bookkeeping system. We doubt its accuracy, but it gave
the monarch some idea of his finances, though this knowledge did not curb
the royal extravagance.

Louis XIV had a religious policy consistent with his secular absolutism.
Not only was he a sincere Catholic, but the toleration of religious differences
would have been inconsistent with the national unity and order he epito-

mized. Indeed, if Catholicism sufficed for "God's image on earth," why not for every Frenchman! Protestants had been tolerated since Henry IV's time, but in the seventeenth century, the soldiers of the Counter Reformation had made effective gains in much of Europe. The Jesuits, clearly allied with papal power, were suspected in France as a threat to the liberties of the Gallican (French national) Church, which was then dominated by royal power. But the Catholic revival gained headway nevertheless with an emphasis upon freeing spiritual authority from secular control. The revival also manifested itself in the reform of religious orders, in the introduction of such new orders as the Carmelites into France, in many celebrated conversions brought on by genuine changes of heart, and in the spirit of charity of which St. Vincent de Paul was the finest example. In 1685 the King revoked the Edict of Nantes, ending toleration for Protestants. He may have believed that the Catholic revival, the many conversions, and the trend toward unity and order had prepared the way for religious absolutism. The exodus of Protestants was immediate and harmful. Many were artisans, important out of proportion to their numbers, and because colonial charters prohibited non-Catholics from settling in French areas abroad, they went to England, Holland, and Brandenburg.

The Protestants, however, were not the only sect to run afoul of Louis XIV. Cornelius Jansen (1585–1636) had taught the Augustinian doctrine of Predestination to a small following, which grew when the Abbey of Port-Royal near Paris became a Jansenist center. But unlike Calvin, Jansen challenged neither the authority of the Roman Church nor the Eucharist. Predestination gave Jansenism the same rigorous quality it had given to Calvinism, which suited neither the Jesuits, who were noted for their flexible moral theology wherever they went as missionaries, nor Louis XIV who was no "puritan." The Jesuits fought the Jansenists, whose doctrine was condemned by the theologians of the University of Paris in 1649. The condemnation was confirmed by Rome in 1653. The persecution of the Jansenists was long and bitter, ending in 1709 with the destruction of Port-Royal; though many Frenchmen who disliked the Jesuits remained fond of Jansenism into the eighteenth century.

Another movement within the Roman Church, Quietism, was less controversial but no less threatening to ecclesiastical authority. Quietism, like other pietistic sects of the seventeenth century, was intensely mystical. Bishop Fénelon of Cambrai (1651–1715), the movement's noted leader, was attacked by Bishop Bossuet; and Rome eventually condemned Fénelon. Mystics, because of their private revelations which can contradict orthodoxy, may threaten clerical authority; but since they are deeply devoted to God, grounds for condemnation come hard.

In the time of Louis XIV, French replaced Latin as the diplomatic language, perhaps because French power was growing, but also because of the reputation of French for precision, clarity, and elegance. The King himself was the model for diplomats, so great was his tact, and the French diplomats were widely regarded as Europe's best. Moreover, French diplomats were considered by Louis as his personal representatives, and as such, he insisted they be given precedence over other ambassadors. Backed by the best army in Europe, they usually got precedence.

The army of Louis XIV was the first great modern standing army. The standing army, as we understand it today, was a concomitant of royal power when that power had grown to a point where it was no longer dependent upon feudal levies. In the sixteenth century, the study of Roman military methods gave rise to a more rigid drill and discipline, which became enforceable only because troops were increasingly professional. Greater discipline was prized in an age weary of pillage and disorder. During the Thirty Years War (1618–1648), the great innovator, Gustavus Adolphus, King of Sweden (*1611–1632*), used his cavalry for shock troops, lightening his muskets and making his field pieces more mobile so that his foot soldiers might more swiftly take advantage of cavalry success. Such tactics were copied by Oliver Cromwell in England, and Cardinal Richelieu encouraged the French in their study. The greatest of Louis XIV's generals, the Vicomte de Turenne (1611-1675), was taught by Bernard of Saxe-Weimar, a disciple of Gustavus.

Louis XIV took active interest in military affairs, sometimes appearing with the Army toward the end of a campaign; but he was no strategist and refrained from risking the royal prestige in battle. His fine military organization was the work of the efficient Marquis de Louvois (1641–1691), named Minister of War in 1666, who employed a rigid inspection system to help maintain high standards. Louvois introduced marching in step and worked to provide identical uniforms for the whole army, hoping to enhance order and discipline. Three notable reputations were made in the field: the Vicomte de Turenne, the Prince de Condé, and the Marquis de Vauban. Turenne was a master planner, Condé was better known for his energetic improvisation in the field, while Vauban was the ablest military engineer of his time. Both a designer of fortifications and a genius in the art of siege, he developed the use of parallels for the advance of infantry and ricochet fire to unsettle defensive guns.

Louis XIV may never have said, *"L'Etat c'est moi,"* but the phrase is accurate. Matters of state, in the seventeenth century, were dynastic concerns; the security, power, and prestige of the dynasty coincided with those of the state. For Louis XIV, security meant that France must have her "natural" frontiers—the Alps, the Pyrenees, and the Rhine—as well as what was "rightfully" hers: the territory that had been Roman Gaul. These, his military goals, were often obscured by the pretexts for war concocted by His Majesty's lawyers. His first war, the War of Devolution (1667–1668), came after the death of his father-in-law, Philip IV of Spain. Louis claimed Spanish territory in the Belgian provinces on the grounds that, according to local practice, the daughters of a first marriage inherited before the sons of a second marriage. To the objection that his queen had renounced her inheritance upon marriage, Louis asserted that her renunciation was invalid because her dowry had never been paid. Turenne invaded the Spanish Netherlands while Condé overran Franche-Comté. The Dutch, however, quickly engineered an alliance with England and Sweden, which had the effect of bringing peace. In the treaty of Aix-la-Chapelle (1668), Louis returned Franche-Comté to Spain but retained twelve fortified towns along the frontier of the Spanish Netherlands.

Next he prepared to deal with the Dutch for interfering with his plans. He bought off the willing Charles II of England at the secret Treaty of Dover (1670) and came to an understanding with Sweden in 1672. The isolated Dutch were invaded the same year. Overwhelmed in the south, they saved the province of Holland and Amsterdam by opening the dikes. They were soon joined by Spain and the Holy Roman Empire. The war dragged on until 1678. In the treaties of Nimwegen which followed, the Dutch emerged territorially intact; but Spain was the chief loser, ceding Franche-Comté and more towns on the Netherlands frontier to France. The Holy Roman Emperor gave up Freiburg in the Breisgau. Louis, now at the height of his power, gave Europe peace for nine years; but his intentions were hardly peaceful. The lawyers pressed claims to territories which had once belonged to the newly annexed towns and provinces. These maneuvers led to the seizure of Strassburg, Saarbrücken, Zweibrücken, Luxemburg, and Trier, and to the occupation of Lorraine. And they were taken without a fight because the Holy Roman Emperor, as we shall see, was preoccupied with the Turks.

Meanwhile, the Dutch resolved to build a coalition to block Louis' path. Under William of Orange, the League of Augsburg was formed in 1686; it included the Holy Roman Emperor, Sweden, Spain, Bavaria, Saxony, and the Palatinate. Three years later, William of Orange, now on the English throne, became an even more formidable enemy; but Louis was not intimidated. Even before this event, he found two quarrels to exploit which led to the War of the League of Augsburg in 1688; a disputed succession in the Palatinate and a disputed election to the Archbishopric of Cologne. His troops overran the Palatinate, while in the Netherlands, Marshal Luxembourg inflicted numerous defeats on William III. The French lost command of the sea, however, after the Anglo-Dutch victory off Cap La Hogue in 1692, and the French hopes to restore James II through an Irish invasion were doomed. The war was a draw, for at the treaty of Ryswick in 1697, France, England, and Holland agreed to restore all conquests made in Europe and the colonies. Louis made separate peace with the Holy Roman Emperor: France kept Alsace and Strassburg, but she gave up the territories seized before the war. Lorraine, except for Saarlouis, was returned to its Duke.

THE ENGLISH RESTORATION

In England, meanwhile, the House of Stuart was restored after the Puritan interlude, and, as Sir John Evelyn tells us in his diary, the reaction against puritanical severity was immediate:

May 29, 1660. This day his Majesty Charles II came to London after a sad and long exile and calamitous suffering both of the King and Church, being seventeen years. This was also his birthday, and with a triumph of above 20,000 horse and foot, brandishing their swords and shouting with inexpressible joy; the ways strewed with flowers, the bells ringing, the streets hung with tapestry, fountains running with wine; the Mayor, Aldermen, and all the Companies in their liveries, chains of gold and banners; Lords and Nobles clad in cloth of silver, gold, and velvet; the windows and balconies all set with ladies; trumpets, music, and myriads of people flocking, even so far as Rochester, so as they were seven hours in passing the City, even from two in the afternoon till nine at night. I stood in the Strand and beheld it, and blessed God.[2]

The Restoration settlement left the question of sovereignty unsettled: A parliament had put a king to death, but parliamentary government without a king had failed. Charles II agreed to make no religious changes nor

2. Sir John Evelyn, *Diary* (published 1818).

to levy taxes without consent of Parliament, suggesting the end of divine right; but Parliament conceded that his title should be "King by the grace of God." This ambiguity encouraged Charles II to plot for twenty years, hoping to achieve absolute power.

The Church of England was also restored. The new Parliament, called the Cavalier Parliament because it was strongly anti-Puritan, passed a series of acts for religious conformity. The Corporation Act (1661) excluded dissenters from holding office in municipal governments; the Act of Uniformity (1662) forced clergymen to accept the Anglican prayer-book or resign their livings; the Conventicle Act (1664) penalized those who attended services other than Anglican; and the Five-Mile Act (1665) forbade nonconformist ministers to come within five miles of towns where they had preached. The King would have favored a more tolerant policy, for in his eagerness to emulate Louis XIV, he had become a Catholic. It is illustrative of Charles II, however, that he did not choose to make an issue of his religion, preferring to move cautiously and keeping his religion a secret. He had to be delicate, for as King he was head of the Church of England.

Though the government of Charles II did not recognize any Puritan legislation as legitimate, the mercantilist policies of both regimes were nearly identical and produced similar results. The First Navigation Act of 1651 had prohibited the importation of goods into England except in English ships or in ships of the country producing the goods; it was aimed directly at the Dutch. Several years of naval warfare followed (1652–1654), with the English having the better of it. After 1660, the Cavalier Parliament pursued the same policy with the Acts of Trade and Navigation, adding provisions to exclude foreign traders from English colonies. The Second Anglo-Dutch War (1665–1667) went poorly for the English. Early good fortune vanished, and the English went through the humiliation of a Dutch fleet's operating on the lower Thames. At the Peace of Breda, each power retained captured colonial territory, the Dutch holding Surinam and the English keeping New Amsterdam, and the Navigation Acts were modified to permit goods brought down the Rhine in Dutch ships to be landed in England, the Dutch thereby winning a significant victory. Disaster for the English was compounded, first by a fearful outbreak of bubonic plague, the worst since the Black Death of the fourteenth century: "August 12, 1665. The people die so, that now it seems they are fain to carry the dead to be buried by daylight, the nights not sufficing to do it in."[3] Finally, in 1666, a seven-day fire in London destroyed much of the older section of the city.

The Peace of Breda was followed in six months by the Triple Alliance of England, Holland, and Sweden (1668), which forced Louis XIV to end the War of Devolution prematurely. Charles II ought to have remained loyal to this alliance, for the future threat to England was to come from France; instead, in his gamble to restore Catholicism and absolutism, he signed the secret Treaty of Dover with Louis in 1670, abandoning the Dutch for a subsidy of 200,000 pounds a year and 6000 French troops if needed.

When Louis XIV attacked the Dutch in his second war in 1672, Charles II joined him, suggesting that this was merely the third in the series of Anglo-Dutch maritime wars. Then he issued the Declaration of Indulgence, which suspended the penal laws for religious deviation. His sin was twofold: he had promised to make no religious innovations without the consent of Parliament, and he was arbitrarily suspending laws passed by Parliament. The Declaration of Indulgence showed Parliament the true nature of the war against Holland; smelling a "popish plot," Parliament withheld supplies from Charles until he withdrew his decree.

Pressing its advantage, Parliament next passed the Test Act (1673), forcing high officeholders to take the sacrament as proof of qualification for office. The Test Act compelled the resignation of several of Charles' close advisors, and his brother James, Duke of York, openly Catholic, relinquished command of the Navy. The King was further embarrassed by defeats in the war, such as the Dutch recapture of New York. He withdrew from the war in 1674 and bespoke a pro-Dutch policy, but he did not join the Dutch, who continued to fight Louis XIV until 1678. To mollify his critics, he commanded the marriage of his niece Mary to William of Orange in 1677, but in secret he continued to deal with Louis XIV, from whom he continued to receive annual subsidies.

The King's deviousness hurt him on every front: the Dutch were justifiably suspicious, Louis XIV increasingly annoyed, and the English Parliament thoroughly aroused. The first true political parties developed during the 1670's, in response to the constitutional ambiguities and the King's maneuvers. The Whigs, somewhat in the tradition of the Long Parliament, championed the parliamentary prerogatives against royal encroachment and favored toleration of dissenters. The Tories defended the

3. Samuel Pepys, *Diary* (published 1825).

King against parliamentary attack, both as head of the State and head of the Church; they were a dynastic and Anglican party.

The election of 1679 was the first in England to be contested by organized parties. The Whig victory in part mirrored the King's growing unpopularity, but the Whigs also profited from the suspicion and fear surrounding the campaign. Ever since Charles' Declaration of Indulgence in 1672, rumors had persisted about a "popish plot." The King was not openly accused, but the avowed Catholicism of his brother kept the specter alive. Sincere Anglicans, the Tories were no more pro-Catholic than the Whigs, but the Whigs could not resist the opportunity to exploit the fear of Catholicism at Tory expense. The fear did not spring alone from devotion to Protestantism; ever since Philip II's attempt to conquer England, Catholicism had meant foreign domination to Englishmen.

Had the country known in the 1670's of Charles' understanding with Louis XIV, Charles might have been deposed. As it was, an entirely fictitious plot was invented in 1678 by a discredited clergyman named Titus Oates, who sought to regain stature. His reckless charges of treason and conspiracy in high places were given credence only because the nation was so fearful of Catholicism. Despite an absence of evidence, his charges sufficed to send five Catholic lords to the Tower and the Duchess of York's confessor to his death; and Parliament passed a bill denying Roman Catholics the right to sit in that body. Certainly Oates contributed to the Whig victory in 1679 and made the Tories realize that the Duke of York was a dynastic liability.

> From hence began that Plot, the nation's curse,
> Bad in itself, but represented worse,
> Raised in extremes, and in extremes decried,
> With oaths affirmed, with dying vows denied,
> Not weighed or winnowed by the multitude,
> But swallowed in the mass, unchewed and crude.
> Some truth there was, but dashed and brewed with lies
> To please the fools, and puzzle all the wise:
> Succeeding times did equal folly call,
> Believing nothing or believing all.[4]

The Whigs then raised the question of succession to the throne, a step calculated to underscore parliamentary prerogatives as against those of the King and to embarrass the Tories further. In his seventeen years of

4. John Dryden, *Absalom and Achitophel* (1681), Part I, ll. 108-117.

marriage, Charles II had sired no legitimate heir; plainly, James Duke of York would succeed his brother. The Whigs sponsored an Exclusion Act in 1679, implying that Parliament had the right to alter succession. Charles dissolved his Parliament after the exclusion issue was introduced, as well as in 1680 and 1681 when the Whigs brought the bill forward. Seeing no legal hope, the Whigs then backed the Duke of Monmouth, an illegitimate son of Charles II, who had no right to the throne.

The Tories remained firm for the dynasty and were aided by the privacy of Charles' Catholicism. And while the Duke of York was openly Catholic, his age precluded a long reign and his two daughters, Mary and Anne, were emphatically Protestant. There seemed little likelihood of a Catholic dynasty even should James succeed. By 1683, therefore, political opinion shifted in favor of the Tories because there seemed no reason to champion Monmouth. Indeed, the Whigs were increasingly unpopular, not only for having backed him, but for having backed the now thoroughly discredited Titus Oates. As for Charles II, when in 1685 he did die, he died in possession of his throne.

James II *(1685–1688),* less attractive than Charles, dogmatic about religion and giving evidence of mental decline, did not long capitalize on the reviving strength of his Tory support. He relied on it to support the royal prerogatives and, in his coronation oath, promised to maintain the established church and state. His first grateful Parliament voted him generous funds. Immediately thereafter, when two invasions were in the offing—one by the anti-Catholic Scottish Duke of Argyle and another by the Duke of Monmouth—Parliament quickly voted him an additional 400,000 pounds for smashing the rebellions. James' success in defeating the invaders (both Dukes were easily taken and executed) may have contributed indirectly to his downfall. Had the invasions been better organized or even coordinated, the considerable opposition to James as a Catholic would have had opportunity to coalesce, and the king would have had a truer picture of public sentiment. Misreading his opponents' bad fortune as public indifference, James showed his despotic intentions at once. He might also have been encouraged by Louis XIV's revocation of the Edict of Nantes (1685), which suggested how every aspiring autocrat might deal with Protestants.

James gave Roman Catholics commissions in the Army in a direct challenge to the Test Act, and he proposed the repeal of the Habeas Corpus Act of 1679. When members of his Privy Council opposed these moves, they were replaced by Catholic peers. Parliament, so recently friendly, grew hostile, and James prorogued it for its critical tone. Meanwhile, James continued to appoint Catholics to high positions: in 1686, the Lord Lieutenant of Ireland, the Master of Ordnance, and the Commander of the Fleet; in 1687, a Catholic was made head of Oxford, a direct thrust at Anglicanism and, thus, at the Tories. In 1687, James also sent agents into the country to sample opinion about repealing the Test Act and about a Declaration of Indulgence which he hoped to make (this was the same edict of toleration which had aroused Parliament in 1672). Faced by Tory disaffection, the King calculated to win Whig support by championing freedom of conscience, because the Whigs wished toleration for dissenters. It was typical of James II that, when his agents reported no support for his program, he plunged ahead anyway, beginning in 1688 with a Declaration of Indulgence, which he made required reading from every pulpit. Seven bishops who begged the King to withdraw it were assigned to the Tower. The public greeted their acquittal by jury with great enthusiasm, and the growing opposition to the King was publicly demonstrated.

Mary and Anne, James' daughters by his first marriage to Anne Hyde, were reared as Anglicans and hated their Catholic stepmother, Mary of Este. Furthermore, Mary, the elder daughter, was married to William of Orange, who had engineered the continental alliance against Louis XIV. Afraid that James would become an ally of the French king, William exploited the fear of James in England to prevent an Anglo-French alliance by intriguing with the Whigs to secure his wife's right to the English throne. Before he had moved, however, the crisis became more sharply focused in England: James' wife, Queen Mary, gave birth to a son, who had precedence in the succession. A Catholic dynasty had become probable.

The Tory party split into factions; the majority joined the Whigs in inviting William of Orange to save England from Catholicism. (Those Tories who held the right of succession to be unalterable were known thereafter as Jacobites, Jacobus being the Latin for James). James saw the danger and made a show of reconciliation. Again he promised to uphold the State and Church as established, and he gave assurances that he had no secret agreement with Louis XIV; but he failed to remove any Roman Catholic officers. He fled London late in 1688 at the approach of William, who had been urged to invade by the Whig leaders. In January, 1689, the Whigs and Tories, without the legal right to do so, summoned Parliament. Parliament first resolved that James had tried to subvert the constitution by breaking his contract with the people and had thus abdicated the throne. Secondly, Parliament resolved that it was unsafe to be governed by a "popish prince," and, knowing that Mary would not come to England without William, named them cosovereigns. The question of sovereignty was thus solved: it lay in Parliament as representative of the nation.

THE AGE OF THE BAROQUE

The Age of Louis XIV might equally well be called the Age of the Baroque. Originating in the sixteenth century and living into the eighteenth, the baroque was not only the predominant artistic style of the seventeenth century, but was a spirit which infused the political and social thought of the period. To grasp the baroque spirit, one must first recognize the search for new principles of authority so characteristic of the seventeenth century, principles which would bring order and reason to private and public life. A search for order implies the existence of disorder; and while we should not be trapped by the easy assumption that there have been historical epochs of golden calm, some periods have been more "orderly" than others because they have been guided by generally accepted principles which gave purpose to men's lives and made it possible to distinguish right from wrong.

At the height of the medieval period, Christian principles had generally served to give order and unity to European life; but by the late medieval period, sometimes called the Renaissance, Christendom had become increasingly a fiction. New ideas, new wealth, and new power had disrupted the old order. We think of the Renaissance as the flowering of an old civilization and admire the vitality of its men. But the decline in private and public morality reflected a growing doubt about the validity of the traditional truths of Christendom, and the emphasis upon the things of this world during the Renaissance amounted to a rejection of the spiritual fundamentals of the thirteenth century. The Reformation movement of the sixteenth century is often seen as a reaction against the individualism of the Renaissance, as an attempt to reassert the principles of Christendom so that, presumably, men would devote themselves primarily to God rather than to material things. Paradoxically, the theological doctrines of the Reformers made them children of their own century: they opposed authority save that of the Bible, and in their nonconformity aided unconsciously the disintegration of Christendom. Moreover, the religious differences of the sixteenth and seventeenth centuries, as causes for civil and

international wars, promoted public disorder. Small wonder that the philosophers of the seventeenth century sought new principles to serve as
the basis for universal order. Some, as we have seen, found the answer
in absolutism; others, as we shall see, sought order in the certainties of
mathematics.

When we attempt to relate the spirit of the baroque to the quest for
order in the seventeenth century, we may be easily led astray. We find,
for instance, that many baroque artists and architects were in rebellion
against Renaissance orthodoxy, against the imitation and refinement of
classical art. Rebellion does not sound like a search for order. Yet, the
practice of any orthodox art leads to the overrefinement of details, and
"clutter" is apt to be silly or sterile. An impressive technical perfection
may be achieved, but the work will seem to lack vitality, and the details
strike us as anarchic. The quest for new forms, therefore, is really a demand
for order; though the new order, once found, will itself eventually become
an orthodoxy. Thus the baroque, beginning as a rebellion against Renaissance orthodoxy, became institutionalized in the seventeenth century—
became "official" art sponsored by academies and governments.

Michelangelo seems to have been the earliest Renaissance architect to
sense the approaching sterility and to begin experimenting in the hope of
finding new vigor. He is often called the "father of the baroque." Other
Italians followed, and the baroque spread into Central Europe by the end
of the Thirty Years War and into Western Europe in the time of Louis
XIV. Grandeur was the essence of the new style, contributing to a sense
of monumental unity and order. All details were subordinate to the single
concept underlying the work: they must contribute to, rather than detract
from, its unity. Thus, the baroque spirit was an artistic absolutism with a
passion for greatness, and this outlook accounts for the speed with which
it became the new orthodoxy in the seventeenth century. Without knowing
it, Louis XIV was the baroque spirit incarnate. The details often used by
baroque architects—twisted columns, heavy scrolls, and flying figures—
sometimes became overpowering, destroying the single impact of the
building and defeating the architect's purpose. Almost invariably, functional and structural requirements were mere afterthoughts in the passion
for grandeur and dramatic effect.

The royal centralization of political power made large-scale planning
possible. The baroque architect of the seventeenth century did not plan
merely a room or a building. His edifice was part of a setting; thus, he
saw his building within a garden or park, and the park within the city.

City planning was not new to Europe, but it had not been practiced since Roman times. The details of the city plan were intended to contribute to the monumental whole, the focal point generally being a chateau. Karls-ruhe, designed by the Roman architect Giovanni Lorenza Bernini (1598–1680), called the greatest of his age, is often cited as the ultimate realization of baroque planning: the town was virtually placed at the castle gate, all the major avenues radiating as a great fan from the palace. Across the fan, several longitudinal streets were added in the interest of traffic, producing oddly shaped blocks. If impractical, it was good theater.

Take Versailles: Le Vau was the original architect—Jules Mansard extending it—and André Le Nôtre the landscape designer. They achieved a monumental palace, something over a quarter of a mile long, set in a vast park; the intricate details in both palace and garden were conceived within a single formal pattern, which produced a massive unity. Versailles was a superb symbol of power and unity, and also of rash expenditure; as a residence, we would hardly call it functional but liken it, again, to a setting for a drama. We have Saint-Simon's malicious description of exquisitely mannered aristocrats relieving themselves on its splendid stair-cases for lack of proper facilities.

The spread of the baroque style from Italy was associated with the Catholic or Counter Reformation and, thus, with the Jesuits. Throughout Europe, Jesuit architects built churches recalling their mother church in Rome, the Gesú. Considering that the baroque represented individualism and lack of restraint, when compared to the classical, it is ironic that it became Church architecture; but the Jesuits, as we have seen in their quarrel with Jansenism, represented a certain resistance to austerity. In their wake, European architects went to Italy to study, in particular to Rome, where Bernini, architect at St. Peter's beginning in 1629, had built its piazza and great colonnades. Returning home, they usu-ally blended the Italian baroque with the local style. The earliest French baroque architects, for instance, in the time of Louis XIII, strove to unite the native French Renaissance forms with the newer baroque. The Chateau de Richelieu was baroque in its size, its gardens, its richness, its "pom-posity"; but there was little ornamentation, so that it retained a sense of the classical.

Prussia, unaffected by the Jesuits, got its baroque at second hand by copying things French, and French architects were hired for buildings in Berlin and Potsdam.

The baroque of the Iberian Peninsula, in contrast to the French, emphasized ornamentation and achieved, on occasion, fantastic elaborateness. The extremism of Spanish and Portuguese baroque may be laid to the merger of three separate artistic strains: the Saracenic, the Latin American, (Indian), and the baroque; each strain alone was noted for ornateness, and their combination produced a riot of elegant fussiness.

On the whole, the English resisted the baroque, perhaps because they associated it with Catholicism and French autocracy. An Italian style known as Palladian, introduced to England early in the seventeenth century by Inigo Jones (1573–1652), remained the dominant architectural influence into the eighteenth century. The Palladian style was a classicism which endeavored to resist the exaggerations of the baroque; it was restrained where the baroque strained for effect. One of the best examples of Jones' work was the Banqueting Hall at Whitehall; completed in 1622, its lower floor was Ionic, the upper floor Corinthian, the whole edifice crowned with a classic balustrade. After the great fire of London in 1666, Charles II's court architect, Sir Christopher Wren (1632–1723), commissioned to reconstruct the old Gothic cathedral, drew plans which were baroque in the grandeur of their conception: a great central domed area surrounded by eight smaller chapels, all the details adding up to a massive unity. Neither His Majesty nor the clergy were pleased, however, preferring something more traditionally English, with a long nave, side aisles, transepts, and a central tower. Wren then achieved in St. Paul's a magnificent compromise: the old Gothic form with a Renaissance dome system. Despite the persistence of the Palladian influence, a few truly baroque houses were built toward the end of the century and in the early eighteenth. They were often the work of Sir John Vanbrugh (1664–1726), architect also for Blenheim Palace, who broke up rigid lines with clusters of chimneys and trophies of arms, for which he was much criticized.

Like the architects, the painters of Europe studied in Rome, often living there in national groups or colonies. A few, such as Claude Gelée called Lorrain (1600–1682) and Nicholas Poussin (1594–1665), resisted the new baroque style, but the majority accepted the influence of the leading Italian schools, of which there were two. The Dutch and Spanish artists of the seventeenth century were most impressed by Caravaggio (1568–1609): his chiaroscuro (the distribution of lights and shades), simplicity, and picaresque subjects. Even a hurried study of the leading Dutch painters (Rembrandt, Frans Hals, Jakob van Ruysdael, and Jan Vermeer) and Spanish painters (El Greco, Velazquez, Francisco Zurbaran, Jose Ribera, and Esteban Murillo) will reveal that whether they were concerned with portraiture, landscapes, or domestic scenes, the problems of light and space were their greatest passion and led them to their most notable triumphs.

The second Italian source of baroque inspiration was Correggio (1494–1534), whose highly decorative work established him as the leading painter in Parma. Here there was no concern for simplicity or chiaroscuro, but a delight in overdecoration, and the European artists in this tradition, often French, rarely measured up to the Dutch and Spanish of the century. An exception was the Flemish painter Peter Paul Rubens (1577–1640), who brought overdecoration and monumentality to its highest development. The Correggio influence in France was largely the responsibility of Charles Le Brun (1619–1690), named head of the French Academy of Arts by Louis XIV. Originally a discussion group of artists and architects, the Academy developed classes in painting, sculpture, and architecture, which had the effect of giving the arts a stylistic unity—an official style financed by the state. It was Le Brun's responsibility to organize many painters to decorate royal buildings, including Versailles; the vast numbers of ideal landscapes, floating figures, and flying draperies are suggestive of his administrative ability, his taste, and the significance of the centralization of culture with political power. It was he who established the Academy's School in Rome (1666) and inaugurated the annual salons the following year.

In matters musical, the Italians again led the way in the seventeenth century; their innovations in harmony, form, and the technical improvement of instruments made music a major concern for men of affairs before the end of the century. Baroque music, perhaps more clearly than any other baroque art, suggests the search for order and unity through symmetry and harmony. The key musical revolutionary was Claudio Monteverdi (1567–1643). Like the scholars and artists of the late medieval period, composers sought the inspiration of antique models, but since Greek music had disappeared and there were no classical remains, the composers could do no more than read about Greek music. One thing they found was the Greek combination of drama and music to make each more effective, and Monteverdi, who had read Plato, came to the conclusion that to make music more dramatic and appealing, both concord and discord were required. Music needed more harmonic possibilities to permit greater individual expression, to make music more subjective and less objective than the old polyphony.

He found the answer in unprepared discords, the most important of which was a minor seventh over a major third. His madrigal "Cruda Amarilla" (published in 1605, though known somewhat earlier) aroused a storm, so radical was the use of discord. When we note that the word *cruda* means cruel, Monteverdi's method becomes clearer: the essence of "cruelty" in his madrigal was heightened when he combined the word with discord. He opened the way for greater dramatic possibilities with his chromatic harmony, his musical revolution contributing enormously to the opera and the oratorio, to great Church music—both Catholic and Protestant—and to the development of instrumental music.

In the sixteenth century, Italian composers developed opera to unify music and drama. As a musical form, it was not immediately popular in Europe, accepted in France only after the middle of the seventeenth century. Louis XIV, ever the baroque absolutist-mercantilist, granted the privilege of an Academy of Music and the monopoly on opera to Pierre Perrin (1620–1675) in 1669. Three years later the monopoly was transferred to Jean Baptiste Lully (1633–1687), presumably a better courtier than Perrin; but Lully was not without talent and, until his death, he was the chief musical figure in Europe. Originally at court in 1651 as a member of the King's twenty-four violins, he was charged the following year with the formation of a second band of twenty-four violins.

As master of the opera from 1672 until 1687, Lully developed the form of the overture: a slow, dignified introduction followed by a fast movement and, finally, by a shorter movement in some dance form. This became the overture style for European opera and was copied even by the Italians. Lully's second contribution lay in music for the ballet (His Majesty was inordinately fond of the dance); he scored for a much larger group of instruments than had been the custom.

French music penetrated England, where the nation's leading Francophile, Charles II, was its patron. The greatest English composer of the day, Henry Purcell (1648–1695), was English trained, but his teacher had been a pupil of Lully and was aware of the French and Italian styles. Like Monteverdi, Purcell's work was known for its expressive dissonances. His best-known work is his first opera, *Dido and Aeneas* (written between 1688 and 1690).

Italian Baroque music was introduced to Germany largely by Heinrich Schütz (1585–1672), who for over a half-century was in charge of music at the Saxon court chapel in Dresden. He made several trips to Italy, but he did not borrow wholesale. His religious works—he developed the oratorio form in particular—showed the new Italian harmonic method, but their simplicity, seriousness, and piety was of native German origin, a forecast of the music to come from Buxtehude, Bach, and Händel.

Baroque music was increasingly difficult and forced the technical improvement of musical instruments. We do not know the great organ craftsmen of the period, but the organ became a more elaborate, versatile instrument. Stringed instruments were notably refined, and here the families of Italian craftsmen are known. During the last half of the seventeenth century and into the eighteenth, the Amati, Guarneri, and Stradivari families produced stringed instruments virtually never since equaled. The growing importance of instrumental music is seen in the use of the word sonata, dating from about 1650 and meaning something sounded, in contrast to the word cantata, which referred to something sung.

More than any of the fine arts during the baroque period, literature resists generalization; yet, even if there was no school of baroque literature, much of the literature had characteristics in common with the other art forms. Clarity and order were prized, leading to the admiration of symmetry, balance, and design, to a passion for "correctness." Such a spirit was not unrelated to that which designed a Versailles and regularized the elegances of its daily life or which sought to regularize and embellish music for greater expressiveness. Just as the musical supremacy of Europe passed to France from Italy in the time of Lully, so did the literary supremacy.

The movement for order in language and literature also reached its peak in France. François de Malherbe (1555–1628) contributed greatly to the well-known precision of French through his attempt to purify the language by defining "correctness." If the spirit of Malherbe seems absolutist, his definitions were neither those of arbitrary whim nor those of an esoteric crank. His goal was a practical one: a disciplined language which would serve as a vehicle for concise ideas and would avoid ambiguities. A year after Malherbe's death, a small literary society was formed privately, which Richelieu reorganized in 1635 as the state-supported Académie française. The Academy, in the tradition of Malherbe, was a regulating body, and membership was not so much a reward for literary merit, as is often believed, as it was recognition of literary authority. The members hoped to produce a dictionary of literary usage, a book on rhetoric and poetics, and a grammar, but only the first of these was completed. Even today, the latest edition of the dictionary of the French Academy is the last word in usage, and though new editions are rare—one appears only every seventy years or so—the result has been a uniformity of language in France unequaled by the other European countries.

The "codification" of the French language was extended later in the

Left: Charles II
Right: Louis XIV
Below: Arising of Louis XIV

Above: View of Versailles, before
1668, by Patel
Right: La Galerie des Glaces in
Versailles

Above: Le Grand Trianon at Versailles
Below: Church of the Gesu, Rome

Above: St. Paul's Cathedral, London
Right: Spanish baroque sacristy at Cartuja, Granada

Right: *The Lace Maker* by
Jan Vermeer van Delft
Below: *Marine* by Salomon
van Ruisdael

Left: *The Bohemian Girl* by
Frans Hals
Below: *The Triumph of Truth* by
Peter Paul Rubens

Above: *Galileo Presenting His Telescope* by Luigi Sabatelli
Right: *Study of an Old Man* by Rembrandt van Rijn

Left: *St. Francis and a Novice*
by El Greco
Below left to right: Johannes
Kepler, Sir Isaac Newton

seventeenth century to literature itself. In both England and France the literary tradition of the Renaissance continued: a classicism which aped the antique and possessed an aura of dignified worldliness. Nicholas Boileau-Despréaux (1636–1711) was the arbiter of taste through his book *Art poétique* (1674). In the interest of symmetry, for example, he recommended the closed couplet: two riming lines of iambic pentameter with the second line completing the thought. The style was not new, having been used by Chaucer and Ben Jonson among others, but it was suitable to an age which sought order and balance.

The passion for analysis, characteristic of much literature, was especially admired in the dramatic literature of the Baroque Age. Jean Baptiste Poquelin, called Molière (1622–1673), delighted in laying bare hidden motivations, especially those of sex, so that his revelations were often regarded as shocking. His goal was moral reform, and not a traffic in the sensational, but his moral standards were unorthodox in a period of Catholic revival. Another analyst was Jean Racine (1636–1699). He dwelt on the problem of passion, especially in women, and his great heroines— Phèdre, Andromache, Iphigénie—were all helpless in the trap of relentless passion, which led them inexorably to tragic ends.

One associates sex with Restoration tragedy in England, too, but in the reaction against Puritanism, comedy was the favored form. Since most of the writers had been Cavaliers, often in exile, French influence upon English writing was powerful. Charles II was a leading patron of the playhouses. A comedy of repartee was developed by Sir George Etherege (1635?–1691?), and its portrayal of the insolent fops of Restoration society set the stage for the two best-known writers of comedy: William Wycherley (1640–1716) and William Congreve (1670–1729). Their plays are usually boisterous and ribald, and it is difficult to be sure whether they were intended as a mirror in which a decadent society might see itself or whether the authors merely pandered to a society sunk in baseness. The lines from Congreve's *The Old Bachelor* (1693) were typical: "Come, come, leave business to idlers, and wisdom to fools; they have need of 'em; wit be my faculty and pleasure my occupation, let Father Time shake his glass."

The greatest figure of Restoration literature, however, wrote prose and poetry in serious vein: John Dryden (1631–1700). Given the poet-laureateship by Charles II in 1670, Dryden went in for political satire, defending the King and the Tories, and was inevitably accused of opportunism and insincerity. His *Absalom and Achitophel* (1681) was an attack upon the Whigs over the attempt to exclude James from the succession, and the suspicion of opportunism deepened in 1685 when Dryden became

Catholic. It is notable, though, that he held firm to Catholicism after 1688, and this action cost him the laureateship.

THE REVOLUTION IN SCIENCE

When one thinks of science in the sixteenth and seventeenth centuries, it is usual to recall immediately the opposition of religious authority—both Catholic and Protestant—to the new astronomy and physics. The opposition was real enough, but many assumptions about it have been erroneous. The errors are doubly unfortunate because they have obscured an understanding of both the typically medieval and the modern outlooks on science. For example, it is widely assumed that the opposition stemmed from the fact that there had been no science in medieval Europe; or that the medieval period had been a centuries-long night of superstition and ignorance, serving the theologians as the basis for their power, which must inevitably collapse in the face of the new scientific awakening. Historians of science reject such notions and offer us explanations which seem more tenable to anyone who, having seen a Gothic cathedral, may wonder how such an intricate and durable structure could have been raised at a time when there was no knowledge of science or engineering.

Medieval science differed from modern science in its world view; medieval scientists, therefore, asked different questions than do modern scientists because they sought different answers. The increasing secularization of life, which came with the declining Middle Ages, changed men's views; thus, the new science was more an effect of the secularization than its cause. Medieval Scholastics, such as St. Thomas, could think of theology as the "queen of the sciences," because they were primarily concerned about *why* things happen. Not satisfied to measure, weigh, analyze, or describe, as would be more characteristic of the modern scientist, the Scholastic sought qualitative answers rather than quantitative ones. The answers he got were consistent with his world view, which did not separate physics from metaphysics. Indeed, the scholastics mustered all knowledge in their quest for God, and the result was a gigantic intellectual construct in which, for example, the Aristotelian explanation of physical motion served also to explain why men, by their natures, must seek God; in which the Aristotelian theory of gravity, requiring the earth to be the center of the universe, was clearly compatible with the theological notion of the central importance of the earth as the stage upon which man worked out his salvation. When the modern scientist asks why something happens, he is asking for a fundamental description in physical terms alone; metaphysics has no place.

This medieval unity of knowledge, if an intellectual triumph, was seriously vulnerable: it had to function as a whole, and an attack upon any feature of it was threatening to the whole. More specifically, doubts about the validity of Aristotelian physics and the Ptolemaic system were disturbing to Christian orthodoxy, though usually not so intended. The scientists of the sixteenth and seventeenth centuries shared the growing individualism and independence of their time, but if they were willing to challenge orthodoxy, it did not mean that they were impious. Toward the end of the seventeenth century, we find Sir Isaac Newton (1642–1727) convinced that his science supported his faith. Indeed, the scientists of the sixteenth and seventeenth centuries challenged religious orthodoxy much less than has been generally assumed, even when, as in the case of Galileo, they denied Aristotelian physics. The opposition of the Scholastic theologians, then, derived neither from a disdain for science nor from the scientists' hostility to religion. In the first place, men are essentially conservative and resist new ideas, especially when they seem to subvert the old order. The new physics and astronomy threatened the unity of the scholastic universe, and the scholars feared that religion would be the chief sufferer.

Indeed, the new scientific spirit was humanistic and increasingly dedicated to harnessing Nature to serve man. Francis Bacon (English, 1561–1626) wrote: "Now the true and lawful goal of the sciences is none other than this: that human life be endowed with new discoveries and powers." Similarly, René Descartes (French, 1596–1650) believed that knowledge ought to be useful to life so that we might "render ourselves the masters and possessors of nature." Theirs was the new world view, a world in which man, served by science, sought Godly powers.

GOOD ANGEL.	Sweet Faustus, leave that execrable art.
EVIL ANGEL.	Go forward, Faustus, in that famous art.
FAUSTUS.	Contrition, prayer, repentance—what of them?
GOOD ANGEL.	O they are means to bring these unto heaven!
EVIL ANGEL.	Rather illusions, fruits of lunacy,
	That makes men foolish that do trust them most.
GOOD ANGEL.	Sweet Faustus, think of heaven and heavenly things.
EVIL ANGEL.	No, Faustus, think of honor and of wealth.[5]

There were, it needs to be added, many nontheological objections to the Copernican system when it was made known in 1543. For one thing,

5. Christopher Marlowe, *Doctor Faustus* (ca. 1588), Scene V, ll. 15-22.

scientists could not measure any change in the relationship between the earth and the fixed stars, which presumably would be possible if the earth actually moved around the sun. Copernicus insisted that no change could be measured because of the "incredible" distances between the earth and the fixed stars, but his assertion sounded lame indeed. Over a half-century later (1609), when Galileo (Italian, 1564-1642) first directed his telescope toward the heavens, he became convinced that the fixed stars were more distant than he had supposed, but the novelty of such vastness was then too much for the imagination. And then, as Tycho Brahé (Danish, 1546-1601) reasoned, if the earth really moved, one ought to be able to fire a canonball appreciably farther in the opposite direction; or, similarly, if one dropped a ball from a tower, presumably the base of the tower would have moved before the ball would strike the ground. In fact, the evidence to support Copernicus was slim, and the majority of scientists hesitated to credit his findings on scientific grounds alone.

Some evidence, however, helped cut the ground from under the Aristotelian-Ptolemaic universe, though not necessarily confirming Copernicus. A new comet appeared in 1577; cutting eliptically across the orbits of the various planets, it did serious damage to the assumption that the planets were supported by impenetrable crystal spheres. As a result, Giordano Bruno (Italian, 1548-1600) theorized that the heavenly bodies must float, but he did not explain how. Another Aristotelian assumption, that the universe was in a state of perfect and eternal rest, was upset in 1572 by the sudden appearance of a nova (exploding star), which suggested that new heavenly generation was possible. Similarly, when Galileo saw the changing nature of sunspots through his telescope, the notion of rest again suffered. The same telescope also revealed the devastating news that Jupiter possessed satellites—or more pointedly, that bodies other than earth could be centers of motion. Galileo was forced to conclude that the planets are terrestrial bodies like earth and not celestial bodies made up of an element unknown on earth, as in the Aristotelian view, and thus subject to the same physical laws of motion as the earth.

Tycho Brahé attempted a compromise between Ptolemy and Copernicus in suggesting that the planets revolve about the sun but that the whole system revolves around the earth. In England, however, William Gilbert (1544-1603) was working with magnets; and in postulating that the earth is a magnet—in fact, that gravity is a form of magnetism—he could account for the "floating" planets, the absence of the crystal spheres, and the working of the Copernican system. Gilbert's work was critical in that he saw magnetic attraction as the cause of gravity; and since every body was a magnet, gravity was a characteristic of all bodies. To put it another way, it was becoming necessary to regard gravity as a matter of *attraction* between bodies rather than the attempt of a body to seek its proper place in the Aristotelian sense. Gilbert went so far as to suggest that the attractive force of a body was proportional to its weight, but even as he was providing ideas which would account for the operation of the Copernican system, he shrank from the logical conclusion of his work, believing that magnetic attraction could not operate at such great distances.

It fell to Johann Kepler (German, 1571–1630), a student of Brahé, to develop Gilbert's ideas. Recognizing that the planets move in elliptical orbits rather than in perfect circles and that they do not move at a uniform speed around their orbits, Kepler concluded that a planet's speed is regulated by its nearness to the sun. This meant, of course, that the sun is responsible for all motion in the solar system, and Kepler sought to describe mathematically the relationship between the sun and its satellites. It is revealing of Kepler that he expected to find constant factors present in the operation of the universe, for even as a rebel against the theological notion of the universe, he thought of the universe as a perfect, mechanistic system: God would do no less. To describe the harmonious working of the solar system, Kepler concluded that the squares of the period of the orbit are proportional to the cubes of their mean distances from the sun. Then, to get the constant factor, he divided the square of the period by the cube of the mean distance from the sun.

$$p^2 \approx d^3$$
$$p^2 = d^3 \cdot k$$
$$k = \frac{p^2}{d^3}$$

The increasing evidence that Copernicus' system was workable served to heighten the conflict. Kepler fled from his Protestant colleagues at the University of Tübingen in 1596, taking refuge with Jesuits; yet, Catholic authorities burned Bruno at the stake in 1600 for speculating about the plurality of solar systems. If the sun was the center of our system, could not other stars serve as similar centers? And if so, would one planet be designated by God as a "unique" platform for men to work out their salvations? Best known of all was the lengthy controversy between Galileo and Rome. Galileo's attack upon the Ptolemaic system involved risk because the Copernican theory had been placed on the Index in 1616; but it is too often forgotten that Galileo invited trouble by using Scripture as evidence for his scientific ideas, solicitous as he was to reconcile orthodoxy with the "new science." The evidence for his ideas was not scriptural, and he put himself on false ground by debating scriptural interpretation with the clergy. Beginning in 1632, he was brought before the Inquisition four times, but the threat of torture ultimately applied to secure his recantation did not change his views.

After Alphonso Borelli (Italian, 1608–1679), who agreed with Kepler that the sun was responsible for motion in the solar system but who added that the sun's attraction was counterbalanced by centrifugal pull, came Isaac Newton (English, 1642–1727) to give mathematical description to both the forces of gravity and centrifugal pull. His law of gravitation, which he had discovered at the age of twenty-four but did not prove to his satisfaction until 1685, was a triumph of synthesis. A century and a half of scientific contributions were reduced to a simple formula, which, in describing gravitation, revealed the operation of our universe. Moreover, unlike the Aristotelians, Newton demonstrated that all bodies—celestial and terrestrial—are subject to one set of principles. In his *Principia mathematica* (1687) we find that "every particle of matter in the universe attracts every other particle with a force varying inversely as the square of the distance between them and directly proportional to the product of their masses."[6]

In the search for new principles of authority in the seventeenth century, theological thought was as vigorous as scientific thought, and the two currents often crossed. The scientists were in the vanguard of the increasing secularization of European life and thought, but it did not necessarily follow that they had lost faith. They found God in the rationality of the universe, a universe understandable by the use of human reason, which led them to be increasingly doubtful that revelation was the one source for the most profound truths. No one more clearly reflected the new scientific attitude than René Descartes (1596–1650); his ideas represented a break with both the traditions and the prejudices of the past. In his *Discourse on Method* (1637), skepticism was the starting point. One must not, according to Descartes, accept traditional opinions or the information given by the senses, for it is in the power of each individual, using the proper method, to discover truth for himself. We must see Descartes, then, as a rebel against authority and, in particular, against the authority

6. Sir Isaac Newton's *Mathematical Principles of Natural Philosophy,* Florian Cajori ed., (Berkeley, University of California Press, 1934), p. 13.

of the Scholastics. His "method" was scientific, and he believed it could be used to solve all problems, not merely those of science.

In discussing his method, Descartes divided the world into two parts, the world of experience and the world beyond experience, sometimes called the worlds of thought and extention. Within the world of experience or thought, one must reject the knowledge dependent upon sense perception and accept as real only qualities and ideas verifiable by reason; in the world of extention, he accepted the existence of God as fundamental, arguing that we could not conceive of perfection unless it had been put into our minds by God. As for the proof of his own existence, Descartes found it in the fact that he was doubting: *"Cogito, ergo sum"*—"I am thinking; therefore I am." Cartesian dualism divided the thinking self from the bodily senses; and this separation of mind and matter, of reason and experience, was one basis for theological criticism, since traditional Christianity regarded man as whole, not separating the mind or the soul from the body. The Jewish philosopher, Baruch Spinoza (1632–1677), while he would have agreed with Descartes that the universe is subject to rational explanation, balked at Cartesian dualism. Spinoza, who could not separate the creator from the creation, or God from nature, would not admit a distinction between mind and matter. Not only was Descartes' method a break with tradition, but his dualistic view of man was such a radical departure from the past that he has often been called the father of modern philosophy. His thought was revolutionary, not only because it upset applecarts, but because the division of reality into two parts has challenged many subsequent philosophers to seek "one world," some maintaining that everything is "really" matter and others insisting that everything is "really" mind.

Like Descartes, Blaise Pascal (French, 1623–1662) began as a skeptic, but whereas Descartes was able to rationalize the existence of both himself and God, Pascal's intellectual speculation left him doubtful about the power of reason. He could not find God through his reason but did not deny the existence of God; for Pascal, His existence was merely most likely. Pascal's life was a search for God, and he did not find God until he achieved a faith that God is a mystery quite beyond human understanding. "It is the heart that knows God and not the Reason." But while denying the unlimited powers of reason, Pascal was one with Descartes in affirming the nobility of human reason:

Even should the universe crush him, man would be yet more noble than that which kills him, because he knows that he is dying and knows the advantage that the universe has over him. The universe knows nothing of this.[7]

The vogue of science led to scientific societies. Organized privately at first in Italy, the most notable obtained official recognition in the seventeenth century. A London group organized the Royal Society in 1660 out of the older Oxford Society and received a charter from Charles II in 1662. His Majesty was an amateur chemist, but his financial interest in science was limited to his own laboratory, there being no evidence that he contributed to the Royal Society. In contrast, the French Academy of Sciences (1666) was an agency of the government; Colbert recognized the desirability of governmental protection and financing of science. Members of the Academy were subsidized and often assigned specific scientific researches, and the membership was international. One leading member, for example, was Christian Huygens (1629–1695), the Dutchman who invented the pendulum clock and reduced the error in clocks to less than ten seconds a day (at a time when the best clocks erred 1000 seconds a day).

THE RISE OF RUSSIAN AUTOCRACY

The medieval Russian (or Kievan) state, overwhelmed by the Tartars in the thirteenth century, endured foreign occupation for nearly two and a half centuries. While not the longest suppression of a European people by an oriental conqueror, the occupation left a significant cultural mark on the Russians: the "besieged-city" psychology said to be characteristic of them, a traditional fear of Asiatic military power, and a taste for oriental philosophy. Even during the occupation, however, the Russian rulers of the city-principalities, all claiming descent from the ancient house of Rurik, retained their domains through sufferance by the Tartars, and in the fourteenth century, the princes of Moscow connived to make their house pre-eminent. Their campaign was clever. They began with a feigned subservience to the Tartars and were rewarded with administrative responsibilities on behalf of the Tartars; with this advantage, Moscow gradually and secretly organized Russian resistance to Tartar rule. In the fifteenth century, the ambitions of the princes of Moscow were as royal as their counterparts in Portugal and Spain.

7. Pascal, *Pensées* (published 1844), XXIII. My translation.

Ivan III (the Great, *1462–1505*) was the first Prince of Moscow to assume the title Sovereign of All Russia. During his reign, the Tartar invaders were finally expelled, and the reintegration of Russia got well under way. Much credit must go to his wife, who not only was stronger-willed than he, but who brought important heritages to Russia. She was Zoë Palaeologus (niece of Constantine XIII, last of the Byzantine emperors) and had been reared in Rome. Thus a Roman Catholic, her marriage was planned by Rome as the first step toward uniting Russia with the Latin faith. Upon arrival in Moscow, however, she returned to the Orthodox faith of her fathers and was renamed Sophia. The marriage had, in fact, quite the opposite effect from Rome's anticipation: Moscow began to pose as the heir to the Byzantine Empire and as the "third Rome." Sophia, knowing the artistic pre-eminence of the Italians in the fifteenth century, imported architects from Rome, and the Kremlin Palace remains as a notable example of their work. Curiously enough, the "westernization" of Russia began at a moment when Russia was becoming the champion of the eastern European faith.

Great things were accomplished in the reign of Ivan III, but he hardly lived up to the name "Great." His personal weakness nearly permitted the Tartars in Russia a lease on life, but Sophia proved to be more coura-geous, forcing a strong stand against them. In the end, the appearance of Russian strength was sufficient to force the Tartars to withdraw, for they were internally divided and unable to make an effective fight. The basic pattern of the new Russian foreign policy, which was followed by the successors of Ivan III, began to emerge. In the east, it meant constant pressure against the weakening Tartars, forcing them ever eastward; toward the west and southwest, the Russians hoped to expel Poland-Lithuania from territories lost during the time of Tartar domination.

The centralization of the monarchy at the expense of the boyars (nobles) was another policy of Ivan III which was continued by his successors, in particular by Ivan IV (the Terrible, *1533–1584*). The first Russian monarch to take the title czar (Caesar), Ivan IV brutally broke the resistance of the old boyars and created an entirely new upper class, the *oprichniki*. Of common origin, the *oprichniki* gave service to the crown and were rewarded with fiefs, generally at the expense of the older boyars. The Czar's deliberate program of terror to crush opposition was intensified by his periods of half-madness when he indulged in fantastic orgies. Against the Tartars, Ivan IV enjoyed success; his conquest of Kazan and Astrakhan freed the Volga River entirely from Tartar control. Toward the end of his reign, the Stroganov family had established itself to the east of the Ural Mountains, and Cossack pioneers were beginning the conquest of Siberia from the Tartars. In the west, however, his efforts against the Poles gained nothing in White Russia.

Ivan was succeeded by his second son, Fedor (*1584–1598*) who was mentally deficient and unfit to rule. It was the beginning of what the Russians have called their "Time of Troubles," which lasted until the accession of Michael Romanov in 1613. Not only did the power of the monarchy suffer, but in the west the Poles and Swedes made serious inroads. The weakness of the crown was the opportunity for boyar reaction, and the consequent struggle for supremacy in Russia threatened the unity of the state. Rival factions accepted foreign support: a Swedish force reached Moscow in 1610, and the following year, the King of Poland occupied the city, hoping to become czar. This threat of a Roman Catholic monarchy produced a national awakening to the seriousness of the situation, and in 1612, a national militia, inspired by Orthodox clergymen, drove the Poles from Moscow. Then a national assembly elected Michael Romanov (*1613–1645*) to be czar, inaugurating a period of greater order.

The chaos had cost Russia Smolensk, which the Poles retained, and Carelia, which the Swedes occupied in 1608. The "westernization" of Russia was promoted in this period, however, by the usurper Boris Godunov (*1598–1605*), who had no right to the crown but who was an able, intelligent ruler. Though not well-educated himself, he believed in education and sent Russian students abroad to study western culture. The emerging centralized state needed to investigate the latest bureaucratic, military, and economic notions in the the West; to speed up their importation, foreigners were often hired to come to Russia. Boris Godunov not only sent students abroad; he also engaged a personal bodyguard of Germans. In 1631, Michael Romanov employed a Scotsman to levy 5000 infantrymen in Sweden, and the following year he put six Moscow regiments under foreign instructors. Simultaneously, 16,000 muskets were purchased in Sweden, but to avoid indefinite dependence upon foreign sources, a Dutchman named Vinius was hired to establish an iron foundry at Tula, the goal being a national ordnance factory. Two years later (1634), copper-mining experts from Saxony were employed to examine Russian mineral resources.

A section of Moscow was set aside for these foreign residents and was known as the German suburb. Its effect was twofold: Here the Russians could see the comforts and luxuries of the West; westerners demanded and received greater personal respect and freedom, indeed larger salaries, than was customary for Russians, so that "westernization" was envied. On the negative side, the foreigners antagonized the Russians. The foreign population increased in particular during the Thirty Years War, the new influx consisting largely of German Protestant refugees. As Protestants, they were indifferent to Russian religious ceremonies, and their cultural superiority easily led to arrogance. In sum, the westerners were unloved, but "westernization" was highly prized.

Modernization, oddly enough, coincided with a worsening of the peasants' status. In the time of Ivan the Terrible, the large-scale expropriation of boyar estates and their redistribution to the *oprichniki* produced an agrarian crisis. Peasants, though not directly involved in the political transformation, were victims of the resulting instability. Traditionally an immobile population, they were unsettled by the Czar's revolution; sometimes they wandered, sometimes they were kidnaped by landowners needing labor. Finally, to prevent an agricultural collapse, Ivan IV tied the peasants for short terms to the land where they were. In the seventeenth century these terms of forced tenure were gradually extended by the crown until, by the new law code of 1649, complete serfdom was a fact.

The pressure for education came not only from the need to modernize, but also because the Russian Church, in its new role as the champion of Greek Orthodoxy, had to meet the intellectual challenge of western humanism and the vigorous missionary work of the Jesuits. Kiev, chief city of the Ukraine, served as an outpost for Jesuit activity. (Annexed to Lithuania in the fifteenth century, Kiev became a center of Polish influence after the union of Lithuania and Poland in 1569). The Jesuits built schools, introducing the classical languages, western architecture, and music, along with Roman Catholicism. Their success was such that Terlecki, Bishop of Lutsk, hoping at least to save the Greek Orthodox rite, came to terms with Rome. The compromise, known as the Union of Brest (1596), produced the Uniat Church, which retained the Orthodox rite while it accepted the headship of Rome. Some Orthodox communicants did not accept the Uniat Church, but organized themselves into brotherhoods. Persecuted by the Poles, they found aid and comfort from the Cossacks of the Dnieper, who resented the presence of Poland-Lithuania in the Ukraine. In the seventeenth century, the Cossacks turned to the rising Russian state for support and furnished Russia ample pretext for war on Poland, an opportunity which Czar Alexis (*1645–1676*), second of the Romanov rulers, could not resist.

The Russo-Polish War (1654–1667) was really part of the First Northern War (1655–1660). Sweden, already in possession of Pomerania after the Treaty of Westphalia in 1648, took advantage of Poland's pre-occupation with Russia and the Cossacks in the Ukraine to invade Poland. The avowed goal was to make the Baltic a "Swedish lake." In alliance with the Elector of Brandenburg, the Swedes won a great victory over the Poles at Warsaw in 1656, but simultaneously they aroused the fear of all the Baltic powers. The Poles bought off the Elector of Brandenburg by recognizing his sovereignty in East Prussia; Denmark, the Empire, and Russia, all declared war on Sweden. This pressure forced the Swedes out of Poland, but in the Treaty of Oliva (1660), Poland gave up Livonia, the last of her Baltic territories, to Sweden. The Russians, meanwhile momentarily successful against the Swedes in Estonia, were now driven out, and the Russo-Swedish Treaty of Kardis (1661) was a *status quo ante bellum* peace. The Russo-Polish conflict dragged on until 1667 when, by the Treaty of Andrussovo, the Poles surrendered the Smolensk region and the eastern portion of the Ukraine, including Kiev.

The humanistic learning introduced to Russia through Kiev produced a religious controversy reminiscent of the controversies stirred up earlier by humanism in the West. Uniat scholars trained in the Jesuit schools ultimately found their way to Moscow; employed in a printing firm which published religious books, they recognized errors in the texts and proposed corrections to restore the original Greek purity. The proposed reforms were bitterly attacked by a group led by the priest Avvakúm: the Zealots of the Faith, sometimes called the Old Believers. They challenged the purity of the Greek Church, raising the specter of Constantinople in Turkish hands, and insisted on the maintenance of Russian religious traditions. When Nikon became Patriarch of Moscow in 1652, he decided to back the reformers, whose program triumphed; but the victory was costly. The Old Believers did not become reconciled to the innovations; the schism between them and the official Church deepened with the years, the Old Believers gradually breaking into sects, many of which were anticlerical. Further, the schism transcended religious matters, for the reformers were westernizers and the Old Believers were champions of native traditions. In another sense, the schism was social and intellectual, tending to separate the intellectuals from the Russian masses.

Finally, the official Church suffered even as its reform program was winning. Nikon's growing unpopularity enabled Czar Alexis, who backed the religious reforms, to remove Nikon from the patriarchate in 1666 and to subject the Church to an increased secular control, which inevitably cost the Church in spiritual authority. Thus, popular resistance to the reforms of the official Church was increasingly directed against the state. Small bands of dissenters, *Raskolniki,* were forming religious communities which served as focal points for political discontent. The confusion of spiritual and secular authority was seen between 1668 and 1676, when the troops of Alexis besieged the Solovetsk Monastery, whose monks were Old Believers. Finally captured, the monastic leaders were hanged.

THE REVIVAL OF TURKEY

The overseas expansion of the western European countries in the seventeenth century has often obscured the fact that Europe itself was still threatened with invasion by an Asiatic power. True, Turkish leadership was not what it had been in the sixteenth century, since the Sultans, now brought up in the degenerating atmosphere of the harem, were no longer awesome generals. But Turkey still controlled the lower Danube and the shores of the Black and Caspian Seas and was a third party in the contest for the Ukraine. The rapid decline of Turkish prestige in the first half of the seventeenth century was suddenly reversed with the appointment of Mohammed Kiuprili (*1656–1661*) as grand vizier. A vigorous, reforming administrator of obscure Albanian origin, Kiuprili established his family as an administrative dynasty within the imperial dynasty. His military and financial reforms paved the way for a Turkish regeneration that ultimately made Turkey a new threat to Venice, Poland, Russia, and the Empire.

Under Ahmed Kuprili (*1661–1678*) the Turks overran Transylvania, Hungary, Moravia, and Silesia, and the Venetians were forced on the defensive, losing most of Crete in 1670. Pope Alexander VII called for a Holy League of Christian powers to meet this threat of Islam, the crusade to be led by Emperor Leopold I (*1658–1705*). Louis XIV offered the Emperor 30,000 French troops, an offer too generous for the Emperor not to suspect Louis of ulterior motives. In the end, the Imperial Army under Count Raimondo Montecucculi included only 9,000 French out of a total strength of 20,000. Yet, in 1664, this tiny force scored a victory over 240,000 Turks, many of whom must have been noncombatants, at St. Gotthard, and a twenty-year truce was signed at Vasvár. The Turks lost no territory, merely being forced to recognize the right of the Transylvanian Estates to elect their own prince. It is evident that the Austrians preferred to be free to meet the rising power of France rather than to pursue their advantage over the Turks.

The Poles, recently weakened by losses to Sweden and Russia, were the next to feel Turkish pressure. Constant raiding led to declared war from 1672 to 1676, and twice deep penetrations of Polish territory by the Turks were repulsed by King John Sobieski (*1674–1696*). His victories won back territories lost during the initial years of the campaign, but in the treaty of Zuravna (1676) the Turks retained a small portion of the western Ukraine. Within a year, they were at war with Russia (1677-1681) over control of the Ukraine, the first of many Russo-Turkish wars. The Turks fared badly, and in the treaty of Radzin (1681) they gave up a large share of the Turkish Ukraine to the Russians.

Turkish interest shifted, then, to Central Europe, where a revolt against Austrian rule in Hungary was under way. The rebellion (1682) against Leopold I was led by Emeric Tölölli, who hoped to become King of Hungary. The Turks swept into Hungary, despite their truce with Austria, and some early victories encouraged them to strike at Vienna itself. The common danger to Austria and Poland ought to have produced an immediate alliance, but as Sobieski had earlier encouraged the Hungarian rebels, the Austrians avoided an understanding with him until virtually the last minute. Then, with Vienna menaced, they came to terms, promising Sobieski a subsidy in exchange for 40,000 troops.

The Turks were commanded by Kara Mustafa, third of the Kuprili grand viziers, whose abilities were not equal to his ambitions. He settled down to besiege Vienna on July 16, 1683. The city was defended by only 13,000 regular troops and a citizen militia, all commanded by Rüdiger von Stahremberg. North of the city, a relief army was formed of both Austrians and Poles under the command of Charles of Lorraine and King John Sobieski. But they did not appear for nearly two months, and the Turks were most wasteful of their opportunity, preferring a leisurely siege to an assault. Suddenly, on September 12, the relief army descended upon the Turks, who were surprised in their siege trenches and in camp. Easily overrun and driven off, the Turks were saved from complete disaster by bickering in the Allied camp.

Not until 1684 did the Austro-Polish army begin pursuit of the Turks, but personal antagonism between the Allied commanders soon led the Poles to withdraw from the campaign. Alone, the Austrians were able to capture Pest in 1684, but Buda did not fall to them until 1687. In the same year, the two armies fought the Second Battle of Mohacs, clearly giving Austria control of Hungary, and shortly after, the Hungarian Diet granted the hereditary Hungarian monarchy to the House of Austria. The Venetians, meanwhile, took advantage of the Turkish reverses to invade the Morea successfully. Moving north to besiege Athens in 1687, Venetian guns set off an explosion in the Parthenon, where the Turks stored munitions, largely destroying one of the greatest architectural masterpieces of all times.

The outbreak of the War of the League of Augsburg diverted the Austrians, allowing the Turks to consolidate their positions in Bulgaria, Transylvania, and Serbia. But the war in the West ended in 1697, and, under Prince Eugene, the Austrians struck hard at the Turks. Eugene's great victory at Zenta was decisive and led to the treaty of Karlowitz (1699). Here Turkey surrendered most of Hungary, Transylvania, Croatia, and Slavonia to Austria. Venice retained the Morea and most of Dalmatia, while Poland received the province of Podolia. The last great effort of the Ottoman Turks to conquer Central Europe had failed.

SUGGESTIONS FOR FURTHER READING

❧

General and Political History

*Frederick L. Nussbaum, *The Triumph of Science and Reason 1660-1685* (New York: Harper and Bros., 1953), a distinguished volume reprinted as a Harper Torchbook (1962) which contains extensive bibliography.

New Cambridge Modern History, V, *The Ascendancy of France: 1648-88* (Cambridge University Press, 1961).

David Ogg, *Europe in the Seventeenth Century* (London: A. and C. Black Ltd., 1931), brilliant work, notably biased against Louis XIV.

Laurence B. Packard, *The Age of Louis XIV* (New York: Henry Holt and Co., 1929), brief survey.

*George N. Clark, *The Seventeenth Century* (New York: Oxford University Press, 1961), arranged topically; a distinguished history.

*Stuart Hampshire, *The Age of Reason* (New York: Mentor, 1956), good study of the chief philosophers.

*William F. Church, ed., *The Greatness of Louis XIV, Myth or Reality?* (Boston: D. C. Heath, 1959), an anthology of diverse interpretations.

G. N. Clark, *The Later Stuarts* (Oxford University Press, 1934).

*Maurice Ashley, *England in the Seventeenth Century 1603-1714* (London: Penguin, 1952), good brief survey.

*W. H. Lewis, *The Splendid Century* (Garden City: Doubleday-Anchor, 1953), a delightful and informative study of France in the last half of the 17th century.

Colin R. Lovell, *English Constitutional and Legal History* (New York: Oxford University Press, 1962).

Maurice Ashley, *Louis XIV and the Greatness of France* (New York: Macmillan, 1948), brief.

E. F. Heckscher, *Mercantilism, 2 vols.* (New York: Macmillan, rev. ed., 1955), a highly-regarded work.

The Baroque

Sir Banister Fletcher, *A History of Architecture* (New York: Charles Scribner's Sons, 1924), technical and authoritative.

Talbot Hamlin, *Architecture Through the Ages* (New York: G. P. Putnam's Sons, 1940), excellent survey.

Albert Guerard, *The Life and Death of an Ideal* (New York and London: Charles Scribner's Sons, 1928), a study of French classicism.

*Carl J. Friedrich, *The Age of the Baroque 1610-1660* (New York: Harper and Bros., 1952), see Chapters II-III and extensive bibliography; reprinted as a Harper Torchbook (1962). Note also the volume in this series by F. L. Nussbaum cited above.

*Basil Willey, see below, [relates the intellectual and literary currents].

S. Sitwell, *Southern Baroque Art; A Study of Painting, Architecture, and Music in Italy and Spain of the 17th and 18th Centuries* (London: G. Richards, 1924).

S. Sitwell, *German Baroque Art* (London: Duckworth, 1927).

Harold Busch and Bernd Lohse, *Baroque Europe: Buildings of Europe* (New York: Macmillan, 1962).

The Scientific Revolution

*Herbert Butterfield, *The Origins of Modern Science* (New York: Macmillan, 1952), brief but learned.

*Basil Willey, *The Seventeenth Century Background* (Garden City: Doubleday-Anchor, 1953), brilliantly suggestive.

*A. R. Hall, *The Scientific Revolution 1500-1800* (London and New York: Longmans, Green, 1954), highly authoritative.

John H. Randall, *The Making of the Modern Mind* (Boston: Houghton Mifflin, 1926), a much-admired survey of the history of ideas.

E. A. Burtt, *The Metaphysical Foundations of Modern Science* (New York: Harcourt, Brace, 1925).

*Alfred North Whitehead, *Science and the Modern World* (New York: Mentor, 1948).

* Available in paperbound editions.

҂ 2 ҂

Europe at War:
1689–1715

THE SEPARATION of domestic and foreign policies, which we often make for organizational convenience, is quite artificial; and nowhere is that artificiality more apparent than in this period when dynastic issues were at once domestic and international. This chapter is organized around two great contemporary conflicts, the Great Northern War in eastern Europe and the War of the Spanish Succession in western Europe, wars which were fought independently, but which affected each other. To examine only the military details—which we keep at a minimum—would be relatively untaxing, and the difficulties are only slightly increased when we include an examination of how the wars affected each other. The true complexity of the situation can be realized only when we add the causes for the wars from the points of view of the countries involved; a study which soon broadens to include not merely war aims but also the effects of the fortunes of war on political decisions at home.

Thus we begin by presenting political events in various nations whose development was to be much affected by the wars: the England of William of Orange, where the new community of Anglo-Dutch interests soon ran headlong into the problem of maintaining the Revolutionary Settlement of 1689; Poland, where the rise of aristocratic power proved to be inconsistent with a strong foreign policy; and Russia, where revolutionary internal changes under Peter the Great contributed to victory in war. For the English, even the problem of ending the war became snarled in party politics, furnishing us with a later example of this unity of domestic and foreign matters.

After our survey of the wars themselves and their general consequences for Europe, we turn to a special situation, the rise of the Kingdom of Prussia, whose skillful, but limited, participation in both great wars capped many decades of slow progress by the House of Hohenzollern toward achieving a place amongst the great powers—all the while forging an absolutist government at home.

ENGLAND

The offer of the English crown to William of Orange (*1689–1702*) and Mary (*1689–1694*) in 1689 had been accompanied by a Declaration of Rights, which defined both parliamentary prerogatives and the liberties of Their Majesties' subjects. The contract was clear: the crown had no right to make or suspend laws, nor to levy taxes or maintain a standing army, without consent of Parliament; as a further guarantee, parliamentary sessions had to be called frequently. Later in 1689, Parliament converted the Declaration into the Bill of Rights, adding the proviso that no Roman Catholic was eligible for the crown. The Revolutionary settlement did more than establish the sovereignty of Parliament; in settling the issues originally dividing Whigs from Tories, it transformed party politics. Henceforth, party strife no longer centered upon such questions as sovereignty and prerogatives: now each party tried to win the crown's support for its particular policies.

The Revolutionary settlement of religious questions was an important step toward toleration. Two factors combined to modify the earlier restrictions: William III (the title of William of Orange as King of England) came from Calvinist Holland and favored toleration for all Protestants; secondly, the apparent danger from Roman Catholicism in 1688 had drawn English Protestants together. Thus, the Toleration Act of 1689 permitted nonconformist clergymen to perform their offices if they subscribed to thirty-four of the Thirty-Nine Articles (the creed of the Anglican Church). The Catholics and Unitarians were virtually the only denominations unable to meet this requirement. A further step would have been the removal of the Test Act of 1673. Originally designed to keep Catholics from holding civil and military office, it had barred Dissenters, too, and now that the Catholic danger seemed removed, the King and the Whigs (who continued to be champions of Dissent) hoped for repeal. The Anglican Tories, however, wished to preserve their political monopoly by saving the Test Act. As the issue grew hot, William dissolved the Parliament which had made him king and commanded new elections (1690). But the voters returned a Tory majority, assuring the continuation of the Test Act.

For a time, foreign developments threatened the Revolutionary settlement in England. The third of Louis XIV's wars (the War of the League of Augsburg) had begun in 1688, and since William had been the chief architect of the alliance against Louis, it was inevitable that England should be brought into the lists against France. All the more embarrassing, then, that an equally inevitable rebellion, led by the deposed James II, had broken out in Catholic Ireland against the new Protestant regime in London. James' position in Ireland was hardly more comfortable than it had been in England, for he was unable to protect the Protestants in Ireland from attack and so compromised himself even more in English and Scottish eyes. To crush this threat, William himself went to Ireland in 1690 and routed James at the Battle of the Boyne. James fled to France, but the final Irish surrender did not come until the following year, when Limerick fell to the English. The subsequent treaty, known as the Pacification of Limerick, was moderate, offering a general amnesty, the right to carry arms, and religious liberty, and it was ratified by the Parliament in London. The Irish Parliament in Dublin, however, where Catholics were denied the vote as in England, rejected the treaty and went on to legislate severe anti-Catholic measures.

Meanwhile, the lengthy war against France made heavy financial demands, leading the government, in 1693, to sell one million pounds' worth of bonds bearing an interest rate of 10 per cent—the beginning of the national debt. The following year, the Whig ministers (who strongly supported William III's policy) granted a charter to a group of merchants to organize the Bank of England, a private agency from which the government might regularly borrow. These financial measures were recommended by Isaac Newton, who was made Master of the Mint in 1695, and by John Locke (1632–1704), the unofficial philosopher and apologist for the Whig party. In the long duel with France, beginning under William III and carried on intermittently until the final defeat of Napoleon in 1815, the ability of the English government to raise money in moments of crisis was in sharp contrast with the growing financial chaos besetting the French monarchy.

That William was able to secure the extraordinary funds needed for war was not accidental. He came to realize that if he selected his ministers from the dominant parliamentary party, his measures had a better chance of being passed by Parliament. Thus, it was during his reign that the principle of cabinet solidarity was established and that it became customary for the cabinet to reflect the will of the majority in Parliament. Happily for the King, who favored the Whigs for their leading role in the Revolution of 1689, the voters usually gave him a Whig majority. As a consequence, however, Tory hostility to William deepened and became even more intense after the death of his Stuart consort, Mary, in 1694.

The war against France ended indecisively with the Treaty of Ryswick (1697). William's position was strengthened, however, because Louis XIV, by the treaty, recognized him as rightful King to the detriment of James II. But because William and Mary had produced no heir, the matter of succession remained an issue. Princess Anne, Mary's sister, was Anglican and shared Tory sentiments; nevertheless, after Mary's death, when it became certain that she would be William's heir, Anne was reconciled to the King. And since it seemed improbable, even before Anne's accession, that she would produce an heir, Parliament passed an Act of Settlement in 1701 providing that after Anne, the throne was to go to Sophia, Princess of Hanover, a granddaughter of James I.

WILLIAM OF ORANGE AND THE DUTCH REPUBLIC

William of Orange remained Stadtholder of the Dutch Republic when he became William III of England. His transfer to London, however, was symbolic of England's rising importance and the relative decline of the Dutch. He remained a Dutchman at heart, but his visits to his homeland were rare. The struggle for Dutch independence from Spain in the sixteenth and seventeenth centuries unfailingly has won the admiration of generations reared on the story of David and Goliath; but it must be admitted that the naval and commercial power, which produced this independence and gave the Dutch their moment of pre-eminence in Europe, was for a time virtually unchallenged by neighbors absorbed in domestic difficulties, neighbors whose natural resources would inevitably allow them to push the Dutch into a secondary position once political order had been re-established at home. The English Navigation Acts and Colbert's mercantilist policies were designed to reduce Dutch prosperity, the costly defense against Louis XIV was both successful and ruinous, and the vigorous and able leadership supplied by the House of Orange ended with the death of William III in 1702.

RUSSIA UNDER PETER THE GREAT

Czar Alexis of Russia, who died in 1676, was succeeded by the two sons of his first marriage, Fedor (*1676–1682*) and Ivan V (*1682–1689*). The latter being mentally incompetent to rule, the Patriarch Joachim arranged to have Peter (later, Peter I, the Great, *1682–1775*), issue of Alexis' second marriage to Natalie Narishkin, named coczar, a situation of doubtful legality. Natalie was appointed regent, Peter being ten and Ivan sixteen. Ivan's sister, Sophia, however, was ambitious for power and connived to unseat Natalie. Having close friends in the Palace Guard (the *strelitzi*), a center of Old Believer, antigovernment sentiment, Sophia engineered a palace revolution and took the regency herself. Once in power, she held the Old Believers in check and proved to be an able ruler, though her attempts to expand southward against the Khanate of the Crimea were unsuccessful. Clearly she was dissatisfied to be merely regent, but there was no precedent for a woman on the throne. Natalie, meanwhile, removed Peter from Moscow for safekeeping and settled near the German suburb, which gave Peter the opportunity to learn of the West and its technology from the neighboring foreign residents.

In 1689, when Peter neared eighteen and his majority, Sophia determined to kill him, but she found her plans blocked when many of the regiments, especially the foreign troops, refused to back her for the throne. Peter entered Moscow, deposed Sophia, and appointed his mother regent. Ivan V was allowed to remain coczar until his death in 1696, but his power was purely nominal. Natalie proved much less able than Sophia, but her regency provided Peter with the leisure to pursue his technological interests, especially his concern for shipbuilding. He had come to regard the sea as the best route to the West, for Poland-Lithuania and Sweden controlled the land routes and were often at war with Russia. In the 1690's, Peter spent much time at Archangel, on the White Sea and Russia's only outlet to the sea, where ships from Holland and England called.

In 1695, Peter renewed the campaign to drive Turkey from the region of the Black Sea. He struck at Azov, but the fortress, supplied by the

Turks from the sea, resisted successfully. Breaking off the siege, Peter set about building a fleet on the Don River; in 1696, he renewed the attack from land and sea, and this time Azov fell to the Russians. As the Turks were retreating elsewhere before the Austrians and the Venetians, Peter thought it opportune to go abroad, in the hope of organizing a Christian crusade which would deal with the Turks once and for all, giving Russia water access to the Mediterranean through the Dardanelles. He went incognito in the hope of continuing his technological education, but whether visiting iron foundries in Brandenburg or shipyards in Holland and England, his six-foot-six frame was quickly recognized. His diplomatic mission was unsuccessful, for the Hapsburgs in Vienna were increasingly concerned with the problem of the Spanish succession and were preparing to free themselves of Balkan entanglement. And before he reached Venice, word came that Sophia had aroused the *strelitzi* against him, playing on their fear of further reforms.

The *strelitzi* had not been misinformed in fearing that Peter intended to modernize Russia. On his return in 1698, his celebrated "westernization" began, the *strelitzi* being the first to pay the penalty for resistance to reform; hundreds of them were executed. As an outward sign of advancement, Peter forced his friends to shave their beards, for the fashions of the West, set by the court of Louis XIV, prescribed a smooth face. He put a tax on beards and proscribed the Old Believers from his presence. More significant, however, was his constitutional reform, which, by the end of his reign, left Russia a truly totalitarian state. He created the senate to replace the boyar duma; comprising ten members appointed by Peter, the senate was charged with drafting legislation requested by the Czar, served as the final court of appeal, and was granted regency powers. The ministerial system, then developing in the West, Peter regarded as unsuitable for Russia, because of the absence of trained, reliable public servants. Instead, he adopted the Swedish "college" system: each Russian ministry was governed by a board of thirteen directors, including three foreigners. To enhance the centralization of royal power, Peter overhauled local government. He divided the country into eight provinces (subsequently expanded to ten), appointing a governor for each. The gentry still retained the right to elect advisors to aid the governor, but it was Peter's intention to force the gentry into service in the Army and in the central government.

The measure of his totalitarian scheme was that Peter regarded everyone, including himself, as a servant of the state. Birth counted for nothing, and the nobility was reconstituted on the bases of ability and service. Those who served the crown were recognized as gentry, and their continued service was compulsory. Promotion was governed by a table of ranks, which was subdivided into three categories: military, civil, and court service. Each category comprised fourteen grades, the top eight carrying the rank of gentry; hereditary ennoblement could be achieved only by the attainment of the first rank. To force education upon the gentry, Peter made an educational certificate a prerequisite for marriage. The burdens of service fell on others besides the gentry: forced peasant labor was used in state mines, to build fortifications, to dig canals, and to build a new capital, Petersburg, on the swampy site the Czar selected. Recruiting for the army also hit the peasantry hard. The army had to be built almost from scratch, especially after Peter had decorated the Kremlin walls with the corpses of the *strelitzi,* and it was a rare year that recruitment took fewer than 30,000 men into service. Especially hated were the fiscals, the tax spies employed by Peter to report earnings and tax evasions. Taxes had earlier been levied on households, but since peasants often merged households to avoid taxation, Peter instituted the poll tax, a personal tax. He not only increased government revenues, but by collecting the taxes efficiently also forced the peasants to cultivate more land to meet increasing taxes.

Since the time of Czar Alexis, the Russian Church had been split on the question of modernization. In smashing the *strelitzi,* Peter struck at a stronghold of the Old Believers, but even though the official Church seemed to support reform, it was inevitable that the growing secular power would seek to dominate the spiritual authorities. Peter I was certainly not irreligious, but like Louis XIV, he was jealous of his absolute power. The Patriarch Adrian was not sufficiently zealous for reform to suit Peter, and, after Adrian's death in 1700, Peter postponed the appointment of a successor with the excuse that such a serious decision must be carefully pondered. Twenty-one years later, with no patriarch yet appointed, Peter extended the "college" system of government to the Church. Henceforth, it was to be governed by a Holy Synod, whose presiding officer, a layman called the procurator-general, was appointed by the Czar. This move, in secularizing the Church one more degree, contributed to the demoralization of the clergy and to a reduction in the Church's popularity. Peter also arranged that the Holy Synod should share the regency with the senate, and in the following year, 1722, he issued a new decree empowering the reigning sovereign to select his own successor, a right he failed to exercise before his death in 1725. But he left Russia an autocracy whose basic structure remained essentially the same until the Revolution of 1917.

POLAND

In the seventeenth century, when the major monarchies, including Russia, were moving toward a high degree of centralization, the opposite tendency in Poland brought her to the brink of extinction. Poland had reached her zenith with the Jagellon dynasty (*1386–1572*), under which she became the dual monarchy of Poland-Lithuania. In theory the monarchy was elective, but under the Jagellons the hereditary principle prevailed. When their line failed to produce an heir, the National Assembly (known as the Sejm) reasserted the principle of election. The first post-Jagellon king elected was Henry of Valois (*1573–1574*), who, as the price for the crown, signed an agreement recognizing constitutional limitations to his authority, the first of the so-called *pacta conventa* which each succeeding monarch was required to accept. Every nobleman was granted the right of *rokosz*—that is, the constitutional right to organize armed opposition to the crown, sometimes known as the right of confederation. A partiotic noble such as John Zamoyski might hope to keep Poland strongly united, while preventing the rise of royal despotism, by reminding the nobility of its duties as well as its rights; but more usually, the noblemen, in limiting the monarchy, were solely concerned to protect the "golden liberties" of the gentry. Some Polish historians have hailed this limitation of absolutism as a cornerstone of liberty and democracy roughly comparable to the limitation of Stuart absolutism in the late seventeenth century, but for outsiders the sorry spectacle of noble selfishness and political irresponsibility has made the "golden liberties" seem fools' gold.

It is only fair to emphasize, however, that seventeenth-century Poland was faced by an unhappy foreign situation which would have tried the strength of the most soundly organized monarchy. First Sweden and then Russia emerged to challenge Polish supremacy in the eastern Baltic, and to the south, the Turkish threat was revived. In the Polish Ukraine, the Cossacks of the Dnieper River resisted incorporation, became Greek Orthodox as a measure of their resistance, and ultimately placed themselves under the protection of Czar Alexis of Russia, providing him with a welcome pretext to challenge Poland. To the west, the Poles faced their traditional German-speaking enemies, the Holy Roman Emperors in Vienna, and watched the ominous growth of Brandenburg in North Germany. Their isolation during the First Northern War almost cost the Poles their national identity, and only a surprising revival in 1655 drove the enemies back and prevented a partition of the kingdom. In his enthusiasm, the King, John Casimir (*1648–1668*) proclaimed that this national revival should be capped by liberating the serfs, but the "golden liberties" did not stretch so far. Nothing was done to emancipate the peasantry, and this failure certainly contributed to the national decline.

The most astounding of the gentry's "golden liberties" was the *liberum veto;* using this right, any deputy in the Sejm could block a piece of legislation by his single negative vote and produce the dissolution of the assembly. In principle, unanimity had long been claimed necessary for major decisions in the Sejm, but the principle was not unreasonably applied before the seventeenth century. The Sejm of 1652 was the first to be "exploded" by a single deputy, and of the subsequent fifty-five biennial sessions, forty-eight were destroyed in this fashion. Small wonder that John Casimir abdicated in disgust in 1668, for the Polish constitution threatened the national survival by inviting political chaos. Even a victorious king such as John III Sobieski (*1674–1696*) could not stem the tide of decentralization. His decision to go to the aid of the Austrians in 1683 (see page 40) was wise, for if Vienna had fallen to the Turks, Poland most likely would have been the next Turkish target. Yet, the King was poorly supported at home, and later, Polish historians would criticize Sobieski for saving a power which would soon participate in partitioning Poland, as if he could have had foreknowledge of that sorry eventuality or of the imminent decline of Turkish military power.

EASTERN EUROPE AND THE GREAT NORTHERN WAR

Europe, in 1700, was on the verge of two great wars, which, though fought simultaneously, essentially remained separate conflicts. The long campaign against the Turks in the late seventeenth century by the Holy Roman Empire was terminated at Karlowitz in 1699, for the Emperor Leopold I wished to turn his full attention to the problem of the Spanish Succession. Peter I of Russia then had to reconsider the advisability of remaining at war with Turkey, and his decision to make peace in 1700 derived both from his doubts of further success on that front and from a new possibility of rich plunder on another front. He had visited the new King of Poland, Augustus II (the Strong, *1697–1733*), who was also Elector of Saxony, and the two monarchs, so much alike in the robustness of their appetites, took an immediate liking to each other. (Augustus' title should not be construed as descriptive of moral strength; he was more notable for fathering 365 children.) Over great quantities of wine, they plotted the partition of the Swedish Empire, and, in 1699, invited the King of Denmark, Frederick IV (*1699–1730*) to join into secret coalition against Charles XII (*1697–1718*) of Sweden. All three powers were interested in reducing Sweden's Baltic hegemony: Poland hoped to recover Livonia, Peter wanted direct access to the Baltic, and the Danes hoped to put an end to Swedish interference in a quarrel between Denmark and the Duke of Holstein-Gottorp.

Known to history as the Great Northern War, the conflict was ignited in 1700 with a Polish invasion of Livonia and a Danish invasion of Schleswig. Charles XII of Sweden, high-minded and puritanical, was outraged by what he regarded as treacherous attacks, and one of his avowed war aims was the dethronement of Augustus the Strong. Perhaps more to the point was the essential unsoundness of Augustus' policy, for in 1700 Poland needed peace for the consolidation of monarchical power, and even the temptation of Swedish territory ought not have blinded the Polish king to the consequences of aiding Russian aggrandizement. Swedish wrath, however, fell first on Denmark, not Poland. Confident that their naval power would prevent Swedish landings on Danish soil, the Danes concentrated their forces against Swedish Pomerania. They at once ran afoul of an alliance which Sweden had entered with William III, who was the designer of the coalition holding Louis XIV in check. In exchange for Swedish support against the French King, William had promised to help maintain the *status quo* in the Baltic; so that with the Danish declaration of war against Sweden, an Anglo-Dutch fleet moved into the Baltic to give the Swedes command of the sea. Charles XII immediately concentrated troops against Copenhagen, and, completely outmaneuvered, the Danes were forced out of the war (1700).

Charles XII struck next at the Russians, landing a small force of 8000 men to relieve Narva (in Ingermanland), which the Russians were besieging. Though the Russian forces greatly outnumbered the Swedes, Charles knew that the Russians were not sufficiently modernized to fight on equal terms with his splendid troops, and he took advantage of a blinding snowstorm (which concealed his true strength) to launch a fierce attack. Charles was further assisted by Peter's last-minute panic, which led him to relinquish command of his troops to General de Croy, adding to the confusion. The Swedes won a brilliant victory at Narva over an opponent five times their number, and then they turned southward to clear the Poles and Saxons out of Livonia. In 1701, Charles crossed the Dvina River into Polish territory, where he was occupied for the next six years. Though repeatedly defeated, Augustus II avoided surrender by retiring in the direction of Saxony. Finally, in 1704, Charles XII declared him deposed from the Polish throne.

Under the auspices of Charles, Stanislas Leszczyński (*1704–1709, 1733–1735*) was illegally elected King of Poland, an election which Augustus II refused to recognize. As a result, the Swedes invaded Saxony, forcing Augustus II to renounce his rights to the Polish throne in 1707 by the Treaty of Altranstädt. Only the Russians remained to oppose Charles XII. Ever since Narva, Peter had been working furiously to rebuild his military strength, and during the years when Charles was occupied in Saxony-Poland, the Russians had been nibbling away at Swedish positions on the Baltic coast. Nyenschantz was captured in 1703 and renamed Petersburg, and though it was technically on Swedish soil, the city was selected by the Czar as his new capital. Now he had achieved direct water communication with the West.

In 1707, Charles XII turned his attention once again to the Russians. Peter's forces were soon driven from Latvia, and Charles prepared an invasion of Moscow in alliance with the Cossack hetman, Ivan Mazeppa (*1640–1709*). The latter agreed to provide 30,000 cavalrymen, in the expectation that a Russian defeat would enable him to organize an independent Ukrainian state. When the campaign of 1709 began, Mazeppa appeared with only 1500 cavalry, and a Swedish reserve force, coming to join Charles, was crushed before its arrival. Despite these setbacks, the Swedish monarch pressed on to besiege Poltava; but outnumbered nearly four to one, the Swedes were finally overwhelmed, most of the army surrendering. The King escaped to Turkey, but his troops were herded into Peter's labor camps. Stanislas Leszczynski, on receiving the news of Poltava, recognized the advisability of relinquishing the Polish throne, which Augustus II reclaimed. Worse for Sweden, he brought Saxony-Poland back into the war and was joined by Denmark.

After 1709, the Swedes were on the defensive and desperately needed an ally, but Louis XIV (whom the Swedes had earlier disdained as a persecutor of Protestants) was himself hard pressed by then and could lend no aid. It remained for Charles XII to maneuver the Turks into a war against Russia, which he accomplished in the following year. Encouraged by his success against the Swedes, Peter moved too impetuously against the Turks and soon found himself surrounded, along the Pruth River, by superior forces of Turks and Crimean Tartars—vassals of the Sultan of Turkey. To avoid a complete disaster, Peter bought off the Grand Vizier, Mehemet Baltadji, who was thankful to win an important victory and a bribe without a fight. Through the treaty of Pruth (1711), Russia gave up lands recently acquired by Peter along the Black Sea and the Sea of Azov, but Charles XII was furious that the Turks had been wasteful of an opportunity to destroy a Russian army. He remained in Turkey until 1712, when his intrigues wearied the Turks to the point of driving him from the country. He crossed Europe in disguise to regain Sweden.

Along the Baltic coast, the Russians enjoyed great success after Poltava, occupying the area from Livonia to Finland. Prussia and Hanover joined the alliance against Sweden, making the odds against her tremendous, but Charles XII kept the field until his death in battle at Friedrichshall (Norway) in 1718. There has been much speculation that the King was not cut down by an enemy bullet, but by an assassin. Certainly there was much discontent in Sweden over the long and increasingly disastrous war, and after its conclusion, the nobility successfully infringed upon the royal power. Sweden ended the Great Northern War by signing separate treaties with her numerous foes. Denmark received a portion of Schleswig; Prussia took Stettin and a bit of Pomerania; Hanover got Bremen and Verden; and Poland, the principal war theater, was rewarded by Sweden's recognition of Augustus the Strong. Russia, not Poland, was the true victor: the treaty of Nystadt (1721) gave Estonia, Livonia, and the Karelian peninsula to Peter. He returned Finland to Sweden and paid her an indemnity, but he had broken her power while reaching the Baltic, and Poland, who should have been his enemy, had aided him to her everlasting regret.

Meanwhile, to the south, the Turks, encouraged by their success on the Pruth in 1711, renewed the quarrel for control of the Balkans in 1714. The Venetians were swept out of the Peloponnesus, or Morea, and from the Balkan mainland, forcing the Austrians to join the struggle. They reversed the Turkish tide, taking Belgrade in 1717; this move led to the treaty of Passarowitz the following year. Austria kept a portion of North Serbia, including Belgrade.

WESTERN EUROPE AND THE
WAR OF THE SPANISH SUCCESSION

Western Europe did not long enjoy peace after the treaty of Ryswick (1697) that ended the third of Louis XIV's aggressive wars which had been fought to achieve French security by obtaining the natural frontiers. But as the century approached its end, a new conflict developed over the succession to the Spanish throne—a conflict in which Louis's interest was primarily dynastic. On the Spanish throne sat one of the truly pathetic figures of the seventeenth century: Charles II (*1665–1700*). Genuinely pious and concerned for the integrity of his empire, he was the physical product of Hapsburg inbreeding; of his numerous ailments, the most serious derived from his "Hapsburg chin," which made the chewing of food nearly impossible. That he remained alive as long as he did both astonished and dismayed Europe, for the powers plotted and counterplotted the partition of the Spanish Empire in the event of his death. But one thing was certain: Charles II could not produce a child to succeed him.

The question of the Spanish succession hinged on a legal matter. Since two of the three rival claimants were already powerful, the balance of power on the Continent was at stake. The latter factor explains why the European powers dared not regard the issue as simply a question of whose claim was most valid. As for the claims, all three were through females, and at least the claims of Louis XIV and Leopold I were complicated by a series of renunciations of inheritances and denials of the validity of the renunciations. Louis XIV's claim was based on the fact that he was the son of Anne, elder sister of Philip IV, and that he had married Philip IV's elder daughter, Maria Theresa. Since the reigning Charles II was the son of Philip IV, it meant that Louis was simultaneously Charles' cousin and his brother-in-law. Leopold I, the Holy Roman Emperor, enjoyed exactly the same relationship with Charles II: son of Philip IV's younger sister, he had married Philip IV's younger daughter.

The third claimant was Joseph Ferdinand, the Electoral Prince of Bavaria, born in 1692, grandson of Leopold I, whose daughter had married Maximilian Emmanuel of Bavaria. The child's claim was favored by many statesmen, not only on legal grounds, but also because his inheritance of the Spanish crown would prevent on the one hand the merger of the Franco-Spanish kingdoms and on the other hand the reconstruction of the vast empire of Charles V. The English and the Dutch were especially nervous about either of those possibilities because their independence would be jeopardized by the emergence of a single power able to dominate the Continent. To soothe this fear, neither Louis nor Leopold claimed the Spanish throne for himself, but rather for relatives not likely to inherit their native thrones. Leopold put forth his second son, Archduke Charles; Louis XIV championed his second grandson, Philip of Anjou.

Yet, Louis XIV showed himself willing to compromise even further to avoid war when approached by William III of England. The two monarchs negotiated the First Partition Treaty (1698), settling the future of the Spanish Empire. Spain, the Indies, the Netherlands, and Sardinia were to go to the infant Electoral Prince of Bavaria, or to his father in case of an untimely death. As compensation, Louis the Dauphin was to get the Kingdom of the Two Sicilies, while the Archduke Charles was to receive the Duchy of Milan. The negotiators had intended keeping this arrangement secret, but news of it leaked out, and Charles II of Spain was understandably furious that the partition of his territories was being arranged without his participation. He responded by drawing up a will late in 1698, making the Electoral Prince of Bavaria his *sole* heir. The English and Dutch readily agreed to this provision, since it safeguarded their own interests. Perhaps the question would have been thus resolved had not the infant Prince of Bavaria died three months later.

Louis XIV and William III then negotiated a second partition treaty (1700), designating the share originally intended for the deceased Bavarian prince to the Archduke Charles and providing Louis the Dauphin with the Duchy of Lorraine as well as the previously promised Italian territory. The dispossessed Duke of Lorraine was to receive Milan. But the Emperor Leopold, demanding the entire inheritance for Archduke Charles, refused to recognize the treaty, while the King of Spain remained opposed to the partition of his empire. He drew up a second will, and, concluding that the Spanish possessions would most likely remain intact if Louis XIV were pleased, Charles II left his empire to Philip Duke of Anjou, who was separated from the French throne by two other heirs with prior claims. In default, the will left the throne to Philip's younger brother, the Duke of Berry, with specific instructions that the thrones of France and Spain were never to be united. Shortly afterward, Charles II ceased to suffer from his humiliating infirmities, and the crowned vultures awaited Louis XIV's move.

Louis' grandson was proclaimed Philip V of Spain (*1700-1746*).

Perhaps Louis' decision to renounce his treaty with William III and accept the second will of Charles II was encouraged by the Tory victory in the elections of 1699, which had been followed by parliamentary measures unfriendly to William. The Tories chose to interpret the partition treaties as likely to produce war rather than to prevent it. Had Louis been able to content himself with a diplomatic victory, it is unlikely that a war would have developed, since the English were unimpressed by William's alarm over the new ties between Paris and Madrid. But Louis' ambitions led him into two mistakes. He first declared that Philip V had not lost his rights in the French succession—a violation of the will of Charles II and a distinct threat that a great continental block might develop in the future. Then, when English opinion reversed itself, permitting William to develop his Grand Alliance against France, Louis countered by recognizing the rights of James II's son as King of England, with the effect of strengthening the war party in England. William's Grand Alliance included England, Holland, and the Empire, many of the small German states joining in; but Bavaria fought on the side of the French and the Spanish Bourbons. This, the War of the Spanish Succession (*1701–1713*), was hardly under way when William III died, to be succeeded by his High Church sister-in-law, Anne (*1702–1714*).

If the military power of France was great, the coalition against her could put more men in the field and had far greater naval power. Bavaria promised Louis 10,000 men in exchange for his support for the Bavarian Elector's candidacy for the Holy Roman throne (the Hapsburgs to be deposed); but this was small compensation for the fact that France had to fight a two-front war against superior enemies. The key military campaign developed in 1703–1704 with Louis' attempt to smash the Grand Alliance by capturing Vienna. The Franco-Bavarian forces joined in the Danube valley, only to be embarrassed by the unexpected defection of the Duchy of Savoy, which had briefly adhered to the French side. Prince Eugene of Savoy was thus able to bring an Imperial army into Germany from Italy to join the Anglo-Dutch forces under the Duke of Marlborough. At Blenheim, they brilliantly blocked the French advance upon Vienna, a victory which came only ten days after the English capture of Gibraltar and which inaugurated an era of serious French defeats. Bavaria was occupied by the Allies, and to the south, the Archduke Charles landed in Spain to make good his claim by right of conquest.

In early 1706, Marshal Villeroi pushed a French drive north into the Low Countries, but once again Marlborough parried the blow at the

Battle of Ramillies and forced the French to evacuate. To save France from an invasion from the North, Marshal Vendôme was brought up from Italy; but his departure from that front quickly led to a new disaster there when late in 1706 the Austrians and Savoyards under Prince Eugene routed the French force besieging Turin and forced the evacuation of Italy. By the end of the year, the French were reduced to the defensive, and it appeared that Philip V was in imminent danger of losing the Spanish throne. He had lost Madrid to Archduke Charles, who called himself Charles III, but an overwhelming and unexpected victory by the French general Berwick over the Allies at Almanza (1707) gave Philip V a lease on life. By and large, the Spanish people favored him over Archduke Charles because Philip represented the will of their late king and legitimacy; the Allied position in Spain was therefore exceedingly uncomfortable.

In 1708 Marshal Vendôme tried for a victory in the Lowlands, but was no more successful than Villeroi had been two years earlier. Defeated first at Oudenarde by Marlborough and Eugene, the French then lost Lille, opening up France to invasion. Louis XIV was now ready for peace; his offensives beaten back, his finances in a chaotic state, and a food shortage threatening thanks to a bad harvest, he offered, in 1709, to abandon Spain and all Spanish territory and to surrender Strassburg and some of the fortresses along the Netherlands frontier. Louis' proposal was reasonable, but his opponents, confident that one more campaign would leave France helpless, insisted that the French also agree to help drive Philip V from Spain. As they had foreseen, Louis disdained peace on this basis, and hostilities resumed; what the Allies could not foresee was a French revival, which, in retrospect, made the Allied ardor for war most unwise.

Retribution was not long in coming. The Anglo-Dutch army invaded France in September, 1709, but the nation made a remarkable response to Louis XIV's appeal for a vigorous defensive effort. At Malplaquet, a new French army under Villars set itself to block Marlborough's advance and inflicted such a slaughter upon the Allies that the invasion ended. Malplaquet was technically an Allied victory, since the French retired; but they retired unbeaten and in good order, having destroyed the best part of the Dutch army. In Spain, the Bourbon cause fared well because in 1710 Louis was able to send Vendôme with 25,000 men to help Philip V, and the Allies' armies were sharply reduced by two defeats and by guerrilla warfare. To cap Allied embarrassment, the Archduke Charles became Holy Roman Emperor in 1711, making his candidacy for the Spanish throne no longer an Anglo-Dutch interest.

DIFFICULTIES IN ENDING THE WAR

The problem of making peace had become snarled in English party politics, since important domestic issues were by implication involved. The Whigs had been regarded as the war party for their support of William III and for their defense of the Revolutionary settlement of 1689, which Louis XIV no longer recognized when he denied William to be the rightful King. The accession of Anne in 1702, however, encouraged the Tories. Her High Church sentiments led them to hope for the support of the crown on domestic issues, particularly in their desire that the tolerance granted Dissenters in 1689 might be withdrawn. The Tories were in the embarrassing position of recognizing the danger from France, while also realizing that the defeat of Louis XIV would be a great victory for the Whig principles of religious toleration and parliamentary supremacy. Accordingly, the Tories were lukewarm for a war which could not be avoided, while the Whigs argued that the war was necessary to defend the principles of 1689 against the probable tampering of the Tory Queen. A further ambiguity was the position of the Duke of Marlborough, chosen to command the troops sent to the continent in 1702. Nominally a Tory, he was Anne's chief advisor. Yet, he favored the Whig policy of total war against the French and used his nominal Toryism to prevent his party from obstructing his military plans.

In preparation for the first general election of her reign, Queen Anne reconstituted her cabinet in favor of the Tories, in the hope of influencing the election in their interest. The stratagem worked, gave Parliament a Tory majority, and forced Marlborough to persist in his nominal Toryism. Immediately, the Tories began their assault on Dissenters with the Occasional Conformity Bill, a measure designed to bar from public office men who satisfied the Test Act by taking communion "occasionally" in an Anglican church but who regularly attended some nonconformist service. The measure failed in the House of Lords, where the Whigs remained a majority; but the Tories brought up the measure again in 1703, threatening to withhold military supplies if it were not passed—an action which put Marlborough squarely on the spot. He voted for the bill but secretly encouraged the Whigs to block it, so that it was again defeated in the House of Lords. The issue festered for several years, with Marlborough finally opposing the bill openly in 1705, the year in which the Whigs won control of Commons. Queen Anne was resentful and resisted Whig demands to shuffle the cabinet to reflect their parliamentary victory, though she gave in by 1708. Marlborough, in the meantime, now openly regarded as a Whig, lost his favor at court, though not his military command.

Thus, the Whigs were in control in 1709 when Louis XIV offered peace with terms that would have signaled a clear victory for the Allies, but which the Whigs rejected, as described above. Too eager to crush France completely, the Whigs bared themselves to the charge that they promoted the war for party advantage alone, a charge which the Tories did not hesitate to make. In 1710, the Whigs raised further doubts about their moral position—as the presumed champions of religious toleration —by impeaching Dr. Henry Sacheverell, a political preacher, before the House of Lords for a sermon he had delivered attacking the religious principles of the Settlement of 1689. The impeachment proceedings were highly unpopular, and the theologian escaped with a mild sentence, encouraging Queen Anne to turn the Whigs from office, to recall the Tories, and to order new elections. As she foresaw, the Tories were victorious, and they moved at once to withdraw England from the war. The Whigs threw what obstacles they could in the path of peace, even allowing the Occasional Conformity Act to pass, in the hope of compromising with the Tories, and holding as their trump a majority in the House of Lords. This later threat the Tories dealt with by getting Anne to create twelve Tory peers, thus packing the House of Lords to prevent it from obstructing the will of Commons. The move not only made peace possible, but also created an important constitutional precedent. Marlborough was relieved of his command the very day that the House of Lords was packed, and a few months later, in 1712, the army was withdrawn from the Continent. Deprived of English support, the Dutch and Austrians, though outnumbering Villars two to one, were badly mauled by him at Denain; this victory culminated the Bourbon revival beginning in 1709. Peace was clearly necessary, and two treaties were required to produce it.

TREATIES OF UTRECHT AND RASTADT

England, Holland, Savoy, Prussia, and the Bourbon powers made peace at Utrecht in 1713, the Austrians coming to terms with France the following year at Rastadt. If England was the chief gainer, it must be added that the Allied military reverses after 1709 permitted Philip V to retain the Spanish throne, and Louis XIV emerged from the conflict

Below: William III
Bottom: Peter the Great of Russsia

Right top to bottom:
Frederick William,
the Great Elector,
Queen Anne, John Locke

Right:
Gilles by Antoine Watteau
Below: Sans Souci, Potsdam

without territorial loss. Yet, French expansion had been blocked and, in the process, Louis' absolutism suffered a loss in prestige from which the monarchy never fully recovered. The Allies prevented the formation of a great Bourbon empire, and Spain lost continental territories which were really beyond her resources to control: Austria took over Milan, Naples, and the island of Sardinia, while the Spanish Netherlands were first given to the Dutch, who turned them over to the Austrians, hopeful that this arrangement would be the best guarantee of their frontiers against future French expansion.

Except for Gibraltar, which Spain ceded to England, the latter's gains were not in Europe. She received Minorca from Spain and Newfoundland, Nova Scotia, and the Hudson Bay region from France. Spain also granted England the assiento, a monopoly on providing the Spanish colonies with African slaves. The lesser states, Savoy and Prussia, became the preeminent national states in their respective regions: Savoy annexed Sicily, while Prussia received Neuchâtel. Moreover, the Powers recognized the royal title in Prussia. In that all parties benefited, the Peace of Utrecht was a reasonably good settlement; the balance of power was restored on the Continent, and France recognized both the separation of the Spanish and French thrones and the Protestant monarchy in England.

ENGLAND: UNION WITH SCOTLAND AND THE HANOVERIAN SUCCESSION

The war was hardly finished when the succession to the English crown was again in question. Immediately before Anne's accession, Parliament had taken steps to provide for her successor, for as early as 1701, the date of the Act of Settlement, it was clear that she could not provide an heir to the throne. In the spirit of 1689, Parliament named the Electress Sophia of Hanover as Anne's heir. Sophia, a granddaughter of James I, was the ranking Protestant Stuart, though the Catholic James II and his son—in exile—would have had prior claims had the right of dynastic succession been strictly adhered to. Parliament also had to face up to a second problem relating to the succession: The Stuarts, after all, ruled in Scotland as well as England, and the Act of Settlement, conferring the crown upon the House of Hanover, pertained to England alone. The possibility remained that upon Anne's death, the Scots would remain loyal to their native house and invite James II or his son to return to Edinburgh. England would lose the advantage of the close Scottish tie, and the presence of the Catholic pretender north of the border would be a constant menace. Small wonder, then, that the Whigs, who regarded the Revolution of 1689 as a victory for their principles, were determined to assure the Hanoverian succession in England by keeping the Stuarts out of Scotland. In 1707, they proposed the union of England and Scotland and carried the measure through Parliament; the Act of Union created Great Britain by unifying the English and Scottish Parliaments in London, and, automatically, the Hanoverian succession applied in Scotland as well as in England. The Presbyterian Church remained the established church in Scotland.

After 1689, the Tories endured the embarrassment of conflicting principles. Champions of Anglicanism and the unalterable right of dynastic succession, they were driven to the wall in 1688 when a Roman Catholic dynasty seemed likely unless Parliament interfered with the succession. This dilemma agonized the Tory party for the next half-century and prepared the ground for a long Whig ascendancy. In 1701, for instance, the Tories could not really approve the Act of Settlement as it altered the succession to the throne; but to have opposed it successfully would have given the Anglican Church a Catholic governor. Inevitably, the Whig politicians saw to it that the House of Hanover was made aware of the lack of Tory enthusiasm for the Hanoverian succession, and Tory misery deepened with the realization that the Hanoverians would govern through the Whigs.

Anne lay dying in 1714 before the Tories made a move in their own interest. The Queen had done her patriotic best to implement her Tory sentiments, but none of her seventeen children had survived. Led by Viscount Bolingbroke, the Tories rose from their political paralysis to negotiate with the son of James II, apparently preferring to risk a Francophile Catholic king than the political oblivion to which the Hanoverian succession would relegate them. We can only speculate as to whether Tory chances to repeal the Act of Settlement would have been better in 1710, when the Whigs were somewhat discredited for their prolongation of the war; but in 1714, the Tories moved too late. Anne died before they could complete their maneuvers, and the Hanoverian succession was a fact. As Sophia of Hanover had died several months before Anne, the heir was Sophia's son George, the first of his name to rule (*1714–1727*).

THE RISE OF PRUSSIA

In recognizing the royal title in Prussia by the treaty of Utrecht in 1713, the Western Powers declared their acceptance of Prussia as a significant member of the European power structure. The title applied to Prussia alone, though the king also had lesser titles deriving from other territorial possessions; he was Elector of Brandenburg, Duke of Pomerania, Magdeburg, and Cleve, Count of Mark and Ravensburg, and Prince of Halberstadt and Minden. These territories had been slowly collected by the Hohenzollern family, and only in the seventeenth century was the royal power consolidated at the expense of the estates (legislatures) in the various territories.

The Prussian state traced its origins to the Teutonic Knights, a medieval crusading order which had seen service against Islam. In 1226, a Polish nobleman, eager for assistance against the native Prussian population, invited the Knights to subdue and convert the Prussians. This campaign completed, the Knights extended their operations northward along the Baltic coast until they claimed sovereignty over the coastal regions from the Vistula to the Gulf of Finland. A fighting aristocracy, the Knights brought in German peasants to work the land, and the void between these colonists and their landlords remained vast. The union of Poland and Lithuania in 1386 produced an enormous state which constituted the first serious threat to the Knights' position along the Baltic. War came in 1409, and Poland-Lithuania found considerable support from the native Prussian population. At Tannenberg, in 1410, the Slavs broke the power of the Knights, whose authority continued to weaken in the fifteenth century. The cession of West Prussia to Poland in 1466 cut off East Prussia from the rest of the German world and forced the East Prussian Knights to become vassals of Poland.

Early in the sixteenth century, the Knights fell upon the expedient of electing as their grandmasters relatives of powerful German princes, for they hoped that such dynastic ties would invite German help against the Poles. In 1511, for example, the Knights elected Albert of Hohenzollern, a cousin of the Elector Joachim I of Brandenburg. Ironically, it was Albert who actually dissolved the Teutonic Order in 1525; he had become a Lutheran, and the order had, of course been Catholic. The Poles were only too willing to permit him to dissolve the order and gave him the title of Duke of Prussia to replace the title of Grandmaster. After the death of Albert in 1568, the Prussian estates were able to make serious inroads on the power of his successors and were inspired by the success of the Polish nobility in limiting central power in Poland.

Nearly a century later, in 1618, the Hohenzollern tie became more significant when the Elector of Brandenburg, John Sigismund, also became Duke of Prussia. His territories were not contiguous, it is true, but the very fact of separation served as a spur to make the personal union a geographical and political reality. Yet, his accession coincided with the Thirty Years War, and its turbulences prevented further political progress. Only with the accession of Frederick William (*1640–1688*) as Elector of Brandenburg and Duke of Prussia do we see the deliberate attempt to consolidate executive power at the expense of the liberties of the estates. Known to history as the Great Elector, Frederick William shared the faith of absolutism common to the rulers of his century; and to establish absolutism, he followed the general pattern already sketched out by those who had earlier reduced the power of the nobility. He must have, first of all, an efficient bureaucracy, which would usurp the obligations of local government, a bureaucracy loyal to the crown; he must have an efficient standing army, both to free himself from dependence upon the fighting aristocracy and to support his foreign policy; and that foreign policy must be aggressive, to aggrandize the crown territorially.

These North German territories, over which the Great Elector presided so ably for forty-eight years, were poor of soil, while inadequate port facilities limited the possibilities of trade. These factors, together with the wreckage resulting from the Thirty Years War, had kept economic development low. When he assumed power in 1640, much of Brandenburg was occupied by Imperial and Swedish troops, who were even more destructive than the Elector's own unreliable, rapacious mercenaries. But Frederick William was equal to these liabilities; as fond of physical exercise as he was of learning, he went to Holland as a young man to study military science and Dutch agricultural and commercial techniques, preparing himself well for his princely obligations.

The Westphalia settlement (1648) was a disappointment for Brandenburg. The Swedes kept much of Pomerania, Brandenburg being awarded only less valuable bits of the province, for at that point Frederick William's dependable standing army, begun in 1644, numbered only 8000. Even so, after 1648 the Hohenzollerns ranked second only to the Hapsburgs in the German world. In 1655, when the First Northern War broke out, Frederick William still felt himself too weak to resist Swedish invasion, even though, as a vassal of the Polish King in Prussia, Frederick William had an obligation to side with Poland against Sweden. He declared his neutrality and went on with military improvements, but found himself financially obstructed by the Brandenburg estates, which resented the logic of voting funds for the defense of East Prussia against Sweden. The Elector responded by collecting taxes with force, successfully intimidating the estates and establishing an ominous precedent for their future.

The early defeat of Charles X (*1654–1660*) of Sweden by John Casimir of Poland (*1648–1668*) led Frederick William to abandon his neutrality in favor of a Swedish alliance. He joined in an attack upon Warsaw in 1656, but though the Allies were momentarily successful, the Poles showed signs of a notable recovery. To maintain the Brandenburg alliance, Charles X formally recognized Frederick William as sovereign in Prussia; but despite this concession, Frederick William switched sides in 1657 upon Poland's willingness to recognize his full sovereignty in East Prussia. This arrangement was more suitable to Hohenzollern ambitions, for it was their desire to drive the Swedes out of Pomerania. When peace came in 1660 at Oliva, Frederick's sovereignty was recognized in Prussia. In Brandenburg, he remained part of the Holy Roman Empire, but in Prussia he was an independent ruler.

Meanwhile, the Brandenburg estates had been increasingly reluctant to grant the collection of taxes after the inauguration of the standing army in 1644. By 1653, with tempers growing thin all around, the estates granted annual tax collection for the succeeding six years, and the monarch employed this six-year interim cleverly by accustoming local tax collectors to serving him. For six years, they collected taxes at his command, though by consent of the estates; after 1659, Frederick William commanded the collection of taxes without summoning the estates for their consent. The Prussian estates proved more stubborn than their Brandenburg counterpart, especially after 1660, when Frederick William's sovereignty had been recognized in East Prussia by Poland. The East Prussian nobility, having been enthusiastic for the liberties enjoyed by the Polish nobility, connived with the Poles, in the hope of resisting Hohenzollern absolutism, and provoked Frederick William to imprison one of the leaders of the noble opposition. In 1663, the Prussian estates yielded and recognized his sovereignty; in turn, he recognized their traditional rights except in cases where those rights infringed upon his own. Opposition, however, did not cease and led, in 1671, to the torture and execution of a leading nobleman, von Kalckstein. His death helped the Prussian nobility see the wisdom of submission, and the estates shortly became impotent, finally disappearing as an instrument of government in 1705.

In matters religious, the developing Hohenzollern absolutism was notably more tolerant than the other European despotisms. Toleration derived in part from the fact that the Hohenzollerns were Calvinist, while most of their subjects were Lutheran. Moreover, toleration was part of a deliberate policy of encouraging immigration in the seventeenth century. The new standing army was at first largely recruited abroad, which had the ultimate effect of increasing the foreign-born population of Brandenburg, and during the last thirty years of the century, nearly 20,000 Huguenot refugees from France were welcomed. Many of them were artisans and professionals, skilled beyond their Brandenburg-Prussian contemporaries, and Frederick William was enthusiastic for the stimulation they could provide for the development of his low-level economy.

The royal title was acquired not by the Great Elector but by his successor, Frederick III (*1688–1713*), who, crowned "King of Prussia" in 1701, restyled himself as Frederick I. This was made possible by the international crisis over the Spanish Succession in 1700, in which Frederick offered to support the Imperial claim to the Spanish throne with 8000 troops in exchange for Imperial recognition of the royal title in Prussia. Since Prussia was outside the Empire, the royal title did not affect the Imperial electoral system, which would have been the case had the Elector of Brandenburg become king. Accordingly, the coronation took place in Königsberg in Prussia, not in Berlin, capital of Brandenburg and the real center of the monarch's power. (Indeed, Berlin was becoming a center of cultural distinction as well, if we remember that 1700 saw the establishment there of the Academy of Sciences with Leibniz as its first president.)

Brandenburg-Prussia, with territories scattered in western and eastern Europe, was concerned with both the great European wars which broke out at the turn of the eighteenth century. Territorially, Frederick stood to gain most in the East from Sweden and Poland, but neither Charles XII nor Peter the Great found the subsidies necessary to secure an alliance with Frederick. As a result, Frederick joined the Grand Alliance against Louis XIV, fulfilling his coronation oath to the Emperor Leopold and throwing himself into the role of protecting German interests in the West against French expansion. Prussian contingents joined the Allied armies, fought with distinction, and won several bits of territory, including Neuchâtel, for Prussia at the Peace of Utrecht (1713). Under Frederick William I (*1713–1740*), Prussia joined in with the powers fighting the Great Northern War, allying with Peter the Great against Sweden in 1714. The reward for this was the eastern part of Swedish Pomerania and the port of Stettin (1720).

Frederick William I continued the deliberate absolutist policy of his two predecessors and contributed to the military atmosphere of his state. Often wearing a military uniform himself, he insisted that young noblemen regard military service in the royal army as obligatory, an attitude reminiscent of Peter the Great. The aristocracy, earlier hostile to the rise of royal power, became accustomed to royal service in this period, in part because the social distinction of the military had been considerably enhanced by the example of the King.

PHILOSOPHY AND SCIENCE

At the turn of the eighteenth century, after a century of scientific and theological genius and of political innovation, European intellectual life was centered in Britain and France. Moreover, these two nations illustrated the political antitheses of the seventeenth century, inviting vigorous political analysis. If we dared to list one quality characteristic of most thought after the publication of the *Principia mathematica* and the Revolution of 1689, it would be *optimism*—no matter whether the speculation was political, scientific, or about the nature of man himself.

In 1690, one of the important Whig politicians, John Locke (1632–1704), published his *Second Treatise on Government*. It was, first of all, an apology for the Revolution of 1689, a philosophical statement demonstrating that Parliament had had every right—in fact, an obligation—to depose James II; but so effective was his demonstration that it was to be used more generally in the eighteenth century by the critics of royal despotism in America and France. Earlier, both Hobbes and Filmer had denied the right of a people to overthrow its ruler (though they differed greatly in their reasons for deploring rebellion). Locke, in affirming the right to rebel, chose to attack Filmer, possibly because Filmer's views on divine right were shared by James II, possibly because Hobbes—an atheist—was not taken seriously in the seventeenth century. Yet, Filmer's arguments were losing their relevance by the end of that century, while

Hobbes' ideas became increasingly influential with the passage of time. Furthermore, a "debate" between Hobbes and Locke would have been more revealing, since as they began on common ground: the acceptance of the social-contract theory.

Both Hobbes and Locke agreed that men were free in the state of nature and that governments were freely instituted by consent of the governed; but they differed about human nature. Hobbes was pessimistic, Locke optimistic. Hobbes, holding that man's nature made him rapacious, saw the state of nature as a state of war. Locke, considering man as fundamentally reasonable, concluded that he was aware of the inadvisability of harming other people or their property. Consequently, Hobbes was much more fearful of a return to the state of nature than Locke, arguing that even the most tyrannical of governments, because they preserve order, must be preferred to the anarchy which would follow rebellion. Locke, in emphasizing man's natural right to life, liberty, and property, saw reasonable men organizing governments to protect these natural rights. And believing that government was an instrument to preserve these natural rights of men and not simply an instrument to preserve order at all costs, Locke justified rebellion when government had ceased to protect those natural rights. Locke had the advantage, of course, of writing after the Revolution of 1689; he knew that a change of government could be achieved without dissolving the bands of society.

The Stuart "Leviathan," in his view, had overstepped his boundaries, threatened the natural rights of Englishmen and their representatives in Parliament. There must be some way, in establishing a government, to make it difficult for that government to violate the natural rights of men. Locke's proposal became the standard answer for the eighteenth century: keep separate the three governing powers—the executive, legislative, and judicial—so that they would act as checks upon each other. This separation would in particular facilitate the overthrow of the executive authority if it became abusive.

Locke's views on private property also became part of the gospel for enlightened men of the eighteenth century because Locke had made property part of the trinity of natural rights. According to him, since God gave the earth to men in common, nobody originally had any private property. But a man's labor was his own, and Locke suggested that a man acquired property by "mixing" his labor with it, and that every man had an equal right to appropriate what he *needed* from the state of nature; no one, however, should take more property than he can use, for God did not create anything to be wasted. In this way Locke justified large landholdings as long as the land was being cultivated properly—a concept as pleasing to the great Whig landowners as the notion that common land might be enclosed as private property without its being called theft. In this light, it is notable than the many Enclosure Acts by Parliament in the eighteenth century were generally justified on the grounds that enclosing common land would lead to its more productive use. It is also well to note that Locke wrote at a time when, thanks to America, the opportunities to acquire new land seemed unlimited.

Like Hobbes, John Locke was interested in how we acquire knowledge, and though Locke is often called the "father of empiricism" (the belief that knowledge comes from experience), he really popularized ideas already held by Hobbes. Fundamental was the notion that we are born without innate ideas:

Let us suppose the mind to be, as we say, white paper, void of all characters, without any ideas:—how comes it to be furnished? . . . To this I answer, in one word, from EXPERIENCE. In that all our knowledge is founded; and from that it ultimately derives itself. Our observation employed either about external sensible objects, or about the internal operations of our minds perceived and reflected on by ourselves, is that which supplies our understandings with all the *materials* of thinking. These two are the fountains of knowledge, from whence all the ideas we have, or can naturally have, do spring.[1]

The question of acquiring knowledge raised the problem of divine revelation. Were there some things beyond the ken of human reason which must, therefore, be revealed to men by God? Locke, who was both a serious Christian and a student of Descartes and Newton, shared the scientific optimism of his time. Certain that the world is a perfect machine operating according to God-given laws and confident in human reason's capacity to understand those laws, Locke could see little "need or use of revelation." As he put it, "God [has] furnished us with natural and surer means to arrive at a knowledge of them."[2]

Locke's scientific optimism was shared by his great German contemporary, Gottfried Wilhelm von Leibniz (1646–1716), and for essentially

1. John Locke, *An Essay Concerning Human Understanding* (1690), Book II.
2. *Ibid.*, Book IV.

the same reason: he saw the rationality of the universe and concluded that of all the logically possible worlds, a benevolent God had inevitably made the best. As the greatest poet of that age put it:

> If plagues or earthquakes break not Heaven's design,
> Why then a Borgia, or a Catiline?
> Who knows but He, whose hand the lightning forms,
> Who heaves old Ocean, and who wings the storms;
> Pours fierce ambition in a Caesar's mind,
> Or turns young Ammon loose to scourge mankind?
> From pride, from pride, our very reasoning springs;
> Account for moral as for natural things:
> Why charge we Heaven in those, in these acquit?
> In both, to reason right is to submit.
>
> . . .
>
> All Nature is but Art, unknown to thee;
> All Chance, Direction, which thou canst not see;
> All Discord, Harmony not understood;
> All partial Evil, universal Good:
> And, spite of Pride, in erring Reason's spite,
> One truth is clear, WHATEVER IS, IS RIGHT.[3]

With his faith in the rationality of the universe and God's logic, Leibniz believed that human reason should be an imitation of God's logic; and he saw no distinction between logic and mathematics. As for Kepler, Descartes, and Newton, so for Leibniz: mathematics was the rational discipline that held the key to the universe. With clear, uniform notation, all the necessary truths could be established by mechanical calculations. The first problem was to find a few principles, universal and eternal, from which hypotheses could be deduced.

To find such universal truths, Leibniz suggested the use of several "axioms." The first was the Law of Non-contradiction: A given proposition and its opposite cannot both be true; therefore, any proposition which permits contradiction is absurd. To put it another way, the predicate must simply state the properties of the subject, and nothing more. This is the test for truths of reason. His second "axiom" was the Principle of Sufficient Reason, in which he stated that for every truth a reason must be given, "or, in the common phrase, that nothing happens without a cause."[4] This was his test for truths of fact.

3. Alexander Pope, *Essay on Man* (1733), Epistle I, ll. 155-164, 289-294.
4. *New Essays on Human Understanding* (1703-04), first published 1765, pp. 83, 99.

Leibniz was one of the most universal men of his time, writing in three languages, working in science, mathematics (he and Newton both discovered the calculus), politics, and theology. For a time he corresponded with Bossuet, in the hope of reuniting the Christian sects into one Church; he persuaded the Elector of Brandenburg to found an Academy of Sciences in Berlin (1700) and became its first president; his efforts to have similar institutions founded in Dresden and Vienna failed, but his letters to Peter the Great undoubtedly contributed to the establishment of the Russian Academy of Sciences somewhat later.

A distinctive feature of Leibniz's thought was his monadology, which led to disagreement with John Locke on the question of innate ideas. In his observations of Nature, Leibniz had been struck by the gradations of organisms—fish with wings, for instance, and birds which lived on the water. Even drops of water, when placed under the new microscopes, seemed to be teeming with life. He came to regard the universe as composed of tiny particles—a kind of atomic theory, except that he believed the particles to be living, unlike lifeless atoms—and he called them monads (life principles), the ultimate substances of life. He regarded the perceptions of a monad as innate, as part of its inner nature.

Bernard de Mandeville (1670–1733) was a younger contemporary of Locke and Leibniz. A Dutchman, Mandeville had come to England in 1691. In 1705, he turned out a piece in two hundred couplets entitled *The Grumbling Hive, or the Knaves Turn'd Honest,* which is more generally known as the *Fable of the Bees.* A political satire on government in England, it criticized the Whigs for pushing the war against France for personal reasons. Apart from the political implications of the fable, its view of human nature was highly irritating to a generation fired with optimism and certain that the rationality of the universe guaranteed the progress of mankind. According to Mandeville, virtue is hypocrisy, and man advances only through his vices and selfishness; "private vices are public benefits." He depicted the society of the hive, full of contented and honest bees living in rational order, as the prelude to apathy and decay.

In Bernard Le Bovier de Fontenelle (1657–1757), a Frenchman, science enjoyed a great popularizer; his work was the bridge between the science of the seventeenth century and the science-based philosophy of the eighteenth century. A literary man, he hoped to make science amusing reading, even for ladies. His *Discussions on the Plurality of Worlds* (1686), a series of chats between an astronomer and a lady, was an understandable description of the Cartesian universe in which the suns and planets were sustained by a mysterious celestial fluid, the sun being the center of a vortex around which the planets revolved. This Cartesian cosmology was outdated the following year with the publication of Newton's *Principia mathematica,* but Fontenelle had succeeded in making the heliocentric theory comprehensible to the public. Deservedly titled Permanent Secretary of the Academy of Sciences, Fontenelle held the post from 1699 to 1741. One of his obligations was to write funeral orations for scientists who died during that period, summarizing their lives and works. Nowhere is Fontenelle's literary skill and scientific knowledge better seen than in these eulogies, which were never hypocritical paeans of unrelieved praise, but included subtle, tactful exposés of the weaknesses of a man's ideas or work. Finally, he wrote many popular books recording scientific advancement.

Fontenelle believed that each generation would continue to derive advantages from the advances made by its predecessors. If there were not some unforeseen physical or mental degeneration in man, or if such adverse environmental conditions as wars, epidemics, famines, and persecutions did not hinder the development of the great men in a given age, the advance of human knowledge ought to be limitless. He was much more pessimistic about the possibility of improving human nature, for the laws of nature are unchanging. Some historians believe that Fontenelle's pessimism derived more from literary than from scientific sources, from Machiavelli and Montaigne in particular.

JOURNALISM AND LITERATURE

With the triumph of parliamentary prerogatives and the rise of political parties in England came the development of periodical literature. The earliest newspaper is said to have been the *London Gazette* (1665), but not until the turn of the eighteenth century did journals achieve political, social, and literary significance. Presenting essays and commentaries on the questions of current interest, the journals were primarily concerned with criticism and satire; but they also served as important outlets for creative writing. The *Daily Courant,* which appeared in 1702, was the first daily journal, and two years later Daniel Defoe (1659–1731) began publishing the *Review* (1704–1713), which appeared two or three times a week. Something of an opportunist, Defoe wrote many pamphlets in support of William III, but in moments of Tory supremacy, he managed to switch sides. Defoe, of course, is better known as a writer of realistic fiction, a form leading directly to the novel: *Robinson Crusoe* (1719), *The Fortunes and Misfortunes of Moll Flanders* (1722), and *Roxana, or The Fortunate Mistress* (1724).

Most of the satirical writers of this period were Tories; indeed, satirists are likely to be conservative in any age. Two exceptions were the Whig writers Joseph Addison (1672–1719) and Sir Richard Steele (1672–1729). In 1709 Steele brought out *The Tatler,* which succumbed two years later to a combination of financial and political pressures. In 1711 Steele joined Addison in a new venture, *The Spectator,* the purpose of which, as Addison put it, was "to banish vice and ignorance out of the territories of Great Britain. . . . I shall endeavor to enliven morality with wit and to temper wit with morality."[5] Many other writers, including Swift, contributed to *The Spectator,* but Addison remained the pre-eminent figure.

Jonathan Swift (1667–1745), the most embittered of the Tory satirists, despised mankind in general and Irishmen in particular. Born in Ireland, he lived much of his life among the Irish, whose miserable lot he worked to improve. He served for a time as secretary to Sir William Temple, a retired politician, and thus came to the attention of William III, who gave him an ecclesiastical living in Ireland in 1695. In 1704, Swift achieved notoriety with his *The Tale of a Tub,* a polemic on the weaknesses of mankind in which he attacked Catholics, Calvinists, and Anglicans alike; the work offended Queen Anne. Yet, he attained the height of his prestige in 1710 when the Tories came briefly to power. He favored immediate peace with France and castigated the Whigs for their military policies, a theme to which he returned somewhat later in *Gulliver's Travels:*

His Majesty desired I would take some other Opportunity of bringing all the rest of his Enemy's Ships into his Ports. And so unmeasurable is the Ambition of Princes, that he seemed to think of nothing less than reducing the whole Empire of *Blefuscu* [France] into a Province, and governing it by a Vice-Roy; of destroying the *Big-Endian* [Jacobite] Exiles, and compelling that People to break the smaller end of their Eggs [to take communion in the fashion of the dissenters], by which he would remain the sole Monarch of the whole World. But I endeavoured to divert him from this Design, by many Arguments drawn from the Topicks of Policy as well as Justice. And I plainly protested that I would never be an Instrument of bringing a Free and Brave

5. *The Spectator,* March 1, 1711.

People into Slavery. And when the Matter was debated in Council, the wisest part of the Ministry were of my opinion.[6]

His pamphlets on behalf of Tory policies earned him the Deanship of St. Patrick's in Dublin in 1713, but the following year, when the Tories fell from power, Swift lost his political influence and became increasingly disillusioned. *Gulliver's Travels* was projected as early as 1714, though it was not finished until 1726, and contained some of the purest hatred for mankind ever penned:

I replied that England (the dear place of my nativity) was computed to produce three times the quantity of food, more than its inhabitants are able to consume, as well as liquors extracted from grain, or pressed out of the fruit of certain trees, which made excellent drink, and the same proportion in every other convenience of life. But, in order to feed the luxury and intemperance of the males, and the vanity of the females, we sent away the greatest part of our necessary things to other countries, from whence in return we brought the materials of diseases, folly, and vice, to spend among ourselves. Hence it follows of necessity that vast numbers of our people are compelled to seek their livelihood by begging, robbing, stealing, cheating, pimping, forswearing, flattering, suborning, forging, gaming, lying, fawning, hectoring, voting, scribbling, star-gazing, poisoning, whoring, canting, libelling, freethinking, and the like occupations: everyone of which terms, I was at much pains to make him understand. . . .

By what I could discover, the Yahoos [men] appear to be the most unteachable of all animals, their capacities never reaching higher than to draw or carry burdens. Yet I am of opinion this defect ariseth chiefly from a perverse, restive disposition. For they are cunning, malicious, treacherous, and revengeful. They are strong and hardy, but of a cowardly spirit, and by consequence, insolent, abject, and cruel.[7]

Jean de La Bruyère (1645–1696) was the French counterpart of Addison, Steele, and Swift. He wrote "in miniature," his chapters being hardly more than paragraphs, and his French usage was notable for its correctness. Best known today for his maxims, he also wrote literary and ethical criticism and sarcastic sketches of individuals, Fontenelle being one of his noteworthy victims. The nobility, whom he castigated as a useless social group, were also stung by his thrusts. The influential retaliated by defeating his candidacy for the Academy, to which he was not admitted until 1693. (His *Caractères* had appeared in 1688). Somewhat earlier than La Bruyère we find the most famous of all French epigramists, the Duc François de

---

6. Jonathan Swift, *Gulliver's Travels* (1726), "A Voyage to Lilliput," Ch. V.
7. *Ibid.*, "A Voyage to the Houyhnhnms," Chs. VI, VIII.

La Rochefoucauld (1613–1680). Best known for his *Réflexions ou Sentences et Maximes morales* (1665), La Rochefoucauld expanded his masterpiece through several editions until, by 1678, it contained more than five hundred maxims. Regarding every human action as selfish, he denied the possibility of disinterestedness, and stressed that even our generous acts are selfish: "We are so accustomed to disguising ourselves before others that we end in deceiving ourselves."[8] An examination of La Rochefoucauld's career will verify that he, at least, was incapable of disinterested acts; but no one denies the brilliance of his wit.

Alexander Pope (1688–1744), the greatest English poet of the early eighteenth century, was inclined to Toryism like so many of his literary contemporaries. Born a Catholic, he was excluded from regular schools on religious grounds and received his education from tutors and wide reading. He became an admirer of Dryden and Boileau and used the closed couplet form which they had made fashionable. His *Essay on Man* (1733) remains the most famous of his works, and since it is the epitome of eighteenth-century philosophic optimism, it has been customary to think of Pope as the Leibniz of verse. Yet, his fame was made much earlier with *An Essay on Criticism* (1711), which revealed him as a master of the closed couplet. His didactic verses are particularly quotable:

> First follow Nature, and your judgment frame
> By her just standard, which is still the same:
> Unerring NATURE, still divinely bright,
> One clear, unchanged, and universal light,
> Life, force, and beauty, must to all impart,
> At once the source, and end, and test of Art.
>
> . . .
>
> A *little learning* is a dangerous thing;
> Drink deep, or taste not the Pierian spring;
> There shallow draughts intoxicate the brain,
> And drinking largely sobers us again.[9]

THE ROCOCO: ARCHITECTURE, ART, AND MUSIC

Around the turn of the eighteenth century, a new decorative style, the rococo, developed on the Continent. At first, rococo merely influenced

8. Maxim 119. My translation.
9. Alexander Pope, *An Essay on Criticism,* ll. 68-73, 215-218.

interior decoration, but soon its spirit spread to architecture, painting, and, to a lesser extent, music. In essence, rococo was an attempt to give color, privacy, and comfort to the massive, theatrical, impersonal structures of the baroque period. The desired effects were first achieved in great houses by using large windows, opposing mirrors, and cool colors; for privacy, smaller dwellings were built in the vicinity of the great houses and palaces. At Marly, for example, Pierre Lepautre redecorated the apartments of the French royal family to achieve a lighter, more intimate atmosphere. Then, this rather simple house was surrounded by twelve small private houses for guests. Similarly, the Grand Trianon and the Petit Trianon were built as "refuges" from Versailles, and in Munich the Amalienburg was built to give relief from the Nymphenburg.

As the rococo style was a reaction against the formality of the baroque, it was inevitably a reaction against the academic standards in architecture and design. Greater variations in style were soon evident, but if the trend was away from pomposity, the end result was not simplicity, but increased luxury and comfort. The revolt against the rigid baroque forms produced a lavish decoration, often characterized by dainty and exotic designs. It is notable that in France there was no "dictator" of the arts from Le Brun's death in 1690 until the time of Jacques Louis David during the French Revolution. Decorative fads flourished unblighted by academic control: sometimes Gothicisms, more often *chinoiseries* (decorations based on Chinese scenes and objects), and for a time *singeries* (decorations featuring humanized monkeys).

In Germany, the baroque and the rococo styles were often combined. The Residenz in Würzburg, for instance, begun as late as 1720, is often considered second only to Versailles as a baroque masterpiece; its interior decoration alone shows rococo influence. Later in the century, Frederick the Great built massively at Potsdam, permitting only his personal residence, Sans Souci, to be an intimate rococo structure. When rococo was used in Germany, the extravagance of ornamentation was generally greater than in France, often creating a heavy, rather than the desired light, effect. The English remained loyal to the architectural traditions of Jones and Wren, but the French rococo influence can be seen in the celebrated furniture designs of Chippendale, especially in his use of the C-scroll.

It has been claimed that medieval houses were more comfortable than those of the seventeenth century, because baroque architects were indifferent to functionalism. A great banquet at Versailles would have been spectacular theater, but the food would have been cold, so great was the distance between kitchens and dining hall. By contrast, the desire for private life, characteristic of rococo, led architects to value comforts in the home. Consequently, the house became more functional—more rational —in the eighteenth century and showed a greater concern for cleanliness and decency. The water closet originally invented by Sir John Harington during the reign of Elizabeth, did not find acceptance until the early eighteenth century. By 1740, it was standard equipment in most great houses and was known on the continent as *chaise à l'Anglais,* the English-style chair.

The lightness of the rococo spirit invaded the realm of painting too, and the massiveness of Le Brun's school gave way to more delicate works by men such as Antoine Watteau (1648–1721), works which are suggestive of the frivolous society which characterized the eighteenth century. This period also saw two great portrait painters who, between them, have furnished us portraits of nearly every great political and military figure of the late seventeenth and early eighteenth centuries: Hyacinthe Rigaud (French, 1659–1743) and Sir Godfrey Kneller (1648–1723), regarded as English though German-born.

Musicologists rarely recognize the rococo as a separate and distinct period in the history of music. Yet, the harpsichord sonatas of Domenico Scarlatti (1685–1757) are an excellent example of the lavish ornamentation characteristic of the rococo, and a contemporary harpsichordist, Domenico Alberti (1717?–?1740) popularized a type of bass, still bearing his name, which broke massive chords into an ornamental pattern.

The splendors and frivolity of rococo overdecoration and artificiality strike us as entirely incongruous with an age deeply committed to a vision of universal order and to a faith in the rational simplicity of nature. The irony of rococo should warn us against forcing cultural syntheses too far.

SUGGESTIONS FOR FURTHER READING

≥≤

General and Political History

John B. Wolf, *The Emergence of the Great Powers 1685-1715* (New York: Harper, 1951, excellent study supported by extensive bibliography.

Also see Ogg, Clark, and Ashley, works cited in Chapter 1.

G. M. Trevelyan, *England Under Queen Anne,* 3 vols. (London and New York: Longmans, Green, 1930), magnificent historical literature.

Sidney B. Fay, *The Rise of Brandenburg-Prussia to 1786* (New York: Henry Holt, 1937), dated but still useful.

Cambridge History of Poland: From Augustus II to Pilsudski 1697-1935 (Cambridge University Press, 1941), the best available.

Oscar Halecki, *A History of Poland* (London: J. M. Dent and Sons, rev. ed., 1955), brief and not notably objective.

Sir Bernard Pares, *A History of Russia* (New York: Alfred A Knopf, 5th ed. 1950), a classic work in this field, now somewhat dated.

Keith Feiling, *A History of the Tory Party* (Oxford: The Clarendon Press, 1924), an important counterweight to the Whiggish tradition represented by Trevelyan, Ogg, and Clark.

B. H. Sumner, *Peter the Great and the Emergence of Russia* (New York: Macmillan, 1951).

Cultural and Intellectual History

*Sir Isaiah Berlin, *The Age of Enlightenment* (New York: Mentor, 1956).

*See also the works of Willey, Hampshire, Randall, and Butterfield cited for Chapter 1.

G. N. Clark, *Science and Social Welfare in the Age of Newton* (Oxford: The Clarendon Press, 1937).

S. F. Kimball, *Creation of the Rococo* (Philadelphia Museum of Art, 1943), see especially for architecture.

P. Hazard, *The European Mind 1680-1715* (Yale University Press, 1935), a major work.

Arno Schönberger and Halldor Soehner, *The Rococo Age* (New York: McGraw-Hill, 1962).

* Available in paperbound editions.

❧ 3 ❧

The Enlightenment
and the Old Regime
in the Eighteenth Century

THE PHILOSOPHES AND THE ENLIGHTENMENT

The brilliant successes in science during the seventeenth century led the men of the eighteenth to apply scientific methods to the solution of problems not strictly scientific; the science of the seventeenth century led directly to the science-based philosophies of the eighteenth century, an era known as the Enlightenment. Repeatedly in history one finds this tendency to apply a successful method or technique to an unrelated problem or problems, perhaps reflecting our deep-seated hope that all mysteries can ultimately be unraveled by a single key. Even the great Newton, so complex himself, was persuaded that the universe was simple and subject to simple analysis.

Enlightenment! The very word suggests optimism, and the hopefulness derived from the intellectual revolution summed up in the work of Newton and Locke. The universe was seemingly a rational mechanism; and man, happily a rational creature, possessed, through mathematics, the power to comprehend and describe the universe. Moreover, man, too, was part of this geometrical, mechanical nature, and thus subject to rational analysis; it followed logically that once the mechanical laws governing man and his societies were discovered, just and virtuous societies could be created. It remained, of course, to discover the various natural laws governing all aspects of life, but the intellectuals of the eighteenth century (we often

79

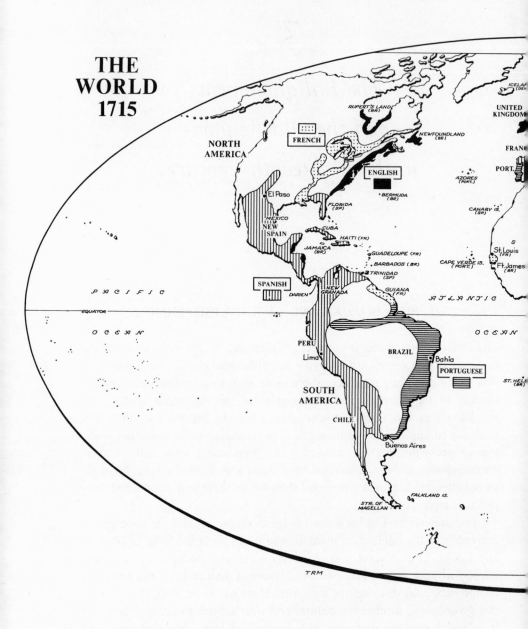

THE
WORLD
1715

NORTH
AMERICA

FRENCH

ENGLISH

RUPERT'S LAND
(BR)

NEWFOUNDLAND
(BR)

ICELAND
(DEN)

UNITED
KINGDOM

FRANCE

PORT.

AZORES
(PORT.)

BERMUDA
(BR)

El Paso

MEXICO

NEW
SPAIN

FLORIDA
(SP)

CUBA

CANARY IS.
(SP)

HAITI (FR)

JAMAICA
(BR)

GUADELOUPE (FR)

BARBADOS (BR)

CAPE VERDE IS.
(PORT.)

S

St. Louis
(FR)

Ft. James
(BR)

SPANISH

DARIEN

NEW
GRANADA

TRINIDAD
(SP)

GUIANA
(FR)

PACIFIC

EQUATOR

ATLANTIC

OCEAN

PERU

Lima

BRAZIL

Bahia

PORTUGUESE

OCEAN

ST. HELENA
(BR)

SOUTH
AMERICA

CHILE

Buenos Aires

STR. OF
MAGELLAN

FALKLAND IS.

TRM

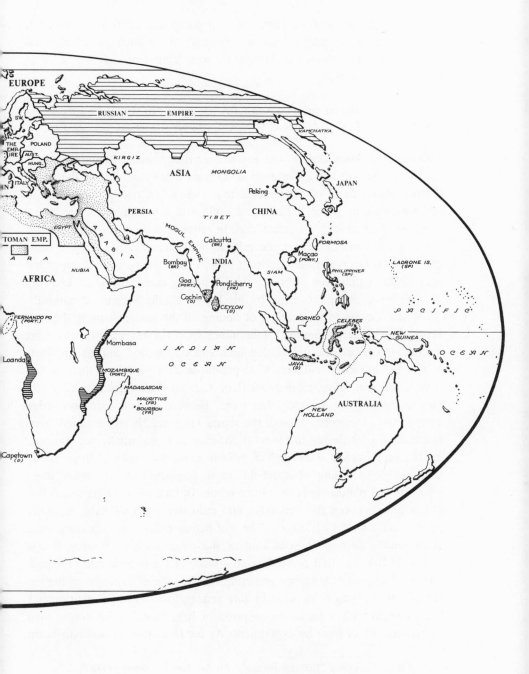

EUROPE

RUSSIAN EMPIRE

SW.

THE
EMP.
IRE

POLAND

AUST.
HUNG.

KIRGIZ

ASIA

MONGOLIA

JAPAN

N

ITALY

PERSIA

CHINA

Peking

KAMCHATKA

EGYPT

MOGUL

TIBET

TOMAN EMP.

ARABIA

EMPIRE

Calcutta
(BR)

FORMOSA

Macao
(PORT.)

LADRONE IS.
(SP)

A R A

NUBIA

Bombay
(BR)

INDIA

Philippines
(SP)

AFRICA

Goa
(PORT.)

Pondicherry
(FR)

SIAM

P A C I F I C

Cochin
(D)

CEYLON
(D)

BORNEO

CELEBES
(D)

FERNANDO PO
(PORT.)

Mombasa

I N D I A N

NEW
GUINEA

O C E A N

Loanda

MOZAMBIQUE
(PORT.)

O C E A N

JAVA
(D)

MADAGASCAR

MAURITIUS
(FR)

Capetown
(D)

BOURBON
(FR)

NEW
HOLLAND

AUSTRALIA

call them the *philosophes,* a freewheeling group interested in science, art, politics, and philosophy), fired by Newton's description of all physical motion, whether celestial or terrestrial, were confident that further successes were imminent:

> Nature and Nature's Laws lay hid in Night;
> God said, 'Let Newton be!' and all was Right.[1]

The moment when man would know everything about his universe was apparently near at hand. Certainly there were a few doubters in the eighteenth century, those who suspected that men might not be analogous to other animals or other objects; but optimistic rationalism remained the dominant note to such an extent that, in retrospect, the eighteenth century seems the last in our history generally to hold human omniscience obtainable. Here is Georges-Louis Buffon (1707–1788) giving us the faith of the age: "What enthusiasm is nobler than believing man capable of knowing all the forces and discovering by his labors all the secrets of nature!"[2]

When it came to the *method* of finding all the laws governing the universe, the eighteenth century's inheritance from the seventeenth was a bit more clouded, because it included both rationalism and empiricism. Descartes, for instance, had taught suspicion of data perceived through the senses, recommending mathematical or rational demonstrations of truth. Hobbes and Locke, on the other hand, believed that all our knowledge comes from experience, through the senses (they are therefore called "sensationalists"). Believing in observation, they were essentially recommending the experimental method. Yet, we can make too much of these differences in method and obscure the more important views which these scientists and philosophers held in common. In fact, even the hard-and-fast distinctions between the deductive and inductive methods have generally been overdrawn by historians. The distinction exists, but scientists were never wholly dependent upon one or the other method. Francis Bacon (1561–1626), so often revered as an apostle of the experimental method, was no champion of evidence gathering for the sake of evidence gathering. He held that experiments must be directed, and therefore the exprimenter had to begin with a *logical* assumption or hypothesis, which might then be proved true or false by experiment. As for Descartes, in order to begin

---

1. Alexander Pope, "Epitaph intended for Sir Isaac Newton" (1727).
2. Quoted in Randall, *Making of the Modern Mind* (New York, Houghton Mifflin, 1926), p. 279.

deducing truths, he began by proving his own existence on the grounds that he was thinking; and such a consciousness must be classified as *sensory* evidence.

We can lump these rationalists and empiricists together and speak of the scientific revolution, because, in beginning as skeptics with "minds washed clean of opinion"—to use Bacon's phrase which might equally well have come from Descartes—they rejected the past and looked forward to the day when man would know all. Furthermore, to refer back to something discussed earlier, these seventeenth-century scientists had a new view of the role of science. Knowledge was directed toward endowing human life with greater comfort and power rather than toward an other-worldly salvation. This world view, rather than the method, was the revolutionary aspect of the new science. As we have already seen, this revolutionary spirit had not seemed incompatible with religion in the seventeenth century; but in the eighteenth, the relations between religion and science became increasingly strained.

When we call the eighteenth century the Enlightenment or the Age of Reason, we somewhat misrepresent eighteenth-century science; for the scientists of that era were increasingly empirical in their methods. The vogue of reason, the faith in reason, was more the property of the literati than of the scientists, and for the most part, the *philosophes* were literary men. They translated the triumphs of seventeenth-century science into the mechanistic optimism of the Enlightenment. The experimental method, having not been much used, could not point to anything comparable to Newton. Indeed, as the experimental method came into its own in the subsequent century, scientific optimism waned. Though experimental science did solve problems, it disconcertingly uncovered deeper mysteries, until the expectation of imminent human omniscience began to appear premature.

An occasional *philosophe* such as the eminent Voltaire (1694–1778) advocated empiricism, but Fontenelle, the popularizer of science discussed earlier, and his followers gave the century its intellectual cues. This may account, not only for rationalism's vogue, but for the religious quarrels of the eighteenth century, since the origin of the skepticism of the period seems to have been more literary than scientific, especially in France. These quarrels were carried on by the *philosophes,* not by the scientists, with many of the clergy who had not yet accepted the new world view of the scientific revolution. Ultimately, in France, the monarchy drew fire from the *philosophes* for its alliance with the Church.

But whatever the vogues of the literary world, eighteenth-century science was increasingly empirical in method, and there was an apparent shift from mathematics to the natural sciences. Evidence collecting was a fad for monarchs and *philosophes,* and among the scientists the classification of collected specimens was a major occupation. Certainly the most celebrated classifier of the era was Carl von Linné, called Linnaeus (1707–1778), who believed in the immutability of species. At least he did early in his career, when his reputation was made; but later in his life, he did much hybridizing in his garden—work which must have changed his earlier assumptions but which did not affect the scientific world. Buffon, whose *Histoire Naturelle* appeared in 1749, accepted neither Linnaeus' notion of the immutability of species nor classification as an end in itself. His goal was a universal history of life in which he depicted the evolutionary development of the earth and the improvement and degeneration of species.

Like Buffon, John Baptist de Monet, called Lamarck (1744–1829), was a student of fossils and accepted the notion of the slow evolution of life forms. But he did not think that species died out unless they had been exterminated by man. Lamarck is best known for his assumption that acquired characteristics that are a response to some special environmental condition can be inherited. George Cuvier (1769–1832), however, held that species did not change owing to special environmental conditions, but that great catastrophes destroyed species from time to time. Whatever their differences, the work of these natural scientists departs from the notion that the earth and its creatures appeared suddenly on a given date and full-blown in their development.

The origin of life itself was also the subject of dispute. Buffon, rather like Leibniz, believed that all living objects are composed of tiny particles, what we might call life principles. Regarding life as somehow inherent in the nature of things, he did not regard creation as necessary to begin life and accepted the ancient notion of spontaneous generation. In this, he was supported by his British contemporary, John Needham (1713–1781), founder and director of the Academy of Sciences in Brussels. His experiments showed that living creatures generated spontaneously in liquids which fermented. In Italy, however, at the University of Pavia, Lazaro Spallanzani (1729–1799) taught that spontaneous generation is impossible, that life can only be generated by something living; and he attributed Needham's results to germs in the air and not to spontaneous generation. Until the time of Louis Pasteur, however, spontaneous generation was generally accepted by scientists.

The experimentalists of the eighteenth century had their philosophers, too, even though their methods did not yet have rationalism's great prestige. John Locke favored empiricism, though he was inconsistent in that he also sought a deductive system of religion; this inconsistency can be further seen in that Locke remained a good Christian, yet his *tabula rasa* (blank slate) theory really disposed of original sin.[3] He was challenged by George Berkeley (1685–1753), Bishop of Cloyne in Ireland from 1734 to 1752, who thought that Locke's ideas led inevitably to materialism and determinism. Berkeley was a Christian believer and something of a mystic. We can say that he was a kind of sensationalist in that he thought material objects do not exist independent of the mind; it followed that he regarded spiritual activity alone as real, saying that the universe depends upon God, who perceives all ideas and is the cause of them.

In David Hume (1711–1776) empiricism found a more consistent philosopher. He was, first of all, a skeptic, arguing that the contrary or opposite of every fact is possible; therefore, deductive reasoning will not necessarily prove what will actually happen in nature, experience alone providing such knowledge. In Hume's view, we cannot be certain about any natural laws, and experiments alone will reveal the truth to us. Hume's contemporary in France, Denis Diderot (1713–1784), also was a champion of experimentalism, and his Baconian views can be found in his *Thoughts on the Interpretation of Nature* (1754). The extremes are perhaps best drawn by a comparison of Liebniz and Hume, the former convinced that absolute truths could be found by using his "axioms," the latter insisting that absolutes are impossible.

Early in his career, Voltaire had shared the optimism of Leibniz, but apparently the Lisbon earthquake of 1755, which took thousands of lives, and the bloody early years of the Seven Years War (1756–1763) combined to convince him that philosophical optimism was a convenient justification of evil. He related his conversion in the most celebrated of his many works, *Candide, or Optimism* (1759), in which the Leibnizes and Alexander Popes of the eighteenth century fared poorly:

Pangloss taught metaphysico-theologo-cosmolonigology. He proved admirably that there is no effect without a cause and that in this best of all possible worlds, My Lord the Baron's castle was the best of castles and his wife the best of all possible Baronesses.

3. See Penfield Roberts, *The Quest for Security: 1715-1740* (New York, Harper, 1947), p. 142.

" 'Tis demonstrated," said he, "that things cannot be otherwise; for, since everything is made for an end, everything is necessarily for the best end. Observe that noses were made to wear spectacles; and so we have spectacles. Legs were visibly instituted to be breached, and we have breeches. Stones were formed to be quarried and to build castles; and My Lord has a very noble castle; the greatest Baron in the province should have the best house; and as pigs were made to be eaten, we eat pork all the year round; consequently, those who have asserted that all is well talk nonsense; they ought to have said that all is for the best." . . .[4]

An amusing book—and deadly serious. Asked to define optimism, Voltaire has Candide say, "Alas! it is the mania of maintaining that everything is well when we are wretched."[5] At the end, he has no solution to the problem of evil in the world, but merely advises each of us to "cultivate our gardens." Since he had forsaken metaphysics, like so many other eighteenth-century thinkers, the problem of evil was beyond his arena of speculation.

But Voltaire, even if he could not explain why there is evil in the world, was the constant enemy of suffering and injustice, and it might be argued that anyone who pursues practical reforms, as he did, is really an optimist despite himself. Here we arrive at a fundamental characteristic of the eighteenth-century intellectuals: whether rationalists or empiricists, whether optimistic or seemingly pessimistic, they were concerned for the progress of man on this earth and regarded such progress as possible. The Abbé de Saint-Pierre (1658–1743), though not the most profound or interesting of the *philosophes*, typifies the progressive spirit of his century; his projected reforms ranged from a plan for perpetual peace (1713) to a design for an improved armchair.

When the good *philosophe* of the eighteenth century spoke of the progress of man, he did not merely mean the inevitable improvement of our material culture, but the progress of humanity toward perfection. The Marquis de Condorcet (1743–1794) has furnished us one of the best statements of this faith in progress:

All the causes which contribute to the improvement of the human species . . . must, from their very nature, exercise an influence always active, and acquire an extent forever increasing. The proofs of this have been exhibited, and from their development in the work itself they will derive additional force: accordingly we may already conclude, that the perfectibility of man is indef-

4. Voltaire, *Candide, ou l'Optimisme* (1759), Modern Library ed., Ch. I, p. 4.
5. *Ibid.,* Ch. XIX, p. 83.

inite. . . . Would it even be absurd to suppose this quality of melioration in the human species as susceptible of an indefinite advancement; to suppose that a period must one day arrive when death will be nothing more than the effect either of extraordinary accidents, or of the flow and gradual decay of the vital powers; and that the duration of the middle space, of the interval between the birth of man and this decay, will itself have no assignable limit?[6]

A heavenly vision, indeed, to use the idiom of a distinguished historian;[7] but an earth-bound heaven peopled with angelic, deathless men, the vision of a *philosophe* who, presumably, regarded a belief in miracles as passé.

Yet, Condorcet was clearly a man of faith, and his was the faith of those who regarded the rationality of the universe as proof of the existence of God. The perfect mechanism implied the Master Mechanic. Furthermore, the rationality of the universe bared it to analysis by man, so that using his reason, man would ultimately know everything about the universe. Such a view brought the *philosophes* into sharp conflict with the more orthodox Christian assumption that some things are beyond the minds of men and must be revealed to them by God. Could reason and revelation be reconciled? While some thinkers abandoned religion entirely, most of the *philosophes* found deism a useful compromise: they could not be called atheists, and their belief in God conformed with their mechanical notion of the universe. We have Voltaire's famous quip: "In the opinion that there is a God, there are difficulties; but in the contrary opinion there are absurdities."[8]

Of course, some theologians defended orthodoxy and, as the century unrolled, increasingly stressed the emotional aspects of religious faith in their zeal to denounce reason as the source of the most profound truths. This "enthusiasm," along with miracles, was denounced by other theologians, who sought to reconcile religion with reason by emphasizing the reasonableness of Christian ethics. In this reconciliatory camp was the Anglican Bishop Joseph Butler (1692–1752). He attacked deism in his book *The Analogy of Religion, Natural and Revealed* (1737) on the grounds that revelation does not contradict reason, as both come from God. Inevitably, then, revelation and reason must support each other. What bothered many rationalists about Butler, however, was his insistence that God's governance of the universe is quite beyond our comprehension,

6. Condorcet, *Outlines of an Historical View of the Progress of the Human Mind* (London edition, 1795).
7. Carl Becker. *The Heavenly City of the Eighteenth-Century Philosophers* (New Haven, Yale University Press, 1932).
8. Voltaire, *Treatise on Metaphysics,* II. My translation.

for they were too thrilled by the prospect of human omniscience to admit any limitations. The Deists, as compromisers, had their difficulties too. If the universe be the perfect, rational creation of the Master Craftsman, how to explain the unpleasant flaws which evil and misery constitute? Deists like Voltaire could only side-step the issue.

The religious issues were further confounded by anticlericalism. Having themselves lost faith in Christianity, the *philosophes* were inclined to suspect the clergy of only cynically adhering to its principles. Certainly there were notable instances of corrupt or atheistic clergymen who retained their livings. Father Etienne Bonnot de Condillac (1715-1780), a follower of John Locke, was an example of a priest in France who was a materialist, and an atheist. The Jesuits were especially hated by the *philosophes,* who regarded them as diabolical agents of the papacy and advocates of religious and political absolutism. Those who espoused political liberty in the eighteenth century had only to recall the history of England in the seventeenth century to demonstrate their belief that political liberty was inextricably tied to the right to dissent, and some, like Thomas Jefferson, went farther by stating that priests had always been enemies of liberty. It is difficult to say at this late date how much irreligion and deism contributed to anticlericalism in the eighteenth century or, for that matter, how much anticlericalism contributed to irreligion or deism; but the embittered controversies do serve to illustrate how the new world view emerging from the scientific revolution affected men's notions as to what constitutes a moral and worthwhile life. As an example of the passion engendered, here is a passage from Voltaire:

> Every man of sense, every good man, ought to hold the Christian sect in horror. The great name of Deist, which is not sufficiently revered, is the only name one ought to take. The only gospel one ought to read is the great book of Nature, written by the hand of God and sealed with his seal. The only religion that ought to be professed is the religion of worshiping God and being a good man. It is as impossible that pure and eternal religion should produce evil as it is that the Christian fanaticism should not produce it.[9]

David Hume (1711-1776), the greatest of the eighteenth century empiricists, represents the shift to the modern outlook better than any other thinker of his day. His *Treatise of Human Nature* (1735) was not well received, and he did not make his mark as a philosopher until 1748 when his *Enquiry Concerning the Principles of Morals* appeared. In his

9. Voltaire, *Bolingbroke.* My translation.

own time, however, he was more admired for his *History of England* (published between 1752 and 1761) than for his philosophy. His feeling that the perceived world is real enough for all practical purposes led him to insist that all valid ideas must be preceded by a sense perception. Thus, experience was his measure, and he refused to reason from axioms. The analogy between the world and the clock, of which the rationalists were so fond, he rejected on the grounds that we have not seen worlds, only clocks. Furthermore, he denied that the existence of a creator could be rationalized simply from the existence of the earth, saying that it could as easily be assumed that the earth is self-existent. Such views put him at odds, of course, with the rationalists and the Cartesians.

He was an enemy of theology, too, as is especially evident in his *Essay on Miracles* (1748). Here the main point was that a miracle, as a super-natural occurrence, cannot be satisfactorily established. He insisted that everything which occurs does so for natural reasons, that even the most extraordinary events have a natural explanation. Quite logically from this position, he was an atheist. The modernism of his outlook, then, is seen in his insistence that man cannot explain but can only observe and describe.

Finally, in reviewing the Enlightenment, we must note the political ideals of the rationalists. Because of the close association of religion and politics in the seventeenth century, it is not surprising that the *philosophes,* when they wrote of liberty, generally lumped freedom from ecclesiastical control with their opposition to secular absolutism. To put it another way, thanks to English experience under the later Stuarts and to French experience under Louis XIV, freedom to worship (or not to worship) meant opposition to absolutism and even opposition to the mercantilist policies of the absolute state (see Chapter I). We come across the expression *laissez faire* in the eighteenth century and generally associate it with the growing demand that governments refrain from interfering with trade; but *laissez faire,* really meaning that government must not interfere with the liberty of the individual, applied equally to the political and religious realms.

Among others, John Locke had proposed that man in his natural state was free, and in an age which equated the natural with the rational —and hence with the good—it was but a step to the supposition that God intended man to be free. Such an ideal was not necessarily revolutionary and threatening to the old regimes, for the philosophers of liberty also held that all things in the world, including men's lives, are governed by immutable laws. They were therefore apt to see liberty guaranteed more

well-ordered, rationally administered state than through
h might radically enhance the role of the individual by
authority of the state.

ʼas a practical politician before he was a disinterested, logical
ʼ. His definitions must be read with James II and 1688 in mind,
for Loc... was a Whig and a champion of the perogatives of Parliament;
this makes clear why he should advocate that sovereignty lay in the
nation as represented in Parliament in place of royal sovereignty. Voltaire
was an enthusiastic proponent of Locke, regarding the Whig program of
parliamentary prerogatives and toleration as long overdue in France. The
government of Louis XV responded to Voltaire by ordering his *Philosophical Letters on the English* burned in Paris in 1734. Obviously, both
Locke and Voltaire hoped to increase the liberty of individuals by checking
the power of the European leviathans, but one might argue that the
national sovereignty which they espoused led to the nation-states of today,
which interfere directly in the lives of citizens much more than did the
governments of the eighteenth century.

Locke's theory that individual liberty is to be guaranteed by keeping
the three governing powers separate was borrowed and expanded in the
eighteenth century by the Baron de Montesquieu (1689–1755). The
following are extracts from his *The Spirit of the Laws* (1748), often called
the most significant political treatise of the first half of the eighteenth
century; here we find the rationalist of that day, believing both in individual liberty and that men are governed by "invariable laws".

God is related to the universe, as Creator and Preserver; the laws by which
He created all things are those by which He preserves them. He acts according
to these rules, because He knows them; He knows them because He made them;
and He made them because they are in relation to His wisdom and power.

Man, as a physical being, is like other bodies governed by invariable laws.
As an intelligent being, he incessantly transgresses the laws established by God,
and changes those of his own instituting. He is left to his private direction,
though a limited being, and subject, like all finite intelligences, to ignorance
and error: even in imperfect knowledge he loses; and as a sensible creature, he
is hurried away by a thousand impetuous passions. Such a being might every
instant forget his Creator; God has therefore reminded him of his duty by the
laws of religion. Such a being is liable every moment to forget himself; philosophy has provided against this by the laws of morality. Formed to live in
society, he might forget his fellow creatures; legislators have therefore by
political and civil laws confined him to his duty.[10]

10. Charles Louis de Secondat, Baron de la Brède et de Montesquieu, *The Spirit
of the Laws* (London edition, 1858), Ch. I.

In summing up the Enlightenment, we must admit that its faith in the simplicity of the universe and in mankind's imminent omniscience proved unfounded. Yet, the spirit of that age remains admirable, as do its thinkers. One is impressed by their hatred of oppression, intolerance, and superstition; their intellectual courage and their hope for the progress of mankind.

THE ARTS IN THE EARLY EIGHTEENTH CENTURY

A people who see the universe as rational, who have faith that the mysteries of the universe will soon be known and expressed in unchanging laws, will also have a feeling for conventionalized art forms. Already, in the seventeenth century, we have seen that the search for political and religious order impinged upon the artistic world, and the attempt to reduce art to rules and regulations, to somewhat overstate the situation, reached its peak in the first half of the eighteenth century. Classicism (or neoclassicism), dealing with universals and generalities, harmonized completely with the spirit of the Enlightenment; and this love for the universal, the general, gave the era a cosmopolitanism which Europe has not known since the eighteenth century. George Frederick Händel (1685–1759), for instance, was German-born, was Italian-trained, and spent the greater part of his creative life in England; the French-born Voltaire went to Berlin in 1750 at the invitation of Frederick the Great (*1712–1786*) and presumably would have stayed indefinitely had he not quarreled with the King several years later; and a hundred years after Frederick the Great, it would be inconceivable for a German monarch to write his principal works in French, as in the case of Frederick.

If our equation of rationalism with classicism has been extended to include cosmopolitanism, it needs to be added that this cosmopolitan society of the Enlightenment was sharply limited in size. The arts were meant to adorn the lives of those few who had the leisure time to acquire knowledge of the techniques and the forms of the arts. Because classicism deals with universals, the appreciation of classical art requires an understanding of the forms and techniques used to achieve universal expression. The virtues and the sins of classicism are closely related: the initial reasons for the control of form and technique can be lost sight of, and the art then degenerates into techniques for the sake of technique and ornamentation for the sake of ornamentation. The result is an artificiality which robs the art of meaning. But, as Pope and Bach demonstrated, a feeling for the conventional form, such as the closed couplet or the fugue, need not end sterilely.

Finally, in generalizing about the arts in the eighteenth century, let us note that for those happy few of the upper classes, the arts were a part of life, adornment for their daily lives. Pictures hung on the walls of private houses, not in museums; music was performed by small ensembles in the drawing-room, in small theaters, and in churches—not in the massive concert halls and opera houses of a later day. This intimacy with art makes Talleyrand's celebrated remark the more understandable: "Whoever did not live before 1789 did not know the real charm of life."[11]

Architecture

After 1700, there was an increasing demand in England and France for illustrated books on architecture, and the demand was met by engravers of great skill, the best known of whom was Giovanni Battista Piranesi (1720–1778). His most important plates were published between 1748 and 1765, and two works, *Opere varie di architectura* and *Le Antichità romane,* were studied by eighteenth-century architects and decorators as sources for classical inspiration. This vogue for the antique, which should more properly be called neoclassicism, contributed to a renewed enthusiasm for the study of ruins in Rome and Athens.

When it came to the actual design of buildings in the first half of the eighteenth century, styles varied throughout Europe. The Germans and Italians continued to favor the baroque, while the English persisted in the Palladian style and tended to ignore the baroque forms introduced by Wren in the previous century. The Palladian style (see Chapter I) featured simple classical lines, and the resistance of the English to embellishment seems to have been an expression of political antagonism to France, where ornamentation (rococo) was in vogue. Rococo was also favored in Poland during this period, but in Russia the French and Italian styles competed for favor. In the time of Peter the Great (*1689–1725*), the French influence dominated, but under the Empress Elizabeth (*1741–1762*), Italian baroque had its day. Carlo Rastrelli was the architect for the Tsarskoe Selo in 1752, and two years later he built the Winter Palace. The French vogue returned with Catherine II in 1762. It will be noted, however, that save for the rococo, these architectural styles were not of

11. Frantz Funck-Brentano, *The Old Regime in France,* p. 117.

eighteenth-century origin. Jacques Gabriel's plan for the Place de la Concorde (1754) revealed a splendid feeling for the classical, and his achievement remains today one of the most noble sights in Paris; but his very success reminds us that the early eighteenth century was not a period of architectural originality.

Painting

The first half of the century saw French painters dominate European art, the dainty rococo fantasies of Watteau (1684–1721) remaining the model long after his death. His chief successor, François Boucher (1702–1770), was a master of brilliant coloring and voluptuousness and, as such, characteristic of the court of Louis XV. His work comprised vast numbers of classical Venuses, goddesses, and shepherdesses, and he himself left the best commentary on the painters of his age: "We have no common sense, but we are charming."[12] Similar magnificence characterized portraiture, Nicolas de Largillière (1656–1746) being the best known painter in that medium. Indeed, in portraiture especially we see the results of conventionalism: portraits were not really likenesses, and many of the subjects look alike and are often clothed in theatrical costumes. An artist's success depended upon his adherence to formal patterns and his skill as a craftsman; and a painter such as William Hogarth (1697–1764), who went in for realism in portraiture, found himself unpopular in that realm. The fashionable preferred the conventional skills of Jean-Baptiste Van Loo (1684–1745) and Louis Tocque (1696–1772).

In England, the great name was Sir Joshua Reynolds (1732–1792). When young he studied in Rome and was thrilled by the draughtsmanship of the artists of the Renaissance. Later, as first president of the Royal Academy (1768), he delivered fifteen discourses in which he defined the ideal artistic education and what he called "grand style." Like his contemporary Thomas Gainsborough (1727–1788), Reynolds urged the imitation of nature and revealed himself a true neoclassicist of his age by explaining that it is in nature that one finds unchanging ideas and perfect beauty. He believed that the great artists of the past had dealt with such universals, and therefore it was possible to study nature indirectly by studying the masters of the past, the artists of antiquity and of Italy in particular. He did not mean copying the masters, but learning the nature of beauty from their works. Finally, he noted that every great

12. Walter L. Dorn, *Competition for Empire, 1740-1763* (New York, Harper, 1940), p. 247.

artist will inevitably transcend "the rules"; but the assumption was that he would first know the rules.

Reynolds' ideas were echoed in Germany by Johann J. Winckelmann (1717–1768), an art historian rather than an artist, who had studied in Rome:

I believe that imitating the Greeks can teach us to become wise more quickly, since in their works we find not only the essence of whatever is beautiful throughout nature but also the extent to which even the highest form of natural beauty can be wisely and boldly transcended.[13]

Obviously a neoclassicist, Winckelmann had great influence on artistic thought well into the nineteenth century. He is also known for his assertion that style is a quality of an historical period and not merely an individual matter. Hence he saw the study of style as a key to the study of civilization.

Although neoclassicism was the primary artistic current for the first half of the eighteenth century, an artistic revolution was in the making. Jean-Baptiste Greuze (1725–1805), for example, sought to criticize and reform the very society to which Boucher catered. His was a moralizing art, and it is significant that he chose his subjects from common people and milieux. Similarly, Jean-Baptiste Chardin (1699–1779) seemed a "democratic" artist in his disdain for classical subjects. This new trend towards moralizing art was applauded by Denis Diderot (1713–1784), who began, in 1759, to publish annual appraisals of art. For him, art was a rather simple matter of ethics and not of aesthetics; accordingly, he greeted Boucher as a decadent and cheered on Greuze.

England's rebel against tradition was William Hogarth. Yet, even he tried to demonstrate that there is an unchangeable standard of beauty that is the basis of all ornament—the serpentine line:

In the year 1745 [I] published a frontispiece to my engraved works, in which I drew a serpentine line lying on a painter's pallet, with these words under it, The Line of Beauty. The bait soon took; and no Egyptian hieroglyphic ever amused more than it did for a time, painters and sculptors came to me to know the meaning of it.[14]

Aside from this aspect of universalism, Hogarth was opposed to neoclassicism and was in the tradition of social criticism as represented in France by Greuze. The series *A Harlot's Progress,* a *Rake's Progress,* and

13. Elizabeth G. Holt, *A Documentary History of Art,* Vol. II, p. 344.
14. *Ibid.,* Vol. II, p. 266.

Marriage à la Mode are illustrative of his antagonism. His skillful engraving from his originals enabled him to enjoy large-scale production, perhaps a bourgeois answer to the aristocratic patronage system which he hated.

Music

In an age when a portrait was more esteemed for its technique than its faithfulness, we may assume that expressiveness was not necessarily closely related to a specific subject or meaning. This can be demonstrated in music, too, where we find both Johann Sebastian Bach (1685–1750) and George Frederick Händel (1685–1759) employing identical passages in both secular and spiritual music. The conventions of music were even more clearly spelled out than were the conventions of painting. The innovations in baroque music since the time of Monteverdi had become an arbitrary set of limitations in the eighteenth century. These rules of harmony can be found in Jean-Philippe Rameau's *Treatise on Harmony Reduced to Its Natural Principles* (1722). In the same year, the first part of Bach's *Well-Tempered Clavichord* appeared, a set of twenty-four preludes and fugues in each of the twelve major and minor keys then regarded as musically feasible.

Bach was not only the greatest composer of his day, but perhaps of all time. Yet, during his life he was most admired as an organist, and much of what he wrote was merely intended for use in his own church and was not published until after his death. His command of technique and form was so nearly absolute that they had ceased to be arbitrary limitations for him, while his expressiveness was of a superb quality which defies explanation and is therefore termed genius. Bach was an accomplished organist and wrote much for that instrument; even when writing for other instruments or ensembles, we find him "organ-minded." With its multiple manuals and pedals, the organ is especially well-adapted to polyphonic music, to the weaving of independent figures and ornamentation. The organs of Bach's day were far simpler instruments, of course, than those in the modern theater, which are meant to substitute for a full orchestra and which can enthrall us with an assortment of stops, including gongs and whistles, unavailable to composers of the eighteenth century. Part of Bach's keyboard skill, incidentally, came from his innovation of using the thumbs.

Bach worked with church music from the beginning of his career, but Händel was fascinated by opera and only turned to the oratorio as the popularity of opera waned. Neither man invariably adhered to strict form, but their music always creates the impression of strong structure. Rational formalism, contrary to popular belief, did not prevent their music from having a strong emotional impact, Bach's *St. Matthew Passion* and *Goldberg Variations* being fine illustrations. And everyone is familiar with the story of the first London performance of Händel's *Messiah,* when the audience, led by George II (who allowed that he hated "bainting and boetry"), was swept to its feet by the "Hallelujah" chorus.

The versatility of stringed instruments was supreme by the eighteenth century, thanks to the innovations of the Italians, but the woods and brasses remained comparatively simple. Opera singing was still dominated by the *castrati,* male sopranos and contraltos, the former taking the female roles. Apparently the *castrati* could produce more powerful and brilliant tones than the female voice. Most of them were Italians, the best-known being Farinelli (or Carlo Broschi, 1705–1782), who performed throughout Europe and finally settled at the court of Spain for twenty-five years, singing daily for Philip V and his successor, Ferdinand VI. This school of singing did not long survive the eighteenth century, Girolama Crescentini, born in 1766, being one of the last representatives.

Literature

The literary vogues of the first half of the eighteenth century offer a rough parallel to those in painting and science; rational neoclassicism, cosmopolitanism, and optimism comprised one dominant trend. But literature, much more than painting or science, was related closely to the political and social facts of the day. In England, for instance, the heat of political controversy in the late seventeenth century, which produced the first political parties, also drove people to read pamphlets; and one of the liberal derivatives of 1689 was the abolition of censorship in 1695. Nothing more clearly demonstrated the superiority of English governmental institutions over their French counterparts in the eyes of French writers, who enjoyed no such liberty. Again, the rise of the coffee house in England was a feature of this era of intense political controversy (there were over 3000 of them in London alone by 1713) and helped to promote a reading public by providing places for discussion. The new journals, discussed earlier, generally began as political organs, then evolved to include literary matters. It has been pointed out that the rise of the coffee houses and clubs was not solely owing to the political climate of the time, but also to the housing shortage in England, then especially bad. Men desired to escape their hovels and took refuge in pleasant company. In retrospect, these coffee houses, in providing hundreds of arenas for the exchange of political and literary opinions, seem to have been harbingers of political democracy many decades before the actual reforms making such democracy possible.

The first half of the eighteenth century saw poetry and drama supplanted as the favored literary forms by novels and works of history, especially novels with their moral lesson. Perhaps this fad reflected a reading public engrossed by "practical" political and philosophical questions. The novels also revealed a new interest in the lives of common men and suggest a new climate of opinion in the making—humanitarianism—which recalls immediately the art of Hogarth or John Gay's *Beggar's Opera* (1728). Samuel Richardson's *Pamela* produced a sensation in 1741; it was followed by his *Clarissa* (1747–8) and *Sir Charles Grandeson* (1753–4). Then there were Henry Fielding's *History of Tom Jones, a Foundling* (1749) and the novels of Tobias Smollett, such as *Roderick Random* (1748) and *Peregrine Pickle* (1751), all accounts of common life.

The increasing demand for reading materials in England was accompanied by an increase in popular literacy, though the educational advances made in the eighteenth century were peculiarly limited to primary education. English universities decayed after 1689 for reasons which are still clouded and debated; but in the late seventeenth century, a charity-school movement was responsible for the growth of primary schools. The movement originally was a Dissenter crusade, the Anglicans joining it after the turn of the century. Here again, the interest of commoners was served, for the new schools trained children of shopkeepers and artisans, though certainly not in great numbers. This educational movement was significant, too, in that it comprised people whose standards were those of the Puritans of the seventeenth century: godliness, hard work, and thrift (qualities which characterized the Methodist movement later in the eighteenth century).

This woman had also had a little school, which she kept to teach children to read and to work; and having, as I have said, lived before that in good fashion, she bred up the children she took with a great deal of art, as well as with a great deal of care.

But that which was worth all the rest, she bred them up very religiously, being herself a very sober, pious woman, very housewifely and clean, and very mannerly, and with good behaviour. So that in a word, excepting a plain diet, course lodging, and mean clothes, we were brought up as mannerly and as genteelly as if we had been at the dancing-school.[15]

The kinship of literature and politics in the early eighteenth century is also seen in the large body of writing critical of the political and social order of the day. We have earlier noted Swift's *Gulliver's Travels* (published in 1726 though belonging somewhat earlier) and, of course, Voltaire's *Candide* (1759). Another celebrated bit of acid commentary was brought out by Montesquieu in 1721, *The Persian Letters,* actually a novel involving a harem intrigue. But its barbs lay in the visit of two Persians to Paris and their comments on life in the French capital. Their analysis of Christianity left them, as one might suspect, anticlerical rationalists. Every age no doubt has its protest literature, but the volume and quality of it in the eighteenth century, especially in France, bears special notice. The causes were numerous. The scientific revolution by then had bred its philosophical offspring, rationalism, which contested with Christianity; the bourgeois were well enough established politically to vie with the aristocracy (as already seen in the embittered remark of the Duc de Saint-Simon to the effect that the seventeenth had been the century of the "vile bourgeois"); and having risen so far, they were the more conscious of "irrational" inequalities remaining. The eighteenth century was a time of rapidly increasing private fortunes, deriving from overseas trade and the beginning of industrialization; and with vast fortunes went a vast dissipation, to furnish a further conflict with the rigid, tight-fisted piety of the less well-to-do. Finally, the relative liberty in England, both political and religious (which are the parents of most other liberties) put most of the continent in sorry contrast.

The foreign milieu of such works as *The Persian Letters* and *Candide* immediately suggests that their authors sought to avoid censorship and prosecution. But this is not sufficient explanation, since authors who had no need to hide—such as Swift for *Gulliver's Travels* or Defoe for *Robinson Crusoe* (1729)—used alien settings. We have here another aspect of the cosmopolitanism of the age, and certainly the overseas expansion of the western states lent interest to the exotic.

Despite the tendency of the French literati to venerate English literature along with English liberty and science, the French novel of the

15. Daniel Defoe, *The Fortunes and Misfortunes of the Famous Moll Flanders* (1683), Chap. I.

eighteenth century really had an independent origin. Much earlier than Richardson, the notable French religious figure, Fénélon, had written *The Adventures of Telemachus* for the instruction of his pupil, the Duc de Bourgogne, grandson of Louis XIV. The novel was a new episode to the *Odyssey*—Telemachus being the son of Ulysses—and was published without the author's consent in 1699. By then, however, Fénélon's Quietism (See Chapter I) had earned him the hostility of Bishop Bossuet and the subsequent loss of his pupil. With the later ideas of Rousseau in mind, it is arresting to find Fénélon teaching his royal pupil the utopian virtues of primitive times as a direct contrast to the virtues of Versailles. And little imagination is required to guess His Majesty's reaction to the thesis that kings are below the law.

When we come to Alain-René Lesage (1668–1747), we find a novelist concerned with character portraits; and as such, Lesage ranks as one of the originators of the modern novel. Most of his works had a Spanish setting (the exotic again), and like his English contemporaries, the chosen subjects were often picaresques. *Gil Blas de Santillane* (1735), Lesage's best work, had such a setting though its intent was clearly a blast at conditions in France. Tobias Smollett, among the English, acknowledged his indebtedness to Lesage. In reverse, another important French novelist, the Abbé Antoine-François Prévost (1697–1763) translated Richardson's *Clarissa* into French. He is better known, of course, for *Manon Lescaut* (1731), a novel in which he hoped to demonstrate "the disastrous effects of the passions." The book enjoyed a sensation and contributed to novel writing north of the Rhine. Probably Prévost's work, including his translation, deeply affected Jean-Jacques Rousseau (1712–1778). Rousseau's *Julie ou la Nouvelle Heloïse* (1761) portrayed his affair with Mme. d'Houdetot and ran through seventy editions in the eighteenth century alone.

The revolt against neoclassicism in literature, affecting both subject and form, was evident by the 1730's in both France and England. The early novels, while they usually housed a moral lesson which would have satisfied the neoclassicist, were a new literary form which had popular appeal and, aside from literacy, required no disciplined knowledge for appreciation. In poetry, James Thomson (1700–1748) deliberately abandoned the closed couplets of the neoclassical and returned to the blank verse of Milton. Here is a passage from *Winter* (1726), the first of four poems known collectively as *The Seasons*:

> With frequent foot,
> Pleased have I, in my cheerful morn of life,
> When nursed by careless solitude I lived
> And sung of nature with unceasing joy,
> Pleased have I wandered through your rough domain;
> Trod the pure virgin-snows, myself as pure;
> Heard the winds roar, and the big torrent burst;
> Or seen the deep-fermenting tempest brewed
> In the grim evening-sky. Thus passed the time,
> Till through the lucid chambers of the south
> Looked out the joyous Spring—looked out and smiled.[16]

Thomson was the first of the "nature" poets—that is, poets who viewed nature sensually rather than as a masterpiece of geometry. This growth in what was called "sensibility" soon produced a rash of melancholy (often called "graveyard") poems, of which Thomas Gray's (1716–1771) *Elegy Written in a Country Churchyard* (1751) is by far the best-known today. Here he did not forsake couplets, but his feeling for nature and his pessimism were not in the rational tradition:

> The boast of heraldry, the pomp of power,
> And all that beauty, all that wealth e'er gave,
> Awaits alike the inevitable hour:
> The paths of glory lead but to the grave.[17]

Hence one can affirm that in the heyday of reason, the romantic movement came alive, just as empiricism was then supplanting reason as the scientists' more revered method.

Around the middle of the eighteenth century, two literary projects deserving of attention were under way. First was the *Encyclopédie,* authorized by the publisher Le Breton, who hired Denis Diderot (1713–1784) to produce a French version of an encyclopedia published earlier in England. As editor, Diderot produced an entirely new work, gathering around him writers dedicated to science and the latest philosophy: Jean d'Alembert (1717–1783), for instance, who served as assistant editor for a time; the sensationalist Abbé de Condillac (1714–1780); and Helvetius (1715–1771). Many articles, as a result, amounted to propaganda for the new intellectual order. Sixteen volumes were completed between 1751 and 1765, and supplementary volumes followed later. The name, Encyclopaedists, was used later on in reference not only to the contributing

16. Lines 6-16.
17. Thomas Gray, "Elegy Written in a Country Churchyard," ll. 31-34.

writers, but also to those who sympathized with the rationalist spirit of the century.

The second project was Samuel Johnson's (1709–1784) famous *Dictionary,* which he began in 1747, hoping to complete it in three years. The manuscript was not completed, however, until 1755, but he had compiled it singlehandedly. His use of the illustrative quotation was borrowed from the practice of the continental academies; but some of the definitions in his *Dictionary* were capricious and humorous: *"Lexicographer,* a writer of dictionaries, a harmless drudge."

In sum, we can say that by 1750 western Europe not only possessed a ready public for the new journals and novels, which in itself suggests the significance of the middle class by then, but also harbored a few writers who were actually able to earn their livings from writing alone. Lesage was one of the first in France to live off his novels, and Samuel Johnson managed, too, though we know from his celebrated letter chastizing Lord Chesterfield that patronage would have been welcome:

> When, upon some slight encouragement, I first visited your Lordship, I was overpowered, like the rest of mankind, by the enchantment of your address, and could not forbear to wish that I might boast myself *Le vainqueur du vainqueur de la terre;*—that I might obtain that regard for which I saw the world contending; but I found my attendance so little encouraged, that neither pride nor modesty would suffer me to continue it. When I had once addressed your Lordship in public, I had exhausted all the art of pleasing which a retired and uncourtly scholar can possess. I had done all that I could; and no man is well pleased to have his all neglected, be it ever so little.[18]

Not all writers, of course, were favored by financial independence coming from their works, and they required patronage. The rise of the reading public, however, clearly marked the decline in the patronage system.

THE ARISTOCRATIC REVIVAL UNDER THE OLD REGIME

Western Europe did not calm down at once after the Utrecht peace settlement in 1713. Seven years were required to smooth the remaining difficulties, and the period saw remarkable reversals in policy. The Whigs, originally the war party in Britain and opposed to peace before the absolute defeat of Louis XIV, soon came to regard the maintenance of the

18. John Bailey, ed., *A Shorter Boswell,* pp. 44-45.

treaty as a bulwark for the new Hanoverian dynasty, whose welfare they regarded a special Whig interest. Fear for the future of that treaty arose largely out of Spanish resentment over the loss of territories in Italy, which Spain revealed by her refusal to make peace with Austria during the general negotiations in 1713. Though denied any claim to the French throne by the Treaty of Utrecht, Philip V of Spain openly aspired to the union of the thrones of Paris and Madrid. Dynastically speaking, he was next in line for the French throne and was galled, in 1715, when he was necessarily by-passed for Louis XIV's sickly five-year-old great-grandson. Worse, the Duke of Orleans, named Regent, was despised by Philip V. Under the circumstances, it was inevitable that Europe wondered if the Spanish monarch proposed to violate the treaty.

Thus, the second political reversal: In 1716, the chief ministers of Britain and France, James Stanhope and Guillaume Dubois, signed an alliance in an honest effort to maintain the peace. The Dutch adhered to it the following year and the Austrians in 1718, thus constituting a formidable bloc against Spain. Meanwhile, however, a Spanish expedition seized Sardinia in 1717, taking advantage of Austrian preoccupation with Turkey and the fact that Austria had no navy. The next year, a second Spanish expedition landed on Sicily, forcing the British to assist Austria with naval strength in order to pressure Spain into accepting the 1713 settlement of the Italian territories. The French, too, applied pressure, sending an army into Spain, though skillfully avoiding any unpleasantness with the Spanish army. Philip V could do little in the face of such gestures. Pulling in his horns in 1719, he adhered to the Quadruple Alliance in 1720. His aggressiveness, however, in producing a reconciliation between Britain and France was responsible for a major diplomatic revolution which was especially unpopular in Bourbon France.

It is customary to refer to the governments of eighteenth-century Europe collectively as the *ancien régime*—the old regime. These governments, rudely shaken at the end of the century by the revolutions in America and France, have also suffered subsequently at the hands of historians, who, reared in more democratic epochs, have harped on the tyranny and exclusiveness of the *ancien régime*. Most certainly there was social inequality, and innumerable injustices derived therefrom. But aside from the fact that the *ancien régime* cannot be shown to have had a monopoly on such injustices, the inefficiency of these governments in general (though there were notable exceptions) precluded well-organized sorties into the privacy of the lives of their citizens. Inefficiency, indeed, was a major factor leading to the failure of the *anciens régimes* by the end of the century. In contrast to his eighteenth-century counterpart, today's man in the West feels the power of the state more heavily and immediately.

For all their haughtiness, eighteenth-century monarchs were not isolated from their subjects. We tend to forget that the average Frenchman had access to the king. Every subject, if decently clothed, could walk into Versailles to view the king at dinner or hand him a petition, a situation comparable to the simplicity of White House etiquette in the time of Thomas Jefferson. The evident exclusiveness and irresponsibility of the eighteenth-century nobility is another cliché of the history books. Yet the record also tells of noblemen performing services for commoners as an obligation of rank—*noblesse oblige*. The existence of such a code of conduct, which implies a social hierarchy, has annoyed a later age brought up to believe in the equality of all men. Thanks to John Locke and his followers, the sanctity of the individual has carried the day against caste or corporate sense. But if individualism has brought western man invaluable guarantees of personal liberty, we have too often felt the absence of individual responsibility in times when *noblesse oblige* has vanished. Yet, who would seriously deny that talent has its responsibilities, not merely its license?

In the seventeenth century, the philosophers of despotism had justified absolutism as essential to produce an orderly society (See Chapter I). Except in Britain, absolutism was the predominant political form in the great powers, but it was accompanied by a series of vast wars which produced financial as well as military chaos, certainly on a scale to equal the disorders produced by the religious controversies of an earlier century. By 1715, therefore, we see an inevitable reaction against absolutism, which had not procured the promised peace. In the main, the reaction took the form of an aristocratic revival, though it was not an organized European movement. The tendency was to limit the power of the crown and not to permit any one group or class to dominate. In other words, by 1715 the fear of the "leviathan" state, which Locke had so ably discussed in 1690, was reflected in most European states.

SWEDEN

In Sweden the most clearly defined reaction took place. A strong and brilliant king, Charles XII (*1697–1718*), had led his country into military disaster and left her impoverished and sharply short of males.

As the King was unmarried and childless at the time of his death in battle, the Swedish Estates-General had the opportunity to assert itself by naming a new sovereign and reforming the constitution to favor aristocratic power. Swedish historians refer to this era as the Time of Freedom, beginning with the appointment of Charles XII's sister, Ulrika Eleonora (*1718–1720*) as sovereign and lasting until 1772. Ulrika revealed absolutist ambitions and was soon persuaded to abdicate in favor of her husband, Frederick I (*1720–1751*), who was a Hessian with no dynastic right of his own. More dependent upon the Estates than his wife had been, he readily signed the new constitution of 1720, which considerably reduced royal authority. Neither he nor his successor, Adolphus Frederick II (*1751–1771*) were Swedish-born, and both were elected on the condition that they would abjure absolutism.

Under the new constitution, the executive power was vested in the Council of the Estates, a body made up of nobles and bureaucrats, presided over by the king, whose influence was limited to two votes. The work of the Estates-General itself was directed by a committee of 100 members, comprising fifty nobles, twenty-five clergymen, and twenty-five bourgeois. (After 1740, peasant members were included.) This committee was in fact the real power, as the Council governed only when the Estates-General (or Riksdag) was not in session.

The aristocratic revival in Sweden brought about a situation not unlike that in eighteenth-century Poland; factious nobles, vying for power, accepted bribes and foreign support—a situation which could have led to the partition of Sweden as it did to that of Poland. Underneath all other quarrels lay the festering issue of Sweden's decline as a Baltic power. The war-of-revenge party—called the "Hats," in reference to military headgear—ached to take on Russia once more; but for twenty years after the death of Charles XII, the peace party, known as the "Caps" (nightcaps—sleepy cowards!), held sway. In 1738, the Hats finally brought about the fall of the Caps' leader, Count Arvid Horn, and turned to military preparations. First securing a French alliance, they then manufactured a war with Russia (1741–1743) at the end of which Russia was in occupation of Finland.

The subsequent Treaty of Abö (1743) not only measured Sweden's defeat, but also illustrates the habit of European powers of interfering in Swedish domestic matters during the "Time of Freedom." In order to get back most of Finland, the Riksdag was obliged to name Russia's candidate for the Swedish throne, Adolphus Frederick of Holstein-Gottorp-

Eutin, as heir to the reigning king. Then Prince-Bishop of Lübeck, Adolphus Frederick was a cousin of the Empress Elizabeth's own heir to the throne of Russia. As compensation, Sweden lost only a bit of Finland to Russia, but the threat to Swedish independence was clear.

FRANCE: THE REGENCY, THE MISSISSIPPI BUBBLE, AND LOUIS XV

The aristocratic reaction after 1715 in France, though perhaps less thorough-going than in Sweden, was nevertheless important and one of the factors in the development of a revolutionary situation in the eighteenth century. When Louis XIV breathed his last in 1715, his great-grandson, Louis XV (*1715–1774*), was a sickly infant of five, likely to die before adulthood. The dynastic picture was threatened by Philip V of Spain, who had been obliged to renounce his right to the French throne but who avowed that his hereditary right, being divine will, could not be set aside by mere men. As it happened, not only was the divine will violated, but that of Louis XIV was, too. He had provided for a multiple regency[19] for his great-grandson, but the Duke of Orleans secured a monopoly on the regency by getting the Parlement de Paris to set aside the will. Orleans, son of Louis's only brother and known as Monsieur, obtained the regency by restoring the Parlement's right of remonstrance to the royal edicts—a right which Louis XIV had ended in 1672. It was the first advance in the battle to contain royal absolutism. No royal decree was valid without being registered by the Parlement de Paris, and this body might protest a decree before registering it.

Until recently, the Duke of Orleans has suffered severely at the hands of historians. Failures in domestic policies were probably less responsible for his bad reputation than were his atheism, his addiction to the grape, and his open homosexuality. Nevertheless, he was an able and intelligent man; the unpopular alliance with Britain was necessary to maintain the peace, and peace was essential if French financial stability was to be recovered. His radical financial reforms failed, it is true, but the Regency was the only pre-Revolutionary government of eighteenth-century France to attempt drastic, fundamental reform of the financial structure.

The aristocratic revival is seen in the Regent's system of government

19. A regency is a temporary government established during the minority of the monarch or during a period of his incapacity to rule.

by committee. The Council of Regency contained eleven members and was advised and supported by six subcouncils of ten men each, representing the six major departments of government. Membership was recruited largely from the nobility and to a lesser extent from the professional bureaucracy. Aside from the return of the nobles to positions of importance, the cumbersomeness of the system amounted to decentralization. Indeed, it never worked and had to be abandoned after three years. The councils were jealous of each other and were largely occupied with bickering over precedence and etiquette, a preoccupation inherited from the baroque minds of the preceding century. In 1718, the Regent had to return to the forms of Louis XIV; six ministers, supported by professional bureaucrats, replaced the six councils, and it is clear from contemporary memoirs that the nobility lost heavily in prestige from its apparent inability to govern. Two men now emerged as the chief advisors of the Regent: the Abbé Guillaume Dubois (1656–1723) and the Scotsman John Law (1671–1729).

The French government was only one of many insolvent governments in 1715, thanks to the great wars, and John Law had been unsuccessfully peddling his schemes for financial recovery about Europe for the ten previous years. Actually, his fundamental ideas were sound and were inspired by the successes of the Bank of England and the East India Company. Law saw that a national debt could be paid off by increasing foreign commerce through great government-chartered trading companies. The Duke of Orleans was convinced Law was correct and gave him a charter to found the Banque Générale in 1716. The temptation to repudiate the government debt was great, especially in a day when many were inclined to regard such indebtedness as the monarch's personal obligation and not as a national responsibility. John Law argued correctly that repudiation would make the situation worse, by destroying public confidence; the solution lay in increasing trade.

The Banque Générale was a private joint stock company with an authorized capital of 6,000,000 livres, which got off to something of an ominous start when only a quarter of its stock was subscribed. The notes which the bank issued did not bear interest, but they were redeemable in specie of fixed, unchangeable monetary value. Thus, the notes were certificates of deposit, and the government accepted them in payment of taxes. The bank also became a convenient depository for government funds. Toward the end of 1718, the Regent bought out all the stockholders, making the crown sole stockholder, and a number of branch banks were opened in major cities. The fatal flaw in the system was the failure to regulate the printing of banknotes. Printing simply catered to the demand for currency and was not restricted to reflect any gold and silver reserves; any amount of cash could, therefore, be provided, and it is estimated that by 1720 the currency in circulation was double that of 1716.

As for the other facet of John Law's scheme—increasing trade—he was granted a charter to found the Company of the West (commonly called the Mississippi Company) in 1717—the same year, incidentally, in which the Banque Générale was renamed the Banque Royale. As was usual in the days of mercantilism, the company received a monopoly, first of trade with Louisiana and later of the beaver trade with Canada. Expecting that tobacco would be grown in Louisiana, Law thoughtfully bought up the monopoly on the manufacture and sale of tobacco in France. Two years after its birth, the Company was reconstituted, absorbing five other important trading companies with their monopolies. A vast amount of France's foreign trade was thus controlled by Law, and his bank was now a royal institution.

As for the fundamental problem of the overwhelming government debt: government bondholders were asked, and in some cases forced, to trade their bonds for stock in the Company; and to ease this transfer, Law began to paint an enticing picture of the enormous profits to be gained by owning such stock. In this way, the government greatly reduced its indebtedness without repudiating the debt, and its creditors had the happy prospect of greater profits than the bonds would have brought in interest. After all, the well-known success of the British and Dutch East India companies augured favorably for the French, and the debt of the London government had been successfully refinanced through just such an exchange of government bonds for trading-company stock. The whole scheme, in short, was not the product of wild-eyed irresponsibility, and John Law was not guilty of an attempt to defraud.

Yet, the crash was not long in coming, and Law, though still possessing the Regent's confidence, was in flight toward exile by the end of 1720. Two factors must be especially noted as having produced the crash. Law's tremendous financial position threatened the whole class of French financiers, who were joined in opposing Law by all those whose political revival had been cut short in 1718 when the Regent had abolished the system of Councils as Law and Dubois emerged as chief advisers to the Regent. Such significant opposition drove Law to promote his company's stock unduly and to glorify the immense profits likely to be won, so that he cannot be held unaccountable for the wild speculation which developed. Shares originally valued at five hundred livres ultimately reached fifteen thousand livres—and could be bought on the installment plan. To make disaster certain, the Banque Royale turned out vast numbers of banknotes to help finance the boom. No one had foreseen this fever for speculation, and the only event which brought it to a halt was a slowly growing suspicion, in 1720, that the shares could not possibly earn enough to justify the prices then being paid for them. Frantic selling replaced frantic buying, and the stock sank despite Law's reiterated guarantees of a bright future. The end came when the mob, which once had gathered outside the company offices to demand stock, trampled on each other in their enthusiasm to wreck the company offices. Orleans had to dismiss Law under the circumstances, though he was convinced that Law's scheme had been sound.

Meanwhile, the Regency had taken other steps to reduce the government's debt. These steps were, in effect, concealed repudiation in defiance of John Law's warning. As an economy, the interest on government bonds was reduced to 4 per cent, a factor which then made it easier for many bondholders to agree to convert their holdings into "Mississippi" stock. During the wars, government bonds had often declined in value, so that the Regency could rightly claim that many of the bondholders had bought below par. But that is part of the game and hardly a justification for reducing the interest rate. More defensible was the abolition of many unnecessary public offices, created and sold for income during the wars; if proof existed that they had not been paid for in full, the offices were closed and the holders were also deprived of the exemption from taxation which usually went with public office.

In the same spirit, the Regency created a special court, a Chamber of Justice, charged with prosecuting those who had speculated in government notes, buying them up cheap in expectation of full payment. Such expedient measures, decreed during the short period of council government, reveal an inability to recognize, first, that wars must be waged on credit; second, that financial manipulations of this sort are an inevitable part of the risk of war; third, that the aristocrats then in power were indifferent to the financial losses endured through these decrees, because the losses hit the bourgeois far more than the nobility; and, finally, that public credit must suffer, as Law had pointed out, when governments have recourse to repudiatory tactics.

Thus it was that the financial expedients of the Regency, discriminatory and uneconomic, crowned by a major financial panic, had social and political significance as well. This is not to say—as has been said by many writers—that the "Mississippi Bubble" completed the ruin of both France and the *ancien régime*. On the eve of the Revolution in 1789, France was the most prosperous country in Europe, a country where most men drew their livelihood from the soil and had been little touched by the acrobatics of the money market. Certainly many of those caught in the epidemic of speculation suffered financial disaster, and their anger and bitterness had political consequences; but we also know that many got out of the market before its crash and lived on to display their *nouveau riche* charms. Finally, let us not forget that enterprising hunchback who passed the weeks of the boom in the marketplace and made his fortune by renting his deformity as a writing desk for those frantic to buy and sell securities. The meek, indeed, shall inherit the earth!

In 1726, sixteen-year-old Louis XV announced that he would govern as well as reign; there would be no chief minister. Officially, at least, there was a return to absolutism, divine-right monarchy under which His Majesty was the final authority in all legal and constitutional matters. The King's tutor, Bishop Fleury (1653–1743), ever kind to his charge, was a natural adviser under the circumstances, and his elevation to the cardinalate that year gave him the rank to stand up against other notables in the royal councils. He was in fact, if not in name, a new chief minister and was ascendant from 1726 until 1743. His administration continued the twin policies of peace and prosperity set down earlier by the Duke of Orleans, and the economic recovery over which Fleury presided did much to win his master the title Louis the Well-Beloved. The currency was stabilized in the first year of Fleury's regime, and the relationship of gold to silver remained constant from that date until 1785, with no changes in the bullion content of the coins. Foreign trade developed rapidly, practically doubling between 1715 and 1740. The highway system was greatly improved. (This involved, incidentally, the *corvée royale,* a much resented new tax which was payable in service; the peasants paid by working on the roads, while the more wealthy had to provide horses and building materials.) In foreign affairs, Fleury maintained Dubois's alliance with Britain, though unable to control French foreign policy after 1740, as we shall see.

After Fleury's death in 1743, the King again made a show of governing in his own right, perfectly aware that in a divine-right state the king must rule and not merely reign. Louis XV offers us a complex character which has resisted analysis: though intelligent and possessed of a fine memory, the King was bored by the details of administration and indulged himself largely in hunting and women. Yet, he doted on his prerogatives and was increasingly reluctant to delegate authority. Many failures of his later reign, especially in foreign affairs, were partly caused by the flaws in the King's character. For one thing, he was irresolute, and his incapacity for decision not only stalled the machinery of government, but also opened the way for court factions, intrigues, and the political machinations of his many mistresses. *L'état, c'est moi* may have been the theory, but such a system in fact requires a Louis XIV, a man whose presence and ability to command leave no doubt that he is the first man of the realm.

While it is true that the King's inabilities cost the monarchy in prestige and that he died hated rather than "well-beloved," it must also be pointed out that the intellectual climate of the eighteenth century was undermining divine-right monarchy even more effectively than Louis XV's incapacities destroyed it. For one thing, divine-right monarchy necessarily assumed the acceptance of a Christian base for society, but in the age of rationalism and empiricism, in the age of Locke and Montesquieu, one would be hard put to demonstrate that the intellectuals were enthusiastic for Christianity as the social fundamental. Furthermore, the division of France for political purposes into three estates (clergy, nobles, and commons) was a far cry from a realistic division. Recent research clearly has demonstrated that each of the three estates comprised numerous, and often incompatible, economic and social groups, so that it will no longer do to speak simply of "the nobility" in the eighteenth century. And obviously the gap between the rich and poor commoners was vast. The whole political system, in sum, was out of step with the intellectual, social, and economic development of the country, and the failure to modify political institutions, as the English did after 1688, led the French government into absolute financial collapse by 1789.

GREAT BRITAIN

In Great Britain, oligarchy had triumphed in 1689. After 1715, as part of the general reaction against monarchs, we find legislation in Britain which further guaranteed the power of Parliament against royal intrusion. George I (*1714–1727*) was not only the creature of Parliament, but he also required its continued support against the constant intrigues of the displaced Stuarts. Scotland was the scene of a Stuart uprising (1715) known as The Fifteen, and though it was easily suppressed, the Whigs had been alarmed and were uncertain as to the extent of Stuart sympathies in the realm. The Septennial Act of 1716 was therefore passed. In giving Parliament a duration of seven years, it prevented an immediate election which might have reflected a Stuart tide and simultaneously gave Parliament a bulwark against arbitrary dissolution by the King. A second measure reflecting the ambitions of the oligarchy was the Peerage Bill, which the Whig leader, James Lord Stanhope (c. 1673–1721), brought before the House in 1719. Stanhope wanted to restrict the crown's right to create peers, for although the recent example of packing the House of Lords had only temporarily favored the Tories, the experiment could be repeated to defeat the will of the House of Commons. The bill would have passed but for a split in the Whig party, engineered by Robert Walpole (1676–1745) in his bid to replace Stanhope as party leader. The maneuver succeeded, Walpole entering the government the following year to begin his long career.

The ultimate measure of the oligarchy's victory, however, was the flowering of the cabinet system of government in the eighteenth century. We have already seen the origins of party and cabinet government in the seventeenth century and how, under Queen Anne, cabinets were shuffled by the monarch so as to influence parliamentary elections (see pp. 59-60). Here we see, if in reverse fashion, the working of the notion that the cabinet and Parliament ought to represent the same opinion—if only for the practical reason of getting legislation passed. Ultimately, we find that cabinets are constituted to reflect the majority in Parliament, and there has been debate amongst historians as to just how this reversal from Queen Anne's practice came to be.

Formerly, it was common to ascribe the development of true cabinet government and the prime ministry to the inability of the first two Georges to speak English. We were given the picture of a dozing King, inattentive at best during cabinet meetings, forcing the ministers to choose one of their own number to preside. Yet, both these German-born kings did occasionally preside over cabinet meetings, and when they did, French was the language spoken. While it is correct to name Sir Robert Walpole as Prime Minister from 1721 to 1742, it would be incorrect to assume that he was responsible solely to Parliament in the sense that a twentieth-century prime minister is. The ministers were chosen by the monarch, not by Sir Robert, and they were responsible to the monarch. Furthermore, a survey of the ministers would reveal that they were largely peers and not members of Commons; and even the House of Commons in the early eighteenth century tended to regard itself as a guardian against the abuse of royal power rather than as the sovereign power. Certainly it is one way to read the events of 1688 that Parliament blocked royal despotism; and only much later are men in general aware that the long-range significance of that revolution was its redefinition of sovereignty.

By the end of the eighteenth century, true cabinet government had been realized and the House of Commons was supreme, but this situation did not come about overnight in 1689; virtually an entire century was required, and the causes were many. More important than the first two Georges' lack of English was their inexperience with British politics and institutions; they were actually more concerned for the continental politics of their Hanoverian homeland than for British problems. They had to rely on experienced British politicians, just as they had to rely on Parliament to maintain the dynasty against Stuart pretentions. It fell to Walpole, as the greatest of the Whigs, to be the monarchs' advisor and to lead the government in their absence. George I recognized Walpole to be a first-rate statesman, but despite this esteem, Walpole sometimes found it necessary to enforce his will by managing the King through his mistress, the Duchess of Kendal (known to the English public as Elephant[20]). Later, he similarly managed George II through Queen Caroline.

Walpole's political career resembled that of Fleury, though they emerged from far different backgrounds. Fleury was the clergyman and tutor who became a cardinal, while Walpole was the practical politician, untroubled by ideals, rising from the vigorous country gentry and addicted, like most of his class, to fox hunting and the bottle. Their careers were roughly contemporary, Fleury ruling from 1726 to 1743, Walpole from 1721 to 1742. They both stood for peace and prosperity, largely for the same reason: the need to recover from the great wars and to re-establish financial order. The Stuart menace gave Walpole's task a unique dimension and forced him to maintain a reasonable harmony between the various social and economic groups in Britain lest the Stuarts find support out of internal conflicts. Under the circumstances, his skill as a compromiser served him well and, as in the case of Fleury, he is not remembered as an innovator. "Let sleeping dogs lie" could have been their watchword.

In one realm, that of taxation, Walpole was an innovator, largely because British financial recovery demanded it. He recognized that prop-

20. Named Elephant and Maypole for their distinctive physiques, the two German mistresses of George I offered the English considerable amusement.

erty assessments, made during the reign of William and Mary, undervalued urban capital, so that the rural classes bore an unfair share of the tax burden and the revenues to be gained were larger than the government actually enjoyed. Walpole's intial proposal of an excise tax on wine and tobacco stirred up a storm of protest. Among the many arguments used to combat the bill was the assertion that Walpole really intended to replace the land tax with a multitude of excise taxes, a situation presumably favorable to the gentry. Recognizing the likelihood of defeat, Walpole withdrew the measure from the House. Out of apparent defeat, however, he won a political victory. He prevailed upon George II (*1727–1760*) to dismiss those ministers who had fought the tax bill in 1733, an event which helped to establish the principle that the cabinet ought to reflect unanimity and that the ministers owed responsibility to the prime minister as well as to the king. Such a precedent was significant in the gradual flowering of true cabinet government.

THE DUTCH REPUBLIC

The aristocratic revival in the early eighteenth century can also be seen in the Netherlands, where the Dutch failed to elect a new national stadholder after the death of William III of England in 1702. Actually, central power had always been weak, the sovereignty lying in the provinces that comprised the union. In the case of William, his central authority really derived from the fact that he was stadholder of five of the seven provinces as well as King of England. The national executive office was regarded as a temporary one and filled only in times of great emergency, but, of course, in the age of Louis XIV, the Dutch lived almost continually in a state of alarm. In emergency, the stadholder could act arbitrarily; but in more normal times, every decision of the central government had to be ratified by the provincial governments and even by the local governments within the provinces. This cumbersome system prevented the rise of a strong monarchy and suited the oligarchs who controlled the country's economic life.

The United Provinces were insolvent by 1715 like most of the other great powers, and they continued to decline after that date as a military and naval factor. Part of this decline was relative, since in the seventeenth century when the Dutch loomed so large in European affairs, their neighbors were temporarily engrossed with internal difficulties. But part of the decline must be attributed to the inefficient and clumsy governmental system, whose constitutional frailties were made increasingly worse in the eighteenth century by the absence of vigorous leadership. The businessmen who dominated Dutch economic and political life seemed unable to devise the imaginative reforms necessary to recover from the financial losses of the war years, and Dutch government was increasingly characterized by nepotism and the creation of superfluous offices. The result was a necessary resignation from the arena of the great powers and a sharp reduction in the armed forces as a matter of economy. Here again, "Peace and Prosperity" was the watchword after 1715, and the Dutch let commercial goals dominate their foreign policy, staying aloof from the balance-of-power wars of the later part of the century. Accordingly, Amsterdam remained the financial capital of Europe well into the eighteenth century, long after Dutch naval power had declined.

RUSSIA

Even Russia, though not yet part of the political life of Europe as a whole, experienced an oligarchic reaction in this period, after the death of Peter the Great in 1725. We have already seen (see pp. 48-50) Peter's disciplining of the nobility, which that group naturally resented; and after 1721, when Peter substituted the Holy Synod for the patriarchate, the clergy opposed the increase in royal power. The Czar's mania to westernize Russia through the agency of strong central power meant that in the eighteenth century the oppositions to strong monarchy, to modernization, and to religious innovation went hand in hand, as they had in the previous century. After Peter's death, no Russian monarch controlled the nobility until the time of Catherine II in 1762, and the nobles' reactionary bent made them fail to provide the nation with highly trained military and civil leadership in the very era when Russia was replacing Sweden and Poland as the outstanding Baltic power. This fact will account for the increased use of foreign officials after 1725, especially evident during the reign of Anne (*1730–1740*), when Germans were conspicuous in the Russian service.

Peter the Great himself helped prepare the way for the revival of noble authority by failing to name his own heir. Had the Senate been allowed to exercise its authority, it probably would have chosen Peter's grandson. Instead, a conspiracy on the part of many officials, supported by the guards regiments, nominated Peter's second wife, who reigned as Catherine I (*1725–1727*). She was the first woman sovereign of Russia, and the nobility expected to dominate her completely. In fact, Catherine I was dominated by Prince Alexander Menshikov (1672–1729), whose mistress she had once been. She named Peter's grandson as her heir, but he died of smallpox after a short reign as Peter II (*1727–1730*).

The precedent for palace intrigue had already been set. In 1730, a few nobles conspired to set up Anne as Empress on terms that would have made her regime a true limited monarchy. (She was the daughter of Ivan V, earlier coczar with Peter I.) The terms: She must not remarry (she was a widow) nor name her successor; she must not arbitrarily declare war, impose new taxes, or create nobles. It is said that Prince Golitzin, primarily responsible for this attempt to limit royal authority, was a student of John Locke. While Anne accepted these limitations at first, she soon became aware that the nobility commanded no great popular following. Taking care to secure the support of the guards regiments, she repudiated the terms. Her advisors were mostly Baltic Germans, whom the Russian nobles resented and hated.

Ordinarily, however, the guards regiments were inclined to back the nobles against the monarch; this is not surprising when we remember that in these regiments even most of the private soldiers came from the nobility. Under Anne's successor, the Empress Elizabeth (*1741–1762*), the hatred of the German officials of Anne's time had the effect of driving the Russian nobility in search of French culture, really bringing them into the stream of western thought for the first time. Elizabeth was more friendly to her nobles than Anne had been, extending their authority in local government and granting them a monopoly of their "inhabited estates." Essentially this freed the nobles and marked the end of Peter the Great's attempt to mold the nobility into a serving class.

In contrast, the peasants did not fare as well; at least, the reforms affecting the peasants had as their aim an increase in tax revenues. The practice of redistributing lands on the crown and noble estates was begun in the time of Elizabeth. The system provided for a periodic shifting of the parcels of land on a given estate, so that each peasant would have his turn at both the best land and the worst. The real purpose of the reform was to equalize the burden of taxation upon the peasants. The redistribution was administered by the village or *mir,* and each peasant had to belong to a *mir.* The *mir,* in turn, owed allegiance to a local noble. The ownership of property was not, therefore, extended to the peasantry at the time it was to the nobility. And merely trying to equalize the tax burdens did nothing in the end to increase the tax revenues of the government, for the collection system—wildly inefficient—was not reformed simultaneously. It is estimated that only about one-third of the taxes collected ever reached the treasury.

CENTRALIZATION OF THE MODERN STATES

After all that has been written here about the aristocratic or oligarchic reaction after 1715, it is important to emphasize that this movement to decentralize governmental authority turned out to be only a temporary reversal of the main current of European history. One of the safe generalities about the course of modern Europe is that in the long run central governments have become more powerful, and even in this period of temporary reversal, the centralization process proceeded in several important states without hindrance. The reasons are not hard to find. Governments were inevitably becoming more complex and, in consequence, required the services of trained bureaucrats; and bureaucracies were a feature of strongly centralized states. Noblemen were rarely specially tutored in the ways of state service, and as a group they favored decentralization at a time when the obligations of government seemed to require greater coordination from the capital. Therefore, even in those states which experienced a definite aristocratic reaction, the centralizing tide was not long halted.

Prussia

· Prussia was the most notable example of a state in which the aristocratic revival made no inroad at all. Quite the opposite, for under Frederick William I (*1713–1740*), the aristocracy found itself virtually compelled to serve the royal cause, especially in the army, and seems to have been perfectly loyal to His Majesty throughout. Of course, Prussia was a small state with a population not exceeding two and a half million, a fact which made centralization easier and made it possible for the King to operate his realm almost as a business. Yet, we would not do justice to Frederick William I if we omitted all mention of his devotion to his job. He worked long hours and had a passion for detail, so much so that in a larger state he would easily have become a bottleneck in the administrative machinery. Economy was his watchword, for his chief concern was to provide as large a share of the budget as possible for the army. Similarly, he squeezed every-thing possible out of the royal domains through careful management and increased his revenues significantly. The end result, by 1740, was an army of 80,000, more than double that of his predecessor; not the largest army in Europe, to be sure, but relative to the total population of Prussia, the army was stupendous. No other country in Europe was remotely com-parable in its devotion to the military establishment, a situation which makes understandable the celebrated remark that Prussia was not a state with an army, but an army with a state.

Spain

Spain, so often in history out of step with the rest of Europe, had seen the aristocrats improve their position in the seventeenth century—the age of absolutism elsewhere. Government was carried on through a series of great councils staffed by noblemen, and the authority of the monarchs shrank in comparison to that enjoyed by Philip II. The Bour-bon succession, however, reversed this trend, and the powers of the monarchy increased at the very moment when much of Europe was expe-riencing the aristocratic revival. Thanks to the territorial losses inflicted upon Spain by the treaty of Utrecht, the Councils of Flanders and of Italy were no longer required, and as the Council of Aragon had had the bad luck to side with the Hapsburgs during the war, Philip V had a good pretext for abolishing it. The remaining councils were not obliterated, but the crown undermined their work. Ministries in the French style were adopted, and a system for training bureaucrats was inaugurated, so that Spain soon had a more professional type of government, and the crown could dispense with the services of the nobility. At first, the ministers were largely foreigners, but as Spaniards received the necessary training and experience, they began to supplant the foreigners.

The Hapsburg Empire

The empire of the Hapsburgs in Central Europe seems unique in this period after 1715 in that it experienced neither a notable aristocratic revival nor a pronounced increase in the centralization of royal power. During his reign, Charles VI (*1711–1740*) revealed his strong reaction to the loss of the Spanish succession in 1713 by his single-minded endeavor to keep intact the remaining provinces in his empire and pass them on to his daughter, Maria Theresa. This female succession was without prece-dent, and Charles first had to secure the consent of his family, which, when obtained, was made known to the world in 1719 as the Pragmatic Sanction. This represented a major constitutional change, and Charles VI spent the remaining twenty years of his reign getting the European powers to recognize the validity of Maria Theresa's right to the throne. He succeeded to the extent that she did follow him in 1740.

Historians have often criticized Charles VI for his devotion to the succession problem and his consequent neglect of the power of the monarchy —indeed, his failure to strengthen the army in the face of Prussian military expansion. It is only fair to point out, however, that he did not make any notable concessions to the nobles in getting them to recognize the Pragmatic Sanction, even though they were already entrenched in their provincial Diets. Under the circumstances, they might well have extorted additional privileges from the Emperor. The three chief provinces of the empire—Austria, Bohemia, and Hungary—each had a strong Diet. Aristocratic liberties in many instances dated from the era of the Catholic Reformation, when Protestant nobles lost their estates, which were thereupon distributed by the crown to loyal Catholic nobles. Their loyalty was further rewarded through the extension of considerable authority to the provincial Diets; this authority was not easily retrieved by the central monarchy. Even so, we see in the eighteenth century the development of a trained bureaucracy, a clear sign that greater royal power was in the making.

SUGGESTIONS FOR FURTHER READING

Intellectual History

Penfield Roberts, *The Quest for Security 1715-40* (New York and London: Harper, 1947), good general study including extensive bibliography.

Walter L. Dorn, *Competition for Empire 1740-1763* (New York and London: Harper, 1940), same as above.

The New Cambridge Modern History, VII: The Old Regime, 1713-63 (Cambridge University Press, 1957).

*Carl Becker, *The Heavenly City of the Eighteenth-Century Philosophers* (Yale University Press, 1959), a controversial but brilliant interpretation.

*Louis L. Snyder, *The Age of Reason* (Princeton, N.J.: Anvil Press, 1955).

*Basil Willey, *The Eighteenth Century Background* (Boston: Beacon, 1961), good brief account.

J. B. Bury, *The Idea of Progress* (London: Macmillan, 1920), especially good on Fontenelle.

Ernst Cassirer, *The Philosophy of the Enlightenment* (Princeton University Press, 1951), often cited as the most penetrating study of the subject.

See also the works of Randall, Butterfield, and Berlin cited for Chapters 1 and 2.

Paul Hazard, *European Thought in the Eighteenth Century* (Yale University Press, 1954).

George R. Havens, *The Age of Ideas: From Reaction to Revolution in Eighteenth Century France* (New York: Henry Holt and Co., 1955).

Daniel Mornet, *French Thought in the Eighteenth Century* (New York: Prentice-Hall, 1929).

The Arts

*Geoffrey Brereton, *A Short History of French Literature* (London: Penguin, 1954).

*Elizabeth G. Holt, *A Documentary History of Art, II* (Garden City: Doubleday-Anchor, 1958).

Paul H. Lang, *Music in Western Civilization* (New York: Norton, 1941), good general history.

D. N. Ferguson, *A History of Musical Thought,* 2nd ed. (New York: Appleton-Century-Crofts, 1948).

F. Fosca, *The Eighteenth Century: From Watteau to Tiepolo* (New York: Skira-World, 1952).

Political History

*J. N. Plumb, *England in the Eighteenth Century 1714–1815* (London: Penguin, 1950), first-rate survey.

Basil Williams, *The Whig Supremacy 1714-1760* (Oxford: The Clarendon Press, 1939), highly recommended.

J. B. Perkins, *France Under the Regency* (Boston: Houghton Mifflin, 1892); and *France Under Louis XV,* 2 vols. (Boston: Houghton Mifflin, 1897), dated, but the best treatment.

W. H. Lewis, *The Scandalous Regent* (New York: Harcourt, Brace, 1961).

M. S. Anderson, *Europe in the Eighteenth Century 1713-1783* (New York: Holt, Rinehart, and Winston, 1961), best single volume now available.

See also the Roberts and the *New Cambridge Modern History,* VII, cited above.

G. P. Gooch, *Louis XV* (London and New York: Longmans, Green, 1956).

A. Goodwin, ed., *The European Nobility in the Eighteenth Century* (London: A. and C. Black, 1953), good essays.

* Available in paperbound editions.

❧ 4 ❧

Empires, at Home and Abroad

1733–1763

BEGINNING with the War of the Polish Succession in 1733, the great opowers engaged in a series of wars, which, by 1763, cost France her overseas empire and left Poland a state doomed to extinction. As Poland declined, her two neighbors, Russia and Prussia, emerged as significant factors in the balance of power. The Hapsburgs viewed their emergence with alarm and began the serious centralization of their empire in order to avoid the fate of Poland. The rapid shifting of alliances during this period, always baffling to those who live in democratic America, can only partly be explained by the arrival of new powers into the fray. The armies of that day did not involve the population as a whole, and, as the continental rulers were relatively unchecked by public opinion, they could use their armies freely as instruments of royal policy without fear of popular indignation. Consequently, when one looks at the complications of international politics in the eighteenth century, he realizes the close association between the form of government and the nature of warfare.

THE PRINCIPLES OF LIMITED WAR

Eighteenth-century warfare often appears highly mechanical and rational to the twentieth-century student; and, in fact, it was. Just as in the seventeenth century, when the general movement to create greater find that the love for the rational, the orderly, produced an attempt to order had influenced military science, so in the eighteenth century do we make warfare as rational as possible. If warfare could be regulated, the argument went, then the atrocities of the Thirty Years War could be avoided. The regulation of warfare included, first of all, a deliberate attempt to produce a system of fighting under which decisive actions could be fought with forces of limited size and with a minimum of casualties, where the civilian population would neither take part nor even have their daily lives disrupted, and where the soldiers recruited to do the fighting came from the unproductive elements of society. As Frederick the Great put it:

> Useful hardworking people should be guarded as the apple of one's eye, and in wartime recruits should be levied in one's own country only when the bitterest necessity compels.[1]

Secondly, the deliberate attempt to limit military action, to restrict the conflict, helped to maintain the balance of power on the Continent, for the notion of annihilating an enemy in battle was inimical to the ideal of limiting the engagement.

To put these principles of limited warfare into practice required, in the first place, the recruitment of the least useful and least reliable elements of society into the army. This, in turn, meant that the troops required constant supervision and a fierce discipline, for being the riffraff of Europe, they were inclined to desert, to loot, and to lack the self-discipline essential to a good fighter. Ruthless drilling not only provided the discipline needed, but made possible the rational formations and movements so dear to the hearts of eighteenth-century generals and so in keeping with the philosophical vogues of that day. Such soldiers as these could not be allowed to roam the countryside when on campaign, which meant that foraging had to be abandoned and magazines had to be established, sharply reducing an army's mobility. This, of course, contributed to the protection of the civilian population. The recruitment of soldiers was not limited to one's own nationals, and many "recruits" were kidnaped and pressed into service or released from prison on condition that they enlist. Voltaire, with his usual acidity, related the capture of Candide by two Prussian recruitment officers:

> They immediately put irons on his legs and took him to a regiment. He was made to turn to the right and left, to raise the ramrod and return the

1. R. R. Palmer in E. M. Earle (ed.), *Makers of Modern Strategy* (Princeton, N. J., Princeton University Press, 1943), p. 54.

ramrod, to take aim, to fire, to double up, and he was given thirty strokes with a stick; the next day he drilled not quite so badly, and received only twenty strokes; the day after, he only had ten, and was looked on as a prodigy by his comrades.[2]

Given their social origin, it is not surprising to find the soldiers of the eighteenth century despised. In France, it was not uncommon to find signs in public places which read: "No dogs, lackeys, prostitutes, or soldiers."[3] When they were lost in battle, the resulting lamentations were largely financial; regarded as useless in society, their value soared in the army due to the lengthy training period required to teach a recruit the intricate drill necessary to make the regiments smoothly functioning units. The system made costly professionals out of sows' ears, and the eighteenth-century commander necessarily maneuvered to keep his losses small, though hardly for humanitarian reasons. Economy was the watchword and accounts for the defensive nature of much eighteenth-century warfare, the campaigns of Frederick II and the French Marshal Maurice de Saxe being notable exceptions.

Even so successful a general as Frederick II had little respect for his troops, believing that they should stand in greater fear of their own officers than of the enemy, a view which led Frederick to insist on a fiercer discipline than was common in the Catholic countries of that day. Frederick's own instructions will illustrate:

If a soldier during an action looks about as to flee, or so much as sets foot outside the line, the non-commissioned officer standing behind him will run him through with his bayonet and kill him on the spot.[4]

The savagery of Prussian discipline was such that a contemporary wit remarked that the native-born half of the Prussian army was charged with the task of preventing the foreign-born half from deserting. An examination of Frederick's battles will show he rarely pursued a fleeing foe nor sought the type of engagement where his troops would be on their own. The opportunity to desert might prove too tempting. Such a problem reduced the mobility of Frederick's army and left it a relatively inflexible instrument. But the inflexibility did contribute to the sense of regulated order so characteristic of eighteenth-century war, just as the inability to

2. Voltaire, *Candide,* Modern Library ed., Ch. II, p. 8.
3. Palmer, *op. cit.,* p. 50.
4. *Ibid.,* p. 56.

pursue a routed foe halted battles short of annihilation of the enemy, which saved lives and helped to maintain the balance of power.

The French army, without peer in the time of Louis XIV, deteriorated under Louis XV. In part, the army suffered from its successes, falling into an easy acceptance of its tactics and practices as beyond the possibility of improvement. The indifference of the monarch to military affairs contributed to the decline by opening military decisions and appointments to court intrigues. Accordingly, high-ranking officers found it necessary to play the game at court rather than to devote themselves to the instruction and improvement of the army. The financial difficulties of the *ancien régime* inevitably led to the sale of commissions, with a twofold effect: It enabled middle-class men to enter the officers' ranks, which angered the aristocrats, jealous of their time-honored monopoly of military offices; and it produced considerable bickering and noncooperation. Furthermore, the sale of commissions perpetuated, or made worse, a promotion system where real merit could not easily rise. The proof lies in the fact that the French army possessed some brilliant officers who never achieved a significant command, while mediocrity was too often rewarded. Under Louis XV, only one general repeatedly won both at court and in the field, the Marshal de Saxe, the double task proving insuperable for lesser men.

All this was the more serious in a day when, as Frederick II saw, the behavior of troops under fire depended on the officers more than on the fighting qualities of the soldiers. Though the soldiers were professionals, the system of warfare made the men into automatons who responded without fail to orders. The Prussian army had the great advantage, of course, of being commanded by its king. Frederick II lived as a Spartan, hardly the life of Louis XV, and all the requirements of government went toward the improvement of the army. One gets the impression that the state played second fiddle to the army. For all its inflexibility in battle, the Prussian army under Frederick was the best-drilled in Europe and, hence, the most mobile, since the drill of the parade ground approximated the formations used in actual battle. It was the final justification for drill that the soldier could expect to maneuver on the battlefield exactly as he maneuvered on parade.

On the whole, there was little difference between the rank-and-file soldiers serving the great powers, and their military organizations were similar. It was Frederick's officers who made the difference. His faith in them was justified not only because eighteenth-century warfare placed such a burden on their courage and discipline, but also because they proved superior in battle to their Austrian and French counterparts. Fredericks's officers came from the rural nobility, now accustomed to serving the royal power loyally and having a class solidarity unknown to the officer corps in France. Frederick suspected that middle-class officers would be neither dependable nor heroic. Coming from a commercial background, they would be corruptible; and they would lack the class solidarity, the corporate loyalty, which inspires individuals to sacrifice themselves and perform heroic deeds. In other words, they would not understand *noblesse oblige*. Whether right or wrong, Frederick refused to employ bourgeois officers until late in the Seven Years War, when his casualties gave him no other choice. He even preferred his officers not to marry, believing that a celibate corps would devote itself more completely to his cause. The reward for such devotion was the pre-eminence the officers enjoyed in the kingdom. They were unquestionably the elite.

We initially noted that eighteenth-century warfare seems rational, mechanical, and orderly, at least in comparison to the wars of earlier and later centuries. The armies were highly professional, costly to train, and necessarily limited in size to enable them to be maneuvered efficiently. To avoid losses, defensive warfare was favored, and it followed that most commanders preferred sieges to pitched battles. Not only was the assault upon a fortified place governed in detail by regulations, but its surrender was also so governed. A French commander, for instance, was required by the rules to repulse only one assault upon his fortress once the enemy had made a breach in the defensive walls with artillery. He literally satisfied his honor in repulsing the first attack, after which a surrender would be a *reasonable* response. To besiege a fortified place, a commander usually began by opening a parallel at six hundred yards—that is, an entrenchment to shelter the assaulting troops, which ran parallel to the fortress to be taken. This completed, trenches and tunnels were dug to permit an advance to within four hundred yards of the fortress, where the second parallel was opened. This procedure was then repeated to permit the opening of the third and last parallel at one hundred yards, from which distance the final assault could be made. The conduct of a siege made it possible, therefore, for the attacking force to fight what amounted to a defensive battle even while on the offensive.

The three parallels of siege warfare had their counterpart in pitched battles. Infantry was usually arrayed in three lines. Each line fired separately on command, then knelt to reload and to clear the way for another line's fire. This type of formation was obviously vulnerable to an attack from the rear and especially from the flanks, and a commander had to seek a position which made an attack from those sides impossible and forced his enemy to make a frontal attack. A frontal attack was a risky matter, and many an eighteenth-century commander refrained from giving battle when he found his enemy in a strong position. Constant maneuvering came to be a feature of eighteenth-century war, every commander working for a defensive position superior to that achieved by his opponent, giving battle only when a *reasonable* possibility of victory seemed assured. A near-classic example of such tactics is furnished by the Duke of Berwick, who defended southern France from invasion from Spain during the War of the Spanish Succession for over three years without ever actually fighting a pitched battle. To be prepared for such battles and carry out intricate maneuvers, the forces needed to be limited in size; and no less an authority than the Marshal de Saxe, regarded as the greatest general of his day, held that an army ought not to be larger than 46,000 men for the utmost effectiveness. Moreover, anything larger would not only have been clumsy in battle, but would also have presented serious supply problems in a day when an army was supposed to live off its magazines rather than off the countryside.

But let us not suggest that eighteenth-century armies never fought. Persistent maneuvering ultimately led to fighting, and the casualties were often high in comparison to the numbers engaged. The lines of infantry advanced in perfect order at a cadence of sixty steps a minute, the attacking force generally withholding its fire so that the first volley could be decisive. If the officers could keep their advancing troops from firing though under fire from the enemy, the first volley could be delivered in the very teeth of the enemy and could be followed by a bayonet attack, which would catch the enemy still staggered by the blast. Of course, the defensive force could also withhold its fire. The ideal was for the first volley to be decisive, to destroy the enemy morale and quickly put an end to the fighting. He who fired too soon often lost the advantage, and this will explain the action of the British officer at the Battle of Fontenoy who politely shouted to his enemy, "Gentlemen of the French Guard, fire first!"[5]

Naval practices in the eighteenth century show a marked resemblance to military operations. Defensive operations occupied the fleets for much

5. Usually attributed to Capt. Lord Charles Hay. The French declined the invitation—and won the battle.

of the time, thanks to the need to protect commercial vessels from privateers, and the rules governed the fleets at sea as much as they did armies on land. In the case of warfare at sea, however, the problem of communication between ships was serious, and standard signals referred to standard maneuvers which every captain presumably understood. But an admiral who wished to undertake an unorthodox maneuver in battle had no safe way to convey his wishes to his captains. Just as for infantry, the line was the basic formation for ships: the single line ahead. Naval battles were a series of duels between individual ships ranged in long lines, and the actual fighting was usually preceded by considerable maneuvering as each fleet sought to gain the advantage of the wind. The rules on not breaking out of the line were strict, so that a victorious ship rarely pursued a beaten foe. Victory lay with him who maintained the integrity of his line, clear indication of the defensive strategy governing naval fighting. It is not surprising to find, therefore, that fleet actions for much of the eighteenth century were indecisive. Victories were won, of course, but the defeated enemy was practically never crushed. This defense-mindedness stemmed also from the close relationship between naval power and overseas commerce; that is, the Navy and the merchant marine were associated in function, in training, and in material requirements. Since the primary function of the fleets was to protect the merchantmen from privateers, a large portion of the navy was tied down by purely defensive operations.

Britain and France were the chief naval rivals in the eighteenth century as Spain and Holland were declining in importance. Britain, in fact, seemed overwhelmingly predominant. Her navy, by 1740, was more than double that of France, and her merchantmen outnumbered those of France six to one. This meant a greater supply of trained seamen, too, than France could muster. In one area only were the French at an advantage: in naval architecture. Their ships were not only stouter, but also did not heel as sharply as those of the British, which could not take full advantage of their fire power. France's chief trouble lay in her dual role as a land and sea power. Unlike Britain, she had both coasts and borders to defend and could not afford to neglect one branch of the services as the British neglected the army in favor of the navy. Neither could France neglect her overseas trade; her exports were important, and her textile factories required cotton from abroad. The wonder is not that Britain ultimately eclipsed the French in the race for overseas empire, but that the French persisted so long against formidable odds.

It might be argued that British supremacy in numbers was considerably offset by the clear superiority of the French ships, so that a third factor must be introduced to account for the ultimate British triumph. Just as the Prussian corps of officers made the real difference between the army of Prussia and the armies of the other powers, so did the ultimate superiority of British naval power lie in Britain's naval officers. They came largely from the gentry—again, in analogy with Prussia—though gentle birth was not necessarily a prerequisite. While a Royal Naval Academy had been established in 1732, most naval officers began their training as captains' servants; and their promotion to midshipmen was the responsibility of the particular captain whom they served. They were commissioned only after six more years of experience and the successful passage of a lieutenant's examination. Thus, it was not unusual for a boy to go to sea at thirteen, literally grow up at sea, and become an officer in his late teens or early twenties. French naval officers in the eighteenth century, like French army officers, came from both the aristocracy and the bourgeoisie; and in both services, the social distinctions promoted hostility and non-cooperation. Worse, a French naval officer's training was largely theoretical, and he often went to sea as an officer with little practical experience. Naval theory was predicated on the assumption that the French navy would always be numerically inferior to the British. It was an easy matter, then, to advocate tactics which avoided seeking out the enemy fleet but encouraged raiding of the enemy commerce and coasts. The trouble with such a theory is that, while it can be momentarily successful, it cannot be successful in the long run without the destruction of the enemy fleet. And the British, who had no well-developed system of naval theory, at least operated on the assumption that the enemy fleet must be brought to a fight and destroyed.

As for the recruitment of seamen, the French system made every merchant seaman liable for navy service in time of war. For all its practicality, this was an unfair system. Had every Frenchman been liable for some kind of service in the armed forces, it would have been a different matter. But the army was professional and, thus, the obligatory service fell on the maritime population alone. There is reason to believe that this recruitment policy acted to discourage men from entering the merchant marine. British merchant seamen were not subject to compulsory naval service, so that in time of war, navy press gangs seized merchant seamen, as well as the nation's riffraff—again a procedure reminiscent of Prussia. The impressment of merchant seamen was usually done at sea, navy ships halting merchantmen to seize a part of their crews, to the great dismay of both ship masters and crewmen. The sailors resented navy service in particular because pay was better on the merchantmen. A merchant captain who had lost part of his crew usually sought foreign sailors as replacements. In sum, neither the British nor the French system of recruitment was enlightened, and the two navies had to exercise the discipline and surveillance common to the armies of that day to prevent desertion.

THE WAR OF THE POLISH SUCCESSION

We have already seen the causes for Poland's decline as a great power and found her, by the eighteenth century, a fatally decentralized state, unfortunately surrounded by powerful and ambitious neighbors. Her participation in the Great Northern War under Augustus the Strong contributed to the destruction of Sweden's Baltic monopoly, but it also contributed to the rise of Russia and Prussia. Under the circumstances—surrounded as she was by enemies—the salvation of Poland lay in a strongly centralized state and in an alliance with a strong continental power, presumably France. The Poles recognized the logic of the alliance; but the nobility, obstinately jealous of its "golden liberties," refused the constitutional reforms required to make Poland a centralized national state. Moreover, the Polish monarchy being elective, the kings were at the mercy of the nobles, and this circumstance invited the interference of various foreign powers ready to bribe the nobles to secure the election of the candidate who might best serve the interests of the particular power. Foreign interference became notably evident when the time neared to elect a successor to the aging Augustus the Strong.

Elected in 1697, Augustus was head of the Saxon House of Wettin, and through his elevation to the Polish throne, he had suddenly become a major figure in the German world. Aspiring to challenge even the Hapsburgs and Hohenzollerns, he had achieved a measure of dynastic success by the marriage of his son and heir to the eldest daughter of Joseph I (*1705-1711*) of the Holy Roman Empire. Later, the House of Wettin was to try to use this connection to push the candidacy of its heir for the imperial title. Thus, Augustus the Strong, though criticized for failing to promote constitutional reforms in Poland, tried to make Poland strong by building a Saxon-Polish-Hapsburg bloc. Yet, his unpopularity in Poland was extreme after the dismal results of the Great Northern War, so that he faced the unhappy likelihood that his son would not be elected to succeed him on the Polish throne, which would in turn damage the family ambitions in Germany.

The rising fear of Russia and Prussia in Poland expressed itself in a wave of antiforeignism. This, added to the increasing hostility toward the House of Wettin, favored the election of a native Pole once the old king should die. The obvious candidate was Stanislaus Leszczynski, the man who had already ruled briefly after 1704 as a Swedish puppet. In his favor was the marriage of his daughter Maria in 1725 to Louis XV, a connection which could easily bring the French alliance which Poland so desperately needed. The French, eager for a strong Poland on the flank of Prussia and Austria, poured money into the 1733 election in support of Leszczynski. Meanwhile, the Russians and Austrians had cooperated in a scheme to dump the Wettins, as too ambitious and potentially dangerous, in favor of a Portuguese prince; but the possibility of a Polish national revival led by Leszczynski and financed from Paris made the Portuguese venture an unreasonable countermove. Consequently, the Russians and Austrians reversed themselves to back the Wettin candidate, Frederick Augustus, who, as the price of Austrian support, agreed to recognize the Pragmatic Sanction (see pp. 133-40) and abandon his claim to the imperial throne.

As it happened, Stanislaus Leszczynski won the election in 1733, thanks to antiforeign sentiment more than to French money. The Russian reaction was immediate, 30,000 troops being dispatched to Poland to back up the Austro-Russian determination to prevent any revival of the Polish state. Leszczynski retired from Warsaw to await French help at Danzig, where he was besieged by the Russian force. In the meantime, the Russians assembled a rump Diet which dutifully elected Augustus III (*1734–1763*). The French relief force of 2000 men, which ultimately tried to reinforce Leszczynski at Danzig, was obviously insufficient, and the city was soon obliged to capitulate. Since France did go to war on behalf of Leszczynski, one might well wonder why she supported him so poorly at Danzig, sending an expeditionary force which had no hope of success.

The answer lies in the pacific policies of Cardinal Fleury. Like Walpole, he needed to maintain the peace for domestic reasons; yet he could not afford to stand by while France's natural ally, Poland, was being bullied by Russia and Austria, His strategy, then, was to limit the scope of the war as much as possible, above all to keep the British out. This precluded the sending of a large force into the Baltic, an action which probably would have alarmed the British. Fleury thus sacrificed Leszczynski for the moment, ignored what the Russians were up to, and merely declared war against Russia's ally (and France's traditional enemy), Austria. To make the situation even odder, this war, known as the War of the Polish Succession, was largely fought in Italy, with Spain and Sardinia joining France against the Austrians. This was Spain's opportunity to recover territories lost at Utrecht, and Sardinia also hoped to expand in Italy. The war went badly for Austria in Italy, where the Allies won repeated victories, and along the Rhine, where, despite some Austrian successes, the French occupied the Duchy of Lorraine. Here the pretext for the French attack lay in the marriage between Francis Duke of Lorraine and Maria Theresa, heir to the throne of Austria, which promised that the future of Lorraine would be tied to that of the House of Hapsburg.

Peace was achieved in 1735 through a series of treaties signed in Vienna, but only after long negotiation. In exchange for his renunciation of the Polish crown, Stanislaus Leszczynski was given the duchies of Lorraine and Bar for his lifetime, after which they were to devolve upon France. Francis, the ousted Duke of Lorraine, received the vacant ducal throne of Tuscany. In turn, the French guaranteed the Pragmatic Sanction —ever the concern of Emperor Charles VI. Italy was literally divided between the Hapsburg and Spanish Bourbon families: in addition to Tuscany, the Austrians retained Parma and Piacenza, while in the south, Don Carlos of Spain was granted the royal title to reign over the Kingdom of the Two Sicilies, with the qualification that the Neapolitan crown was never to be united with that of Spain. Sardinia got little for her efforts —only a few border rectifications to her advantage. And the Poles got nothing except the hated Augustus III, who was to spend most of his time in the more congenial atmosphere of Saxony.

Of greater seriousness for the Poles, however, was the revelation of their weakness, for they had been utterly powerless against a small Russian invading army. This weakness was not only recognized by Poland's ambitious neighbors, but also by friendly France, where the astute old Cardinal Fleury saw that continued Russian interference in the affairs of Poland and Sweden could deprive France of her traditional allies. He further saw that the deep penetration of Russian troops into Europe for the first time marked the beginning of a new power factor, especially since at the moment, the Russians cooperated with France's traditional enemy. "Russia," he wrote, "in respect to the equilibrium of the north has mounted to too high a degree of power and its union with the House of Austria is extremely dangerous."[6] In actual fact, the War of the Polish Succession did not significantly alter the balance of power in Europe, because the French victory had not been overwhelming, the Austrians were far from crushed, and the Russians withdrew from the scene without annexing territory.

THE WAR OF JENKINS' EAR

The next upset of the continental peace was preceded and complicated by a clash of colonial interests, involving Britain on the one hand and Spain and France on the other. Although after the treaty of Utrecht Britain and France had acted in concert to maintain the peace by checking Spain, this alliance was unpopular in France, where Bourbon Spain was regarded as a natural ally and Britain as the traditional enemy. The collaboration of France and Spain in the War of the Polish Succession in 1733 seriously weakened the Anglo-French alliance, especially when it soon became clear that the two Bourbon states had pledged themselves to cooperate in advancing their colonial and commercial interests at the expense of Britain; this agreement is called the Bourbon family compact.

On the one hand, the overseas expansion of these powers had enlarged the scope and intensity of their continental rivalries. On the other, it spread to the New World, not only their conflicting ambitions, but also their diverse philosophies of government and economic practices. The key to the antagonism between Britain and Spain lay in Spanish colonial policy, which was anachronistic in comparison to that of Britain. Spain regarded the trade with her colonies as a government monopoly, and charters to trade within that empire were sold only to Spaniards—and for a high price. Britain on the other hand, while she still practiced mercantilism in the form of Acts of Trade and Navigation, nevertheless granted charters to trading companies, which included not only the commercial rights in a given colonial area, but rights of self-government as well. These divergent colonial policies reflected the natures of the home governments, Britain having for some time enjoyed freer politicial institutions.

Unhappily for Spain, she could not produce ample goods to meet the colonial demand; this state of affairs inevitably invited the smuggling of

6. Fleury in secret instructions to La Chétardie, French Ambassador to St. Petersburg, in *Cambridge Modern History* (1909), VI, p. 308; and in *New Cambridge Modern History* (1957), VII, p. 205.

non-Spanish goods into the empire by foreigners. Britain, then beginning to industrialize, was able to supply the needed goods, and not only in quantity, but also at lower prices, for the British trader had not had to pay a high price for the right to trade and could sell his goods more cheaply than his Spanish competitor. Increasingly unable to halt smuggling, Spain began to search foreign vessels, most of them British, cruising in her colonial waters. British ships did have the right, dating from the treaty of Utrecht, to supply the Spanish Empire with slaves, and in addition, one British ship a year was allowed to call in the Spanish Empire, though it was limited to a cargo of 650 tons. This monopoly had been given to the South Sea Company by the British government, but the company was not careful to stay within the limit of 650 tons. Nor did the British government pay any heed to protests from Madrid when British subjects violated the legitimate rights of Spain.

On the contrary, as incidents became more numerous, the British public supported their sea captains, resenting the Spanish regulations, insisting on freedom of navigation, and eagerly swallowing all tales of Spanish atrocities supposedly committed during the search of ships. The most famous of these concerned a trader named Jenkins, who presented his ear in a box, presumably separated from his head by a Spanish coastguardsman, for the edification of the House of Commons. Sir Robert Walpole, eager to maintain the peace, realized that Spanish grievances were well-founded and tried to negotiate. Faced with a popular clamor for war, however, Walpole dared not uphold the Spanish right of search, which would have settled the issue, and so was pushed into a war. Whether one calls it the Anglo-Spanish War of 1739 or by its more popular title, the War of Jenkins' Ear, it has been called the purest trade war in British history.[7]

It was also one of the most miserably conducted of Britain's wars. The strategy was to capture the principal terminal ports in the Spanish Empire: Porto Bello, Cartagena, Changres, and La Guayra. The attack on Porto Bello in Panama succeeded, but that on Cartagena went awry and wrecked the total offensive. At that point, the war expanded, with new participants and new issues, both colonial and continental. France, for instance, was far from disinterested in the Anglo-Spanish struggle. For one thing, many of the goods shipped by Spain to her colonies originally came from France; moreover, there was reason to believe that France

7. See Walter L. Dorn, *Competition for Empire,* 1740-63 (New York, Harper, 1940), p. 126.

would ultimately lose her few colonies in the West Indies if Britain defeated Spain. On the Continent, the succession of Maria Theresa in 1740 was followed by an assault upon her empire, which quickly embroiled France and Spain and ultimately Britain. The Anglo-Spanish War had become the War of the Austrian Succession (1740–48).

THE WAR OF THE AUSTRIAN SUCCESSION

In the previous chapter we noted that the Hapsburg monarchy was not a strongly centralized state. It consisted of a collection of provinces, the possession of the Hapsburg family, each having Diets with considerable local authority. The head of the Hapsburgs had for many generations also been elected to the throne of the Holy Roman Empire, a title carrying considerable prestige but precious little power. But the prestige was important, especially in the Hapsburg's own domains, where their actual authority was seriously limited by the provincial Diets. Thus the failure of Charles VI to produce a male heir threatened the dynasty's future. There was no precedent for a woman's succession either to the Hapsburg lands or to the imperial crown.

Nevertheless, thanks to the Pragmatic Sanction, Maria Theresa did assume the Hapsburg domains in 1740, and she hoped that her husband, Francis, formerly Duke of Lorraine but now Duke of Tuscany, would be elected Emperor. Of all the powers, only Bavaria, whose King trotted out a most dubious claim to the imperial crown, refused to recognize Maria Theresa; but this was not overly serious because Bavaria's chief ally, France, did recognize her. Indeed, all seemed well. Russia had been cooperating with Austria for some years in a common desire to push back the Turks from the southern frontiers, and they had recently acted in concert to keep Poland weak. It is true that Austria had been watching the rise of Prussia with some concern, but in 1740, Prussia, too, had a new monarch, Frederick II (*1740–1786*), and any difficulty from that quarter seemed to be precluded, at least for the moment.

Frederick II, however, was not the man to stand aside simply because he was new to office. His predecessors had created a fine army and a strongly centralized state for its support; he had also inherited their absolutist outlook and their tendency to justify all actions and policies which enhanced the power and well-being of Prussia. A moment had come when it was opportune to strike at Austria, and he moved without any great prepa-

ration, either military or diplomatic, though he anticipated a French alliance. The target was the province of Silesia, an acquisition which would enrich Prussia economically and in population and which had the further advantage of being in a part of Germany which did not directly concern the interests of France, Britain, or Holland. His invasion of Silesia came as a surprise to Austria, for knowing that he had no valid claims, Frederick had not bothered with any prior negotiations. He occupied the province with little opposition and then offered to pay Maria Theresa three million gulden as compensation and to support her husband for the imperial title. In short, he offered himself as an ally, and since many of the Austrian ministers feared the Bourbon powers more than Prussia, they advised her to accept Frederick's offer.

Maria Theresa, young and inexperienced, was outraged by this unprovoked attack. Overruling her ministers, she gave orders to clear the Prussians out of Silesia, but the attempt failed at Mollwitz in 1741. While the Austrians were not crushed, their check encouraged all those whose interest it was to ignore the Pragmatic Sanction. A month later, Bavaria entered into a new alliance with the Bourbon powers, an alliance which Prussia and Saxony soon joined. Charles Albert of Bavaria put forth his claim to the imperial crown; the Spaniards hoped to regain more Italian territories lost at Utrecht; and Saxony-Poland saw an opportunity to expand in Bohemia and Moravia. Along with France, such a coalition against Austria seemed overwhelming.

In France, meanwhile, old Cardinal Fleury argued against an attack upon Austria, even though it might drive her out of Italy. Just as in the time of the Polish Succession, when Fleury had seen the significance of Russia's appearance on the European stage, so in 1741 he saw that the traditional French antagonism toward Austria was no longer politic. Since Utrecht, France had no longer had to face the nightmare of Hapsburgs in both Austria and Spain. Britain was the real enemy, he argued, and it would be well to cooperate with Spain overseas against Britain and not against the Austrians in Italy. Friendship for Austria, however, was more than most French statesmen could swallow, and the war party at court, led by the young Count of Belle Isle, put pressure on Fleury until he gave way. The decision to back Bavaria and Prussia proved disastrous in the long run, for the failure to concentrate on Britain ultimately cost France much of her overseas empire. It is the more ironical that this traditional French policy was advocated by the young at court, while the forward-looking policy had the backing of a Cardinal of nearly ninety.

A Franco-Bavarian invasion of Austria began in 1741 and extended into Bohemia with the aid of the Saxons. These successes led to the election of Charles Albert of Bavaria to the imperial throne as Charles VII (*1742–1745*) and to the thrones of Austria and Bohemia. In desperation, Maria Theresa threw herself upon the mercy and gallantry of her Hungarian estates, appealing to them as an outraged woman. The real loyalty of the Hungarians to the Hapsburg dynasty was certainly doubtful, but in this crisis, the nobles responded as gentlemen. She promised, in return for their support, to avoid all legislation injurious to them as a class.

Maria Theresa was further assisted by Frederick's resentment against his allies. He thought the French were carrying on a listless campaign in Austria, and he worried over the possibility of having to share Silesia with Bavaria and Saxony. In the summer of 1742, he suddenly abandoned his allies and signed a separate peace with Austria, which had to surrender Silesia. Saxony then necessarily gave up the struggle, leaving the French position in Central Europe dangerously exposed. The French vainly protested to Frederick and then began a speedy evacuation of Bohemia and Austria. Disgusted, the French allowed Bavaria to be overrun by the Austrians while negotiations for peace went on. Maria Theresa, however, would hear of no peace which did not allow Austria to annex Bavaria as compensation for Silesia, and this Paris would not permit. Thus, the war continued, and Austria made plans to invade Alsace and Lorraine. Furthermore, the British, who had helped negotiate the Austro-Prussian peace, now entered the European war to help Austria against the French. Since the war in the West Indies, as we have already seen, was not going well for Britain, it made sense to strike France on the Continent now that the opportunity was so clearly offered.

Prosecution of a war on the Continent and overseas simultaneously proved more complicated than the British had bargained for. Having had little experience with such a two-front war, they had no well-developed notion of how to proceed. Even on the Continent alone, they could not muster the coalition which had checked Louis XIV, for Holland no longer participated. Worse, Marlborough was long in his grave, and it was now the French who had the most gifted field commander, the Marshal de Saxe. The British government was further embarrassed by Austria's insistence on Bavaria, a demand threatening to Frederick II of Prussia who had let it be known that Austria's compensation must come from outside Germany. To gain compensation for Austria elsewhere and, thus, keep Prussia from re-entering the war, Britain moved to focus the war on Italy, where Spain had made notable gains in the War of the Polish Succession. Defeat for the Bourbon powers in Italy seemed the best guarantee for a quick peace, and Britain began negotiations with the little Kingdom of Sardinia, in the hope of securing her support for the Hapsburg cause against that of the Spanish Bourbons.

The Sardinians quickly recognized the opportunity to expand in Italy and negotiated with both sides for concessions. To head off a possible disaster, the British then promised Sardinia a large subsidy and brought pressure to bear on Vienna to make a major concession to Sardinia: the southwestern portion of Lombardy. The balance of power in Italy, then, shifted in favor of the British-Hapsburg-Sardinian coalition, and the situation looked bad for the Bourbon powers. Yet, all the precautions to keep Prussia from re-entering the war were in vain, for despite the Italian locale of the new operations, Frederick became convinced that the defeat of the Bourbon powers would end with Austria's renewing her claim to Silesia. In 1744, having revived his treaty with France and Bavaria, Frederick re-entered the war with an invasion of Bohemia. Prussian troops violated the Saxon frontiers in the process, bringing Saxony back into the war, but on the Austrian side.

As in the earlier part of the war, Franco-Prussian efforts were not coordinated. With Frederick in Bohemia, the French failed to move on Austria, but occupied themselves in driving the Austrians out of Bavaria. As a result, Frederick suffered a major defeat and had to evacuate Bohemia, while the Franco-Bavarian recapture of Munich led to a separate peace between Austria and Bavaria (1745). Frederick's plight was desperate— he was facing invasion by the Austrians and Saxons; but instead of marching to his rescue, the French moved against an Anglo-Austrian force defending the Austrian Netherlands. Here Marshal de Saxe won a great victory at Fontenoy and moved on into the Netherlands. Frederick, in the meantime, had been learning from his military failures, and at this critical moment in the summer of 1745, he showed great generalship for the first time. He turned back the Austrians twice and managed to reoccupy Saxony. Then he abandoned the French for the second time by signing a separate peace with Maria Theresa at Dresden (1745), Prussia keeping Silesia. The Austrians were reluctant to sign the treaty of Dresden but were pressured to do so by Britain, who was anxious to see the full force of the alliance turned against the Bourbon powers. One favorable result for Austria in the treaties ending the war with Prussia and Bavaria was their acknowledgement of Francis' right to the imperial crown. He was elected Emperor (*1745–1765*) in place of Charles Albert of Bavaria.

Two months after the victory at Fontenoy, the French succeeded in depositing the Stuart pretender to the British throne, Prince Charles, on the Scottish coast. This compelled the withdrawal of the British force from the Netherlands, leaving their Austrian, Hanoverian, and Dutch allies helpless in the face of de Saxe's advance. (The Dutch had entered the war only to help stem the French drive.) The French occupied the Austrian Netherlands, and only the continued British control of the Channel prevented them from supporting Charles Stuart directly with an invading army. As it was, Charles gathered only a small army of Jacobites, his support coming mainly from the Highlands, and his invasion of England was smashed at Culloden early in 1746. He fled to France, ending the last serious Stuart effort to regain the crown.

The colonial theaters of war never became paramount in the War of the Austrian Succession, despite British preoccupation with the commercial issues which had originally caused the break with Spain. The scope of the war had quickly broadened to include many issues and states, and the balance of power on the Continent was obviously at stake. This balance required the primary attention of the great powers if they were to remain great powers, and few troops were spared for service in the colonies. The British navy, for example, had to operate in the Mediterranean to prevent the Bourbon powers from freely supplying their armies in Italy by sea, and later in the war the navy had to guard against a possible invasion from France. This preoccupation of the great powers with continental issues explains the great temptation for the colonists in New England to seize French Canada, at a time when Canada could expect little reinforcement from France. William Shirley, the Governor of Massachusetts, organized an expedition for the conquest of Canada which achieved one notable success: the capture of Louisburg on Cape Breton Island (1745); this base guarded the entrance to the St. Lawrence valley. Had British aid arrived, this victory might have been enlarged to include all Canada; without help, the colonists were unable to continue their offensive. A similar situation developed in India, where the British and French East India Companies accepted the European war as an invitation to demolish its rival in India. In this case, it was the French governor, Joseph François Dupleix, who mounted an offensive which captured the British post at Madras in 1746. The British counterattacks upon French positions in India all failed.

Negotiations for peace were carried on chiefly by France and Britain, without much consultation of Austria, largely because the French hoped such a procedure would provoke the Austrians into an angry rupture with Britain for apparently being willing to sign a separate peace—much as France had been angered by Prussia's conclusion of a separate peace on two occasions. There had been a slow realization in Paris that the old Cardinal had been right; Austria was no longer the dangerous enemy of yesteryear, and the chief menace to France came from Britain, especially overseas. The treaty of Aix-La-Chapelle (1748) did produce the effect desired by the French, for even though the Austrians adhered to it, they were furious at Britain for having agreed to a peace which ignored Austria's interests. It was, in fact, a peace with no clear-cut victory, and it did not even resolve the initial issue dividing Spain and Britain overseas—the right of search. Britain and France gave up their overseas conquests, Britain receiving Madras in India and France gaining Louisburg in Canada. France returned the Austrian Netherlands to Austria, which, in turn, ceded Parma to Don Philip of Spain and confirmed the earlier cessions of Silesia to Prussia and southwest Lombardy to Sardinia. Spain reconfirmed the assiento (see p. 132) in Britain's favor, while France agreed to recognize the Hanoverian dynasty in Britain and to withdraw further support from the Stuarts.

If Britain and France returned to the *status quo ante bellum* at Aix La-Chapelle, they left Austria as the war's chief loser, for she lost Silesia, Parma, and part of Lombardy. All she could point to in 1748 was the confirmation of the Pragmatic Sanction and the election of Francis as Holy Roman Emperor. Prussia, Sardinia, and the Spanish Bourbons were the victors. It is interesting that more than a century later, Prussia and Sardinia would unify the German and Italian peoples into national states after the further defeat of Austria.

CENTRALIZATION IN THE HAPSBURG EMPIRE

The loss of Silesia to upstart Prussia was a bitter pill for the Hapsburg monarchy, and Maria Theresa's response was to begin the reform of her administration so that the resources of her empire could be efficiently mustered for a war of revenge. The war just concluded had demonstrated only too painfully that the high degree of decentralization prevented the monarch from utilizing the real strength of the empire; it is therefore not

Above left to right:
Marquis de Condorcet
y Jean Antoine Houdon,
David Hume
Right: *Voltaire* by Jean
Antoine Houdon

Above: *Les Prisons* by Piranese   Top: Place de la Concorde, Paris

Left: *Master Hare* by Sir Joshua
Reynolds
Above: Philippe, Duke of Orleans
Below: *The Humours and Diversions
of Southwark Fair* by William Hogarth

Below: George I of England
Bottom: Cardinal Fleury

Above: Robert Walpole, First Earl
of Oxford
Top: *The Painter in His Studio* by
François Boucher

surprising that the reforms beginning in 1748 should have aimed at greater centralization. This meant the creation of a larger, highly trained bureaucracy, as well as a reduction of the authority of the provincial Diets. To direct the reforms, Maria Theresa summoned Count Haugwitz, a Silesian. Her other principal adviser, Prince Wenzel Anton von Kaunitz (1711–1794), was ordered to direct Austrian foreign policy toward the recovery of Silesia. To this end he set about isolating Prussia, relinquishing the traditional hostility to France and seeking that reconciliation already predicted earlier by Cardinal Fleury.

Haugwitz's early reforms were confined to Austria and Bohemia because Maria Theresa's obligation to the Hungarian nobles for their loyalty in the recent war meant that she could not infringe upon their liberties without being ungracious and violating her pledge to them. Haugwitz estimated that the monarchy must support a standing army of 108,000, requiring an increase in the military budget from nine to fourteen million gulden annually. His problem was twofold: he must get the Diets of Austria and Bohemia to grant the additional money, which could only be raised by extending the property tax to include the estates belonging to the great nobles; and in the process he must reduce, rather than increase, the authority and privileges of the provincial Diets. Traditionally, the Diets expected more, not fewer, privileges when they agreed to provide more money or greater services; but in 1748, the need for administrative reform was so obvious that the Diets realized that refusal to cooperate would lead to further military disaster.

Haugwitz did not mean to eliminate the provincial Diets completely, as the Prussian monarchy had succeeded in doing by the beginning of the eighteenth century; but he wanted to transfer their administrative functions to officials appointed by the central government—officials who would represent the interest of the monarchy and not that of the locality or the local nationality. This is not to say that Haugwitz meant to Germanize the empire and destroy the identity of the many nationalities it comprised. Only much later would the Germanization of the empire seem to be a logical concomitant of greater centralization. It is true, however, that most of the civil servants being trained were of German rather than Hungarian or Bohemian origin.

In cutting into the authority of the provincial Diets, Haugwitz did employ a device reminiscent of the Prussian monarchs' tactics of the previous century. He persuaded the Diets of Austria and Bohemia to grant increased taxes for the following ten years, thus giving the monarchy a ten-year period to govern without provincial interference. Then he proceeded to reorganize the administrative units of Austria and Bohemia into ten districts without regard for provincial borders. To put it another way, he really merged Austria and Bohemia by reconstituting the western half of the monarchy into ten administrative districts, and he did so without the consent of the Diets. He underscored the significance of the reform by then eliminating some of the tax exemptions enjoyed by the nobility and clergy in the western half of the empire. Even though the peasantry continued to pay more than its share of the taxes, the tax reform was a step in the right direction, and the central government soon began to realize revenues from the Bohemian taxpayers which were double the amount coming in from Hungary.

An entirely different course was followed in Hungary. Here the policy was to tie the country closer to the Hapsburg monarchy without touching the rights of those nobles who owned virtually 80 per cent of the land in Hungary but who were nearly tax exempt. They had demonstrated their loyalty to the monarchy during the War of the Austrian Succession; the monarch would now shower honors, titles, and offices upon them, ostensibly giving testimony of her gratitude, but really capturing them for further services to the empire. Many were given court positions in Vienna, so that they shortly began to identify themselves with Vienna rather than solely with the Hungarian Diet in Budapest. The fact is that Maria Theresa, whose inexperience and poor preparation gave so little promise upon her accession, gave the monarchy a degree of centralization far beyond that which any of her predecessors had been able to accomplish. Though her military and administrative reforms were not sufficiently perfected to bear fruit when she sought to recover Silesia in 1756, her second military failure spurred her to even greater reforms after 1763.

RENEWED COLONIAL STRIFE

It will be recalled that our study of the War of the Austrian Succession (1740–1748) was made especially complex by the necessary inclusion of colonial factors which had nothing directly to do with the Austrian succession and the fate of Silesia. In fact, Spain and Britain had come to blows over colonial issues a year before the struggle extended to the Continent. This same juxtaposition of colonial and continental problems confronts us in the study of the Seven Years War (1756–1763); and in many respects, the second war was really a continuation of the first after an uneasy truce of eight years, during which alliances were shifted and France, rather than Spain, furnished Britain with the causes for colonial strife. Just as the earlier squabble between Britain and Spain was in part related to the differences in the structure of their empires—differences which simply increased the rivalries and hostilities normal between national states —so do we find that the differences in the structure of the British and French empires in the 1750's made for trouble. This is not to say that the differences in political organization alone made the conflicts, but rather that the differences acted to complicate the economic rivalry and introduced causes for war which were not strictly economic.

The economic and political freedom granted the British colonies by the mother country contrasted sharply with French practices just as they did with those of Spain. The contrast was even greater in the eighteenth century than it had been in the seventeenth because after 1689 British political institutions became even freer than before; and British commerce moved towards *laissez faire*—that is, toward actual freedom from governmental regulation. The British Empire remained mercantilistic in form, as the unrepealed Acts of Trade and Navigation guaranteed, and many economic theorists were still delighted with the vision of the self-contained empire whose economic self-sufficiency was presumably the foundation of the nation's strength. But in actual fact, British commerce moved away from mercantilism, because the closed economy of the mercantilists was never satisfactory in either absorbing all the produce of the empire or providing all the commodities required. The practice of mercantilism produced a situation in which uneconomic items were produced and protected rather than being imported from outside the empire, where they might be economically produced. As we have already noted in the case of the Spanish Empire, illicit trade was the inevitable result of mercantilism.

The British colonies were not only remarkably autonomous in the eighteenth century, but their indifference to the trade regulations passed by the Parliament in London amounted to economic freedom. Even manufacturing developed in the colonies, and illicit trade was so common that historians now doubt that trade regulation by Britain had much to do with the coming of the American Revolution. In contrast, the administration of the French Empire reflected the highly centralized and autocratic French monarchy. Far from being given local autonomy, the French colonies were administered through the Ministry of the Marine in Paris, almost, as one writer put it, as if the colonies were ships and all alike.[8] There was little reason for Frenchmen who opposed the political and religious institutions of their country to go to a French colony. They stayed at home to make trouble, while many English Dissenters went to English colonies in the expectation of greater freedom. The failure of the French to attract colonists was not the least of the reasons why the French failed in the New World. Furthermore, the English colonists in North America recognized the political advantages of being English rather than French colonists, so that their hostility to French expansion in North America cannot be written off as mere economic rivalry.

But economic rivalry there was, too, and despite the Peace of Aix-la-Chapelle in 1748, British and French traders and colonists argued and privateered wherever their interests collided: in the West Indies, in India, and in Canada. Most serious of all was the French expansion on the North American continent. French Canada had a population hardly in excess of 65,000, whereas the population in the thirteen British colonies exceeded one million. On the other hand, the French were encouraged by the very fact that the British colonies had no political unity and were relatively defenseless. Moving into the Ohio and Mississippi valleys in the eighteenth century, the French gave the appearance of hemming in the British colonies along the eastern seaboard; but the French advances were more spectacular than real because exploration was not followed by settlement. The bulk of the French population remained in the narrow St. Lawrence valley between Quebec and Montreal, so that when British colonists began to push across the mountains into the Ohio valley, they were opposed not by French colonists but by the French military.

The French recognized the seriousness of the situation, holding that the Ohio valley was the key to control of the American interior. The British colonist must be kept out at all cost, for wherever he went, he settled down to develop agricultural communities, and British political control of the area soon followed. To prevent British penetration, the French built a long series of forts which stretched from the St. Lawrence in Canada to the Illinois country. The most strategic of these forts was at the forks of the Ohio where the Allegheny and Monongahela Rivers merged. Here, in 1754, Governor Duquesne drove off a group of Virginians under George Washington and completed the fort begun by them, leaving

8. *Ibid.*, p. 258.

the French in such a strong position that the government in London could no longer stand aside.

It would be a mistake to conclude that the British decision to use force in America derived primarily from a desire to protect British commercial interests from French encroachment; nor were the British especially moved by the plight of the frontiersmen exposed to French operations. The well-developed colonial resistence to British authority, the open flouting of the Acts of Trade and Navigation, not only irked the London government but inevitably also raised the question of the value of the colonies to Britain. But French expansion in North America, seen from London, was related to the expansion of French power in Europe, and that the British were determined to block. In short, it was a new phase in the old campaign to contain the ambitions of absolutist Catholic France.

Neither government was eager for a resumption of hostilities. The British experience in the War of the Austrian Succession did not recommend taking on the combined forces of France and Spain again; and in India, where the rival East India companies bickered, the French government actually shrank from supporting its company for fear a war would develop. Yet, both governments got war, drifting into it against their will. It had been suggested that if either government had possessed a well-formulated colonial policy that could have been the basis for negotiation, perhaps a settlement could have been reached. But indecision and confusion led to war for lack of any other way to settle the issues. The fighting began in America in 1754 without a declaration of war, the responsibility falling on the British for their decision to send 2000 troops under General Edward Braddock to clear the French from Fort Duquesne and the Ohio valley. Getting word of British preparations, the French immediately assembled reinforcements for Canada; whereupon, the British Navy was ordered to see to it that the French reinforcements would not land in Canada. The British failure was twofold; Braddock's little army was ambushed and slaughtered as it approached Fort Duquesne, while the French evaded the British fleet and landed reinforcements in Canada. At this point, the colonial fighting merged with continental issues, producing the Seven Years War.

THE SEVEN YEARS WAR

One of the striking features of the War of Austrian Succession had been the incompatability of allies: Frederick had been suspicious of French failure to give him direct support; France had resented Frederick's repeated desertions from the alliance. Britain, whose chief interest had been overseas, had several times sacrificed Austria's interests in Italy, and the alliance had failed to recover Silesia for Austria. These factors alone might have produced a revision of the alliance systems, but as it happened, other factors were added to produce, by 1756, what historians have called the Diplomatic Revolution. Much earlier, Cardinal Fleury had argued that the traditional antagonism between France and the Hapsburgs was no longer tenable, thanks to the decline of Austria's European position; she was no longer a threat to France as she had been in the sixteenth and seventeenth centuries, when Hapsburgs ruled in Madrid as well as in Vienna. The loss of Silesia by 1748 proved the accuracy of Fleury's argument.

Thinking in Vienna, after 1748, ran along similar lines. Prince Kaunitz, Maria Theresa's primary adviser in foreign matters, had to recognize that Prussia had replaced France as Austria's most dangerous enemy. Moreover, as long as France supported Prussia, there was little hope of recovering Silesia; the recent war had demonstrated that the British alliance was inadequate to offset the Franco-Prussian alliance. Finally, that war had also revealed Austrian inability to defend the provinces in the Netherlands against French attack. The Netherlands, of course, had been the one area where Austrian and British interests had coincided, but British assistance to Austria in that theater had been slim. And Austrian help for the defense of Hanover against Prussia had been nonexistent. With the approval of Maria Theresa, Prince Kaunitz set out to reconcile Paris and Vienna.

Frederick II, in the meantime, recognized the possibility of a Franco-Austrian reconciliation; this eventuality was alarming to him despite the fact that he had come to doubt the efficiency of the French army, which no longer possessed its superb captain, the Marshal de Saxe. Worse for Prussia was the possibility that Russia, already a long-term ally of Austria against the Turks, would now support Austria in Central Europe. For some time in the eighteenth century, Russian interference into Polish affairs had demonstrated her keen interest in Poland and the Saxon dynasty; and since Frederick's ambitions seemed to include Saxony and West Prussia, Russia's interest in Poland would be served by the defeat of Prussia. Fearful of a great coalition against him, Frederick reached an understanding with Britain in 1756 to the effect that they would maintain the *status quo* in the German world.

The news of the Anglo-Prussian *entente* provided the shock necessary to convince Louis XV's government of the need for the Austrian alliance to maintain the balance of power. The French were uninterested in a continental war for the recovery of Silesia, but they felt that this defensive alliance would allow them free rein to deal with Britain overseas. Kaunitz plotted a war against Prussia, but felt certain that he could make Prussia appear to be the aggressor and, thus, require France to come to Austria's aid. The desire of Russia to adhere to the alliance was embarrassing for France, who had alliances with Sweden, Poland, and Turkey—all enemies of Russia—but the three-party alliance was made complete when Russia agreed that France need not give up her alliance with Turkey. The Austrians understood that Russia would supply 80,000 troops for a war to recover Silesia, but the French still regarded the new alliance system as an instrument for peace through the maintenance of the power balance. And war need not have come had Frederick kept his head and waited to see if an attack upon him would develop. Instead, he anticipated trouble and invaded Saxony in the summer of 1756, thus activating the defensive alliance against him. This made general the colonial war which had been openly declared between Britain and France earlier that same year.

Britain's chief theater in the war was, of course, colonial, since she had no great army to be sent to the continent. Her strategic problem was thus quite clear: keep Frederick II in the field against such a formidable alliance, while winning victories against France overseas, where British seapower could provide the margin of victory and where the small British military forces would be effective all out of proportion to their size. The monarch's concern for Hanover, however, forced the British to be more directly involved on the continent than most strategists thought wise, and George II was criticized for subordinating British interests to those of Hanover. William Pitt (1708–1778), chief British policy maker from 1757 on, would have sacrificed Hanover to the French for the moment, helping Frederick with subsidies and concentrating British armed strength overseas. Instead, he was persuaded to employ some troops for the defense of Hanover and for raids on the French coast to supplement his major operations; since these supplementary campaigns were miserably conducted, they were ultimately scored as a shameful waste, especially in comparison to what the subsidies to Frederick and the British operations overseas accomplished.

Continental hostilities had been opened by Frederick's invasion of Saxony in August, 1756. The Saxon army capitulated near Dresden in October and was incorporated wholesale into the Prussian army. Augustus

III, who had commanded the Saxons, retired to Poland, while an Austrian force under Count Maximilian von Browne, attempting to come to the aid of the Saxons, was beaten off. Meantime, a large French force under Marshal Louis Charles d'Estrées began its advance against Hanover, where the Duke of Cumberland held out a few months before surrendering in 1757. Though his capitulation opened up Prussia's western flank to invasion, Cumberland had kept the French occupied for a time when Frederick had more than his share of troubles without having to deal with the French. The Swedes had landed in Pomerania, the Russians had moved into East Prussia, and the Austrians were concentrating their strength in Bohemia for invasions of Saxony and Silesia.

To deal with these threats, Frederick fought four battles in 1757, earning a military reputation which far outshone that of any other commander in the Seven Years War. The Swedes were rather easily repulsed, whereupon Frederick turned upon his more major enemies, judging the Austrian menace the most pressing. He moved into Bohemia from Saxony and defeated the Austrians near Prague, into which they then retired and had to be besieged. An Austrian relief force then approached under Count Leopold von Daun and took up excellent position at Kolín. To attack Daun, Frederick had to maneuver in the open, enabling the Austrians to counter his every move, so that he was ultimately compelled to make a frontal attack. The attack failed and a Prussian evacuation of Bohemia followed. It is generally held that if the Austrian army had been capable of a rapid pursuit, the war could have been decided then and there. But Daun failed to follow up his advantage, and Frederick escaped with the lesson that successful flank attacks upon an enemy cannot be launched in the open. Surprise is necessary. The Austrians then occupied Silesia and even moved into Berlin. Even so, Frederick had scored two victories against one defeat.

He next had to meet the threat of two hostile armies cooperating in Thuringia: a French force under the Prince de Soubise and a Holy Roman Imperial force under Prince Joseph of Saxe-Hildburghausen. Soubise's initial positions were so strong that Frederick dared not attack, for the memory of Kolín was still fresh. Then Soubise selected new positions for the allied armies, positions which were not only strong, but would also threaten Frederick's communications. As so often happened in the eighteenth century, the cooperation between the allied armies was more nominal than real. Prince Joseph bided his time, while the French got under way in the direction of the new positions. Realizing what was afoot, Frederick ignored the imperial forces and hid his own men behind hills across the path of the French advance. He delivered a surprise attack on November 5 at Rossbach, and the French had no time to form their lines to meet the assault. Their rout was complete and the invasion broke down.

In December, Frederick was ready to take on the Austrians again to force their evacuation of Prussia and Silesia. The Battle of Leuthen was similar to that at Rossbach in that Frederick again hid his main force from the enemy. He toyed with the Austrian front with a covering force while he developed his main attack on the Austrian left flank. His victory was complete, causing the enemy to evacuate Prussia and most of Silesia.

These four victories in 1757 so encouraged the British that they repudiated the earlier truce over Hanover and in 1758 granted Frederick a much larger subsidy. A new Anglo-Hanoverian force was put in the field under Prince Ferdinand of Brunswick to divert the French, allowing Frederick to concentrate on the Austrians and Russians in 1758.

Anglo-Prussian optimism for 1758 was short-lived. Frederick moved into Moravia to strike at the Austrian base at Olmütz, but had to abandon the campaign for two reasons; his supply lines were too long and vulnerable to Austrian action, and the Russians had finally begun to move from East Prussia into Brandenburg and could no longer be ignored. In August, he blocked the Russians at Zorndorf, but only at great cost in lives; and while he was so occupied, the Austrians reinvaded Saxony and Silesia. In desperation, Frederick rushed to Saxony, only to find Daun ensconced in excellent positions. Aware of the risk, he felt there was no alternative but to give battle. The Austrians beat him (at Hochkirch) but, as in the previous year, were unable to pursue. Frederick's dilemma would have been even greater but for the astonishing successes won that year by the Anglo-Hanoverian forces over the French, whose generalship was proving incredibly bad. Ferdinand of Brunswick drove the French out of Hanover and Brunswick, then out of Hesse and Westphalia, and finally across the Rhine.

In 1759, the French resumed the attack under the Duc de Broglie and recovered some of their losses, but they were finally halted by Brunswick at the Battle of Minden. The important aspect was that the French were kept occupied and could not help the Austrians at a moment when Frederick was on the run. The Prussians were suffering further reverses in the summer of 1759, which culminated in a catastrophic defeat by the Russians at Kunersdorf and by the Austrian occupation of Dresden. Had the two powers coordinated their efforts at that point, they could have brought the war to a conclusion. But Prussia was saved for the third time in the war by Austrian inaction, which made the Russians angry and suspicious, so that they withdrew temporarily and did not follow up their great victory.

Meanwhile, the Duc de Choiseul (1719–1785) had been named French foreign minister and was determined to revise French policy. Despite the French gains in western Germany early in 1759, he thought quite correctly that French strength was being dissipated to little avail in that theater. Britain, he argued, was the real enemy, and her subsidies alone kept Frederick in the field. An invasion of Britain was the answer, and even a small army would suffice for the task if the Channel could be crossed. The problem was to gain control of the Channel with inferior naval forces. Choiseul's plan required that the British fleet be decoyed off to the Irish coast by a small French squadron which would sail from Dunkirk. The Toulon and Brest fleets would then sail into the Channel unopposed, to cover the invasion forces, one to land in Essex for a drive on London, the other to land in the Clyde estuary to march on Edinburgh. Unfortunately for the plan, the British got wind of it and refused to be led off to Ireland. When the Toulon fleet sailed for its rendezvous, it was intercepted at Lagos and driven back; and shortly after, late in 1759, the Brest fleet was beaten by Sir Edward Hawke in Quiberon Bay.

The overseas war also went badly for the French. In America, the British superiority began to tell by 1758, and lacking seapower, the French were virtually cut off from aid from Europe. Louisburg, Frontenac, and Fort Duquesne all fell in 1758. General Montcalm lost Quebec to General Wolfe in 1759, and the capture of Montreal the following year gave Britain control of Canada. The forces of the French East India Company were similarly overwhelmed by the British in 1759, and what French help could be sent arrived too late to save India.

Yet, despite their inability to invade Britain or hold the overseas empire, owing to naval inferiority, France and her allies were near to victory on the Continent by 1760. That was a year of relative military stalemate; France continued to make gains against Brunswick in Germany, though unable to crush him; Austria and Russia failed to cooperate, as usual, and hence could not take advantage of their victories over Frederick. But clearly the game was up for Frederick, and he knew it.

Then came the miracle which Frederick needed. In January, 1762, the Empress Elizabeth of Russia died, to be succeeded by her nephew, Peter III, who reigned only six months, but long enough to take Russia out of the war. Peter idolized Frederick and made his decision without any consideration of Russia's true interest in the war. Having grown to respect Russia's power, the Swedes also left the war, leaving Frederick free to deal with the Austrians. Peter III did not long survive to enjoy his alliance with Frederick. Resentful army officers overthrew and murdered him, and he was succeeded by his wife, Catherine II (*1762–1796*); but the damage to the Austrians was already done. Frederick drove them out of Silesia that same year.

Choiseul ought to have been discouraged at this point; instead, he sought to give the war a new dimension to intimidate the British. He threatened to bring Spain into the war and, when the British stood firm, was obliged to do so. The price was the island of Minorca, which the French had captured in 1756. He devised a second invasion plan, more intricate than the first, which involved naval feints at Gibraltar and Jamaica, and a Spanish invasion of Portugal. Troops assembled for the invasion of Britain were to be earmarked for a new drive into Germany, so as to mislead the British. But all came to naught, and Spain's entry into the war in early 1762 gave the British an excuse to seize some Spanish possessions overseas. Peace had become as necessary for France as for Austria, and the negotiations late in 1762 were ratified at Paris in 1763, only five days before Austria and Prussia formalized their peace at Hubertusburg.

The treaty of Paris was an imperial triumph for Great Britain. France ceded Canada and Cape Breton Island, Granada in the West Indies, and her bases on the Senegal in Africa; the British East India Company remained dominant in India, the French recovering only Chandernagor and Pondichery. From Spain, the British received Florida, but returned the Spanish bases taken late in the war. France had earlier given Louisiana to Spain as compensation for the probable loss of Florida. The Mississippi River was recognized as the boundary between Louisiana and the English colonies to the east. In other words, the Bourbon powers lost their claim to the Ohio valley and the lands beyond the Appalachian Mountains.

In Europe, the treaty required France to give up territories in Hanover, Brunswick, and Hesse, which she had won late in the war. She was to retain the Prussian Rhenish territories she had occupied only until peace was made between Austria and Prussia. And Spain, finally, had to evacuate Portuguese territory. Frederick II, suspicious by nature and quick to make the claim that he had been betrayed by the British, did not see that his interests had been protected. Britain returned bits of French territory overseas in order to force the French evacuation of Rhenish Prussia, which took place once Prussia, Austria, and Saxony signed the Treaty of Hubertusburg. It is true that the British made a separate peace, but Frederick

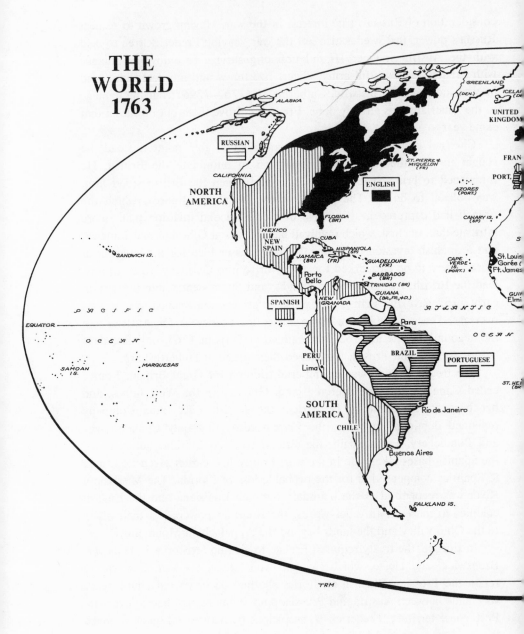

THE WORLD 1763

GREENLAND (DEN.)

ICELAN

ALASKA

UNITED KINGDOM

RUSSIAN

FRAN

ST. PIERRE & MIQUELON (FR.)

PORT.

CALIFORNIA

AZORES (PORT.)

NORTH AMERICA

ENGLISH

FLORIDA (BR)

CANARY IS. (SP)

SANDWICH IS.

MEXICO NEW SPAIN

CUBA

HISPANIOLA (SP.)

S

CAPE VERDE IS. (PORT.)

St. Louis Gorée Ft. James

JAMAICA (BR)

GUADELOUPE (FR.)

Porto Bello

BARBADOS (BR)

GUIL Elmi

TRINIDAD (BR)

SPANISH

NEW GRANADA

GUIANA (BR, FR, +D.)

ATLANTIC

EQUATOR

PACIFIC

Para

OCEAN

OCEAN

SOUTH AMERICA

PERU

Lima

BRAZIL

PORTUGUESE

SAMOAN IS.

MARQUESAS

ST. HE (BR

Rio de Janeiro

CHILE

Buenos Aires

FALKLAND IS.

TRM

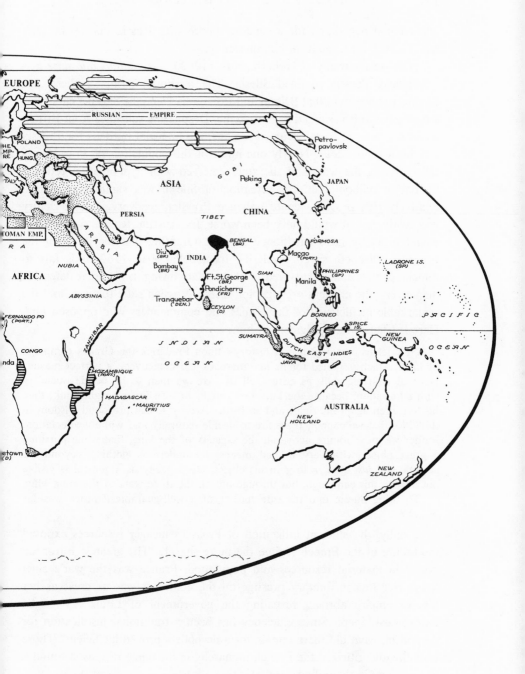

himself had negotiated for a separate peace with Russia during the war, making such a charge from him unseemly.

Because the treaty of Hubertusburg (1763) was a *status quo ante bellum* peace, Prussia retained Silesia. The territorial terms of these two treaties left no doubt that Britain and Prussia had won the Seven Years War, but the cost to Prussia had been extreme. Despite the subsidies from Britain and the exactions from occupied regions, the financial burdens for Prussia had been tremendous. Nearly one-ninth of the population of Prussia was killed during the war, and the state emerged with a population reduced by half a million. Yet, the retention of Silesia was significant; such a relatively rich province could enhance Prussian recovery. But if victory was costly, defeat would have been worse, for Austria, Russia, and Saxony would probably have partitioned Prussia. Granting that the death of the Empress Elizabeth saved Frederick from collapse in 1762, it is fair to remember that he had survived until that date owing to his great defensive maneuvers, the efficient organization of the Prussian state for war, and the remarkable inefficiency of the armies and commanders who opposed him. Here is Clausewitz's judgment of him:

> Now let us cast a glance at history—upon Frederick the Great's campaign of 1760, which is famed for its fine marches and maneuvers; a perfect masterpiece of strategic skill, as critics tell us. Are we then to be beside ourselves with admiration, because the king first sought to turn Daun's right flank, then his left, then again his right, and so forth? Are we to see profound wisdom in this? No, that we cannot, if we are to decide naturally and without affectation. Rather we must admire above all the sagacity of the king, that while pursuing a great object with very limited means, he undertook nothing beyond his powers, and *just enough* to gain his object. His sagacity as a general is visible not only in this campaign, but through-out all the three wars of the great king.
>
> To bring Silesia into the safe harbor of a well-guaranteed peace was his object.[9]

Finally, the efficient utilization of Prussia's meager resources exposed the failure of the French regime the more sharply. The greatest European power in material resources and population, France was the war's chief loser. Her loss in military prestige on the continent was as great as her loss of empire abroad, revealing the government of Louis XV to be outrageously inept. Since efficiency has been a traditional justification for despotism, what did there remain for a despotism proved inefficient? Those who already criticized the French monarchy in the name of reason found a new weapon in the military and maritime disasters of the Seven Years War.

9. Karl von Clausewitz, *On War* (New York, Modern Library, 1943). Originally written between 1818 and 1830. O. J. Matthijs Jalles, translator.

SUGGESTIONS FOR FURTHER READING

⚜

General Political History

The three principal volumes cited for the preceding chapter remain appropriate here: *The New Cambridge Modern History, VII, The Old Regime;* Penfield Roberts, *The Quest for Security;* and especially Walter Dorn, *Competition for Empire.*

W. E. Lunt, *History of England* (New York: Harper and Bros., 4th ed., 1957), a good survey with excellent bibliography by chapter.

W. B. Wilcox, *Star of Empire: A Study of Britain as a World Power, 1485-1945* (New York: Alfred A. Knopf, 1950), particularly good for its synthesis of political and military history.

Robert Kerner, *Bohemia in the Eighteenth Century* (New York: Macmillan, 1932).

H. Marczali, *Hungary in the Eighteenth Century* (Cambridge University Press, 1910).

F. Veale, *Frederick the Great* (London: H. Hamilton, 1935), *Cambridge History of Poland: From Augustus II to Pilsvdski 1697-1935* (Cambridge University Press, 1941).

Lawrence Henry Gipson, *The British Empire before the American Revolution* (Caldwell, Id., The Caxton Printers, 1936).

Richard Pares, *War and Trade in the West Indies 1739-1763* (Oxford: The Clarendon Press, 1936), definitive.

H. H. Dodwell, *Dupleix and Clive* (London: Methuen, 1920).

Military History

Edward Mead Earle, ed., *Makers of Modern Strategy* (Princeton University Press, 1943).

Karl von Clausewitz, *On War* (New York: Modern Library, 1943), a classic, the original edition being 1831.

Alfred Vagts, *A History of Militarism* (New York: W. W. Norton, 1937), highly regarded.

Alfred T. Mahan, *Influence of Sea Power Upon History 1660-1783* (Boston: Little, Brown, 1889), another classic.

Gordon A. Craig, *The Politics of the Prussian Army 1640-1945* (New York: Oxford University Press, 1955).

❧ 5 ❧

Despotism and Sentimentality:
The Later Eighteenth Century

WE HAVE already noted (see pp. 72-75) that the rational view of nature so dear to the neoclassicists was increasingly challenged during the first half of the eighteenth century, both consciously and unconsciously, by such men as Swift and Voltaire, whose acid literary comments suggested that all was not the best in this best of all possible worlds. It was challenged too by men whose aesthetic tastes were increasingly repelled by the mathematical descriptions of nature common to the Age of Reason and who turned to more sensual descriptions. And it was challenged by scientists who turned more to the empirical method and away from a single dependence upon mathematics as the rational method to discover truth. Thus we have an example of one of the difficult problems facing all students of history: any given era or century, like the eighteenth, seems characterized by dominant ideas, forces, currents, and tastes; but it is important to take into account that era's minority opinion, not only because it existed, but also because those who are out of step with their own time *may* be the heralds of the future.

To make our analysis even more difficult, the last half of the eighteenth century saw simultaneously the climax of the Enlightenment and the full flowering of the revolt against it. The safest generalization about the eighteenth century, then, is that the dominant intellectual vogue was rationalism, with its emphasis upon the classical and the universal, and that this

dominant vogue necessarily bred its own antagonists, who saw nature
sentimentally rather than mathematically and who were concerned for the
individual's rights and feelings rather than for the universal. Historians
have seen fit to give this revolt against reason the ambiguous title "the
Romantic Movement."

A classical age necessarily breeds its own antagonists because the universal style, at which the classicist aims, beyond being a brand of con-
formism, will also defeat all but its masters in expressing the truth about
something unique, especially about the self. True enough, the great masters
of any classical art form, including the neoclassicists of the eighteenth
century, inject themselves into their works through their mastery of the
form; but strict adherence to classical form can be the salvation of artistic
hacks, and the history of eighteenth-century art is full of works hopelessly artificial in their formalism and in their absence of emotional depth.
(Musicologists have a delightful term to describe such works: *Zopf* [wig]
music, the metaphor recalling the artificiality of the bewigged society of
the eighteenth century.) Here is Jean-Jacques Rousseau (1712–1788), one
of the fathers of the Romantic Movement, telling us how he intended to go
about writing his *Confessions*:

> I shall not try to render the style uniform; I shall ever use the one which
> comes to hand; I shall change it without scruples, in accordance with my
> moods; I shall say everything as I feel it, as I see it, without art, without shame,
> and with no thought of decoration.[1]

As it developed, the romantic spirit became much more than an artistic
revolt, infusing the political and social thought of the later eighteenth
century and the nineteenth. The eighteenth century, for all its love of
order, was a revolutionary age; and we shall see in subsequent chapters
that the vast social, economic, and political upheavals wrought by the
agricultural and industrial revolutions on the one hand, and the American
and French Revolutions on the other, shook the old order to its foundations and opened the way for *innovation* in every realm. Just as rationalism
had embraced almost all aspects of early-eighteenth-century life, so did
romanticism shoot its threads through the whole fabric of society by the
early nineteenth century.

1. Rémy G. Saisselin, "Buffon, Style, and Gentlemen," *Journal of Aesthetics and
Art Criticism,* Vol. XVI (March, 1958), p. 360; quoted from Rousseau's *Ecrits bio-
graphiques* (Paris, 1955), p. 9.

JEAN-JACQUES ROUSSEAU

For the individualism and sentimentality of the romantic movement, and for that movement's political and social implications, no writer of the later eighteenth century surpasses Rousseau in importance. His highly subjective and sentimental novel, *La Nouvelle Héloïse* (1761), was the story of his own unrequited love, but his subsequent works were of greater significance for defining what we might call the romanticists' world view. When the rationalist looked at nature, he sought the universal, impersonal laws of nature; but Rousseau looked at nature in an individual, personal manner. The opening paragraphs of his *Confessions* reveal him faithfully:

> I am commencing an undertaking, hitherto without precedent, and which will never find an imitator. I desire to set before my fellows the likeness of a man in all the truth of nature, and that man myself.
> I alone. I know my heart, and I know men. I am not made like any of those I have seen; I dare to believe that I am not made like any of those who are in existence. If I am not better, at least I am different. Whether Nature has acted rightly or wrongly in destroying the mould in which she cast me, can only be decided after I have been read.[2]

Since Rousseau was not a rationalist looking for those natural laws so basic that every man must obey them, since he respected the intuition and the inner life of every individual, he has sometimes been accused of favoring anarchy. Furthermore, a loose reading of his recommendation that we return to our "primitive dispositions" has too often been interpreted as an invitation to dissolve the bands of society and to return to the woods and forests. Such charges becloud Rousseau's meaning. First, he regarded nature as a state of freedom and virtue, and like John Locke before him, he thought of man as free in the state of nature. Secondly, he saw that when men emerged from the freedom of the state of nature into society and the political state, their new environment had to house harmoniously many different human qualities and impulses. And, finally, he realized that the older the society became, the more likely it would be that individual uniqueness would be smothered by complexity and artificiality. If we can remember that the society about which Rousseau was writing was that of

2. Rousseau, *Confessions* (published posthumously, 1783), Vol. I, p. 1; see edition revised by Lester G. Crocker, The Pocket Library, 1957.

eighteenth-century France, which was neither free nor virtuous but astonishingly rigid and artificial, we can better understand what he meant when
he advised a return to nature. And who among us has not at one time
echoed Rousseau's sentiments when we have felt cut off from nature and
padded from reality by the speed, the complexity, and the conventions of
modern life? To despise artificiality, however, is not to advocate the overthrow of society, and, in fact, Rousseau was at one with John Locke in
believing that society exists to guarantee individual rights:

> The passage from the state of nature to the civil state produces a very
> remarkable change in man, by substituting justice for instinct in his conduct,
> and giving his actions the morality they had formerly lacked. Then only, when
> the voice of duty takes the place of physical impulses and law succeeds appe-
> tite, does man, who so far had considered only himself, find that he is forced
> to act on different principles, and to consult his reason before listening to
> his inclinations. Although, in this state, he deprives himself of some advantages
> which he got from nature, he gains in return others which are very great; his
> faculties are stimulated and developed, his ideas enlarged, his feelings ennobled,
> and his whole soul so uplifted, that, did not the abuses of this new condition
> often degrade him below that which he left, he would be bound to bless con-
> tinually the happy moment which took him from it forever, and instead of a
> stupid and limited animal, made him an intelligent being and a man.[3]

The abuses of this new condition, then, are the problem. Rousseau goes
on to relate what he calls the "general will" to sovereignty:

> The general will alone can direct the state according to the object for which
> it was instituted, that is, the common good; if the clash of private interests
> made the establishment of societies necessary, the reconciliation of those very
> interests made societies possible. That which those different interests have in
> common makes the social bounds; and if there had been no point on which all
> interests could agree, no society could exist. It is solely on the basis of this com-
> mon interest that society must be governed.
>
> Therefore, I hold that sovereignty, being nothing less than the exercise of
> the general will, can never be alienated, and that the sovereign, who is nothing
> but a collective being, only represents the sovereignty: Power can indeed be
> transmitted, but not the will.[4]

If sovereignty is the exercise of the general will and can never be alienated,
any government which rules in defiance of the general will may be legally
overthrown. Not only does Rousseau's theory justify revolution; but if

3. Rousseau, "Le Contrat Social" (1762), in *Oeuvres* (Paris, 1838), Vol. VI, p.
48. My translation.
4. *Ibid.*, Vol. VI, p. 54. My translation.

we think of sovereignty resting in the people, in the nation as a whole, then the theory can—and did—become the basis for political democracy and nationalism.

GERMANY

Rousseau's thought initially found a more enthusiastic audience in Germany than elsewhere, probably because it was received at a moment when Frederick the Great's victories had awakened a national consciousness, a national pride. To rebel against things French was to rebel against neoclassicism, and ironically enough it was a Frenchman who showed the way. The earliest of the significant "cultural patriots" was Gotthold Ephraim Lessing (1729–1781), who gained a reputation as a critic in Berlin about 1750. He urged German writers to abandon French neoclassicism and turn to English literature for models. In 1755, he followed his own suggestion by writing and producing a play called *Miss Sara Sampson,* its setting taken from everyday life in the fashion of the contemporary English novels, complete with tear-jerking sentimentality and heavy-footed dialogue. Not a masterpiece, it at least pointed the way for others.

During the decade of the 1760s, Lessing engaged in combat with the great classical scholar, J. J. Winckelmann (1717–1768), a man well-known for his hatred of the rococo. The controversy arose over the Laokoön, the sculpture in the Vatican representing the Trojan priest, Laokoön, and his two sons in the coils of snakes. Winckelman compared Virgil's poetic treatment of the Laokoön story unfavorably with the sculptor's image of more moderate suffering. His point, as a neoclassicist, was that highly disciplined, serene art is necessarily superior to more passionate artistic outbursts. Nothing better illustrates Lessing's moderation than his response to Winckelmann:

Since the artist can use but a single moment of ever-changing nature, and the painter must further confine his study of this one moment to a single point of view, while their works are made not simply to be looked at, but to be contemplated long and often, evidently the most fruitful moment and the most fruitful aspect of that moment must be chosen. Now that only is fruitful which allows free play to the imagination. The more we see the more we must be able to imagine; and the more we imagine, the more we must think we see. . . .

But when Virgil's Laocoön screams, who stops to think that a scream necessitates an open mouth, and that an open mouth is ugly? . . . Furthermore, nothing obliges the poet to concentrate his picture into a single moment. He can take up every action, if he will, from its origin, and carry it through all possible changes to its issue. Every change, which would require from the painter a separate picture, costs him but a single touch; . . . Who blames the poet, then? Rather must we acknowledge that he was right in introducing the cry, as the sculptor was in omitting it.[5]

Without ever stooping to the argument that personal taste alone can justify an artistic expression, Lessing was saying that the expression of passion did not necessarily make a work of art inferior. The importance of his essay goes beyond this, however, in that he advanced the opinion that not all subjects are equally suitable to all art forms, and that, as a literary critic, he advised poets not to attempt descriptive themes for which the plastic arts are better suited.

Germany was the scene, from the mid 1760's until the mid 1780's, of a rash of literary works which substituted emotional fervor for the rigidity and authority of French neoclassicism, a movement known to historians as *Sturm und Drang* (Storm and Stress). These writers reacted not only against neoclassical forms; they tilted against authority in general— against convention—and saw themselves as the champions of humanity. In short, they reflected the humanitarianism common to much of the literature of the Romantic period. *Die Räuber* (The Robbers, 1781), by Johann Friedrich Schiller (1759–1805), which has been called the greatest revolutionary drama in German literature, was a Robin Hood-style poetic drama challenging the political tyranny of the day. Since Schiller was an army surgeon in the service of the King of Würtemberg, the drama was published anonymously; but Schiller soon felt it expedient to flee, and he went to Mannheim.

The best example of the *Sturm und Drang* spirit, however, was the novel *Die Leiden des jungen Werthers* (The Sorrows of the Young Werther), published in 1774 by Johann Wolfgang von Goethe (1749– 1832). In form and in theme, Werther reveals the influence of Rousseau's *La Nouvelle Héloise:* a sentimental, lachrymose story, put in epistolary form, of unrequited love ending in suicide. Its impact on Germany, England, and even France was such that it has been styled "Werther fever." Goethe also produced in this early period of his long career a fragmentary *Faust* (1775) true to the spirit of the age. It preached a return to nature to find the truths unobtainable in books and from schools. The magnificent analysis of the philosophical dilemmas of modernity for which *Faust* is

5. G. E. Lessing, *Laocoön: An Essay upon the Limits of Painting and Poetry,* (1766), see Noonday Press edition, Ellen Frothingham, translator, 1957, pp. 16-21.

known was injected by Goethe only in later incarnations of the work, which was not completed until after the turn of the nineteenth century (see pp. 296-297).

For an understanding of German political history, it is important to note that for all their humanitarianism and their revolt against tyranny and convention, the literary revolutionaries of the *Sturm und Drang* era were virtually isolated from the social and political realities of German life.[6] More than one historian has emphasized that these writers knew nothing of the poor and the downtrodden, and that *Werther* revealed not only class consciousness, but even naked snobbery. This divorce between literature and practical politics stands in sharp contrast to their close marriage in England by the time of Milton, Dryden, and Swift.

History, as a branch of literature, provides another example of rationalism and the romantic reaction during the later eighteenth century. Edward Gibbon (1737-1794) can well serve as a fine example of a historian in the rationalist tradition—those historians, in other words, who think of human nature and human problems as substantially unchanging, because natural law is unchanging. These men are moralists and use the past to enlighten the present about itself. Gibbon shared the anti-Christian sentiments common to eighteenth-century rationalists, and his prejudice led him to regard Christianity as the poison which ruined imperial Rome. His own words reveal him:

> It was at Rome, on the 15th of October 1764, as I sat musing amidst *the ruins of the Capitol,* while *the bare-footed friars* were singing vespers in the temple of Jupiter, that the idea of writing the decline and fall of the city first started to my mind. [My italics.][7]

The suggestion was that Christianity could also corrupt European civilization. He did not actually begin writing until four years later, and the first volume appeared in 1776. The sixth and final volume of *The Decline and Fall of the Roman Empire* was published twelve years later. That it was an immediate success owed more to Gibbon's irony and epigrammatic style than to the religious views of his readers. The fifteenth and sixteenth chapters have always been the most famous and controversial, for there, with sublety and irony to avoid possible prosecution, he described the

---

6. See Leo Gershoy, *From Despotism to Revolution: 1763-1789* (New York, Harper, 1944), p. 251.

7. Quoted by John B. Bury in *Encyclopedia Britannica* (11th ed., 1910), Vol. XI, p. 932.

growth of Christianity in Rome and the government's attitude toward the faith. The thesis was climaxed with his description of the Middle Ages as "the triumph of barbarism and religion" (an indictment which has not stood the test of subsequent research). However prejudiced and inaccurate, Gibbon's work remains a masterpiece of elegant literature.

The reaction against the universal history of the rationalists centered in Germany, where Johann Gottfried von Herder (1744–1803), another disciple of Rousseau, emphasized the changing rather than the unchanging. For him, the proper study of history was the discovery of the uniqueness of national communities. Each nationality had a *Volksgeist* (folk spirit) originating in the dim past and distinguishing that nationality from all others. One studied, then, the evolution or organic growth of nations in order to understand their history. If Herder studied in particular the growth of the German "nation" and "culture," from the Middle Ages to the eighteenth century, he also honored equally all nations and their languages. He held that each nationality, thanks to its distinctive history, had a particular genius; that just as each individual is part of a nation, so is every nation part of humanity. While it is true that Herder's ideas were used in the nineteenth century to justify nationalist political ambitions, in particular the unification of nationalities into self-determining states, he did not project his views so far. His was a benevolent nationalism, which rejected the notion that some nationalities are superior to others:

It would . . . betray the ignoble pride of a barbarian to . . . regard the Germans as God's chosen people in Europe, destined by its innate nobility to rule the world and to enslave other peoples. The barbarian rules and dominates; the educated conqueror educates.[8]

All nationalities, in sum, have their unique contributions to make toward the main stream of civilization.

PHILOSOPHY AND RELIGION

The revolt against formalism and rationalism had its religious side, too, in the later eighteenth century, but the revolt was an expression of many disparate views rather than a unified movement. In England, for instance, David Hume (1711–1776) attacked religion based on Reason,

8. Herder, *Materials for the Philosophy of the History of Mankind* (1784), quoted by Hans Kohn, *Nationalism: Its Meaning and History*, p. 109.

because he was an empiricist and rejected rational argument from axioms (see pp. 88-89). In France, Baron Paul Henri Dietrich d'Holbach (1723–1789) also rejected rational religion because, as a materialist, he denied the existence of God and immortality, and thus, could not accept the First Cause of the Deists. A third attack on rational religion came from Immanuel Kant (1724–1804) in Germany, but whereas the ideas of Hume and Holbach served to weaken religion itself, Kant's work provided an intellectual basis for a religious revival which came later in the nineteenth century and which was part of the romantic movement. His *Critique of Pure Reason* (1781) included the following lines:

> I assert, then, that all the attempts at a mere speculative use of reason in the field of theology are entirely fruitless and in their very nature null and void.[9]

He held that reason is valid within limits, meaning that we may use reason to describe only the world in which we can have rational experience. But to use reason to describe the world beyond our rational experience is the very essence of unreason and is, accordingly, quite useless. Kant, however, did not deny the existence of reality beyond the realm of reason or human science. On the contrary, he maintained that there are things beyond the realm of human science which science can neither prove nor disprove, and in that realm there is nothing left for us but intuition—or faith. Against the predominant rational vogue of the eighteenth century, Kant maintained that man is not merely a rational creature, but that emotion and intuition are also part of man's nature.

Kant's work reached only the intelligentsia and was unrelated to the revival of emotional religion in his own time. In Germany and Central Europe, under the heading of Pietism, and in England where it was called Wesleyanism or Methodism, there was a resurgence of faith which recalled many of the sixteenth-century Protestant doctrines. The University of Halle in Saxony was the center of continental Pietism in the eighteenth century, though after 1750 many of its professors were in the rational tradition. Until then, however, Halle was the scene of popular religious literature and hymn writing, a center of biblical translations into many languages, and the base for the first waves of Protestant overseas missionaries. A new sect, the Moravian Brethren, was founded on the estate of a pietistic Saxon noble, Count Ludwig von Zinzendorf, in 1722. Spiritually akin to their Central European predecessors, the Bohemian Brethren, the Mora-

9. Quoted in J. H. Randall, *Making of the Modern Mind*, p. 305.

vians built a community called Herrnhut, which was rigidly supervised by Count Zinzendorf. Their missionaries went first to the New World, to Labrador, Greenland, and the new colony of Georgia, where John Wesley first saw them and was impressed by their piety.

John Wesley (1703–1791) was an Anglican clergyman whose ministry in Georgia had been a notable failure. When he returned to England in 1738, he sought out some Moravian missionaries, and under their influence he saw that the old Protestant doctrine of justification by faith alone was the answer to his spiritual dilemma. The doctrine was not alien to his own Church historically, but the vogue of rationalism had swept up much of the Anglican clergy in its train, so that the emotional fervor of faith was hardly fashionable. Wesley began to emphasize the notion that with faith, the divine spirit would suddenly manifest itself in the individual, making him aware that his sins had been forgiven and that salvation was possible for him. He presented his ideas at Oxford in a famous sermon, saying that faith is not "barely a speculative, rational thing, a cold lifeless assent, a train of ideas in the head, but also a disposition of the heart."[10] A majority of the Anglican clergy recoiled from this return to emotionalism—this "enthusiasm," as they called it; the Wesleyans therefore had to use separate chapels and even to preach in open fields, and finally to form a new sect: the Methodists. It is notable that the separation of the Methodists from the Anglicans was not a doctrinal matter, but a difference in spirit. Ultimately, thanks to their great successes among all classes —most notably among the poor, whose morality they notably improved— the Methodists forced the Anglicans to make a stronger spiritual appeal.

MUSIC

When we come to music in the later eighteenth century, we find that our cultural terminology veils the reality of the changes which took place after 1750. Music, in fact, was consistent ₓwith the other arts in shifting away from strict rational formalism of the early century. Not only had opera deteriorated, but the polyphonic music of the baroque era was also ceasing to satisfy, and a growing demand for melody both produced new styles and methods and revealed the more sentimental taste of the later century. What confuses the issue, however, is the label pinned on this

10. R. W. Greaves, "Religion," *The New Cambridge Modern History*, Vol. VII, p. 138.

new melodic form: classical. And the name is not necessarily a misnomer. The crux of the problem lies in the fact that classical music, while the ultimate refinement of formalism, contained the seeds of highly individual expression characteristic of romanticism.

Of the composers who produced the changes which led from Bach to Mozart, the Bavarian Christoph Willibald Gluck (1714–1787) is the best known. To achieve his operatic innovations, he first secured a librettist willing to write a more flexible libretto, no mean assistance in helping Gluck to break with operatic conventions. His operatic revolution was first evident in *Orfeo ed Euridice* (1762), and he actually spelled out his novelties in the preface to his second important opera, *Alceste* (1767). He avowed that Italian opera had become "tiresome and ridiculous," because complacent composers and vanity-ridden singers were solely concerned with "useless and superfluous ornaments." As for Gluck, he refused

to stop an actor in the heat of a spirited dialogue for a tedious *ritornello;* nor to impede the progress of passion by lengthening a single syllable of a favorite word purely to display agility of throat; and I was equally inflexible in my resolution not to employ the orchestra to so poor a purpose as that of giving time for the recovery of breath sufficient for a long and unmeaning cadenza. . . . In short, I tried to banish all those vices of the musical drama against which good sense and reason have in vain so long exclaimed. . . .

Lastly it was my opinion that my first and chief care, as a dramatic composer, was to aim at a noble simplicity in favor of clearness; nor have I sought or studied novelty if it did not arise naturally from the situation of the character and poetical expression; and there is no rule of composition which I have not thought it my duty to sacrifice in order to favor passion and produce effects.[11]

What could be more illustrative of the romantic spirit? No artificialities: only nature and passion, clarity and expressiveness. It is further revealing that Gluck, in hoping to extend his initial successes from Vienna to Paris, prepared for his assault upon the French capital by reading Rousseau, as well as by writing a new opera with a French text, *Iphigénie en Aulide* (1774). The work received the support of Rousseau, and its presentation was successful.

Johann Stamitz (1717–1757) was another important innovator. His significant career began in 1745 when he was appointed director of the court orchestra in Mannheim (Baden). His unique instrumentation be-

11. Preface to *Alceste* (1767), quoted in T. M. Finney, *A History of Music,* p. 357.

came the model for a standard orchestra. He began with ten first and ten second violins, four violas, four violoncellos, two contrabasses, and two each of flutes, oboes, horns, and bassoons; one trumpet, organ, and kettledrums. Somewhat later, he augmented the winds by adding two more flutes, another oboe, two horns, two bassoons, and three or four clarinets. This was the orchestra which made a great impression upon Mozart and in association with which the word "symphony" was first used, to describe both the orchestra and new compositions for it. Symphony was used to mean a major nonoperatic work in several movements, and most of the symphonies played by the Mannheim orchestra were written by Stamitz. He followed a set routine, and his form is the more important because it contained the outline of what we call sonata form. The first movement was generally *allegro;* the second movement, showing the influence of the operatic aria, was generally slow; the third was often the final movement, either *presto* or *vivace,* though on occasion the composer slipped a short minuet or trio between the second and last movements to complete the four-movement symphony familiar to today's concertgoers.

The piano, so much a part of home decoration today and a symbol of filial oppression to the young, was little appreciated before the time of Carl Philipp Emanuel Bach (1714–1788), a son of the great baroque composer. He first revealed the instrument's capacities in a theoretical work published in Berlin between 1759 and 1762: *Essay on the True Way to Play the Piano.* He also wrote sonatas for the piano, not only creating a body of literature for the instrument, but also setting the style for others.

We come finally to the greatest figures of Classical music, Franz Joseph Haydn (1732–1809) and Wolfgang Amadeus Mozart (1756–1791), who brought the monophonic style of the postbaroque to its perfection. Much late-eighteenth-century music, it is true, was unvarnished formalism: dainty, delicate hollowness. But Haydn and Mozart brought an independent expressiveness to their works which formalism could not suffocate. Theirs was not *Zopf* music, not mere decoration, but highly personal art. Though the audiences of the day were enthusiastic for melody and the simple lines of monophonic style, Mozart ultimately experimented with the polyphonic methods of the baroque period and began the use of chromatic elements, which greatly increased the tonal possibilities of music. He further challenged the formal rules by using dissonance, the most notable example of which is in the Quartet in C major, one of the six quartets dedicated to Haydn.

ENGLAND

The increasing interest of the general public in literature and journalism, which we noted in discussing the rise of the newspaper and the novel, was also influential in the development of the Romantic Movement. Classical formalism was not suitable to the new interest and taste, and it is notable that the early romantic novels reveal a concern with the lives of common people and with the social dilemmas of the eighteenth century. The novelists moralized in sentimental tones, this tendency reaching its peak in the works of the English writer Lawrence Sterne (1713–1768), best-known for *The Life and Opinions of Tristram Shandy* (1759–1767) and *A Sentimental Journey Through France and Italy* (1768). His contemporary, Oliver Goldsmith (1728–1774), also wrote a celebrated sentimental novel, *The Vicar of Wakefield* (1766), but he is further interesting in that he reveals to us the writer in transition from the classical to the romantic. In his poem *The Deserted Village* (1770), he employed the heroic couplets of the neoclassicists to express his feelings on a sentimental subject. Admittedly he employed couplets rather freely, as in the following instance:

When lovely woman stoops to folly,
   And finds too late that men betray,
What charm can soothe her melancholy,
   What art can wash her guilt away?

The only art her guilt to cover,
   To hide her shame from every eye,
To give repentance to her lover,
   And wring his bosom—is, to die.[12]

The release from neoclassical confinement produced not only romantic individualists, but some highly individual eccentrics. In literature, the so-called Gothic novel, another product of the reaction against rationalism, verged on the eccentric. The setting was usually medieval—hence the epithet Gothic—and the plots revelled in the mysterious, the horrible, and the supernatural. Most closely identified with the Gothic Revival in England was Horace Walpole (1717–1797), for two reasons: he wrote the most notable of the Gothic novels, *The Castle of Otranto* (1764), and he built at Strawberry Hill a home which epitomized the architectural

12. "Stanzas on Woman" from *The Vicar of Wakefield* (1766), Ch. 24.

elements of the Gothic Revival. Actually, a liking for the Gothic had never totally expired in England, and even the greatest of the classical architects of the seventeenth century, Wren and Vanbrugh, had used Gothic features in their plans. In the eighteenth century, many years before Horace Walpole built at Strawberry Hill, the Gothic enjoyed a revival in house architecture, especially amongst the *nouveaux riches*.

Walpole wrote that he was "imprinting the gloomth of abbeys and cathedrals" at Strawberry Hill, while furnishing it with "a thousand plump chairs, couches and luxurious settees.[13] Such a concern for comfort and for ornamentation was not only allied to the rococo spirit of the earlier part of the century, but also suggests again a major departure from seventeenth-century attitudes about household comforts and conveniences. Louis XIV thought comfort to be contemptible and certainly not the proper aspiration for gentlemen, but we find the gentlemen of the eighteenth century valuing highly their *agremens*—their amenities—especially during the 1780's, when the age of eccentricity, with Horace Walpole as its greatest figure, reached its peak. "I did not mean," he wrote, "to make my house so Gothic as to exclude conveniences and modern refinements in luxury."[14]

Historians have treated the eccentrics of this period unkindly, regarding them as useless fops, cold-heartedly devoted to their own pleasures. Many of them, however, including Walpole, were given to unostentatious charities, were champions of justice, and were in harmony with the humanitarian spirit of their time. We have Walpole's revealing aphorism to the effect that this world is a comedy to those who think, a tragedy to those who feel.

ECONOMIC THEORY: THE PHYSIOCRATS AND ADAM SMITH

This chapter has, up to this point, been concerned with the rejection of rationalism in the late eighteenth century; but this rejection was by no means universal, as an examination of economic theory will show. In the France of the 1750's, a court physician, Dr. François Quesnay (1694–1774) wrote articles on economics for the *Encyclopédie* which won him a group of disciples. Quesnay's ideas were developed and better

13. R. W. Ketton-Cremer, *Horace Walpole,* pp. 153-159.
14. T. H. White, *The Age of Scandal,* p. 36.

expressed by two disciples, P. S. Du Pont de Nemours (1739–1817) and Mercier de la Rivière (1720–1793), and their school of thought reached its greatest influence about 1770. Their aim was to rationalize the economic life of France and, ultimately, that of Europe according to the "rule of nature," or physiocracy—hence their name: the physiocrats. The disciples of Dr. Quesnay called him "the Confucius of the West," a reminder that eighteenth-century rationalists tended to think of China as an empire perfectly governed in harmony with the laws of nature. How unlike their own dear France under Louis XV—and, indeed, had they only known the truth, how unlike China under the Ch'ing dynasty.

As economic theorists, the physiocrats opposed mercantilism on two grounds. First, they argued that governments ought not to interfere with the production and distribution of economic goods, for such interference was artificial rather than natural. They adopted a phrase which had been used earlier in the century to attack mercantilism: *Laissez faire la nature"*—leave nature alone, or let the natural laws operate without interference. In the long run, *laissez faire* was the only physiocratic principle to enjoy wide acceptance.

Secondly, the physiocrats were critical of the mercantilists for having fostered the development of industry and commerce with government protection and subsidies. The physiocrats argued that this was another violation of nature, in that land and its produce alone (including metals) are true wealth. Industry merely combines those materials which have been produced from the soil, and commerce is merely the transfer of this wealth to new hands. Admittedly, commerce and industry might be useful, but the physiocrats insisted that they were also sterile. Consequently, they saw the trading classes gaining at the expense of the nation. The landowners were thus defined as the only productive class, while *net product* was defined as the return from the soil over and above the cost of seed, fertilizer, and labor; and this net product was called a "gift of nature." The notion that agriculture was virtuous and industry sterile may have appealed to a few who had utopian visions of the goodness of nature, but when the physiocrats pushed their views to include a proposal that landowners alone should be taxable as the only productive class, the illogicality of physiocracy became immediately apparent to anyone with any economic sophistication.

It is true that the French state was increasingly impoverished in the eighteenth century and that the landowners escaped taxation more than any other class. All economic reformers in eighteenth-century France, whether physiocrats or not, recognized that there could be no significant economic recovery without a reform of the tax structure. But to argue that the welfare of the nation depended upon keeping the profits of industry and commerce small, because of their sterility, while insisting that industry and commerce ought not to be taxed, did not make much sense. Le Mercier de la Rivière's *L'Ordre naturel et essential des sociétés politiques* (1767) devoted nearly one-third of its pages to tax theory. He proposed a single tax on land (in place of the tangle of inequitable taxes then plaguing France), as a matter of rational, orderly administration, recognizing that his proposal meant a complete reassessment and listing of landed property. He also recognized that this rational system of equal taxation would strike at the vestiges of feudalism.

Nothing more reveals the physiocrats as rationalists than their faith in natural law. For them, order in society comes from a government under an enlightened prince who understands natural law, who recognizes natural wealth alone and devises a tax system to tap natural wealth, and who favors free trade—without artificial barriers—so that agricultural products will find their natural markets and prices. This equation between nature, good government, learning, and morality does recall the precepts of Confucius, but the equation was also inherent in rationalism. For two years beginning in 1774, the much-admired Chief Minister in France, A. R. J. Turgot (1727–1781) tried to practice physiocracy. He attacked monopolies in industry, gild controls, and the restrictions on the grain trade, but the protectionist opposition proved too strong. But, as we shall see, his master, Louis XVI, was not counted among the enlightened despots of the later eighteenth century and could not be expected to force the royal administration into the framework of nature.

The best-known and most influential economist of the eighteenth century was surely the Scotsman, Adam Smith (1723–1790). If he did not share the physiocrats' preoccupation with agriculture, he was influenced by them and shared their faith in an economy controlled by natural law. Furthermore, they were in common agreement that the right to hold property was a natural right of man, and Adam Smith emphasized that government, in defending the individual's right to property, was defending the individual's liberty:

The property which every man has in his own labor, as it is the original foundation of all other property, so it is the most sacred and inviolable. The patrimony of a poor man lies in the strength and dexterity of his hands; and to hinder him from employing this strength and dexterity in what manner he thinks proper without injury to his neighbor is a plain violation of this most sacred property. It is a manifest encroachment upon the just liberty both of the workman and of those who might be disposed to employ him. As it hinders the one from working at what he thinks proper, so it hinders the other from employing whom they think proper. To judge whether he is fit to be employed may surely be trusted to the discretion of the employers whose interest it so much concerns. The affected anxiety of the law giver lest they should employ an improper person is evidently as impertinent as it is oppressive.[16]

The notion that labor is the foundation of all other property should recall the earlier ideas of John Locke, who also associated the right to own property with individual liberty (see pp. 89-90). This economic liberalism, by which we really mean the rejection of mercantilism, reached its classic definition in Smith's statement of free trade:

To give the monopoly of the home market to the produce of domestic industry, in any particular art of manufacture, is in some measure to direct private people in what manner they ought to employ their capitals, and must, in almost all cases, be either a useless or a hurtful regulation. If the produce of domestic industry can be bought there as cheap as that of foreign industry, the regulation is evidently useless. If it cannot, it must generally be hurtful. It is the maxim of every prudent master of a family never to make at home what it will cost him more to make than to buy. The tailor does not attempt to make his own shoes, but buys them of the shoemaker. The shoemaker does not attempt to make his own clothes, but employs a tailor. The farmer attempts to make neither the one nor the other, but employs those different artificers. All of them find it to their interest to employ their whole industry in a way in which they have some advantage over their neighbors, and to purchase with a part of its produce, or what is the same thing, with the price of a part of it, whatever else they have occasion for.

What is prudence in the conduct of every private family can scarce be folly in that of a great kingdom. If a foreign country can supply us with a commodity cheaper than we ourselves can make it, better buy it of them with some part of the produce of our own industry employed in a way in which we have some advantage. The general industry of the country, being always in proportion to the capital which employs it, will not thereby be diminished, no more than that of the above-mentioned artificers; but only left to find out the way in which it can be employed with the greatest advantage.[17]

Influential long after his own time was Smith's assertion that society in general will benefit from each individual's pursuit of his own best interest, though only under conditions of free trade, which force capital

16. Adam Smith, *An Inquiry into the Nature and Causes of the Wealth of Nations* (1776), Book I, Ch. 10.
17. Smith, *op. cit.*, Book IV, Ch. 2.

and labor to find their most economic employment. Everyone, presumably, profits when the economic life of a nation is regulated solely by the "natural laws" of supply and demand, and it was to express this idea that the phrase "enlightened self-interest" was coined. Thus, for Adam Smith, both economic well-being and personal liberty were dependent upon governments surrendering their habit of interference into economic affairs, and it is not difficult to see why to this day *The Wealth of Nations* has been regarded as Holy Writ by the commercial classes in the English-speaking countries.

POLITICAL IDEAS OF THE RATIONALISTS

Not everyone in the late-eighteenth-century rationalist tradition, however, favored the weakening of government authority, as did the advocates of *laissez faire*. In our own history, it is quite rightly pointed out that there was a close connection between the criticisms of the *ancien régimes* in Europe, made by the rationalists in the name of liberty, and the revolutions in America and France, where the demand for *liberty* figured prominently. It comes as something of a shock, then, to discover that the liberal political ideas held by the *philosophes* did not necessarily imply political democracy; that, in fact, their ideas could—and did—justify autocracy. The rationalists argued that all human institutions ought to be rationalized—that is, put in harmony with natural law; it followed that when such harmony had been achieved, it made men free as they had been in a state of nature. If the *ancien régimes* were despotic, the cause lay in their irrationality; they were inefficient and chaotic. For the rationalist, then, freedom and good order were identical.

The contrast between Rousseau and the rationalists reveals that such words as liberty and nature meant different things to different people in the eighteenth century, just as they do today, and these distinctions must be observed if we are to understand how the desire to make men as free in society as they had been in nature led some to champion democracy and others, autocracy. This ambiguity is a further illustration of the difficulty in characterizing historical periods. As noted above, Rousseau's idea that the people is sovereign, that sovereignty is inalienable, and that the monarch who does not govern according to the general will may be overthrown, logically led to political democracy. The rationalists, in contrast, sought to promote liberty by urging the European monarchs to reform their states along more rational lines. The cure for despotism—that is, inefficiency and chaos—was "enlightened" despotism: rational despotism. In one respect, the rationalists and Rousseau were as one; they believed that all men and all institutions should be subject to natural law. Natural order and freedom seemed to them an indissoluble marriage.

But the rationalists were not revolutionaries, as seen in the words of Anne Robert Jacques Turgot when he became Controller-general of finance in 1774: "Give me five years of despotism and France shall be free."[18] Nor were they democrats:

Liberty does not consist, as some imagine, in a supposed equality between fellow-citizens: this chimera, adored in democratic states, is totally incompatible with our nature, which makes us unequal in our faculties of body and mind. . . . True liberty consists in conforming to the laws which remedy the natural inequality of men, that is, which protect equally the rich and the poor, the great and the small, sovereigns and subjects. . . . In a word, to be free is to obey only laws.[19]

What was needed was a Kepler or a Newton for the social sciences, a man who could describe the universal principles that ought to govern man's institutions. Kant put it this way:

We will see if we can succeed in finding a cipher to such a universal ground-plan for society and then leave it to Nature to produce the man who can solve it. So once, she brought forth a Kepler, who reduced the eccentric orbits of the planets to an orderly formula in unexpected fashion, and a Newton who clarified the universal principles governing the natural order.[20]

Between 1763 and the outbreak of the French Revolution, a number of European monarchs, including Frederick II of Prussia, Joseph II of Austria, Charles III of Spain, Gustavus III of Sweden, and Catherine II of Russia, paraded as reformers according to the dictates of the Enlightenment. Whatever their intentions, their results would not lead us to call any one of them the "Newton of the Social Sciences."

THE COMMON-SENSE SCHOOL

Having reviewed the intellectual and artistic dualism of the eighteenth century (that is, conflict between the rationalists and the empiricists, and,

18. Quoted in G. Bruun, *Europe and the French Imperium,* New York, Harper, 1938, p. 4.

19. Baron d'Holbach, *Système sociale ou principes naturelles de la morale et de la politique* (1772-3), as quoted in Randall, *Making of the Modern Mind,* p. 338.

20. Immanuel Kant, *Idea of a Universal History on a Cosmo-Political Plan* (1784), quoted in G. Bruun, *op. cit.,* p. 4.

in matters artistic, conflict between the neoclassicists and the romanticists), we must look to Scotland to see a remarkable attempt to reconcile the two antagonistic traditions through the development of a synthetic philosophy, that of the common-sense school. Scotland enjoyed a burst of intellectual and literary activity in the eighteenth century, which, oddly enough, coincided with the end of political independence and the resulting decline in Scottish political activity. As David Hume wrote in 1757:

> Is it not strange, that, at a time when we have lost our Princes, our Parliaments, our independent Government, even the Presence of our chief Nobility . . . is it not strange, I say, that in these Circumstances, we shou'd really be the People most distinguish'd for Literature in Europe?[21]

One can argue correctly that the Act of Union (1707), which ended Scottish independence through the merger of the Edinburgh and London Parliaments, was not only the logical outcome of the Reformation, which turned Scotland away from France and toward England in the time of Elizabeth, but that the merger was beneficial to both nations in the long run. At the time, however, the merger was a national humiliation for the Scots, even though the settlement was moderate and the Presbyterian Church remained established in Scotland. In time, many Scots recognized the advantages of the union, but these were by no means equally divided. The Lowlands, for example, realized the commercial benefits of the union, though the Highlands did not. This disparity was the more significant in the light of a further schism between the Lowlanders and the Highlanders; the former had taken to Protestantism, while the Catholic strongholds remained in the Highlands; the political and religious settlement after 1689 was therefore resented more fiercely in the Highlands than in the Lowlands. The attachment to the Stuart cause, accordingly, was more profound in the Highlands, while Jacobitism elsewhere in Scotland was largely sentimental and patriotic rather than an expression of political and religious belief. One finds in Robert Burns (1759–1796), for instance, a loyalty to the Scottish dynasty coupled with expressions of democratic idealism which the Stuarts most certainly did not represent.

Despite these schisms and the loss of political independence, the Scots refer to the years between 1740 and 1830 as their "golden age." The literary and intellectual outburst was not unified in spirit, however, and one finds contrary currents within the mainstream of the Scottish renascence. One group seems to have reacted to English political supremacy

21. M. A. Goldberg, *Smollett and the Scottish School* (Albuquerque, N. M., University of New Mexico Press, 1959), p. 7.

Above: Wolfgang Amadeus Mozart
Right: *Jean-Jacques Rousseau* by
Jean Antoine Houdon
Below: Maria Theresa and Her Children

Above: Joseph Haydn
Right top to bottom:
Catherine the Great of Russia,
Christoph Gluck, Frederick the Great

by accepting English culture enthusiastically and setting out to make Edinburgh an even greater center of that culture than London was. This included the acceptance of English speech and an emphasis on philosophy, science, history, and medicine; and the names that come to mind as representing these disciplines reveal that their Scottish renascence was European in its significance: Tobias Smollett and James Boswell in literature, David Hume in philosophy and history, Adam Smith in philosophy and economics, Joseph Black and James Watt in science and technology, and William Cullen in medicine.[22]

A second group of Scots reacted to English political domination by emphasizing the native traditions and Gaelic speech, but these men were not responsible for Edinburgh's intellectual reputation. Here we find Robert Burns, Scotland's greatest poet, a patriot, sentimentalist, democrat, and humanitarian:

> The cheerfu' supper done, wi' serious face,
> They, round the ingle, form a circle wide;
> The sire turns o'er, with patriarchal grace,
> The big ha'-Bible, ance his father's pride.
> His bonnet rev'rently is laid aside,
> His lyart haffets wearing thin and bare;
> Those strains that once did sweet in Zion glide,
> He wales a portion with judicious care,
> And "Let us worship God!" he says, with solemn air.
>
> They chant their artless notes in simple guise;
> They tune their hearts, by far the noblest aim;
> Perhaps *Dundee's* wild-warbling measures rise,
> Or plaintive *Martyrs,* worthy of the name,
> Or noble *Elgin* beets the heavenward flame,
> The sweetest far of Scotia's holy lays.
> Compar'd with these, Italian trills are tame;
> The tickl'd ear no heart-felt raptures raise;
> Nae unison hae they with our Creator's praise.
>
> . . .
>
> From scenes like these old Scotia's grandeur springs,
> That makes her lov'd at home, rever'd abroad:
> Princes and lords are but the breath of kings,
> "An honest man's the noblest work of God;"
> And certes, in fair virtue's heavenly road,
> The cottage leaves the palace far behind;

22. See David Daiches, *Robert Burns* (New York, Holt, Rinehart & Winston, 1951), pp. 1-9.

What is a lordling's pomp? a cumbrous load,
Disguising oft the wretch of human kind,
Studied in arts of hell, in wickedness refin'd![23]

The facet of the Scottish intellectual revival which concerns us most here, however, was the attempt of the common-sense school of philosophy to compromise the intellectual and artistic dualism of the eighteenth century. Adam Ferguson's *Essay on the History of Civil Society* (1767) was representative of the common-sense views. He objected, first of all, to the construction of a philosophical system such as Hobbes, Locke, and Rousseau had offered, based upon the supposed emergence of man from a state of nature into society. Ferguson held that, as we have no evidence of man living in anything but a social state, it makes sense to conclude that society is man's natural state. His middle-ground position was also revealed in his reaction to the question of whether man is a rational or a passionate creature. His answer was that man comprises both reason and passion, and that "superiority of mind" derives from their combination In this light, the main characters in Tobias Smollett's novels illustrate the common-sense opinion that we all possess antipodal characteristics, and that it is foolish and unreal to look at mankind in any other way.[24] Nevertheless, in the main the eighteenth century preferred to look at mankind from one of two extreme positions: either with a faith in reason, or with a faith that truth is knowable through the senses alone.

THE "ENLIGHTENED" DESPOTS

Frederick II of Prussia

On August 8, 1736, the Prince Royal of Prussia mustered his courage and sent off an admiring letter to the great Voltaire. Thus began a correspondence which was to cover forty-two years and which has preserved for us a notable example of a *philosophe* instructing a monarch in the interest of enlightened government. Voltaire quickly responded to the Prince's initial letter:

Monseigneur,
   One should have to be without feelings not to be greatly touched by the

23. Stanzas from *The Cotter's Saturday Night* (1785).
24. See Goldberg, *op. cit.*, pp. 4-16 and 184-185.

letter with which Your Royal Highness has deigned to honor me. I have been highly flattered; but the love of mankind, always close to my heart, and which, I dare say, forms my character, has given me a pleasure a thousand times purer when I have seen that there is a prince on earth who thinks as a man, a philosopher-prince who will make men happy. . . . Remember that the only truly good kings are those who, like you, began by instructing themselves, by learning of others, by loving truth, by hating persecution and superstition. Any prince so thinking can lead his state into a golden age. . . .[25]

As king, Frederick II never sought to justify himself on the grounds of divine right, a theory he had rejected in a work entitled *Anti-Machiavel,* but he justified himself as an enlightened, efficient ruler. His military successes were dazzling and made him the pre-eminent figure on the Continent by 1763, though his Spartanism hardly made him a popular person. He called himself the first servant of the realm, not its master, and his awesome self-discipline in the service of the state contributed mightily to the prestige of enlightened despotism, especially outside Prussia. It has to be emphasized that his greatest admirers were pleased not to live within his kingdom. Liberty in Prussia was defined by the King himself: his subjects might *say* anything they pleased, especially about religion, to which he was indifferent; and the King might *do* anything he pleased. Lessing, whose poetic drama *Nathan the Wise* (1779) extolled religious toleration, was not misled into believing that the King's indifference to religion was a measure of liberty in Prussia:

Do not talk to me of your liberty of thought and the press; it reduces itself to the liberty to let off as many squibs against religion as one likes.[26]

After the wars ending in 1763, Frederick devoted himself to peace and the necessary economic revival of his stricken country. Despite the new economic doctrines preached by the physiocrats, Frederick remained a mercantilist; but this is not surprising when we think of the Prussian monarchy's presiding over the country almost as if the state were a business enterprise. National economic planning was inherent in the system rather than being a matter of economic philosophy. Under Frederick's direction, the swampy lower valley of the Oder River was drained, and 50,000 colonists were attracted to the region from neighboring countries by the offer of land on easy terms. This "colonial" policy was followed

---

25. *Oeuvres complètes de Voltaire* (1817 ed.), Vol. XII, p. 5. My translation.
26. Letter from Lessing to Nicolai (1769), quoted in C. P. Gooch, *Germany and the French Revolution,* p. 5.

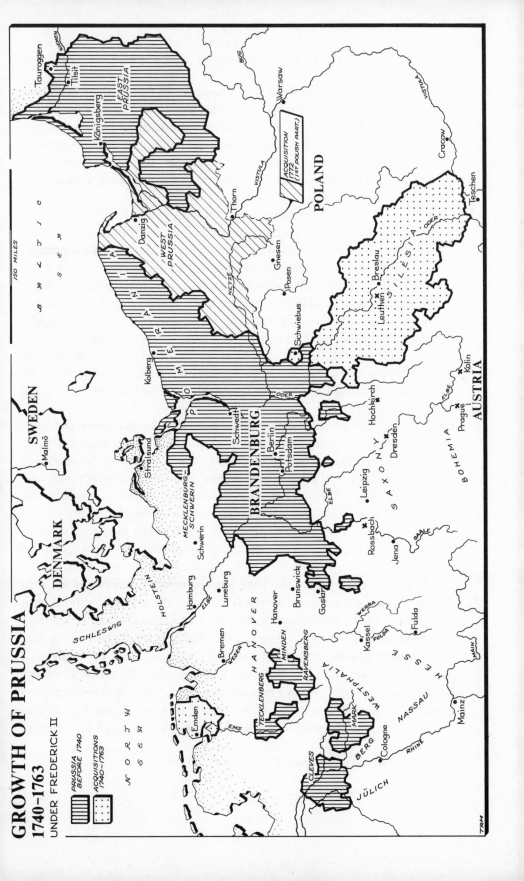

GROWTH OF PRUSSIA
1740–1763
UNDER FREDERICK II

PRUSSIA
BEFORE 1740

ACQUISITIONS
1740–1763

150 MILES

SWEDEN

Malmö

DENMARK

SCHLESWIG

HOLSTEIN

Hamburg

Bremen

Luneburg

HANOVER

Hanover

Brunswick

Goslar

MINDEN

RAVENSBERG

TECKLENBERG

WESTPHALIA

Emden

EMS

MARK

BERG

CLEVES

JÜLICH

Cologne

NASSAU

Mainz

HESSE

Kassel

Fulda

FULDA

WERRA

RHINE

MAIN

SAALE

Jena

Rossbach

Leipzig

SAXONY

Dresden

Hochkirch

Kolin

Prague

BOHEMIA

AUSTRIA

ELBE

WESER

VESER

ELBE

MECKLENBURG-
SCHWERIN

Schwerin

Stralsund

Kolberg

P O M E R A N I A

Schwedt

Berlin

Potsdam

BRANDENBURG

Schwiebus

ODER

Breslau

Leuthen

S I L E S I A

ODER

Teschen

Cracow

POLAND

Warsaw

BUG

VISTULA

VISTULA

Posen

Gnesen

Thorn

NETZE

WEST
PRUSSIA

Danzig

B A L T I C   S E A

Königsberg

EAST
PRUSSIA

Tilsit

Tauroggen

NIEMEN

ACQUISITION
1772
(1ST POLISH PART.)

N O R T H
S E A

TRM

later when Frederick acquired West Prussia in the first partition of Poland, most of the peasants coming from within the Holy Roman Empire, and through the forced settlement of German-speaking peoples in the out-lying districts of his kingdom, in particular in East Prussia, Pomerania, and the newly annexed province of Silesia. In all, it is estimated that nearly 300,000 peasants were resettled on Prussian territory during Fred-erick's reign to increase agricultural output.

He did little, on the other hand, to improve the lot of the peasants whom he shuffled about so ruthlessly in the interest of the state. It is true that during the Seven Years War he used money from his British subsidies to aid the victims of military devastation, but he did this for national rather than charitable reasons. Serfdom persisted in Prussia, though Frederick professed to hate it. Moreover, though he recognized that the tax burdens fell largely on the peasantry, his financial reforms in 1776 did not signifi-cantly change this state of affairs. The trouble was that the landowning aristocracy gave the crown such loyal service that the King shrank from more than a token increase in its financial obligations to him. Thus, the peasantry remained a seriously depressed class, which had no love for its enlightened ruler.

Prussia was overwhelmingly agricultural until the annexation of Silesia, whose coal, iron, lead, and textile production was a rich industrial prize. Frederick encouraged industrial development by granting subsidies and monopoly rights, and the government even established factories which were sold to private entrepreneurs once a profitable operation was achieved. Though foreign trade was undoubtedly limited by the high tariffs enacted to protect Prussian industry, Frederick left Prussia's industry and com-merce notably greater. Yet, impressive arguments have been presented that Prussia's economic development would have been even greater under a freer economic system. The King was omnipresent, supervising all, even to a point where the royal busybody discussed the merits of various ferti-lizers and breeds of chickens in his letters to Voltaire, whose competence in such matters must have been equal to His Majesty's. The king, in fact, really managed the nation's life so that the army could be strong, and there was much truth in Mirabeau's witticism that "the national industry of Prussia is war."[27] When Frederick died, he left the royal treasury piled high—a mercantilist's dream come true. But Adam Smith had already made clear that the wealth of a nation cannot be measured by the coins

27. Attributed to Mirabeau by Albert Sorel.

in the royal coffers. A freer economic system would have given the profits of agriculture and industry to the entrepreneurs for capital development, and Prussia would have been economically stronger than Frederick left her.

Nothing more clearly demonstrated the vulnerability of the enlightened-despotic state than the swift decline of Prussia after the death of Frederick II in 1786. Prussia had not possessed, in the eighteenth century, the resources which make a great power; but Frederick's genius, the ineptitude of his opponents, and a fair measure of luck had created the impression of greatness. His successor, Frederick William II (*1786–1797*), a nephew who had hated his brilliant uncle, mismanaged the state almost by design in his attempt to reverse the policies of Frederick II. The new monarch was easygoing and self-indulgent, sensual to an extreme, and given to periodic bouts of piety. Frederick the Great having been a Francophile, Frederick William was necessarily a Francophobe and, in particular, rejected deism and naturalism as wicked French ideas. The Prussian court was transformed from its former austerity into a den of intrigue and license, the bureaucracy lost its discipline, government expenses soared, and even the army was allowed to decay, paving the way for its shabby showing in the 1790's against the French.

The Hapsburg Empire

The rationalization of the Hapsburg Empire was complicated by a multitude of factors never faced by Frederick II in Prussia. In the first place, the monarchy was still far from centralized, thanks to Maria Theresa's unwillingness to infringe upon the rights of her loyal Hungarian subjects. Yet, just as defeat in 1748 led directly to the first centralizing energy, so did defeat in 1763 point the way to further efforts. The Empress shrank from what seemed obviously necessary to the reforming party: incorporating Hungary into a highly centralized, rationally administered monarchy. Two years later (1765) the reform party found a champion in Joseph II (*1865–1890*), the son of Maria Theresa, who took the imperial title and became coregent with his mother. They quarreled incessantly over the reform question, with the Empress successfully preventing a raid upon Hungarian liberties.

Joseph, however, had the Enlightenment in his eye. Blocked on the Hungarian front by his mother, he turned his reforming zeal upon the crown lands in Bohemia. He abolished serfdom on these estates and made it possible for the emancipated peasants to buy small plots of land on easy terms. Anticipating a more general emancipation of serfs, he established commissions of inquiry, which began to review the serf problem in Austria and Bohemia. Unfortunately, the peasantry allowed itself to believe that the appointment of the commissions meant an instantaneous emancipation, and when this did not come immediately, they broke into angry revolt. The peasants were joined by Hussites, secret Protestants, who welcomed every opportunity to undermine the authority of their Catholic Hapsburg oppressors. To his sadness, the humane Joseph II had to use the army to suppress the uprising and had to face the rebuke of his mother in Vienna. The revolt may have confirmed Maria Theresa in her conservatism, but Joseph II rightly saw the revolt as further proof that serfdom must be eliminated.

From 1780 to 1790, he was sole ruler. The reform movement went into high gear, and the Hungarians were no longer exempt. The elimination of serfdom was not accomplished in one stroke, but came about through a series of decrees between 1781 and 1785. By the latter date, the serfs were no longer bound to the soil, and they could marry without a lord's consent, choose their own vocations, and seek the legal protection of the crown against a lord. In the meantime, and under the influence of physiocratic thought, the Emperor had ordered the surveying and reappraisal of all lands within his empire for the purpose of tax reform. This vast enterprise was not completed until 1789, when Joseph II abolished the existing tax system. With one decree, he wiped out the financial vestiges of feudalism, for with the old tax system went the tithe and all service obligations, including the *robot*—compulsory labor. In exchange, Joseph inaugurated a single tax on all landed proprietors. The nobility, inevitably, was furious, but Joseph II was not granted the time to enforce his reforms. Leopold II (*1790–1792*) came to the throne in 1790 and succumbed to aristocratic pressure. He abandoned the new tax program and restored the *robot,* so that serfdom remained in the Empire. Peasant confusion and anger was manifested in violence, and troops were again required to restore order.

The influence of the physiocrats on Joseph II is also evident in his industrial legislation, though he never completely removed all artificial barriers to trade. He disapproved of monopolies and exclusive economic rights and eliminated the power of guilds to regulate manufacturing, but protective tariffs against foreign goods remained and often provoked serious tariff reprisals, especially from Prussia, Saxony, and Turkey. On the other hand, while governmental aid was extended to new industries, the total amount of governmental subsidies to industry was sharply reduced. The government not only realized the financial benefits from its decreased activity, but also benefited from the notable increase in commerce, which produced taxable wealth. It has been calculated that the commercial expansion would have been even greater had the tariff policy been more enlightened. Unfortunately, the greater tax income of the government was offset by large military budgets, which the Vienna government, after two unsuccessful wars, deemed necessary.

But the reforms of Joseph II were political as well as economic. He had long disapproved of his mother's softness toward the Hungarians, and after her death, he resumed the centralization of the empire, a policy which had as its final goal the reduction of the polyglot empire into a German state. He began by stripping the powers from the Diet in Budapest, so that provincial autonomy was lost as it had earlier been lost in Bohemia. The Hungarian chancellery merged with the chancellery in Vienna, and German became the official language throughout the empire. Even municipal government was taken over by officials appointed from Vienna, giving us once again a demonstration that strong central government and bureaucracy went hand in hand. The Germanization program was extended to the Belgian Netherlands and Lombardy as well, so that when Joseph's reorganization was complete, the entire realm was divided into thirteen provinces (*gubernia*), and each *gubernium* was subdivided into numerous districts (*Kreise*). He also revised the administration of justice to correspond with the new political boundaries. Legal cases were to be heard in the first instance in the municipal courts; each *Kreis* had a court of second instance, each *gubernium* a court of third instance, with the supreme court in Vienna.

It would be hard to find a better example of enlightened despotism than the regime of Joseph II; he tried to rationalize the organization of his realm—to bring order—and he tried to eliminate serfdom as a crime against humanity. Yet, by the end of his reign in 1790, disaster threatened from all sides, and his reforms came to nothing. The Hungarian nobility was in a rage, the land reforms had infuriated the gentry without satisfying the peasantry, and the Belgians were in angry revolt. No one doubts the sincerity and the energy of the monarch, but it does appear that his despotism, his very arbitrariness, raised opposition to his reforms from people who might otherwise have shown enthusiasm for his ends. His goal, after all, was highly patriotic, and he sought the welfare of his subjects. Certainly he would have met opposition to reforms as sweeping as he envisioned, but had he possessed an ounce of political acumen, he might have seen a part of his program succeed.

Catherine the Great of Russia

Historians still debate the issue of Catherine II's (*1762–1796*) right to be styled an enlightened despot, and a review of her reign will reveal the contradictions basic to the argument. Clearly she was enlightened and despotic, but the question remains as to whether she sincerely tried to reform her vast empire according to the dictates of reason. Her accession to the throne, to which she had no dynastic right, was made possible by a palace revolution which unseated her husband, Peter III. Palace revolutions had become, in the eighteenth century, a serious hindrance to orderly government and the consolidation of royal power in Russia; it is also true that Peter III, during his few months as Czar, gave ample evidence of his unfitness for power. He completed the aristocratic reaction, under way since the time of Peter the Great, by relieving the gentry from any further obligatory state service. This was all the more subject to criticism as Peter III did not simultaneously free the serfs. In the eighteenth century, the official justification for serfdom was that it freed the gentry for state service. Under the circumstances, it is not suprising to find the peasantry growing dangerously restless within the next decade.

Presumably the gentry was pleased, but the Czar's remaining deeds failed to satisfy any major section of the population. He began by withdrawing the Russian troops from the Seven Years War, for the simpleminded reason that Frederick the Great was his idol and without the slightest concern that Russia had expended her treasure and troops for a cause which was inconsistent with a Prussian victory. (A Prussian defeat would have given Russia a freer hand in dealing with declining Poland.) To cap the humiliation of the Russian army, whose victories had been so cavalierly cancelled, the Czar introduced Prussian uniforms and drill. Next, he planned a war against Denmark, which was having trouble with Peter's native Holstein—a war in which no Russian interest would be served. At home, he publicly insulted the clergy, confiscated all ecclesiastical lands, and gave his enemies their opportunity by threatening to divorce Catherine. She became part of a plot, led by the three Orlov brothers—Grigori, Alexis, and Fedor—to force Peter's abdication. He was imprisoned and, several weeks later, came to a violent end. The official report was that he had died of hemorrhoidal colic, but the evidence was that he had been murdered by Alexis Orlov. As one French wit noted, hemorrhoids were surprisingly dangerous in Russia.

Despite this impolitic beginning, Catherine II soon revealed herself as an astute politician. She worked hard to create the impression that she was a liberal, and there seems little doubt that she did admire the intellectual leaders of the Enlightenment; but her liberal pronouncements were rarely transformed into liberal actions, and this fact has led some historians to deny that she should be counted among the enlightened despots. Her correspondence with Voltaire began in 1763, though he had earlier been impressed by her offer, in 1762, to have the *Encyclopédie* printed in Russia, since it was provoking the disapproval of the royal censor in France. Finally, Voltaire sent an offering of verses to Catherine as an expression of his admiration, and she answered:

For the first time I regret that I am not a poet and that I must reply to your verse in prose, but I may tell you that since 1746 I have been deeply in your debt. I had only read novels when by chance your books came into my hands. Since then I have never ceased to read them, and have had no craving for anything less well written or less instructive. But where are such writings to be found? So I came back to you. If I possess any knowledge I owe it to you alone. I am now reading the *Essai sur l'Historie Générale,* and I wish I knew every page by heart.[28]

The two correspondents never met, but their messages were mutually flattering; and we may safely assume that the Empress thought she was paving the way for Russia's cultural advancement.

Early in her reign, Catherine announced that she intended to preside over the rationalization of Russia's tangled legal customs and the remnants of feudal law. To produce a single law code for the entire Empire, she would call at national assembly—to be called the Great Commission—representing all classes. In preparation for this, she worked hard for over a year on a manifesto which would guide the Commission's deliberations. Her *Nakaz* (Instruction) of 1766 included roughly 500 paragraphs, nearly half of of which were borrowed from Montesquieu's *The Spirit of the Laws* (1748) and another fifth from the Italian Cesare Beccaria's *Crimes and Punishments* (1764). Some of the principles she set down made her an idol for the rationalists, and the French government deemed the *Nakaz* too radical for publication in France. She asserted that a government should be more concerned with preventing crime than with its punishment—that

28. G. P. Gooch, *Catherine the Great and Other Studies,* p. 58.

is, that education is better than punishment. She also asserted the equality
of all men before the law, that the sovereign is only the servant of the
people, and that serfdom was an evil which could be justified only for
reasons of state. Voltaire had this to say to her:

Lycurgus and Solon would have signed your work, but they could not have
performed it. It is clear, precise, equitable, firm, human. Legislators occupy the
first place in the temple of glory. The conquerors only come after. Assuredly
no one will have a greater name in days to come than you.[29]

Even discounting the polite flattery characteristic of eighteenth-century
address and the possibility that Catherine paid for such adulation with her
financial assistance to the *philosophes,* there is no denying that the intelligentsia had reason to be enthusiastic. Frederick the Great, who had no
need of her largesse, nominated her to membership in the Academy in
Berlin.

The Great Commission was elected and set to work on the new code,
but the outbreak of the First Turkish War in 1768 was the excuse for
suspending work, and the code was never completed. There remains the
well-founded suspicion that Catherine never intended its completion, but
that the project was a good example of her mastery of what we today call
good public relations.

Catherine's expressed solicitude for the serfs similarly was not followed
by their emancipation, and the peasantry, its grievances redoubled by
Peter III's earlier generosity toward the nobility, rumbled into serious
revolt in 1773. The uprising began among the Cossacks of the Don under
the leadership of an escaped convict, Emilian Pugachev, who posed as
Peter III. Soon, a variety of elements, including Old Believers, joined in,
and the government was embarrassed with a shortage of troops to deal with
the rising. By 1774, much of the Volga valley was in rebel hands, Kazan
and Nizhni Novgorod were captured, and the capital itself was menaced.
Only with the end of the Turkish War were more troops available. Pugachev was then beaten and forced to retreat down the Volga, until he was
betrayed to the government. Catherine's justice was brutal: Pugachev was
taken in a cage to Moscow, where he was drawn and quartered. As for
the serfs, their lot deteriorated, the government permitting their public
sale, so that there was little to distinguish them from slaves.

Catherine's record in economic expansion again gives us an ambiguous

29. *Ibid.,* p. 63.

policy to illustrate the difficulty in classifying her as an enlightened despot. Officially, she favored freer trade, an end to monopolies, and the construction of canals to supplement Russia's rivers. Foreign trade was expanded through Catherine's military policy, for after the First Turkish War, Russian traders could move by water from the Black Sea to the Mediterranean. Even so, the Baltic ports remained pre-eminent, and Britain was Russia's most important buyer and supplier. In contrast to Catherine's principles, the China trade remained a government monopoly, and much of the labor employed in factories was far from free. Factories were still on a small scale, often built on a manor and operated with serf labor. Entrepreneurs who manufactured goods of importance to the state, particularly military and naval supplies, were often given state serfs to labor in their factories, even though the factories were privately owned. The evident increase in commerce and industry did mean the rise of taxable incomes, but the wild inefficiency in tax collection, ever the curse of Russian government, meant that the state realized far less than its due. And in the time of Catherine, the crown was notably wasteful: the court was lavish, and the large army was a serious financial burden. In lieu of adequate revenues, the government fell back on borrowing, most of the money being raised abroad. The whole financial picture, in short, does not suggest the administration of a Rationalist.

Sweden, Spain, and Portugal

Three lesser powers which saw enlightened despotism in the late eighteenth century were Sweden, Spain, and Portugal. The accession of Gustavus III (*1772–1792*) brought to an end the period of aristocratic reaction which the Swedes called their "Time of Freedom." As we have earlier seen, it was a period of party strife which had enabled foreigners, the Russians in particular, to influence Swedish policies unduly. The fate of Poland was too threatening for the new king's taste, and he engineered a military *coup d'état* in 1772, to re-establish strong monarchy. The new constitution, modeled on the British monarchy, did not give the king dictatorial powers, but the monarch was far stronger than he had been during the period of Riksdag supremacy, after the death of Charles XII. Under the new constitution, he convoked and dismissed the Riksdag and had the power of initiation. The Riksdag could reject legislation initiated by the crown and even had the right to vote the budget, but since royal displeasure meant less frequent meetings of the Riksdag, it is understandable that its members were dissatisfied with their new lot.

The claim of Gustavus III to be an enlightened despot stems from liberal reforms early in his reign, when he was under the influence of the physiocrats in particular. In the interest of free trade, he opened a number of Baltic ports to unrestricted commerce, he removed the internal barriers to the grain trade, and he forced the abandonment of many guild regulations. The press was remarkably free for that era, and, beginning in 1781, he granted religious toleration for all Christians. The restrictions upon Jews were lifted to the extent that they might live and worship freely in three designated towns. Later, in the 1780's, the tide turned toward absolutism as the King wearied of mounting criticism from jealous parliamentarians. Though he was vulnerable, thanks to the high cost of his lavish court and heavy military expenditure, demands for economy really masked a constitutional issue. In 1792, Gustavus III was assassinated as a result of an aristocratic conspiracy against him.

The slow decline of Spain was momentarily checked during the reign of Charles III (1759–1788), who has been counted among the enlightened despots. He was genuinely interested in reform and had the advantage of twenty years' experience in Naples before coming to the Spanish throne; furthermore, his Bourbon predecessors had prepared his way through the consolidation of royal power. There was ample work to be done if Spain meant to return to the first rank of the powers: her agriculture was primitive, and her peasantry was notoriously poverty-stricken; she had an unfavorable balance of trade, and her commercial activity was feeble; finally, the Spanish Church was determined that the ideas of the rationalists should not penetrate Spain. Charles III, while a devout Catholic, was equally determined that his secular authority should be supreme in Spain, just as he was convinced that the rationalization of his kingdom required that more Spaniards be trained in secular matters. His support of secular education led him into conflict with the Jesuits, whom he suddenly expelled from Spain in 1767 without prior warning. Numbering nearly 10,000, they were deported to the Papal States.

The King's economic reforms were at once physiocratic and anti-aristocratic. In the interest of the peasantry, he tried to halt the enclosure of the commons by the great sheep ranchers, and he forced the breakup of a number of great estates, in the hope of giving peasants an opportunity to become landowners. If he did not eliminate the internal tariffs, he at least reduced them, and he further stimulated Spanish commerce by providing a uniform coinage for the first time, by standardizing weights and measures, and by giving the country a national postal system. And if he could have produced an heir equal to himself in vision and energy, the Spanish revival might have produced impressive results.

In many respects, the best example of an enlightened despot in the eighteenth century was not a monarch at all, but the courageous and vigorous Portuguese Secretary of State, the Marquis of Pombal (1699– 1782). He served the government of Joseph I (*1750–1777*), but in reality he exercised complete authority over the King. Portugal's dilemma in the eighteenth century was similar to Spain's: she was a clerical country with a powerful aristocracy, whose population was declining and whose prestige in international affairs had vanished while she still retained an impressive empire overseas. Pombal's problem was not so much that of a Frederick the Great or a Catherine, but the problem of the monarchs of the preceding century, whose task had been to consolidate royal power at the expense of Church and nobility. This circumstance will account for the fact that he was a mercantilist, not a physiocrat, and that much of his legislation was directed toward enhancing the royal power rather than rationalizing the administration of Portugal. Yet, by attacking the Church's resistance to eighteenth-century secular thought, by expelling the Jesuits from Portugal in 1759, and by sponsoring the teaching of natural science at the University of Coimbra, Pombal gave evidence that he was of the enlightenment, too.

The sin of the Church, from Pombal's point of view, was economic as well as intellectual. Great wealth from the empire, especially from Brazil, found its way into ecclesiastical coffers, and Pombal hoped to divert this golden flood toward His Majesty. His attempt to make the Brazil trade a royal monopoly raised a storm of clerical and aristocratic protest, and his troubles were compounded by the Lisbon earthquake of November 1, 1755, which took 15,000 lives. The earthquake had international repercussions, for it was a shock to a complacent European society which had achieved a happy confidence in its harmonious world. Voltaire, as usual, laughed loudest at such optimism:

"Men," said he [Jacques], "must have corrupted nature a little, for they were not born wolves, and they have become wolves. God did not give them twenty-four-pounder cannons or bayonets, and they have made bayonets and cannons to destroy each other. I might bring bankruptcies into the account and Justice which seizes the goods of bankrupts in order to deprive the creditors of them."

"It was all indispensable," replied the one-eyed doctor [Pangloss], "and private misfortunes make the public good, so that the more private misfortunes there are, the more everything is well." While he was reasoning, the air grew dark, the winds blew from the four quarters of the globe, and the ship was attacked by the most horrible tempest in sight of the port of Lisbon.[30]

The courage and humanity which Pombal showed during and after the earthquake earned him enormous popularity and contributed to the success of his assault upon the aristocrats and the clergy. He was further assisted by an attempt upon the King's life in 1758, which he used as an opportunity to indict his most dangerous political enemies and the Jesuits. Their expulsion followed during the next year, while the aristocracy was terrorized through the slaughter of its leaders.

Pombal emerged as a dictator to begin new administrative reforms. The tax system was more highly centralized, producing an immediate increase in governmental revenues, and he abolished many government offices. Aristocrats driven from office were replaced by bureaucrats chosen for merit. He also worked to revive Portuguese military and naval strength. While everywhere one could see the revitalizing effect of Pombal's energy, it is true that his reforms were only accomplished by the use of naked force, and that even in his own lifetime the mercantilist policy failed. (Much of Portuguese trade was carried in foreign ships.) With the death of Joseph I, he fell from power, and his reforms hardly survived him.

The Partitions of Poland

The story of Poland in the late eighteenth century has always been a bitter one for Polish patriots. Internal chaos, largely the result of a highly decentralized state, had gradually reduced Poland to insignificance as an international factor, until a few of the more enlightened of the gentry had recognized that constitutional reform was the only alternative to extinction. These men were reformers, not only because Poland's desperate plight demanded it, but also because they had been influenced by the enlightenment. The Czartoryski family led the way, pointing out that the reform movement could best be based on the election of a native Pole as King when the throne should next be vacant. As the Czartoryskis openly called for the abolition of the *liberum veto,* they were opposed by the great majority of the gentry (the szlachta).

The Polish problem was complicated by the rise of aggressive neighbors who were ambitious to exploit Polish weakness and by the religious issues separating Poland from her neighbors. For both Prussia and Russia,

30. Voltaire, *Candide* (1759), Modern Library, Ch. IV.

POLAND
1772
*FIRST
PARTITION*

RUSSIA

PRUSSIA

Warsaw

Kiev

AUSTRIA

250 MILES

POLAND
1793
*SECOND
PARTITION*

RUSSIA

PRUSSIA

Warsaw

Kiev

AUSTRIA

POLAND
1795
*THIRD
PARTITION*

PRUSSIA

RUSSIA

Warsaw

Kiev

AUSTRIA

250 MILES

POLAND
1771

*JUST BEFORE THE
FIRST PARTITION*

ESTONIA

LIVONIA

COUR-
LAND

Riga

BALTIC SEA

Memel

Kaunas

LITHUANIA

Vilna

Minsk

DVINA

Smolensk

Moscow

OKA

Tula

RUSSIAN

TO
RUSSIA
1667

EMPIRE

PRUSSIA

Danzig

EAST
PRUSSIA

VISTULA

NIEMEN

DNIEPER

Posen

Warsaw

POLAND

Brest-
Litovsk

PRIPET

Breslau

ODER

SILESIA

Lublin

BUG

MORAVIA

VISTULA

Cracow

GALICIA

Lemberg

Kiev

DNIESTER

Brünn

PODOLIA

Vienna

DANUBE

AUSTRIA

BUKO-
VINA

DNIESTER

BESSARABIA

Budapest

PRUT

HUNGARY

MOLDAVIA

Jassy

Odessa

BLACK SEA

SEA
OF
AZOV

POLAND
1808-1814
*GRAND DUCHY
OF WARSAW*

BOUNDARY OF
POLAND, 1772

PRUSSIA

RUSSIA

Warsaw

Cracow

Kiev

AUSTRIA

250 MILES

POLAND
1815-1831
*CONGRESS
POLAND*

*K. OF POLAND
UNDER RUSSIA
1831-1922*

BOUNDARY OF
RUSSIA, 1914
POLAND, 1772

PRUSSIA

Warsaw

RUSSIA

Kiev

AUSTRIA

POLAND
1922-1939
*BETWEEN THE
WORLD WARS*

BOUNDARY OF
POLAND, 1772

E. PRUSSIA

Danzig

LITH.

Vilna

Minsk

GERMANY

Warsaw

RUSSIA

Cracow

Kiev

CZECHOSLOVAKIA

RUMANIA

Poland was an ancient enemy, and Russia especially found a long-term grievance in the Greek Orthodox population subjected to intolerant Polish rule. If many of the antagonisms were of a religious origin, by the eighteenth century the issues were largely political and economic. None of Poland's strong neighbors could afford to allow Poland to fall intact to another power. As early as 1763, during negotiations for the treaty of Hubertusburg, Frederick II had raised the question of Poland's partition. Out of this came an understanding between Frederick and Catherine that they would act in concert to control the next Polish royal election. The opportunity was not long in coming: Augustus III (*1734-1763*) died later that year.

The formal understanding between Russia and Prussia to support the candidacy of Stanislas Poniatowski was reached in April, 1764. As a nephew of Prince Czartoryski, Poniatowski was acceptable to the reform party in Poland; and since he was one of Catherine's discarded lovers, she flattered herself that she would be able to manage him without difficulty. In fact, she rejected Frederick's preference for partition because she thought Poniatowski would make Poland a Russian puppet, so that she would not have to share Poland with Prussia. Austria and France would have preferred the election of the son of Augustus III because the union of the Polish and Saxon thrones offered a barrier to Prussian expansion, but Catherine sent sufficient military forces to Warsaw to ensure the election of Poniatowski (*1764-1795*). After the election, the Russian troops were not withdrawn but remained to give the Russian ambassador, Nikolai Repnin, the power to intimidate the Polish government.

Stanislas Poniatowski proved more difficult to manage than Catherine had anticipated, and his willingness to promote the reform movement for the regeneration of Poland was the last thing either Russia or Prussia desired. The abolition of the *liberum veto* in the Sejm (Diet) was a forecast that the Czartoryski program was to be implemented, which meant to the gentry the probable loss of its tax privileges and the emancipation of the serfs. Recognizing the likelihood of Russian displeasure over these reforms, a number of the gentry appealed to Catherine to protect its liberties against Poniatowski's centralization, and several confederations of armed resistance to the King were organized with Russian encouragement.

Repnin showed himself to be a master of the diabolical in his exploitation of the growing chaos. Feigning a great solicitude for the rights of the gentry, he seized a number of the reformers and packed them off to Siberia;

following which, he forced on Poniatowski a new Russo-Polish treaty (1768) in which all the old constitutional liberties of the gentry, including the *liberum veto,* were restored with a Russian guarantee. Also in the name of liberty, Repnin forced the Polish government to guarantee equal rights to Greek Orthodox and Protestant subjects, a clause calculated to infuriate the gentry and make the treaty satisfactory to neither the Polish government nor the gentry. It left Catherine in the position of apparently championing liberty and toleration, while the gentry, now despairing of Russian support, retired to Bar to organize a new confederation of armed resistance. Led by Count Joseph Pulaski and Bishop Krasinski, the Confederation of Bar asked for French help to drive the Russians from Poland. They would have to deal with the Russians before they could turn on the reform party.

The French response, little more than token, revealed the weakness of Louis XV's government. French agents were authorized to purchase 22,000 muskets for the Poles, but otherwise there was little sign that Paris was seriously alarmed, even though a surprising expression of friendship between Austria and Prussia in 1769 was ominous for the future of Poland. Thus, the Confederation of Bar was swiftly defeated by the Russians under Alexander Suvorov—then holding his first command—and the foreign policy of France was revealed to be bankrupt. Faced with the King's indecision, the Duc Etienne de Choiseul fell upon an old French trick: he ordered Count de Vergennes, his ambassador in Constantinople, to urge the Turks to take this opportunity to attack Russia while she was preoccupied with Poland. It was not hard to stir up the Turks who, since the time of Peter the Great, were aware that Russia meant to expand southward at their expense.

Using a border violation by Cossack troops during the suppression of the Confederation of Bar as a pretext, the Turks opened the war by launching a Tartar invasion of Russia from the Crimea (1768). Their attack was too late to do anything for the Poles and failed to accomplish anything for Turkey. Against great odds, the Russians advanced into Turkish Moldavia in 1769, and by 1770 they were winning repeated victories in the region of the Black Sea and the Sea of Azov. Catherine sent the Baltic fleet, under Alexis Orlov, to the Mediterranean, where it won a notable victory over the Turks at Chesme Bay; and though the fleet did not attempt the Dardanelles, its operations in the Aegean excited both fear and admiration in Europe. Voltaire, who chose to see the conflict in Eastern Europe through Catherine's eyes, grew dithyrambic over the spectacle of Islam, allied with

Catholicism, being defeated by the champion of toleration. Thus he could write, "She who establishes science and makes the arts flourish has punished their enemies."[31]

The governments of Austria and Prussia were less inspired by these Russian successes, Austria having a stake in the Balkans, where Russian armies were winning victories, and Prussia being anxious to forestall any Russian attempt to settle the Polish question without Prussian participation. With this idea in mind, Frederick II proposed to Catherine that she compensate herself in Poland for the victories she was winning over Turkey, pointing out the possibility of Austrian aid to Turkey. Their negotiations were enlarged to prevent the Austrians from going to the aid of Turkey, and on August 5, 1772, the three powers signed the Partition Treaty, which deprived Poland of nearly one-third of her territory and five-twelfths of her population. The official justification for this brutal seizure was the chaos in Poland; and the Polish Sejm, threatened by Russian troops, ratified the galling treaty in 1773.

Catherine's war with Turkey, momentarily bogged down, revived in 1774, when her troops crossed the Balkan Mountains and were in a position to approach the Turkish capital. This state of affairs led to the peace settlement at Kuchuk Kainarji, and the treaty terms revealed not only a major Russian victory, but also the fact that Catherine was careful to take compensations from Turkey in areas least likely to arouse Austrian alarm. Russia, for instance, returned the provinces of Moldavia and Wallachia to Turkey, but with the proviso that the Christian population of the provinces be given moderate government under a Russian guarantee. In this spirit, Turkey also gave Russia the right to build an Orthodox church in the foreign quarter of Constantinople, with the right to make representations on its behalf. In the Black Sea region, Russia took three key points: Kerch, Kinburn, and Yenikale; she obtained free navigation for Russian commercial ships in Turkish waters; and the Crimean Tartars were declared independent.

The treaty of Kuchuk Kainarji, while giving Russia bases on the Black Sea, did not remove Turkish control over most of the northern coast of that sea. Though Catherine II desired to sweep the Turks entirely out of the area, she recognized that Turkey would try to avenge her recent defeat and would court Austrian suspicions in hope of an alliance. Thus, Catherine set out to woo Austria, whose enemy, after all, Turkey had long been.

31. Gooch, *op. cit.*, p. 64.

Joseph II visited Russia on Catherine's invitation in 1780, and she presented her "Greek Plan" for the partition of the Ottoman Empire by the two powers. As the Austrian government showed itself definitely interested in such a scheme, negotiations continued over the ultimate disposal of Turkish territories; but by 1783, no definite partition treaty had been signed, largely because the Austrians had come to recognize that Catherine intended large gains for Russia and only vague ones for Austria. Furthermore, the Austrians were rightly doubtful of the wisdom of allowing Catherine to make her grandson, Constantine, the ruler of an independent Constantinople.

The Empress promoted difficulty with Turkey that year (1783) by annexing the Crimea to Russia; subsequently, the ruler of Georgia put himself under the protection of Catherine, and this was a threat that the Turks could not ignore. In 1787, they sent an ultimatum to Russia demanding the withdrawal of that protection, the restoration of an independent Crimea—in fact, the cancellation of the Treaty of Kuchuk Kainarji; Catherine, of course, rejected the proposal. The war which followed offered more than the usual amount of diplomatic confusion. Initially, the Turks showed surprising strength, and the Russian drives broke down. Gustavus III of Sweden was thereby encouraged to strike at Russia in the north, in the hope of ending Russian interference into Swedish affairs, and there is little doubt that he had been inspired by Frederick of Prussia, who was eager to compel Catherine to give up her Turkish ventures in favor of further surgery on Poland.

The Russo-Swedish war (1788–1790) was largely fought in Finland, where the Swedes scored several victories, but Gustavus III was seriously hampered by the disloyalty of many of his aristocrats, who worked to weaken royal power. Furthermore, Sweden's ability to sustain a long war was dubious, forcing the king to make a *status quo ante bellum* peace with the treaty of Wereloe (1790). In the meantime, Austria joined Russia against Turkey in 1788, honoring a commitment Joseph II had made to Catherine after his visit to Russia. After early Austrian reverses, the war in the south began to favor Austria and Russia in 1789. Even so, after the death of Joseph II in 1790, the Austrians decided to withdraw, in part because the new Emperor Leopold II was seriously concerned about the revolutionary situation in France; and in part because the Austrian government, weary of opposition and revolt in the Austrian Netherlands, had been engaged in negotiations with the ruler of Bavaria, in the hope of getting him to swap Bavaria for the Netherlands. This proposed trade angered Prussia, who did not wish to see Austria expand in Germany, so that war threatened between those two powers. Beset by these problems, Austria abandoned Russia in 1791 by signing the separate peace of Sistova with the Turks; by its terms, the Austrians retained only a slice of northern Bosnia. The Russians, nevertheless, continued to hold the advantage over the Turks, scoring a number of new successes. Early in 1792, the Turks gave up the fight and signed the treaty of Jassy. Russia not only retained the Crimea, but also advanced her southwestern frontier from the Bug River to the Dniester. In two wars, Catherine had cleared the Turks from the northern shores of the Black Sea.

Since the first partition in 1772, meanwhile, the Polish government had promoted domestic reform with deadly seriousness. Progress was soon evident in an expanding educational system and in agricultural and industrial advances, while in 1788, a new Diet was convened for the purpose of considering constitutional reform. Prussia, anxious to put pressure on both Russia and Austria in this period, encouraged the Poles with hints of support, though certainly not with any degree of sincerity. The result was a courageous new constitution in 1791, which abolished the *liberum veto* and made the monarchy hereditary, thereby creating a ministry responsible to the legislature. The Saxon dynasty was to succeed Stanislas Poniatowski.

Inevitably, some of the nobles could not accept these changes and went into confederation at Targowitz. They appealed to Catherine for aid, and she, now nearly free of her Turkish quarrel, answered with 100,000 troops. The Poles then turned to Prussia, only to be denied assistance. Poniatowski tried to save the constitution by offering to accept Catherine's grandson, Constantine, as his heir, but she was unmoved. Russian troops occupied Warsaw, while Prussian troops moved into western Poland (1792), following which the two powers shared in the second partition in early 1793. They left Poland only four million people, one-third of the population before 1772.

Just as the first partition had excited a reform movement, the second partition gave birth to a wild anti-Russian outburst (1794), led by Thaddeus Kosciuszko (1746–1817). The Poles enjoyed a number of local successes against isolated Russian garrisons, giving the Prussians the opportunity to intervene to save the situation. Ultimately, new Russian forces were sent in, and the uprising was smashed. Prussia tried to exploit the situation by making extraordinary demands in negotiations for a third partition, which Catherine countered by backing Austria's claim to Polish territory. In the end, the three powers signed the Third Partition Treaty in 1795, and Poland disappeared from the map.

SUGGESTIONS FOR FURTHER READING

⤜⤝

General and Political History

Leo Gershoy, *From Despotism to Revolution 1763-1789* (New York and London: Harper, 1944), excellent study with good bibliography.

G. P. Gooch, *Germany and the French Revolution* (London: Longmans, Green, 1920).

G. P. Gooch, *Frederick the Great* (New York: Alfred A. Knopf, 1947), for Frederick as an enlightened despot.

G. P. Gooch, *Catherine the Great and Other Studies* (London and New York: Longmans, Green, 1954).

Geoffrey Bruun, *The Enlightened Despots* (New York: Henry Holt, 1929), brief but wise.

S. K. Padover, *The Revolutionary Emperor: Joseph II* (New York: R. O. Ballou, 1934).

The Cambridge History of Poland, from Augustus II to Pilsudski (Cambridge University Press, 1941).

C. Hallendorf and A. Schuck, *History of Sweden* (Stockholm: C. E. Fritze, 1929).

Sir George Young, *Portugal Old and Young; An Historical Study* (Oxford, The Clarendon Press, 1917), good introduction.

Frederick L. Nussbaum, *History of the Economic Institutions of Modern Europe* (New York: F. S. Crofts, 1933).

Herbert Heaton, *Economic History of Europe* (New York and London: Harper, 1936).

Overton H. Taylor, *A History of Economic Thought* (New York: McGraw-Hill, 1960).

Eleanor Barber, *The Bourgeoisie in Eighteenth Century France* (Princeton University Press, 1955).

S. Konovalov, *Russo-Polish Relations: An Historical Survey* (Princeton University Press, 1945).

Cultural and Intellectual History

G. R. Havens, *Age of Ideas* (New York: Henry Holt, 1957).

John H. Randall, *The Making of the Modern Mind* (Boston: Houghton Mifflin, 1940).

Jacques Barzun, *Romanticism and the Modern Ego* (Boston: Little, Brown, 1943).

*Basil Willey, *The Eighteenth Century Background* (Boston: Beacon, 1961).

Alfred Cobban, *Rousseau and the Modern State* (London: Allen and Unwin, 1934).

Robert E. Ergang, *Herder and the Foundations of German Nationalism* (Columbia University Press, 1931).

W. J. Warner, *The Wesleyan Movement in the Industrial Revolution* (London and New York: Longmans, Green, 1930).

Milton A. Goldberg, *Smollett and the Scottish School* (Albuquerque: University of New Mexico Press, 1959).

Frederick C. Green, *Minuet. A Critical Survey of French and English Literary Ideas in the Eighteenth Century* (London: J. M. Dent and Sons, 1935).

John G. Robertson, *A History of German Literature*, rev. ed. (New York: G. P. Putnam's Sons, 1930).

Paul Henry Lang, *Music in Western Civilization* (New York: W. W. Norton, 1941).

W. H. Bruford, *Germany in the Eighteenth Century: The Social Background for the Literary Revival* (Cambridge University Press, 1952).

Frederick C. Green, *Jean-Jacques Rousseau: Critical Study of His Life and Writings* (Cambridge University Press, 1955), rated as the best biography.

* Available in paperbound editions.

≽ 6 ≼

Industrialization:

Economic and Social Change

THE PHRASES "agrarian revolution" and "industrial revolution" are so well established in historical usage that it may seem caviling to point out that they are misleading in significant ways. Originally, they were used to characterize a period of remarkable technical innovation thought to have begun roughly in 1760 and to have slackened off about 1830. Now it appears that rapid technical change was not confined by these dates and that the technical changes affected far more than the economic structure of Western Europe. In the first place, we shall see that the conditions which made these "revolutions" possible were a long time in preparation, so that the notion of a sudden burst or sudden change seems too arbitrary; in the second place, while the period of technical change most certainly altered the economic organization of Europe, the most revolutionary aspect of the technical changes was their impact upon the social order. We look at Britain in the eighteenth century as *the* industrializing nation, and there the record is both that of inventions and new sources of power and of a change in the countryside and the way of life. Fields were enclosed, hamlets grew into industrial towns, highways were improved, and the population not only increased notably but also shifted geographically from the traditional centers to the midlands and the north. "

History, especially as taught by contemporary historians, is the record of change. We look for the differences characteristic of historical eras to such a degree that we often fail to record those things which have been relatively unchanging. Given this qualification, it is nevertheless true that the eighteenth century was an era of extraordinary change. There is evidence not only of normal, evolutionary changes, but also of a coincidence of drastic technical and economic changes—in tune with the intellectual and political climate—which uprooted patterns that had served Europeans for many centuries. Granted that life in the seventeenth century was not the same as life in the twelfth, it is arguable that the average man of the seventeenth century would have had more in common with his twelfth-century counterpart than with a factory worker of the late eighteenth century. Is it any wonder, then, that historians have been so ready to affix "revolution" to the agrarian, industrial, and political changes of the eighteenth century?

One outward sign that the conditions of life were changing notably in Britain was the sudden growth of population, in particular after 1740. It is estimated that the population of England and Wales was 5.5 million in 1700, 6.5 million in 1750, and 9 million in 1801 (the first census). Yet, there was no appreciable increase in the birth rate, and even Irish immigration, while important, was largely offset by the emigration of Englishmen, either as colonists or as transported criminals. Mainly responsible for this 40 per cent increase during the last half of the eighteenth century was a decline in the death rate, for which we must list a number of contributing causes: a better knowledge of medicine and improved midwifery, thanks to the school of medicine in Edinburgh; greater numbers of lying-in hospitals and orphanages, which meant the survival of more children from middle- and lower-class families; a better supply of fresh meat and an increased consumption of fresh vegetables; greater supplies of soap and the availability of cheap underwear for the first time; the removal of a number of injurious manufacturing processes from homes to factories; and, finally, the replacement of thatched by slate roofs, reducing the pests which had contributed to infection and disease.[1]

The coincidence of this population increase with the innovations in industry has led to various theories which suggest that the "industrial revolution" was the necessary answer to a rapidly increasing population's demand. Such theories seem to fall short of adequacy if we look beyond Britain in the eighteenth century to discover that other nations also experienced a population increase without a subsequent industrial revolution;

1. See J. H. Plumb, *England in the Eighteenth Century* (London, Penguin Books, 1950), p. 78, and T. S. Ashton, *The Industrial Revolution, 1760-1830* (New York, Oxford, 1948), pp. 3-4.

that, in fact, an increasing population in some countries has meant a lowering of the standards of living and often starvation. But in Britain one sees not only a rise in food production, but also that fewer and fewer people were required to raise more and more food. This would clearly have been impossible had not agricultural techniques both reduced labor and increased the yield per acre. This suggests the important part played by the agricultural revolution in the development of the industrial revolution in Britain. And the agricultural revolution, in turn, was tied to the enclosure movement. Since the traditional open-field system did not lend itself to experimentation, innovations in agricultural techniques would have been impossible without the enclosures.[2]

Enclosures were an old story in Britain and continued until the middle of the eighteenth century; but whereas formerly enclosures were designed to increase wool production, those of the late seventeenth and eighteenth centuries reflected a desire to increase the food supply. Larger-scale farming, with its possibilities for more rational or scientific methods, obviously appealed to the men of the enlightenment and seemed to justify the enclosures, though for the poorer proprietors they were a disaster. The small farmers soon found themselves unable to compete with the great landowners, and they often lost the right to use the common. Many sold out and became wage earners, and their living conditions deteriorated whether they remained in the country as farm laborers or moved to the towns. Roughly one-fifth of the English lived in towns in 1700; by 1760, one half of them did.[3]

Investment, whether in land or in industry, means capital, and one of the most perceptive historians of this period has related the power to accumulate capital and the willingness to invest it to the political stability which Britain experienced after 1689. No other European country had achieved a government as enthusiastically supported by the governed as Britain. And the financial stability of the British government after that date, so much in contrast with the continental powers, contributed to public confidence. As the dangers of investment lessened, interest rates

2. Enclosures were generally accomplished by act of Parliament. A large landowner, desiring to enclose his property, petitioned Parliament to have all the village land in his locality enclosed. Parliament, reflecting the interests of the large landowners, generally overrode the protests of the small freeholders in the village. Lands would then be resurveyed and redistributed to give all freeholders in the village compact holdings (thus ending strip-farming), after which the holdings were enclosed.

3. See W. E. Lunt, *History of England,* 3rd ed. (New York, Harper, 1946), pp. 567-571.

declined markedly, providing greater supplies of cheap capital than had been hitherto known.[4]

Beyond this, we must note that peculiar British practice of primogeniture, by which only the eldest sons inherited titles and properties. For many generations, second and third sons of gentle families, having no expectation of inheritance, married for money, often into the middle class. Class distinctions remained, but intermarriage considerably lessened class hostilities, especially when compared to the social cleavages on the Continent, and probably made it easier for an English gentleman to consider investing in commercial enterprise. That the two classes sat side by side in the House of Commons, rather than in exclusive estates, was the political manifestation of this social and legal phenomenon. (One must be careful to distinguish the nobility from the gentry, the former represented in the House of Lords, the latter in Commons.)

The period of the "industrial revolution," thus, does not offer itself to a simple cause-and-effect analysis, for one finds a complex and peculiar coincidence of many factors—technical, intellectual, economic, political, and demographic—which provide a problem of historical causation about which there is still a large measure of disagreement. The complexities and disagreements do not end there; many of the inventors and industrialists of the eighteenth century were Dissenters rather than Anglicans, and for this circumstance there remain various explanations. It is said that those who were concerned for novelty in religion would be innovators in other lines too. Others have argued that the exclusion of Dissenters from politics drove them into other fields. And most debated of all is the theory—originally stated by Max Weber at the beginning of the twentieth century and later altered by R. H. Tawney—that the ethics of the more radical Protestant sects harmonized with the ethics of business. While there is a measure of truth in each thesis, there are also serious qualifications which render each suspect. That the Nonconformists were a better-educated group than the Anglicans in the eighteenth century there seems little doubt, especially if one looks at the middle class in England or at Presbyterian Scotland, where both primary schools and universities were the widely copied example for the rest of Europe. The original impetus for education among the Nonconformists had been, it is true, the zeal for their novel sects; but their curricula were soon expanded to include mathematics, history, geography, French, and bookkeeping. Could it be, then, that the simplest

4. See Ashton, *op. cit.*, pp. 7-11.

explanation for the preeminence of the Nonconformists in invention and industry lies in the modernity of their education?[5]

Finally, when all the economic, political, religious, and demographical factors contributing to this age of invention have been surveyed, it is important to add the most obvious and the least considered of all the factors: that inventions are the products of men's minds. Our children read stories of great inventions which leave the impression that most inventions are the result of accidents, that the inventive process is a matter of luck and is evidently irrational. We obscure from them three important matters: first, that it is only the mind prepared by long, arduous work, the mind which is capable of making a synthesis, which sees the significance of the accident; and second, that an invention, while perhaps the work of one man, is part of a stream of ideas and inventions which are the work of many men; which leads us to the final matter:

Invention . . . is more likely to arise in a community that sets store by things of the mind than in one that seeks only material ends. . . . Newton, indeed, was too good a philosopher and scholar to care whether or not the ideas he gave to the world were immediately "useful"; but the belief in the possibility of achieving industrial progress by the method of observation and experiment came to the eighteenth century largely through him.[6]

With these generalities in mind, we can turn to a more detailed consideration of this age of innovation.

INNOVATIONS IN AGRICULTURE

The enclosure movement preceded the introduction of agricultural machinery not only in Britain; on the Continent, where enclosure lagged behind that in Britain, the introduction of machinery also lagged. Traditionally, the open-field system prevailed. A village was surrounded by two or three large, unfenced fields which were divided into strips. The strips were owned and worked by individuals, but the crops and livestock were controlled by a community of owners through the village. Enclosure meant individually owned fields and the result that crops and livestock were controlled by the owner alone. One can immediately see that the enclosure movement was not merely agricultural in significance, but was social as

5. See Ashton, *op. cit.,* pp. 18-20.
6. *Ibid.,* pp. 15-16.

well. In England, permission to enclose was granted by Parliament, and the number of Enclosure Acts passed by Parliament in the eighteenth century reflects the enthusiasm for investment in large-scale food production and scientific agriculture:[7]

1700-1710:	1	1750-1760:	156
1710-1720:	8	1760-1770:	424
1720-1730:	33	1770-1780:	642
1730-1740:	35	1780-1790:	287
1740-1750:	38	1790-1800:	506

It required capital, first to carry out agricultural experiments, and, second, to adopt the new inventions; and the failure of many of the smallholders to partake of the latest agricultural wisdom should not be indiscriminately ascribed to conservatism. Even some of the experimentists seem less than wise in retrospect. Take Jethro Tull (1674–1741), for instance, whose work marked the first significant step towards eliminating manual labor in the fields. He invented a number of drills to permit him to sow field crops in a manner to make frequent cultivation of those crops possible while they were growing—something impossible where the older broadcast sowing was used. His drills were used to plant crops in parallel rows, and he introduced the horse hoe for their cultivation. He had found, of course, that cultivation improved crops and that the horse-drawn hoe was more efficient than hoeing by hand. Yet, his enthusiasm for cultivation derived from his notion that plants were nourished by tiny particles and that their nourishment was simply made easier by disturbing the soil. He thought the use of manures as nourishment to be madness, and some economic historians write him off as a crank.[8]

In any case, the experiments carried out during the same years by Charles, Viscount Townshend (1764–1738), were of far greater significance. He was known as "Turnip" Townshend, for his work concerned crop rotation. Here the problem was to find fodder crops with which animals could be fed over the winter, for until that was possible, the animal-raising industry could not develop. Such an industry was vital, not only to increase the food supply, but also to provide the manures for crops which most farmers, Jethro Tull to the contrary, recognized as necessary. It is uncertain where fodder crops were first grown, though they were

7. See Plumb, op. cit., p. 82.
8. See Singer et al., eds., A History of Technology (New York, Oxford, 1958), Vol. IV, pp. 5-6; Ashton, op. cit., p. 27; Lunt, loc. cit.

known on the Continent in the seventeenth century, clover, turnips, and buckwheat in particular. Grass and root crops were grown for animals, and their manure was carefully saved. This was on a limited scale, however, and in England the open-field system was, again, the barrier to agricultural advancement. Under that system, all the village farmers had the right to graze animals on the stubble after harvest and on the fields lying fallow. Only with enclosure was it possible to improve the livestock through controlled breeding, and, equally important, to raise fodder crops on land previously left fallow. Lord Townshend worked out a four-course rotation involving wheat, turnips, barley, and clover, eliminating the need to let land lie fallow every third year and leading to an impressive increase in farm production.[9] The smallholders, who through enclosure lost their grazing rights and often, thereby, the means to an independent rural existence, understandably did not view the enclosures as a blessing. But there is no doubt that the British population in the long run had a far better food supply. The displaced country folk, migrating to towns, provided a labor force for the new factories. The profits from agriculture, moreover, increased sometimes as much as 400 per cent in the quarter-century following Townshend's innovation; these profits could not indefinitely be reinvested in agriculture, but served as capital for investment in industry.

The new root and grass crops, which made it possible to keep herds alive during the winter, set a number of breeders to experimenting. Of these, Robert Bakewell (1725–1795) of Leicestershire was the best-known. Before his time—that is to say, before 1750—animals had not been primarily grown for their meat; sheep were raised for wool and cattle for dairy products. Their meat was of poor quality. While little is known of Bakewell's methods, it is known that they involved intensive inbreeding to produce the characteristics he wanted, and the New Leicester sheep was his creation. He also improved horses and Longhorn cattle. His followers and imitators were even more successful in developing sheep of greater weight, Dutch cattle were often imported for breeding purposes, and even Chinese pigs were imported to improve the native stock. Herefords, Ayrshires, Shorthorns, and Devon cattle were the results of this controlled breeding, and there is good evidence that the average weight of carcasses sold between 1750 and 1800 roughly doubled. We have figures of animals sold at Smithfield:[10]

9. See Singer *et al., op. cit.,* Vol. IV, pp. 13-18.
10. Plumb, *op. cit.,* pp. 82-83.

	1710	*1795*
Oxen	370 lbs.	800 lbs.
Calves	50 lbs.	150 lbs.
Sheep	38 lbs.	80 lbs.

Just as science had its great popularizer in the eighteenth century in Fontenelle, the new agricultural methods had their publicist: Arthur Young (1741–1820). Between 1766 and 1775, he traveled extensively to observe agriculture, finally establishing a monthly magazine in 1784, the *Annals of Agriculture*, to which even George III (under the name Ralph Robinson) contributed articles.

This year (1791) His Majesty had the goodness to present me with a present of a Spanish ram. The world is full of those who consider military glory as the proper object of the ambition of monarchs, who measure regal merit by the millions that are slaughtered, by the public robbery and plunder that are dignified by the title of dignity and conquest, and who look down on every exertion of peace and tranquillity as unbecoming those who aim at the epithet great, and unworthy the aim of men that are born for masters of the globe. My ideas are cast in a very different mould, and I believe the period is advancing with accelerated pace that shall exhibit character in a light totally new, and shall rather brand than exalt the virtues hitherto admired, that shall pay more homage to the prince who gave a ram to a farmer than for wielding the sceptre.[11]

"Farmer George's" enthusiasm mirrored the agricultural vogue of that day, and in 1793 his government created the Board of Agriculture, of which Arthur Young became the first secretary. The Board's duty was to publicize rather than to control, and while a governmental institution, it was largely supported by private subscription from those agricultural enthusiasts who hoped to popularize horse hoeing, four-course crop rotation, the use of fertilizers, and the draining of fields. The Board advocated the use of new machinery, a wheeled plough and a threshing machine in particular, and it sponsored both Sir Humphry Davy's (1778–1829) *Lectures on Vegetable Chemistry* and Erasmus Darwin's (1731–1802) *Phytologia*. The new methods were also publicized through annual sheepshearings, sponsored by the great landowners, where animals, implements, and new varieties were on display. Even though there were important agricultural developments elsewhere in the eighteenth century, Britain had become the model, and visitors came from abroad for these annual fairs.[12]

11. Arthur Young, *Travels in France*, 3rd ed. (London, 1890), p. XLII.
12. See Plumb, *op. cit.*, p. 152.

As for agricultural developments in the German world during the eighteenth century, it is remarkable that the innovations were usually sponsored by governments rather than by individuals, as in Britain; this situation surely furnishes us with more evidence that the technical innovations of that age were caused and conditioned by factors far transcending the economic realm alone. The losses in population suffered during the Thirty Years War meant that many fields were abandoned and reverted to grass and forest. In the eighteenth century, some of the German governments, notably Prussia, sponsored colonial migrations to recover these waste lands and encouraged the adoption of new crops and methods of cultivation. Frederick the Great, as the best example, championed the cultivation of potatoes, encouraged the planting of orchards, and imported dairy stock from Holland and merino rams from Spain to improve the Prussian livestock. In general, the tradition for fallow was strong, and the three-field system prevailed during the century. Complete rotation did not become usual in Germany until the nineteenth century. In the eighteenth, new crops from America were the principal innovations: potatoes, tobacco, and corn.

French agriculture lagged behind that of Britain, too. Aside from the enlightened Turgot, who secured a few merino rams in 1776 for the royal flock at Rambouillet, the government was little concerned for agricultural reform. The merino was famous for its silky wool but was poor for food, a fact which will account for why the English farmers of the period did not favor it; but Turgot's efforts led to the great improvement of wool production in France. As in Germany, the three-field system prevailed, though late in the century corn was used in the south to replace fallow. Large areas, however, remained in waste, and there was no serious pressure from the population to force large-scale food production. Improvement of the livestock for food was similarly delayed, and, worse, animal diseases seem to have been more prevalent in France than elsewhere in Europe, leading to the establishment of Europe's first veterinary school at Lyons in 1762. The backwardness of the French in agricultural matters is the more strange when one remembers that the philosophers of agriculture in the eighteenth century—the physiocrats—were French. What innovations were made, it is true, were made by men like Turgot under the influence of physiocratic ideas.[13]

While one finds an occasional farmer in the eighteenth century who did

13. See Singer *et al., op. cit.,* Vol. IV, pp. 22-32.

not believe in fertilizing the soil, European planters, as early as the sixteenth century, had generally recognized that the soil must be replenished with minerals if fertility is to be maintained. Scientists had not been overly concerned about this, perhaps in part because chemistry had not attracted the greatest scientific minds in the seventeenth century. The great advances in knowledge during that century had been in astronomy, mechanics, and physics; the revolution in chemistry came later, in the eighteenth century, and even then the chemists who were interested in the soil and the nutrition of plants had less influence on fertilization than did the farmers who were experimenting. Such experiments, however, did not explain how plants receive their nutrition, nor were the farmers aware of the startling fact that the plant world is not dependent upon the animal world for survival.

In the light of current knowledge, the problem can be simply stated: our world "runs" on solar energy, which we largely derive from plants. Plants are responsible, directly or indirectly, for all our food, and they supply our principal fuels: wood, coal, and petroleum. The nuclear energy from the sun comes to the earth as radiant energy (or light), where it is transformed by plants into chemical energy. Only plants can utilize radiant energy; animals require chemical energy, which the plants furnish; animal life can therefore not survive without plants. Yet, plants could survive without animals, since decaying plants can produce the carbon dioxide used by plants to produce oxygen and food. Though the carbon dioxide used by plants often comes from animal metabolism and also from combustion, the point is that the plants could survive without them. It is further true that until the chemists of the eighteenth century could learn more about the properties of the air and the nature of combustion, they could not know the nature of plant life.[14]

ADVANCES IN CHEMISTRY

The key problem in the chemical revolution of the eighteenth century was that of combustion. It was traditional to believe that when anything burned, something was streaming out of it—struggling to escape—which accounted for the fluttering of the flame; and it was the escape of this subtle ingredient which reduced the burned object to more elementary ingredients; hence, decomposition. This ancient explanation was called

14. See J. B. Conant *et al.*, eds., *Harvard Case Histories in Experimental Science* (Cambridge, Harvard University Press, 1957), Vol. II, pp. 325-327.

"phlogiston theory" by the German physician and chemist G. E. Stahl (1660–1734). "Phlogiston" referred to the fiery principle which was presumably lost during burning, and that which remained after burning was called the ash or, in the case of a metal, the calx.

Doubts about the phlogiston theory were not long in coming, because the weight of the ash or calx was often greater than that of the object before burning. If something had escaped during the burning, the residue would presumably be lighter. Most chemists also suspected that the nature of the air had something to do with combustion, but tradition had it that air, like water, is a simple substance, an irreducible element; furthermore, air was regarded as too subtle to be "fixed," by which was meant that air could not be forced to combine with a solid substance to form a compound. Such preconceptions blinded some of the chemists to the significance of their own experiments. In 1754, for instance, the Scottish scientist Joseph Black (1728–1799) noted an "air" or gas which was attracted to quicklime —unlike common air—but he did not recognize that he had demonstrated the existence of separate gases in the air, for such a thing could not be. (He was dealing unknowingly with carbon dioxide and had discovered "fixed air.")

Joseph Priestley (1733–1804) was another example. A believer in the phlogiston theory, he directed the sun's rays through a burning glass onto some mercuric oxide, which, in his day, was called calx of mercury (1774). He found that mercury was formed and that a gas was given off. According to the phlogiston theory, the calx should have been unaffected by the heat, and he was baffled by the reaction. As for the gas given off, he found that a candle placed in it burned more brightly than in common air, but like Black, he did not recognize that he had isolated a gas (in this case oxygen).

In France, however, A. L. Lavoisier (1743–1794) had been carrying on similar experiments and had studied the work of others. It fell to him to see the significance of various experiments and to be a synthesizer —the Newton of Chemistry. Recognizing the difficulties inherent in the phlogiston theory, he heated metal in a sealed flask and found that there was no change in weight until the flask was opened and air allowed to enter, whereupon the flask would increase in weight. He reported his discovery to the Secretary of the French Academy on November 1, 1772:

About eight days ago I discovered that sulfur in burning, far from losing weight, on the contrary, gains it; it is the same with phosphorus; this increase of weight arises from a prodigious quantity of air that is fixed during combustion and combines with the vapors.

This discovery, which I have established by experiments, that I regard as decisive, has led me to think that what is observed in the combustion of sulfur and phosphorus may well take place in the case of all substances that gain in weight by combustion and calcination; and I am persuaded that the increase in weight of metallic calxes is due to the same cause.[15]

Thus it was that Lavoisier, having demonstrated that calcination was not a matter of decomposition but a combination of a metal with air or gas, saw that Priestley had undoubtedly isolated that component of the air involved in combustion. This meant that the air was not an element, but that it must consist of at least two gases, and he gave the name oxygen to the active component associated with combustion. The following year (1775), Lavoisier published a paper revealing the significance of Priestley's work: *On the Nature of the Principle that combines with Metals in Calcination and that increases their Weight.*[16] Recognizing the air to be a compound proved to be one of those major discoveries in science which open up many new possibilities for inquiry. As an illustration, we need merely recall that an understanding of plant life requires the use of words such as oxygen and carbon dioxide.[17]

INDUSTRIAL INNOVATIONS

In turning next to technical innovations in eighteenth-century industry, we find that, as in agriculture, the implications were social as well as economic, in large part because the technical advances led to the factory system and to rapid urbanization. The textile industry was an early example of the transition in manufacturing. Before the establishment of factories, textiles were produced in homes, a method known variously as the domestic system, the cottage industry, and the putting-out system. Here, the key figure was a merchant or clothier who hired putters-out to distribute material to spinners and weavers. Many of these worked full time in their homes, though some were partially engaged in farming. The textile industry was far more important than the clothing industry because most families

15. *Ibid.*, Vol. I, pp. 72-73.
16. See Herbert Butterfield, *The Origins of Modern Science: 1300-1800* (New York, Macmillan, 1952), pp. 150-161.
17. See Singer *et al., op. cit.,* Vol. IV, pp. 218-200.

either made their own clothes or hired seamstresses—at notoriously low wages.

In 1717, Thomas Lombe established the first true factory to house machines for throwing silk, a technique he had learned in Italy. He employed about 300 workers on his premises and used water power to operate the machines. Beginning with the silk industry, technical innovations spread to the manufacture of other textiles, the innovations making man's energy more efficient, but taking him from his home to the factory, where new sources of power could be mustered to operate the machines. The woolen industry received its first technical innovation in 1733, when John Kay invented the labor-saving flying shuttle, but its adoption was slow, thanks to the hostility of the workers who feared it would contribute to unemployment; and the cotton industry did not use Kay's shuttle until after 1760. Others worked to improve the spinning technique, but the spinning machines were imperfect and also encountered the workers' hostility.

Meanwhile, the mining industry was pushed to find more efficient methods. Coal had become important in the seventeenth century as Brittain's timber famine became acute, and the outcroppings were used initially. By the eighteenth century, it had become necessary to sink shafts and dig underground galleries. Coal mines were developed by the great landowners, and many of the early miners were part-time farmers, though after 1750 there was an increasing use of women and boys to drag the coal baskets and carry them up the ladders to the surface; this practice continued well into the nineteenth century. Working conditions were not only unhealthful but even dangerous because of water and gas in the tunnels and galleries. Despite many devices to explode gas and to force fresh air into the shafts, accidents were routine. It was not unusual to line the shafts with sheepskins to hold back spring water, and hand pumps and bucket chains were used to expel water which did seep in.

A pumping engine was an obvious necessity, and there were numerous experiments before Thomas Newcomen (1663–1729) invented an engine, driven by steam power, which was clearly superior to the others. In the first engine, built in 1712, the steam was introduced from a boiler into the bottom of the cylinder; the piston then rose to the top of the cylinder, though the weight of the pump rod was chiefly responsible for this. Finally, the connection between the boiler and the cylinder was closed, and a steam of cold water was used to condense the steam in the cylinder. A vacuum was thus produced, and the atmospheric pressure forced the piston back to the bottom of the cylinder, raising the pump rod.[18] Newcomen's engine may have been the best of its day, but it was seriously inefficient because of the necessity of alternating the temperature in the cylinder to produce the strokes of the pump rod; this entailed a great loss of energy. A group of scientists at the University of Glasgow, recognizing the problem, urged a local instrument maker, James Watt (1736–1819), known by them to be an ingenious mechanic, to improve the steam engine. His solution to the problem (1765) was to have a separate condenser, which could be kept permanently cool while the cylinder was kept hot. It required nearly another ten years before Watt could find craftsmen sufficiently skilled to build his engine, which was about four times more efficient than Newcomen's atmospheric engine had been. The improved engine was used not only to pump water from mines, but also to power the wheels in the developing iron industry; its bellows, hammers, and rolling mills.

Coal production was small in the eighteenth century, it is true, and was a factor limiting the growth of industry; but the figures suggest a notable increase in coal production: 2.50 million tons in 1700, 4.75 million tons by 1750, and 10.00 million tons by 1800. Earlier, charcoal had been used for smelting iron; but in 1709 Abraham Darby managed to produce pig iron by smelting with coke; from that time on, furnaces and foundries were built in the neighborhood of coal fields rather than near forests. The timber supply, by the eighteenth century, had, of course, been seriously depleted.[19]

The pace of technical improvement increased as the century developed, and both the benefits and the dilemmas created thereby seem especially measurable after 1760, which may account for the tendency of the earlier historians to date the "industrial revolution" from that year. Townspeople, for instance, had a better diet: meat was no longer a rarity, and wheat and potatoes were more generally available. And other things being equal, the improved nutrition meant better health for factory workers. There remains, however, the question of whether conditions of work and housing facilities were equal in health-giving units to what the workers had known as countrymen, a question which we can postpone for the moment.

Meanwhile, we must note some of the technical improvements after 1760. In the textile industry, spinning techniques were at last improved by two men: James Hargreaves (?–1778) produced a hand machine called

18. See *Ibid.,* Vol. IV, p. 175; and Ashton, *op. cit.,* pp. 34-37.
19. See Ashton, *op. cit.,* pp. 38-41, 67-69.

Above: Richard Arkwright
Left: The Jacquard Loom
Below: Hargreaves' Spinning Jenny

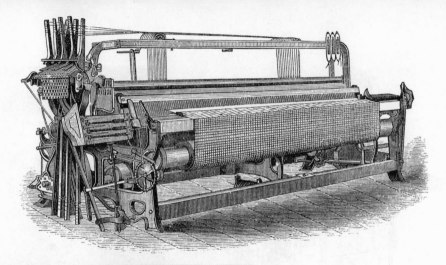

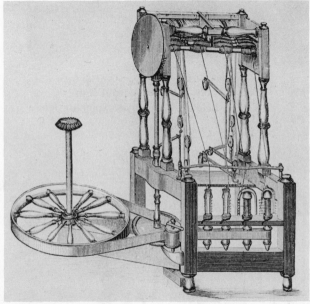

Above: Crompton's Fancy
Loom
Left: Arkwright's Spinning
Frame
Below left to right:
Joseph Priestley, James Watt,
Antoine Lavoisier

the jenny which made it possible for a woman to spin more than one thread at a time. The first jenny could handle six threads, and later models held up to eighty; but the yarn so spun was suitable only for the weft. The warp was spun on a machine called the frame, which Richard Arkwright (1732–1793) invented in 1768. Unlike the jenny, the frame could not be operated by hand, but required water power. The speed-up of spinning in the 1760's created a demand for more wool which the old methods of carding could not meet. Arkwright next produced a power-driven carding machine (1775). In the 1780's a new machine called the mule came into use: it combined the spinning features of the jenny and the frame, and though it was often powered by water, steam engines of the Watt variety were increasingly used.

These textile innovations after 1760 were first applied to the cotton industry, which, by then, had gained the inventive precedence from the silk and woolen industries. Probably the nature of these latter materials hindered technical progress, but it is also true that the cotton industry benefited from new techniques of bleaching and dyeing—in short, from the chemical advances of the eighteenth century—developed in both Britain and France. Cottons were relatively cheap, and were popular, not only because of their price, but also because they were suitable for garments previously beyond the reach of the public, underwear in particular.

Unlike the advances in the textile industries which were associated with new sources of power, the notable improvements in the pottery industry had little to do with new sources of power. Here there were two factors: the growing shortage of the metals—tin and lead—traditionally used for utensils, and an increasing use of tea and coffee, which made metal utensils less desirable than pottery. We have noted earlier that the Europeans of the eighteenth century were greatly impressed by China, and Chinese porcelains were the model for those who sought better clays, glazing materials, and methods of decoration. In Britain, family industries were the rule, the Wedgwoods for example. In the eighteenth century, Josiah Wedgwood (1730–1795) was their greatest experimenter; it was he who developed the jasper ware so famous today: the white figures in relief against a colored background, generally blue or green.

Even the briefest survey of technical improvement in the eighteenth century requires some mention of the advances in transportation, and it is striking to note that most of the innovations were sponsored by men who required better transportation facilities to serve the new industries. Canal building was clearly related to the need to bring coal to the new factories, and, beginning about 1760 and reaching near mania by 1790, one can find some astonishingly bold projects which were financed by private individuals. The era of canals was short, ending about 1830, but in that period canals, far more than highways, served to reduce the cost of transporting heavy industrial materials, making them more readily available. Furthermore, the technical problems faced by the canal builders gave rise to a new profession in Britain: civil engineering. It would be unfair to ignore the improvements made in roads during the eighteenth century, even though their commercial importance was less than that of the canals. Highways were notoriously poor and unsafe, and before 1750, the government tried ineffectively to regulate traffic for its protection. After 1750, commercial and industrial requirements led individuals and companies to build roads for heavier traffic, so that in time wagons replaced pack horses. The best road surfaces were made by John McAdam (1756–1836), a Scottish engineer, with fragments of granite packed down into a hard roadbed, a type of construction still known as *macadamizing*.

Railroads had their origin in the eighteenth century as part of the movement to build more stable roads, especially roads to bring iron and coal from the mines to the canal docks. The first rails were made of wood; then the wood was fitted with cast-iron plates at points of exceptional wear; finally, in 1767, all-iron tracks were built, with flanges to hold the wheels in line. The flanges were first transferred to the wheels in 1789. The trains were drawn by horses, though as early as the 1760's, when Watt was improving the steam engine, there were suggestions in both Britain and France that the steam engine would replace the horse. But James Watt thought the idea to be utterly ridiculous, and his prestige was sufficiently great to discourage experiments, retarding this development until the nineteenth century.[20]

To sum up these sections on technical change, it is important to add that economic historians have studied the progress of inventions in the eighteenth century by charting the patents taken out. Their findings have done some damage to the popular impression that technical improvement throughout history has been mothered by war, a generalization which is neither wholly right nor wrong. The peak years of inventions, not only in the late eighteenth century but in the early nineteenth, were invariably years of peace; and, what is more revealing, they were years when the interest rate was low (generally not true of war years) and the expecta-

20. For a more detailed account of technical improvement after 1760, see *Ibid.*, pp. 60-87.

tion of profit high. Though this approach is a suggestive generalization, it is no more infallible than the one above. Yet, to harken back to the early part of this chapter, it is well to remember, in discussing any age of invention, that capital must be available as well as a willingness to invest it. In eighteenth-century Britain, that capital came first from land and overseas trade, and as industry expanded, its profits were ploughed back for expansion. Furthermore, the increasing political stability under the Hanoverians meant that the interest rate on public securities fell during the century, making other investments more attractive. Thus the suggestion, again, that the economic, political, social, and intellectual realities cannot be so neatly packaged and separated as is sometimes done.[21]

Nowhere on the Continent were there present sufficient factors necessary to promote industrialization until the nineteenth century; then each industrializing nation varied in its experience from that of Britain. Sometimes, as we shall see, industrialization did not come to a country as a matter of natural development, and governmental encouragement and subsidies were required to secure the advantages of industrialization.

THE EFFECTS OF INDUSTRIALIZATION

The phrase "industrial revolution" was not of eighteenth-century origin but became common only after 1884, following the publication of a famous series of lectures given at Oxford by Arnold Toynbee (1852–1883). He held that the "industrial revolution" was a moral disaster in that it led both to the degradation of the workers and to increasing class consciousness and hostility. The debate as to whether the "industrial revolution" was good or bad has gone on ever since, though, if we remember Oliver Goldsmith (1728–1774), the issue was not new:

> Ill fares the land, to hastening ills a prey,
> Where wealth accumulates, and men decay;
> Princes and lords may flourish, or may fade;
> A breath can make them, as a breath has made;
> But a bold peasantry, their country's pride,
> When once destroyed, can never be supplied.
>
> A time there was, ere England's grief began,
> When every rood of ground maintained its man;

21. See *Ibid.*, pp. 91-98.

For him light labor spread her wholesome store,
Just gave what life required, but gave no more;
His best companions, innocence and health;
And his best riches, ignorance of wealth.

But times are altered; trade's unfeeling train
Usurp the land, and dispossess the swain;
Along the lawn, where scattered hamlets rose,
Unwieldy wealth and cumbrous pomp repose;
And every want to opulence allied,
And every pang that folly pays to pride.
Those gentle hours that plenty bade to bloom,
Those calm desires that asked but little room,
Those healthful sports that graced the peaceful scene,
Lived in each look, and brightened all the green—
These, far departing, seek a kinder shore,
And rural mirth and manners are no more.[22]

Whatever the debate over the merits of industrialization, there is little doubt that the enclosures, which promoted industrialization, made rural poverty worse; in fact, the attention given to the plight of urban workers in the new factory towns has often obscured the plight of the rural workers, who are generally believed to have been worse off. That many of the destitute moved to towns to seek employment does not account for the destitutes who remained behind and sought relief from their parish—for the parish was still responsible for poor relief. Toward the end of the century, the rural situation was publicized in William Eden's *The State of the Poor* (1797), but rational opinion too often held that misery and poverty were facts, or laws, of nature and therefore inevitable. Inevitable or not, the poor were surviving in greater numbers by the end of the century.[23]

There is also reason to believe that the urban workers of the eighteenth century were far from enthusiastic about the new concentration of population which the factory system demanded, and certainly the factory system owed its existence to factors not concerned with their welfare. Sometimes a factory was necessary to manufacture a product, such as iron, which could not be produced satisfactorily on a small scale; sometimes the advantages of power machinery, as in the textile industries, justified the factory system; and from the point of view of the employer, the concentration of workers permitted a closer supervision both of the quality of output and of the materials of production. Furthermore, the increasing

22. *The Deserted Village* (1770), ll. 51-74.
23. See Plumb, *op. cit.,* pp. 153-154.

complexity of the machines of production made it desirable for employers who gave workers special training to make it difficult for the workers to leave their job. The very fact that the workers had been brought to a factory town, where they were usually dependent upon the local industry, was a controlling factor, and it was not unusual for employers to put their laborers under long-term contracts. Some manufacturers even established secondary industries for the employment of their workers' families to further embroil their lives with his economic requirements.

Thus, the moral tradition condemning the "industrial revolution" has been promoted by such recent historians as Paul Mantoux and John and Barbara Hammond, who have argued that the technological triumphs led to slavelike conditions of labor and living: "Treadmill cities where the daylight never broke upon the beauty and the wisdom of the world."[24] They are opposed by a later group of historians—including Thomas Ashton, W. W. Rostow, and J. D. Chambers—who believe that the "industrial revolution" must be studied and judged through economics and not through social and political history; and that on economic grounds, the "industrial revolution" has been a blessing. Ashton, in particular, believes that some of the distressingly inhumane conditions of the late eighteenth century would have existed with or without industrialization, and he cites uneven harvests and the wars which forced prices and interest rates up and were so destructive of the national resources. He admits that some of the baleful conditions were due to industrialization: the drab city life, the smoky skies, the decline in taste, and the absence of charm in towns that grew too fast; but he also points out that the living conditions in Britain were not uniformly lowered by industrialization, that in the north they were improved, and that in the southeast they were little changed.

And we must remember that the principal commodities whose production was revolutionized by technology—textiles and food in particular—were commodities of general consumption, benefiting all in the long run. The distribution system may indeed have been faulty, but certainly the average man ate and dressed better in the nineteenth century, thanks to the innovations. His working hours may have been long, and the working conditions in the early factories were clearly conducive neither to good health nor good morals; but the argument runs that, because industrialization offered the possibility of better standards of living, it gave impetus to protest against bad conditions. In other words, as long as the condition of

24. P. A. M. Taylor, *The Industrial Revolution in Britain: Triumph or Disaster?* (Boston, Heath, 1958), p. xii.

the mass of the population remained low and apparently fixed by the *status quo,* there was little likelihood of protest. Once the possibility of change, of drastic improvement, became clear, then the bad conditions were protested. It is, furthermore, unfair to imply that all the evils of material existence were showered upon Britain after 1760 by industrialization. There had been ample malnutrition and bad housing before that date.

This is not to say, as the Hammonds would be quick to insist, that eating and dressing better makes a man necessarily happier and freer, nor that a study of economics and technology is the touchstone for life. Herein lies a paradox for our own century as well as for the eighteenth and nineteenth: he who argues for industrialization can point to examples in modern times where the population has increased enormously without an accompanying mechanization, and the result has been appalling misery and mortality. What then of those societies which do mechanize and end by making better eating and dressing their gods?[25]

HUMANITARIAN MOVEMENTS

Throughout Europe, in the late eighteenth century, a humanitarian movement gathered force from several sources. It is a commonplace that the social and economic abuses of that period focused men's minds on poverty and disease, not because the industrial revolution created them for the first time, but because the industrial revolution, holding the promise of raising standards of living for all, offered the hope that these traditional evils could be eradicated. This was true especially in Britain, where the economic changes had meant sharp geographic and communal dislocation and where inhuman working and living conditions were the subject of increasing criticism. Indeed, when we learn that it was not unusual to employ children beginning at age seven, and work them twelve to fifteen hours a day six days a week, we are aghast at the callousness of an era whose manners and arts were the epitome of refinement, and it has been only too easy to finish by castigating the gentlemen of that day as hypocritical, selfish, and cruel. To do so means that we have judged the late eighteenth century according to the standards of our own day, and it is most important, for an understanding of both centuries, to note that our standards were made possible by the industrial revolution. Long before the

25. See *Ibid.,* p. 86; and Ashton, *op. cit.,* pp. 156-161.

factory system attracted attention to child labor, children were apprenticed at an early age to merchants and craftsmen; and the truth about the late eighteenth century is that there was greater—not lesser—concern for human misery than before.

This humanitarianism gave rise to statements defining the obligation of the "more fortunate" to be benevolent toward the "lower ranks of society," but not to remedial legislation which was delayed until the nineteenth century; which is another way of saying that humanitarian concern did not breed criticism of industrial and business practices, the obvious sources of many of the evils. The best possible explanation for this lies in the fact that eighteenth century humanitarianism derived not so much from an observation of appalling conditions as from the intellectual and sentimental climate of the age. Even John Wesley's Methodism, which, as we have seen, was a religion for the poor, was an emotional reaction against rationalism. Wesley had nothing to do with political radicalism and believed that the evils in society would be reformed only through the spiritual transformation of individuals. Describing thrift, hard work, and abstinence as those virtues which would lead to individual salvation, Wesley's movement was actually anti-intellectual. In his espousal of hard work, he probably inadvertently fostered child labor in the industrial areas where he preached. Even more ironical, Wesley himself saw that the virtues he championed often led to materialism and the erosion of spiritual values:

The Methodists in every place grow diligent and frugal; consequently they increase in goods. Hence they proportionably increase in pride, in anger, in the desire of the flesh, the desire of the eyes, and the pride of life. So, although the form of religion remains, the spirit is swiftly vanishing away.[26]

It is primarily to rationalism, therefore, that we turn for the sources of humanitarianism. Rationalism was the philosophical vogue of the eighteenth century, and the rationalist looked for moral law just as he looked for the other natural laws. What was natural was both right and good, and in Rousseau, who went even beyond the rationalists in his concern for the natural, we get the most telling criticism of society's mutilation of human nature:

All is good which comes from the Maker of things, but degenerates in man's hands. Man forces one soil to nourish the products of another soil, a tree to bear another tree's fruit; he mixes and confuses conditions and places; he

26. Quoted in Plumb, *op. cit.,* p. 97.

alters (*mutile*) his dog, his horse, and his slave; he unsettles and disfigures everything; he loves deformity and the monstrous; he wants nothing in the form nature made it, not even man. . . . We are born impressionable, and, from the moment of birth, we are influenced in various ways by things which surround us. As soon as we have an awareness of our sensations, we are inclined either to seek out or flee from those objects producing them, at first according to whether they are pleasant or unpleasant, later according to selfish expediency, and finally according to our judgment of goodness or happiness which reason gives us. These dispositions are strong or weak to the degree that we become more sensitive and enlightened; but, warped by our habits, these dispositions become altered by our opinions. Before this alteration, they (dispositions) are what I call the nature in us. It is to these primitive dispositions that we must return.[27]

Joseph Priestley (1733–1804), chemist and Nonconformist minister, was a leader in the humanitarian movement. His humanitarianism was not really benevolent—that is, he was not emotionally concerned for the lot of the poor. He saw poverty and crime as destructive of social order and wanted them abolished as hindrances to the development of a rational society. Thus, his humanitarianism was derived from his science rather than from his religion. The natural definitions of goodness, whether from Rousseau or Priestley, were secular in that they were independent of theological or metaphysical principles; and the secularization of ideals led both to naturalistic ethics and to a demand to improve man's lot on earth. Asceticism and self-denial were hardly valued by a society whose temper was hedonistic, for if one is abandoning eternal life as a goal, it makes sense to live as pleasantly as possible. Here is Diderot ridiculing the celibate priest in the South Seas who had indignantly refused the offer of a chief's daughter:

I do not know what the thing you call religion is, but I cannot help thinking ill of it, since it prevents you from enjoying the innocent pleasure, to which nature, our sovereign mistress, invites us all.[28]

To rationalism and secularism must be added the sensibility of the later eighteenth century as a humanitarian factor, since the dictates of the heart led to benevolence and to compassion for the human race—a happy supplement, indeed, for those rationalists like Condorcet (see pp. 86-87) who foresaw the perfectibility of human nature. For all their important

27. Jean-Jacques Rousseau, *Emile, ou de l'Education* (1841 edition), Vol. I, pp. 17-23.
28. J. H. Randall, *op. cit.*, p. 370.

differences, the rationalists and the romanticists were as one when it came to their enthusiasm for liberty and happiness as expressed in secular terms. One group of rationalists even related humanitarianism to self-interest, sometimes called "enlightened self-interest"; the idea being that the more we promote private interests, the more we contribute to the general welfare. But the assumption was, as in the case of Adam Smith, that private interests were to be promoted in a "natural state," where there would be no artificial restraints or barriers; and that natural regulation, since "the natural" was equated to "the good," necessarily made the private and general interests identical. From the ideal of "enlightened self-interest," it was but a step to the utilitarianism of the early nineteenth century: the justification of actions which led to the "greatest good for the greatest number."

One of the best examples of a rationalist-humanitarian was the Marchese Cesare di Beccaria (1738–1794), whose book, *Essay on Crimes and Punishments,* was utilitarian in spirit. To protect society from crime— indeed, to reduce the amount of crime—Beccaria held that punishments ought to fit the crime because he believed that suitable punishment would deter the would-be criminal.[29] His views were not merely humane, but were also grounded in the common eighteenth-century assumption that an orderly (rational) code would remove evil from this earth. Evil was, after all, social and unnatural; nature, which was the state of goodness, was also perfectly rational; hence, a rational code would return man to nature and inevitable goodness. Small wonder that we may think of the Age of Reason as an age of faith.

29. See Leo Gershoy, *From Despotism to Revolution* (New York, Harper, 1944), pp. 218-219.

SUGGESTIONS FOR FURTHER READING

Technical and Scientific History

T. S Ashton, *The Industrial Revolution 1760-1830* (London and New York: Oxford University Press, 1948, a brief but brilliant study.

Conant and Nash, eds., *Harvard Case Histories in Experimental Science,* 2 vols. Harvard University Press, 1957), a stimulating approach for the general student.

Singer, Holmyard, Hall and Williams, *A History of Technology,* Vol. IV (New York and London: Oxford University Press, 1958), an indispensible source, though somewhat difficult to read.

Herbert Butterfield, *The Origins of Modern Science, 1300-1800* (New York: Macmillan, 1952), especially useful for the revolution in chemistry. William E. Lunt, *History of England* (New York: Harper, 4th ed.,1957), see Chapter XXXI for a general survey.

Social History

*J. H. Plumb, *England in the Eighteenth Century* (London: Penguin, 1950), brief but extremely valuable.

W. E. H. Lecky, *History of England in the Eighteenth Century,* 7 vols. (New York: D. Appleton, new ed., 1891-93), a dated classic, but still valuable if used with more recent works.

Leo Gershoy, *From Despotism to Revolution* (New York and London: Harper and Bros., 1944), see Chapter VIII on humanitarianism.

M. Dorothy George, *England in Transition* (London: G. Routledge, 1931), a good summary of this period of rapid change.

J. L. and Barbara Hammond, *The Rise of Modern Industry* (New York: Harcourt, Brace, 5th ed. rev., 1937), brilliant but controversial work.

*P. A. M. Taylor, ed., *The Industrial Revolution in Britain: Triumph or Disaster?* (Boston: D. C. Heath, 1958), an excellent summary of the varied interpretations of the Industrial Revolution.

* Available in paperbound editions.

≈ 7 ≈

Revolution in America and France

BRITAIN'S DOMESTIC PROBLEMS UNDER GEORGE III

The Peace of Paris (1763) left Great Britain on a lofty pinnacle of power and prestige; it also left her dangerously isolated in her exalted state. Not that she was the *only* mistrusted nation of the great powers; but since her interests in the two major wars before 1763 were both continental and colonial, her diplomacy in defense of those interests was necessarily more complicated than that of the continental powers whose overwhelming concern was in Europe. The early alliance with Austria and the later one with Prussia had both ended in alienation, while the Bourbon powers, severely mauled overseas by the British, plotted revenge to restore Bourbon prestige. Furthermore, the British victory overseas, by removing the French from Canada, also removed a principal reason for American colonial loyalty to Britain.

The natural military complacency spawned by victory was a convenience for those who had to repair the financial damage resulting from two great wars fought on credit, and the armed forces were allowed to decay for the sake of economy. By 1775, the British had fewer than 15,000 troops ready for service, while the fleet steadily declined under the administration of an incompetent minister. However unwise such economies proved to be, it is certainly clear that Britain's financial state was precarious in 1763. A greatly increased empire might well mean greater power and wealth in the future, but it also meant an increase in immediate administrative costs—and just at a time when increased taxes were already required to reduce the war debt. It fell to the ministry (1763-1765) of George Grenville (1712-1770) to solve the financial dilemma, and for so grave a situation, success required that the ministry receive ardent parliamentary support. Unfortunately for Grenville, however, such support was lacking, and the root of the trouble was the monarch.

George III (1760-1820) was the first of the Hanoverians to be primarily concerned for British rather than for Hanoverian affairs. As a result, he was eager to recover the authority sacrificed through indifference and inexperience by his two Hanoverian predecessors and to exercise the powers enjoyed by William III in 1689. Under the first two Georges, the Whigs, ever the champions of parliamentary prerogatives, had dominated the parliamentary scene and had consistently won elections by the careful use of patronage—in short, corruption. Learning from them, George III realized that he, too, must "buy" parliamentary votes if he were to recover the initiative in government and secure a docile Parliament. There followed a constitutional struggle that profoundly affected British attitudes and policies during the 1760's and 1770's, especially the issues of imperial administration and taxation.

COLONIAL POLICY UNDER GEORGE III

We noted earlier that, in contrast to the Spanish and French colonies, the English colonies had always possessed a large measure of self-government. The colonists regarded themselves as Englishmen with constitutional rights identical to those enjoyed by the citizens of the mother country.

Colonial government had, in fact, evolved from its origins in the seventeenth century in the direction of even greater popular participation. Government by chartered company, as known earlier in Virginia and Massachusetts, had disappeared in favor of royal administration before the eighteenth century. The proprietorships gradually disappeared, too, New York, New Jersey, and Maryland becoming royal provinces after the Revolution of 1689, with South Carolina, North Carolina, and Georgia following in the first half of the eighteenth century. By the time of the American Revolution, Pennsylvania and Delaware alone remained proprietorships, and even there elected assemblies checked proprietory authority. While the details of royal administration varied in the eleven royal colonies, the pattern of government was similar. Each colony had its bicameral assembly, the lower house being elected locally, the upper house being a group of councillors appointed by the King. Governors were also appointed by the King. (Rhode Island and Connecticut were notable exceptions, electing their own governors.) Generally, the governor had the authority to veto laws passed by his colonial assembly, and the King retained the right to veto laws assented to by the assemblies and the governors. In sum, the period between 1689 and 1763 in America reflected the constitutional struggle in Britain: legislative authority, representing local rights and views, rubbed against executive authority which represented the imperial British point of view; and there is little question that the longer the colonists exercised the powers of government, the greater their sense of political independence from His Majesty.

The economic basis of the European notion of empire—and here the British and Bourbon powers held similar views—was mercantilistic. The empire was considered a self-contained geographic unit for purposes of profit and defense. In theory, colonies were not merely exploited, but also profited within the framework of economic unity. If in practice the profits seemed mostly to flow to the mother country, this could be justified by the fact that the mother country supplied much of the capital for economic development and all the money for imperial defense. The earliest laws to regulate the economic unity of the empire were the Acts of Trade and Navigation of the seventeenth century, which were directed toward economic isolation and self-sufficiency.

Economic unity and harmony within the empire implied regulation from London, and it was inevitable that economic legislation passed by Parliament for the empire as a whole would infringe upon the rights of self-government cherished by Englishmen in the various colonies. Before 1763, however, the imperial economic legislation had been laxly enforced, so that the colonies had developed a measure of economic independence virtually equivalent to their political autonomy. It was just this laxity that had to be corrected, after 1763, if the British were to meet the burdens of the war debt and the defense of an expanded empire. Furthermore, the need to reform—or shall we say, to rationalize—the administration of the empire found sanction in the tenets of the Enlightenment, though applying reason to politics was hardly the traditional British way. Britain's constitutional development (the origin of the cabinet, parliamentary supremacy, and the prime ministry, for example) shows a faith in what is workable rather than in what is theoretically ideal.[1] But those who set out, in 1763, to rationalize the administration of the empire were not only ignorant of, but also indifferent to, colonial opinion. Proceeding logically rather than politically, the Grenville ministry was soon in deep trouble for failing to distinguish between mathematics and politics.

When the British government determined to tax the colonies to help pay for frontier defense, it did so in the certain knowledge that the colonial assemblies would not act together harmoniously to raise a colonial army for defense; attempts to get them to do so had produced little but friction during the Seven Years War. A great Indian reaction to the British victory in 1763, Pontiac's Rebellion, which swept up all the frontier posts save Detroit and Fort Pitt, showed that new defensive measures were immediately necessary in the west, and the British prepared to station six thousand men in the American colonies. Whatever the military necessity, the presence of unusual numbers of regulars, coinciding with the new British decision on taxation, could not help but raise the specter of despotism. Did the King, through his Parliament and under the guise of meeting defensive requirements, seek to destroy the authority of the colonial legislatures? Even in Britain, the Whigs, ever sensitive to legislative rights and aware of George III's personal ambition, saw the constitutional issues at stake.

The Proclamation of 1763, issued by the British government, was a temporary measure to prevent further colonization west of the Appalachian watershed; it was at once a defensive and a financial device. By protecting the Indians from further colonial encroachment, the British hoped to end the frontier clashes; they would, in the meantime, develop a permanent policy for the peaceful settlement of trans-Appalachian lands. The sale of this land might well prove a financial blessing to a government anxious to reduce its war debt. It is also true that the British were anxious to preserve the American tobacco industry, which was plagued by increasingly serious financial ills; a colonial expansion westward might provide the opportunity for the tobacco growers to make a new start with new crops. But these obvious issues should not obscure the constitutional aspects of the Proclamation. Virtually half the colonies had claims to western lands—lands which clearly had economic importance; even more fundamental, in the

1. See W. B. Willcox, *Star of Empire: A Study of Britain as a World Power, 1485-1945* (New York, Knopf, 1950), pp. 142-147.

long run, was the question of the King's right to assume the direction of the western lands and their ultimate disposition. Those colonies with western claims saw the Proclamation as a challenge to the authority of their assemblies; and five years later, when the British modified the Proclamation by adopting the Hillsborough Policy, colonial fears were justified. Under that policy, the western lands were opened to gradual settlement as treaties for Indian removal could be negotiated; significantly, the land grants were to come from the King and not the colonial assemblies.[2]

Meanwhile, the actual taxes devised for the colonies by the Grenville ministry were a further grievance. The initial move was an attempt to enforce the old Molasses Act (1733), which placed a duty of sixpence a gallon on molasses imported from non-British plantations to the continental colonies, as well as a duty on refined sugar. It may be noted in passing that the Molasses Act, while a revenue measure, also protected the British colonial sugar growers in the West Indies. The following year (1764), the Sugar Act replaced the Molasses Act, reducing the duty on molasses to threepence a gallon but raising the duty somewhat on refined sugar. Even though molasses was more important than sugar to the continental colonies —to the New England rum industry especially—this more liberal law caused greater annoyance because it contained provisions for enforcement.

In 1765, Grenville brought the Stamp Act before Parliament, where it passed with great majorities. Under this act the colonists were to purchase stamps for all newspapers and legal documents; revenues from this tax were specifically earmarked for the support of the British troops stationed in America for defense. Most of the colonial leaders recognized the justice of the tax, but it was disliked by the lawyers, among them Patrick Henry (1736–1799) of Virginia, who rose in the House of Burgesses to make the earliest of the revolutionary speeches: "Caesar had his Brutus; Charles the First, his Cromwell, and George the Third—" Here he was interrupted by shouts of "Treason!" But he concluded, "—may profit by their example."[3] The House ended by resolving that no other assembly could lay taxes upon Virginia, again pointing up the constitutional issue; hostility to the stamps quickly spread to the other colonies. The Stamp Act, in short, served to remind the colonists of the ancient English principle of no

2. The increasing friction between Britain and her colonies is well presented in Curtis P. Nettels, *The Roots of American Civilization.*

3. O. P. Chitwood, *A History of Colonial America* (New York, Harper, 1958), p. 628.

taxation without representation; and the colonists were not represented in Parliament. The fact also remained that they showed precious little inclination to tax themselves through their own assemblies.

Colonial reaction to the new taxes soon became sufficient to make the collection of the stamp tax in particular impossible, and even the trade between Britain and the colonies was in jeopardy. Some of the American leaders sought to make a distinction between "internal taxes" and "external taxes"—that is, those collected within the colonies and those collected at ports; so that when a new British government, under the Marquis of Rockingham, succeeded Grenville's in 1765, it seemed politic to repeal the Stamp Act and devise new taxes which would not offend the colonists' "internal" rights. The repeal passed Parliament in 1766, but it was accompanied by the Declaratory Act, which asserted an unlimited parliamentary jurisdiction in America.[4] The Sugar Act was revised the same year, again lowering the tax on molasses, this time to one penny a gallon, but now to include molasses from British as well as foreign sources; it was clearly a revenue measure.

Charles Townshend, who assumed the direction of the cabinet in 1767, was thus forced to look for new sources of revenue that could be collected in America without raising a storm. His answer was a duty on glass, lead, paper, and tea imported into the colonies; this duty was to be collected at the ports. In other words, he was proposing "external taxes" by the colonial definition. But the colonists met the Townshend acts with a new objection: that these revenues went to defray the costs of imperial administration in the colonies and, as such, tended to make the royal governors independent of the colonial assemblies. This constitutional issue was heightened the same year, when the British arbitrarily suspended the New York Assembly for refusing to provide billeting for troops. Opposition to the new taxes was heaviest in the commercial centers, where the merchants agreed to reduce imports from Britain. In response, the British brought troops into Boston, where the bad feeling between the population and the troops led to the "Boston Massacre" (1770). Provoked by a jeering crowd, the troops fired, killing five; but the most revolutionary of the colonial leaders, notably Samuel Adams (1722–1803) of Massachusetts, spread greatly distorted reports of this incident throughout America. Frederick, Lord North, meanwhile, had taken the direction of the cabinet from Charles Townshend, and by coincidence called for the repeal of the Townshend taxes on the very

4. See J. R. Alden, *The American Revolution: 1775-1783* (New York, Harper, 1954), pp. 4-5.

day of the "Boston Massacre." Lord North retained only the tax on tea, not because he had any hope of revenues from it, but to save the principle that Parliament had the right to tax. For all practical purposes, however, the colonists had won the battle of the taxes.

The coming of Lord North to power in 1770 not only coincided with this colonial victory, but heralded the victory of the King over the Whigs in the struggle for the control of Parliament. Lord North led a group in Parliament known as the "King's Friends," whose votes, thanks to the resources of the royal coffers, were sure. The Whigs were increasingly embarrassed by a double dilemma: if they posed as knights of parliamentary reform, they would destroy the very instruments of corruption and advantage which they themselves had perfected earlier in the century and which they required if they were to regain power in the constitutional battle with the King. As for the American issue in the 1760's, they, as the champions of parliamentary prerogatives, wished to retain the colonies under parliamentary control; but they also saw that if they backed the colonists against the King on the constitutional issues at stake, parliamentarianism *everywhere* would benefit. Certainly, the leading Whigs were not friends of American independence, but in their critical battle with the King, the Whigs had to give the colonists significant help. William Pitt (1708–1778), for instance, had denounced the Stamp Act as unconstitutional, and in Edmund Burke (1729–1797) the colonists had a superb advocate, distinguished both for his constitutional knowledge and oratorical skill:

... The people of the colonies are descendants of Englishmen. England, Sir, is a nation which still, I hope, respects, and formerly adored, her freedom. The colonists emigrated from you when this part of your character was most predominant; and they took this bias and direction the moment they parted from your hands. They are therefore not only devoted to liberty, but to liberty according to English ideas and on English principles. Abstract liberty, like other mere abstractions, is not to be found. Liberty inheres in some sensible object; and every nation has formed to itself some favorite point, which by way of eminence becomes the criterion of their happiness. It happened, you know, Sir, that the great contests for freedom in this country were from the earliest times chiefly upon the question of taxing. ... On this point of taxes the ablest pens and most eloquent tongues have been exercised, the greatest spirits have acted and suffered. In order to give the fullest satisfaction concerning the importance of this point, it was not only necessary for those in argument defended the excellence of the English Constitution to insist on this privilege of granting money as a dry point of fact, and to prove that the right had been acknowledged in ancient parchments and blind usages to reside in a certain body called a House of Commons. ... They took infinite pains to inculcate as a fundamental principle, that in all monarchies the people must in effect themselves, mediately or immediately, possess the power of granting their own money, or no shadow of liberty could subsist. The colonies draw from you, as with their life-blood, these ideas and principles.[5]

Thus, it was not enough that Lord North had withdrawn most of the taxes obnoxious to the colonists, for the constitutional principles at stake had still to be resolved; principles, as Burke saw, which underlay the whole question of taxation both at home and abroad.

The complexity of the issue can be seen in the crisis which grew out of the Tea Act in 1773, which was actually passed to help relieve the financial embarrassment of the East India Company. The Company had large stores of unsold tea in Britain; the new legislation exempted the Company from the heavy tax on tea in Britain, so that it might easily undersell its competitors within the empire. From a much earlier date, the East India Company had had a monopoly on the sale of tea within the empire, but the colonists had long undermined this by smuggling tea from Holland. Lord North's measure was clever in that it struck on two fronts. Not only did the Tea Act threaten to upset this established (and illicit) trade by making East India Company tea cheaper than smuggled tea, but in addition, if the colonists bought East India tea and paid the small Townshend tea tax at the port, they would admit Parliament's right to tax. The economic and the constitutional issues were thus joined again, and most colonial merchants refused to pay the tea duty, and the East India tea could not be landed. One tea ship was burned at Annapolis, but it was the "tea party" in Boston harbor that forced the British government to crack down.

A number of punitive measures passed Parliament in 1774: the port of Boston was closed until the dumped tea was paid for; the royal governor for Massachusetts was given authority over the legislature; and in every colony, the governor was given power to requisition quarters for troops. The measures harkened back to the time of Charles I and were delivered with four new regiments to back them up. Clearly the time had come for the colonists to confer, for the new laws seriously threatened colonial autonomy. In late 1774, the First Continental Congress met in Philadelphia, with only Georgia unrepresented, and the debates revealed that colonial leadership was far from united. There were radicals, especially in the Virginia and Massachusetts delegations, who preached resistance to the

5. From Burke's *Speech on Conciliation with the Colonies,* March 22, 1775.

new British regulations; but conservative opinion, which advocated a policy of reconciliation with Britain that would safeguard colonial rights within the empire, had the better of the argument, as reflected in the Declaration of Rights and Grievances which the Congress adopted. Their rights to "life, liberty, and property" were guaranteed, according to the declaration, by the principles of the English constitution, their colonial charters, and "the unchanging laws of nature." They even admitted that Parliament had the right to regulate external commerce, but only so long as there was "no idea of taxation, external or internal." To give this declaration teeth, the congress announced that the colonies would boycott British goods. In sum, however, the statements were conservative rather than revolutionary and suggest that most colonists would have been satisfied to return to the *status quo ante* Grenville.[6]

In Massachusetts, however, those patriots more disposed to resistance than to conciliation began to collect arms at Concord, only eighteen miles from Boston, obliging the British commander in Boston, Thomas Gage, to send out a small force for the destruction of these arms. The mission was accomplished, but colonial militia fired on the troops all the way back to Boston (April, 1775), so that by the following month, when the Second Continental Congress met, the spirit of resistance was stronger and encouraged more radical opinion to dominate the assembly. While the Second Congress still avowed its loyalty to the King, it nevertheless appointed a commander-in-chief; but since there was no declaration of independence, the initial months of the conflict might best be described as a civil war. Indeed, the impression of civil war was further heightened because in Britain itself the leading Whigs opposed the King's colonial policies and supported the Americans.

Faced by these developments, the British government remained unyielding, choosing to regard the colonists as rebels. General Gage repeatedly reported to London that the situation in America was far more desperate than the government realized; but his reports were regarded as proof of his timidity, and after his costly victory at Bunker Hill (summer of 1775) over the patriots surrounding Boston, he lost his command to General William Howe, from whom the British looked for both a more optimistic and, if necessary, more positive and successful approach. On the one hand, a general contempt for colonial troops made Gage's alarms seem

6. See Alden, *op. cit.*, p. 16.

unrealistic; and on the other, whether Gage's estimate was right or wrong, the home government needed to bring the rebels to heel for the sake of the King's prestige in his battle with the Whigs.

The initial British plan was to subdue the Americans by commercial rather than by military means. There were several reasons for this attitude. For one thing, there was obviously no general enthusiasm for the conflict on either side of the Atlantic; therefore, the more violent the campaign, the more the King alienated opinion on both shores. A British war of blockade made further sense because the colonists had no sea power, and because, being a cheap form of war, it would subject His Majesty to less parliamentary interference than would a costly land campaign. Garrisoning several bases for the operation of the fleet would suffice to enforce the blockade, and it was believed that the systematic destruction of American commerce would soon bring the rebels to see the error of their ways.

THE DECLARATION OF INDEPENDENCE AND WAR

Unfortunately for the British, the colonists had had long experience as smugglers, and nearly two years were wasted before the government accepted the unpleasant necessity of a land campaign. Thus, the colonists won precious time to consolidate their forces while, even more important, the drawing out of the crisis encouraged Britain's enemies in Europe to consider intervention. The Bourbon monarchies, for instance, were hardly champions of rebellion, but they were anxious to set matters square with Britain after their losses in 1763. And the Americans knew it. After they had been declared in a state of rebellion, it made increasingly little sense to declare their loyalty to the King, especially since there was little hope of foreign help or alliance until they had made the decision for independence. Thus came their celebrated declaration on July 4, 1776, nearly fifteen months after the opening of hostilities. Written by Thomas Jefferson (1743–1826), the Declaration of Independence was somewhat revised by the Second Continental Congress to focus the American attack on the King rather than the British people, suggesting a clear recognition of the constitutional nature of the struggle. Indeed, the basic premises of the declaration were quite the same principles which John Locke had used nearly a century earlier to justify the Glorious Revolution of 1689.

Meanwhile, the blockade failing to crush the rebellion, the British considered a number of schemes for ending the war with an invasion from

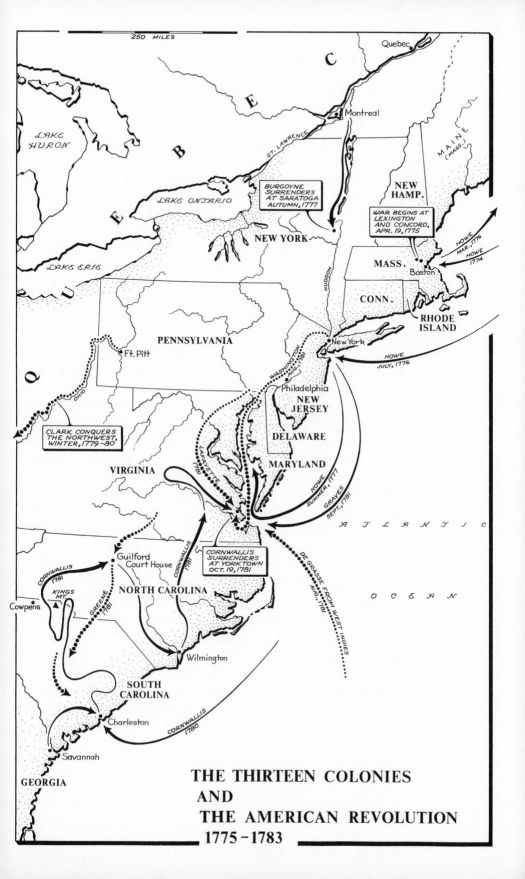

THE THIRTEEN COLONIES
AND
THE AMERICAN REVOLUTION
1775-1783

Canada. What followed, in 1777, remains the most debated and studied phase of the Revolution—a campaign which has fascinated historians, because it encompassed so many factors calculated to produce failure. The elementary conception of the campaign was sound enough: to strike southward from Canada along the water line of Champlain, Ticonderoga, and the Hudson, to isolate New England from the rest of the rebellious colonies. The implementation of the basic plan, however, was another matter and furnishes us with an almost classic example of how ambitious, bickering generals and ministers can destroy the effectiveness of a sound plan.

A divided command was the first unwise ingredient. General Howe, who commanded at the British base at New York, did not command in Canada; General Guy Carleton, who commanded in Canada and expected to be placed in charge of the expedition, was furious when he was passed over in favor of young General John Burgoyne; that choice was made in London. Considering the difficulty in communicating between New York, London, and Canada, a well-conceived plan, understood by all parties, was essential; but General Howe, whose responsibility the plan was, engendered pure confusion by dispatching frequent alterations and suggestions, and he was not brought to heel by the Colonial Secretary, Lord George Germain. In consequence, when "Gentleman Johnny" Burgoyne marched southward, he had no precise assurance from Howe of what he could expect in case he encountered serious resistance; presumably Howe would march up the Hudson to his rescue. Burgoyne, a rash and overconfident soldier, found his route blocked at Saratoga by an army nearly three times his size, only to receive the disconcerting news that General Howe had attacked Philadelphia and that no help was forthcoming. He ended by surrendering his army. General Howe, who captured Philadelphia but failed to pursue the retreating Americans and gave no aid to Burgoyne, tacitly admitted that the mess was his responsibility by resigning his command early in 1778.[7]

For the British, the loss of an army at Saratoga was only the first blow, for it convinced the French that the time had come to intervene by providing substantial military and moral aid to the colonists. The moment for Britain to settle with the Americans had also come, for the simple reason that Britain had never before successfully fought the French except with the aid of allies; and in 1778, Britain was isolated, while the French fleet had been greatly improved after 1763. But to settle with the Americans meant recognizing their independence, which the King, for political reasons

7. See *Ibid.*, pp. 112-118.

at home, could not afford to do. There was, in fact, little British enthusiasm for American independence, for those who gave the Americans support in Parliament were largely concerned for constitutional and political principles. Spain joined France in 1779 and the Netherlands late in 1780, but the brunt of the fighting overseas fell on the French. After Saratoga, parliamentary hostility to George III increased: the poor state of the fleet meant that Britain was in constant danger of invasion from France, other colonial areas were endangered, and the costs of war were particularly unwelcome. In 1780, a declaration passed Commons which was threatening to His Majesty: "... that the influence of the crown has increased, is increasing, and ought to be diminished," but the Opposition was unable to turn out Lord North until Britain suffered a second disaster.

Having failed to cut off New England from the remainder of the colonies in 1777, the British launched a new campaign in 1780 to detach the south from the north. Still holding New York, they sent a seaborne force under Charles, Lord Cornwallis, to the Carolinas. Such an invasion was far more risky than the invasion from Canada had been three years earlier, for the presence of the French fleet in American waters threatened British communications between New York and Charleston. To make matters worse, Cornwallis, marching northward into Virginia, broke contact with his base at Charleston, further isolating himself. General George Washington at once recognized the opportunity and, with General Jean Baptiste Rochambeau, prepared a masterful trap for Cornwallis.

They proposed to move the Franco-American army from the Hudson valley southward, both to block Cornwallis's advance and to prevent his retreat. In the meantime, they summoned the French fleet from the West Indies to the Virginia coast, to prevent his evacuation by sea. The British in New York were slow to learn of Washington's sly departure, and getting word of it to Cornwallis was made the harder by his having broken all communication with Charleston. When he got the news, it was both too late and horrifying: not merely colonial troops whom the British had lately been whipping in South Carolina and Georgia, but also substantial numbers of regulars from France were in his path. He retreated immediately to the coast, in the expectation of an evacuation by ship, only realizing the extremity of his position when he saw the French ships. The British fleet, sent from New York, was helpless in the face of the superior French numbers and had to leave Cornwallis to his inevitable fate: his surrender at Yorktown.

Parliamentary opposition to the King increased seriously after Yorktown and finally forced the resignation of Lorth North early in 1782. Recognizing the defeat of the "royal experiment," George III considered abdication, but in the end accepted an opposition ministry led by Rockingham. When it came to negotiating peace with the Americans, the Whigs soon revealed that if they had been pro-American on constitutional issues, they did not favor American independence. They understood, for instance, that the interests and ambitions of an independent American nation would be incompatible with Spain's possession of Louisiana and her claim to the Floridas and that in any clash between America and Spanish interests, France would be most likely to support her Bourbon ally. Thus, the British negotiators stressed the likelihood of future American trouble with the Bourbon powers in the hope that the Americans would abandon their claim to independence.

Benjamin Franklin, the chief American negotiator, also saw that America would have trouble with the Bourbon powers, especially since Spain claimed land to the east of the Mississippi as part of Louisiana; but he argued that if the British granted America independence and would recognize the Mississippi as the western boundary of America, the Americans would consider a separate peace. In other words, France and Spain would be abandoned. In view of Britain's woeful military position in America, the separation of her enemies was an achievement, and she seized the opportunity to work out separate peace treaties with America and the Bourbon powers. The French, especially, were embittered by the defection, and it is notable that they realized practically nothing in the peace settlement. Britain returned Florida, however, to Spain, but recognized the Mississippi as the western boundary of the new American state whose independence she granted. In exchange, the Americans abandoned all claims to Canada, and both powers agreed to champion the principle of free navigation on the Mississippi. While the terms represented a clear American victory, they were also calculated by Britain to produce future tension between America and the Bourbon powers and to prepare the way for better Anglo-American relations—perhaps even a reunion with Britain. These Anglo-American terms were put in final form on September 3, 1783, in the treaty of Paris.

Yorktown did more than guarantee American independence; it brought defeat to the King's hope of reviving royal power. In a real sense, the American Revolution underscored the significance of the Glorious Revolution of 1689. Parliament, in that year, had demonstrated its ability to unseat a monarch and nominate his heir; but during the eighteenth century, it proved difficult to legislate in defiance of the monarch's will, even though the early Hanoverians were often indifferent to policy and exercised only limited authority. The emergence in 1760 of a strong monarch who was determined to "be a King" brought the constitutional issue into focus, and the failure of his American policy gave the logicians of politics the occasion to redefine the parliamentary rights and powers as of 1689. The issue of royal absolutism was thus clarified in Britain less than a decade before the French undertook a solution of the issue in Paris.

THE FRENCH REVOLUTION

The analysis of the French Revolution and its causes is not an activity of recent origin. From the outset, the Revolution was recognized as one of the great pivotal events of modern history, and analysis, both within and without France, began while the Revolution was still in its infancy. The analysis continues to this day. The historiography of the background of the Revolution, of the Revolution itself, and of its impact upon France during every generation up to the present, has the aspects of a minor industry.[8]

Few historical periods, indeed, have been the subject of such intense scrutiny as that of the French Revolution; but whatever their differences, the examining historians recognize—at least implicity—that there developed in eighteenth-century France both a revolutionary situation and a revolutionary spirit. By the latter we mean the growth of hostility to the *ancien régime,* especially to the inefficient absolutism of the Bourbon monarchy, · which could be criticized by the rationalists as irrational and by the libertarians as illiberal. Furthermore, the official Catholicism of the regime was obnoxious to the rationalist intelligentsia, which, for the most part, had lost faith in divine revelation as the source for the most profound truths. Finally, the regime tolerated a privileged, but selfish, nobility (this will be discussed at greater length below), a class which no longer gave the nation the services which had earlier warranted a privileged status. In sum, the revolutionary spirit amounted to a recognition that the regime was an anachronism, unable to meet the responsibilities of government, and that it must be reformed.

The revolutionary situation derived from many factors, none of which the government faced up to either in time or with skill. The most pressing

8. S. J. Idzerda, "The Background of the French Revolution" (Washington, D.C., American Historical Association, 1959), p. 1.

problem of the century was a rapidly increasing inflation. Two elements contributed to it, the influx of large amounts of precious metal into Europe from the New World, half of which ended up in France; and the increase in French population from eighteen to twenty-five million within the century. Production failed to keep pace either with the increasing money supply or with the demands of the rising population. As a result, prices rose markedly, while wages, as usual, lagged behind. The consequent inflation not only brought misery and resentment, but equally important, it brought a decrease in the government's revenues. This leads us directly to the second factor in the revolutionary situation: the deepening financial embarrassment of the regime.

The tax administration had been recognized as inefficient and inequitable long before 1789. First, the tax system varied from province to province, depending upon the circumstances under which a particular province had been annexed to the realm, so that the tax rate actually was inequitable. Secondly, the first two estates were exempt from most taxation, a privilege dating from the medieval period and granted in exchange for crucial spiritual and military services rendered to the realm. The French population of roughly twenty-five million was divided politically into three estates, but more than twenty-four million of the people were in the third estate. A vast majority of them were rural, only about two million of the third estate living in towns and cities; and it has been too often ignored that a great many of the peasants were small freeholders. Some were tenants, others were hired rural workers, but certainly more than 90 per cent of the peasantry was free of actual serfdom. The two million living in towns included the upper bourgeoisie, the lower bourgeoisie (both groups being property owners), the professionals, and salaried people. Though a small proportion of the total French population, the urban dwellers were significant far beyond their numbers. The towns were increasingly the centers of intellectual life, and thus of the revolutionary spirit, while the salaried people—we often call them the proletariat—were the first to feel the pressure of economic dislocation and were easily mobilized into an angry mob. But upon the entire third estate fell the major burden of taxation. The difficulty was that, though small in numbers, the first two estates controlled vast amounts of property. Just how much is still a debated question, but there is no doubt that a significant amount of property went tax-free.

The clergy, or first estate, comprised only about 130,000 people, of whom nearly 60,000 were regular clergy living under orders. It is generally agreed that as individuals the clergy fulfilled its functions faithfully, especially in the case of the lower clergy. The hierarchy, however, was vulnerable to criticism. A recent study by a French clergyman of the 130 French bishops suggests that only about fifteen of them could be classified as "virtuous"; and since the hierarchy did not enjoy the esteem of the lower clergy, the Church was seriously divided when faced with outside criticism. And it was the Church as a corporation, rather than the clergy as individuals, which was rightly subjected to criticism for using its power and privileges (the control of censorship and education in addition to exemption from much taxation) to avoid the financial responsibilities commensurate with its wealth and for fostering intolerance and obstructing the traffic in new ideas. ·

The second estate, or nobility, numbered about 200,000, only a minority of whom were descendants of the proud fighting nobles of the Middle Ages. All nobles, however, were exempt from most taxes, and they had easy access to the best judicial, military, and administrative posts. It is estimated that nearly one-fourth of the government's income went into salaries and pensions for the nobility—far beyond the value of services rendered. In the face of the mounting inflation in the eighteenth century, the landed aristocrats pressed their claims to manorial dues even more vigorously than before. Such dues, part of the "vestiges of feudalism," were paid by the French peasantry as a matter of custom but increasingly resented as unwarranted now that the peasants were largely freeholders.

Above all, to be "privileged" meant to be exempt from taxation. A few reformers sought ways to remove financial privilege in order to subject the property of the first two estates to equitable taxation, while the majority of the third estate dreamed of achieving a privileged status. But what better proof that France had reached a constitutional crisis by 1789 than the fact that the wealthiest country in Europe possessed a bankrupt government which was seemingly powerless to revise its governmental machinery in its own interest?

Finally, the revolutionary situation included a much-debated social factor, which, on the surface, appears as much political as social. The Estates-General, the French parliamentary institution, where the aristocrats had traditionally curbed the royal powers, had not been summoned by the kings since 1614 for precisely that reason. It had become usual in the seventeenth century to fill the highest of the administrative and judicial posts with men drawn from the bourgeoisie. Though these men of middle-class origin did not have social equality with the aristocracy, and though the crown expected them to be docile servants of royal power, the middle class, through its judicial and bureaucratic position, exercised a far greater check upon the royal authority than did the aristocracy.

We have earlier seen that the French aristocracy enjoyed a political revival after the time of Louis XIV, a revival which became especially apparent in the reign of Louis XVI (*1774–1792*), when all but one of the ministers were nobles. It is not surprising that many of the bourgeoisie were alarmed; and not merely because, obviously, their gains were threatened. For another issue was at stake as well: if they, the real check upon royal authority, were removed, would not royal absolutism prevail? The nobles had repeatedly demonstrated political ineptitude after 1715, and, given the weakness of Louis XVI, royal absolutism might well end in chaos.

It is well to remember that men are rarely single-minded creatures, easy of analysis, but are driven by both mean and disinterested motives, which are disentangled only at peril of distortion and error. As one of the most distinguished historians of the French Revolution has put it:

> Scholars have showed quite rightly that the revolutionary spirit originated in a social and economic movement, but they too often omit the fact that there is no true revolutionary spirit without the idealism which alone inspires sacrifice. The interest of the bourgeoisie, which was the first to profit from the new order, can easily be detected beneath the philosophy of the eighteenth century. The bourgeoisie believed sincerely that it worked for the good of humanity.[9]

In fact, when one warns against oversimplification, he must at once add that the very terms *nobility* and *bourgeoisie,* which are necessarily used when the French Revolution is discussed, are generalities—both real and unreal. The study of the class structure in France has revealed such a hodgepodge of hostile factions within each class that the notion of class solidarity has evaporated. In particular, the bourgeoisie has been studied and reduced to countless categories. A great banker, whose sumptuous life resembled that of a great noble more than that of a greengrocer, found himself, nevertheless, a member of the third estate along with the greengrocer; but it is doubtful that their political or social aspirations were identical. Yet, class distinctions there were, and we are in debt to the wit who raised his glass and said, "To the bourgeoisie, whoever they were."

9. Georges Lefebvre, *The Coming of the French Revolution* (Princeton, Princeton University Press, 1947), p. 50.

If the American Revolution excited the French liberals, it also put a further burden on the royal finances. The government borrowed to carry on the war, and when increased taxation failed to keep pace with the deepening debt, the government had to continue to borrow. By 1786, nearly 50 per cent of the royal expenditures was being absorbed in interest payments on the debt, obviously a ruinous practice. It was also evident that raising taxes would produce nothing, and should the crown end by repudiating its debt, its credit would vanish. Worse, the creditors of the crown, mostly bourgeois, were powerful through their domination of the courts of law, where they obstructed the royal will. The aristocracy showed no willingness to surrender privileges unless the crown began by surrendering much of its local authority, so that in 1789 there was nothing left but to summon the Estates-General to consider the crisis; this was its first meeting in 175 years.

THE NATIONAL ASSEMBLY

The Estates-General was tricameral, the three houses representing the three estates or class divisions: the first estate being the clergy, the second estate the nobility, and the third estate the remainder of the nation. Traditionally, each estate sat separately for deliberation, expressing its will as one vote. The leaders of the third estate argued, in 1789, that the traditional procedures must be altered if the government was to achieve financial reform. After all, the privileges of the first two estates, most important their tax exemptions, were at the root of the government's inability to tax effectively; and if each estate had one vote, the first two estates could block every reform detrimental to their privileges. The third estate therefore asked the crown to double the membership of the third and to decree voting "by head" instead of by order. It is revealing of Louis XVI that, in this crisis, he allowed the doubling of the third estate but nullified the reform by refusing the vote "by head."

The third estate was obstinate in its refusal to accept the King's compromise, and bickering over procedure and etiquette went on for weeks until, on June 17, 1789, the third estate declared itself the National Assembly and invited the clergy and nobility to join it. Only a few liberal nobles and clergy complied. Faced with this defiance, the royal government hesitated; but the third estate, finding its hall closed for repairs and fearing that the King meant to disperse the National Assembly, convened in a royal tennis court on June 20, to pledge that it would remain in session until a new constitution had been framed. Hoping to regain the initiative, the government began to concentrate troops near Paris, giving rise to popular fear that the King meant to abolish the Assembly. A few radicals took advantage of this fear to direct the Parisians against the Bastille, a fortress where arms and munitions were presumably stored, and the governor, having only a tiny garrison, soon surrendered. The dramatic gesture was effective; if the National Assembly did not plot the attack upon the Bastille, it profited through the subsequent royal decision to accept the existence of the Assembly. The Estates-General passed out of the picture, and the Revolution had made a half-turn to the left. This new parliamentary structure implied that sovereign power was vested in the nation as a whole —along with the crown—a more egalitarian and fraternal structure, obviously, than the Estates-General had had. Future decisions would be made in the name of the nation; and later, when the power of France would bear heavily upon other countries, the latter would conclude that the French owed their successes to their mobilization of the whole nation and would respond in kind. Modern nationalism, in other words, was at its birth. The assault upon the Bastille had a further result. It established the precedent that political deadlocks could be broken by violence.

The task of the National Assembly, now including most former members of the first two estates as a result of the King's retreat, was to write a new constitution for the monarchy—to make orderly, financially sound government possible. But how to eliminate those privileges, those "vestiges of feudalism" as the bourgeoisie called them? The course was set in August, 1789, through two parliamentary maneuvers. On the night of August 4, a special session of the Assembly was organized by a group of liberal members of the privileged class; it was realized that the session would be poorly attended because of the hour. The strategem worked, and the liberal minority, led by the Viscount de Noailles and the Bishop of Nancy, proceeded to vote the surrender of many privileges enjoyed by the first two estates. We may doubt, however, that this group's claim to have entirely destroyed the feudal regime was strictly accurate. It is true that they abolished without compensation all obligations of personal servitude, such as *corvée* (unpaid labor), and that they decreed that there should be equality of taxation. But they also declared that manorial dues must be redeemed by a money payment—a procedure which would take time to work out—and while they abolished tithes, they also declared that the tithes should be collected until the assembly could provide other means to provide for the Church.

Having destroyed privilege and inequality in principle, the Assembly soon began the draft of a Declaration of the Rights of Man and of the Citizen, which was adopted on August 26. Its basic assumptions harken back to Rousseau: "Men are born and remain free and equal in rights; social distinctions may be based only upon general usefulness."[10] The rights enumerated were to liberty, property, security, and resistance to oppression, and sovereignty was defined as resting in the nation, with the law the expression of the general will. Moreover, the Declaration was couched in universal terms: these were the rights of man, not merely of Frenchmen.

The significance of the August legislation should not blind us to the fact that the National Assembly had really been driven to its enactment by the violence of the Parisian mob and by a series of peasant uprisings during the summer of 1789, when peasants had taken advantage of the new order to burn local and manorial archives in the hope of destroying the records of their obligations. In short, the Assembly was driven faster than many delegates liked, and some of the patriots withdrew from the revolutionary party to form a group called Anglomaniacs. In the interest of conservatism, they advocated a bicameral parliament along British lines and favored giving the king an absolute veto; and had the sulking aristocrats consented to back the Anglomaniacs on these issues, they might have won out against the more radical patriots who wanted to weaken executive power and insisted on a suspensive (temporary) veto and a unicameral parliament. As it was, the radicals carried the vote on these significant constitutional issues against a divided opposition. The King, meanwhile, had been encouraged by the apparent divisions in the Assembly to withhold his sanction from the August legislation, and when the patriots offered him a suspensive veto in exchange for his acceptance of the principles laid down in August, he refused. The bargain was a fair one, for a vetoed measure would have to pass three successive assemblies to become law; and it is a fair measure of Louis XVI's lack of political acumen that he did not recognize the necessity of compromise.

The precedent of force had already been set, and the leaders of the Assembly determined to coerce His Majesty to accept the new principles. On October 5, they let loose from a poor quarter in Paris a horde of women who marched to Versailles to demand bread; these ladies were reinforced

10. John Hall Stewart, ed., *A Documentary Survey of the French Revolution* (New York, Macmillan, 1951), p. 114.

later in the day by a detachment of National Guardsmen, the Guard having been previously raised by the Assembly for its protection. By coincidence, the King had already decided to give provisional approval to the desired legislation pending completion of the constitution. He was, nevertheless, asked to return to Paris to take up residence; by complying, "the baker, the baker's wife, and the baker's little boy," as the women called the royal family, put themselves at the mercy of their Parisian subjects.

Meanwhile, in the process of making France a constitutional monarchy, the Revolution was becoming an international problem. In the summer of 1790, the National Assembly finished that portion of the new constitution which regulated relations between Church and State. Ever since the night of August 4 of the previous year, it had been understood that the Church would be provided for, but the new arrangement really subjected the Church to the State as defined in the Civil Constitution of the Clergy. The clergy became little more than civil servants devoted to the state, and there was to be no papal authority in France. Several months later, a new decree commanded the clergy to prove its devotion to the state by taking an oath to support the Civil Constitution of the Clergy and the new constitution. All but seven of the French bishops and about half the lower clergy refused the oath; but more significant, the Papacy was necessarily led in 1791 to condemn the Revolution, making it impossible for orthodox Catholics to accept the Revolution. Among the latter was Louis XVI, who signed the religious legislation as politically necessary, but who began making plans to escape from Paris.

The second international problem was caused by the so-called *emigrés* who had left the country in the wake of the political changes. Had they merely bided their time, their departure would not have become an issue; but many of the aristocrats among them actively recruited for a counter-revolutionary army and sought assistance from foreign governments. Their own defection—many had been officers in the royal army—and that of their recruits seriously weakened the French army; while their counter-revolutionary activities abroad soon identified the enemies of the Revolution with the traditional enemies of France. This situation was more sharply focused in the summer of 1791, when Louis XVI slipped out of Paris and fled northward toward the Austrian Netherlands. He was recognized short of his goal, however, was captured at Varennes, and was returned to Paris. By identifying himself with the *emigrés,* and thus with the enemies of France, he hopelessly compromised himself and the monarchy.

THE LEGISLATIVE ASSEMBLY

Shortly after this event, the new constitution was completed and, under its electoral provisions, new elections were ordered to provide for the first regularly elected assembly of the constitutional monarchy: the Legislative Assembly, which first met on October 1, 1791. The new government was threatened, or at least felt itself threatened, from the outset by a declaration (the Declaration of Pillnitz) signed by the Emperor of Austria and the King of Prussia, following the capture of Louis XVI, to the effect that the restoration of the French monarch to his full powers was their mutual interest.[11] We know today that the European monarchs were not seriously alarmed yet by the Revolution and only hoped to warn the French Assembly against overthrowing the monarchy, but it is little wonder that the Assembly saw their declaration as a threat of invasion.

Furthermore, the possibility of war was agreeable to one faction in the Legislative Assembly: the Girondists, who were then counted among the Jacobin party. The Jacobins were the leftist minority in the new Assembly, and by the end of 1791, they were dedicated to the establishment of a republic. With their heaviest support coming from Paris, they championed a strongly centralized regime. The Girondists were that part of the Jacobin party whose delegates came largely from the provinces rather than from Paris and, thus, hoped to preserve much local authority. If both factions of the left were republican, they were also both ambitious for power; and the Girondists became identified as the war party in their bid to seize the leadership of the Revolution. No doubt they were also sincere in their revolutionary idealism and saw in the tenets of the Declaration of the Rights of Man a mandate to carry the principles of liberal government to peoples other than French; in short, they were crusaders. Despite the group's minority, the brilliance of such Girondist orators as Jacques-Pierre Brissot and Pierre Vergniaud gave them the initial leadership in the Legislative Assembly, and they moved for a showdown with Austria and Prussia.

Early in 1792, they engineered an ultimatum to the Austrian Emperor, demanding that he abandon his understanding with Prussia and return to the earlier Austro-French alliance of 1756. His reply was conciliatory, but he included hostile references to the Jacobins and failed to renounce

11. See the Declaration of Pillnitz, *Ibid.*, p. 223.

the Declaration of Pillnitz. The Girondist-led Assembly then declared war on Austria alone and followed it with an invasion of the Austrian Netherlands. Since the French Queen, Marie Antoinette, was Austrian, the republicans hinted that the court was in treasonable correspondence with Austria—which was true, though the republicans probably had no real evidence of it. When the initial invasion proved a fiasco, the Girondists therefore tried to blame the royal couple. The remainder of the Jacobins, however, saw in military disaster the opportunity to smear and supplant both the monarchy and the Girondists. For this reason, in the summer of 1792, the Girondists, though sincerely republican, suddenly hesitated in their attack upon the King, leaving the Jacobins as the clearest champions of republicanism.

Once again a foreign pronouncement (the Brunswick Manifesto), this time from Prussia alone,[12] offered the chance for the advancement of a French party. Louis XVI, in the knowledge that the Prussians were going to join Austria in the war, tried to present himself as the champion of moderate monarchy by pleading for a Prussian repudiation of both the Jacobins and the *emigrés,* the latter popularly regarded in France as traitors. But the Prussians ignored His Majesty's wishes and couched their manifesto in strict anti-French terms, further weakening the King's position at home. Several weeks later, the Jacobins instigated a mob attack upon the Tuileries Palace (August 10, 1792), and after nearly 900 of its defenders were killed, the King commanded an end to the defense. (He had, meanwhile, taken refuge with the Legislative Assembly and had become a virtual prisoner.) Such an attack would have been impossible had not popular suspicion of the King's correspondence with the enemy deepened. This recourse to popular violence intimidated those who shrank from overthrowing the monarch (especially the Girondists) and was a sign that the Jacobins were about to replace the Girondists as leaders of the Assembly. Indeed, coincident with the attack on the palace, the Jacobins seized control of the Paris Municipal government (the Paris Commune), and Girondist efforts in the Assembly failed to stem the Jacobin tide. Worse for them, the Assembly felt obliged to accede to Jacobin demands that a convention be authorized to modify the constitution; this action clearly prefigured a republic.

The King was brought to trial before the end of the year in response to Jacobin pressure, and a sentence of death was meted out to him as a

12. See The Brunswick Manifesto, July 25, 1792, *Ibid.,* pp. 307-311.

counterrevolutionary. His noble bearing on the scaffold, early in 1793, did much to redeem his reputation.

THE CONVENTION

In the meantime, the Assembly named an executive committee to function in place of the king, and one of the leading Jacobins, Georges-Jacques Danton (1759–1794) became its virtual head. Shortly afterward, word arrived of the long-anticipated Prussian invasion under the Duke of Brunswick, and the news gave rise to near panic in Paris. Danton kept his head: "We must be bold, bold anew, always bold, and France will be saved!"[13] But as the elections for the Convention also coincided with the invasion news, the Jacobins encouraged the frightened mob to massacre people thought to be opposed to the Revolution. An indiscriminate slaughter took place, many people feared to go to the polls, giving the Jacobins a great victory in Paris. Many Girondists were returned from the provinces, however, because the rural voters increasingly associated the Jacobins with irresponsible violence.

The Convention, the third legislative body to govern France since the summoning of the Estates-General in 1789, had to prosecute the war while drawing up a new republican constitution. These two important tasks, which affected each other, were further complicated by struggles within the Convention. First, the Jacobins had a final showdown with the Girondists in the spring of 1793; secondly, the victorious Jacobins again split into warring factions; and, finally, the surviving Jacobin faction was overthrown by a majority in the Convention bent on reaction. It is well to keep these general problems in mind when reviewing the history of the Convention.

After the engagement at Valmy in the fall of 1792, the troops of the young Republic enjoyed a series of successes, leading to the occupation of Rhenish territory, of Savoy, and of the Austrian Netherlands. To avoid the appearance of conquest, the Convention issued a series of "propaganda decrees," to the effect that the French people were eager to help all peoples recover their liberties; these sentiments were perhaps consistent with the idealism in the Declaration of the Rights of Man, but they were also threatening to all established regimes. The Revolution, already condemned

13. Speech in the Legislative Assembly, September 2, 1792. My translation.

by the papacy and at war with Austria and Prussia, quickly added to its list of enemies by these conquests and by the harsh financial exactions demanded from the "liberated" Belgians. The British and Dutch entered the war early in 1793 and were shortly followed by Spain, Sardinia, and Naples. Extraordinary military measures were decreed by the Convention to meet the grave danger of multiple invasion, but even so, it is small wonder that military reverses were not long in coming. Every able-bodied, unmarried man between eighteen and forty was decreed liable for military service, in an attempt to field an army of 300,000 men. This decree was followed, in the summer of 1793, by a levy *en masse,* which amounted to a complete national mobilization:

Henceforth, until the enemies have been driven from the territory of the Republic, the French people are in permanent requisition for army service.

The young men shall go to battle; the married men shall forge arms and transport provisions; the women shall make tents and clothes, and shall serve in the hospitals; the children shall turn old linen into lint; the old men shall repair to the public places, to stimulate the courage of the warriors and preach the unity of the Republic and hatred of kings.[14]

While the conscription was generally successful, it was resisted by ortho-dox Catholics who rose against the Convention in the Vendée and in Brittany, two Catholic strongholds.

To invasion and revolt must be added the deepening economic dislo-cation, which forced the Jacobins to move toward economic controls. They were the logical economic counterpart to the levy *en masse;* but since the Jacobins also required the support of the Parisian proletariat, they were vulnerable to the charge that they were a proletarian party anxious to use the crisis to confiscate private property. There is no reason to believe that the Jacobins were any less "bourgeois" than the Girondists who made the charge, but the Jacobins did have to deal with an extremist minority in Paris—the *enragés*—who advocated price controls and income taxes on the wealthy to provide for poor relief. If Danton agreed to support more rigorous economic measures in 1793, he did so for political expediency and because the war demanded it, and not because he hoped to achieve a social revolution. The resulting *enragé* support helped the Jacobins in their final struggle with the Girondists.

The military and economic crises of 1793 also led the Convention to establish a Committee of Public Safety, an executive body of twelve mem-

14. Decree of August 16, 1793, *Ibid.,* pp. 472-474.

bers to supervise the ministers. Danton, again, was the leading member, and not one of the leading Girondists was named to it. The committee members were elected for one-month terms by the Convention and were eligible for re-election. In the meantime, tension and rivalry between the Jacobins and the Girondists had festered for nearly a year, and in early June, 1793, the latter were outmaneuvered in the Convention and destroyed. In part, they had been fatally compromised by the defection of General Charles François Dumouriez, appointed through their influence to command in the Netherlands, who had gone over to the Austrians when the military reverses began. But this occurrence was merely a pretext used by the Jacobins to discredit the Girondists and should not be allowed to obscure the issues really dividing the rival republican factions. Oddly enough, it was essentially the same question which had always divided the king from the aristocracy, and in both cases those championing centralization won the day.

It is also well to remember that history is made by human beings, and one should not be content to ascribe historical causation to extrahuman factors alone:

All political struggle is a struggle among human beings, creatures at times capable of extraordinary consistency of purpose, whether determined by ideas or by interests, but also at times subject to whims, to inconsistencies, above all to the strangest and most inexplicable feelings of attraction or repulsion towards certain of their fellows. The grandest philosophy of history must make room for these personal emotions. The neatest theory of the Terror will fall flat if it omits the crescendos of hatred—hatred of persons, not just hatred of ideas— which accompanied the logical development towards a dictatorship of the elect.[15]

Through all the struggles, the Convention gave some attention to its intended task: the formation of a republican constitution. An early draft was presented by the Marquis de Condorcet, one of the Girondists, but the project fell victim to the party strife. Its principles were hardly radical, defining liberty as the sanctity of the individual and his property and discriminating against the urban proletariat. After the fall of the Girondists, the Jacobins whipped together a revised constitution which was more democratic in that it provided for universal manhood suffrage and required no property qualifications for either voters or candidates, but which still

15. Crane Brinton, *A Decade of Revolution 1789-1799* (New York, Harper, 1934), p. 137.

Left top to bottom: George III, Edmund Burke, William Pitt
Above: George Washington, Jean d'Alembert

Above: *The Arrest of Louis Capet at Varennes, June 21, 1791* by Prieur
Below left to right: Marie Antoinette, Maximilien Robespierre

emphasized property rights. The Constitution was ratified by popular vote in July, 1793, but the vote was tiny, owing to the chaos throughout the land. In fact, the Constitution of 1793 was not put into effect because of the national emergency, the argument being that it was a poor time to dissolve the Convention and hold elections for a new assembly. This permitted the Committee of Public Safety to continue as the executive body, and it shortly became a virtual dictatorship, with its Jacobin personnel simply being re-elected every month.

With the Girondists out of the picture in June, 1793, the struggle for power shifted to the factions within the Jacobin party itself. The Dantonists were both the most moderate, the most practical, and the least idealistic of the Jacobins; they are, indeed, difficult to characterize as a group because they included enthusiasts for moderate republicanism and cynical opportunists who sought little more than power and wealth. They were the first to profit from the decline of the Girondists. A second group of Jacobins, the Hebertists, named for their leader (Jacques René Hebert, 1775-1794), are equally difficult to characterize, but in general they were given to violent slogans and notions. While they had no program that could be dignified under the heading of social or economic philosophy, they irresponsibly agitated for all measures beneficial to the urban workers and inevitably attracted the lunatic fringe. Finally, the Robespierrists, followers of Maximilien Robespierre (1758-1794), were the true idealists of the party, men who hoped to preside over a rational, natural government in the eighteenth-century sense, whence goodness and virtue would necessarily flow. As idealists with a faith in eighteenth-century philosophy, the Robespierrists were outraged by the opportunism of the Dantonists and were contemptuous of the Hebertists as cranks.

The active conflict—known as the Terror—began in October, 1793, and lasted until the following midsummer. It was directed initially against suspected royalists and Girondists, who had, after all, been guilty of armed opposition to the regime in time of war. After the turn of the year, the Hebertists took advantage of a particularly bad food shortage in Paris to stage an insurrection in the hope of absolute power. The bid failed, and the leaders were soon seized and sent to the guillotine. Shortly afterward, the Robespierrists charged Danton with a plot to restore the monarchy, the charge was sustained, and Danton went to the scaffold. His last fine phrase was: "Better a hundred times to be guillotined than to guillotine." With Robespierre now supreme, France experienced a few months of his "Republic of Virtue."

For one thing, the judicial procedures were modified in the interest of speed, leading to a notable expedition in executions. The Revolutionary Tribunal in this period defined the enemies of the Revolution in moral terms, so bent were the Robespierrists on establishing a society of virtue and goodness. Indeed, their definitions were so narrowly puritan that few men could flatter themselves into feeling safe. The new morality was institutionalized through a new state religion, the Cult of the Supreme Being, a deist but non-Christian faith, making atheism as sinful as vice or folly.[16] Such a dictatorship was both uncomfortable and dangerous, and since dictatorship had been permitted by the Convention only as an extreme measure to meet the appalling threat of invasion and insurrection, the notable improvement in France's military position during the spring of 1794 should have been a warning that a dictatorship could not long be justified. Robespierre himself set off the reaction on July 26 by revealing in vague terms the news of a conspiracy of wicked men against the Republic. No one in the Convention could any longer deem himself safe; even the Jacobins, whom he presumably led, felt vulnerable and took the lead in voting his imprisonment. Two days later he was guillotined. The "Republic of Virtue," which marked the most extreme moment of the French Revolution, came to an end, and the Convention embarked upon a more moderate course.

Even when occupied with war, insurrection, party strife, and constitution making, the Convention had found time to consider education and the arts, and nothing better reveals the intention of some of the revolutionaries to uproot the old regime than the proposals made to modernize the former and control the latter. By the eighteenth century, France was a treasure house of art objects, a great many of which necessarily reflected social, political, and religious values of prerevolutionary eras. Shortly after the fall of Louis XVI, all symbols of "ostentation, prejudice, and tyranny" offensive to the principles of liberty and equality were condemned for destruction. Only after many months did some members of the Convention realize that the artistic evidence of France's greatness was being systematically destroyed. The next step was to devise a compromise through which the symbolism of the old regime could be erased while the artistic monuments were preserved. The solution was both ingenious and significant: to remove the art objects from houses, churches,

16. For a brilliant study of the Jacobins as religious fanatics, see Crane Brinton, *The Jacobins.*

and public places where they were a part of daily life and to put them in museums to become a part of history and education.[17]

The anticlericalism evident in the early stages of the French Revolution led first to the subjection of the French Church to the state and then to the state's assuming responsibility for education. The proposals made by the Marquis de Condorcet to the Legislative Assembly for free, universal, compulsory, and secular education, which were acted on later by the Convention, were full of statements reflecting modern educational attitudes and ideals:

Neither the French Constitution nor even the Declaration of Rights will be presented to any class of citizens as tables which are handed down from Heaven and must be worshipped and believed. Enthusiasm will not be founded on prejudice or the habits of childhood; . . .

Gymnastics will not be overlooked. Care will be taken to direct the exercises in such manner that all the powers will be equally developed, and the ill effects of habits produced by certain types of work will be corrected. . . .

As industrial processes are perfected, their operations become more and more subdivided, or there is an increasing tendency to give each individual a purely mechanical task, limited to a few simple movements, a task which is better and more easily done, but through habit alone, and in which the mind functions but little. Hence, the perfecting of industries will become, for a part of the human race, a cause of stupidity, will produce in every nation a class of men incapable of rising above the grossest interests, will introduce both a humiliating inequality and the seed of dangerous troubles, unless more extensive education offers to individuals of this same class a resource against the inevitable effects of the monotony of their daily occupation. . . .

A prolonged and assiduous study of the languages of ancient peoples, a study which would require the reading of the books which they have left us, might perhaps be more harmful than useful. In education we seek to make truths known, and these books are full of errors. We seek to train the mind, and these books may lead it astray. We are so far removed from the ancients, we are so far ahead of them on the road to truth, that we must have well-fortified minds if these precious relics are to enrich them without corrupting them. . . .

Each religion must be taught in its own temples by its own ministers. Parents, whatever their opinion, concerning the necessity of one religion or another, may, accordingly, without reluctance, send their children to the national schools; and the government will not have usurped rights over consciences under pretext of enlightening and guiding them. Besides, how important it is to base morality on the principles of reason alone! . . .

17. See Stanley J. Idzerda, "Iconoclasm During the French Revolution," *American Historical Review,* Vol. LX, No. 1 (October, 1954), pp. 13-26.

After having freed education from all kinds of authority, let us be careful not to subject it to public opinion, which it should anticipate, correct, and form, but neither follow nor obey. . . .[18]

In conclusion, Condorcet reminded the Assembly that this educational program anticipated the day when error and prejudice would vanish, when enlightenment would be universal, when men would be delivered from superstitions and false doctrines; indeed, when every man would be so sufficient by his knowledge alone that the new educational institutions could be abolished.

It fell to the Convention to implement Condorcet's principles, though many of them went unheeded. In late 1793, education was made free and public, parents being required to send their children to primary school for a minimum of three years.

Young people who, on leaving the primary schools, do not apply themselves to working the land, shall be required to learn a science, art, or craft useful to society. Those . . . who, at the age of fully twenty years, have not [so] complied . . . shall be deprived of the enjoyment of the rights of citizenship for ten years.[19]

After the fall of Robespierre, the Convention pursued its educational legislation (1794–1795). Among other measures, an attempt was made to regulate qualifications for teaching, and communities were required to make primary schools available in proportion to their population. The old royal academies having been abolished, the Convention created many government-supported schools of higher learning, such as the Ecole des Beaux-Arts and the Ecole Polytechnique, a number of which survive to this day.

EUROPEAN REACTION TO THE FRENCH REVOLUTION

The European reaction to the French Revolution is an important story in itself. Faced with the revolutionary "crusade," Europe was left to distinguish between French propaganda and French expansionist intentions. The new ideals of liberty, equality, and fraternity had international appeal, and it is understandable that a Europe grown accustomed to think

18. Stewart, *op. cit.,* pp. 346-361.
19. *Ibid.,* p. 518.

of France as the spawning ground of political and philosophical novelties regarded the ideas of 1789 as the latest model coming from the usual source. In the regions bordering on France, Jacobin clubs sprang up and petitioned the French government for annexation; but when war came in 1792 and many of these adjacent regions were in fact invaded and occupied, the subsequent irritations and troubles considerably reduced popular enthusiasm for the French Republic. A good example is furnished by the Belgian experience. Austrian rule in the southern Netherlands had never been popular or successful, and in 1792 the French were in a position to appear as liberators. Soon, the financial exactions, seemingly justified by the requirements of war, and the religious policy of the young republic infuriated the Catholic Belgians into opposition, and when the Austrians drove General Dumouriez's forces southward in 1793, the Belgians were delighted. It is revealing that in 1794, when the French reinvaded the Austrian Netherlands, they made little attempt to appear as liberators.

It would be wrong to assume that the new French ideas were largely spread by secret agents of the French Republic, though this was commonly believed by other European governments. Nor did the ideas necessarily catch fire where local social and economic conditions were most vulnerable, but only where the local discontented or ambitious took the lead in organizing radical societies to spread the word. It is small wonder that by 1793 and 1794, when the Revolution had not only revealed its annexationist tendencies but had also slain a king as a prelude to bloody party strife, much of Europe recoiled in horror. This was not the cultivated, cosmopolitan France they had learned to admire; the ideals of the Revolution perhaps still attracted many non-Frenchmen, but the Republic's military program smacked of Louis XIV. For others, the violence of the Revolution negated its ideals.

The reaction against things French in Prussia actually antedated the Revolution, for as we have already seen, Frederick William II, hating his exalted predecessor, had worked to reverse his policies and the evidences of his French taste. As for the Prussian peasantry, they remained relatively untouched by the revolutionary events in France, apparently owing to the depths of their serfdom. Compared to their French counterparts, they were not yet sufficiently emancipated to organize demands for greater liberty. Austria, too, had an anti-French, anti-Enlightenment policy under Francis II. This was due in part to the Austrian government's hostility to the liberal, anticlerical measures of the French Republic and in part to the unsuccessful reform program, based on the tenets of the Enlightenment, that had been initiated by Joseph II and then reversed by Francis II after it had produced widespread dissension and even rebellion (see pp. 181-183). Although the social and political ideas of the Enlightenment were generally unpopular, there were isolated groups of Jacobins in both Austria and Hungary; but they ran the risk of severe penalties if they were caught. Catherine II of Russia, earlier the enthusiastic patron of the *philosophes,* changed her mind about the beneficial effects of French ideas upon hearing of the attack on the Bastille and the march on Versailles in October, 1789. Russian social conditions being what they were, and having already faced a fearful rebellion during her reign, Catherine tried to seal the country off from further French influence. Her efforts were largely successful, leaving Russia almost as untocuhed by the Revolution as was clerical Spain.

ENGLISH REACTION

Before tackling the reaction to the French Revolution in the British Isles, it is necessary to note the prior reaction to defeat in America. Yorktown spelled the defeat of George III's attempt to reassert the royal prerogatives; it also meant the necessity of calling the Whigs to power, since Lord North could no longer command a majority. The King so abhorred his long-time opponents that he contemplated abdication, but in the end he brought them to power. He soon discovered that the Whigs were disunited, the leaders jockeying for positions of pre-eminence, and he exploited Whig dissension in an attempt to ruin the party's governmental effectiveness. A rapid succession of Whig prime ministers followed, until, in 1784, young William Pitt (1759–1806) succeeded to office, ushering in eighteen years of stable government.

Britain's financial position, already precarious before the American Revolution, had deteriorated to the point where her credit was doubtful. Financial reform was a necessity, and Pitt set himself to the task. Many sinecures were abolished, and government income was further increased by the simple expedient of reducing the number of taxes to economize in their collection. Tariffs on articles commonly smuggled into Britain were reduced, to take the profit out of smuggling and to bring an income from customs. In 1786, Pitt flew in the face of mercantilist opinion by negotiating a commercial treaty with France which greatly reduced duties. The reform movement extended into politics when Pitt proposed to reform

Parliament by redistributing the seats in the House of Commons to reflect the shifting population. Many rural constituencies, depopulated by the development of the factory system—the "rotten boroughs"—were still represented in Parliament, while the new towns were often unrepresented. Since many of the Whigs had been elected by the same rotten boroughs he proposed to eliminate, Pitt did not push the reform bill hard, and it was not passed. Nevertheless, Britain did possess a reform-minded government when the news of the Revolution in France arrived.

The English were at first favorable to the Revolution; after all, the *ancien régime* in France was regarded as the home of tyranny, where the enemies of the English system of government had often found haven. In Ireland the favorable reaction was even greater, for the Irish hatred of tyranny had been intensified by the harsh settlement dating from the reign of William III.

William Pitt, still in his reforming mood, honestly tried to improve the Irish situation. His bill of 1793 secured the right to vote for the Irish Catholics, but it did not give them the right to sit in the Dublin Parliament; this remained a monopoly of the Anglo-Irish. The latter refused to surrender any of their prerogatives, forcing Pitt to recognize ultimately that he could solve the Irish problem only by eliminating the Dublin Parliament and uniting the two parliaments in London. Of course, the Anglo-Irish opposed the plan, but Pitt got the support of the Catholic Irish by pledging that such a union would be accompanied by Catholic emancipation, giving all Catholics the right to vote and to hold public office. The Act of Union (1800) passed both Parliaments, but only because Pitt bought off the Anglo-Irish with offices, peerages, and pensions. Union became a fact in 1801, but Pitt found to his dismay that he could not obtain the monarch's approval of Catholic emancipation. He resigned the prime ministry as a point of honor, but the Irish Catholics felt betrayed. Many had never trusted Pitt's sincerity anyway and had plotted cooperation with the French Republic against Britain.

In the meantime, British attitudes were hardening against the Revolution, in particular against the French tendency to devise a new order according to rational, abstract principles, without concern for the practical realities of political life. Edmund Burke's pronouncement against the Revolution (1790) lent emphasis to the reaction, though his ideas also split the Whig party. In opposing the Revolution, Burke made it clear that he was no enemy of reform:

A state without the means of some change is without the means of its conservation. Without such means it might even risk the loss of that part of the constitution which it wished the most religiously to preserve. The two principles of conservation and correction operated strongly at the two critical periods of the Restoration and Revolution, when England found itself without a king. At both those periods, the nation had lost the bond of union in their ancient edifice; they did not, however, disolve the whole fabrick. On the contrary, in both cases they regenerated the deficient part of the old constitution through the parts which were not impaired. They kept these old parts exactly as they were, that the part recovered might be suited to them. They acted by the ancient organized states in the shape of their old organization, and not by the organick *moleculae* of a disbanded people. At no time, perhaps, did the sovereign legislature manifest a more tender regard to that fundamental principle of British constitutional policy, than at the time of the Revolution, when it deviated from the direct line of hereditary succession. The crown was carried somewhat out of the line in which it had before moved; but the new line was derived from the same stock. It was still a line of hereditary descent; still an hereditary descent in the same blood, though an hereditary descent qualified with protestantism. When the legislature altered the direction but kept the principle, they shewed that they held it inviolable.[20]

Thus, for Burke, reforms had to be consistent with the spirit and the experience of a given nation if they were to be true reforms. He was no rationalist:

In the famous law of the 3d of Charles I called the *Petition of Right,* the parliament says to the king, "Your subjects have *inherited* this freedom," claiming their franchises not on abstract principles "as the rights of men," but as the rights of Englishmen, and as a patrimony derived from their forefathers. Selden, and the other profoundly learned men, who drew this petition of right, were as well acquainted, at least, with all the general theories concerning the "rights of men," as any of the discoursers in our pulpits, or on your tribune; full as well as Dr. Price, or as the Abbe Sieyes. But, for reasons worthy of that practical wisdom which superseded their theroetick science, they preferred this positive, recorded, *hereditary* title to all which can be dear to the man and the citizen, to that vague speculative right, which exposed their sure inheritance to be scrambled for and torn to pieces by every wild, litigious spirit. . . . You will observe, that from Magna Charta to the Declaration of Right, it has been the uniform policy of our constitution to claim and assert our liberties, as an *entailed inheritance* derived to us from our forefathers, and to be transmitted to our posterity; as an estate specially belonging to the people

20. Edmund Burke, *Reflections on the French Revolution* (1790), Cambridge University Press, 1912, pp. 21-22.

of this kingdom, without any reference whatever to any other more general or prior right. By this means our constitution preserves an unity in so great a diversity of its parts. We have an inheritable crown; an inheritable peerage; and a house of commons and a people inheriting privileges, franchises, and liberties, from a long line of ancestors.

The policy appears to me to be the result of profound reflection; or rather the happy effect of following nature, which is wisdom without reflection, and above it. A spirit of innovation is generally the result of a selfish temper, and confined views. People will not look forward to posterity, who never look backward to their ancestors. . . .[21]

Though Burke's ideas did not rule out reform, they were conservative in the face of the French Revolution and became a rallying point for those Englishmen, including the Prime Minister, who were increasingly alarmed by the course of the Revolution. Conservative Whigs and Tories alike rode into Pitt's camp, inaugurating a period of fear which bred political repression and brought to an end the reform legislation. It is true that a minority of the liberal Whigs followed Charles James Fox in remaining enthusiastic for the Revolution, but even they disapproved of the Jacobins and their violence. Though some radical societies corresponded with French Jacobin clubs, their movement made little headway in Britain and hardly justified the fears of the ruling classes.

Burke was answered by a barrage of pamphlets from the pro-French radicals, the most significant being Thomas Paine's (1737–1809) *Rights of Man* and William Godwin's (1756–1836) *Political Justice*. Paine was a republican who had lived in America from 1774 to 1787, and his hopes of seeing Britain become a republic were fired by the rise of Jacobinism in France. His argument with Burke was a classic example of reason *versus* experience, Burke arguing for what is possible within the limits of a nation's experience, while Paine upheld what is humane and ideal— according to reason—without any compromise with the actual situation.

Before anything can be reasoned upon to a conclusion, certain facts, principles, or data, to reason from, must be established, admitted, or denied. Mr. Burke, with his usual outrage, abuses the *Declaration of the Rights of Man*, published by the National Assembly of France as the basis on which the constitution of France is built. This he calls "paltry and blurred sheets of paper about the rights of man." Does Mr. Burke mean to deny that *man* has any rights? If he does, then he must mean that there are no such things as rights anywhere, and that he has none himself; for who is there in the world but men? But if Mr. Burke means to admit that man has rights, the question then will be: What are those rights, and how came man by them originally? . . .

21. *Ibid.,* pp. 32-33.

Every history of the creation, and every traditional account, whether from the lettered or unlettered world, however they may vary in their opinion of belief of certain particulars, all agree in establishing one point, *the unity of man;* by which I mean that men are all of *one degree,* and consequently that all men are born equal, and with equal natural rights, in the same manner as if posterity had been continued by *creation* instead of *generation,* the latter being only the mode by which the former is carried forward; and consequently every child born into the world must be considered as deriving its existence from God. The world is as new to him as it was to the first man that existed, and his natural right in it is of the same kind.[22]

After his attack upon the most sacred of British institutions, Paine thought it expedient to flee to France in 1792; there he was elected to the Convention.

William Godwin was both more radical and less influential than Paine. We find in his *Political Justice* a demonstration of the eighteenth-century notion of the perfectibility of man, an extreme statement that man is by nature good and reasonable. To leave the individual free, Godwin would have wiped away as artificial restraints most social institutions, including the family and the state. Godwin's following was not large. The British working class, which might have been susceptible to the radicals' egalitarian tracts, was largely unmoved; and it has been suggested that it was the progress of Methodism among the workers which prevented their conversion to the rationalist, anti-Christian tenets of the French revolutionaries and their British friends. In any case, the government's anti-Jacobin campaign, begun in 1794, seems to have been neither necessary nor consistent with the liberties to which every Englishman had a right. The government packed juries to insure convictions, used spies and *agents provocateurs,* and gave subsidies to friendly newspapers. Pitt now completely dropped his project to reform the distribution of seats in Parliament, with the result that this urgent reform was postponed for many decades.

THE POETIC REACTION

England's greatest poets during the revolutionary era applauded the events in France, and through their love of liberty and their lack of political experience, they were led into poetic pronouncements and projects which can most politely be termed unrealistic.

22. Thomas Paine, *The Rights of Man* (1791), (New York, Everyman's Library, 1915), pp. 40-42.

Shall France alone a Despot spurn?
  Shall she alone, O Freedom, boast thy care?
Lo, round thy standard Belgia's heroes burn,
  Tho' Power's blood-stain'd streamers fire the air.
And wider yet thy influence spread
Nor e'er recline thy weary head,
  Till every land from pole to pole
  Shall boast one independent soul!
And still, as erst, let favour'd Britain be
First ever of the first and freest of the free![23]

In 1794, when many of the conservative Whigs (including Burke) had rejected Fox's leadership in favor of Pitt, Coleridge (1772–1834) was convinced that they had been bought, since he could not conceive of them honestly opposing Jacobinism:

As late I lay in Slumber's shadowy vale,
  With wetted cheek and in a mourner's guise,
  I saw the sainted form of FREEDOM rise:
She spake! not sadder moans the autumnal gale—
  'Great Son of Genius! sweet to me thy name,
    Ere in an evil hour with alter'd voice
    Thou had'st Oppression's hirelling crew rejoice
Blasting with wizard spell my laurell'd fame.
  'Yet never, Burke! thou drank'st Corruption's bowl!
    Thee stormy Pity and the cherish'd lure
    Of Pomp, and proud Precipitance of soul
Wilder'd with meteor fires. Ah Spirit pure!
  'That Error's mist had left thy purged eye;
  So might I clasp thee with a Mother's joy![24]

In the same year, Coleridge met another radical poet, Robert Southey (1774–1843). They hatched a plan to found an ideal community on the banks of the Susquehanna in Pennsylvania, to be called a pantisocracy. Southey invented the name, which meant to him the equal government of all. It was to be an agricultural community with no private property. We have a brief statement of their dream from Thomas Poole, a fellow radical:

Twelve gentlemen of good education and liberal principles are to embark with twelve ladies in April next. Previous to their leaving this country they are

23. S. T. Coleridge, *Destruction of the Bastille* (ca. 1789), 6th verse.
24. S. T. Coleridge, *Burke* (1794).

to have as much intercourse as possible, in order to ascertain each other's dispositions, and firmly to settle every regulation for the government of their future conduct. Their opinion was that they should fix themselves at—I do not recollect the place, but somewhere in a delightful part of the new settlements; that each man should labour two or three hours a day, the produce of which labour would, they imagine, be more than sufficient to support the colony. As Adam Smith observes that there is not above one productive man in twenty, they argue that if each laboured the twentieth part of time, it would produce enough to satisfy their wants. The produce of their industry is to be laid up in common for the use of leisure hours to be spent in study, liberal discussion, and the education of their children. . . .[25]

The two even collaborated on a poetic drama, some of the lines of which suggest a certain uneasiness over the course of the French Revolution:

> Was it for this we hurl'd proud Capet down?
> Is it for this we wage eternal war
> Against the tyrant horde of murderers,
> The crowned cockatrices whose foul venom
> Infects all Europe? was it then for this
> We swore to guard our liberty with life,
> That Robespierre should reign?[26]

Like Coleridge and Southey, William Wordsworth (1770–1850) was influenced by Rousseau and Godwin; but one also detects a deep humanitarian strain in him. He wrote a lengthy autobiographical poem called *The Prelude* (1799–1805) which revealed his great expectation that the Revolution would eliminate inequality. By 1802 he had been disillusioned by events in France, but he continued, quite rightly, to condemn the repressions in Britain by a fearful government:

> Milton! thou should'st be living at this hour:
> England hath need of thee: she is a fen
> of stagnant waters: altar, sword, and pen,
> Fireside, the heroic wealth of hall and bower,
> Have forfeited their ancient English dower
> Of inward happiness. We are selfish men;
> Oh! raise us up, return to us again;
> And give us manners, virtue, freedom, power.
> Thy soul was like a Star, and dwelt apart;
> Thou hadst a voice whose sound was like the sea:
> Pure as the naked heavens, majestic, free,

25. Jack Simmons, *Southey* (New Haven, Yale University Press, 1948), p. 44.
26. S. T. Coleridge and Robert Southey, *The Fall of Robespierre* (1794), Act II.

So didst thou travel on life's common way
In cheerful godliness; and yet thy heart
The lowliest duties on herself did lay.[27]

It was similarly true that the most notable writers of France in the late eighteenth century were inclined to radicalism, though not necessarily to revolution. Pierre-Augustin Caron (1732–1799), known as Beaumarchais, expressed liberal and democratic sentiments in some of his comedies; though it is thought that he was catering to contemporary opinion rather than airing genuinely held opinions, for his career reveals him to have been an adventurer and an opportunist. *The Barber of Seville* (1775) and *The Marriage of Figaro* (1778) remain his best-known works. The following lines appeared in the latter play: "Because you are a great lord you think you have a great talent. . . . What have you done to deserve all these things? You took the trouble to get born, nothing more." The play was banned until 1784, when some of Beaumarchais' liberal patrons succeeded in having the ban lifted. In contrast, the poet André Chénier (1762–1794) was enthusiastic for the Revolution. Often regarded as the greatest French poet of the eighteenth century, Chénier held a post in the embassy in London at the outbreak of the Revolution. With the beginning of the Terror in 1793, however, he became disillusioned. Finally he was arrested, held for four months, and then executed. While in prison, he wrote *Les Iambes,* expressing the sadness of his fate and his regret that the Revolution had been betrayed:

As a last ray of light, as a last zephyr
Animates the end of a beautiful day,
In the shadow of the scaffold I again sound my lyre.
Will it not soon be my turn![28]

27. William Wordsworth, *London, 1802.*
28. André Chénier, *Les Iambes* (1793), my translation.

SUGGESTIONS FOR FURTHER READING

The Revolution in America

Curtis P. Nettels, *The Roots of American Civilization* (New York: Appleton-Century-Crofts, 1938), a good survey.

John R. Alden, *The American Revolution, 1775-1783* (New York: Harper, 1954), probably the best one-volume study.

William B. Willcox, *Star of Empire: A Study of Britain as a World Power 1485-1945* (New York: Alfred A. Knopf, 1950), by a specialist in Anglo-American relations in the eighteenth century.

L. B. Namier, *The Structure of Politics at the Accession of George II,* 2 vols. (London: Macmillan, 1929).

L. B. Namier, *England in the Age of the American Revolution* (London: Macmillan, 1930).

Alfred Cobban, *Edmund Burke and the Revolt Against the Eighteenth Century* (London: Allen and Unwin, 1929).

The Revolution in France

*Georges Lefebvre, *The Coming of the French Revolution* (Princeton University Press, 1947), a brief but learned summary which is close to definitive.

Crane Brinton, *A Decade of Revolution 1789-1799* (New York and London: Harper, 1934), beautifully written and includes a fine bibliography.

John Hall Stewart, *A Documentary Survey of the French Revolution* (New York: Macmillan, 1951), a monument of careful editing.

Leo Gershoy, *The French Revolution and Napoleon* (New York: Crofts, 1933), a standard text.

Crane Brinton, *The Jacobins* (New York: Russell and Russell, 1930), a brilliant piece of work, which is controversial.

M. J. Sydenham, *The Girondins* (London University, Athlone Press, 1961).

*Edmund Burke, *Reflections on the Revolution in France* (New York and Toronto: Rinehart, 1959), a major interpretation, originally dating 1790.

Thomas Paine, *The Rights of Man* (New York and London: Everyman's Library, 1915), the answer to Burke, the original edition dating 1791.

*Alexis de Tocqueville, *The Old Regime and the French Revolution* (Garden City: Doubleday-Anchor, 1955), a classic interpretation, dated but penetrating and useful, the original published in 1856.

Francois V. A. Aulard, *The French Revolution, A Political History, 1789-1804,* 4 vols. (London: T. F. Unwin, 1910), another classic; in the moderate Jacobin tradition.

Albert Mathiez, *The French Revolution* (New York: Alfred A. Knopf, 1928), a classic Marxist interpretation.

Louis Madelin, *The French Revolution* (New York: G. P. Putnam's Sons, 1916), the classic Bonapartist interpretation.

Paul Farmer, *France Reviews Its Revolutionary Origins* (Columbia University Press, 1944), a study of the histories about the period.

Robert R. Palmer, *Twelve Who Ruled* (Princeton University Press, 1941), a fine study of the Committee of Public Safety.

* Available in paperbound editions.

❧ 8 ❧

The Napoleonic Age:
1795–1814

THE EXECUTION of Robespierre on July 28, 1794 (10th Thermidor on the Revolutionary calendar), marked the major turning point in the French Revolution, but the reaction against the Robespierrists neither ended the Terror nor brought to an abrupt end the innovations of the Revolution. The Thermidoreans—those who overthrew Robespierre—represented a momentary alliance of different factions united by common fear of Robespierre. This alliance included Jacobins, more moderate Republicans, and latent royalists—men whose brief loyalty to the republic had been alienated by its democratic "excess." The Jacobin element hoped to preserve the democracy won by 1794; but once under way, the reaction gained momentum, and we see the emergence of moderate republicans, such as Emanuel Siéyès, who worked to restore the Republic to its pre-democratic stage. (The royalists, of course, hoped to turn back the clock at least to 1791—if not farther.) In short order, the Thermidorean reaction became an anti-Jacobin movement, and since the alliance of the moment had served its purpose, the Jacobins were pushed from the government. A few of them, notably Paul François Barras and Jean Tallien, realized the situation in time to adjust their principles in the direction of moderation. By 1799, the continuing reaction had produced a military dictator, who, by 1804, had restored hereditary monarchy.

THE CONSTITUTION OF 1795—THE DIRECTORY

Following the 10th Thermidor, 80,000 prisoners awaiting the verdict of the "Republic of Virtue" were released as part of a general amnesty. Ninety Jacobin members of the Paris Commune were arrested and executed, and the Convention assumed control of the Paris municipal government. The Committee of Public Safety lost its dictatorial powers, while the Revolutionary Tribunal was directed to confine itself to normal court methods. Toward the end of 1794, the Jacobin club in Paris was closed, and early in the following year, religious liberty was restored.

Meanwhile, the Convention abolished the Constitution of the Year I (1793), which had never been implemented, and in 1795 produced a constitution from which the political democracy of 1793 was absent. The suffrage was sharply limited by property qualifications and the executives were selected by the parliament. Furthermore, the elections for the new bicameral parliament in 1795 were rigged to guarantee that two-thirds of the seats would be won by members of the Convention. Such maneuvers did not go unprotested.

The executive power under the new constitution was vested in a five-man board of directors; hence, the regime is remembered as the Directory. With the exception of one man (Barras, a supreme opportunist), the initial Directors were sincere republicans and men of integrity, which was not true of many parliamentarians. The heyday of revolutionary idealism was past, and the political life of the Directory was soon characterized by corruption, self-seeking, and a willingness to employ any method to remain in power. The regime soon became unpopular and lost public confidence, making it harder to deal with the discontent engendered by the hardships of war, the dislocation of trade, and an unusually bitter winter (1795–1796). Finally the government had to resort to force, using an army now grown to 800,000 to crush both Jacobin and royalist uprisings. In the third insurrection of the year, young General Napoleon Bonaparte was second in command to Barras of the artillery used to disperse a mob in Paris.

In the spring of 1796, the government got wind of a new plot led by a revolutionary journalist named François Noel Babeuf (1760–1797). His doctrine was both a call to revolution, in the hope of reestablishing the Jacobin Constitution of 1793, and a rather crude expression of opposition to private property. Most of the Babeuvists were concerned solely with the restoration of the Constitution of 1793, but Babeuf himself has been called the first truly class-conscious leader of the proletariat in Europe.

Article 10:   The aim of the French Revolution is to destroy inequality and to re-establish the general welfare.

Article 11:   The Revolution is not complete, because the rich monopolize all the property and govern exclusively, while the poor toil like slaves, languish in misery, and count for nothing in the State.[1]

The Army nipped this budding insurrection, too, with General Bonaparte now commanding, but Babeuf's trial was postponed for a year, so as to coincide with the elections to renew Parliament. The government hoped that publicizing this threat to property would frighten the electors into voting for the incumbent defenders of property and order.

Meanwhile, the French military position seemed increasingly strong. The Directory had inherited this improved military situation from the Convention, the same improvement which had made the emergency dictatorship of the Convention intolerable. Holland, Prussia, and Spain all withdrew from the war in 1795, leading the Directory to concentrate its efforts against Austria in 1796–1797. Twin offensives were launched against Vienna, one down the Danube valley and the other, under Bonaparte, through northern Italy. Both drives pushed forward toward the goal, and it is revealing of Bonaparte that when he suspected that the cooperating army under Louis Lazare Hoche and Jean Victor Moreau might reach Vienna before him, he hastened into armistice with the Austrians without consulting the home government. Though he granted the Austrians terms highly advantageous to France, the terms were nevertheless contrary to French foreign policy of that moment and contrary to the agreement that France had earlier reached with Prussia. French policy was not merely to secure the Austrian Netherlands for France, but also to secure German territory for Prussia, after which Prussia would openly recognize the Rhine as the French frontier. Austria was to be compensated for her losses by grants of Italian territory. Given the unpopularity of the Directory, however, the furious Directors dared not renounce so favorable a peace, especially since the treaty of Campo Formio gave both Lombardy and the Austrian Netherlands to France.

The unpopularity of the Directory was fast undermining faith in the republic as was soon revealed in the national election; only 13 of the

1. The "Doctrine of Babeuf" in John Hall Stewart, ed., *A Documentary Survey of the French Revolution* (New York, Macmillan, 1951), p. 657.

216 deputies standing for re-election in 1797 were returned. As the election was clearly a royalist victory, the frightened Directorate used armed force to purge the parliament of the newly elected deputies. A revolutionary dictatorship was thus re-established. New elections were then held in 1798, but the results were again unsatisfactory to the Directorate, since mostly royalists (from the country) and Jacobins (from the city) were victorious. This time, the government found pretexts to annul many of the Jacobin elections—an action which only heightened the anger against the Directory. Worse, the military situation was once again deteriorating, and increasing demands were heard in Paris for a Jacobin dictatorship, presumably the key to military victory as it had been in 1793–1794.

Meanwhile, in the attempt to force the British out of the war, Bonaparte invaded Egypt in 1798 and threatened to overrun the Turkish Empire; but the defeat of the French fleet at Aboukir Bay cut French communications and doomed the campaign to defeat. With Bonaparte bottled up in Egypt, the foreign opponents of the Revolution rallied. Russia, Turkey, Naples, and Austria reached an understanding with Britain; and in 1799 an Austro-Russian counteroffensive dislodged the French from Italy, while an Anglo-Russian force landed in Holland. The efforts of the coalition were plagued by the inability of the Allies to trust each other and to cooperate effectively. Having swept the French from Italy, the Austrians and Russians fell to bickering; the Austrians did not properly support the Russians moving into Switzerland, and each ally separately fell victim to French attack. In Holland, the poorly directed offensive was also beaten by the French, and the British commander agreed to evacuate the continent. The Russian Czar, Paul I (1796–1801), furious at what he called the disloyalty of his allies, withdrew from the coalition.

In the meantime, General Bonaparte, having already shown his independence and ambition in 1797, became party to a plot to overthrow the Directory, to reestablish strong executive control, and thus to halt the rise both of royalism and Jacobinism—the latter in particular. He abandoned his fruitless campaign in Egypt and returned to Paris. On November 9, 1799 (18th Brumaire), the conspirators used a rumor of a Jacobin plot to frighten the deputies. The parliament then asked for military protection, and Bonaparte was named commander of the forces in the Paris region. The Directors were then persuaded to resign; but when some of the deputies asked for further proof of the Jacobin plot, Bonaparte lost his nerve, and the maneuver bordered on failure. At this critical point, his brother, Lucien Bonaparte, kept his head and used troops to clear out the protesting deputies. A rump parliament replaced the Directors with a Consulate of three, with Napoleon Bonaparte as First Consul, and a parliamentary committee was formed to draft a new constitution.

THE CONSULATE

Officially the Republic had not been overthrown but merely preserved by the *coup d'état* of the 18th Brumaire, and if the French overwhelmingly accepted the new order, it can be attributed both to their disgust at the crassness of the Directory and to their weariness after ten years of uncertainty and turmoil. Bonaparte promised both glory and order. The Constitution of 1799 (Year VIII) provided the appearance of democracy by granting the vote to every male over twenty-one who could prove a year's fixed residence, while a highly indirect system of election diluted the possibility of real democracy. In fact, the new constitution was a diabolical document, whose liberal clauses were mere pretense and hardly hid the dictatorship created for General Bonaparte. Executive power was vested in three consuls, but the other two, Siéyès and Pierre Roger Ducos, were really advisers to the First Consul; a legislature was permitted, but it was divided into four houses, each with such a limited function as to be powerless.

The new constitution was supplemented in early 1800 by two laws reorganizing local administration and the judicial system; each law enhanced central power and, hence, the power of the First Consul. The first law virtually ended local responsibility for the administration of the national law: the Prefect for each department, the subprefect for each district, and the mayor for each community were appointed from Paris rather than elected locally. In the reorganization of the judicial system, all the judges on the district and departmental level—that is, the courts of first instance, the courts of appeal, and the criminal courts—were appointed by the First Consul. Only the justices of the Supreme Court of Cassation, the highest court of appeal, were independent of him. The centralization was far more complete than anything enjoyed by the *ancien régime,* though it is well to emphasize that, in promoting centralization, the Revolution and Napoleon really completed the work of the *ancien régime.*

The aim of the Revolution was not, as once was thought, to destroy the authority of the Church and religious faith in general. Appearances notwithstanding, it was essentially a movement for political and social reform. . . . It sought to increase the power and jurisdiction of central authority. . . . We find that the chief permanent achievement of the French Revolution was the suppression of those political institutions, commonly described as feudal, which for many centuries had held unquestioned sway in most European countries. . . .

. . .

Far be it from me to deny that this centralization was a glorious achievement and that other nations envy us in this respect, but I do deny that it was an achievment of the Revolution. On the contrary, it was a legacy from the old regime and, I may add, the only part of the political constitution of that regime which survived the Revolution—for the good reason that it alone could be adapted to the new social system sponsored by the Revolution.[2]

Napoleon's handling of the religious question was further evidence that his regime was a compromise between prerevolutionary ideas and institutions and those of the Revolution. Rome resisted his overtures, in the realization that an understanding with Napoleon meant the sacrifice of some ecclesiastical principles. In particular, Napoleon hoped that the Church would recognize the title rights of those who had purchased properties confiscated from the French Church during the revolution. The papacy, hopeful of a more favorable settlement and in a position to tarry because the French had been driven from Italy in 1799, refused Napoleon's terms for the restoration of Catholicism. Then, in 1800, the Austrians, deprived of Russian help, were beaten both in northern Italy and in southern Germany and were forced to leave the war for the second time (1801). Italy was left open to the French, and the papacy had no choice but to come to terms. On paper, the Concordat of 1801 reflected a compromise between Rome and Paris, but in reality the arrangement was far more satisfactory to Napoleon than to the Pope. Roman authority was again recognized in France, in that the bishops, nominated by the First Consul, had to be consecrated by the Pope. On the other hand, the French clergy continued to be paid by the state—that is, the tithe was not restored—and the Church had to recognize and accept the loss of its confiscated lands as final.

Peace was the final ingredient in the First Consul's settlement. After Austria's surrender (1801), Britain stood alone against France; but she was in a position to negotiate, thanks to her occupation of Malta (1800) and Egypt (1801). Furthermore, Pitt resigned that year over the Irish issue, and the new British government felt that an opportune moment to

2. Alexis de Tocqueville, *The Old Regime and the French Revolution* (1856), Stuart Gilbert trans. (Anchor, 1955), pp. 19, 32.

negotiate had come. The two powers came to terms at Amiens (1802), the British handing back most of the conquests overseas and restoring Malta to the Knights of St. John. Consequently, the treaty was highly unpopular in Britain. In France, however, Bonaparte took advantage of having brought peace after nearly ten years of war to further his personal interests. He arranged to have the captive legislature express the nation's gratitude by offering him the First Consulship for life. All that remained was to make the office hereditary in his own line.

EMPIRE

The rise of Napoleon Bonaparte to absolute power—indeed, to a power greater than Louis XVI ever enjoyed—seems almost incomprehensible in the light of the previous enthusiasm for liberty, equality, and fraternity. To assume that he rose to power against the wishes of the French would be an error. If the Revolution brought a more popular and modern political and social order by "abolishing feudalism," it also brought war and insurrection; it brought a division in the nation's conscience through the religious settlement of 1790; and it brought internal chaos when idealists and opportunists alike contested for the right to replace the *ancien régime*. Is it strange that, after so many years of uncertainty and rapid change, the French accepted with relief a man who seemed to guarantee order and whose political settlement seemed a satisfactory compromise between the old monarchy and the democratic republic?

When one looks at France between 1800 and 1802, one sees not merely the re-establishment of peace and the modified ties with Rome, but also a more highly rationalized central administration. In a world where the rationale of enlightened despotism was not yet dead, it could be argued that the despotism of the rational administrator was a better guarantee of liberty than democracy would be. The merits of democracy, after all, had been sullied by the guillotine. Part of Napoleon's appeal lay in his being all things to all people. Could the Jacobins fear him too much when one of their own, Joseph Fouché, was his minister of police? Could not the old nobility rally to a regime which the artful Maurice de Talleyrand—himself of the nobility—served as foreign minister? If censorship silenced liberal critics, it could be justified to the multitude—if not to the intelligentsia—as a wartime requirement. And Bonaparte's encouragement of industrial development, along with his willingness to protect French industry from British competition, contributed to full employment and higher wages than had been previously known. Thus he got enthusiastic support from both employers and employees. Napoleon's popularity, indeed, seems to have been genuine enough; his military prowess, a guarantee against further invasion, fed the national pride.

His popularity was, in fact, international, because he seemed the incarnation of the romantics' ideal, an "artist of action." Here was a man of obscure origin who, having imagination and intuition, faith in his "star," and no fear of appearing ridiculous, had shattered conventions and social limitations to rise to the top.[3] He was both the guarantor of liberty in France and its generator elsewhere. Already, in 1800, Napoleon revealed his concern for rationalizing French legal codes. The new Civil Code of that year (not promulgated until 1804) assumed the equality of all citizens before the law, granted freedom of conscience, and guaranteed each citizen the right to choose his own profession without fear of social limitations. There is the oft-repeated story of Ludwig van Beethoven (1770–1827), who finished his third symphony in 1804 and subtitled it "Eroica" in his enthusiasm to dedicate the work to Napoleon. Then came the unpleasant realization that the order brought by the enlightened despot was not to be liberty after all, that enlightened despotism was still despotism. And so the dedication page was ripped from the symphony. Had Beethoven, or anyone else for that matter, looked further into the Civil Code of 1800, he would have found clauses disturbingly inconsistent with its profession of liberty and equality. In a civil case, the court was to prefer an employer's testimony to that of a laborer; all workers were required to carry employment cards for identification; and the Code incorporated the Chapelier law of 1791, making it illegal for workers to combine or form unions.

In foreign matters, the First Consul also had a mixed record. His first reorganization in Germany (1803) did indeed appear to be the work of an enlightened despot. No German state, no German ruler, had ever been able to unite Germany into a nation; Germany had remained a collection of states loosely grouped and under the feeble leadership of the Holy Roman Emperor. Napoleon's plan, which was accepted by the Imperial Diet as a necessary rationalization of the German world, meant the obliteration of 112 small German states. It also gave France the left bank of the Rhine as her frontier—the "natural frontier" which Louis XIV had failed to achieve. The German powers which lost Rhineland territory were

3. Elie Faure, *Napoleon* (New York, 1924), perhaps carried this thesis to an extreme, but it has merit.

compensated elsewhere in Germany at the expense of the 112 obliterated petty states. When one discovers that Prussia and Bavaria received five times the territory they lost in the Rhineland, that Austria picked up several bishoprics, and that Würtemberg and Baden (with close dynastic ties to Russia) profited greatly by the exchange, their willingness to see France expand too becomes quite understandable.

The honeymoon was shorter for the British, however. In 1802 Napoleon inaugurated a new colonial policy and a new tariff policy and gave hints of new expansion; all of these actions held grave consequences for Britain. When Spain had withdrawn from the war in 1795, she had given up the island of Santo Domingo to France, but at the time the French were too busy to occupy it. Later, in 1801, when all the Continent gave way before French arms, the Spaniards had found it necessary to appease Napoleon with Louisiana. Using these two territories as bases, he hoped to recover the great American empire lost by France in the eighteenth century. The Haitians, having become virtually independent as a result of French neglect, resisted Napoleon's decision to implement the French claim, and a sizable expedition was sent to the island (1802). The venture proved an utter fiasco. Three-quarters of the troops having fallen victim to yellow fever within a year, Napoleon cut his losses and gave up the colonial dream. Clearly, this loss affected his decision to sell Louisiana in 1803, for in the probable renewed war against Britain, he was likely to lose that territory anyway.

The British were further agitated by a new French tariff in 1803, directed against British goods in particular, and to apply not only in France but in the French empire and in those states allied to France. In fact, the closer the British looked at their peace with Napoleon, the more they realized it could be more ruinous than war. French possession of Holland, following the Anglo-Russian evacuation, gave France control over the Cape Colony in Africa, putting her in position to control the trade routes to Asia. And when Napoleon hinted that he might renew his efforts to occupy Egypt, the British feared to evacuate the island of Malta. By not doing so, they violated the Amiens agreement and inadvertently gave Napoleon a pretext to renew the struggle (1803) without appearing to be the aggressor.

Naturally, the British sought to revive a European alliance against France, and Napoleon's high-handedness after the renewal of war with Britain irritated the continental powers and drove them into Britain's arms. For one thing, using Britain's position in Malta as an excuse, Napoleon occupied three Neapolitan ports—Naples being one of the few remaining Italian states not under French domination. Not only was this a violation of Neapolitan neutrality, but any French move in the direction of the eastern Mediterranean caused Russia anxiety, just as the Egyptian campaign had brought Russia to arms earlier. The Russians had ambitions in the region of the Dardanelles and did not wish to see a weakening Turkey replaced by a powerful France.

Then, in 1804, Napoleon violated the territory of Baden to seize a French *emigré,* the Duc d'Enghien, who was accused of participating in a royalist plot to overthrow the regime. He was brought to Paris and shot, presumably as a warning to royalists, but in reality as part of a contrived campaign by Napoleon to convince the French that the republic was in danger. This violation of a country's frontier was a lawless act, threatening to every European country. In this case, the close dynastic ties between Baden and Russia led Alexander I to construe the incident as an insult to Russia. European anger only mounted when Napoleon used the royalist "plot" to convince the legislature of the need to "complete the work of the 18th Brumaire"—in other words, to bring the Consulate to an end and name him Emperor! The institutions of the Life Consulate required little alteration to provide for a hereditary monarchy, and a new Constitution (1804) was sanctioned by plebiscite. The Revolution had gone full cycle. In northern Italy, the French-dominated republics were merged into the Kingdom of Italy, Napoleon taking the royal title. These events induced Russia and Austria to join Britain in the Third Coalition (1805), but Prussia maintained her neutrality. Baden, Würtemberg, and Bavaria signed alliances with France, in the hope of additional territory in Germany.

Napoleon moved against the Third Coalition on a grand scale (1805). He proposed first to gain naval control of the Channel in order to invade Britain, after which he would turn his attention to defeating the armies of Austria and Russia. The first part of this plan was frustrated when his Mediterranean fleet, sailing for a rendezvous with the Atlantic fleet, was intercepted off Cape Trafalgar and badly beaten by Admiral Horatio Nelson (1758–1805), making French control of the Channel impossible. On land, however, the French were more fortunate. The Austrian General Karl Mack, waiting in the fortified city of Ulm for the approach of his Russian ally, found himself suddenly surrounded by the faster-moving French. His consequent surrender opened the way for a French occupation of Vienna; but the Russians, hearing of the Austrian defeat, retired into Moravia to await the arrival of a second Austrian force which was being withdrawn from the Italian front to meet the French challenge. Napoleon's position was actually dangerous, operating as he was in Central Europe between two enemy armies, always with the possibility that Prussia would enter the campaign against him. Yet, he pressed against the Russians, forcing them to battle at Austerlitz and crushing them in the most perfectly executed movements of his military career. He deliberately weakened his right wing to invite Russian attack; the Russians accommodated him, weakening their center in order to strengthen their left wing for attack. Once that attack was well under way, the French struck the Russian center and then wheeled to the right to envelop the Russian attacking force.

This disaster forced the Russians to retire from the campaign, though they signed no peace. The Austrians, on the other hand, for the third time came to terms with Napoleon. They gave up Venetia and the Dalmatian coast to the Kingdom of Italy and their remaining territories in southern Germany to Baden, Bavaria, and Würtemberg. Meanwhile, Prussia, which had dickered with both sides, decided that the safest course was to accept Napoleon's terms. Britain had offered Prussia a large subsidy and territory on the left bank of the Rhine (then French), while Napoleon had offered her Hanover. Upon the news of the Prussian annexation of Hanover, Charles James Fox reflected British opinion when he characterized it as "a compound of everything that is detestable in servility with everything that is odious in rapacity."[4] Since the Hanoverians and British crowns were united, Britain necessarily declared war on Prussia.

Napoleon then took his second step in reorganizing the German world. The Holy Roman Empire was dissolved (1806), the Hapsburg Emperor remaining Emperor of Austria, and nearly seventy small German states (in addition to the original 112) lost their identity. A Confederation of the Rhine was sponsored by Napoleon; it initially comprised fifteen states, Bavaria, Würtemburg, Saxony, and Westphalia among them; both Prussia and Austria were excluded. The idea was to create a third German state which would be closely allied to France. Other German states adhered to the Confederation, so that by 1808 it had thirty-eight members. Its existence was a fair measure of Austria's defeat and Prussia's supineness.

As in 1801, so again in 1806 the British found themselves virtually alone; and once again Napoleon sought peace on terms highly favorable to himself. To get the British out of Malta and Sicily, he offered to get Hanover back for them—presumably compensating Prussia elsewhere. But since

4. From a speech in Parliament.

he had not consulted Prussia about this exchange, the British used the proposal to alienate Prussia from France. The furious Prussians reached a secret understanding with Russia and declared war on France. It was a rash move and was severely paid for at the Battle of Jena (late in 1806). Berlin was occupied ten days later. Napoleon then turned eastward, to force Russia to terms. The initial engagement at Eylau in East Prussia (1807) was costly to both sides and indecisive; but the subsequent battle at Friedland was ruinous to the Russians and forced them to agree to peace.

The treaties of Tilsit were negotiated by Napoleon and Alexander I on a raft anchored on the river Nieman, while Frederick William of Prussia paced the riverbank in anxiety over his fate. The terms, to which Prussia had to adhere, included a recognition of the territorial and political changes engineered by the French in Italy, Germany, and the Netherlands. Thus, Prussia admitted the loss of her Rhenish lands and recognized the Confederation of the Rhine. Both Russia and Prussia consented to the formation of the Grand Duchy of Warsaw, a miniature Poland created out of Prussia's share of partitioned Poland, with the King of Saxony as Grand Duke. Both powers also agreed to close their ports to British goods. Finally, Russia agreed to try to mediate the war between Britain and France and, in case peace was not possible, to join France against Britain. Similarly, France promised to put pressure on the Turks, who had taken advantage of Russia's preoccupation in 1806 to try to recover territories lost in the eighteenth century; and to join Russia against Turkey in case the Turks failed to see reason. Apparently, too, Napoleon hinted that he would consider the partition of the Turkish Empire with Russia's assistance.

The Tilsit terms seemed a great victory for Napoleon in his attempt to isolate the British, for he had begun, in late 1806, to implement his so-called Continental system. If he could not invade Britain, he would reduce her through economic warfare by closing the Continent to her goods. By the nineteenth century, her industrialization had developed to such a degree that her prosperity required overseas markets for her manufactured goods. A sharp reduction in exports would force the shutdown of factories, and the resulting unemployment would soon produce sufficient misery among the working class to give the British government the choice between revolution and making peace. Napoleon's estimate of the effectiveness of this economic warfare was not far off. The Continental system posed such a serious threat to Britain that she was driven to extreme measures to counter it—her attempt, for instance, to prevent neutral shipping from reaching the Continent, which led to war with the Americans. And had she not developed new markets for her goods, in Latin America in particular, she surely would have succumbed. Shrewdly, Napoleon did not forbid the sale of agricultural products to the British, since this was helpful to continental agriculture; such products, however, had to be paid for in gold or silver, and this manner of payment would help deplete Britain's reserves and make subsidies to a continental ally increasingly impossible.

However ingenious the Continental system, it made trouble for Napoleon, too. British manufactured goods, often cheaper than continental manufacture, thanks to the factory system, were highly desired in Europe; even regimes friendly to Napoleon were reluctant to cooperate to make the blockade effective. Beginning in 1807, French policies designed to extend and police the blockade did much to inflame Europe against Napoleon. The economic unity of Europe, when seen in the light of the political adjustments dictated by Napoleon, suggested that the entire continent was becoming a vassal to France. More precisely, Europe appeared more and more to be a prize for the Bonaparte family; but it is notable that, in finding suitable thrones for his relatives, Napoleon placed them in spots critical for the success of the Continental system—localities favorable to smuggling in British products.

Naples, for instance, whose Bourbon government had necessarily been opposed to the Revolution and Napoleon, was completely occupied in 1806 and the crown was given to Joseph Bonaparte. In the same year, the republican government of Holland, established by the French during the Directory, was converted into a monarchy for the benefit of Louis Bonaparte. To Napoleon's great annoyance, Louis, in his desire to please the Dutch, failed to enforce the ban against British goods. In the second shuffling of German territories that year, two new states were created along the Rhine for Bonapartes; the Duchy of Berg for Caroline Bonaparte and her husband, Marshal Joachim Murat; and the Kingdom of Westphalia for Jerome Bonaparte. Both of these states became members of the Confederation of the Rhine. Lucien, the brother who had made Napoleon's seizure of power on the 18th Brumaire possible, married a commoner against Napoleon's wishes and was thus denied an imperial title.

The Baltic seemed the only remaining artery by which British trade could reach the Continent; the British were therefore understandably fearful that Napoleon would try to block that route by bringing pressure on Denmark, or perhaps even by seizing the Danish fleet. This accounts for Britain's offer of an alliance to Denmark—and the request that Denmark turn over her fleet to the British for safe-keeping for the duration of the war. This the Danes refused to do, and rather than see the fleet fall to the French, the British bombarded the fleet at Copenhagen (1807) and forced its surrender. Such a decision suggests the desperation in London in facing the facts of the Continental system. Of course the Danes then entered that system, but the fleet had been rendered useless to France.

Sweden was also in an awkward position in those years. Having been an opponent of France (Gustavus IV had refused to recognize Napoleon's title and called him Mr. Bonaparte), Sweden was caught short by Russia's reversal in 1807; and when—in compliance with the Tilsit terms—Russia declared war on Britain the following year the Swedish King refused to follow suit. Russia promptly took advantage of his stubbornness to invade and occupy Finland (1808). Gustavus IV was then overthrown by his angry compatriots and a settlement presumably pleasing to Napoleon was achieved. The ex-king's uncle, the aged Charles XIII, became the monarch and, because he was childless, the Swedes invited the French Marshal Jean Baptiste Bernadotte to be heir-presumptive. This arrangement was comfortable just so long as Russia and France remained friends.

Napoleon recognized that the Iberian Peninsula was imperfectly integrated into the Continental system and could be increasingly troublesome. Portugal had a long history of friendship for Britain, while Spain, technically allied to France, was unreliable. The alliance had been forced on Spain after military defeat, her fleet had been appropriated by Napoleon, and now, thanks to naval isolation and alliance with France, the British were able to penetrate the Spanish Empire for purposes of trade. Even had Spain been pro-French, the inefficiency of the Spanish government was such that a vigorous enforcement of the Continental system would have been impossible. The regime in Madrid, unfortunately, was in no position, in 1807, to reap the benefits of public indignation against France. Charles IV (*1788–1808*) was inept and unperceptive, probably even unaware of his Queen's outrageous and notorious affair with Manuel de Godoy, whom she had sponsored as chief minister of the country which, of all European countries, was least likely to tolerate such a spectacle. Napoleon was not the sort of man to resist such an opportunity for intervention.

He began by proposing that France and Spain partition Portugal, a third of which was to go to Godoy personally. When the Spanish government fell in with the scheme, it gave permission for the French army to cross Spanish territory to attack Portugal. Napoleon hoped to seize the Portuguese fleet, but the fleet and the royal family escaped to Brazil. In the meantime, the partition arrangement had further compromised Godoy

NAPOLEONIC
EUROPE
1810

FRENCH
EMPIRE

DEPENDENT
STATES

ALLIED WITH
NAPOLEON

NORTH
SEA

UNITED
KINGDOM

IRELAND

ENGLAND

London

Dover

Brus.

Boulogne

Cherbourg

SEINE

Paris

Valmy

Versailles

FRENCH

LOIRE

EMPIRE

Lyons

Bordeaux

RHONE

Marseilles

Oporto

DOURO

Almeida

EBRO

Saragossa

Barcelona

PORTUGAL

SPAIN

Talavera

Madrid

TAGUS

Ocaña

Lisbon

Elvas

BALEARIC IS.
(SP.)

Baylen

M E D I T E R

TRAFALGAR ×

GIBRALTAR
(BR.)

MOROCCO
(INDEP.)

ALGERIA
(TURK.)

in the eyes of Spaniards, and Napoleon used the resulting unrest as a pretext for sending an occupying army into Spain. At that, the furious Spaniards overthrew Godoy, and Charles IV was persuaded to abdicate in favor of his son, Ferdinand VII, the latter having been part of the anti-Godoy party. The French army, meanwhile, occupied Madrid while Napoleon invited both Charles and Ferdinand to visit him in Bayonne to discuss a solution to the situation. Once there, he tricked both father and son into signing abdications (1808), and they remained prisoners of the French. Napoleon's brother Joseph was then elevated from the Neapolitan to the Spanish throne, and Marshal Murat replaced Joseph in Naples. Spanish fury was now complete: No matter that King Joseph might prove an efficient and enlightened ruler; such tricks by foreigners must not be tolerated. And when, that same year, the French occupied Rome after the Pope's refusal to enter the Continental system, the Spaniards added this event to their list of grievances against France. Spain, in sum, proved impossible to digest and had to be held down by a large army. It was the first sign of serious opposition to Napoleon and an intolerable drain on his resources. He rightly called it a "running sore."

INTERNATIONAL REACTION TO FRENCH DOMINANCE

With our advantage of hindsight, we can see that the balance was shifting away from Napoleon in 1808, even though, on the surface, he seemed master of Europe. Spain was to prove an insoluble problem, which ate up troops and supplies to no avail. A fearful omen was General Junot's failure to prevent the landing of a small British expeditionary force in Portugal under Sir Arthur Wellesley (1808).

Napoleon's alliance with Russia was also in trouble. Russia had declared war on Britain and closed her ports to British goods, in compliance with the treaty of Tilsit, but France intended doing nothing about her promised war against Turkey. Alexander I came to understand that his alliance with Napoleon would not produce a partition of the Ottoman Empire, which the Russians had anticipated as the chief benefit of the alliance with France, while the loss of British trade won the Czar considerable criticism from the nobility. Though the two emperors met at Erfurt (late 1808) to renew the alliance, Alexander I secretly encouraged Austria by promising not to aid Napoleon in any future Austro-French conflict.

Prussia

This growing resistance to Napoleon, however, was not merely a military matter. Those responsible for devising new barriers to French aggression were coming to the conclusion that France's recent invincibility was to be explained by the militant devotion of the entire nation to its government's causes; and that the French government had won this popular support through the revolutionary reforms, which promised a better life for all. In other words, the logical defense against the French was to beat them at their own game; national sentiments had to be mobilized, and the most effective method to achieve this would be to grant liberal reforms. As Karl August Hardenberg (1750–1822) put it to the King of Prussia:

> It is an illusion to think that we can resist the Revolution effectively by clinging more closely to the older order, by proscribing the new principles without pity. This has been precisely the course which has favored the Revolution and facilitated its development. The force of these principles is such, their attraction and diffusion is so universal, that the State which refuses to acknowledge them will be condemned to submit or to perish. . . .
>
> Thus our objective, our guiding principle, must be a revolution in the better sense, a revolution leading directly to the great goal, the elevation of humanity through the wisdom of those in authority and not through a violent impulsion from within or without. . . .[5]

Hardenberg was joined by Karl, Freiherr vom Stein (1757–1831) in promoting a program of social and political reform in Prussia. The way had been prepared, partly by the ideas of Herder who, we have already noted, urged the study of the national past and the development of indigenous national qualities, as against the rational universalism of the eighteenth century; and in part by the swift defeat of the Prussian army at Jena (1806), a defeat which revealed the decay of the administrative and military system left by Frederick the Great. In the wake of shocking defeat, Johann Gottlieb Fichte (1762–1814) delivered a series of addresses to the "German nation" in which he advocated educational reforms that would produce a vigorous German patriotism. To realize a "free fatherland," it was not enough to advocate the ideal, said Fichte, it was also necessary to inculcate a firm conviction that the ideal must be obtained through action.

5. Geoffrey Bruun, *Europe and the French Imperium* (New York, Harper, 1938), p. 174.

Of the reforms inspired by Hardenberg and Stein, the most revolutionary was the Law of October 14, 1807, which abolished serfdom and all the personal obligations of feudal relationships. No longer were vocational opportunities to be limited by class restrictions, and many peasants, despite the protests of landlords, gained title to the lands they worked. Military reforms were also necessary, not only because the old system was obviously ineffective, but because a military system reflects the social order. Note for instance that the levy *en masse* in France came at the height of Jacobin democracy, while Frederick's army reflected the social caste system of Prussia. Thus, the social reforms of October 14 made a more liberal army system necessary. As Fichte argued, military service should be regarded as a patriotic duty, and the military reforms promoted by the Prussian generals Gerhard Johann von Scharnhorst, August von Gneisenau, and Hermann von Boyen were dedicated to producing a truly national army. The peace settlement after Jena allowed Prussia an army of only 42,000 men, but the military reformers evaded the treaty's intention through a system of short-term enlistments followed by a period of reserve status. As a result, Prussia was able to field an army of 270,000 by 1814 while technically fulfilling the treaty. In that year, with Napoleon in full retreat, Prussia threw off the wraps and decreed compulsory military training.

Russia

Like Prussia's, Alexander I's (*1801–1825*) government responded to the threat of Napoleonic domination of Europe by projecting reforms, though in this case the reforms were more political than social. The Czar is correctly remembered as a liberal, and it is true that he had promoted liberal reforms in Russia long before he signed his uneasy peace with Napoleon at Tilsit. It is necessary to add, however, that his liberalism was reminiscent of his grandmother's, Catherine the Great's: it was the liberalism of the enlightened despot, not of the Jacobins; so that it is hardly surprising that the constitutional reforms he sponsored were directed toward achieving rational, efficient government rather than more democratic government. The following description of Alexander I, by one of his liberal advisors, could have applied equally well to Catherine II:

The Emperor liked forms of liberty as he liked the theatre; it gave him pleasure and flattered his vanity to see the appearances of free government in his Empire; but all he wanted in this respect was forms and appearances; he did not expect them to become realities. In a word, he would willingly have agreed that every man should be free, on the condition that he should voluntarily do only what the Emperor wished.[6]

In the first year of his reign, Alexander I met regularly with his Private Committee, which he had organized to advise him on necessary reforms. One notable change, recommended by the Committee, was the conversion of Peter I's "college" system into western-style ministries, making one minister, rather than a committee, head of each governmental department. The Czar also pronounced on the need to expand educational opportunities and backed a number of new universities, including an Institute of Pedagogy in St. Petersburg.

Russia's adherence to the Continental system in 1807 was not only catastrophic for her economy, but also had the inevitable effect of reducing the government's income; and insufficient income had already been a long-time governmental problem. The Czar appointed Michael M. Speransky (1772–1839) to find an answer to the dilemma, and by late 1809, he came up with a proposal to reorganize the national administration. Though his plan was accepted only in part, in its totality it reflected both the thinking of the rationalist reformer and the attempt to rally the entire nation for the coming struggle with Napoleon. As an indication of the limits of Alexander's liberalism, it is significant that he found acceptable only that portion of Speransky's proposal which dealt with governmental departments appointed by the Czar; he ignored Speransky's suggestions for the creation of representative institutions. More specifically, it was agreed that the Council of State should serve as an advisory committee, presided over by the Czar and appointed by him, with the obligation to help formulate legislation. Secondly, the ministers were to meet together as a committee to advise on governmental policy; appointed by the Czar, they were responsible only to him. Finally, the appointive senate was to act as a supreme court. Speransky's most startling innovations, none of which were acceptable, would have constituted a pyramidal edifice of representative institutions in four degrees. He proposed local, district, provincial, and national dumas, which would be complemented by a judicial system, also to be graded in four degrees. Not only were the representatives to the dumas to be elected, but Speransky even espoused the election of judges and trial by jury. But if the reforms were incomplete, they did provide the central administration with more rational, regularized procedures.

6. From the *Memoirs* of Prince Adam Czartoryski, in Warren B. Walsh, ed., *Readings in Russian History* (Syracuse, Syracuse University Press, 1950), p. 247.

In 1810, Speransky devoted himself to financial reforms in the hope of increasing governmental income. Russia's withdrawal from further participation in the Continental system was one of the few popular measures of his program. But when he turned his attention to the national debt and to taxation, he aroused increasing hostility. In brief, Speransky tried to rationalize the government's financial position by calling in the outstanding paper, redeeming it, and floating an entirely new, properly secured loan. This meant operating the government on a balanced budget, and in order that the debt be properly retired, Speransky insisted both on economy in governmental expenditures and on increased taxation. Accordingly, new taxes were levied and fell in particular on the gentry, who, inevitably, complained bitterly. And when, in violation of Speransky's directions, the new taxes were used for current expenses instead of for the retirement of the debt, the debt mounted—along with criticism of Speransky. In 1812, he fell from power, sacrificed by Alexander I to aristocratic opinion in a manner which did the Czar's reputation little credit.

Austria

Meanwhile, Austria, driven from the war three times already (in 1797, 1801, and 1805), planned a war of revenge. As in Prussia, the military revival was accompanied by a deliberate campaign to make the cause national rather than dynastic. Not only was the standing army increased in size, but regiments of civilian militia were conscripted and trained, in an apparent acceptance of the levy *en masse*. All men between the ages of eighteen and forty-five became subject to military service, and the government launched in the Austrian press a campaign designed to whip up patriotic enthusiasm. In 1809, with half the French army concentrated in Spain, and with secret assurances from Alexander I that he would not aid Napoleon, the Austrians believed the time right to strike.

The Austrian declaration of war was not as mad as it seems in retrospect. Not only was the national mobilization encouraging, but the Austrians expected—and did receive—British subsidies; and they expected that their initial victories would rally Prussia to the "German" cause at stake. Furthermore, they had word of defeatism in Paris; there were those in high places who were increasingly doubtful of Napoleon's ultimate success— those, in the words of the Austrian Ambassador, "who have fortunes to preserve," for whom the news from Spain seemed the harbinger of total ruin. The time had come to reconsider loyalties, to readjust one's principles, to insinuate oneself into the camp of Napoleon's foreign opponents. At the

Erfurt meeting (1808), one of Napoleon's chief advisors in foreign affairs, Maurice de Talleyrand-Perigord (1754–1838), had tipped his hand by remarking that France was civilized, but her ruler was not. Another opportunist was Joseph Fouché, the minister of police, who was caught in secret negotiations with Britain. Both men were removed from positions of authority, Talleyrand with the famous stinging rebuke: "S——t in a silk stocking."[7]

Napoleon met Austria's challenge immediately. Within a month, after three quick victories, he was in Vienna. The remainder of the campaign proved more rugged, but at Wagram, the Austrians were beaten though not destroyed. The game seemed up, and they accepted terms in Vienna in the treaty of Schönbrunn. Austria agreed to enter the Continental system and to reduce her army to 150,000. Her greatest territorial loss was the province of Galicia, which was annexed to the Grand Duchy of Warsaw, the enlargement of which was a violation of the Tilsit settlement. Finally, there was a war indemnity. As an aftermath, Napoleon took as his second wife the Austrian Grand Duchess Marie Louise (1810). He was concerned for an heir, and the Empress Josephine had borne him no children. Since the future of the dynasty was at stake, there was nothing to do but divorce her. Napoleon had first sought a Russian princess, and the Czar's refusal had been a clear indication that the Tilsit alliance had deteriorated. Austria was in no position to refuse, and anyway, such an alliance was in harmony with the new Austrian Chancellor's policy of feigning friendship for France. Klemens von Metternich (1773–1859) was convinced that Napoleon's time was running out and that the national revivals in Austria, Prussia, and Russia, with support from the British, would soon prevail.

DOMESTIC POLICIES IN FRANCE

Whatever the growing resistance to Napoleon in Europe, the French Empire appeared an impressive edifice after 1804: a glittering court, a superb army, an increasing population, general prosperity, and an administration dedicated to public works and the rationalizing of the legal codes. We have already noted the Civil Code of 1800, which was promulgated in 1804. If its clauses were not uniformly democratic, most of them could have been counted liberal by the definitions of that day; and the assumption

7. Albert Guerard, *Napoleon I* (New York, Knopf, 1956), p. 105.

that all citizens were equal before the law and had the right to freedom of conscience and to choice of vocation was a measure of the success of the French Revolution in altering the fundamental structure of the state. On the other hand, the supplementary legal codes were reactionary, suggesting that the Napoleonic settlement was a compromise between the old regime and the Revolution. The Code of Civil Procedure (1806), for example, revived the court procedures of the old regime, while the Code of Criminal Procedure (1810) stiffened the penalities for crimes against both property and persons, prescribing special severity for cases of political offenses. It could be argued, however, that whether the codes were liberal or illiberal, they gave uniform law and legal procedure to the entire country and, hence, produced order.

The civil liberties guaranteed by the *Code Napoléon* must also be judged in the light of constant police surveillance, the seriousness of which was underscored by the legality of arbitrary arrest (1810). It has been estimated that Napoleon held nearly 2500 political prisoners at the time of his fall from power; this figure may seem petty in comparison to the achievements of the police states of the twentieth century, but it seemed huge when measured against the arbitrary arrests in the time of Louis XVI (the Bastille, a symbol of royal tyranny, held seven political prisoners on July 14, 1789). Censorship of the press and the theater was continual and thorough. Of the seventy newspapers in Paris at the time of Napoleon's rise to power in 1800, only four remained by 1810. Even the ideal of free education suffered under the Empire. Napoleon did extend the public-school system by establishing a number of state-supported secondary schools (the *lycées*), but he thought that the goal of education was the production of loyal citizens and devoted soldiers. To that end he brought public education more directly under state supervision by creating the Université de France (1808), which was nothing more than the corporate name for all public-school teachers; it made all teachers civil servants under the direction of the minister of public instruction.

It is remarkable that, with all the military campaigns, France remained quite prosperous, at least until 1810. We notice, in fact, that the date 1810 recurs in describing the cracks appearing in the imperial edifice. It was then that a breakdown of trade, resulting from the Continental system, began to be felt, and the growing insecurity of the regime was reflected in the beginning of arbitrary arrests. Opposition came from all sides—no longer merely from intellectuals unable to stomach the police state, or from parliamentarians who longed for true parliamentary government, but also from the middle class, which shuddered at the prospect of economic stagnation, and from the peasants, who increasingly sought to avoid military service now that the war was going sour in Spain. Even so, the French did not suffer from the increasing costs of war and empire until 1812. Until then, the high costs had been met by indemnities charged to defeated opponents and by forced contributions of supplies and troops. But beginning in 1812, and just at a time when the economic health was declining, the burden began to shift to the French themselves, in the form of increased taxation. Worse, by 1813, the military losses required drastic levies of manpower, not so much for new offensives, as for defense against probable invasion. Equally ominous, the opponents of France had in the meantime adopted French military methods as demonstrably more successful than their own and were no longer at the disadvantage they had been in earlier campaigns.

It would be unfair, however, to ascribe the French military superiority to Napoleon alone; the reorganization of the French army had begun considerably earlier. We have already seen the decline of France's military efficiency in the time of Louis XV, culminating in the military and naval humiliations of the Seven Years War, and noted the determined efforts after 1763 to repair the naval establishment, which redounded to the benefit of the Americans at Yorktown. Reforms in the army were similarly overdue, and the government cashiered many inefficient or aged officers as a beginning. The main problem for the new army chiefs was to find new tactics which could undermine those of the Prussian army, which, under Frederick II, was the model for all Europe. The reformers saw correctly that the movements of an eighteenth-century army were very slow. An army marched in column, it is true, but it fought in line; and the canons of eighteenth-century warfare required that the deployment from column to line be carried out slowly and in perfect alignment. The result was both a rational perfection and a static, immobile fighting force once positions were taken. Under the direction of Jacques Antoine de Guibert, the French determined to sacrifice rational perfection in order to achieve mobility. Presumably, if an army deployed from column to line in haste, unmindful of ragged ranks, its consequent mobility gave it a decided advantage over a more static enemy. French artillery was also improved to give it a faster rate of fire and greater mobility. The keynote, in short, was speed and efficiency.

These innovations of the old regime survived the opening years of the Revolution, despite the defection of many officers, because they were consistent with the requirements of the young republic. Men with little or no military experience found themselves in positions of command; they were ignorant of traditional maneuvers and had no time to learn them. Similarly, there was no time to train the new recruits to perform intricate movements, and poorly trained troops are always inclined to seek cover and use skirmishing tactics. Some of the early engagements after 1792 resemble not so much battles between eigtheenth-century armies as a horde of undisciplined enthusiasts swarming locustlike over the neatly arrayed and helpless enemy. Even so, indefinite military success required greater discipline, and by 1794, the French government had achieved a marriage between the tactics of Guibert and the relative indiscipline of mobility and the possibility of using great numbers of conscripted civilians. Under the new system, the French not only advanced in column but attacked in column charge with fixed bayonets: the aggressive "mass" against the thin line.

Eighteenth-century armies were kept small; compactness was essential if their intricate maneuvers were to be controlled. In contrast, the French army, having abandoned rational refinement, could afford to increase the size of a field army; and the levy *en masse* provided soldiers in quantities unavailable to the old regimes of central Europe until they, too, after 1805 and 1806, recognized the necessity of raising national armies. Meanwhile, larger-scale warfare led the government of the young Republic to create new military units, since the field army was becoming too large. The new basic unit was the division, which contained 10,000 to 20,000 men; several divisions were grouped to form a corps; and an army was made up of several corps. The corps was designed to be a self-sufficient fighting force, resembling the field army of the old regime, which contributed to the mobility of the army on campaign. Inheriting this superb organization, Napoleon proved to be the first great master of warfare on the grand scale. His ability to coordinate the movements of his corps, his perception of the weaknesses in the enemy positions, and his sense of timing once the battle was under way were qualities unmatched by any of the commanders he opposed. Unfortunately for him, however, the French methods of organization and attack were increasingly understood and copied, and the French appeared increasingly vulnerable, owing to their inability to bring Spanish resistance to an end.

THE DECLINE OF THE NAPOLEONIC EMPIRE

The Franco-Russian alliance, shaky from the start, received a new blow in 1810 when Napoleon declined to promise that he would never restore

Poland. As he had already taken the Prussian and Austrian portions of Poland in creating the Grand Duchy of Warsaw, his refusal was an unveiled threat to Russia, whose response was to cease cooperation with the Continental system. The possibility of a Franco-Russian rupture made the Swedes in particular uneasy, but Marshal Bernadotte, heir presumptive and real ruler, argued successfully that it would be more dangerous to be anti-Russian than anti-French. This led to the treaty of Abo (1812), in which Russia obtained Swedish support in exchange for backing Sweden's claim to Norway—as a compensation for having earlier lost Finland to Russia. (Norway was Danish, and Denmark had been an ally of Napoleon ever since the British bombardment of Copenhagen.) Thus did the opportunist Bernadotte repay his debt to opportunist Bonaparte! The balance against France was further tipped in 1812 when the Russians succeeded in ending their war with Turkey (treaty of Bucharest). Russia retained the province of Bessarabia but evacuated both Moldavia and Wallachia.

Napoleon, in the meantime, had been massing an enormous army for his invasion of Russia. Italian, Bavarian, Polish, Saxon, Würtemberger, and Westphalian contingents were drawn from the Empire, while Austria and Prussia, still apparently subservient, agreed to supply contingents in exchange for favorable modifications of their treaties with France. Added to the large French army, they gave Napoleon a fighting force of nearly 400,000 backed by 200,000 reserves. Russia, in contrast, was able to field only about 200,000 men to meet this formidable threat, but she could take some comfort in the secret knowledge that the Austrian force pledged to France would not cooperate effectively. Presumably, too, the Prussian contingent would be unreliable in case of French reversals.

As for invasion strategy, Napoleon planned to march from the Grand Duchy of Warsaw to Vilna, where he would announce the creation of a Lithuanian state and proclaim the complete independence of Poland. The Russians, not certain of the exact invasion route, planned to withdraw eastward, avoiding battle, until French designs were clear; whereupon the Russian forces would be concentrated to meet the French drive. In actuality, Napoleon postponed the announcements in favor of the Lithuanians and the Poles, recognizing his Austrian ally's sensitivity in the matter of Poland; and the Lithuanians were, if anything, alienated by the presence of the gigantic French army, which proved undisciplined and inclined to pillage.

When Napoleon turned eastward from Vilna to seek out the Russian field army in the hope of crushing it as he had at Friedland in 1807, the

Russians recognized the danger and withdrew toward Smolensk. Even that city was evacuated after only a rear-guard action, and Napoleon found it half-burned, deliberately destroyed to deny him haven. Since his army was already dwindling, owing chiefly to disease and desertion, a successful campaign became increasingly problematical. If the Russians could not be brought to fight, did it not make sense to veer northward, capture St. Petersburg, and use it as a pawn either to bring the Russians to a decisive battle or to peace terms? St. Petersburg was defended only by a small covering force, and its possession would give the French a base easily supplied by sea. Instead, Napoleon garrisoned Smolensk and chose to follow the retreating Russians in the direction of Moscow. The Czar, in the meantime, determined that Moscow must be defended, and General Mikhail Kutuzov selected as the most defensible site an area of low hills near Borodino, some sixty miles west of Moscow. The subsequent battle was fiercely contested, and losses were great on both sides. Rather than face the uncertainties of continued fighting, the Russians abandoned the field, opening up Moscow to the French. They entered the city in mid-September. Even here victory eluded Napoleon, and unforeseen calamities quickly made his position untenable. A great fire broke out in Moscow, which burned unchecked for a week and destroyed three-quarters of the city. Napoleon waited nearly two months for Alexander I to come to terms, but in spite of momentary reverses, the Russians recognized that the French could not remain indefinitely in Moscow. Their evacuation began on October 19, 1812, about 100,000 strong. Napoleon's first thought, to winter in the Ukraine, was countered by Kutuzov, and rather than fight his way southward, Napoleon turned westward in the direction of Smolensk. There, at least, were food supplies and the garrison of 100,000 he had left behind. Kutuzov harried the retreat with nerve-racking and costly raids, but the French reached Smolensk reasonably intact—just as the snows began. To their utter dismay, half the expected garrison force had vanished and the food stocks were exhausted. The retreat must continue.

A complete debacle was soon in the making. Hounded on the flanks and from the rear, exposed to the appalling snow and cold, the retreating army fought its way toward Poland. Fewer than 20,000 of the original invading army recrossed the frontier into Poland, there to rejoin the Franco-Polish garrison and the Austrian contingent. The reunited forces numbered about 100,000, roughly one-sixth of the original Grand Army. That Napoleon's career and prestige survived the disaster was not the least astonishing part of the story. To make an impossible situation worse, the French in Spain had been equally unsuccessful. An all-out attempt to drive the British from the Iberian Peninsula had failed, and, beginning in 1811, the French slowly gave way before British attack and guerrilla fury. Napoleon returned to Paris to organize new forces, as energetic in defeat as he had been in victory, but the new recruits were a far cry from the seasoned veterans left behind in foreign fields. On paper, he achieved a new army of 600,000, but too much of it included overage and underage men.

The inevitable defection of "allies" began at the end of 1812, when the Prussian General Hans von Yorck, commanding the Prussian contingent pledged to France, signed a cease-fire with the Russians. This was soon converted into an open alliance, Prussia declaring war on France (1813). Sweden was next to enter the lists against France, leaving Austria, alone of the great powers, uncommitted. She did sign an armistice with Russia but, unlike Prussia, did not immediately join in the alliance against France. We must remember that Austria, for all her determination to unseat Napoleon, had other cares, dating from the eighteenth century. Prussia was her rival for domination of the German world and Russia for spoils at the expense of the declining Ottoman Empire. To weaken France too much might expose Austria to other losses engineered by Russia in close cooperation with Prussia. This situation accounts both for Chancellor Metternich's watchful waiting in 1813 and Austria's half-hearted military measures once she joined the other powers later that year.

In the late spring of 1813, Napoleon struck twice at the gathering strength of Prussia-Russia, defeating them twice at Lutzen and Bautzen, but he found himself unable to follow up his victories because he lacked sufficient cavalry. The apparent stalemate encouraged the Austrians to advance themselves as mediators in the hope of a favorable peace without the necessity of crushing France militarily. Having first consulted Russia and Prussia, Austria was to offer France a settlement satisfactory to the three powers and, in case of French refusal, to join the alliance against France. Before this maneuver could be completed, however, the French suffered a new defeat at Vittoria in Spain, opening up the southern French frontier to invasion. As a result, the allies saw no reason to consider a negotiated peace, and there was nothing for the Austrians to do but to join the alliance. A prolonged neutrality would have been regarded as hostility, which was worse than the uncomfortable alliance.

There followed the treaty of Töplitz (1813) between Austria, Russia, and Prussia. Each promised to make no separate peace with Napoleon, and, as war aims, agreed that the Grand Duchy of Warsaw and the Confederation of the Rhine should be obliterated, Prussia should be restored to her pre-1806 frontiers, and the French should be removed from Holland, Italy, and Spain. Napoleon replied with renewed attacks (autumn of 1813), but while he won victories against his opponents, he failed to prevent the convergence of the four allies at Leipzig. Austrians, Russians, Prussians, and Swedes, commanded by the Austrian Karl Philipp von Schwarzenberg, overwhelmed the French in a four-day battle. The defeat left Napoleon no choice but to abandon Germany. Equally bad news came from the south, where Arthur Wellesley, Duke of Wellington, crossed the frontier from Spain, and from the southeast where the French forces in Italy were in retreat.

The allies pressed on to invade France, but not without misgivings. It was impossible to forget the vital defense of France in 1793, which had checked the advance of four invading armies. But in 1814, the French were war-weary and far from enthusiastic for increased sacrifices. Napoleon's tactical brilliance, not the national resistance, proved to be the stumbling block in 1814, and the allies did not improve their chances by insisting on maintaining the separation and command of their respective armies on a national basis. Napoleon therefore had the opportunity, after Leipzig, to tangle with his opponents individually, and his defense of France in 1814 remains a classic example of successful operations against larger forces which maneuvered under divided command.

Indeed, Napoleon's victories over the Austrians on the Seine and over the Prussians on the Marne led to talk of armistice, but the allies were held in the field by the anxious British, who offered large subsidies to those remaining in the fight. In the treaty of Chaumont, the allies once again pledged to fight until Napoleon was unseated—a victory for British diplomacy. Meanwhile, a group of French royalists, led by Talleyrand, had been negotiating with the allies for a restoration of the Bourbon monarchy as a basis for peace. On March 31, 1814, they surrendered Paris to the allies without allowing Napoleon an opportunity to defend it. Four days later the Senate deposed him, which Napoleon tried immediately to counter by abdicating in favor of his infant son, the King of Rome. The maneuver failed, and the French government exiled Napoleon to Elba, allowed him to keep the imperial title (Emperor of Elba), and agreed to provide an income of two million francs a year. The great adventure was seemingly over, and the way was open for a Bourbon restoration.

Above: *The Coronation of the Empress Josephine* (detail) by Jacques Louis David
Right: *Napoleon Crossing the Alps* by Langlois after a painting by Jacques Louis David

Above left to right: Maurice de Talleyrand
Johann Wolfgang von Goethe by Rauch

Left: *Ludwig van Beethoven* by Bourdelle
Below: The Battle of Trafalgar

THE ROMANTIC REACTION

We noted, in a previous chapter, the rise of the cult of sensibility during the late eighteenth century, but we found that sensibility still competed with neoclassicism for predominance. By 1800, romanticism was clearly gaining the ascendancy, especially outside France; and when one looks for the reason, the impact of the French Revolution looms large in most explanations. Defining the "romantic spirit" is a necessary prelude to understanding the "romantic reaction." It will be recalled that the rational-neoclassicists of the eighteenth century held a mechanistic view of man and his universe; they emphasized the universal, the eternal and unchanging aspects of reality. Nature was seen as a perfect mechanism, and if one could rationalize—that is, make natural—the lives of men in society, one would have legislated perfection and goodness.

In contrast, the romantic spirit, growing out of the sensibility and sentimentality of the eighteenth century, rejected this mechanistic, rigid view of things in favor of a more subjective, individualized, complicated view. The eternal and universal gave way to the changing and the personal; the notion of set values gave way to relative values. Perhaps the most distinctive philosopher of this reaction was G. W. F. Hegel (1770–1831), whose idea that being is a process of becoming epitomizes the changing, or revolutionary, view of life. To exist, according to Hegel, is to change, to grow, to evolve toward a goal, and it is notable that he believed that the striving for a goal gave to life its significance and meaning; not believing that the attainment of the goal was likely, he could not offer the vision of a perfect order which had so often inspired the *philosophes* of the eighteenth century. Not a literary stylist, Hegel stated his emphasis on the becoming rather clumsily: "Universal history is the exhibition of Spirit in the process of working out the knowledge of that which it is potentially." And that which the "Spirit" is potentially is *free* or, in his own words, man's evolution is the "progress of the consciousness of Freedom."[8] To put it another way, this emphasis on the changing suggests that for the romantics it was the approach of Herder, as a historian, rather than that of Gibbon that was meaningful; that they found themselves in sympathy with the ideas of Edmund Burke, who had argued that perfect institutions cannot be rationalized, but that they must grow of their own accord.

8. From Hegel, *Philosophy of History* (1832), in J. H. Randall, *Making of the Modern Mind,* p. 423.

Consciously or otherwise, Napoleon represented an attempt to reconcile the twin political currents of the eighteenth century. A Jacobin as a young man, he retained, even as a dictator, the universal suffrage of Jacobin democracy; and that particular democracy derived from Rousseau's teaching that sovereignty resides in the General Will. Hence, governments must express the will of the governed, and under the Empire the will of the governed was presumably expressed in the plebiscites. On the other hand, Napoleon was also a lawgiver, the architect of the various codes which bear his name, and in this work he was the enlightened despot of the *philosophes* —the ruler who would bring liberty by establishing rational order. If we recognize that a plebiscite is not an honest expression of the general will, because it calls upon the people to judge an accomplished fact rather than to sanction policies suggested by the government, we may conclude that Napoleon's definitions of liberty were, in fact, those of the enlightened despot, and that the element of democracy in his system was a façade behind which he could pose as a "crowned Jacobin." Nevertheless, this posture had its usefulness because it gave Bonapartism a legitimacy. In seeming to reconcile the political currents of the eighteenth century, and in seeming to reconcile the monarchy of the old regime with the democratic institutions of the Revolution, Napoleon appeared to be the alternative to chaos, the necessary compromise between two extremes.

It was precisely Napoleon as a lawgiver whose career forced the recognition that a despot, however his title is modified, will necessarily be despotic; in other words, that liberty is not necessarily a product of the order he legislates. We have earlier noted the gradual alienation of those who originally hailed Napoleon as a savior, as a universal legislator, and this reaction against his despotism became part of the general reaction against rationalism. Burke, never an enthusiast for the political rationalism of the French revolutionaries, had already cautioned against the attempt to order society on the basis of the presumed order in nature. Similarly, F. K. Savigny (Prussian, 1779–1861) attacked the Napoleonic codes, in particular the assumption that a law code, rationally derived, was universally applicable:

Men sought new codes, which would assure by their completeness a mechanical certainty in the administration of justice. The judge, spared the exercise of private opinion, was to be limited to a stark and literal interpretation. At the same time the codes were to be delivered from all historical variations, and to possess equal utility for all nations and all ages. . . .

All law . . . is first produced by custom and popular faith, then through jurisprudence; everywhere, that is through internal, silently working forces, not through the arbitrariness of a lawgiver.[9]

In consequence, Savigny concluded that one could undertake legal reforms in any given nation only after having carefully studied that nation's traditions and history.

There were religious and moral aspects, also, to the rejection of rationalism. The charge was made that, as nature is an amoral state, a society based on nature's laws would be amoral. Kant, as noted earlier, had wrestled with this problem in the late eighteenth century and had finished by insisting that man is not merely a rational creature and that there are realms into which man's reason cannot penetrate. This left the way open for intuition and for faith. In his conclusion that each man has an *intuitive* ethical sense, Kant introduced into his philosophy a measure of individualism, or subjectivity, qualities which were the roots of romanticism. At the same time, if Kant was correct about man's intuitive ethical sense, a rational society would not necessarily be an amoral society.

While Kant argued for the existence of God and the individual soul as necessary—if not provable—postulates, he was not the leader of a religious revival, even though his ideas contributed to such a revival. One aspect of the rejection of rationalism was the assumption that, as "enlightened" laws had *not* produced peace and order, a spiritual awakening was the key to man's dilemma. This emphasis on personal salvation, on the individual rather than on the universal, leads us to note a further characteristic of the romantic spirit: the general disenchantment felt by so many of the intelligentsia by the end of the century. Reason had failed to produce the perfect society of their dreams; instead, it had brought war, the guillotine, and dictatorship. Their expectations had been for a society founded upon the certainties of natural law, where great security and happiness would derive from order. But, seemingly, the Revolution had destroyed traditions and standards and had produced a chaos which was only faintly veiled by the order imposed by Napoleon. Under the impact of this external disorder, their minds turned inward in pursuit of personal salvation, of an inner order as a defense against the shambles around them. The Vicomte René de Chateaubriand (French, 1768–1848) is an excellent example of the disillusionment and the melancholy of the time. Resigning public office the year Napoleon proclaimed himself Emperor, Chateaubriand drifted toward the Church and published *Les Martyrs* (1806). Here he summed up the

9. Bruun, *op. cit.,* p. 212.

troubles of his generation as a clash between Christian and pagan standards, avowing that Christianity was the only salvation for mankind. Others were more pietistic or mystical in their religious reaction, notably the Germans Franz von Baader (1765–1841) and Adam Müller (1779–1829), and even Alexander I of Russia was affected by German mysticism.

When one has catalogued the various possible traits of romanticism— individual expression, subjectivity, the rejection of classical rigidity, and the reliance on intuition and the senses—it remains to emphasize that not all romantics shared these qualities to an equal degree. Some were even equivocal in their rejection of rationalism, surely uneasy about the fruit of rampant individualism, yet insistent in the best romantic fashion on the *striving* for a rich personal life, struggling for the noble goal regardless of its attainability. Such was romanticism at its finest, because in its subjectivity, it scornfully rejected the claims of selfish existence. While exalting greatness, it deplored self-indulgence. Johann Wolfgang von Goethe (German, 1749–1832) was one of the greatest of the romantics, yet he shrank from the excesses of subjectivity, leaving, on that topic, a telling epigram: "The classical is health; and the romantic, disease."[10] He did not advocate, let us hastily add, a slavish adherence to classical forms, but recognized that when the security of traditional form is abandoned in the pursuit of greater expressiveness, wild indiscipline may result. Break conventions if necessary, we may infer from Goethe, but only in the interest of revitalizing culture. He had no sympathy for those who lapsed into helpless despair once they recognized that the old forms lacked vitality:

I feel pity for those persons who make so much ado about the transitoriness of all things and lose themselves in the contemplation of earthy vanity. Why, we are here for the very purpose of making the transitory imperishable, and this can be done only if we know how to appreciate both conditions.[11]

In an earlier chapter we noted that as a young man Goethe had been a leader in the German *Sturm und Drang,* movement, at which time he produced a fragmentary *Faust.* Subsequently, he published a poem, *Hermann und Dorothea* (1798), which revealed his renewed interest in classical form; but when the First Part of *Faust* appeared in 1808, it became apparent that Goethe had not completely shed his romanticism. Rather, he had achieved a moderate, more balanced view of reality and the human condition than was common in a day of widespread disillusionment. Com-

    10. Stephen Spender, ed., *Great Writings of Goethe* (New York, New American Library, 1958), p. 277.
    11. *Ibid.,* p. 273.

bining the discipline of classicism with the liberal aspirations of romanticism, Goethe achieved a serenity which is rare in any epoch—an air of unruffled aristocracy, which has been termed "Olympian." The Faustian theme occupied him during much of his long literary life, and as was the case in Christopher Marlowe's earlier treatment of the same theme, Goethe's *Faust* was intended as a warning to mankind. Tragedy is always concerned with human greatness; "Faust's tragedy is that of titanism."[12]

Goethe gives us a Faust who, in yearning for the fullest possible life, seeks to know more than man's natural limits entitle him to know. Thus we have symbolized the likely aspirations of the romantic, along with the implication that there are things beyond the possibility of human knowledge —hence, a criticism of the rationalist's optimism. Faust's ambition leads him into a career of crimes and into illusions; he abandons the traditional disciplines as unfruitful and hopes to find the totality of wisdom in magic. But he discovers late in life that even perfect knowledge is unsatisfying if it is bereft of human experience; he has sold his soul to the devil for superhuman powers, and in overstepping man's natural limits, ends by not even knowing himself. The lesson is that man has to live within natural limits, to strive for fuller knowledge with the realization that he will fall short of fulfillment. There must be no surrender in the realization of this limitation, and herein lies the tragedy; that man must struggle for that which he recognizes is unattainable:

> Worthy alone is he of life and freedom
> This is wisdom's final word:
> Who conquers them anew each day.[13]

If the comparison is not pushed too far, one can be struck by the similarity of Goethe and Ludwig van Beethoven (German, 1770–1827). For although Beethoven's music always revealed his attachment to classical form, it was also more personal, more subjective than that of Mozart and Haydn, especially after 1802 when increasing deafness heightened his isolation and individualism. The love of liberty, which made him admire the French Revolution—at least until 1804—also led him to violate strict musical form, leading some musicologists to call him a romantic. Yet, he never completely abandoned classical form. The romantic spirit is there, nevertheless, and romantic music began with his willingness to

12. Alexander Gillies, *Goethe's Faust: An Interpretation* (Oxford, Blackwell, 1957), p. 1.
13. *Faust,* Part II, Act 5.

depart from strict form to achieve greater expression. We also see it in Beethoven the man: burdened and afflicted as he was, his music reflects his faith that the human spirit can triumph over adversity.

Romanticism had become the predominant note in German and English painting, where the great names were Caspar David Friedrich (1774–1840), John Constable (1776–1837), and Joseph Turner (1775–1851). Rather than adhering to rigid form and precise draftsmanship, their works display misty landscapes. In France, on the other hand, classicism held out much longer. The republicans had imitated the art of republican Rome, and under the Empire the vogue was to copy Imperial Rome. The prevailing style of furniture, which was classically rigid and quite uncomfortable, is still referred to as Empire. The greatest technician among the French artists of the period was Jacques Louis David (1749–1825) whose gigantic canvas depicting the coronation of Napoleon required nearly three years to complete.

THE SCIENTIFIC CLIMATE

For if the trumpet gives an uncertain sound, who shall prepare himself to the battle?

I Corinthians, XIV:8

The romantic reaction against eighteenth-century neoclassicism and rationalism took various forms, as we have just seen, and its spirit was often one of uncertainty and disenchantment. A distinguished philosopher has made the point that all thought in the nineteenth century seems muddled and perplexed when compared to the certainties and clarity of the two preceding centuries.[14] He recognized that there had been "opposing camps" before, but argued that the camps were "whole-hearted." His point is well taken. The nineteenth century was an era of both scientific advance and religious revival—just as the seventeenth century had been; but in the seventeenth, we do not find that the religious and scientific ideas were at loggerheads, as was so often the case in the nineteenth. Moreover, the seventeenth century achieved a remarkable unity in thought and art, which began to dissolve in the eighteenth and is found wanting in the nineteenth. The subjectivity of romanticism might be regarded as compatible with

14. See Alfred North Whitehead, *Science and the Modern World* (New York: New American Library, 1948), p. 83.

the personal religion of the revivalists, but neither spirit was congenial to the mechanistic universe of many of the scientists—a universe whose life was determined by natural laws leaving no room for man's free will or free action. Even the scientific ideas of the century, however, were brought into question by new scientific disclosures. What would happen to the notion of the universe as a perfectly operating mechanism if those suggestions of evolutionary development and change, made by many natural scientists in the later eighteenth century, were scientifically demonstrable?

Chemistry, in the period after Lavoisier, is a good case in point, for its innovations continued to suggest the mechanistic nature of the universe. The first serviceable atomic theory was published by the Englishman John Dalton (1766–1844) in *New System of Chemical Philosophy* (1808). He held, as did earlier atomic theorists, that all physical phenomena resulted from the interaction of small particle, or atoms, which he believed to be indestructible and uncreatable.

Chemical analysis and synthesis go no further than the separation of particles one from another, and to their reunion. No new creation or destruction of matter is within the reach of chemical agency. We might as well attempt to introduce a new planet into the solar system, or to annihilate one already in existence, as to create or destroy a particle of hydrogen.[15]

Dalton suggested, moreover, that each element has its distinctive kind of atom, and that the different atoms have different weights. Finally, he suggested how the *relative* weights of atoms could be established. Water, for example, was known to be a compound of oxygen and hydrogen. Dalton's initial assumption was that a molecule of water contained one atom of each combining gas. When subjected to gravimetric analysis, however, the atoms seemed not of equal weight. As clearly as he could tell, seven parts *by weight* of oxygen combined with only one part *by weight* of hydrogen to form a molecule of water, implying that an atom of oxygen is seven times as heavy as an atom of hydrogen.

Dalton's quantitative analysis to find the weights of atoms was more than a beginning, for, in assuming that a compound would be composed of only one atom of each component element, he reveals to us that age's faith in the simplicity and logic of the universe. Even when he recognized that some gaseous compounds contained more than two atoms, he reasoned that the proportions would be simple: 1 to 1, 1 to 2, 1 to 3, 2 to 3, and so

15. W. P. D. Wightman, *The Growth of Scientific Ideas* (New Haven, Yale University Press, 1951), p. 232.

forth. Thus, in his notation, he represented water as HO, olefin gas as HC; but marsh gas, which seemingly contained more hydrogen, he formulized as H^2C. His formulas were not intended to reveal the relative weights of the atoms. In 1813, Jöns Jacob Berzelius (1779–1848), a Swede, simplified the system of chemical notation: his symbols had the further advantage of making it possible to show the relative weights of elements, essentially the system still used today.

Shortly after Dalton's findings were published, the French experimentalist, Joseph Gay-Lussac (1778–1850), established relationships of atoms by volume rather than weight. He found that gases combine with each other in very simple ratios—by volume, thus lending support to Dalton's assumption that all atomic relationships are numerically simple. It fell to the Italian Amedeo Avogadro (1776–1856), however, to develop Gay-Lussac's work. Avogadro's law (1811) informs us that equal volumes contain an equal number of "molecules," whatever the gas. Dalton, among others, refused to recognize these continental additions and refinements of atomic theory, leaving the world of chemistry in confusion for nearly fifty years. The issues were further confused by Avogadro's use of the word "molecule" when he sometimes meant atom.

The English physician William Prout (1785–1850) remains an interesting example of the rationalist mind at work. In 1815, he published his view that hydrogen is the basis of all matter. The chemical information available suggested to him that the atomic weights of the elementary gases were even multiples of the atomic weights of hydrogen. He started a controversy that occupied chemists for the rest of the century; but though he was ultimately thought to be wrong, the hypothesis is another example of the rationalist's temptation to believe in the simplicity of the universe.

Another Englishman, Humphry Davy (1778–1829), held that chemical and electrical attraction are fundamentally identical, and he thought that substances which had previously resisted attempts to split them might be decomposed by passing powerful electric currents through them. The electric battery had been available to chemists only since 1800, when the Italian Alessandro Volta (1745–1827) had demonstrated it. In 1807, Davy experimented on fused caustic soda and on potash, and the electric currents passed through them did indeed cause them to be decomposed.

When we turn to astronomy and mathematics in this period, we find implications which cast some doubt on the universe as a perfect mechanism. Take the career in France of Pierre Simon Laplace (1749–1827), who was a rationalist, for the most part, and worked in many mathematical realms. He contributed an important essay on probability (1814), and it is hard to imagine a more telling revelation of rational mind than its conviction that even probability—or chance—is a law and, thus, subject to mathematical description. Here is the first of his seven principles laid down to establish a calculus of probabilities:

The theory of chance consists in reducing all the events of the same kind to a certain number of cases equally possible, that is to say, to such as we may be equally undecided about in regard to their existence, and in determining the number of cases favorable to the event whose probability is sought. The ratio of this number to that of all the cases possible is the measure of this probability, which is thus simply a fraction whose numerator is the number of favorable cases and whose denominator is the number of all the cases possible.[16]

Furthermore, Laplace spent many years working on the perturbation problem (the irregularity in the orbits of heavenly bodies) in order to confirm Newton on gravity—the very principle which had been the foundation of the rationalist view of the universe. Newton's law was an expression of the relationship of *two* mutually attracting bodies. As the universe will presumably always contain more than two bodies, and as some irregularity in the presumed orbits of the planets had been observed, it was inevitable that the validity of Newton's law should have been questioned. Laplace studied the movements of three bodies and demonstrated that the discrepancies in their movements could be accounted for by Newton's law. The five volumes of his *Mecanique celeste* appeared between 1799 and 1814.

But Laplace's name has always been associated with the nebular hypothesis, and this hypothesis is "evolutionary" rather than "mechanistic" in its implications. In the best Fontenelle manner, Laplace presented the hypothesis in a delightfully written popular work on astronomy: *Exposition du système du monde*. The crux of the hypothesis, which had been held by Kant as early as 1755, derived from the observation that the planets are notably similar in their motion, in the motion of their satellites, and in the direction of their paths. Assuming that these similarities were not accidental, Laplace believed they suggested a common origin. In brief, the hypothesis proposed that the solar system *evolved* from a rotating mass of gaseous matter (or nebula), which condensed to form the sun. Then the sun threw off a series of gaseous rings which became

16. James R. Newman, *The World of Mathematics* (New York, Simon & Schuster, 1956), Vol. II, p. 1327.

the planets, which, in turn, while still in a gaseous state, threw off rings which became the satellites. This hypothesis remains a hypothesis today, and the origin and nature of the universe remains one of our greatest intellectual challenges.

Another great mathematician of that day also gave some of his time to astronomy: Carl Friedrich Gauss (1777-1855), a German. Gauss has been called one of the three greatest mathematicians of all time, the others being Archimedes and Newton. While still a student at the University of Göttingen, the nineteen-year-old Gauss was the first to prove the law of quadratic reciprocity. At Göttingen, too, he began to work on the theory of numbers, completing his *Disquisitiones Arithmeticae* (Arithmetical Researches) in 1798; the work, which was somewhat revised before publication in 1801, was his first masterpiece and possibly his greatest. But in that year, the discovery of Ceres, first of the minor planets, by the Italian Giuseppe Piazzi (1746–1826), set Gauss off on an astronomical track. The new planet was difficult to observe, and Gauss determined to compute its orbit. His success, using Newton's law of gravity, was further verification of Newton's law.

Yet, when we have surveyed the Napoleonic age, we are struck by its apparent inconsistencies. Not only are we forced to deal with the coexistence of romanticism and classicism, or the conflicting views of the nature of the universe; but we are confronted by an age of titans, by men of extraordinary ability and energy: Napoleon, Pitt, Gauss, Laplace, Dalton, Beethoven, and Goethe, who lived in a world of increasing disenchantment. The Revolution had failed to produce a rational society, and the faith in human reason, which had illuminated so much of the eighteenth century, shone far less brightly. Here is Alfred de Musset (1810–1857), poet and novelist, who tells us that he was stricken in the flower of his youth by an appalling *moral sickness:*

If I alone had been sick, I would say nothing; but as there were many others besides me who suffered the same disease, I write for them without knowing whether they will pay any attention. But in case no one pays any heed, I shall still benefit from my words, being better healed myself. Like the fox in a trap, I shall have gnawed away my captive foot.[17]

As the disease was *uncertainty,* there did not seem a certain answer to

17. Alfred de Musset, *Confession d'un enfant du siècle* (Paris, 1866), p. 2. My translation.

the dilemma of Musset's generation. As Madame de Staël (1776–1817) put it:

I do not clearly know what one must believe; but I know that one must believe. The eighteenth century has only denied. The human spirit lives on belief. Either find certainty through Christianity, through German philosophy, or simply through enthusiasm; but believe something.[18]

18. Emile Faquet, *Politiques et Moralistes du Dix-Neuvième Siècle* (Paris, 1898), Vol. II, p. 232. My translation.

SUGGESTIONS FOR FURTHER READING

Political and Military History

Crane Brinton, *A Decade of Revolution, 1789-1799* (New York and London: Harper, 1934), excellent for the Directory.

Geoffrey Bruun, *Europe and the French Imperium, 1799-1814* (New York and London: Harper, 1938), remains the best single volume covering this period.

E. F. Heckscher, *The Continental System, An Economic Interpretation* (Oxford University Press, 1922).

R. B. Mowat, *The Diplomacy of Napoleon* (London: E. Arnold, 1924).

Sir Charles Oman, *Studies in Napoleonic Wars* (London: Methuen and Co., 1929).

Alfred T. Mahan, *The Influence of Sea Power Upon the French Revolution and Empire, 1793-1812*, 2 vols. (Boston: Little, Brown, 10th ed., 1898), a well-known classic.

F. M. Kircheisen, *Napoleon* (New York: Harcourt, Brace, 1932), rated by some as the best single volume on the subject.

Albert Guerard, *Napoleon I* (New York: Alfred A. Knopf, 1956), brief but crisp, witty, and altogether delightful.

*Warren B. Walsh, *Russia and the Soviet Union, A Modern History* (University of Michigan Press, 1958), contains good material on Napoleon's continental enemy.

Philip Anthony Brown, *The French Revolution in English History* (London: Lockwood and Son, 1918).

W. O. Shanahan, *Prussian Military Reforms 1786-1813* (Columbia University Press, 1945).

Cultural History

Crane Brinton, *Political Ideas of the English Romanticists* (Oxford University Press, 1926).

G. P. Gooch, *Germany and the French Revolution* (London and New York: Longmans, Green, 1920).

Robert Ergang, *Herder and the Foundations of German Nationalism* (New York: Columbia University Press, 1931).

Albert Guerard, *Reflections on the Napoleonic Legend* (New York: Charles Scribner's Sons, 1924).

Alexander Gillies, *Goethe's Faust: An Interpretation* (Oxford: Basil Blackwell, 1957).

*Stephen Spender, ed., *Great Writings of Goethe* (New York: Mentor, 1958).

Jacques Barzun, *Romanticism and the Modern Ego* (Boston: Little, Brown, 1943).

History of Science

W. T. Sedgwick and H. W. Taylor, *A Short History of Science* (New York: Macmillan, 1919).

William P. D. Wightman, *The Growth of Scientific Ideas* (Yale University Press, 1951).

E. T. Bell, *Men of Mathematics* (New York: Simon and Schuster, 1937).

*James R. Newman, *The World of Mathematics,* 4 vols. (New York: Simon and Schuster, 1956).

* Available in paperbound editions.

❧ 9 ❧

Restoration and Reaction:
1814–1830

THE CONGRESS OF VIENNA; THE HUNDRED DAYS;
THE TREATIES OF PARIS

The general peace settlement of 1813–1815 has been rightly called a conservative settlement. Talleyrand, who had betrayed Napoleon and plotted for the restoration of the Bourbons in France, had necessarily argued that the peacemakers should be guided by the principle of legitimacy. He meant that the "legitimate" dynasties—the traditional ruling families—should be restored to their thrones wherever they had been unseated by the Revolution or by conquest. As Talleyrand knew, his proposal had great appeal to the victorious statesmen whose task it was to insure the future peace of Europe. They all represented "legitimate" monarchies; they were all bent on preventing the resurgence of the Revolution; and, finally, the alternative would have been to admit the right of each nationality to determine its future. Excepting Britain, where the sovereignty was regarded as vested in the crown *and* in Parliament, the victorious powers regarded sovereignty the property of the crown, and there was no admission that the people—the nation—shared the sovereignty. Indeed, the liberal notion that "we, the people" are sovereign was one of those dangerous ideas of the eighteenth century which had been used to justify and inspire the revolutionaries of that age. Legitimacy it had to be, to avoid any compromise with revolutionary ideals.

305

In their concern to make the restored Bourbon monarch acceptable to the French, the Allies designed an incredibly soft peace for France: no indemnity, no loss of territory, and no army of occupation. She was simply reduced to her prewar boundaries, those of 1792.[1] Secondly, Louis XVIII (*1814–1824*), brother of Louis XVI, was empowered by the allies to grant the French a constitution; it was recognized by both the King and the allies that a nation that had gone through the liberalizing period of the Revolution would not readily consent to a flat return to the old regime of 1789.

An examination of the Constitutional Charter of June 4, 1814, will reveal that Louis XVIII sought a compromise between the old and the new, between the rights of the crown and the rights of the people. As a result, the charter was not always clear and contained contradictions. Here is an example:

17. Proposed legislation is submitted, at the choice of the King, either to the Chamber of Peers or to the Chamber of Deputies, with the exception of tax laws, which must be submitted to the Chamber of Deputies.

18. Every law must be discussed and passed freely by a majority of both houses.

But Article 14, in discussing the powers of the king, included the following sentence: "He issues the regulations and decrees necessary for the execution of the laws and the safety of the State." The question would soon arise as to how much latitude the monarch had to issue decrees in a parliamentary monarchy, and the constitution was plainly ambiguous.

The compromise inherent in the new constitution could be found in its first article: "Frenchmen are equal before the law, whatever their titles or ranks." Moreover, while aristocrats might retain their titles, the constitution also assured those who had purchased confiscated properties during the Revolution that their rights would be honored. Freedom of religion was guaranteed, yet the Catholic religion was declared to be the "religion of the State." The highly centralized system of local administration, the legal codes, and the educational system of the Napoleonic period were retained, but conscription for the armed forces was abolished. It was, in short, a settlement designed to please everybody, and could therefore hardly avoid displeasing everybody.[2]

---

1. First Treaty of Paris, May 30, 1814.
2. Louis L. Snyder, ed., *Fifty Major Documents of the Nineteenth Century* (Princeton, N.J., Princeton University Press, 1955), pp. 32-34.

①The Constitutional Charter and the First Treaty of Paris pertained to France alone; a far more complex problem②concerned the disposition of the great empire won by the French. Chancellor Metternich, in charge of Austrian foreign affairs since 1809, invited the representatives of the powers to meet in Vienna to tackle the problem, and there they convened in the fall of 1814. All at great expense to impoverished Austria, it may be noted, but Metternich was convinced that an "Austrian peace," a conservative peace, must be obtained whatever the cost. Of all the major peace conferences since that of Westphalia in 1648, the Congress of Vienna is remembered for its lavish entertainments and the brilliance of the delegations. Yet, the major decisions were never made by the representatives sitting together, but by the chief delegates of the four great powers: Metternich for Austria; Alexander I for Russia; Robert Stewart, Viscount Castlereagh for Britain; and Karl August von Hardenberg for Prussia.

Of the "Big Four" only Britain had no territory at stake on the Continent. Yet, she was greatly concerned about the disposition of continental territory, holding the belief that the key to peace lay in maintaining a balance of power in Europe. We must remember that French military power had not been destroyed in 1814, so that there were still four significant military powers on the continent: Russia, Prussia, Austria, and France. The British assumption was that on most critical issues these powers would line up two against two, in which case the uncertainty of victory would discourage the powers from seeking a solution in war. Moreover, in the event that such a balance of two against two were threatened by a growing strength or an evident weakness on either side of the fulcrum, the British could support the weaker alliance in order to restore the balance. From this point of view it was clearly important that no single power emerge from the Congress of Vienna sufficiently powerful to upset the balance of power. This question became relevant as soon as the "Big Four" turned to the problem of Poland.

Poland had been partitioned during the eighteenth century by Russia, Prussia, and Austria. Napoleon had begun Poland's reconstruction when he established the Grand Duchy of Warsaw (1806) under the King of Saxony—out of Prussia's share of Poland. The Grand Duchy had then been augmented in 1809 at the expense of Austria. Now, in 1814, Alexander I asked that all of Poland be given to Russia as compensation for her military efforts, and he carefully arranged in advance that Prussia would back his demand. Instead of their former Polish territories, Prussia would receive Saxony and Austria would be compensated elsewhere in Europe.

EUROPE
1815

AFTER THE CONGRESS OF VIENNA

But Britain and Austria resisted Alexander's demand, because they recognized that the disposition of Polish territory was not merely a matter of shuffling provinces in the hope of compensating all the allies equally; the balance of power on the Continent was at stake.

The reason partly goes back to Russia's expansion toward the eastern Mediterranean at the expense of the Turks in the previous century. In other words, Russian aggrandizement must be curbed. Secondly, the only place where Prussia could be compensated for the loss of Polish territory would be in the German world, and here, again dating from the eighteenth century, Austria and Prussia were anxious rivals. The prospect of a Russo-Prussian bloc, supporting each other's interests, was a bleak possibility for the Austrians to face. Rather than give in to the Russo-Prussian proposals, Britain and Austria sought the support of Talleyrand, the new French foreign minister, early in 1815. There was, for a moment, a distinct threat of war, until the Russians and Prussians thought better of a conflict in which France would have major allies; and, of course, the French were happy to be summoned to break the deadlock, because it ended their brief exclusion from the deliberations of the great powers.

Without doubt, the bickering at the Congress of Vienna encouraged Napoleon to recover his throne, but he also knew that in the ten months that had passed since his exile to Elba, the Bourbon monarchy had aroused considerable opposition in France. His sudden landing at Cannes on March 1, 1815, brought the allies back together as they gathered their forces to deal with him again. Louis XVIII fled northward when the French army revealed its preference for Napoleon, but the more responsible elements in the population had little enthusiasm for a renewal of war against all Europe. Recognizing this, Napoleon sought the support of the urban masses by posing as the defender of the revolutionary ideals. In June, he struck north into the Lowlands, where the British and Prussians were bringing up forces. The Prussians were defeated initially, and with every confidence Napoleon turned on Wellington's British troops at Waterloo. Here, on June 18, the French and British fought indecisively all day until the unexpected arrival of the Prussians, who had been inadequately covered by a French pursuing force. They turned the battle into a French disaster. Napoleon fled, abdicated for the second time four days later, and then put himself into the hands of a British admiral. This time the Allies caged him on the remote island of St. Helena, where he died in 1821.

The revival of Allied cooperation during the so-called "Hundred Days" of Napoleon's return from Elba enabled the great powers to complete the treaty of Vienna (June 9, 1815). Most of Poland went to Russia after all, the Prussians and Austrians receiving out of their earlier Polish holdings only the provinces of Posen and Galicia respectively. As compensation, Prussia received the northern half of Saxony, the city of Danzig, and an enlargement of her territories in Westphalia; while Austria was given the provinces of Lombardy, Venetia, Illyria, and Dalmatia, the Tyrol, and the city of Salzburg. It should be noted that, in this shuffling of frontiers, the Prussians lost Slavic population but gained in German population. Austria traded Slavs for more Slavs and Italians.

If at first it appears that Austria received much more than Prussia, it must be immediately noted that the Austrians agreed to abandon the southern Netherlands which they had governed since the treaty of Utrecht. Austrian rule there, as we saw earlier, had never been popular and had proved a headache for Vienna; worse, the Austrians had proved an insufficient barrier to French expansion into the Lowlands, which had been the pretext in 1713 for the Austrians, rather than the Dutch, taking over the southern Netherlands. Thus, in 1815, the two Netherlands (Belgium and the Dutch Republic) were united as the Kingdom of the Netherlands, and the former Dutch stadtholder became the first king: William I (*1815–1844*) of the House of Orange.

Napoleon's Confederation of the Rhine necessarily had to be scrapped, but the powers could agree neither on a United Germany nor on a revived Holy Roman Empire to replace it. In the end, they created a new confederation, to be called the Germanic Confederation, comprising 39 sovereign states—including Austria and Prussia. This compromise left the form of German unity without its substance, for the member states retained their sovereignty. The delegates that they were to send to the federal Diet at Frankfurt were actually ambassadors only, and the Diet had no effective power. Austria, granted the permanent presidency of the Diet, hoped to use that body to check the growth of German nationalism and to block Prussian ambitions in the German world.

In northern Europe, Denmark was punished for her alliance with Napoleon by the loss of Norway, which went to Sweden as compensation for Finland, earlier lost to Russia. Britain took no compensation in continental territory, but she regarded the restoration of the continental balance of power as a major achievement. As for overseas territories, there she was in an enviable bargaining position, for her navy had captured most of the colonies belonging to France, Spain, and Holland. Most of them were returned in 1815, enabling Britain to take a choice of colonies which seemed especially important for commercial advantage. France gave up Mauritius, Tobago, and St. Lucia; Spain gave up Trinidad; while the Dutch parted with Ceylon and agreed to sell the Cape Colony to the British. In European waters, Heligoland and Malta were retained by Britain, who was also given a protectorate over the Ionian Islands. Finally, Britain secured an agreement that the slave trade would be abolished; this provision was a victory for the British humanitarians.

In Spain and Italy, the "legitimate" governments were restored, except in the provinces of Lombardy and Venetia, which were annexed by Austria. The Bourbon Ferdinand VII (*1814–1833*) was returned to Madrid, the Bourbon Ferdinand I (*1759–1825*) was restored to Naples, and Pius VII (*1799–1823*) came back to the Papal States. To the north, Victor Emmanuel I (*1802–1821*) of the House of Savoy was restored in Sardinia-Piedmont, and in the three small states of Modena, Parma, and Tuscany, the rulers were Austrian-sponsored candidates who could be counted on to support an Austrian, rather than an "Italian," policy. Thus, the momentary unity in Italy under the French had vanished, and the newly awakened "national" ambitions of the Italians were totally ignored by the statesmen at Vienna.

The final defeat of Napoleon coming shortly after the completion of the Vienna settlement, the powers turned for a second time to a settlement with France: The Second Treaty of Paris (November 20, 1815). Understandably, the terms were harsher than those that had been granted the previous year, Prussia even proposing the partition of France; but the majority of the powers preferred to penalize France in a mild manner, so as not to jeopardize further the possibility of stable government under Louis XVIII. France was reduced from her frontiers of 1792 to those of 1790, which meant the cession of a few small fortified districts to Prussia, the Netherlands, and the Germanic Confederation; and a slice of Savoy, retained in 1814, was now returned to Sardinia-Piedmont. More serious was the decision of the allies to charge France a war indemnity of 700,000,000 francs, and to garrison Allied troops in northeastern France —at French expense—for five years.

Napoleon's return from Elba in 1814 had shown the Allies the peril of bickering among themselves and led them to underscore the treaties of 1815 with an alliance designed to keep the peace, the Quadruple Alliance (Britain, Austria, Russia, and Prussia), which was signed the same day as the Second Treaty of Paris. Article VI of the alliance treaty deserves special attention, because it provided for future concerted action by the allies:

ART. VI. To facilitate and to secure the execution of the present treaty, and to consolidate the connections which at the present moment so closely unite the four sovereigns for the happiness of the world; the high contracting parties have agreed to renew their meetings at fixed periods, either under the immediate auspices of the sovereigns themselves, or by their respective ministers, for the purpose of consulting upon their common interests, and for the consideration of the measures which at each of those periods shall be considered the most salutary for the repose and prosperity of nations, and for the maintenance of the peace of Europe.[3]

Accordingly, the great powers did convene periodically after 1815, when issues arose disturbing to the general peace, but they did not meet regularly or systematically in the manner of the United Nations today, nor were the lesser states of Europe invited to join the discussions. Lord Castlereagh was largely responsible for this scheme to maintain the peace through international conference, which has been labeled the Concert of Europe.

In the background was the better-known, but less significant, Holy Alliance, also dating from the autumn of 1815. Proposed by Alexander I of Russia as a basis for international cooperation, the Holy Alliance was not so much a treaty as a statement of principles. As such, it reveals the reactionary intentions of the three powers—Russia, Prussia, and Austria —who initially signed it; but the Holy Alliance did not provide for the Concert of Europe. Rather than stressing specific political aims and tactics, the wording of the text suggests the religious revival of this era, to which the Czar had become the most notable convert. He hoped that the monarchs would regard each other as Christian "brothers" and their subjects as "families." Moreover,

They thus confess that the Christian nation, of which they and their people form a part, has in reality no other sovereign than He alone to whom belongs by right the power, for in Him alone are to be found all the treasures of love, of knowledge and of infinite wisdom, that is to say God, our Divine Saviour Jesus Christ, the word of the Most High, the word of life.[4]

Most of the other powers ultimately adhered to these principles too, but

3. E. Hertslet, *The Map of Europe by Treaty* (London, 1875), Vol. I, p. 377.
4. The Holy Alliance, November, 1815, in Leon Bernard and Theodore H. Hodges, *Readings in European History* (New York, Macmillan, 1958), pp. 364-365.

not Britain, where the sense of practical politics was too well developed to accept what Castlereagh called "a sublime piece of mysticism and nonsense" as an instrument of government.

THE AFTERMATH:
POLITICAL REACTION AND RELIGIOUS REVIVAL

The 1815 settlement leads us to conclude that the peacemakers hoped that Europe could pick up the threads of life as of 1789 and proceed as if the French Revolution had never occurred. This attempt to go backward in time by restoring the old regimes was a fair measure of how remote from reality were many of the statesmen of 1815. One exception was Britain, which had succumbed neither to the Revolution nor to Napoleonic occupation, and where no restoration was necessary. But even in Britain the Revolution had exerted an influence—though a less direct one than on the Continent—in that the reform movement of the late eighteenth century had been stifled as a reaction against Jacobinism.

Life, in fact, was much different in 1815 than it had been before the Revolution, not only in France, but also in much of Europe. It was not so much that the Revolution was the cause of the changes as that the Revolution was *caused* by the changing conditions and ideas in the eighteenth century. Thus, to go back to the political forms of 1789 was to go back to the forms which had shown themselves unadaptable to the social, economic, and intellectual pressures of that age. "Liberty, Equality, Fraternity" may not have been perfectly practiced by the proponents of the Revolution, but the widespread enthusiasm for those ideals indicates the general readiness for major changes—for which the *philosophes* and inventors had prepared the way.

Monarchs and aristocrats, time-honored rivals, drew close after 1815 in defense of an old order of things which they sensed to be in great peril; and they were joined by the Church, which was anxious to repulse those threatening ideas loosely spoken of as "Voltairian." The facts of national life were brazenly published by a social critic in 1819:

Let us suppose that France suddenly loses fifty of her eminent physicians, fifty leading bankers, two hundred of her best merchants, six hundred of her leading planters, five hundred of her skilled ironmasters, [and so on]. . . . Since these men are her indispensable producers, the moment she loses them the nation will degenerate into a lifeless body.

Now let us suppose that France retains her men of genius but, at a given moment, has the misfortune to lose the King, the King's brother, the Duc d'Angoulême, the Duc de Berry [he lists the members of the royal family], all the high royal officials, the councillors of state, the marshals, the cardinals, archbishops, bishops, grand vicars, canons, the prefects and subprefects, the bureaucrats and magistrates, and in addition, ten thousand of the landed proprietors who live as nobles.

Such a loss would certainly sadden the French, who are a kindly-disposed people who would not look indifferently upon the sudden disappearance of so many compatriots. But this loss . . . would arouse only sentimental grief, for it would not cause the nation the least inconvenience.[5]

Since the political order of 1815 was an anachronism, it would be logical to assume that reforming sentiments would soon recover from the setback given liberalism by the excesses of the Revolution. For the moment, however, reaction had its day, with most European governments dedicated to the *status quo* and to the ruthless destruction of liberalism. A major exception was Louis XVIII of France, whose Constitutional Charter of 1814, issued with the blessing of the victorious allies, was granted to the nation in the honest and intelligent recognition that there could be no going back to the regime of Louis XVI. In contrast—and more typical of the era—was Ferdinand VII of Spain. Having initially promised to support the democratic constitution of 1812, he soon was embarked upon a vicious persecution of liberals, with every intention of re-establishing royal absolutism. And when we find, as in Naples, that intellectuals were regarded as dangerous, that such things as street lighting and vaccination were declared revolutionary because they had been introduced by the French, we see reaction pushed to the point of idiocy. In Britain, the coming of peace quickly lowered the price of food as the agricultural output of the Continent was again available. Parliament, whose unreformed constituencies still largely represented the agrarian interests, responded with a protective tariff: the Corn Law of 1815. The consequent rise in food prices not only angered the workers, but also annoyed industrial employers, who were forced to pay higher wages to keep their workers alive. Rioting and agitation were met head-on by the conservative government: rioters found themselves liable to the charge of treason, public meetings were generally prohibited, and periodicals were taxed to limit their distribution.

5. The so-called Parable of Henri de Saint-Simon, published originally by him in *L'Organisateur* (Paris, 1819). My translation.

A notable feature of reaction in Russia was the decision, in 1816, to create military colonies in some of the peripheral areas of the empire. The population in a district to be colonized was not removed but was simply incorporated into the regiment assigned to that district. Alexander's scheme seems to have been an attempt to keep his regiments intact and disciplined while returning them to peacetime family life and employment in agriculture, thus reducing the military expenditure of the crown. Under the administration of General Alexis Arakcheev (1769–1834), the colonies numbered nearly 400,000 soldiers by the end of Alexander's reign. It is probable that the Czar expected that conditions of peasant life would improve under strict government supervision, but the opposite was true. Arakcheev was a martinet and was soon bitterly hated for an administration which combined "the worst features of both serfdom and army barracks."[6] The system also proved seriously uneconomical.

The continental aristocrats, taken as a group after 1815, demonstrated the same hatred of the immediate past and fear of the immediate future as the royal governments of the period. No longer do we find them the frivolous, witty, confident, bold gentlemen of the eighteenth century. (Let us note that the Prussian Junkers had always been a serious lot!) Their new seriousness was not a new-found sense of their obligations as a class, but rather a loss of nerve, an uncertainty as to whether they had a future as a class. They showed a remarkable inclination to enter the religious societies for laymen created by the Church after 1815. If anything, organized Christianity had suffered even more than the aristocrats from the revolutionary upheaval, for behind the Revolution lay a century of intellectual criticism of the Church. Yet, the Church—and Christianity in general—rebounded much more strongly than the aristocrats, and in its opposition to rationalism and the Revolution, the Church was a ready ally to the restoration governments.

It was also true that Pius VII, having long suffered at the hands of Napoleonic secular power, emerged in 1814 as a determined champion of ultramontanism—that is, he favored papal supremacy in doctrinal matters. And ultramontanism was irritating to some of the strong sovereign states, France and Austria in particular, where the national Churches had long enjoyed a measure of independence from Roman jurisdiction, and where, as in the case of France, the state had achieved a sufficient degree of control over the clergy to regard them as civil servants. Thus, the alli-

6. Michael T. Florinsky, *Russia: A History and An Interpretation* (New York: 1955), p. 720.

ances between the Church and the restoration governments, though marriages of convenience, were not without their inconveniences.

Furthermore, making the religious settlement a matter of "convenience" offended the genuine piety of many Catholics, and we have to recall that this was a period of religious revival. Napoleon's arrangement with the Church in 1801, avowedly political rather than religious in intent, seemed a more honest settlement than the cynical piety of many of Louis XVIII's ministers: skeptical politicians who saw the Church as a bulwark against revolution, who paid lip service to the Church, and against whom the genuinely religious fought. For many of the faithful, then, the vigor and purity of the faith could only be preserved by eliminating secular control of religion and clergy, and they threw their support behind the ultramontanism of Pius VII. In 1814 the Savoyard Count Joseph de Maistre (1753–1821) wrote in a letter:

> Never forget this chain of reasoning: No public morality nor national character without religion, no European religion without Christianity, no Christianity without Catholicism, no Catholicism without the Pope, no Pope without the supremacy which belongs to him.[7]

The Abbé Felicité de La Mennais (1782–1854) even more pointedly challenged the independence of the French bishops, by advocating the doctrinal infallibility of the Pope. His insistence that the primary obligation of secular government is to protect and serve religion was regarded as extreme by even the governments of Catholic states.

> Without the Pope, no Church; without the Church, no Christianity; without Christianity, no religion and no society; so that the life of the European nations has its source—its only source—in pontifical power.[8]

The confusion of secular and spiritual issues was deepened by the inevitable demand that the Church recover properties confiscated during the revolutionary era; and just as inevitably, the issue was most sharply focused in France where the confiscation had been most drastic. As noted before, the Constitutional Charter of 1814 had guaranteed the property rights of those who had purchased the confiscated properties from the state, but a clerical-aristocratic coalition known as the Ultras (Extremists) set out to defeat the intentions of Louis XVIII's moderate monarchy. Not

---

7. Quoted in Adrien Dansette, *Histoire religieuse de la France contemporaine* (Paris, 1951), Vol. I, p. 295. My translation.
8. Quoted in *Ibid.*, Vol. I, pp. 294-295. My translation.

only did they demand the return of properties, but asked that the Napoleonic public school system—the Université de France—be abolished and education be given to the Church as a monopoly. Such extreme demands so alarmed the middle class that its recent fear of liberalism began to pale, and for a time the Ultra program lost ground.

Another measure of the clerical revival and ultramontanism was the papal decision to revive the Jesuits, whose order had been abolished in the eighteenth century; and many of the religious societies for laymen, which brought them into work formerly reserved for the clergy, were Jesuit-inspired. The societies were designed, not so much to back the clergy, as to meet the social and political conditions of the day. It is not surprising, then, to find these societies—often called congregations—engaging in political activity on behalf of the faith.[9] In Spain, the Society of the Exterminating Angel devoted itself to the destruction of liberalism; in the Papal States, the San Fedists worked against those Italian liberals who sought a united, free Italy; while in France, one of the societies was the Congregation of the Virgin, of which the Comte d'Artois, the head of the Ultras and the King's brother, was a leading member.[10]

The religious reaction in Britain was somewhat more complicated. Anglican bishops, sitting in the House of Lords, opposed both Catholic emancipation and all measures to reform the constituencies of the lower house. Yet, within the Church, we find a group known as Evangelicals who resembled the Methodists in that they hoped to promote religion among the poorer classes. The Evangelicals were also crusaders against slavery outside Britain and advocated missionary work abroad as well as at home. Those Evangelicals in politics—William Wilberforce (1759–1833) was one—were known as the Clapham Sect. They found themselves in an ambiguous position: they were humanitarian without doubt, but, like the Methodists, they suspected liberalism to be tainted by the irreligion of the French Revolution. Consequently, they refused cooperation with some of the nonevangelical reformers of that day and were open to the charge that they were indifferent to abuses in Britain and concerned for foreign evils alone. Actually, they did favor the reform of Parliament.

The greatest literary figure of the Christian revival on the continent was René de Chateaubriand, whose earlier-noted conversion came during

9. See G. de Bertier de Sauvigny, *La Restauration* (Paris, 1955), p. 426.
10. See F. B. Artz, *Reaction and Revolution, 1814-1832* (New York, Harper, 1934), pp. 12-16.

the Napoleonic era. His Christianity was a religion of the heart, highly emotional and sentimental. An avowed ultramontane and a royalist, he was, in fact, more liberal in his political views than this avowal suggested. An erratic person without political experience, he avoided a cabinet post under Louis XVIII, who made him a peer instead. In 1816, the King suddenly dissolved the lower house and called for new elections, in the expectation that the Ultras would lose strength to the more moderate middle-class liberals with whom he could work; Chateaubriand took the occasion to publish a pamphlet on constitutional monarchy. Both actions had unfortunate results: profiting from the imprecision of the Constitution, the government juggled the electoral regulations to assist in the election of a favorable Chamber; and though this demarche was successful, it set an unhappy precedent for the future of the parliamentary government. As for Chateaubriand personally, his *Monarchy According to the Charter* proved too liberal for the royal taste, and he fell from favor. His main point was that the cabinet, being responsible to parliament, should be responsible for policy; therefore, the king, while having a veto, should not be held responsible for policy and ought not interfere with parliamentary elections.[11]

THE REACTION AND PHILOSOPHY

In Chateaubriand, we see the convergence of many facets of romanticism. His Christianity was not only emotional, but he was sentimental over the aesthetic quality of the medieval Church and moved by the security which came from the Church's long tradition. Friedrich von Schlegel (1772–1829) in Germany was another excellent example of this romantic traditionalism. Beginning as an eighteenth-century rationalist and neoclassicist, Schlegel shed his past during the Revolution and ended as a convert to Catholicism. In his *Philosophy of History* (1829), he rejected the rationalist view of history in favor of the evolutionary, organic view. Like Chateaubriand, Schlegel was an ultramontane.

The pietism and mysticism of the eighteenth century remained in the nineteenth as another religious form of the reaction against reason, the difference being that the mystical prophets of the nineteenth century enjoyed greater acceptance. Most of them were visionaries who believed

11. M. D. R. Leys, *Between Two Empires* (London, 1955), pp. 82-83.

that they had received a divine mandate to save the world. One of the most celebrated was the Russian Baroness Julie von Krüdener (1764–1824). She met Alexander I in 1815, having already learned of his interest in mysticism, and she followed him to Paris after the collapse of the French Empire. The Holy Alliance was one clear sign of the Czar's religious preoccupation in those months.

The world-weariness, disenchantment, and loneliness of the romantics can be seen in the philosophy of the German Arthur Schopenhauer (1788–1860), who saw the world as inherently evil and who had little patience with Hegel's confidence in inevitable progress. Yet, both men may be counted within the ranks of the romantics. In the development of German philosophical thought, Schopenhauer represented something of a return to the ideas of Kant. Kant had recognized that every thesis generates its own antithesis and that such contradictions—especially those relating to the ultimate cause of things—are beyond solution by human reason. Hegel had tried to improve on Kant by suggesting that the thesis and antithesis are both imperfect statements of a higher expression of truth—the synthesis—which will contain elements of both the thesis and antithesis. Each synthesis automatically becomes a new thesis, so that the endless process proceeds. This was the crux of Hegel's dialectic: continual contradiction is the mechanism for change and makes possible our intellectual development in the search for truth. The theory is romantic in that it implies a struggle to find new truths, and optimistic in that the dialectic or method for reaching the truths was laid down.

Such optimism disgusted Schopenhauer, not only because he thought Kant much closer to the truth than Hegel, but also because the Prussian government found in Hegel's ideas the rationale for proving that the Prussian state was the last word in man's evolution toward the idea of freedom. Reality, for Schopenhauer, cannot be divorced from the knowledge we get sensually; in other words, we cannot know the world beyond the senses. And this real world he loathes; it is to be avoided at all cost. This is all the more difficult because he regarded as our basic drive our will to live—our will to live in the world of reality, thus in the world of misery.

If we compare life to a course which we must unceasingly run—a path of glowing coals, with a few cool places here and there; then he who is entangled in illusion is consoled by the cool places, on which he now stands or which he sees near him, and sets out to run the course. But he who sees through the illusion and thus recognizes the whole for what it is, is no longer capable of such consolation; he sees himself at all places at once, and withdraws.[12]

Schopenhauer's was a philosophy of despair. He advocates withdrawal from reality, surrender of this strong will to live, and the giving over of oneself to contemplation, in particular to the contemplation of art. He does not call this a "greater reality," nor does he advocate suicide. He states merely that the world is evil and that one must avoid it.[13]

THE CONCERT OF EUROPE IN ACTION

Beginning in 1818, the politics and philosophies of reaction were implemented by a series of international congresses designed to police the peace and order of Europe. Peacetime cooperation among the great powers had been deemed necessary in 1815 to hold both the French and revolution in check, but the peacetime cooperation turned out to be more tenuous than the allied wartime cooperation had been. The first meeting, the Congress of Aix-la-Chapelle (1818), was the most harmonious of all the congresses, and its issues were the least controversial. The powers convened at the request of the French, the latter's paid-up indemnity was declared settled, and the allied armies of occupation were withdrawn. To symbolize the return of France into the family of nations, a Quintuple Alliance was signed; but as a matter of safety, the allied powers also renewed the Quadruple Alliance of 1815.

The Germanic Confederation was the second instrument of political reaction. Since Austria had the permanent presidency of the Confederation, Metternich was in a position to throttle any German liberal challenge to the settlement of 1815. German patriots had hoped that the social and political reforms in Prussia after 1807, which had led to an impressive national revival, would be crowned in 1815 with genuine constitutional government. But under the influence of Metternich's agents, Frederick William III abandoned the constitutional project—to the great distress of German nationalists and liberals. German university students then formed societies to agitate for liberal reforms and the unification of Germany.

---

12. From *The World as Will and Idea* (1819), quoted in J. H. Randall, *Making of the Modern Mind,* p. 591.
13. Henry D. Aiken, *The Age of Ideology* (New York, Mentor, 1956), pp. 98-104.

Matters came to a head in 1819, when a mentally unstable student murdered a reactionary writer named August Friedrich Kotzebue, who was serving as an agent of Alexander I of Russia. Metternich pointed to this incident as a sign of dangerous political activity in the German universities and called together the representatives of the nine largest German states for a conference at Carlsbad. As he wrote a few months later:

> The first principle to be followed by the monarchs, united as they are by the coincidence of their desires and opinions, should be that of maintaining the stability of political institutions against the disorganized excitement which has taken possession of men's minds; the immutability of principles against the madness of their interpretation; and respect for laws actually in force against a desire for their destruction.[14]

Out of Carlsbad came proposals for repressive decrees, which were quickly ratified by the Germanic Diet at Frankfurt. Not only were the liberal societies outlawed, but the universities came under police surveillance and the press was censored to exterminate liberal opinion. The liberals were again disappointed to see the Prussian king in apparent agreement with Metternich.

Hardly had the German ferment been halted when Metternich found the *status quo* assailed from every side. On the first day of 1820, revolution flamed in Spain in answer to Ferdinand VII's vicious and capricious rule. Leadership of the revolt came from the army, which at that moment was being prepared by the King for an expedition to recover the Latin American colonies; these had claimed their independence from Spain while that country was under French occupation. Ferdinand made haste to restore the liberal Constitution of 1812, but remained a virtual prisoner of the army. A second shock came a few weeks later with the assassination of the Duc de Berri by a fanatic in France. Berri was the second son of the Comte d'Artois, leader of the Ultras, and was thus third in line for the throne. The Ultras chose to regard the murder as proof of revolutionary sentiments in France. Meanwhile, the success of the Spanish army encouraged liberals in the Neapolitan army to rise against the cruelties of Ferdinand I during the summer of 1820. He, too, speedily granted a constitution. Later in the summer, Portuguese liberals overthrew the regency which had been established in 1807 after the flight of the royal family to Brazil.

14. Memorandum to Alexander I from Metternich, December 15, 1820.

In response, the governments of Austria, Russia, and Prussia—the Holy Alliance powers—convened at Troppau in late 1820 to consider intervention, the monarchs attending in person. Britain and France only sent observers, being reluctant to give the Quintuple Alliance the right to intervene into the internal affairs of any nation. As Lord Castlereagh had put it:

> . . . Nothing would be more immoral or more prejudicial to the character of government generally than the idea that their force was collectively to be prostituted to the support of established power without any consideration of the extent to which it was abused.[15]

The decision to intervene into revolutionary situations deemed likely to jeopardize the European peace was announced by the three conservative powers alone, though the two western powers did not openly protest. At a second meeting, at Laibach (1821), Austria was given the mandate to restore Ferdinand I of Naples to his full powers. In the meantime, the revolutionary enthusiasm spread northward through Italy, and in Sardinia-Piedmont the liberals demanded that Victor Emmanuel I either take the lead in the Italian national movement or abdicate. Rather than risk war on behalf of the Italians or face the wrath of the liberals for refusing war against Austria, he gave up the throne to his brother, Charles Felix (*1821–1831*). The reaction in Italy was swift and brutal. In the wake of Austrian arms in Naples, Ferdinand I presided over a furious wave of imprisonment and execution. The Austrians themselves helped Charles Felix crush the uprising in Sardinia-Piedmont and struck hard at the liberals agitating in their own province of Lombardy.

The Spanish revolt was still untouched by the powers when the international scene was further complicated by a rising of the Greeks against the Ottoman Turks in 1821. Britain feared that Russia would profit from the strife to extend her influence into the eastern Mediterranean world unless the powers took up the question in concert. Such a fear was not unfounded in view of Russia's recent expansion at the expense of Turkey, and in this case Russian aggression could be disguised as solicitude for coreligionists. When the representatives of the five powers met at Verona (1822), Alexander I was reminded by Metternich that this was revolution. If revolution was insupportable in Naples, it was equally so in Athens:

> At the very moment when the rebels in Naples and Turin were retiring at

15. Memorandum to the British Government, October 19, 1818.

the approach of legitimate power, a rebellious firebrand was cast into the Ottoman Empire. The coincidence of the events leaves no doubt as to the similarity of their origin. The outbreak of the evil at so many different points, everywhere conducted in the same manner and using the same language, unmistakably betrays the common focus from whence they all issue.[16]

Thus nothing was done for the Greeks, and the representatives turned their attention to Spain.

None of the powers had any stomach for a Russian offer to send an army across Europe to liberate Ferdinand VII, and all save Britain were heartened by a French offer to perform the task. By surrounding the restoration of Ferdinand with as liberal an atmosphere as possible, Louis XVIII's government hoped to strengthen the cause of constitutional monarchy and revive the eighteenth-century cooperation between the two crowns. If the British were not alarmed by constitutional monarchy, they regarded the Bourbon family compact with horror and wanted no part in encouraging French military revival. Spain's lost Latin American empire was also at issue. Britain had developed important trade relations with the newly independent states, and this trade would presumably be severed if Spain's control were resumed. The betting was that Spain was too weak to recover her colonies; but with French military aid and the encouragement of the Holy Alliance Powers, the outcome might be different.

George Canning (1770–1827), long an opponent of concerted action, took over the direction of the British foreign office upon Castlereagh's suicide in 1822. He let the French know that the British fleet would block any attempt to intervene in Latin America, but his hope that the United States would join him in the warning was ill received by the American government. Both governments suspected each other's motives, since neither government had hastened to recognize the independence of the Latin American republics. Canning could not promise that George IV (1820–1830) and the Tories would recognize the republics, while America refrained from irritating Spain during the negotiations for the purchase of Florida. The tactics used to gain Florida and American reluctance to recognize Texas as part of Spanish Mexico left bare the expansionist ambitions of Secretary of State John Quincy Adams' foreign policy, so that he had good reason to suppose that Canning's proposal for a joint declaration had as an ulterior motive the blocking of American expansion in

16. From the Verona Circular (1822) issued by Austria, Russia, and Prussia.

Latin America. There was also room to suspect that Britain might replace Spain in Latin America. At any rate, the particular issue was settled by the French government's response to Canning in 1823, that France had no intention of aiding Spain in recovering her colonies.

The United States, however, did not drop the matter and went on to formulate a unilateral policy statement. Two years earlier, Alexander I had claimed the 51st parallel—well within the Oregon area—to be Alaska's southern border. In the American treaty of 1819 with Spain, the United States had assumed Spain's claims to the Oregon territory. The issue became more inflamed when the Russian minister to Washington tactlessly commented on the evils of republicanism (1823). President Monroe, therefore, favored a statement which would both check European colonization in the Americas and defend the principles of republicanism. His original draft contained a resounding support of Greek independence as a slap at the Quintuple Alliance Powers, but Adams struck that statement from the manuscript and denied the document much of its idealism.

The American continents, by the free and independent condition which they have assumed and maintained, are henceforth not to be considered as subjects for future colonization by any European powers.[17]

The President further stated that we had no interest in European affairs. However candid, the statement encompassed the paradox which has plagued American foreign policy ever since: the pretension of isolation at the very moment of American involvement into world affairs.

Many months before Monroe's pronouncement, a French force had invaded Spain, defeating the rebels by the late summer of 1823. French hopes that the restored Ferdinand VII would consolidate his throne by continuing constitutional government proved vain. Worse, he refused to honor his earlier promise to grant complete pardon to all revolutionaries, and the savage hunting down of liberals had no parallel in Europe—not even in Naples. Disdaining to be a constitutional monarch, Ferdinand had the backing of Austria, Russia, and Prussia. The French were in the embarrassing position of having restored such a monstrous government, while the British had broken with the alliance and remained aloof.

17. The Monroe Doctrine, in the message to Congress on December 2, 1823.

GREECE REBORN

Only in Greece did the liberal hope live on. Of the Christian population within the Ottoman Empire, the Greeks were pre-eminent. The superiority of their culture had forced the Turks to employ them as officials after the conquest of the Byzantine Empire, for the Turks were ill-equipped to govern their conquered territories. These bureaucratic families resided in the Phanariot quarter of Constantinople—the seat of the Patriarchate—and were called Phanariots. Their eminent positions in Turkish administration helped keep the national traditions alive, but also earned them the enmity of the other Balkan Christians. Their ancient instincts for business and trade also served the Greeks well, for the Turks traditionally disdained trade. Especially after the decline of the Italian cities, the commerce of the eastern Mediterranean world was dominated by Greeks, and during the eighteenth century, they built up trading stations outside the confines of the Ottoman Empire. Such bases soon became centers for anti-Turkish plotting. The successes of Catherine II against the Turks inclined the Greeks to look to Russia as the natural ally, and many sons of Phanariot families found employment in the Russian army and civil service. Finally, the liberal ideas of the French Revolution further inspired the Greeks to work for national liberty. Revolutionary committees were formed in the overseas trading stations; the most famous of these groups was the National Hetairia. Founded in 1814 at Odessa, it ultimately attracted nearly 200,000 members throughout the Greek world.

After 1815, the reasonable British rule in the Ionian Islands provided the Greeks with an example which was a far cry from Turkish justice. Moreover, it brought to Greece British travelers who soon associated themselves with Greek aspirations. The uprising began when a Phanariot Greek serving in the Russian Army, Alexander Ypsilanti (1792–1828), accepted the leadership of the National Hetairia. He crossed from Russia into Moldavia in the hope of sparking a general revolt against Turkish rule, but the antagonism of the Moldavians against the Greeks was too great. Worse, Metternich prevailed upon the Russian government to disavow any support for the movement. This came as a particular shock, since the Greeks had counted on Count John Capodistrias (1776–1831), a Phanariot and one of the Czar's principal ministers, to rally Russia against Turkey. When Ypsilanti's scheme failed, he fled northward into the Austrian empire, where he was confined by Metternich's order.

In the meantime, a general uprising took place in the Peloponnese, many small Turkish garrisons being overwhelmed. In retaliation, a Turkish mob massacred many Greeks in Constantinople and on Easter morning hanged the Patriarch Gregory V. The Turks had been caught off guard, however, and for several years the Greeks had the best of the fight. European enthusiasm for their cause spread to America in a movement known as Philhellenism. The educated classes were too steeped in the ancient classics not to be moved by the spectacle of Greeks opposing tyranny. Living as they did in a romantic age and unaware of the realities of Greek politics, they may be pardoned for thinking that they were sending help to Pericles.

> The world's great age begins anew,
>   The golden years return,
> The earth doth like a snake renew
>   Her winter weeds outword;
> Heaven smiles, and faiths and empires gleam,
> Like wrecks of a dissolving dream.
> A brighter Hellas rears its mountains
>   From waves serener far;
> A new Peneus rolls his fountains
>   Against the morning star.
> Where fairer Tempes bloom, there sleep
> Young Cyclads on a sunnier deep.
>   .   .   .
> Another Athens shall arise,
>   And no remoter time
> Bequeath, like sunset to the skies,
>   The splendor of its prime;
> And leave, if nought so bright may live,
> All earth can take or Heaven can give.[18]

By 1824, the balance began to swing against the Greeks. The Sultan Mahmoud II (*1808–1839*) not only gathered his forces to invade Greece from the northeast, but also engaged his vassal, Mehemet Ali, the Khedive of Egypt (1811–1848), for a sea-borne invasion of the Peloponnese. Western excitement was heightened by the death of Lord Byron that year, for though he died of a fever at Missolonghi before he had become much

18. Percy Bysshe Shelley, *Hellas* (1821), ll. 1059-1071, 1084-1089.

involved on the side of the Greeks, the popular poet's "martyrdom" for the noble—and failing—cause proved irresistible.

> The sword, the banner, and the field,
>   Glory and Greece, around me see!
> The Spartan, borne upon his shield,
>   Was not more free.
>
> Awake! (not Greece—she *is* awake!)
>   Awake, my spirit! Think through *whom*
> Thy life-blood tracks its parent lake,
>   And then strike home!
>
> Tread those reviving passions down,
>   Unworthy manhood!—unto thee
> Indifferent should the smile or frown
>   Of beauty be.
>
> If thou regrett'st thy youth, *why live?*
>   The land of honorable death
> Is here—up to the field, and give
>   Away thy breath!
>
> Seek out—less often sought than found—
>   A soldier's grave, for thee the best;
> Then look around, and choose thy ground,
>   And take thy rest.[19]

The accession of Nicholas I (*1825-1855*) to the Russian throne brought the question of intervention to a head. Public opinion in favor of the Greeks was sufficiently great in both Russia and the West to enable the Russians to strike at the Turks under the guise of helping the Greeks. The western governments had to find a way to preserve Turkey as a bulwark against Russian expansion while doing something for the Greeks to appease public clamor. At St. Petersburg, Britain worked out with Russia a protocol (early 1826) which offered a joint mediation of the conflict on a basis of giving the Greeks autonomy under Turkish suzerainty. Because the Sultan declined to make peace on this basis—understandably in the light of continued Turkish military success—the two powers invited France to join them in forcing an armistice, the treaty of London (1827). The Greeks, meanwhile, to give needed unity to their fight, elected Capodistrias as president.

19. George Noel Gordon, Lord Byron, *On This Day I Complete My Thirty-Sixth Year* (1824), ll. 21-40.

When Turkey rejected the three-power demand to grant an armistice in 1827, an Anglo-Russo-French squadron was dispatched to Greek waters under the British admiral Sir Edward Codrington with instructions "to intercept all ships freighted with men or arms . . . without degenerating into hostilities." In carrying out these difficult orders, Codrington's ships engaged the Egyptian fleet in Navarino harbor and in a matter of hours destroyed most of the Egyptian Ibrahim Pasha's ships. The Sultan was understandably furious at this peacetime "incident" and demanded reparation; but public reaction in Europe was so enthusiastic over the incident that an apologetic attitude was awkward for the western governments, particularly for Britain, who hoped to avoid weakening Turkey. Nicholas I took advantage of this embarrassment in the West to promote a war with the Turks in 1828. Not wanting Russia to act alone, Britain and France then forced the Egyptians to evacuate Greece by threatening to intervene. After eight years of chaos, the Greek cause seemed saved.

Though the Russians crossed the Balkan Mountains and approached Constantinople, they did not lay siege. The Turks made peace at Adrianople (1829), where Russia agreed to evacuate all conquered territory in exchange for an indemnity. The objective of weakening Turkey had been achieved, and the disease-ridden Russian army was unfit for a lengthy siege at that moment. A settlement for Greece was reached by the three powers in London in 1832. President Capodistrias, who had been autocratic and unacceptable to some Greek factions, had been assassinated the previous year, leading the powers to insist on monarchy. They finally settled on Otto (*1832–1862*), whose father, Ludwig I of Bavaria, had been a prominent Philhellene. Otto proved to be unpopular. He relied on Bavarian advisors and administrators, not only wounding Greek pride but also preventing the development of a native Greek civil service. The new national frontiers were also a disappointment; Epirus, Crete, and Thessaly remained Turkish, and the British continued their protectorate over the Ionian Islands.

LIBERALISM AND THE ROMANTIC REVIVAL IN THE ARTS

Despite the efforts of the reactionary regimes to turn back the clock, it is only too apparent that the liberal and national currents in Europe remained alive. Indeed, by 1820, it required the concerted efforts of the powers to squelch the liberal fires. The Greek revolution had a special significance because of its simultaneous appeal to the literary romanticists and to the classical sentiments of the educated classes. Philhellenism ultimately forced the powers to intervene on behalf of revolution and, in making a liberal cause respectable, provided the opportunity for the first general European revival of liberalism after 1815.

Many of the literary romanticists, such as Chateaubriand, had favored Christian royalism after 1815, but romanticism in fact had never been clearly tied to one political cause. Hardly any literary figure of the period exercised greater influence than Madame de Staël (1766–1817). Exiled from France by Napoleon for her opposition to his despotism, Madame de Staël had come to despise any form of political extremism, though she was more liberal than conservative. Living in Switzerland, she studied German romanticism, and her thoughts on the subject went far to spread the gospel of romanticism in France—still the citadel of Neoclassicism:

When I began the study of German literature, it seemed as if I was entering a new sphere where the most astounding light was shed on things I had earlier perceived in a confused way. For some time now, little had been read in France except memoirs and novels, and it is not wholly from frivolity that we have become less capable of more serious reading, but because the events of the revolution have accustomed us to value nothing but the knowledge of men and events. We find in German books, even on the most abstract subjects, that type of interest which makes good novels sought for, which is to say that they teach us of our own hearts. The distinctive feature of German literature is that it relates everything to an interior existence; and as that is the mystery of mysteries, an endless curiosity is awakened.[20]

In Britain, the most notable of the romantic poets who had been enthusiastic for the French Revolution—Wordsworth, Southey, and Coleridge—had become increasingly conservative as the drama in France had deepened into despotism. But at the moment of their disillusion, a new generation of romantic poets caught the revolutionary fever. Though most of them came of literary age at a time when to be liberal was no longer to be pro-French, they often scandalized their nation with advanced opinions or, as in the case of George Gordon, Lord Byron (1788–1824), their unusual conduct. Because of marital difficulties, he left England for the Continent in 1816. His greatest achievement was *Don Juan,* an autobiographical poem expressive of his libertarian, adventurous, and restless existence. Percy Bysshe Shelley (1792–1822) was probably an even

20. Baroness de Staël-Holstein, *De L'Allemagne* (1813), (Paris, 1871), Part II, p. 363. My translation.

greater rebel against all authority and convention, leaving England in 1818 when his erratic behavior made his domestic situation intolerable. Brilliant and humane, he was also impractical and naive:

> An old, mad, blind, despised, and dying king—
> Princes, the dregs of their dull race, who flow
> Through public scorn—mud from a muddy spring—
> Rulers who neither see, nor fell, nor know,
> But leech-like to their fainting country cling,
> Till they drop, blind in blood, without a blow—
> A people starved and stabbed in the untilled field—
> An army, which liberticide and prey
> Makes as a two-edged sword to all who wield—
> Golden and sanguine laws which tempt and slay;
> Religion, Christless, Godless—a book sealed;
> A senate—Time's worst statue unrepealed—
> Are graves, from which a glorious Phantom may
> Burst, to illumine our tempestuous day.[21]

John Keats (1795–1821), the third of this generation, was the most tranquil of the three, devoting himself to sensual beauty instead of to reform and revolution:

> A thing of beauty is a joy forever:
> Its loveliness increases; it will never
> Pass into nothingness; but still will keep
> A bower quiet for us, and a sleep
> Full of sweet dreams, and health, and quiet breathing.[22]

In the 1820's, many of the literary romantics can be seen moving more definitely into the liberal camp. In France, Victor Hugo (1802–1885) emerged in that period as a poet and dramatist. Like Chateaubriand, he began as a Christian-royalist, but when the leader of the Ultras succeeded to the throne as Charles X (*1824–1830*), both abandoned the Bourbon cause. After 1830 in particular, we find Hugo an outspoken liberal. Early that year, he produced a romantic drama, *Hernani,* which was the occasion for a minor art war. The neoclassicists were out to destroy it with hisses, while Hugo mustered a crowd of romantics to defend his right to have his play staged. His defenders' names read like a *Who's Who* of nineteenth-

21. Shelley, *England in 1819*. "Stabbed in the untilled fields" is a reference to the military clearing of a mob demanding reforms from St. Peter's Field. "Worst statute unrepealed" a reference to the seventeenth-century law denying Catholics public office.
22. Keats, *Endymion* (1817-18), Book I, 11. 1-5.

century art: Théophile Gautier, Gérard de Nerval, Balzac, Stendhal, Berlioz, and Delacroix. They were not necessarily champions of Hugo's particular views, but as romantics they insisted on freedom from the rigidity of classical form.[23]

France was also the scene of the most intense antagonism in the realm of painting. David, the neoclassicist of the revolutionary and Napoleonic periods, went into Belgian exile with the return of the Bourbons, but his disciple J.-A.-D. Ingres (1780–1867), notable for his superb drawing, kept the tradition alive. Indeed, since France seemed the last stronghold of neoclassicism, it is remarkable that she was the scene of the greatest romantic painting of the period. In 1819, J.-L.-A.-T. Géricault (1791–1824) revealed his large canvas called *The Raft of the Medusa,* his best-known work. The facial expressions were pathetic, a far cry from neoclassical calm and impersonality. Boldness of design and brightness of coloring were characteristic of Géricault, as they were of his devoted follower, Eugène Delacroix (1799–1863). These artists had a fascination for anything which "leaps, writhes, or struggles." After Delacroix produced his famous painting of a scene in the Greek Revolution, *The Massacre of Chios* (1824), the neoclassicists insisted that it was the massacre of painting. Ingres added the remark, "He's a drunken broomstick. . . . Be a friend of his if you want to, but for goodness sake don't imagine he's a painter."[24]

Delacroix's musical counterpart was Hector Berlioz (1803–1869), who hoped to take up music "where Beethoven left it." The German master, who died in 1827, had been the bridge between the classical and the romantic. His French disciple was far more revolutionary in abandoning traditional symphonic form, in the lavishness of his individualism, and in the liberties he took in orchestration. The first great result was the *Symphonie Fantastique* (1830), a vital, intensely dramatic work which still sounds astonishingly modern. The first orchestra to tackle the work had, in Berlioz's words, "to blaze a trail through a virgin forest. Besides many things that are new to them, the greatest difficulty is that of expression, in the first movement especially. . . . It will take angelic patience on the part of the conductor to teach them all the nuances."[25] Meanwhile, Carl Maria von Weber (1786–1826) developed German opera using folk

23. See Jacques Barzun, *Berlioz and the Romantic Century* (Boston, Little, Brown, 1950), Vol. I, pp. 127-129.

24. George Besson, *La Peinture française au XIXᵉ siècle* (Paris, n.d.), pp. 7-8. My translation.

25. Barzun, *op. cit.,* Vol. I, p. 133.

melodies and folk-lore—national and romantic ingredients—of which *Der Freischütz* (1821) and *Oberon* (1826) remain the best known. Like Berlioz, Weber did not shrink from the dramatic and the fantastic, as the famous scene in the devil's glen at midnight in *Freischütz* will attest.

Oddly enough, the national themes and patriotic elements of romantic music did not much affect Italian opera of the period, possibly because the censorship in Italy was sufficiently threatening to intimidate composers. The Italian love for melody and vocal fireworks, however, had survived Gluck's earlier attack upon it, and part of the enormous popularity of Italian opera in the nineteenth century owed to its sensuous qualities. Gioacchino Rossini (1792–1868), producing *The Barber of Seville* in 1816, soon was a European sensation, becoming director of the Paris Opera in 1823. His *William Tell* (1829) did, it is true, encompass a national and patriotic theme, but it is notable that he selected a Swiss story and wrote it in France. Franz Schubert (Austrian, 1797–1828), though neither Italian nor a composer of operas, is also best remembered for his lyrical qualities. Evident in his instrumental music, this lyricism reached its finest expression in his art songs, of which he left hundreds. The art song was a romantic medium in that there were no formal conventions; rather, the music was designed to reach an aesthetic unity with the poetry, suggesting that a new form had to be tailored for each composition.

One notable writer of the romantic period, the Scottish novelist Sir Walter Scott (1771–1832), did not intrude his political views in his works. Yet his subject matter, historical and often patriotic, was characteristic of the period. The nearly thirty Waverly Novels began appearing in 1814. *Ivanhoe* (1820) was set in the England of Richard the Lion-Hearted, *Rob Roy* (1818) was a Scottish Jacobite novel set in the time of George I, while *Kenilworth* (1821) had an Elizabethan setting—to name three of the best-known works. Scott pointed the way for the elder Alexander Dumas (1803–1870) in France and James Fenimore Cooper (1789–1851) in America. In contrast to Scott, the French novelist Marie Henri Beyle, better known as Stendhal (1783–1842), gave his novels contemporary settings and was never more acid than when describing the political and religious reaction of restoration Europe. Here is Fabrice, the liberal Italian hero of his *The Charterhouse of Parma* (1839), being instructed by the Canon Borda as to how liberal leanings are disguised in Italy.

1. Go to mass without fail every day, take an intelligent man as confessor, one devoted to the monarchical cause, and avow to him in the confessional only the most irreproachable sentiments;

2. He must avoid any man regarded as having a good mind, but if that should occur, he must speak of revolution with horror, as something insupportable;

3. He ought never be seen in a cafe, he must never read newspapers other than the official gazettes from Turin and Milan; in general, show distaste for reading, and above all never read any work published after 1720, the novels of Walter Scott a possible exception;

4. Finally, added the canon a bit maliciously, he must openly pay court to one of the pretty local women—of the nobility of course; that will prove that he does not have the unhappy mind of a budding conspirator.[26]

Apparently Fabrice learned his lesson well. Later in the novel, we find him in the company of a nobleman who suspects Fabrice of dangerous ideas. Says Fabrice:

I read the Journal of Parma, which strikes me as quite well written; moreover I share its view that all which has been done since the death of Louis XIV in 1715 is both criminal and mad. A man's first interest is his salvation—there cannot be two ways of looking at that matter—and *that* bliss must last for eternity. Words like *liberty, justice, the happiness of the greatest number,* are infamous and criminal; they condition men's minds to discussion and suspicion.[27]

POLITICAL LIBERALISM IN BRITAIN

The liberal revival, of course, was not confined to the arts, and its political aspects were not limited to Philhellenism. In Britain, we have already noted that the reform movement of William Pitt's time had been stifled by the fear of revolutionary ideas from France, with the result that both the major parties had become more conservative, leaving a vacuum on the left. The cabinets during the Napoleonic Wars were often coalition cabinets—and invariably illiberal. After 1815, the dislocations produced by the change from a wartime to a peacetime economy had aroused popular demand for reform. William Cobbett (1763–1833), a journalist of middle-class origin who had great credit among the workers, pointed the way to peaceful reform: if the constituencies were revised so that representation in the House of Commons truly reflected the nation instead of the few, the necessary social and economic reforms would follow. Cobbett

26. Stendhal, *La Chartreuse de Parme* (1839) (Paris, 1925), Vol. I, p. 117. My translation.
27. *Ibid.,* Vol. I, p. 172.

was a democrat, who saw constitutional reform as the key to all reform, and the fact that men like Cobbett, who were called Radicals, favored nonviolent change helped to remove the revolutionary taint from the reform movement. They were not organized as a political party, practically none were members of Parliament, but they represented respectable families and professions. Cobbett's contemporary, Jeremy Bentham (1748–1832), trained as a lawyer, favored not only universal male suffrage, but also the secret ballot and annual elections for Parliament. Bentham's Scottish friend, James Mill (1773–1836), an officer of the East India Company, went further by advocating the spread of popular education as a concomitant of democracy, and a free press as a critical instrument to check arbitrary government. "Grant, in any quarter of the globe, a reading people and a free press—and the prejudices on which misrule supports itself will gradually and silently disappear."[28]

These British Radicals maintained the eighteenth-century liberal tradition of anticlericalism and were often irreligious as well. In fact, their religious and political ideas were not clearly separated, as was the case with their reactionary contemporaries. James Mill, for example, could not reconcile the idea that a "good" God would create the evil world he saw around him. Yet, he also maintained that it was logically impossible to deny or to affirm the existence of God. But apart from their confusion about the existence of God or the nature of God, the Radicals were inclined to regard organized religion as an arm of secular despotism. That churches had fallen victim to the national states in so much of Europe by the nineteenth century gave weight to their argument.

Jeremy Bentham is best known as the formulator of the political philosophy called utilitarianism. Here the legitimacy of social and political institutions was measured by their "utility"—that is, their social usefulness. Bentham was unconcerned about claims made in the name of tradition, or about divine and natural rights: laws must secure what men *need* and *desire*.

An action may be said to be comfortable to the principle of utility when the tendency it has to augment the happiness of the community is greater than any which has to diminish it.[29]

28. James Mill, "Education," *Edinburgh Review* (1813), quoted in Elie Halévy, *The Growth of Philosophical Radicalism* (Boston, 1955), p. 289.
29. Bentham, *Introduction to the Principles of Morals and Legislation* (1789), quoted in Randall, *Making of the Modern Mind*, p. 360.

From this he derived his best-known principle: "The greatest good for the greatest number."

Bentham did not have a high opinion of man's natural inclinations. He thought that we are motivated only by self-interest, and he boiled down our motives to two: the desire to avoid pain and the desire to secure pleasure. Beginning in 1820, he worked until his death in 1832 on his *Constitutional Code* in an attempt to outline a form of government which would not only bring the "greatest good for the greatest number," but also secure the greatest happiness of the greatest number. The problem was to suggest a political form in which the greatest number of individuals believed their own interests to be best served, a condition which led him to espouse representative democracy as the most utilitarian political form, for it followed that, if each individual best knows his own interest, it could be argued that the general interest can best be judged by the "greatest number" —that is, the majority. His was an ingenious device to reconcile individual egotism with the general welfare, and it recalls the "enlightened self-interest" of Adam Smith.[30]

The average liberal of the post-1815 period was not, however, a democrat. Like his eighteenth-century counterpart, the nineteenth-century liberal emphasized the ordering of man's laws to harmonize with those of nature. Some of the assumptions about nature forecast little happiness for the "greatest number." One example of gloomy thinking is furnished by the Reverend Thomas R. Malthus (1766–1834), a clergyman with an interest in political economy. Considering the growth of population in proportion to the food supply, he came to some depressing conclusions:

> The power of population is indefinitely greater than the power in the earth to produce subsistence for man. Population, when unchecked, increases in a geometrical ratio. Subsistence only increases in an arithmetical ratio. A slight acquaintance with numbers will show the immensity of the first power in comparison with the second.[31]

To be more precise, he figured that a population, if unrestrained, would double every twenty-five years, and given the slower production of food, such a population increase would be catastrophic. He had no faith in men's willingness to limit the birth rate through self-restraint. On the contrary,

30. Halévy, *op. cit.,* pp. 405-411.
31. Malthus, *Essay on the Principle of Population* (1798), quoted in Halévy, *op. cit.,* p. 237.

nature limits the growth of all organisms, and in the case of man, she limits his growth through wars, poverty, and vice. Let the social reformer beware of trying to remove these natural controls lest the population swiftly outstrip the food supply. Let nature be: *laissez faire.*

David Ricardo (1772–1823) was another *laissez-faire* liberal who shared the pessimistic outlook of Malthus, and it was from such pessimism that economics became known as the "dismal science." Economic life, Ricardo believed, was governed by unalterable natural laws. Important among them was the natural antagonism between the three classes: land-owners, capitalists, and laborers. He also believed that there is a fixed amount of goods and a fixed amount of wages to be divided among the workers. Knowing of Malthus' work on population growth, Ricardo insisted that the conditions of life for the workers must inevitably decline, since the supply of workers would increase faster than the demand for them. Only a reduction in their birth rate would improve their lot. All legislation designed to keep more of them alive was in reality an unkindness to them. To the suggestion that workers' standard of living be raised through higher wages, Ricardo answered that this necessarily lowered the capitalists' profits. The reduction of capital earnings in the long run meant smaller investments and fewer jobs for workers. Unable to see any way out of this vicious circle, he named his essay *The Iron Law of Wages* (1817).

If the liberals did not share the radicals' faith in democracy, they were as one when it came to belief in constitutional government. A constitution could limit the power of a despot, a provision particularly pertinent on the Continent; and constitutional reform, as espoused by the liberals and radi-cals in Britain, could lead to economic and social reforms. The credit of Montesquieu as a liberal constitutionalist had not died on the Continent, and the British system from which he had learned was still the model for continental liberals. And Montesquieu had taught that free government is achieved by separating the three branches of government and limiting them constitutionally. Benjamin Constant (1767–1830), dear friend of Mme. de Staël and the most eminent parliamentarian under the restoration, defined the liberal position in a series of public lectures and articles between 1818 and 1820 (*Cours de poltique constitutionelle*). Individual liberty had to be defended against governmental encroachment, he said, because it was to gain liberty that men originally instituted government and society.[32]

32. See Artz, *op. cit.,* pp. 90-94.

The Congress of Vienna, 1815 by Jean-Baptiste Isabey

Below left to right:
Klemens von Metternich, Vicomte René de Chateaubriand, Alexander I

Right: George Gordon, Lord Byron
Below: *Massacre at Chios* by Eugène Delacroix

Above left to right:
Arthur Schopenhauer, Percy Bysshe Shelley, Stendhal (Marie Henri Beyle)

The Raft of the Medusa by Théodore Géricault

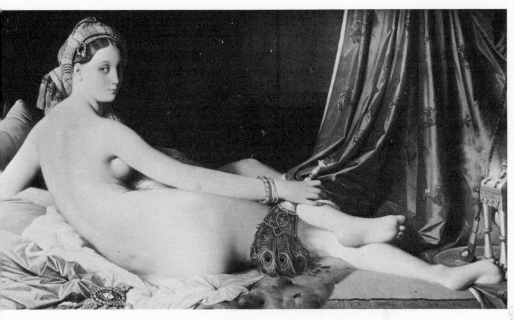

La Grande Odalisque by Jean-Auguste-Dominique Ingres

Right: Madame de Staël
Below: Jeremy Bentham

THE LIBERAL EXPERIMENT IN POLAND;
REACTION AND REVOLUTION IN RUSSIA

The greatest inconsistencies in constitutional practice were to be found within the Russian Empire. Alexander I, who had cut short the development of representative institutions which Speransky had proposed for Russia, allowed the Finns to retain the constitutional regime they had under Swedish rule. This clemency meant virtual autonomy for Finland, with the Czar taking the title of Grand Duke of Finland. Russians were not free to settle in Finland without permission of the Finnish authorities. In Poland, too, Alexander advanced himself as the patron of liberal government. He became King of Poland and gave the Poles a government entirely separate from that of Russia, even permitting an independent Polish army —though putting it under a Russian commander.

Prince Adam Czartoryski (1770–1861), a Polish noble and long an associate of the Czar, directed the writing of a constitution for Poland. It provided for a bicameral Diet. The Senate was appointed by the Czar, but the Chamber of Deputies was elected by broad franchise. Unlike the Finnish example, however, the Polish government found its autonomy constantly hampered by the interference of Russian officials, and Polish irritation was further heightened by the failure of Alexander to include Lithuania in the Polish kingdom. The two countries had been united in earlier centuries, and Polish patriots were eager to make the reborn Poland as large as possible. Conversely, Russian opinion was hostile to making Poland any larger than necessary.

Beginning about 1819, the Czar responded to Polish demands for greater independence and more territory by removing troublemakers from office and substituting men thought to be more conservative and subject to his will. In so doing, he stimulated the national movement for complete independence from Russia. The University of Vilna, an ancient center of Polish culture, harbored student societies which, inspired by the nationalist ideas of Herder, were suspiciously regarded by the government. These student groups, much like their German contemporaries, agitated for the unification of all Polish-speaking people into one nation, and, of course, they wanted liberal, constitutional government. Out of this ferment came a Byronic-style poem, the national epic of the Poles, *Conrad Wallenrod* (1828), by Adam Mickiewicz (1798–1855).

In Russia proper after 1815, we find Alexander I the patron of deepening autocracy. What he allowed the Finns and Poles, and what he regarded as a condition for permitting the Bourbon restoration in France, he did not extend to Russia. Earlier, he had been an educational reformer; after 1815, education was supervised so closely by state inspectors as to lose its vitality, and professors guilty of liberal views were dismissed. Under Prince A. Golitsin, who became head of the Ministry of Religion and Education in 1817, the educational reaction reached its nadir. Word soon went out that all teaching was to proceed from the ideas set down in the Holy Alliance. Finally, there were the harsh and unpopular military colonies noted earlier.

The revolutionary movement first developed among officers who had seen service in France in 1814 and who had been in the occupation force between that date and 1818. The superiority of western conditions of life shocked the more perceptive as they reflected upon conditions in Russia:

> When I look at the brilliant qualities which God has gifted the Russian people, first in the world for glory and power, for its strong melodious language which has not its like in Europe, for the cordiality, kind-heartedness and quickness of mind that are peculiar to it above all others, it grieves me to think that this is all crushed, withering and perhaps dying out without bearing any fruit in the moral world.[33]

The liberal movement began in 1814 with secret societies. Some of these merged in 1816 to form the Union of Salvation, which, in turn, disbanded in 1820. By that date, the revolutionary movement had divided into two principal currents, the more radical of which was the Southern Society led by Colonel Paul Pestel (1792–1896). The Society's program was both democratic and republican, directly inspired by the French Revolution: overthrow of the monarchy, freeing of the serfs, and elimination of all class distinctions. A second, but minor, republican society was the United Slavs, whose chief distinction was a Pan-Slav program. The other principal party was the Society of the North led by Alexander Muraviev (1792–1864), an army officer who favored an English-style constitutional monarchy; by Nicholas Turgenev (1789–1871), a *laissez-faire* liberal who had studied in the West; and by Prince Serge Trubetskoi (1790–1860), commanding colonel of the Preobrazhensky Regiment. The leadership in both societies came from the gentry.

The liberals' first opportunity came late in 1825, upon the death of Alexander I, because the succession of the throne was unclear. Grand

---

33. Sir Bernard Pares, *History of Russia,* p. 313.

Duke Constantine, the next in line, had been serving as Viceroy of Poland. Desiring to marry a Polish commoner, he had abdicated his right to the throne, but that abdication had not become widely publicized. His younger brother, Nicholas, was the heir, but Nicholas preferred a clear statement from Constantine in Warsaw before accepting the crown he knew was rightfully his. Otherwise, the suspicion of unsurpation might prove his undoing. In the meantime, the Society of the North, undoubtedly ignorant of the legal details of the succession, recognized the moment of uncertainty as a time to strike. Colonel Prince Trubetskoi would seize the palace, then force the Senate to grant constitutional government and settle the succession. It was the group's misfortune to have presumed that Constantine was the heir; hence the revolutionaries demanded Constantine as a constitutional monarch. But Nicholas was warned in advance, and the revolution—known as the Decembrist Revolt—was swiftly smashed. Early in 1826, the Southern Society also burst into revolt, but this uprising, too, was easily handled. Thus, the reign of Nicholas I (1825–1855) opened with the shock of revolt, but for once a palace revolution had been unsuccessful.

Nevertheless, Nicholas struck hard and arbitrarily at the conspirators. Five leaders, including Colonel Pestel, were summarily hanged, and another hundred or more were exiled or sentenced to Siberia. There followed a rigid censorship of the press, which was intended "to make printing harmless," in the words of one official. Nicholas attended to these matters personally. To Aleksander Pushkin (1799–1837), who had produced the greatest of all Russian tragic dramas, *Boris Godunov* (1825), the Czar recommended that he reissue the work "with an elimination of superfluous material, a novel after the manner of Walter Scott."[34] It may be noted that Pushkin had been sympathetic to the Decembrists, and that *Boris Godunov* was the most celebrated usurper in the Russian past. The imperial severity was the more striking as there had been no executions under Alexander I, and Nicholas' arbitrariness served to alienate the monarchy even more from the liberal gentry. This meant that the monarchy increasingly depended upon a professional bureaucracy. A further result was the tendency to remember the defeated Decembrists as martyrs in the good fight against absolutism. To meet mounting criticism of the regime, Nicholas created the Third Section, a political police. In short order, the Russian monarchy under Nicholas I was regarded throughout Europe as the best—

34. *Ibid.,* p. 328.

or worst—example of successful despotism, and the maintenance of the Metternichian *status quo* became increasingly a Russian responsibility.

THE LAST OF THE BOURBONS IN FRANCE

Meanwhile, the experience of the French monarchy after 1815 offered Europe another spectacle of growing despotism. Louis XVIII, as noted elsewhere, had made an honest attempt to introduce moderate, constitutional government, but the odds were against him from the start. Parliament contained three major factions: the Ultras, or extreme royalists, on the right; ex-revolutionaries and ex-Bonapartists on the left; and what we might call royalists-of-convenience as the moderate center. Insecurity was inherent in the situation. Neither extreme was devoted to the monarchy as then constituted. Though hating each other, the extremes could cooperate to bring down the center; or, the center could, by alternating concessions to the left and the right, play them off against each other. The King felt it necessary to keep the center in control at all costs. After all, the left could not be counted on to support the monarchy, and the right might well overthrow the Charter of 1814—which would seriously displease the allies and invite foreign intervention. Beginning in 1816, the government altered the electoral laws before elections in attempts to secure success for the moderate deputies. The stratagem was understandable, but the precedent was unfortunate.

The moderate policy was further jeopardized by the embarrassing fact that the leader of the Ultras, the Comte d'Artois, was the King's brother and heir. Even if Louis XVIII managed to maintain moderate government, what would happen when Artois succeeded to the throne? Indeed, if Artois, when king, tried to restore absolute monarchy, would the French tolerate it? This was not merely a French concern but an international anxiety, for who could doubt that a renewal of revolution in France would ignite all the liberal movements in Europe? We do not usually think of Metternich as a liberal, but when he thought about maintaining the 1815 settlement, he saw constitutional monarchy in France as essential.

Metternich is convinced that the general currents throughout Europe for the past thirty years have brought new ideas and new practices, and that representative governments have become a necessity that, sooner or later, must be accepted. . . . He actually recognizes all the advantages which a skillful minister can draw from these representative bodies, and possibly he has enough confidence in these methods to regret not finding himself in such a government. At the same time he feels that the only way to obtain their advantages is through the direction of a strong and skillful ministry, and he recognizes that a weak ministry can only lead to anarchy.[35]

Perfectly aware of Artois's views, Metternich even suggested to the French ambassador that when the powers met at Aix-la-Chapelle in 1818, Artois be informed that he could count on the support of the allies only so long as he followed the moderate path of Louis XVIII. The "established order" in France, Metternich said, was the key to the general European peace. There is no evidence that Artois was impressed.

Richelieu retired as prime minister and foreign minister after his triumph at Aix-la-Chapelle, but the reconstituted cabinet, with Elie Decazes (1780–1860) as its leading figure, remained moderate. Its most important work was in press legislation. The laws of 1819 were significant steps to implement the freedom of the press which the Charter of 1814 had guaranteed. A rash of publications followed. Decazes, however, could not cure the chief political ill of the time—the cooperation of the extremists against the center—and it became increasingly clear that the government must seek a permanent alliance with either left or right. Before a decision could be reached, the Duc de Berri, son of Artois, was struck down by an assassin (1820), an event the outraged Ultras promptly used as the proof of the violence which they claimed liberal government was bound to bring. Louis XVIII, as a result, was driven toward the right.

The first reactionary measures—the renewal of censorship and of arbitrary arrest—were intended to be temporary, but another juggling of the election law increased the political power of the wealthy landowners. Thus, in the elections of 1821, the Ultras won a clear victory, which assured the deepening of the reaction. Press censorship became increasingly oppressive in 1822, the same year that a bishop was named Grand Master of the Université de France, the state-supported school system. The architect of this reaction was the Ultra Joseph de Villèle (1773–1854), actually minister of finance but virtual director of the cabinet from 1821 to 1828. With the accession of Artois to the throne as Charles X (*1824–1830*), the reaction was given new impetus.

One of the questions which had festered ever since 1814 arose over

35. The report of the Marquis de Caraman to the Duc de Richelieu, May 19, 1818, in de Bertier de Sauvigny, *France and the European Alliance 1816-1821* (Notre Dame, Ind., 1958), pp. 61-62.

the failure of the monarchy to idemnify the *émigrés* whose properties had been confiscated during the Revolution. The Charter guaranteed the property rights of those—many of them peasants—who had purchased land which the government had confiscated, but not until 1825 did Villèle succeed in getting legislation to indemnify the despoiled. Whatever the justice of the measure, it proved impolitic. Wanting to avoid special taxes which might alienate the country from the monarchy, Villèle fell upon a scheme to convert government bonds bearing an interest rate of 5 per cent to bonds bearing 3 per cent. The capital holdings of the bondholders was to be increased, but even so, the bondholders stood to lose some income. In answer to their protests, Villèle argued that bonds were then selling for more than their face value, and the bondholders could sell their holdings and reinvest if they chose not to accept the new 3 per cent bonds. Villèle intended that the money saved on interest could be used to indemnify the *émigrés*. Unfortunately, his attempt to close this chapter of revolutionary history coincided with a period of financial instability elsewhere in Europe, and the net effect was an unexpected reduction in the market value of the French bonds. In sum, the bondholders lost more than the government had anticipated.

Many of these bondholders were middle-class people, who felt they were being dunned for the benefit of the landed aristocracy. Their irritation was only heightened by the Law of Sacrilege (1825), for a great many of them were Voltairian when it came to religion. The close association of throne and altar was summed up in this law, which made sacrilege a crime punishable by the state. The death penalty was possible under the law only if the accused committed the sacrilege "knowingly, openly, and out of hatred or contempt for religion." Many of the leading Christians, such as Chateaubriand, were convinced that the law was both unwise and un-Christian, but its proponents reasoned: "The Revolution which began with the Declaration of the Rights of Man, shall finish with a Declaration of the Rights of God."[36]

By 1828, it was evident that the country was committed to policies considerably more liberal than the government represented. Villèle gave up office after the opposition gained control of parliament, and his successor, the Vicomte Jean-Baptiste de Martignac, tried to relieve the tension (1828–1829) by courting liberal opinion. Martignac's was an impossible position. He liberalized the press laws and gave evidence of trying to stop the

36. de Bertier de Sauvigny, *La Restauration,* p. 512.

increasing clerical control of education; but he could not do sufficient to please the liberals, and everything he did displeased the King. In 1829, Charles X replaced him with the Prince de Polignac (1780–1847), a man who had refused to give allegiance to the Charter in 1814. The change of ministers indicated that the King determined to govern in defiance of the parliamentary majority.

The integrity of the Charter was at stake, and there was talk of a "French 1688" among the moderate royalists. They formed a new journal, *Le National,* whose very title was a warning to the monarch that the sovereignty rested in the nation. Yet, Charles X, when he met his new parliament in the spring of 1830, asserted his "sacred rights" and threatened force should they be infringed upon. The majority replied that the King's ministers ought to have the confidence of parliament, thus raising the fundamental constitutional question outstanding since 1814. His Majesty ended by dissolving the parliament and calling for new elections.

In the meantime, the Prince de Polignac had been pursuing a foreign policy designed to increase his regime's prestige. The Greek question having been settled, the French turned their major attention to the Algerian coast, which had been a source of irritation for a number of years. Algerian piracy in the Mediterranean had long annoyed the western powers, and in 1819, Britain and France had jointly informed the Bey of Algeria of their displeasure. In return, the Bey sharply increased the rent for several concessions which French firms had enjoyed on the Algerian coast since the sixteenth century. Another minor matter was a debt which the French government owed an Algerian firm for wheat purchased under the Directory. The price had been so outrageous that Napoleon had refused to pay it, but the Bourbon government tried to negotiate a settlement at a just price. Since the Bey of Algeria was a creditor of the firm trying to collect from France, he regarded the French attempt to scale down the debt as an indirect attack upon him in retaliation for the piracy. His fury, in 1827, led him to strike the French Consul three times with a flyswatter, after which the French began a naval blockade of the coast to force the Bey to make reparation for the insult.

As the blockade produced no results, the French sent a negotiator to Algiers in 1829 in an effort to settle the squabble. The Bey not only disdained to negotiate, but the French suffered the further indignity of having their negotiator's ship fired on as it departed. At that point, the Khedive of Egypt offered to clear up the Algerian situation if he were given four warships and a French subsidy; but Polignac's initial enthusiasm for the scheme faded when French military opinion held serious doubt that Mehemet Ali could sustain a successful campaign across the deserts of North Africa. Indeed, they argued, this was merely a trick to recover some of his losses in Greece. Early in 1830, then, the French informed the great powers of their decision to send an army to North Africa. Nicholas I responded enthusiastically, glad to support a regime which increasingly mirrored his own, but the British were highly alarmed at this new evidence of French military ambition. Opposition was no less great in France, where the opponents of Charles' despotism raised the question of parliamentary consent for money which would be needed for the expedition. The answer came twenty days after the landing in North Africa, when the French army smashed into Algiers and took possession of the Bey's treasury.

Parliamentary elections toward the end of June, 1830, came a few days too soon for the government to profit from the Algerian victory, and the opposition proved to be even stronger than in the previous Chamber. As the King could no longer hope to manage parliament, he decided to have recourse to Article 14 of the Charter, which gave him the power to make "regulations and ordinances necessary for the execution of the laws and for the security of the state." Charles X saw fit to interpret this article as giving him the constitutional right to become a royal dictator, but given the spirit of the entire Charter, it is unlikely that its framers were so motivated. Consequently, the King's decision to invoke Article 14 and issue four repressive ordinances was rightly termed a *coup d'état*. By ordinance he ended the right to publish freely, government authorization being required; the newly elected Chamber was dissolved; and the electoral laws were once again juggled to narrow the franchise and reduce the number of deputies. Charles X affixed his signature on July 24, 1830. Within a week the opposition, liberal monarchists and republicans, had so aroused Paris that it was necessary to withdraw the ordinances, but the gesture came too late. On the 31st, the royal family fled from the Paris area and finally to England. The French Bourbons had fallen for the second and last time.

POSTSCRIPT

Many of the political and cultural currents alive in Europe after 1815 —especially liberalism, democracy, and nationalism—remain alive today. Because the average man in the western world today is aware of these currents, we may easily fall into the error of believing that the same situation obtained 150 years ago. On the contrary, the gap between the educated few and the uneducated many remained vast, and movements and ideas which later became popular were still the concern, in the 1820's, of a comparatively few people. Malthus wrote for a tiny audience, German nationalism was centered in the universities, and the Russian revolutionaries were limited to the classes already in power. The day of mass communication and culture was still in the future.

SUGGESTIONS FOR FURTHER READING

⅏

The Peace Settlement and the Congress System

Charles K. Webster, *The Foreign Policy of Castlereagh 1812-1815* (London: G. Bell and Sons, 1931), a most distinguished work.

Harold Nicolson, *The Congress of Vienna, A Study in Allied Unity* (New York: Harcourt, Brace, 1946).

Henry A. Kissinger, *A World Restored; Metternich, Castlereagh, and the Problems of Peace* (Boston: Houghton Mifflin, 1957).

G. de Bertier de Sauvigny, *France and the European Alliance 1816-21* (Notre Dame University Press, 1958).

H. W. V. Temperley, *The Foreign Policy of Canning, 1822-1827* (London: G. Bell and Sons, 1925).

Reaction and Revolution

Frederick B. Artz, *Reaction and Revolution 1814-1832* (New York and London: Harper, 1934), the best single volume on the period, with excellent bibliography.

Arthur J. May, *The Age of Metternich 1814-1848* (New York: Henry Holt, 1933), somewhat dated but useful.

Wesley M. Gewehr, *The Rise of Nationalism in the Balkans, 1800-1930* (New York: Henry Holt, 1931).

Edward S. Forster, *A Short History of Modern Greece, 1821-1956* (New York: Frederick A. Praeger, 1957).

André A. Lobanov-Rostovsky, *Russia and Europe, 1789-1825* (Duke University Press, 1947).

A. G. Mazour, *The First Russian Revolution, 1825; The Decembrist Movement, Its Origins, Development, and Significance* (University of California Press, 1937).

G. S. Veitch, *The Genesis of Parliamentary Reform* (London: Constable and Co., 1913).

*Elie Halévy, *The Growth of Philosophical Radicalism* (Boston: Beacon, 1955) a distinguished work.

G. de Ruggiero, *The History of European liberalism* (New York: Oxford University Press, 1927) provides good bibliography.

Roger H. Soltau, *French Political Thought in the Nineteenth Century* (London: E. Benn, 1931).

*Hans Kohn, *Nationalism: Its Meaning and History* (Princeton, N.J.: Anvil, 1955) contains short but good bibliography.

Jacques Barzun, *Berlioz and the Romantic Century,* 2 vols. (Boston: Little, Brown, 1950).

A. O. Lovejoy, "Meaning of Romanticism for the Historian of Ideas," *Journal of Ideas,* II (June, 1941).

* Available in paperbound editions.

⚘10⚘

The Liberal Heyday:
1830–1851

LIKE MOST general titles applied to historical periods, the term "liberal heyday" is open to question. Conservative governments held sway over much of Europe at the same time that various radical and socialist theories found their adherents in western Europe. Yet, the period opened and closed with a rash of liberal revolutions; and in between, Great Britain—ever the liberal model—was the scene of important reforms. The various creeds of liberalism found their champions at the rostrum and the barricade, giving the era its character. In 1830, moreover, the Continent was on the brink of rapid technical and economic change, about to experience the "industrial revolution" which Britain had earlier begun. As in Britain, those whose fortunes were made by the new economic opportunities were often in the liberal camp for social and political reasons.

FREE TRADE AND ECONOMIC EXPANSION

We think of a liberal in the nineteenth century as favoring free trade. In theory at least, he disapproved of governmental interference as an artificial regulation of matters which ought to be left to natural regulation. But in practice the economic liberal tempered his enthusiasm for nature with a recognition of hard business realities. It would have been disastrous, for example, to expose the infant continental industries to the competition of the more efficient British industry; and, in fact, even Adam Smith had urged that infant industries be protected from competition until they became well enough established to survive in a free market. This modification of economic liberalism in the national interest was well spelled out by the German Friedrich List (1789–1846) in his *National System of Political Economy* (1841). There should be protection against *external* competition, he argued, until the national industrial economy becomes sufficiently developed to permit free trade. Consequently, most of the European countries worked to remove the *internal* barriers to trade (regional tariffs), while retaining high tariffs against foreign manufacturers, thus developing the home market.

The tariff history of Prussia in this period is the best case in point. Beginning in 1818, she removed the internal barriers while establishing a uniform external tariff. She then proceeded to negotiate tariff treaties with neighboring German states, which culminated with the *Zollverein* (1834), a customs union including seventeen sovereign states. Austria was notably excluded, suggesting that this economic union had political significance. No doubt other factors also worked to increase German trade and unity, but the *Zollverein* contributed, too, and was an example of Prussia's challenge to Austrian leadership in the German world.

In Britain, all the internal tariff barriers had disappeared in 1801 with the Act of Union, but the Corn Law of 1815 protected domestic agriculture and reduced foreign trade. British industrialists, unafraid of foreign competition, increasingly demanded free trade. In 1836, some of the Radical leaders in Parliament began to agitate against the Corn Law, showing that it kept food prices high, and they were soon joined by a group of Manchester manufacturers (the Anti-Corn-Law League) in a great campaign of meetings and pamphlets. Led by Richard Cobden (1804–1865), the League tried to demonstrate to each section of the population how it would profit from the repeal of the Corn Law. The great landowners were able to prevent repeal, however, until 1846 when, owing to a failure of the Irish potato crop and poor harvests in England, it became necessary to import large quantities of *cheap* food. Not only did the Corn Law go, but by mid-century the navigation acts were also abolished. The liberal cause of tree trade had become a fact.

Railway building was another significant factor in the economic expansion of Europe after 1830. Both railroads (horse-drawn) and steam engines had been used in the eighteenth century, but they were not successfully combined until George Stephenson (1781–1848) saw that success lay in avoiding steep gradients in railroad construction. Since the time of James Watt, men had argued that a mobile steam engine was impossible; and the canal and road companies, fearful of railroad competition, conjured up fearful images of a countryside blighted by the passage of smoke-belching engines. After many technical and political difficulties, the steam-locomotive age opened in 1830 with Stephenson's Liverpool and Manchester Railway. The railroad craze quickly caught up the Continent, all the major countries undertaking construction before the decade was out. If the British were the pioneers, the Belgians were the first to tie their national economy to railroad construction. As early as 1834, the Belgian government sought to design the rail network that would make Belgium the commercial center of Europe. Her central position among Britain, France, Holland, and the German world did make her a natural entrepôt. In contrast, political disunity in Germany stood in the way of national planning. Even so, the scattered railway building in Germany did much for economic development, because German roads were notoriously poor. France, on the other hand, was somewhat slower to develop railroads, in part because French roads were among Europe's best. The first Russian railroad was begun in 1838, but the Russian system did not expand as rapidly as those of the other European powers. During the Crimean War after mid-century, the poverty of Russia's internal communications proved fatal, thus revealing the military potential of railroads.

The application of steam power to ships was somewhat slower, even after steamships were technically possible. As long as ships were constructed of wood, keels were limited to 300 feet. Plainly, there was insufficient room for engine equipment, fuel, and a cargo. Worse, the paddle wheels were terribly vulnerable to storms. In contrast the sailing vessel had the double advantage of low-cost construction—there were vast supplies of cheap timber in the New World—and low-cost operation. Beginning in 1832, the British pioneered in the building of iron ships, which ultimately permitted keels longer than 300 feet. Four years later, the screw propeller was invented, while in 1854 the first compound steam engine was used. Triple and quadruple expansion engines reused steam, either saving fuel or making it possible to carry less. Though these innovations made steamships more economical, the sailing vessels nevertheless competed rather successfully until the 1880's.

Iron and coal production has always been a fair measure of the progress of industrialization. Consequently, we should expect to find that in the 1830's and 1840's Britain led in their production. In fact, she doubled her iron output between 1835 and 1848, her two million tons of that year constituting about half the world's supply. In the same thirteen-year period, her coal production rose from 30 million tons to 50 million tons. The industrialized textile industry had from the start furnished the most significant products for export, but in the nineteenth century, cottons replaced woolens as the chief article of trade. It may be noted that British industry as a whole suffered after 1815 during the period of readjustment to peace, but the volume of trade rose sharply again after 1830. Then there was a tremendous increase in the construction of ocean-going trading ships. By mid-century, 60 per cent of all ocean-going ships were British.

In the face of such startling economic expansion, one might well wonder who provided the capital. In the earliest days of the "industrial revolution," it will be recalled, agricultural profits were often invested in industry. Then there appeared a number of great private banks ready to lend capital for business and industry, dominating the banking scene for the first half of the nineteenth century: Barings in London, Hopes of Amsterdam, Bleichröder in Berlin, Mallet Frères in Paris, and most notable of all, the Rothschilds with their various European branches. As the century progressed, the trend was toward joint-stock banks as a better way of amassing the great capital in demand. Of these, the Société Générale of Belgium (1822) was an early example which became a model for many others. A second trend was toward the merger of these joint-stock banks, thus reducing the number of lending institutions and concentrating great economic power.[1]

The social evils of industrialization, already experienced in eighteenth-century Britain, were now visited upon the Continent as well. New industries tended to be heavily concentrated into a few towns, whose rapid growth was unregulated by either national or local authorities and whose living and working conditions set the stage for dehumanizing poverty and murderous waves of cholera and tuberculosis. Between 1830 and 1835, Europe was ravaged by her first cholera epidemic. While no class was immune, the urban poor suffered inordinately because of wretched living conditions. Saint-Etienne was an example of a new factory town in France. In the ten years following 1831, her population rose from 16,000 to 54,000 without a corresponding growth of housing and municipal facilities. Hardships were born of other factors too; the rapid expansion of industry and international trade meant a period of dislocation, uncertainty, and occa-

1. S. B. Clough, *The Economic Development of Western Civilization* (New York, McGraw-Hill, 1959), pp. 360-361.

sional retrenchment. Worse, a crisis of fluctuation in one place had increasingly grave international repercussions. Before this expansion of industry and trade, the nations had been much more self-sufficient economically; but at a time when the British cotton industry purchased much of its raw cotton in America, British employment was obviously affected by the price of cotton in America. When, in the face of widespread misery, we find many employers steadfastly opposed to any economic regulation, we can only wonder to what extent their motives were crass and selfish or to what extent their willingness to exploit cheap labor was a response to those "dismal scientists" who warned against flouting the natural laws of economic life.

REFORM MOVEMENT IN BRITAIN

However indifferent to reform of factory and town, the British manufacturer was not indifferent to the reform of Parliament, where he was inadequately represented. The difficulty lay in the definition of property; land alone was regarded as real property, which, considering the property qualification for the right to vote, had the effect of disenfranchising many of those who owned commercial and industrial property. Moreover, the failure to reapportion the seats in the House of Commons to reflect the shift in population from farm to town meant that many urban centers were unrepresented, while depopulated rural districts—the so-called Rotten Boroughs—retained seats. While the Whigs were traditionally more liberal than the Tories, both parties necessarily represented landed interest; and the issues separating the two parties had always revolved around establishment versus dissent and the prerogatives of the crown versus those of Parliament. In the 1820's, the British manufacturer fell into uneasy alliance with the Whigs, who, thirsting for office after nearly a half-century of Tory government, were finally ready for the reform of Parliament even at the expense of the landed interests; and with the Radicals, whose democratic tendencies were anathema to both the manufacturers and the Whigs. The pressure for reform was great, for it united the political ambitions of the opposition with the liberal and democratic aspirations of employer and employee; and the Tory regime, while it had accepted the necessity of some reform, such as the removal of the political disabilities against Catholics in 1829, did so reluctantly in the face of possible revolt in Ireland rather than from conviction. The Duke of Wellington, furthermore, went on record as believing that the British electoral system was the most perfect ever devised, and he implied that it was beyond improvement.

The death of George IV in 1830 necessitated new parliamentary elections, and the reform party, headed by the aristocratic Whigs, won the right to govern. A two-year struggle was required to get the Reform Bill accepted, partly because of the divisions within the reform party and partly because the House of Lords, with its Tory majority, opposed the bill when passed by Commons. The Radical leaders mobilized public opinion for the bill, while the Whig leaders obtained from William IV (*1830–1837*) the promise to pack the House of Lords with Whig peers in case that body persisted in its obstruction of the wishes of the majority in Commons. This threat was sufficient, and the King was not required to create the new peers. Thus, the passage of the Reform Bill of 1832 reaffirmed the principle that the House of Lords must not block legislation which has popular support. The bill itself reformed the constituencies, redistributing the seats in Commons to reflect the shift in population from country to town, while the property qualifications for the vote were revised. Actually, the reform did not greatly enlarge the electorate, but the total effect of the bill was to give the middle class much greater participation in politics and reinforce the liberal climate.

For some years, humanitarians had been arguing for political reform as the key to social and economic reform, but the reform picture in Britain after 1832 revealed a wide disparity between popular expectations and liberal notions of what constituted reform. Regulation of factory conditions, for example, had been an evident need for nearly a half-century, but as the *laissez-faire* liberals (now the Whig-industrial alliance) opposed governmental interference, the initiative had to be taken by such aristocratic Tories as the Earl of Shaftesbury (1801–1885), and by the Radicals, the most notable after 1832 being John Stuart Mill (1806–1873). Mill, brought up on the utilitarianism of his father and Bentham, never "wavered in the conviction that happiness is the test of all rules of conduct, and the end of life." But after a spiritual or emotional crisis, he saw how insufficient was the utilitarian assumption that mankind's requirements can be met by the avoidance of pain and the reception of pleasure.

I, for the first time, gave its proper place, among the prime necessities of human well-being, to the internal culture of the individual. I ceased to attach almost exclusive importance to be ordering of outward circumstances, and the training of the human being for speculation and for action.[2]

Investigations by parliamentary committees revealed only too clearly that one of the most crying abuses was child labor in the factories and mines. Shaftesbury, backed by public opinion, forced the Whig cabinet to support his bill in 1833, the terms of which suggest the magnitude of the problem. Children under nine were no longer to be employed in the textile factories, and those between nine and thirteen were to be limited to a nine-hour day. Those between thirteen and eighteen might work up to twelve hours. Equally significantly, the law provided for government inspectors for the enforcement of the regulations. A similar law in 1842 sought to end the employment of boys under ten and women in the mines, where the conditions of work were notoriously destructive of health and morals. At the height of the cholera outbreak, municipal governments everywhere had proven incompetent in matters of public health. Local government was in the hands of the few, and taxes were rarely employed for civic improvements. In 1835, Parliament passed the Municipal Corporations Act, designed to remove local government from the control of oligarchies. The local franchise was greatly extended, in the hope that more responsible governments would spend public funds on improving water supplies, streets, sewers, and police protection. Once the principle of governmental regulation was established, it became generally accepted as necessary. In the matter of slavery, the Whigs and the Radicals saw eye to eye from the start. The proposal to end slavery throughout the Empire passed in 1833, to the great annoyance of the colonial planters. Parliament voted, however, a large sum to compensate them for their losses.

Shortly thereafter, Parliament took up the question of poor relief. Pauperism had always been present, of course, but there is every evidence that the economic dislocations of industrialization were made worse by the hardships brought on by the wars beginning in 1793. In the time of Elizabeth, the parish had been made responsible for the administration of poor relief, and the justices of the peace were empowered to ascertain that relief was so administered. But as the population began shifting in the eighteenth century, the machinery of poor relief ceased to be effective. In 1795, the justices of Berkshire met at Speenhamland to seek a solution. They established a dole system by which public funds were

2. John Stuart Mill, *Autobiography,* Ch. V.

used by the parish to make up the difference between a worker's wage and a minimum living wage in that particular parish. Known as the Speenhamland Act, this dole was widely copied. Its long-term effects, however, both economic and moral, were unfortunate. For one thing, it encouraged the employer to pay low wages, since he knew that his workers would be kept alive at public expense; secondly, the employee drew relief according to his dependents, including his illegitimate children, so that there was no encouragement to curtail births; the tax rate for poor relief rose markedly, meaning that the taxpayers were really contributing to high profits for inhumane employers; and worst of all, the employees were losing the sense of independence and personal responsibility necessary to keep people morally strong and free.

The new Poor Law of 1834 proved an effective reform, but it was not calculated to charm the workers. Henceforth, no relief was given to the ablebodied unless they resided in a poorhouse. Not only did the social stigma of such residences work to keep the poor out of them, but the conditions in the poorhouses were kept deliberately wretched, so that a man was likely to accept any kind of work to keep out of them. Employers were pleased by the reform. It enabled them to have a large supply of laborers eager for work—and at low wages—while taxes for poor relief diminished. As governmental interference was consequently lessening, the principle of *laissez faire* was being served. The Poor Law, however, revealed to the workers that the Reform Bill of 1832 had been inadequate to improve the conditions of their life, and the principle of *laissez faire* stood increasingly condemned as a guarantee of inhumanity.

LAISSEZ FAIRE ON THE CONTINENT

In France, the focus of unrest in the 1830's was Lyons, center of the silk industry. Work days were long, averaging more than sixteen hours, but wages were so low that a family could not manage unless the children worked. In 1831, a group of workers succeeded in negotiating better wage rates; but the government, devoted to *laissez faire,* was alarmed at this sign of labor organization and refused to give the force of law to the new wage agreement. The workers were quickly disillusioned, and a near-revolutionary climate prevailed, with fighting between workers and royal troops. When order was restored by force, the government seemed ready to grant the new wage scale. Consequently, the workers agreed to turn in their weapons, whereupon the government reversed itself and declared that the wage scale had no binding force. The incident had the double effect of convincing the government that it could control labor agitation and proving to the workers that the government was indifferent to their welfare. Liberal opinion was deeply divided on the matter, especially in 1834, when a second rising in Lyons in response to a depression was smashed by the military. The liberal wanted *laissez faire*, but he also shrank from the idea of a government based on force.

This ambiguity can be seen in the Education Law of 1833, sponsored by the liberal François Guizot (1787–1874), who was genuinely concerned for the moral improvement of the population. Municipalities were made responsible for establishing primary education for boys, but instruction was not to be made compulsory in order to safeguard the individual's liberty. Freedom to establish private and parochial schools was also decreed, and the law was worded in a way to permit local authorities to hire either lay or clerical teachers. This was Guizot's way of promoting public instruction without removing from it religious and ethical training, and all to be done in the interest of liberty and social order. Note further the Factory Act of 1841: industries employing fewer than twenty workers were no longer allowed to hire children, but no inspection system was established to enforce the law, leaving us to conclude that humanitarian intentions were too often overborn by a faith in *laissez faire*.

Elsewhere in Europe, the liberals seemed even less concerned for social and economic welfare or were willing to leave it to nature. The Belgians did, it is true, enact a requirement for each community to establish a primary school in 1842, but there was no regulatory legislation affecting factories. As for Prussia, the decision in 1839 to limit child labor to ten hours a day for children between the ages of nine and sixteen was hardly prompted by humane considerations. It had been noticed in several of the industrializing countries that army recruits from the industrialized regions were deteriorating physically, and the Prussian decision to limit child labor was really a military measure. Even so, the Law of 1839 did not include provisions for factory inspection, and when that came in 1853, it was bitterly resented by the employers.

The apparent indifference of many liberals to human suffering makes it necessary for us to recall the sources of their beliefs—namely, the natural philosophies of the eighteenth century and the recent experiences with the all-powerful state which denied individual rights. It followed that the nineteenth-century liberal was primarily concerned to define what the state might not do.

The object of this Essay is to assert one very simple principle, as entitled to govern absolutely the dealings of society with the individual in the way of compulsion and control, whether the means used be physical force in the form of legal penalties, or the moral coercion of public opinion. That principle is, that the sole end for which mankind are warranted, individually or collectively, in interfering with the liberty of action of any of their number, is self-protection. That the only purpose for which power can be rightfully exercised over any member of a civilized community, against his will, is to prevent harm to others. His own good, either physical or moral, is not a sufficient warrant.[3]

Mill's formula might condemn the principle of *laissez faire* as injurious to members of the community, but it is also clear that he recoils from the prospect of the state or the majority coercing the individual.

THE REVOLUTIONS OF 1830

France

The plight of the working people after 1830 takes on further dimensions when the economic and social facts are put in political focus. The year 1830 was full of political revolution, and the stand-pat Metternichian order was given a severe shaking. Where the revolutions were successful (Belgium and France), the workers had the same high hopes of reform which the British workers expected from the Reform Bill of 1832. The opening assault upon the old regime came in France, where Charles X, in attempting to rule by decree, provoked an uprising by constitutional monarchists and republicans. The former quickly got control of the revolution and promoted the candidacy of the Duke of Orleans. (The Orleans family descended from Philippe, Duke of Orleans, brother of Louis XIV.) The aging Lafayette (1757–1834), veteran of the American and French Revolutions, and the very symbol of republicanism, was convinced that a monarch chosen by the people would be best for France at that moment, and his adherence to Orleans clinched the throne for the Duke. He became Louis-Philippe I (*1830–1848*), King of the French "by the grace of God and the will of the people"—the title an explicit denial of the theory of divine right.

3. John Stuart Mill, *On Liberty* (1859).

At the outset, Louis-Philippe promised to uphold the Charter of 1814 and to accept the tricolor—symbol of the Revolution—as the national flag. His coronation was a simple ceremony at the Chamber of Deputies and did not include the traditional religious service. The revolutionaries, meanwhile, declared void the titles of all peers nominated by the previous king, seriously weakening the upper house for the moment. Since there was no national plebiscite to sanction the new government, it may be said that the revolution in July of 1830 was the work of the lower-house parliamentarians alone. Their subsequent revisions of the Charter were designed to maintain their supremacy: the upper house lost its hereditary nature, the peers to be appointed for life by the crown; and the electorate was broadened by reducing the voting age and the property qualification for the vote. This was to be a middle-class monarchy and Louis-Philippe was to rule as *"le roi bourgeois."*

It remained to be seen how Europe would accept the fall of the Bourbon monarchy, which had, after all, been re-established by the victorious allies in 1814. The question was whether they would stand by, after all their interventions of the 1820's, and permit revolution to be successful. The coldness with which Louis-Philippe's first envoys were received in the major capitals was calculated to express hostility to the new regime, but there was also precious little sympathy for Charles X, who had been warned by Metternich years before that violations of the Charter would certainly cause trouble. Louis-Philippe's pledge that he would maintain the Charter was calculated to reassure the powers and prevent them from taking any action. Furthermore, the successful revolution in France revitalized revolutionary fires elsewhere, soon distracting other governments from the accomplished fact in Paris.

Belgian Independence

Resentment in Belgium over the forced union with the Dutch had been growing ever since 1815. Though substantially outnumbering the Dutch, the Belgians were governed by William I as if they were a minority. Economic and religious legislation invariably favored the Dutch, and such action had the effect of uniting Belgian liberals and Catholics into a national movement. The revolt against William I began in August, a few weeks after the July revolution in Paris. Dutch troops were forced out of Brussels after violent street fighting. Quickly seeing their dilemma, the Dutch gave way and proposed to give Belgium autonomy, the two countries to be united only through the person of the monarch. The Belgian

nationalists, however, proceeded to draw up a liberal constitution providing for an independent constitutional monarchy, specifically excluding
any member of the house of Orange-Nassau. Since a great many of the
Belgians were Catholic and French-speaking, and since it was likely that
the two new revolutionary governments might draw together for protection against intervention, there was speculation that the Belgians would
choose Louis-Philippe or one of his sons as king.

The temptation in Paris must have been great, but Louis-Philippe was
also aware that Britain would not likely tolerate a French regime in
Brussels. He sent old Talleyrand to London to reach an understanding
with the British, while the Dutch were appealing to the Vienna treaty
powers for help to maintain the 1815 settlement. The Belgian cause was
helped by a number of factors: Britain's new Whig ministry was pledged
to reform and was sympathetic to the plight of the Belgians; France was
glad to see the 1815 settlement ruptured, even if an Orleans prince were
not to become king; and revolts in Poland, Italy, and the German world
helped to occupy the three despotic powers whose inclination was to intervene in the Netherlands. At British invitation, the great powers convened
in London and there recognized the dissolution of the Kingdom of the
Netherlands (1830). A few months later the Belgians elected Leopold
of Saxe-Coburg (*1831–1865*) as their king; this choice was acceptable
to the London conference. It proved far harder to get the Belgians and
Dutch to agree on the territorial terms of their separation, and it was
ultimately necessary for the British and French to expel the Dutch by
force from Belgium (1833). Six more years were required before William
I came to terms (1839), agreeing to the Twenty-Four Articles which had
been drawn up by the London conference in 1831. Article VII of the
treaty recognized Belgium to be "independent and perpetually neutral,"
under the guarantee of the powers.

Germany and Italy

Elsewhere, the uprisings had less happy results for the liberal nationalists. In Hanover, Saxony, Hesse-Cassel, and Brunswick, the rulers were
obliged to grant constitutional government, but Metternich did not mean
to tolerate such innovations in the German world. Backed by Prussia, he
got the Germanic Diet to vote the Six Acts (1832), measures which sought
to re-establish the unlimited authority of the petty princes of Germany.
The following year, a group of students tried to seize the Frankfurt Diet.
Their failure marked a further failure for liberalism.

Far more serious were the uprisings in Italy, where the secret societies plotted for national independence. Having failed in 1820-1821, the liberals were again inspired by the success in Paris. The rising began in Parma and Modena early in 1831 and spread into the Papal States. Knowing he had the backing of Russia and Prussia, Metternich sent Austrian forces to crush these uprisings. Austria, as one wit would have it, was becoming "the fire department of Italy." These abortive revolutions convinced the leading Italian nationalists that the plotting of secret societies reinforced by sporadic uprisings, was ineffective. Giuseppe Mazzini (1805–1872), the most notable of the patriots, fled Italy in 1831 to found the Young Italy movement in Marseilles. His goal was the organization of the entire peninsula to give the national regeneration movement (the *Risorgimento*) unity and direction.

Poland

We saw in the previous chapter how Russo-Polish relations slowly deteriorated after 1815. Autonomy within the Russian Empire was made unsatisfactory for the Poles by the Czar's repeated interference into internal affairs, and neither Russian nor Polish patriotic opinion was satisfied with the frontier between the two states. The contested provinces, taken from Poland in the time of Catherine the Great, were clearly Russian in population, and Nicholas I let it be known that they would remain within Russia. Late in 1830, Polish patriots rose against Russian rule, not only inspired by the events in Paris, but also naively expecting assistance from the new Orleans regime. The movement was poorly planned and lacked both direction and popular support. Had the Grand Duke Constantine not lost his head and evacuated Warsaw, it is probable that he could have crushed the insurrection with ease. His panic contributed to the success of the insurgents, and a large Russian force was required to re-establish order. Poland suffered severely for this rebellion: Nicholas I withdrew the Polish Constitution and abolished the Diet and the Polish army. The country, indeed, really became a province of Russia. The Russian language was introduced into the schools, and the Universities of Warsaw and Vilna were closed. Study abroad was prohibited, while works of social and historical import could not be published. An independent Polish culture was threatened with extinction, and it is notable that Polish refugees abroad, particularly in France, lent their energies to keeping Polish culture alive —all the while plotting another insurrection.

THE REVOLT AGAINST *LAISSEZ FAIRE*

In light of the industrial abuses of the early nineteenth century, the liberal doctrine of *laissez faire* appeared to some observers to be simple inhumanity or indifference. To regulate society by natural laws in the fashion of the rationalists was proving to be the height of irrationality. John Stuart Mill, as we have seen, was one liberal conscious of the dilemma. Jean Simonde de Sismondi (1773–1842), a Swiss liberal, was another who realized that some governmental regulation was necessary. Further, although the slogan "Liberty, Equality, Fraternity" had been coined with political and social reform in mind, the industrial revolution had introduced the possibility of a further application of the notions expressed by the slogan: economic equality. By holding out the promise of a higher living standard for all, the industrial revolution made the economic inequalities of the nineteenth century the more obvious. Europe, in short, was ripe for economic doctrines which would promise greater equality and would reduce the exploitation of human beings.

Count Henri de Saint-Simon (French, 1760–1825) was the first eminent socialist writer of the nineteenth century. He believed that the industrialized society was one in which men should cooperate to exploit nature. The state of the future should be a kind of cooperative which would supervise production and distribution of goods. As for the sharing of goods, he would have each person receive "according to his capacity and according to his services." That which a man accumulated during his lifetime could not be passed on to an heir, all inheritance going to the state for the commonweal. His disciples developed his ideas into a political system which was authoritarian, the assumption being that individual liberty and initiative was the cause of social strife. They were also responsible for developing Saint-Simonian socialism into a religious cult, though Saint-Simon himself laid the groundwork in his last book, *The New Christianity* (1825), the movement being a peculiar example of the religious revival after the Napoleonic era. His Christianity, however, was a moralistic Christianity rather than a mystical matter. Yet, he suggested that he was the messiah for the new cult. Christianity could be summed up in one commandment: The Golden Rule. And Saint-Simon castigated the Catholics as Antichrists for losing sight of this one truth in their development of a vast spiritual and temporal hierarchy.

The spiritual force, the force of morality, the Christian force, the one which bestows frankness and loyalty, is entirely absent. In a word, the Catholic, apostolic, and Roman religion is nothing else but a Christian heresy. It is only a segment of a degenerate Christianity.[4]

The Saint-Simonians carried his doctrine of brotherly love into the economic and social realm. Salvation lay in organizing the means of production so as to improve the lot of the poor as quickly as possible. The cult attracted around 300 members, some of whom became notable social and economic reformers later in the century; but almost from the start, a schism developed over the question of the probable coming of a woman-messiah. And in 1832, Louis Philippe's government cracked down on the cult for its open advocacy of the abolition of private property. Several leaders were imprisoned, and the movement collapsed.[5]

Another French socialist, Charles Fourier (1772–1837), was similar to Saint-Simon in his opposition to the competition of a free society which presumably led to exploitation. Let us have harmony, he said, rather than antagonism; but he thought that this new social harmony would be best achieved through the establishment of small cooperative communities rather than through regulation by the national state in the Saint-Simonian manner. He called these communities phalansteries (*phalanges*). Each individual entering the phalanstery would be given property to give him a stake in the community and to make all members equal as property holders. Moreover, each person would freely choose his own occupation. Fourier believed that harmony would be the result. Where competition and antagonism were removed to make the environment sweeter, human instincts would naturally work for peace and happiness. It should already be evident that these early socialists had inherited the eighteenth-century faith in the inherent goodness of human nature, the belief that it is society which corrupts mankind. Improve man's environment through the reorganization of the production and distribution of goods, and human nature would recover its natural goodness. The first of the phalansteries was established near Rambouillet in 1832, but the movement enjoyed its greatest vogue in America during the 1840's, when sixteen communities were founded, the most notable being Brook Farm.

4. Frank E. Manuel, *The New World of Henri Saint-Simon* (Cambridge, Mass., 1956), p. 335, quoting from *The New Christianity*.
5. See Arthur Louis Dunham, *The Anglo-French Treaty of Commerce of 1860 and the Progress of the Industrial Revolution in France* (Ann Arbor, Mich., 1930), pp. 29-31.

Meanwhile, in Britain, Robert Owen (1771–1858) was developing a third socialist system which was closer to Fourier's than to Saint-Simon's in that he did not advocate abolition of private property. Owen rose from being the manager of a cotton mill in Manchester to become owner of another in New Lanark, Scotland. New Lanark was a typical wretched factory town, an arena of poverty and drunkenness. An environmentalist, Owen worked to turn the town into a model community, where there would be no unemployment. He paid higher wages while reducing the average work day from seventeen hours to ten, and he established a school which children between the ages of five and ten were required to attend. He not only improved factory conditions but also constructed decent houses for his workers. There was also a cooperative store at which they could purchase goods at little more than cost. Owen hoped that his example would lead both the state and other individuals to establish similar communities numbering between 500 and 3000 people. The more self-sufficient the community, he felt, the more the general welfare would be enhanced. Such ideas, even coming from a highly successful manufacturer, failed to impress most of the Whigs and the Tories; but he did stimulate the founding of many cooperative stores in Britain, and a number of Owenite communities were established in America.

In the 1830's, as British workers became increasingly dismayed by the failure of the reformed Parliament to enact legislation directly beneficial to their conditions of life, they joined a movement for political democracy known as Chartism. The "People's Charter" was drawn up by two artisans, William Lovett and Francis Place. This document not only asked for universal male suffrage and the removal of the property qualification for the vote, but, in demanding annual parliamentary elections, it implied the sovereignty of the people. And on that subject, neither Whig nor Tory could go farther than a belief that sovereignty was vested in the Parliament and the crown. When the Chartists presented their petition, which had a million and a quarter signatures, to Parliament in 1839, it was promptly rejected. The Chartist leaders were divided as to whether to use violence or peaceful propaganda to further their cause. Most of them shrank from violent methods, and what rioting there was was handled by the government. Their energies were soon channeled into the anti-Corn Law movement of the 1840's. Chartism did accomplish something, however, in that it focused attention on the shocking conditions of life in the factory towns. An eye-opener for many humane liberals, Chartism weakened their faith in *laissez faire*.

The Frenchman Louis Blanc (1811–1882) was another radical whose ideas amounted to an attack upon free enterprise. Whereas Saint-Simon, Fourier, and Owen had based their social philosophies on the theory of environmentalism, Blanc's theories developed as a direct reaction to the miserable conditions of the workers in the industrial cities. In 1839, Blanc published a book entitled *The Organization of Labor* in which he presented what he called facts—statistics—on the miserable conditions of employment. Unregulated free enterprise, he insisted, meant low wages and long periods of unemployment for the majority of workers, contributing to crime and the destruction of family life. But, he continued, every man has not merely the right to live, but also the right to live by the fruits of his own labor; and any system under which an employed man cannot subsist stands condemned. Finally, Blanc would condemn any government which stood aside and refused to regulate the economy. The obligation of the state was to open factories and to provide full employment at decent wages. Confident that this competition would ultimately ruin private operators, Blanc saw this device as the means of achieving complete nationalization of capital.

His French contemporary, Pierre-Joseph Proudhon (1809–1865), was a far more complex personality whose ideas have often been misinterpreted. He opened one of his early books, for instance, with the following passage:

> If I should be asked to answer the following question: "What is slavery?" and I should answer in one word, "Murder!", my meaning would at once be understood. No further argument would be required to show that the power to take from a man his thought, his will, his personality, is a power of life and death, so that to enslave a man is to kill him. Why, then, to this other question: "What is property?" may I not likewise answer, "Theft?"[6]

It is understandable that Proudhon was understood to mean that private property is evil and that it must be abolished. In fact, he meant to denounce only the property of anyone who used it to exploit the labor of others. Otherwise, the right to own property he—much like John Locke —felt to be inseparable from individual liberty. He denounced socialists and communists for their desire to destroy private property. His own end was "justice, nothing else."

Proudhon called himself an anarchist, probably the first serious thinker of the nineteenth century to adopt the tag. He started with the older

6. Proudhon, *Qu'est-ce que la Propriété?* (Paris, 1840). My translation.

view that man, when he emerged from the state of nature, necessarily organized government to create order. But as man's reason developed and he gained experience, this authority becomes increasingly obnoxious, so that he sought to revolt against government. Thus, rational man, who seeks liberty and equality, will find it through decentralizing political authority, by voluntarily reorganizing society so that authority is self-imposed rather than imposed by the state.

When we come to Auguste Comte (1789–1857), early in his career a close associate of Saint-Simon, we meet a thinker whose ideas seem to epitomize the main currents of mid-nineteenth-century thought. Comte summed up mankind's experience as an evolutionary progress through three main phases. The first he called the theological phase, a period when man's knowledge was so limited that he necessarily ascribed all phenomena to supernatural powers. Next, man progressed to a metaphysical phase, a period in which he sought to discover the causes of phenomena by observing nature and by using his reason. Finally, man had reached the positive phase of his historical development, the period in which he no longer asks *why* things happen but is content with the "scientific" facts —content to know *how* things happen or *what* is happening. Hence the school of thought which Comte founded has been called positivism. The particular kind of scientific fact-finding which engaged the positivists we now call social science. Their purpose was to gather information about man and his society so that our political, religious, and ethical systems could be given scientific foundation. Comte was not merely the founder of sociology as a discipline; he also gave the discipline a strong humanist cast—another indication that the metaphysical or spiritual realm had been abandoned. The study of man in order to give him a better life was soon transformed into a worship of mankind. Like Saint-Simonian socialism, positivism became a religious cult. In both cases, however, the cults did not have the longevity of their social doctrines.

Towards Humanity, who is for us the only true Great Being, we, the conscious elements of whom she is composed, shall henceforth direct every aspect of our life, individual or collective. Our thoughts will be devoted to the knowledge of Humanity, our affections to her love, our actions to her service. . . .

Thus Positivism becomes, in the true sense of the word, a Religion; the only religion which is real and complete; destined therefore to replace all imperfect and provisional systems resting on the primitive basis of theology.[7]

7. Auguste Comte, *A General View of Positivism* (Official Centenary edition of the International Auguste Comte Centenary Committee, New York, 1957), p. 365.

Surely the most famous social philosopher of that day was the German Karl Marx (1813–1883). It was he who dubbed Saint-Simon, Fourier, and Owen "Utopian Socialists" because their systems were not founded upon historical knowledge. He claimed his own system to be historically demonstrable—his thesis borne out by what had happened in the past. While the historian may disagree with Marx's reading in history, Marx did trace the progress of mankind; and he found an evolutionary mechanism which not only explained the past but predicted the future. His *Communist Manifesto* (1848) was, thus, a statement of a philosophy of history as well as a call to arms: "Let the ruling classes tremble at a communistic revolution. The proletarians have nothing to lose but their chains. They have a world to win. Workingmen of all countries unite!"[8]

Marx greatly expanded his ideas later in *Capital* (1867), but their outline appeared in the *Manifesto*. "The history of all hitherto existing society is the history of class struggles."[9] He had borrowed what he thought was the Hegelian dialectic or argument—namely, that the conflict of the thesis with its antithesis, ultimately producing a synthesis, was the key to explaining historical change. As Marx used this dialectic, the conflict was always between the propertied and the propertyless; and since he also believed that reality lies in the realm of matter and things (property), this mechanism was called dialectical materialism. This was another way of saying that the course of history had been determined by economic factors. According to his theory, the class owning the means of production will inevitably become politically ascendant. In the past, when machines and factories became the principal means of production, the bourgeoisie replaced the feudal aristocracy. In the future, the proletariat—the operators of the machines—would replace the bourgeoisie.

The triumph of the proletariat would be brought about by the failure of capitalism—which Marx predicted as the inevitable outcome of the nineteenth-century conflict between labor and the owners of capital. He did not mean that capitalism would fail because it was ethically bad, but rather because the low wages paid to laborers would make it impossible for them to buy the products of their own labor. Prices would not be lowered, because this would be inconsistent with the capitalist's necessary profits. (We see here, incidentally, that Marx was influenced by Ricardo's

8. See, Massima Salvadori, *The Rise of Modern Communism* (New York, 1952), pp. 5-8.
9. E. H. Carr, *Studies in Revolution* (London, 1950), "The Communist Manifesto," p. 17.

inflexible views on wages and profits.) In the long run, then, since Marx could not conceive of bourgeois governments limiting bourgeois profits, he thought that the rich would get richer and the poor poorer. Much of the middle class would fade into the proletariat, which would finally seize the state and the means of production. The proletariat would then provide a temporary dictatorship which would abolish capitalism, organize a cooperative commonwealth, and create the first classless society in history. Necessarily this would be a society without conflict, an earth-bound Eden.

Whereas in Hegel's dialectic, the synthesis becomes a new thesis and the philosophical mechanism grinds endlessly on in the search of higher truths Marx's dialectic foretold a happy ending: the end of class conflict with the achievement of a classless society.

LITERATURE AND THE ARTS

The intellectual and artistic climate of Europe remained predominantly romantic in this period, and even many writers of history were imbued with the Romantic spirit. Jules Michelet (French, 1798–1874), for instance, was frankly partisan and wrote passionately of the greatness of France. We remember him as a nationalist and a liberal too:

Frenchmen, of every condition, every class, every party, remember well one thing! You have on earth but one sure friend, France! Before the ever-enduring coalition of aristocracies, you will always be guilty of one crime,—to have wished, fifty years ago, to deliver the world. They have not forgiven it, nor will they ever forget it. You are always their dread. Among yourselves, you may be distinguished by different party names; but you are, as Frenchmen, condemned together. In the face of Europe, know that France will never have but one inexpiable name, which is her true, eternal designation,—The Revolution![10]

Michelet's English contemporary, Thomas Carlyle (1795–1881), not only sought for the dramatic in history, but in emphasizing the impact of great men upon events, he really thought of history as biography.

For, if we will think of it, no Time need have gone to ruin, could it have *found* a man great enough, a man wise and good enough; wisdom to discern truly what the Time wanted, valour to lead it on the right road thither; these are the salvation of any Time.[11]

10. Jules Michelet, *The People* (London, 1846), p. 16.
11. Thomas Carlyle, *On Heroes, Hero-Worship, and the Heroic in History* (London, 1840), Lecture I.

Another distinguished Englishman, Thomas Babington Macaulay (1800–1859), if less emotional and more careful of facts than Carlyle, did not believe that a cold, dispassionate recitation of facts made for successful history. The individual historian must give meaning to the facts through their selection, arrangement, and lucid presentation:

> No picture, then, and no history, can present us with the whole truth; but those are the best pictures and the best histories which exhibit such parts of the truth as most nearly produce the effect of the whole. He who is deficient in the art of selection may, by showing nothing but the truth, produce all the effect of the grossest falsehood.[12]

In Germany, meanwhile, Leopold von Ranke (1795–1886) was trying to put the discipline of history more squarely in the empirical tradition. The historical way of acquiring knowledge, he said, is "through the perception of the particular."[13] Those particulars must come from primary sources: diaries, letters, memoirs, and diplomatic correspondence; and the historian should be concerned "to show what actually happened." Interpretation of what actually happened will then presumably avoid the pitfall of making the facts fit a preconceived notion of what ought to have happened.

As for religious romanticism after 1830, the Oxford Movement in England is the best example; though the Oxonians certainly did not consider themselves romantics. The earlier evangelical movement in the Anglican Church had lost its vitality, and when the Whigs came to power in 1830, many sincere Anglicans feared that the Church might become completely subject to secular control. Traditionally, after all, the Whigs had been champions of dissent and opposed to the establishment. Beginning about 1833, a group of Oxonians led a revival movement dedicated to infusing greater spiritual strength into the Church. Their emphasis upon faith and, in particular, upon the sacraments, doctrines, and rituals of the ancient Church had the effect of rallying the clergy and raising its morale and standards. But the same emphasis led a few of the Oxford Reformers on into the Roman Church, including, in 1845, the greatest of their number, John Henry Newman (1801–1890). Necessarily he left Oxford, and the whole movement became compromised in Britain. New-

12. Macaulay, "History," *Edinburgh Review,* May, 1828.
13. See Fritz Stern, *The Varieties of History: From Voltaire to the Present* (New York, Meridian Books, 1956), for Ranke, Macaulay, and Michelet.

man became a prominent and popular Catholic and was created a cardinal in 1879.

Many romantic novelists of the liberal era have remained popular to this day. It is remarkable how many of them protested against the conventions of bourgeois society and the conditions of the industrial towns. We see in them as a group the pessimism which had earlier marked those who had become disenchanted with rationalism. Stendhal (1783–1842), a Frenchman, was an extremely sensitive romanticist and a liberal. His *The Red and the Black* (1831) was the story of a young upstart who chose clerical black rather than military red in his scheme to rise in society. His love affairs and his opportunism were Stendhal's way of commenting on the morality of that day. A later novel, *The Charterhouse of Parma* (1839), earlier quoted, was an acid commentary on the illiberal regimes of Italy.

His compatriot, Honoré de Balzac (1799–1850), has even greater historical interest in that he sought to give, through his novels, a detailed survey of French life under the July Monarchy of Louis-Philippe. He gave the over-all title *The Human Comedy* (1842) to this survey and established the tradition of "documentary" novels which Zola was to perfect later in the century. *The Human Comedy,* however, lacked the systematic organization which Zola achieved, so that it was not a complete survey. Balzac's hatred of the society of industrializing, commercial France is continually evident in his books. He had the romanticist's contempt for the unexciting, stingy standards set by *le roi bourgeois* himself, a world in which bankruptcy was the greatest of all possible tragedies. "I adore Louis-Philippe," exclaims Achille Rivet, a bourgeois who has enriched himself by making gold braid for officers' uniforms; "he is my idol, the august and perfect representation of the class on which he has founded his dynasty. I shall never forget what he has done for the gold braid industry by reestablishing the National Guard."[14] Balzac's subjects were taken from real life, though he used his imagination liberally in their rendering, giving us the mixture of romanticism and realism characteristic of the remainder of the century. George Sand's (1804–1876) novels were more romantic in a sentimental sense than Balzac's. A well-known French feminist, she gave her readers heroines who were restless romantics, draw-

14. From *La Cousine Bette,* quoted in Raymond Giraud, *The Unheroic Hero in the Novels of Stendhal, Balzac, and Flaubert* (New Brunswick, N.J., 1957), p. 124.

ing in particular upon her own emotional experiences for *Indiana* (1831) and *Lelia* (1833).

In Russia, N. V. Gogol (1809–1852) fiercely attacked hypocrisy and corruption in high places in his play *The Government Inspector* (1836), a picture which Nicholas I admitted was accurate; while his novel *Dead Souls* (1842) included a sharp denunciation of serfdom. Gogol's sharp characterizations are reminiscent of his English contemporary, Charles Dickens (1812–1870), the most popular of the early Victorian novelists. Here we find, as in Balzac, a mixture of realism and romanticism. His characters were recognizable types set in familiar situations, but this realism was sentimentalized and melodramatized. Because many Victorian novels appeared in installments in the popular magazines, they had a wide public; but this practice sometimes contributed to lengthy, episodic novels rather than highly unified, crisp works. Dickens' *Pickwick Papers* (1836) is a good example. Some of his best-known works are propagandistic: *Oliver Twist* (1838), for instance, which reflected the harshness of the Poor Law, or *Nicholas Nickleby* (1839), which showed the need for school reform. While Dickens was revealing lower-class life, William Makepeace Thackery (1811–1863) portrayed upper-class life. Also a moralist and a social critic, he was always more restrained than Dickens. Furthermore, he worked more painstakingly than Dickens, turning out fewer works. His best-known novel is *Vanity Fair* (1847), but *Henry Esmond* (1852) is generally thought to be superior.

In painting, the leadership in the romantic and the neoclassical schools in France was retained in this era by Delacroix and Ingres respectively, but a new and dynamic figure appeared on the scene: Honoré Daumier (1808–1879). Working most of his life as a lithographer-journalist, he was recognized as a painter and sculptor only at the end of his long career. His subject matter, with few exceptions, was the unpleasant, the ugly, the grotesque, the inhumanity to be found on all sides, and the shallow pompousness of the bourgeoisie. He had that merciless wit found in the most merciful of men. Two other notable talents emerged in this period: Jean-Baptiste-Camille Corot (1796–1875) and Jean-François Millet (1814–1875). Corot, even though sympathetic to the romantics, called himself a naturalist. His earlier paintings had a clarity and precision reminiscent of the seventeenth-century French classicists, Poussin and Claude Lorrain; but toward the end of his life, his landscapes prefigure impressionism. Millet correctly called himself a rustic, for, in sum, if that quality is not revealed in what I have done, I have done nothing at all. . . . I am a peasant of peasants . . . and as for explanations of my styles of painting, that would be difficult to tell because I have not bothered myself with them; and if styles there are, they could only have derived from my having entered, more or less, into my subject, from the difficulties of my life.[15]

Hector Berlioz continued after 1830 to be the most significant innovator in the world of music, though he did not achieve great popularity. His difficulty in being heard derived only in part from his unconventional music; he scored on a Napoleonic scale, so that a performance often required an organ, extra brass and percussion, sometimes choirs, and even brass bands. *Harold in Italy* was completed in 1834, the *Requiem* in 1837, *Romeo and Juliet* in 1839, and the *Damnation of Faust* in 1846. The three important romanticists who emerged after 1830 stood in sharp contrast to Berlioz: two Germans, Felix Mendelssohn-Bartholdy (1809–1849) and Robert Schumann (1810–1856), and the Pole Frederic Chopin (1810–1849). All composed on a much smaller scale, all were intensely lyrical, inclined to be sentimental, and at least the last two were pianistic rather than orchestral in their conceptions. Furthermore, they were popular in their own lifetimes. To ascribe their popularity to "program" music —that is, music whose understanding is presumably enhanced by either title or verbal description—would be a mistake. Their appeal lay in their lyricism, of which Mendelssohn's Violin Concerto (1844), Schumann's Piano Concerto (1845), and Chopin's Nocturnes and Ballads are excellent examples.

Born in Berlin, Mendelssohn was the founder of the Leipzig Conservatory, an able pianist and conductor, and most significantly the discoverer of Johann Sebastian Bach—who had remained obscure after his death. Schumann, a Saxon by birth, went to the University of Leipzig, becoming a member of the musical circle which soon included Mendelssohn. In 1834, a group of romantics founded the *Neue Zeitschrift für Musik* to champion new music, and Schumann was its editor for ten years. Schumann's four symphonies were poorly scored, but when he wrote for the piano, his work was among the century's greatest. Chopin, who was almost exclusively a composer for the piano, also composed some of the greatest music of the time for that instrument. Born in Poland of a French father

15. Paul Gay, *J. F. Millet* (Paris, 1950), p. 3.

and a Polish mother, he came to Paris in 1830. Like all romantics, he chose forms which allowed him great freedom: études, preludes, nocturnes, as well as dance forms—waltzes, polonaises, and mazurkas. His was intensely personal music.

SCIENCE

By 1830 the world of science had come forth with ideas calculated to revolutionize physics. The wave theory of light had been suggested in the seventeenth century but had been rejected by the ultimate authority, Sir Isaac Newton. One of his several objections was his assumption that waves of light would simply bend around corners, the way water swirls around an obstruction. Obviously this does not happen, since we observe shadows. Thus, Newton saw light as rectilinear rays, and he suggested a corpuscular theory of light—a theory, it is true, in which he had no great confidence.

Are not the Rays of Light very small bodies emitted from shining Substances? For such Bodies will pass through uniform Mediums in right Lines without bending into the Shadow, which is the nature of the Rays of Light.[16]

The work of the Englishman Thomas Young (1773–1829) answered this particular objection by Newton, his experiment being the well-known one which involved passing a narrow beam of white light through two pin holes in a screen onto a second screen. If the distance that the two waves of light had to travel to reach a common point on the second screen was equal, then the crests of the waves were superimposed on the screen and the light doubled. But if one wave was given a half wavelength more to travel than the other in order to reach a common point, the crest of one wave coincided with the trough of the other—and there was darkness. In retrospect, Young's demonstration of the wave theory of light is recognized to have been the first breach in the Newtonian system.

In 1820, a Danish physicist in Copenhagen, Hans Christian Oersted (1777–1851), published his observation that a magnetic needle was deflected when a current of electricity flowed through it. Immediately physicists all over western Europe turned their attention to the problem of electromagnetism. Within four months, three important contributions were

16. Quoted in Sir William C. Dampier, *A History of Science* (4th ed., London, 1956), p. 163.

read before the Academy of Sciences in Paris. Let us note in particular, however, the work of Michael Faraday (English, 1791–1867), for he was the synthesizer of these early efforts. He was convinced from the outset that those phenomena he called "the forces of matter" are mutually dependent and have a common origin; in other words, that magnetism, electricity, gravitation, cohesion, heat and light are different manifestations of the same basic power. Consequently, his experiments were designed to find the relation of these "forces." He began by verifying the experiments already done by his predecessors—Oersted, Humphrey Davy, Ampère, and Arago—as the foundation for his own work on electromagnetic induction.

He reported his first successful experiment to the Royal Society on November 24, 1831. He had wound two helices of insulated wire on the same wooden cylinder. One wire was then attached to a galvanometer, the other to a battery. When a current was introduced into the latter wire, there was a momentary slight effect on the galvanometer; there was a similar response when the circuit was broken, though the current had not been introduced into the wire attached to the galvanometer. Furthermore, in between the induction and the cutting of the current, the galvanometer gave no response. Knowing the likely connection between electricity and magnetism from Oersted's experiment, Faraday next substituted a small steel needle for the galvanometer:

On substituting a small hollow helix, formed round a glass tube, for the galvanometer, introducing a steel needle, making contact as before between the battery and the inducing wire, and then removing the needle before the battery contact was broken, it was found magnetized.[17]

Since most practical electrical machinery depends on the principles of the induction of currents, Faraday had laid the ground for a new industrial boom.

The publication of *Principles of Geology* (1830) by Charles Lyell (English, 1797–1875) was a landmark in the development of the natural sciences. By showing that the earth got its appearance from the continual action of geological processes—the rising and sinking of land, earthquakes, volcanic action, and erosion—Lyell contributed important evidence to those who argued for the evolutionary rather than the mechanical view of the universe. Similarly, an important discovery in chemistry in 1828

17. *Ibid.,* p. 222.

Left: *Honoré de Balzac* by Nadar
Above: Giuseppe Mazzini

Above: Louis-Philippe
Right: Karl Marx

The Third Class Carriage by Honoré Daumier

Right: Fedor M. Dostoevski
Below: John Stuart Mill

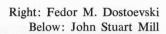

had philosophical implications. Friedrich Wöhler (German, 1800–1882) succeeded in producing urea from the chemical elements making up urea. Previously it had been held that organic matter could not be artificially produced, and now Wöhler was apparently creating living matter in a laboratory. His work proved to be the basis for many synthetic products later in the century.

1848: THE YEAR OF REVOLUTION

The years of 1848–1849 were full of revolutionary turmoil, and, as in 1830, France proved to be the initial focal point. It used to be said that the various revolutions of 1848 were failures—that except in France they failed to overturn existing regimes and that even in France a monarch was soon again on the throne. But would we say, for instance, that the French Revolution of 1789 or the Russian Revolution of 1917 were successes or failures? Or would we conclude that such judgments do not get us very far in understanding what happened?

Looking at 1848, it is more useful to note how many liberal, national, and radical ideas—the heritage of the French Revolution and the industrial revolutions—came to a head in that year. Each group of revolutionaries, whatever its nationality and whether liberal or radical, strove to found regimes reflecting the more advanced ideals of the earlier nineteenth century. Moreover, that these revolutionaries failed to establish durable regimes did considerable damage to the prestige of their ideals and opened the way to a new species of political leadership, a tougher and more realistic leadership on the whole, which revamped the older ideals in its own image. Thus, while the details of the revolutions of 1848 varied according to nationality, subsequent generations came to recognize that year as a significant political and cultural watershed, after which nationalism was more militant, the tenets of liberalism seemingly on the wane, and the proletarian movement increasingly inclined to violent solutions of social and economic problems.

France

As for France, we must remember the revolutionary origin of the July Monarchy of Louis-Philippe and the subsequent disenchantment of the workers when they found that his liberal government was too dedicated to *laissez faire* to permit legislative attempts to improve economic and social conditions. The liberal of that day was largely concerned to protect the individual from the tyranny of the state; but the French worker who could not support his family because of low wages can be excused for not respecting the tact of the state in refusing to regulate minimum wages or to decree an end to miserable working conditions and long hours. His was the liberty to starve to death without governmental interference. He might toy with various socialist and radical schemes, but Louis Blanc's brand of socialism became the usual answer for French laborers in the 1840's. The September Laws of 1835, coming after many months of labor agitation in Lyons and Paris and after an attempt upon the King's life, drove the radical movement underground by providing for swift trials of insurgents and for rigid press control.

Labor was not alone in opposing the July Monarchy. The Legitimists regarded Louis-Philippe as a usurper, the clergy was naturally opposed to the government's official anticlericalism, and patriots in general—including the Bonapartists—were affronted by the spineless foreign policy which suggested peace at any price—or profits without honor. The poet Alphonse de Lamartine (1790–1869) was later to write, in explaining the coming of the revolution in 1848, that France was bored; a remark which contained an element of truth. In the face of general opposition, François Guizot, the chief policy maker from 1840 to 1848, manipulated elections and bought votes in parliament. Property qualifications still limited the electorate sharply, and when the intellectuals demanded an end to corruption and the broadening of the electorate, Guizot advised them to get rich: *"Enrichissez-vous."* Perhaps this would have satisfied the new railroad barons, but as Berlioz said, these were times "when artists ought not to be alive."[18]

Taking advantage of a severe depression in 1846–1847 which led to widespread suffering, the parliamentary opposition (moderate republicans and legitimists) demanded an extension of the suffrage and an end to corruption. To rally support from the general public, the Republicans organized a campaign of banquets, which was to culminate in a giant banquet in Paris. This set off popular demonstrations, which the King hoped to halt by dismissing Guizot as prime minister. Yet, the Republican rioting continued until shots were fired. The following day, Louis-Philippe abdicated and left for Britain. A republic was proclaimed the same day, but the revolutionaries making up the provisional government were hardly

18. Jacques Barzun, *Berlioz and the Romantic Century* (Boston, 1950), Vol. I, p. 343.

of one mind. The moderate republicans, led by Lamartine, had joined with the Radicals, dominated by Louis Blanc (1811–1882), to overthrow the monarchy—the one point on which they could agree. Blanc's followers hoped to establish a socialist republic, and they had the advantage of controlling the Parisian mob. Lamartine's group wanted a liberal republic but recognized the necessity of temporary compromises with the radicals until provincial opinion could be informed of these events in Paris; they expected that rural France would be antisocialist.

Thus, the Moderate and Radical republicans struck a bargain. The Moderates agreed to adopt Louis Blanc's "right to work" principle in exchange for the radicals' agreement to postpone elections for a constitutional assembly until mid-April. The Moderates assumed that immediate elections in the heat of revolutionary enthusiasm would favor the radicals; but let the country think of the socialist implications of the radical program for a few weeks, and the moderates would win. Such was the case. The new National Assembly in April had about 600 republican delegates, with the moderates outnumbering the radicals about 5 to 1. Many of these moderates were nominal republicans. In addition, there were nearly 300 monarchist delegates, a further conservative element. In the meantime, the provisional government established the National Workshops to implement the "right to work" principle. Presumably the government meant to provide work for the unemployed, but the program was threatened from the start when its direction was confined to a man who had little sympathy for its principles. When the antiradical electoral results were known, the days of the National Workshops were numbered; furthermore, applicants for government employment streamed into Paris in such numbers that work could not be supplied.

In June, the government determined to reduce the Workshops to manageable size—as a prelude to dissolving them. Men not resident in Paris for at least six months were immediately dismissed, and those between the ages of eighteen and twenty-five were either to enlist in the army or be dismissed from employment. The radical leaders quickly convinced the Parisian mob that it had been betrayed—indeed, that the revolution had once again been betrayed—and the street fighting which followed was unprecedented anywhere in Europe. Republicans fought republicans for four frightful days (the June Days), leaving over 5000 dead. The army remained loyal to the Assembly and crushed the radical movement. These events explain why the Assembly ultimately produced a constitution far more conservative than one might have expected from a revolutionary assembly.

Late in 1848, the constitution for the Second Republic was ready. It provided for a unicameral assembly to be elected by direct, universal suffrage; a Council of State, appointed by the Assembly to draft bills for the Assembly's debate; and a president, to be elected by direct, universal suffrage. The president was allowed to choose his own ministers, but—in order to check executive power—the framers of the constitution made the ministers responsible to the Assembly. As soon as new elections were held to establish government under the new constitution, they revealed that the Second Republic had limited republican support. The new Assembly contained only 250 republicans out of a total of 750 deputies, the remainder being Orleanists and legitimists. But the greatest surprise came in the presidential election: Prince Louis-Napoleon Bonaparte, nephew of Napoleon I, swamped the moderate and radical republican candidates, beating his combined opposition nearly three to one. Surely his appeal lay partly in his name, especially attractive in the aftermath of the June Days when a man or order seemed required. And a half-century of romanticism had served to remove the odium of Napoleonic dictatorship and had left an aura of glory in notable contrast to the dullness of Louis-Philippe's reign. In this way, the Second Republic was given a mortal blow at its birth.

Italy

Meanwhile, the Italian national movement, led by Giuseppe Mazzini, had been merging with other liberal and national movements. Mazzini had organized his Young Italy movement in Marseilles, where he had fled after the abortive revolutions in 1831. Soon thereafter, he was in London trying to coordinate the efforts of kindred organizations representing other nationalities which had not achieved national unity. For Mazzini, the nation-state was the key to the welfare of humanity in general:

In laboring for our own country on the right principle, we labor for Humanity. Our country is the fulcrum of the lever we have to wield for the common good. If we abandon that fulcrum, we run the risk of rendering ourselves useless not only to humanity but to our country itself. Before men can *associate* with the nations of which humanity is composed, they must have a National existence. There is no true association except among equals. It is only through our country that we can have a recognized *collective* existence.[19]

19. Mazzini, *On the Duties of Man* (a series of articles published originally between 1844 and 1858).

Mazzini's nationalism, in short, was not a selfish, exclusive patriotism. Each nationality had its unique qualities, which could enrich the general stream of civilization only when that nationality was free and self-governing. Mazzini's propaganda from London kept the Italian nationalists in ferment through the 1830's and 1840's.

There were some Italian patriots, however, for whom Mazzini's revolutionary methods and republican anticlericalism were untenable. A Piedmontese priest, Vincenzo Gioberti (1801–1851), promoted a confederation of independent Italian states, which would have made the Pope the national leader:

> The perfect political life of various peoples can and must vary in details and minor matters, but not in generality and essence. These are reduced substantially to three heads: unity, liberty, and independence of the fatherland No public life is perfectly ordered if it is not united, if it is not free of any foreign yoke and strong enough to fear none, and if it does not enjoy full civil liberty.... Now from what I have shown, it is clear that Italy can obtain these benefits without war, without revolution, without offense to any public or private authority. That is to say, unity and liberty can be obtained by a confederaation of the various states under the presidency of the Pontiff, and independence by internal reforms in each state which every prince can effect without peril and without any loss of his own power.[20]

An advantage of Gioberti's scheme was that it solved the Roman question by making possible a united Italy without despoiling the papacy. Mazzini and the republicans meant to seize Rome as the national capital and relieve the papacy of its temporal power. This temporal power, granted to the Popes in the eighth century, was a device to help preserve the independence of the papacy. Thus, temporal power was a means of securing spiritual freedom, and was not an end in itself. By the 1840's, the temporal power of the papacy was insignificant in the face of the great military states of Europe; but the Popes clung to their temporal power as a matter of principle. To surrender it might lead to the loss of Rome itself. Of even greater import was the unwillingness of many churchmen to come to terms with the liberal nationalists, many of whom were suspected of being not only merely anticlerical, but downright irreligious.

A third solution to the Italian question was posed by Count Cesare Balbo (1789–1853) in his book *The Hopes of Italy* (1843), which es-

20. Gioberti, *On the Civil and Moral Primacy of the Italians* (1843), quoted in Mendenhall, Henning, and Ford, *The Quest for a Principle of Authority in Europe, 1715-Present* (New York, 1948), p. 180.

poused the cause of the house of Savoy. His hope was that the King of Sardinia-Piedmont would make his country the nucleus of a united Italy from which Austrian influence would be banished. The Italy he envisioned was a constitutional monarchy—a liberal, progressive state, but not the democratic republic planned by Mazzini. One of Balbo's readers was the Piedmontese aristocrat Count Camillo Benso di Cavour (1810–1861). In 1846, Cavour declared his adherence to "the wise counsels of that enlightened patriot, M. di Balbo," and emphasized in particular that industrialization and railroad building—not conspiracies and plots—would lead the Italians out of servitude. "For them the railroad will be not only a means to greater wealth but also a powerful weapon, by the use of which they will eventually triumph over the reactionary forces that have held them back in a state of industrial and political infancy."[21]

It appeared in 1846 that the leadership of the national movement would devolve upon the new Pope, Pius IX (*1846–1878*). His predecessor had been an associate of Metternich, standing firm against revolution. Pius IX, however, quickly granted amnesty to more than a thousand political prisoners and refugees, and talked of modernizing the administration of his state. The Italians were soon wildly enthusiastic, and Metternich had to admit that the one thing he had not counted on was a liberal Pope. If a gesture must be made, Metternich thought the Pope would be better advised to grant pardons rather than amnesties. A pardon is an act of mercy, while the amnesty might suggest a change in political outlook—which it certainly did to liberal Italians—an acceptance of wicked revolutionary principles. As Metternich put it: "God never grants amnesties, God pardons."[22] Following the amnesty, Pius IX started immediately to outline the modernization of the Papal States. Some of his reforms were material—as in his interest in scientific agriculture, the development of railroads, and the promotion of gas lighting for streets—but he also projected political and constitutional reforms. The press laws were liberalized, the criminal code was revised, and, against the wishes of the cardinals, he began to employ laymen in administrative positions. By the end of 1847, the Pope, to his discomfort, found himself a hero of the Italian revolutionaries.

To counteract the apparent papal advantage in Italy, Charles Albert

---

21. The dated biography by W. R. Thayer, *The Life and Times of Cavour*, 2 vols. (New York, 1911) is still recommended.

22. E. E. Y. Hales, *Pio Nono, A Study in European Politics and Religion in the Nineteenth Century* (London, 1954), p. 57.

(*1831–1849*) yielded to liberal pressure by granting similar reforms in Sardinia-Piedmont. But early in 1848, a purely local revolt in Sicily spread to the Neapolitan mainland, and Ferdinand II (*1830–1859*) appealed for Austrian aid. Pius IX refused to allow Austrian troops passage through papal territory, forcing Ferdinand to grant a liberal constitution. In short order, the Duke of Tuscany, the King of Sardinia-Piedmont, and Pius IX all felt compelled to follow suit. Suddenly came the astonishing news of a liberal uprising in Vienna and the consequent resignation of Metternich. In response, the Milanese rose against the Austrians, forcing them out of the city, while the Venetians declared themselves an independent republic. Charles Albert, though not inclined toward liberalism, recognized that he must further ally himself with the liberal movement if Sardinia-Piedmont were to swallow up the whole of Italy. Thus, he went to the aid of the Milanese, declaring war on Austria.

The first blow to the national hopes came when Pius IX refused to allow his forces to join the Piedmontese. He took this stand because he thought it improper to use his troops except for the defense of the Papal States and because his international spiritual leadership precluded his becoming a national leader in Italy. Whatever the logic of his argument, it infuriated Italian patriots. The Pope's reforms were immediately forgotten, and his appeal to the Austrians to withdraw their troops from Italy went unnoticed. A second national reversal came in Naples, where the King recovered his position in the late spring of 1848 with the aid of Swiss mercenaries. Then, in July, Charles Albert was completely routed by the Austrian General Joseph Radetzky and driven from Lombardy. An armistice followed.

In the meantime, radical protest against Pius IX blossomed in Rome and culminated in the assassination of Count Pellegrino Rossi, the prime minister, a liberal—but not revolutionary—reformer. The Pope fled from Rome to Gaeta and Neapolitan protection. Early in 1849, the Mazzinian republicans sought to take advantage of this vacuum in Rome and the fiasco of "Charles Albert's war" to set up a republic in Rome. This, in turn, put pressure on Charles Albert. To regain his position in the national movement, he renounced his armistice with the Austrians—only to suffer a second and decisive defeat at Novara. Sardinia-Piedmont had to pay the Austrians a large indemnity, and Charles Albert abdicated in favor of his son, Victor Emanuel II (*1849–1878*).

The final actions in the Italian drama were engineered from abroad. Louis-Napoleon Bonaparte, new president of the Second French Republic, sent a small force to overthrow the Roman republic and restore Pius IX. At first blush, one might have expected the two revolutionary republics to be congenial. In fact, as we have seen, the Second Republic was not impressively republican, France was a Catholic country, and the President himself was anti-Austrian. He feared that Austria would move to restore the Pope and make all Italy an Austrian peninsula, and being a Bonaparte—a hater of the 1815 settlement—he was bound to try to balk the Austrians at every turn. Thus it was probably his hostility to Austria, and his assumption that she would intervene if he did not do so first, rather than opposition to the Roman republic itself that guided his actions. The Romans held out for over a month against the French expedition, Giuseppe Garibaldi (1807–1882) commanding the defenders; but the city fell in the midsummer of 1849. Shortly after, the Austrians beseiged Venice and brought down the Venetian Republic. The revolutionary fires seemed suppressed.

The Hapsburg Empire

No doubt the revolutions in Italy would have been more vigorously combatted by Austria in 1848 had she not been in the throes of revolution herself. The peculiar multinational make-up of the Hapsburg Empire had always made the centralization of power difficult, as we noted in discussing the events of the eighteenth century. And in the nineteenth, when the claims of nationalities to the right of self-government were increasingly strident, the Hapsburg Empire had had to stand firm against nationalism everywhere in Europe for fear the disease prove fatal at home. Necessarily a conservative in foreign matters, Metternich had advised the emperors under whom he served to promote internal reforms intended to reconcile the masses to the monarchy; but the principle of Francis I, "Rule, and change nothing," guided the monarchy down to 1848. Meanwhile, liberal ideas seeped in from the West, and the beginnings of an industrial revolution in Austria had the same social and political implications as elsewhere. Hungary had long been a special problem, never having been comfortably blended into the Hapsburg Empire. As Hungarian national feeling grew more intense after 1815, opinion was divided over the benefits of autonomy within the empire as opposed to complete independence. The elections of 1847 to the lower house of the Diet (the Table of Deputies) which represented the gentry, produced an impressive liberal majority. Francis Deák (1803–1876), a leader of those favoring autonomy within the empire, came forth with a reform program called the Ten Points. He asked not only for responsible government with popular representation, but also for religious freedom and the abolition of serfdom. The upper house, comprising the great landowners, haggled over the proposal; at this stage of the deliberations, news came of the overthrow of Louis-Philippe.

The revolution in Paris set off demonstrations and speeches in both Vienna and Budapest, Metternich's resignation being the first consequence. Ferdinand I (*1835–1848*) promised constitutional government for Austria; and when the Table of Deputies in Budapest accepted Deák's Ten Points (the March Laws of 1848) as a basic constitution for Hungary, Ferdinand gave his assent. As a result, Hungary was virtually independent, joined to the empire only through the common monarch. Instead of calling a constitutional convention in Vienna, Ferdinand offered the Austrians a constitution of his own manufacture. He was answered by further rioting, whereupon the imperial family retired to Innsbruck. The constitutional movement, meanwhile, had spread to Prague, where the Czechs demanded a separate constitution for the Kingdom of Bohemia.

Though the Hapsburg monarchy seemed doomed in the spring of 1848, the divisions within its opposition were a cause for hope. The Piedmontese, as we have seen, were hindered by lack of support from Rome. In Bohemia, the antagonisms between Czech and German, and between the conservative landed aristocrats and the urban middle class, made a solid front against Austria impossible. And this the Austrian government knew. Its decision to grant autonomy to Bohemia, therefore, was mere temporizing until troops could be brought up to restore Austrian authority. In June, Prince Alfred zu Windischgrätz (1787–1862) bombarded Prague, crushed the Czech revolutionary movement, and established himself as a military dictator.

The example of the Czechs, however, had inspired other Slavic minorities in the empire to aspire to autonomy. Shortly before the surrender of Prague to Windischgrätz, the Czechs had launched a Pan-Slav movement proclaiming the solidarity of all Slavic peoples against their German oppressors. Thereupon the Croats and Slovenes demanded autonomy from Hungary, hopeful that the new Hungarian liberties would be extended to them. Their appeal was flatly rejected. Here again, then, was an opportunity for the Austrians to "divide and rule." With Prague in hand and the Piedmontese driven into armistice, the Austrian government encouraged the Croatian leader, Baron Joseph Jellachich (1801–1859), to invade Hungary. The scheme backfired with the defeat of Jellachich, and the furious Hungarians turned on Vienna itself.

On the home front, in the meantime, the Austrian government had been forced to call a constitutional assembly, but its deliberations revealed a deep schism between the liberals and the radicals. Windischgrätz took advantage of this split, coming in from Prague to bombard Vienna and smash the revolutionary movement. The Hungarian forces remained idle on the outskirts of this fighting and lost an excellent opportunity to intervene for their own advantage. Prince Felix Schwarzenberg (1800–1852) organized a new Austrian regime, dedicated to restoring the Hapsburg Empire. He obtained the abdication of the inept Ferdinand I in favor of his grandson, Francis Joseph I (*1848–1916*), and almost immediately the efforts of Austria were directed toward a campaign to punish the Hungarians. The most dynamic of the Hungarian liberals, Louis Kossuth (1802–1894), who had foreseen war between Austria and Hungary, had been organizing an army and became the real leader for Hungarian independence. In the first week of 1849, the Austrian invasion of Hungary began.

The Austrians were at first successful, occupying Budapest, but by late spring, the Hungarians had driven them out of Hungary and had declared Hungary to be an independent republic. Nicholas I of Russia had warned Europe after the fall of Metternich that Russia felt threatened by the revolutionary movements, and he had watched the Hungarian successes with increasing alarm, for fear their example would inspire the Poles. Consequently, when Francis Joseph asked for Russian help in 1849, Nicholas readily granted it. Hungary, simultaneously invaded by Austria and Russia, put up a fierce, if short, resistance. After the Hungarian surrender, the Austrian military courts visited brutal revenge upon the revolutionary leaders unable to flee, though many, including Kossuth, escaped. Thus, after a year and a half of uncertainty, the Hapsburg domains were reunited, but the scars left by the revolutions were omens of further upheaval.

The German States

When the news of the February Revolution in Paris reached the German world, liberals and nationalists alike were thrilled. Would this be the opportunity to secure at once a united Germany and representative government?

. . . Since the French had driven away Louis-Philippe and proclaimed the Republic, something, of course, must happen here too. Some of the students

had brought their rapiers, as if it were necessary at once to make an attack or
to defend themselves. We were dominated by a vague feeling as if a great outbreak of elemental forces had begun, as if an earthquake was impending of
which we had felt the first shock. . . .

Now had arrived in Germany the day for the establishment of "German
Unity" and the founding of a great, powerful national German Empire. First
in line the convocation of a national parliament; then the demands for civil
rights and liberties, free speech, free press, the right of free assembly, equality
before the law, a freely elected representation of the people with legislative
power . . .[23]

The swiftness of the revolutionary movement sweeping through the German
states caught the many rulers by surprise. A plethora of promises of reform
followed, and in Prussia the timid Frederick William IV (*1840–1861*) even
felt compelled to promise that he would assume the leadership of the entire
German world. A paternal monarch who wished well for his subjects, he
did not understand their demands for restricting his power; and he feared
the attitudes of Russia and Austria if he seemed to place himself at the
head of revolution. For the moment, however, he ordered his troops out of
Berlin to appease his "Good Berliners."

The national movement soon focused on Frankfurt, where a self-
appointed committee of liberals met to arrange elections for a national
assembly. In May of 1848, this Frankfurt National Assembly, elected by
universal manhood suffrage, convened. It suspended the Diet of the Germanic Confederation—presumably replacing it. Almost simultaneously,
Frederick William IV called a constituent assembly for Prussia. That body
deliberated through the summer and into the fall, its constitutional suggestions becoming increasingly radical. But when the news reached Berlin
that Prince Windischgrätz had seized Vienna from the revolutionaries,
Frederick William took steps against his Prussian assembly, finally dissolving it late in 1848. In Frankfurt, meanwhile, the debates seemed endless
and the problems enormous. First was the question of form of government:
should Germany be a republic or a monarchy, a centralized or a federal
state? Should a united Germany include only territories inhabited by a
majority of German-speaking people, or should it also include areas where
Germans were a minority? Finally, should Austria be included in a Greater
Germany?

The Frankfurt Constitution was not ready until the spring of 1849,
by which time some of the questions had been solved elsewhere. Restored

23. *The Reminiscences of Carl Schurz* (New York, 1907), Vol. I, pp. 111-112.

Austria let it be known, for instance, that no part of the Hapsburg domains could be included in a German Empire. In the Frankfurt Assembly itself, the moderate liberals greatly outnumbered the radicals, which meant that constitutional monarchy was preferred to a republic, that the empire should be a federal union of German states under a hereditary emperor. He was to be given only a suspensive veto, and his ministers were to be responsible to a bicameral parliament. The obvious candidate was Frederick William of Prussia, and the Frankfurt Assembly duly elected him. His refusal stunned the Assembly and made a shambles of the constitutional project. No doubt the conservative powers, Russia and Austria, had warned him against cooperation with a liberal assembly; but probably he would have rejected the throne without their prompting. If he did not mean to allow a constituent assembly to make a constitution for Prussia, it followed that he would not accept a constitution and a throne from the Frankfurt Assembly. He would be a ruler by divine right alone, and not by consent of the governed.

On the other hand, the Prussian government was reluctant to see slip away this opportunity for Prussia to dominate the German world. The House of Hohenzollern, as the House of Savoy in Italy, wanted national unity, but on its own terms. Shortly after he had rejected the offer from the Frankfurt Assembly, Frederick William IV proposed a Prussian union designed to create a large Central European bloc. This confederation was to have two administrative centers, Prussia and Austria, and to include the non-German parts of the Hapsburg Empire. Late in 1849, Prussia called a national assembly at Erfurt, since a number of German states had given favorable response to his Prussian project; but by the time this assembly convened in 1850, Austrian recovery was sufficient for Prince Schwarzenberg to resist. He intended to restore the Austrian-dominated Germanic Confederation. Both states mobilized, though the irresolute Frederick William hardly wanted war. Once again the reactionary influence of Russia was decisive. Nicholas I, still eager to crush national movements, let it be known that he would side with Austria. As a result, Prussia abandoned her scheme and allowed the restoration of the Germanic Confederation at Frankfurt. Thus, in Germany as elsewhere, the ambitions of the liberal nationalists had been blocked, and their prestige suffered accordingly in the aftermath of disappointment.

SUGGESTIONS FOR FURTHER READING

⤜⤛

Economic and Social History

Shepard B. Clough, *The Economic Development of Western Civilization* (New York and London: McGraw-Hill, 1959), contains excellent bibliography.

Overton H. Taylor, *A History of Economic Thought* (New York and London: McGraw-Hill, 1960), good bibliography.

Arthur Louis Dunham, *The Industrial Revolution in France 1815-1848* (New York: Exposition Press, 1955).

W. O. Henderson: *The Zollverein* (Cambridge University Press, 1939).

Adrien Dansette, *Religious History of Modern France. Vol. I, From the Revolution to the Third Republic* (New York: Herder and Herder, 1961), the point of view of a liberal Catholic, which is especially significant in dealing with the conflict between religion and the industrializing society.

Frank E. Manuel, *The New World of Henri Saint-Simon* (Harvard University Press, 1956).

*John Stuart Mill, *Autobiography* (New York: Liberal Arts Press, 1957), a classic revealing the decline of Utilitarianism and the development of an outstanding liberal.

The New Cambridge Modern History. Vol. X, The Zenith of European Power 1830-70 (Cambridge University Press, 1960), contains much excellent material.

Henry W. C. Davis, *Age of Grey and Peel* (Oxford: The Clarendon Press, 1929).

G. M. Trevelyan, *Lord Grey of the Reform Bill* (London: Longmans, Green, 1920).

Elie Halévy, *History of the English People,* 5 vols. (New York: Harcourt, Brace, 1924-34), a near classic, covering the period 1815-1852.

Auguste Comte, *A General View of Positivism* (New York: Official Centenary Edition of the International Auguste Comte Centenary Committee, 1957).

Karl Marx, "The Communist Manifesto," in *Capital* (New York: Modern Library, 1932).

M. Hovell, *The Chartist Movement* (London and New York: Longmans, Green, 1918).

J. D. Chambers, *The Workshop of the World: British History from 1820-1880* (Oxford University Press, 1961), brief but good; contains excellent bibliography.

Cultural and Scientific History

Sir William Dampier, *A History of Science* (New York: Macmillan, 4th ed., 1949).

W. T. Sedgwick and H. W. Tyler, *A Short History of Science* (New York: Macmillan, 1919).

W. P. D. Wightman, *The Growth of Scientific Ideas* (Yale University Press, 1951).

Volume X of *The New Cambridge Modern History*, noted above.

James W. Thompson and Bernard J. Holm, *A Historical Writing*, 2 vols. (New York: Macmillan, 1942).

G. P. Gooch, *History and Historians in the Nineteenth Century* (New York: Peter Smith, new ed., 1949).

*Fritz Stern, *The Varieties of History: From Voltaire to the Present* (New York: Meridian Books, 1956).

Jacques Barzun, *Berlioz and the Romantic Century*, 2 vols. (Boston: Little, Brown, 1950).

Raymond Giraud, *The Unheroic Hero in the Novels of Stendhal, Balzac and Flaubert* (Rutgers University Press, 1957).

Albert Guerard, *French Civilization in the Nineteenth Century* (New York: Century, 1918).

David Owen-Evans, *Social Romanticism in France 1830-1848, With a Selective Critical Bibliography* (Oxford: The Clarendon Press, 1951).

Ernst Kohn-Bramstedt, *Aristocracy and the Middle Class in Germany: Social Types in German Literature 1830-1900* (London: P. S. King, 1937).

The Revolutions of 1848

*Geoffrey Bruun, *Revolution and Reaction 1848-1852, A Mid-Century Watershed* (Princeton, N.J.: Anvil, 1958), brief survey with readings.

Donald C. McKay, *The National Workshops: A Study in the French Revolution of 1848* (Harvard University Press, 1933).

Sir Lewis B. Namier, *1848: The Revolution of the Intellectuals* (New York: Oxford University Press, 1946).

Raymond Postgate, *Story of a Year: 1848* (New York: Oxford University Press, 1956).

Priscilla Robertson, *Revolutions of 1848: A Social History* (Princeton University Press, 1952).

Frederick A. Simpson, *The Rise of Louis Napoleon* (London and New York: Longmans, Green, new ed., 1925).

*Hans Kohn, *Pan-Slavism: Its History and Ideology* (New York: Vintage, 2nd ed. rev., 1960).

*Available in paperbound editions.

❧ 11 ❧

Realism and Realpolitik
1851–1871

THE AFTERMATH OF 1848

Ironically, though the upheaval of 1848 celebrated the fall of Metternich, it also marked the defeat of liberalism. For while it revealed that nationalism and the demand for nation-states was a powerful force, it demonstrated at the same time the failure of liberal leadership to achieve these goals. In Central Europe and Italy, nationalist aspirations had been denied. The liberal hopes of the Second Republic in France had been shattered as soon as provincial opinion declared itself. The era of reaction that had followed 1815 was duplicated after 1848: conservative governments were generally in the saddle and justified themselves as the guardians of "order" in the wake of the uprisings.

This reaction went beyond politics. Romanticism, too, was discredited because the leadership in 1848 had in many cases come from the liberal intelligentsia and literati known for their romantic views. Throughout Europe a new leadership emerged to advance the claims of nationality— tough-minded, skillful politicians. What liberalism and democracy had failed to accomplish they would attempt through diplomacy and war. Otto von Bismarck (1815–1898) sounded the keynote in a speech to the Prussian parliament:

Germany looks not to Prussia's liberalism but to her power. . . . Not by parliamentary speeches and majority votes are the great questions of the day determined—that was the great mistake of 1848 and 1849—but by iron and blood.[1]

Realpolitik—politics based on the realities of power—was becoming the order of the day. Between 1850 and 1870, the marriage of liberalism and nationalism was dissolved, and the idealistic nationalism of Herder and Mazzini passed from the scene. Instead, the belief grew that nationalities were units of hostility, that each nation-state must strengthen itself for inevitable competition with other nation-states.

Austria

Multinational Austria, with her claims in Italy and Germany, seemed increasingly an anachronism. Yet Austria after 1848 was the supreme example of the general European tendency to increase the centralization of the state. Under the direction of the Minister of the Interior, Alexander Bach (1813–1893), the many provinces of the empire were drawn more closely together. The provincial Diets were abolished, the revolts in 1848 being sufficient excuse, and local government came into the hands of officials sent out from Vienna. Since there was no national parliament, the abolition of provincial Diets transformed the Hapsburg monarchy into an absolutism, with the emperor possessing sole right of initiation. Finally, Bach hoped that centralization would lead to the Germanization of the empire and make the Hapsburg domains a true nation-state.

Prussia

One of the results of 1848 in Prussia was a constitution granted by Frederick William IV. Having dissolved the constituent assembly in Prussia and refusing the offer of the Frankfurt Assembly, the King allowed a constitution in Prussia which preserved his ultimate authority. It provided for a two-house parliament, the lower house, or Landtag, being given the power to vote laws and taxes. The Landtag was elected by universal suffrage; but a complicated system of indirect election gave representation to the well-to-do. The upper house was limited to aristocrats, whose seats were hereditary, and to a few individuals appointed for life by the king. But there was no ministerial responsibility, and the king could issue ordinances when parliament was not in session. As in Austria, centralization was enhanced by removing the right of towns and rural districts to par-

1. From Bismarck's budget speech of September 30, 1862.

ticipate in the selection of officials. All officeholders came to be appointed by the crown.

France

When we turn to France after 1848, we find unusual complexities and ambiguities. Not only did the Second Republic fade into the Second Empire by 1852, but in Louis-Napoleon Bonaparte we have the most characteristic leader of the middle years of the century. In an age of transition from liberalism to *Realpolitik,* Louis-Napoleon embodied both traditions. A Bonaparte, he necessarily opposed the Vienna settlement and was, hence, anti-Austrian. This combination made him a champion of nation-states, and he himself was the beneficiary of revolution. Yet, as President of the Second Republic, he sent troops to Rome in 1849 to overthrow Mazzini's republic, thus blocking Italian national ambitions. Given Austria's recovery in Italy that year, she would surely have restored the Pope had not France done so. Louis-Napoleon could argue that he had surrounded the papal restoration with as liberal an atmosphere as possible by blocking Austria, and he knew that French liberals could not rally much support at home in protest, for the elections of 1848 had shown the country to be antirepublican. Certainly the deed pleased French Catholics, and the incident had the merit of showing Louis-Napoleon's policy of trying to please everybody while enhancing his own position.

The Assembly, furthermore, played into his hands by being more conservative than he and allowing him to pose as the representative of popular interests. In 1850 it passed—over his objections—a law designed greatly to reduce the electorate. Louis-Napoleon had been elected president in 1848 as the guarantor of order; by 1850, he seemed the hope of democracy as well. The constitution, however, prevented his re-election, and once again the Assembly assisted by refusing to amend the constitution. His inherited destiny, "his star," was to lead France to greatness, and a four-year term would hardly suffice. Late in 1851, he struck back at the Assembly which had balked him, forcibly dissolving it. Recalcitrant deputies were jailed, and an uprising they had organized in the Paris streets was easily crushed by troops. The President immediately restored universal suffrage and organized a national plebiscite to obtain popular mandate for revising the constitution in his own favor. He received an overwhelming vote of confidence: 7.5 million to 640,000. Then came the constitutional revisions granting the President a ten-year term and making him directly responsible to the nation. Parliament lost the right to initiate or amend legislation; a dictatorship had been established, by popular vote.

Louis-Napoleon's popularity was real, because his program catered to all. The propertied classes saw him as a strong man of order, a guarantee against a renewal of the June Days of 1848; the Catholics saw in him the defender of the Papacy; his pamphlet *The Extinction of Pauperism* (1844) revealed him as a friend of the downtrodden and something of a Saint-Simonian. Thus it was that, in 1852, President Bonaparte saw that he had sufficient popular support to take the final step: to restore empire. Again he received an overwhelming vote from a national plebiscite. A Caesarian democracy was the final act of the Revolution of 1848, and the Vienna settlement, with its provision against a Bonapartist restoration, had been peaceably defied.

Britain

British political parties were notably unstable in the 1850's and 1860's. The Tory-Conservative party had split over the question of the Corn Law in 1846, those for repeal following Sir Robert Peel (1788–1850), while the protectionists rallied behind Benjamin Disraeli (1804–1881). The Whigs were presumably united, but—as in 1832—the party contained disparate elements, making prolonged unity difficult. Both parties suffered in this period from the competition of rival personalities, no single figure being able to unite his party through vigorous leadership. Thus, between 1846 and 1867, little significant domestic legislation was passed, and cabinet changes were frequent.

Yet, one domestic problem was crying for attention: the Irish question. The native Irish were not reconciled to the Act of Union (1801) as they possibly might have been had it been accomplished by Catholic Emancipation—which came twenty-eight years later. Thus, after 1829, the Irish members of Parliament worked for the repeal of the Act of Union. Worse from the English point of view, the Irish nationalities were inspired by the revolutions of 1848 and began to plan armed rebellion in the event that parliamentary efforts by their representatives should fail to secure repeal.

Meanwhile, the need to reorganize and realign political parties was made especially obvious during the maneuvers for a second reform bill. The leaders of both parties had come to recognize that the Reform Bill of 1832 had fixed a property qualification for the vote which was altogether too high. Many artisans were intellectually qualified to vote, yet they did not possess sufficient property or pay sufficient rent to qualify. Proposals for a second reform of Parliament, therefore, were introduced as early as 1851, but all fell victim to the half-hearted politics of that era. It has been rightly claimed that the impact of the American Civil War upon British political opinion finally brought the reform issue to a head. Whereas the gentry saw its way of life at stake in the Southern cause, and the textile manufacturers were concerned for supplies of raw cotton and, hence, annoyed at the Northern blockade of Southern ports, the British urban workers—especially after the Emancipation Proclamation—were enthusiastic for the North as representing the more democratic society. Consequently, the victory of the North was seen as presaging the advance of democracy elsewhere and gave the British workers a reputation for political acumen for having picked the winning side. It is also true that trade unionism had reached a point in the 1860's at which it could exert some political influence through propaganda—and not merely upon the workers.

By that date, the leadership in each party had developed upon one man: William E. Gladstone (1809–1898) of the liberal Whigs, and Benjamin Disraeli (1804–1881) of the conservative Tories. With public opinion prepared for a new reform bill, both men brought forth various proposals, each maneuvering to capture votes from the other's party. Of the bills presented, Disraeli's second bill passed, but only after he had accepted a flock of amendments proposed by the more radical Whigs and had won their backing. The Second Reform Bill (or Act of 1867) reapportioned the seats in Parliament to reflect population shifts, as in 1832. But more important, the suffrage qualifications were lowered so as to give virtual universal suffrage to the urban workers, though the bill had little effect upon the rural workers.

In the aftermath, Gladstone believed that the time had come to consolidate and discipline his party after so many years of wavering and shifting. In 1868, he fell upon the Irish question as *the* issue. He would pronounce for reform in Ireland, especially to advocate the disestablishment of the Anglican Church in Ireland, and would establish a program which would give the old Whig party a truly liberal character intended to be in sharp contrast with the Tories, who had little more than repression to offer as the answer to the Irish question. Gladstone's strength lay not merely in the evident need for reform in Ireland, but in the fact, that though only about 10 per cent of the Irish were members of the established Anglican Church, all were taxed for its support. The injustice was only too evident, and the Tories could only weakly oppose disestablishment with a claim that the Whigs, traditionally anticlerical, would then attempt to disestablish the Anglican Church in England. National elections on the issue held in 1868 were solidly won by Gladstone's party, after which the disestablishment bill easily passed in 1869. As Gladstone had hoped, the Irish issue pried the liberal wing of the Tory party (the Peelites) away from Disraeli once and for all, and the modern Liberal party was born of this fusion of the Peelites with the old Whigs.

Through it all reigned Victoria (*1839–1901*), niece of William IV. Married two years after her accession to Albert of Saxe-Coburg-Gotha, she mothered nine children and became, in her mode of life, her prejudices and enthusiasms, the symbol of the era that bears her name. In matters political she openly preferred her conservative ministers, particularly Disraeli, and showed a desire to play an active role in the conduct of foreign affairs. She demonstrated that the crown could still exercise authority, if only in an advisory capacity.

THE CHURCH

Pius IX, abandoning his liberalism after his experience with the Mazzinian republicans, joined in the general reaction. As a result, the papacy enjoyed better relations with the Catholic states of Europe, and this rapprochement, of course, heightened the hostility between the Church and the liberals. This alliance between Church and State, even closer than in the aftermath of the French Revolution, was an uneasy marriage of convenience. Statesmen who negotiated concordats with the papacy were usually men of little or no faith, who saw the Church as an institution of social control because it placed spiritual values above those of this world. There emerged within the Church in the nineteenth century a group which regretted and resisted this coming to terms with cynical secular power. Calling themselves Liberal Catholics, they argued for a free Church within a free State—meaning that neither Church nor State should impinge upon each other's domains. Earlier in the century, it had been the ultramontanes who had sought the independence of the Church from secular influences, and Liberal Catholicism, oddly enough, made the same demands, though for opposite reasons; the ultramontanes had found the states too liberal, whereas the Liberal Catholics found them too reactionary.

This internal dispute as to the proper attitude toward the secular states brought the official Church to define its position more specifically in the

Encyclical *Quanta Cura* (1864), to which was attached a *Syllabus of the Principal Errors of our Time*. The papal position was extreme and, in its attack upon liberalism, it pronounced against modern civilization, thus alienating the very secular states whose alliance was valued. The eightieth "principal error" summed up the Roman attitude: it is an error to believe that "the Roman Pontiff can, and ought to, reconcile himself, and come to terms with progress, liberalism and modern civilization."[2] Such views were born of Pius IX's recognition that modern civilization had become highly secularized:

And since Religion has been excluded from civil Society, and the doctrine and authority of divine Revelation, or the true and germane notion of justice and human right have been obscured and lost, and material or brute force substituted in the place of true justice and legitimate right, it is easy to perceive why some persons, forgetting and trampling upon the most certain principles of sound reason, dare cry out together, "that the will of the people, manifested by what they call public opinion, or in any other way, constitutes the supreme law, independent of all divine and human right, and that, in the political order, accomplished facts, by the mere fact of having been accomplished, have the force of right." But who does not see and plainly understand, that the Society of man, freed from the bonds of Religion and of true justice, can certainly have no other purpose than the effort to obtain and accumulate wealth, and that in its actions it follows no other law than that of the uncurbed cupidity, which seeks to secure its own pleasures and comforts?[3]

Pius IX's next step was to challenge the omnipotent authority of the modern secular states by summoning a Vatican Council (late 1869). As expected, the Council proclaimed the dogma of Papal Infallibility (1870), maintaining that when a pope speaks *ex cathedra* on matters of faith and morals, he is infallible. This not only marked the final victory of the Ultramontane party within the Church, but was a statement of ecclesiastical independence which most of the Catholic states were not ready to swallow. Those who cried out against this papal authoritarianism seemed little conscious of how much they were insisting upon the authority of the secular state. Most of the liberal Catholics, though notably not those in Germany, now rallied to the papacy. For in the battle between materialism and the Church, the liberal Catholics preferred to uphold papal supremacy, despite the papacy's conservatism.

2. Anne Fremantle, *The Papal Encyclicals in their Historical Context* (New York, Mentor, 1956), p. 152.
3. *Ibid.*, pp. 137-138.

THE SECULAR "CULTS" OF MID-CENTURY

When we speak of the increasing secularization of European life and the claims of the national state in the nineteenth century, we are not merely dealing with matters of political loyalty, but with social, economic, and intellectual phenomena as well. The economic expansion, for example, made possible by the slow accumulation of capital and by advances in technology, inevitably increased men's concern for the things of this world. Factories, which employed women as well as men, contributed to the break-up of family solidarity. Then there was the issue of public education, one of the European heritages of the French Revolution. The liberal wanted state-supported education and the removal of clergymen from teaching. After *Quanta Cura* and the papal attack upon modern civilization, the educational issues were more clearly drawn. Victor Duruy, Napoleon III's liberal minister of public instruction from 1863 to 1869, believed that a modern education could not be achieved until teaching was in the hands of laymen and religious instruction was removed from public schools. The papacy knew that Duruy's point of view was increasingly held throughout Europe; that curricula would emphasize modern languages, history, mathematics, and science; and that in place of religious instruction, children would be subject to patriotic propaganda from a body of techers who owed their positions to the state: As Duruy himself admitted, "the greatness of France is my religion."[4]

It is probable that nationalism, as expressed by Duruy, had become virtually a cult in the nineteenth century, and Napoleon III (*1852–1870*) became its highest priest. Nationalities ought to be free and self-governing —united in nation-states, as we now phrase it—without regard to the principle of legitimacy which had guided statesmen earlier in the century. Liberalism, which since the seventeenth century had been developing its tenets—individualism, *laissez faire,* and humanitarianism; the perfect society to be achieved through the application of nature's laws— was another "cult" to rival Christianity. A further "cult" beginning to attract support was socialism, especially the form advocated by Marx, whose classless society seemed reminiscent of the City of God. Each of these secular cults legitimized itself by offering scientific foundations for the faith. The nationalist assumed that all people speaking the same lan-

4. Victor Duruy, *Notes et Souvenirs* (Paris, 1901), Vol. I. p. 329. My translation.

guage naturally had identical qualities and desires; it was only natural, then, that language and territorial boundaries should coincide. Liberalism was grounded in the faith in a rational universe governed by perfect, natural laws, while Marx believed that he had discovered the scientific explanation of history, his key to the past being also the key to the future. These cults, in sum, were the rivals of Christianity, as Pius IX clearly saw.

One further generality about this period must be noted: socialism began to achieve a new dimension through international organization. The International Working Men's Association, generally called The International, was founded in London in 1864 after the visit of some French laborers to the London Exhibition of 1862. Industrial employers had resisted, as a matter of self-interest, the tendency of laborers to combine in order to bargain for improved wages and working conditions. Collective bargaining was seen as an artificial restraint of trade—a violation of *laissez faire*—so that unions were regarded as conspiracies against both employers and nature. Britain recognized the legality of trades unions in 1825, allowing collective bargaining but forbidding strikes and violence. Continental laborers, enjoyed no such rights until much later. As one example, France adopted legislation (1864) permitting workers to organize trades unions for limited periods for the purpose of bargaining, they might even strike as long as there was no violence; but permanently organized trades unions did not become legal in France until 1884.

At first, the International was a forum chiefly for the discussion of labor questions, but it soon expanded its agenda to include major political and economic problems for which socialism proposed solutions. In so doing, the movement opened the door to increasing dissension within the organization, and this proved its undoing by 1874. In the meantime, the first congress of the International, meeting at Geneva (1866), had voted disapproval of standing armies, preferring the arming of the people, and the issue of peace had also dominated the second congress in Lausanne (1867). It was not until the third congress in Brussels (1868) that a communist majority succeeded in getting the principle of private property condemned. The following year, at Basle, a battle for control of the organization erupted between Karl Marx and the Russian radical, Michael Bakunin (1814–1876). Marx's program included, of course, the dictatorship of the proletariat, implying the seizure of central government, as a preliminary step toward an ideal society in which the state would wither away. Bakunin was an anarchist who desired the immediate destruction of the state—in fact, the destruction of all authority save that of nature:

The liberty of man consists solely in this, that he obeys the laws of nature, because he has himself recognized them as such, and not because they have been imposed upon him externally by any foreign will whatsoever, human or divine, collective or individual.[5]

His ideas suggest those of Proudhon, but Bakunin went beyond him in advocating the violent destruction of existing society. Marx engineered Bakunin's expulsion from the International in 1872, but the movement survived the schism by only two years.

The history of radicalism seemed to parallel that of nationalism in the nineteenth century: a benevolent beginning gave way to a belief in violence after mid-century.

INTELLECTUAL CURRENTS AT MID-CENTURY: THE SCIENCES

On to this scene Charles Darwin (English, 1809–1882) brought forth his immensely important *Origin of Species* (1859), to be followed by his *Descent of Man* (1871). He asserted that species are not permanently fixed as a result of creation, but rather, that all species are in a process of continual change and have evolved from a common source. He offered three mechanisms to explain how differentiation and change occurred: natural selection, sexual selection, and the inheritance of acquired characteristics. Darwin emphasized natural selection, however, by which he meant that in the struggle for life, those individuals within a given species with special variations favorable to survival tended to survive and reproduce. Repeated variations and improvement through many generations resulted finally in a new species.

Theories of evolution had been in the air for a hundred years, not only in natural science but also in philosophy, history, and sociology as well. Darwin knew, for instance, of the evolutionary implications of Lyell's *Principles of Geology,* and he was influenced by Malthus' view that the growth of population is related to the eternal struggle for food. Consequently, we cannot say that Darwin was the first to conceive of evolution; rather Darwin successfully popularized evolution. And if his

5. From *God and the State,* published posthumously in 1882.

ideas enjoyed great vogue, it was not merely that they were plausible, but that other factors had paved the way for their acceptance.

In the first place, European intellectuals had been seeking for many generations the natural laws governing the universe, and those laws which found ready acceptance often did so because they apparently solved problems being posed by the era in question. Darwin's views on variation and survival hit home because they were broached at a moment when hostility and struggle were the main political, economic, and social currents —whether one thinks of nationalism, Marxism, or the individualism of *laissez faire*. Moreover, those who sought evidence for a materialistic explanation of life—and that was a common goal amongst the anticlericals and the irreligious—thought that Darwin had given them a mechanical solution to the origin of life which refuted the Bible in particular. Indeed, those who read Scripture literally saw this as the proof of Darwin's error. In point of fact, Darwin did not tackle the enormous problem of the origin of life itself, but only the origin of the differences demarking the many species.

In the eighteenth century, the static or rational view of the universe had seemed at odds with the evolutionary view. The assumption that the universe is a perfect mechanism was incompatible with the notion of a growing, improving world. Yet, one hundred years later, the theory of natural selection as the crux of the evolutionary mechanism had become part of the mechanical, rational view of the universe. Darwin's theory described the mechanism which presumably governed life itself, a mechanism which involved no choice and no act of individual will and which suggested no purpose to life; that is, unless simple survival be counted a purpose, survival through evolution:

Thus, from the war of nature, from famine and death, the most exalted object which we are capable of conceiving, namely the production of the higher animals, directly follows. There is grandeur in this view of life, with its several powers, having been originally breathed by the Creator into a few forms or into one; and that, whilst this planet has gone cycling on according to the fixed law of gravity, from so simple a beginning endless forms most beautiful and most wonderful have been, and are being evolved.[6]

The romantics of the earlier nineteenth century had rejected a mechanistic view of the universe and had insisted on the ability of the individual to act and triumph in unique ways. It is the more significant, then, when

6. *Origin of Species,* Chapter 15.

we seek to explain Darwin's popularity, that romanticism had been dealt a mortal blow in 1848.

Louis Pasteur (French, 1822–1895) is another example of a scientist whose work had philosophical implications. Trained as a chemist, Pasteur's significant discoveries were in bacteriology, and all of them hinged on his unorthodox view of the origin of life. It was generally held in the mid-nineteenth century that life is generated spontaneously—by heterogenesis—a theory congenial to the materialists of that day because it seemed to abolish the need for creation. By 1860, Pasteur was convinced that heterogenesis was fallacious, and he began a series of experiments to demonstrate that, in the case of fermentation or putrefaction, the alteration was produced by organisms present in the air. If one isolated a putrescible liquid from these "microbes" in the air, the liquid would remain pure indefinitely, because the microbes could not generate spontaneously in the liquid. He showed that by keeping wine at a temperature between fifty and sixty degrees Centigrade for a few minutes, the vitality of all "parasites" could be destroyed. Firmly corked to prevent further contamination from the air, bottles preserved the wine from deterioration. It may be assumed that the resistance of scientific opinion to the demonstrated results of "pasteurization" derived from the desire to defend materialism.

Pasteur, in the meantime, came to see that diseases in animals and in man result from the growth of microorganisms within the host. And if organisms which ruined wines could be controlled, so, presumably could those causing animal diseases. In 1865, he tackled the silkworm epidemic which threatened the destruction of the French silkworm industry. He solved the problem only because he was able to treat the disease as an infectious matter rather than as a phenomenon of spontaneous generation. He went, in short, from fermentations to the germ theory of disease, and the vaccines which he was to develop in the 1870's and 1880's were all grounded in the procedure he used in 1869 in finding a vaccine for chicken cholera.

This raises the incidental, but significant, fact that Pasteur thought it would be a "beautiful" thing if a benign infection could immunize an animal from a more serious attack of the same disease. He knew, of course, of Edward Jenner's eighteenth-century discovery that cowpox, or a cowpox vaccine, gave immunity to smallpox. In that case, a benign disease was induced to protect against a serious disease. Pasteur fell upon the key to his problem when he noticed that chickens inoculated with chicken cholera microbes died quickly; but if the microbe culture was allowed to age so that the microbes became attenuated, the chickens then inoculated became sick—but recovered. From there it was simply a matter of learning how to attenuate the virulence of disease microbes as the bases for vaccines. His work on chicken cholera, therefore, must be regarded as a major contribution to medical knowledge.

Joseph Lister (English, 1827–1912), called the father of antiseptic surgery, was among the first to recognize further implications of Pasteur's work. As a young surgeon, Lister was baffled by the great amount of septic disease which developed in hospitals and the supuration of wounds in particular. Through his microscopic study of tissues diseased with what was called hospital gangrene, Lister concluded that the cause was a parasitic fungus not unlike the fermentation phenomena Pasteur had discovered. He then turned to carbolic acid, which he guessed would be a germ killer because of its effectiveness in deodorizing sewage. Carbolic acid was used to destroy germs on the surface of wounds, and in a spray to clear the air. Early in 1874, Lister wrote to Pasteur:

> Allow me to take this opportunity to tender my most cordial thanks for having demonstrated to me, by your brilliant researches, the truth of the germ theory of putrefaction, and thus furnished me with the principle upon which alone the antiseptic system can be carried out.[7]

The decade of the 1860's was equally significant for advances in chemistry, a field in which confusion had reigned for a half-century after John Dalton presented his atomic theory. In 1858, Stanislao Cannizzaro (1826–1910) of Genoa wrote a pamphlet in which he demonstrated the possibility of harmonizing the data on atomic weights with that on the volumes of gases. His work was unknown until 1860, when an international convention of chemists met at Karlsruhe. Atomic proportions, Cannizzaro suggested, should be established by relative weight, oxygen being assigned a weight of 16. Molecular proportions, however, should be established by gas volume. A molecule of water, for instance, containing two atoms of hydrogen and one atom of oxygen, should be written H_2O, a formula which does not reflect the relative weights of the combining atoms. Cannizzaro's synthesis gave support to Berzelius' earlier system of notation and broke the deadlock stifling the development of chemical theory.

7. René Vallery-Radot, *La Vie de Pasteur* (Paris, 1900), p. 238. My translation.

A dramatic result was the periodic table: the elements arranged according to their atomic weights. Many chemists contributed information in the 1860's, but Lothar Meyer (1830–1895) in Prussia and Dmitri I. Mendeleyev (1834–1907) in Russia led the field. Mendeleyev capped this work in 1870 with his periodic law, a law of nature. When arranged by atomic weights, the periodic sequence of the elements revealed a mechanically perfect progression. The gaps in the chart simply meant undiscovered elements, three of which Mendeleyev predicted would be discovered—and were—in his lifetime.

The great scientific advances of the period 1850–1870 were synthetic: a century of discoveries was organized into systems. Consciously or otherwise, Darwin was a synthesizer of first-rank significance, and the chemists of the 1860's achieved clarity and order for their discipline after a half-century of dispute. Such a breath-catching period may seem in retrospect unproductive of new discoveries, whereas in fact these syntheses—the organization of impressive bodies of facts into systems—served the already great prestige of science enormously. Moreover, there seems to have been an increased practical use of scientific knowledge after 1850 as the industrialization of Europe proceeded. Science did not abandon its search for truth, but it was stealing marches on philosophy and the arts, neither of which produced engines nor domestic comforts.

The field of physics had its great synthesis in mid-century, too, with the statement of the laws of thermodynamics. The study of the motive power of heat had been encouraged by the increasing use of steam engines. In the eighteenth century when heat was believed to have material substance, to be an "imponderable fluid," a New Englander, Count Benjamin T. Rumford (1753–1814), presented a contrary view before the Royal Society in London in a paper entitled *Enquiry concerning the Source of Heat which is excited by Friction* (1798), Rumford, in brief, related heat to motion. The problem was taken up by many researchers in Germany, France, Denmark, and Britain during the first half of the nineteenth century, James P. Joule's (English, 1818–1889) experiments ultimately proving decisive. Finding that water warmed when it was agitated with a paddle, he arrived at a formula which related the rise of the temperature with the amount of work spent on the paddle—thus establishing the mechanical equivalent of heat. If his formula underwent later modifications, the principles he established had revolutionary significance for physics, opening up the field of thermodynamics.

If we state the first law of thermodynamics, also known as the law of conservation of energy, in several possible ways, its philosophical as well as its physical importance can be revealed. The more usual statement is as follows. When heat is transformed into any other kind of energy, or vice versa, the total quantity of energy remains invariable; that is to say, the quantity of heat which disappears is equivalent to the quantity of the other kind of energy produced and vice versa. H. L. F. von Helmholtz (German, 1821–1894) put it this way in his celebrated paper (1847) read in Berlin:

Nature as a whole possesses a store of force which cannot in any way be either increased or diminished ... therefore the quantity of force in Nature is just as eternal and unalterable as the quantity of matter.[8]

The second law of thermodynamics, usually called the law of dissipation of energy, also had enormous philosophical implications. Formulated by William Thomson, Lord Kelvin (1824–1907) in 1851, the second law was a frightening warning. Admitting that the total energy of the universe is constant, Kelvin added that the useful energy was being diminished by its conversion into dissipated heat. Kelvin, in short, prophesied the death of the universe with the gradual cooling of the sun. It required nearly a half-century, however, for Europe to hitch its cosmic despair to the second law.

The hypothesis of an aether—that is, of a subtle substance said to exist in apparently empty space—had been speculated upon for many centuries. In the nineteenth century, after the demonstration of the wave theory of light by Thomas Young, British scientists increasingly believed an aether to be necessary for the propagation of light. Those who continued to espouse the Newtonian, or corpuscular, theory of light were finally undermined in 1850 when J. B. L. Foucault (French, 1819–1868) provided new evidence for the wave theory by showing the greater velocity of light in air than in water. Immediately thereafter, the aether was regarded as the medium not merely for light, but for those phenomena believed to be related to light—electricity and magnetism—by Faraday, Kelvin, and James Clerk Maxwell (1831–1879). Here was one further example of the compulsion for scientific synthesis in the 1860's. But of even greater philosophical import, the notion of space filled by a subtle substance was exceedingly congenial to an age convinced of materialism.

8. Quoted in Robert C. Binkley, *Realism and Nationalism* (New York, 1935), p. 10.

TECHNOLOGY AND ACCELERATED INDUSTRIALIZATION

Surely, however, the increasing prestige of science lay not so much in the triumphs of pure science as in the practical application of the new knowledge to produce useful products. The first of what we would call a world's fair today was the London Exhibition (1851), followed shortly by the *Exposition universelle of Paris* (1855). For the first time the products of technology were brought in an organized manner before the public eye, and ever since, science and technology have been identical in the public mind. Visitors to these early exhibitions saw the latest application of building materials—for instance, the Crystal Palace in London. Farm machinery was another popular section. But in Paris, the exhibit

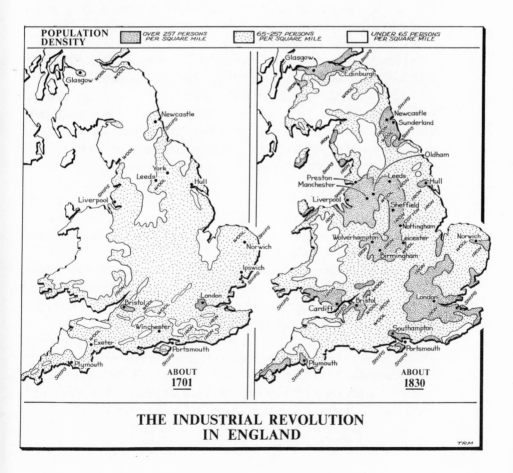

THE INDUSTRIAL REVOLUTION IN ENGLAND

which drew the largest crowds was that called home economy, which featured household items designed to raise the living standards of the poor. Material results, not speculation about the nature of the universe, were the measure of science's pre-eminence.

But one did not have to attend an international exhibition to see the cherished results. The expansion of the railway network in Europe after mid-century was phenomenal, and the attempt to standardize the rail gauge in Britain (1846) at 4' 8½" was a calculated attempt to expand commerce by rail. Canal building fell off after 1850 as a result, except where the canals connected major water routes. The Suez Canal was the most celebrated example of these, and in cutting 4000 miles from the trip to India from Britain, the canal's commercial significance was clearly revealed.

The increasing volume of production and trade in industrializing Europe had a significance which transcended their promise of a higher standard of living for all. It is perhaps obvious that the increasing complexity of European national economies meant a greater division of labor, a deepening of specialization, and an ever-increasing diversification of products. It also meant that a greater portion of the population would be involved in the exchange—rather than the production—of goods: in trade, finance, and transport. A concomitant was a reduced economic self-sufficiency, both for individuals and for national states. With the remarkably improved methods of long-distance transportation, the national state could acquire the goods it lacked from abroad, paying for these imports with the proceeds from the goods it could most easily manufacture or grow for export. This made free trade a logical policy. But the increasing specialization of individuals and the attrition of their self-sufficiency subtly contributed to increasing personal insecurity, which we continue to observe in the industrialized societies of the moment.

A definite movement toward freer trade can be seen in the two decades after 1850. In England, the era opened with the repeal of the Corn Laws in 1846, a victory for the principles of Adam Smith. In 1860, France and Britain signed a commercial treaty providing for lower tariffs if not for free trade. Napoleon III hoped the treaty would cement political relations with the British as well as force French producers to become more efficient. French manufacturers in particular were outraged by the treaty, but the Emperor bought them off with large government loans to help them modernize their factories. Liberal principles, however, were not always employed for liberal reasons. In 1864, Chancellor Otto von Bismarck (1815–1898) of Prussia forced the states of the *Zollverein* to join France in a low-tariff treaty as part of his policy to eliminate Austria from the duel to control the German world. Consequently, Europe's brief romance with free trade seems to have been both the culmination of the liberal heyday and an aspect of the deepening illiberal hostilities of the later century.

The expansion of business had always been accompanied by new instruments of credit or novel banking practices. One of the curious features of mid-century finance was the number of former Saint-Simonians who had evolved from being champions of the morality of production to practical bankers. Their particular innovation lay in investment banking: joint-stock banks which used their money to found new companies. The best-known example was the Crédit Mobilier, founded in 1852 by Isaac and Emile Péreire with the Emperor's backing. They specialized in financing new railroads and backed the development of the French shipping line.

The enormous commercial expansion of Europe was matched by steady population growth, an increase of roughly 30 million people in the two decades after 1850, despite an emigration from Europe estimated at 5.5 million. On the other hand, the birth rate in both France and Ireland was already declining, a tendency which would become general in Europe before the end of the century. Of course the death rate was also declining, and that decline would become more notable after 1870, when the germ theory of disease became accepted and antisepsis was practiced. But one would rejoice to have two demographers agree on the causes for a declining birth rate: No doubt, the causes were many and differed in the various sections of Europe: famine in Ireland, for instance, and the increased practice of contraception in France. In those cases where limitation of family size was deliberate, however, we are never sure what social and economic forces produce the relative infertility.

THE REACTION TO MATERIALISM AND DARWINISM

It is perhaps not out of place to speculate, therefore, that the declining vitality of the European populations in the last half of the nineteenth century was related to the growing insecurity of an era of materialism and violence. We have already noted the psychic effects of specialization in the industrializing society where lack of self-sufficiency becomes a rule.

Add to that the implications of a highly popular book which, like Darwin's *Origin of Species,* was published in 1859: Dr. Samuel Smiles' (1812–1904) *Self-Help.*

Fortune has often been blamed for her blindness: but fortune is not so blind as men are. Those who look into practical life will find that fortune is invariably on the side of the industrious, as the winds and waves are on the side of the best navigators. Success treads on the heels of every right effort; and though it is possible to over-estimate success to the extent of almost defying it, as is sometimes done, still, in any worthy pursuit, it is meritorious. Nor are the qualities necesary to insure success at all extraordinary. They may, for the most part, be summed up in these two,—common sense and perseverance. Genius may not be necessary, though even genius of the highest sort does not despise the exercise of these common qualities. The very greatest men have been among the least believers in the power of genius, and as worldly wise and persevering as successful men of the commoner sort.[9]

This was the first of the success books advising every man not to be content with his lot, but to make money and to rise. No doubt Smiles' words inspired many young men to work hard, in the expectation of prosperity and respectability. But one must ask whether the psychology of success did not have a negative effect for the multitude, since only the few could achieve the kind of success Smiles espoused. His measures of success were accepted by the later century, and in their light, most men were failures. The impossibility of individual success drove many to movements promising collective success, to the claims of national patrotism and socialism in particular—which meant, to be more precise, to the selfish hostility of nationalism and to the materialism of socialism. One must then ask whether the search for personal security in an increasingly violent age was likely to be fulfilled through an appeal to hostility and materialism.

John Ruskin (1819–1900), the English essayist and critic, placed himself in flat opposition to the development of an ethics founded on acquisitiveness:

The fact is, that people never have had clearly explained to them the true functions of a merchant with respect to other people. I should like the reader to be very clear about this.

Five great intellectual professions, relating to daily necessities of life, have hitherto existed—three exist necessarily, in every civilized nation:

The Soldier's profession is to *defend* it.

The Pastor's to *teach* it.

9. Samuel Smiles, *Self-Help* (Boston, 1860), p. 67.

The Physician's, to *keep it in health.*
The Lawyer's to *enforce justice* in it.
The Merchant's, to *provide* for it.
And the duty of all these men is, on due occasion, to *die* for it.
"On due occasion," namely:
The Soldier, rather than leave his post in battle,
The Physician, rather than leave his post in plague,
The Pastor, rather than teach Falsehood.
The Lawyer, rather than countenance Injustice.
The Merchant—What is *his* "due occasion" of death?
It is the main question for the merchant, as for all of us. For, truly, the man who does not know when to die, does not know how to live.[10]

If the right to acquire should become the standard measure, Ruskin predicted, national destruction would follow. His bitter antimaterialism was sufficiently out of joint with the time to provoke an angry outcry which intimidated his publisher and put an end to his articles on political economy.

Another English poet and critic out of step with his time was Matthew Arnold (1822–1888), called "The kid-glove Jeremiah" by those who resented his condemnation of the barbarism of mid-century life. Here he is exposing a Tory and a Liberal politician:

Mr. Adderley says to the Warwickshire farmers:
"Talk of the improvement of breed! Why, the race we ourselves represent, the men and women, the old Anglo-Saxon race, are the best breed in the whole world. . . . The absence of a too enervating climate, too unclouded skies, and a too luxurious nature, has produced so vigorous a race of people, and has rendered us so superior to all the world."
Mr. Roebuck says to the Sheffield cutlers:
"I look around and ask what is the state of England? Is not property safe? Is not every man able to say what he likes? Can you not walk from one end of England to the other in perfect security? I ask you whether, the world over or in past history, there is anything like it? Nothing. I pray that our unrivaled happiness may last."
Now obviously there is a peril for poor human nature in words and thought of such exuberant self-satisfaction, until we find ourselves safe in the streets of the Celestial City.[11]

It is clear that Arnold did not believe Europe or Britain to be on the threshold of the Celestial City:

10. John Ruskin, *Unto This Last,* Essay I, "The Roots of Honor," 1860.
11. Matthew Arnold, *The Function of Criticism at the Present Time,* first published in 1864.

Ah, love, let us be true
To one another! for the world, which seems
To lie before us like a land of dreams,
So various, so beautiful, so new,
Hath really neither joy, no love, nor light
Nor certitude, nor peace, nor help for pain;
And we are here as on a darkling plain
Swept with confused alarms of struggle and flight,
Where ignorant armies clash by night.[12]

To return to Darwinism, we must ask whether the new biological dogma brought hope or fear? Between the publication of the *Origin of Species* in 1859 and the defeat of France by Prussia in 1870, Darwin had his popularizers, Thomas Henry Huxley (English, 1825–1895) and the German naturalist Ernst Haeckel (1834–1919) in particular. At Oxford in 1860, the former was engaged in debate by Bishop Samuel Wilberforce (1805–1873), who sought to crush the evolutionists with ridicule. Having assured his audience that pigeons had always been pigeons,[13] Wilberforce asked Huxley whether it was through his grandfather or his grandmother that he was descended from a monkey. This witty sally was well parried by Huxley:

I asserted—and I repeat—that a man has no reason to be ashamed of having an ape for his grandfather. If there were an ancestor whom I should feel shame in recalling it would rather be a man—a man of restless and versatile intellect—who, not content with an equivocal success in his own sphere of activity, plunges into scientific questions with which he has no real acquaintance, only to obscure them by an aimless rhetoric, and distract the attention of his hearers from the real point at issue by eloquent digressions and skilled appeals to religious prejudice.[14]

The reader may guess that such debate solved few scientific questions, but it did reveal the reluctance of the public to accept the evolution of man from lower forms. The theory of evolution seemed to underscore our brutish qualities:

If my body come from brutes, though somewhat
finer than their own,
I am heir, and this my kingdom. Shall the
royal voice be mute?

12. Matthew Arnold, *Dover Beach* (1867).
13. Darwin included numerous observations on pigeons in the *Origin of Species*.
14. Quoted from Eugen Weber, *The Western Tradition* (Boston, 1959).

No, but if the rebel subject seek to drag
   me from the throne,
Hold the scepter, Human Soul, and rule the
   province of the brute.

I have climbed to the snows of Age, and I
   gaze at a field in the Past,
Where I sank with the body at times in the
   sloughs of a low desire,
But I hear no yelp of the breast, and the Man
   is quiet at last.
As he stands on the heights of his life with a
   glimpse of a height that is higher.[15]

In fact, when the English banker-journalist Walter Bagehot (1826-1877) sought to apply Darwinian biology to human affairs, he necessarily came to measure progress as advancement in the military arts. He stated not only that civilization is made possible by military advantage, but that the fittest to survive will have that military advantage. In fairness to Bagehot, he was too liberal to feel comfortable with his own equation, which seemed to make might equal right, but he evaded the knots of the problem by citing the victory of English colonists in Australia over primitive people and ignoring the struggles in Europe of the 1860's. Darwin had stumbled over a similar dilemma: wars presumably should be a good thing, since they enable the fitter nation to survive. But we recruit the fit to fight them, leaving the unfit home to survive. What the dilemma really illustrates is that nature and society are not identical and not subject to the same laws. Yet we shall see that after 1870, Darwinism was applied to politics and sociology, and the merger of Darwinism with nationalism gave the latter its illiberal code for the remainder of the century. In recalling the sequence of events after 1848, it is well to remember that Darwinism proved a convenient justification for *Realpolitik* but was not the cause of *Realpolitik*.

REALISM IN THE ARTS

The defeat of the romantics in 1848 and the consequent emergence of the "blood and iron" politicians had its artistic counterpart in realism.

15. Alfred, Lord Tennyson, *By an Evolutionist* (1889), ll. 13-20.

A close examination of realist literature and painting often reveals that the artists strayed less far from the romantic pasture than they claimed; but it is also true that they deliberately chose subjects from the everyday world and strove to be impersonal in recording what they saw. In eschewing the personal and the individual, they did not retreat to the ideal or the rational; instead, in their eagnerness to be true to life, they became collectors of facts. One can see immediately that the spirit which drove the realists was that which guided the materialists as well. They saw life as brutish, its conditions appalling, and mankind as weak. It followed that much realist art was social criticism, for more often than not, it portrayed the wretchedness of man in his environment. Only through science and technology could man's lot be improved, for the realists had no faith in anything beyond the material universe. Gustave Flaubert (French, 1821–1880), whose brilliant novel *Madame Bovary* (1857) revealed the destruction of a country doctor's wife whose lovers inevitably deserted her, put his faith in science this way:

The moral of the present regime will be to prove that universal suffrage is as stupid as divine right, though a little less odious.

The problem shifts, therefore. It is no longer a question of striving for the best form of government, since one form is as good as another, but of making Science prevail. That is the most urgent. The rest will follow inevitably. Pure intellectuals have been of greater use to the human race than all the Saint Vincent de Pauls in the world! And politics will continue to be absurd until it becomes a province of Science. A country's government ought to be merely a section of the Institute—and the least important one of all.[16]

The Russian realist school included three well-known novelists: Ivan S. Turgenev (1828–1883), Fedor M. Dostoevski (1821–1881), and Leo Tolstoy (1828–1910). All were concerned for the social evils in Russia and were at odds with the autocracy. Turgenev lived most of his creative life in France, having earned the anger of Nicholas I's government with a note written on the occasion of Gogol's death. *Fathers and Sons* (1862) remains his most notable work; a novel of the revolutionary movement in Russia, it has for its hero a nihilist. Dostoevski is more difficult to characterize than Turgenev. Sentenced to exile in Siberia in 1849 for membership in a revolutionary society, Dostoevski lived four terrible years among the empire's most vicious criminals. His subsequent novels were notably

16. Letter from Flaubert to George Sand (1869), quoted in Francis Steegmuller, *The Selected Letters of Gustave Flaubert* (London, 1954), p. 206.

concerned with the good and evil in man, and with the Russian character. They are more admired for their psychological insights than for their literary polish, *Crime and Punishment* (1866) being held the greatest. Here he develops the theme that the purification or expiation of a crime can only be achieved through suffering. Tolstoy departed in major respects from the principal tenets of realism, yet he was an enemy of serfdom, thought of himself as a defender of the helpless, and, as *War and Peace* (1866) plainly shows, could do painstaking research to give his work reality. Tolstoy, however, must be regarded as a peculiar mixture of realist and mystic. If he saw life in its realistic detail, he also struggled to transcend that detail in order to find a larger meaning or pattern in life. He wrote in 1877, "I have been thinking about the Divinity of God for a long time. Don't say that we must not think about it. Not only we must, but we ought. In all ages the best people, the true people, have thought about it."[17]

In Britain, Charles Dickens continued his social criticism through novels, especially with *Hard Times* (1854), a blast against the *laissez faire* liberals. Mrs. Gaskell (Elizabeth G. Gaskell, 1810–1865) achieved a charmingly realistic picture of English village life in her novel *Cranford* (1853). Two years later she published *North and South,* which she intended as an exposé of the evils of the factory system. In George Eliot (Mary Ann Evans, 1819–1880), Victorian England had her best novelist of human nature—of psychological problems. Her earlier novels dwelt on the life of laborers, *Adam Bede* (1859) and *Silas Marner* (1861) being examples. With *Middlemarch* (1872) she won fame as an analyst of English character.

On the Continent, even Victor Hugo, long the leader of the French romantics, turned to realism in 1862 with the publication of *Les Misérables,* an enormous canvas of social evils. The best German novel of that era was *Soll und Haben* (1855) by Gustav Freytag (1816–1895), a humorous portrait of middle-class life. Freytag's novel not merely lauded the sound qualities of the German middle class, but was also a vehicle for his German patriotism expressed in anti-Slavic, anti-Semitic sentiments. He became well-known as a champion of Prussian hegemony over Germany.

Such a brief survey of the first-rate novelists of the 1850's and 1860's, while it will suggest that the period was of outstanding literary excellence,

17. See the brilliant essay by Sir Isaiah Berlin, *The Hedgehog and the Fox,* New York, Mentor, 1957.

hardly reveals the massive quantity of literature produced. Second- and third-raters were beginning to turn out inferior novels for the mass audience, so that popular opinion was coming to exercise a control over the arts as never before. Such an audience was not interested in questions of aesthetics or philosophy of art. It doted, instead, on the syrup of sentimentality, where virtue was invariably rewarded and sweetness and light triumphed over oppression and godlessness. When Flaubert dared to suggest a contrary view of reality in *Madame Bovary*—which was, incidentally, a literary masterpiece—he was invited to court to face a charge of outraging public morality—as if he had invented the evils he reported. Despite his acquittal, such a public attitude was a restraining influence on the artists of the day, and many of them were disinclined to experiment with new forms.

In retrospect, the decades after mid-century proved to be the great age of the novel. The reading public had increased immensely in the nineteenth century, and many of the novels first saw the light of day serialized in newspapers. This made them readily available at a cheap price, though the increasing public for newspapers was in itself evidence of growing popular literacy and wealth. Since news agencies concentrating on the news of the day were still in their infancy, newspaper readers were still more concerned for lead articles and literary pieces than for the political and sensational news of a later day.

We have yet to account for the moralism which pervaded much Victorian and continental literature. Here the problem was not so much realism *versus* romanticism nor sensuality *versus* scientific materialism, but the expression of a social dimension: the insistence on respectability so characteristic of Victorian England. One might make the favorable point that this empahasis on morality was another aspect of that age's predilection for social criticism; yet, it was the same insistence on morality that brought *Madame Bovary* into court, though the novel was a powerful piece of social criticism. We are thus left with a social, rather than an artistic, phenomenon. The cult of respectability was a middle-class enthusiasm and became a mark of legitimacy. Aristocrats, no matter what their financial or moral position, never feared for their social rank; but members of the middle class, necessarily upstarts, sought to demonstrate their worthiness of social preeminence through lives of rigid restraint. Self-denial and priggishness too often lead to self-righteousness and smugness, qualities of which the Victorians were not entirely free. This middle-class moral earnestness became such a pervading force that we find it affecting the aristocracy and working people as well. It is hard to say whether the Queen or Tennyson embodied these middle-class virtues the more: Victoria, the devoted wife and mother of nine; or Alfred, Lord Tennyson (1809–1892), her poet-laureate for forty-two years, who lived a life of almost unrelieved high-seriousness.

Robert Browning (1812–1889) was less a moral teacher than Tennyson, and undoubtedly a greater poet. Yet, even through the impressive intellectuality of Browning, moral purpose can often be discerned. Living for many years in Italy, Browning was inspired by the Renaissance and things Italian. His poetry, like many of the novels of that day, showed an interest in psychology and character portrayal.

> What I love best in all the world
> is a castle, precipice-encurled,
> In a gash of the wind-grieved Appenine.
> Or look for me, old fellow of mine,
> (If I get my head from out the mouth
> O' the grave, and loose my spirits bands,
> And come again to the land of lands,
> In a sea-side house to the farther South,
> Where the baked cicala dies of drouth,
> And one sharp tree—'tis a cypress—stands,
> By the many hundred years red-rusted,
> Rough iron-spiked, ripe fruit-o'ercrusted,
> My sentinel to guard the sands
> To the water's edge. For, what expands
> Before the house, but the great opaque
> Blue breadths of sea without a break?
> While, in the house, forever crumbles
> Some fragment of the frescoed walls,
> From blisters where a scorpion sprawls.
> A girl barefooted brings, and tumbles
> Down on the pavement, green-flesh melons,
> And says there's news today—the king
> Was shot at, touched in the liver-wing,
> Goes with his Bourbon arm in a sling—
> She hopes they have not caught the felon.
> Italy, my Italy!
> Queen Mary's saying serves for me—
>   (When fortune's malice
>   Lost her, Calais)—
> Open my heart and you will see

Graved inside of it, "Italy."
Such lovers old are I and she;
So it always was, so shall ever be![18]

More than Browning, a group calling themselves the Pre-Raphaelite Brotherhood were the rebels against realism and the earnestness and moralism of Victorian literature. Poets and painters, they were led by Dante Gabriel Rossetti (1828–1882). Theirs was a romantic return to the late medieval, and their art was sensual rather than spiritual or realistic. The Victorians, of course, attacked them as immoral, but John Ruskin defended them as rebels against the barbarism of the industrial age.

Like Ruskin and Arnold, the French poet Charles Pierre Baudelaire (1821–1867) was appalled by the apparent decline in the vitality of European culture, a decline which the cultural pundits of that day dated from the vast commercial and industrial expansion of Europe, from the rise to social supremacy of the middle class, which could not distinguish comfort from pleasure. "Comfort subtly usurped the place of pleasure —a passive for an active thing."[19] Instead of individual greatness he saw "general animality," and predicted for the near future a time when

the son will desert his family, not at the age of eighteen, as at present, but at the age of twelve, emancipated by his gluttonous percocity; he will run away, not in search of heroic adventures, not to deliver a beautiful prisoner from a tower, not to immortalize a garret with his sublime thoughts; but to start a business, to grow rich, to enter into competition with his vile papa, founder and chief shareholder of a journal that will spread enlightenment and make the one-time *Siècle* seem like a pillar of supersition. . . . Those times are perhaps quite close at hand. Who knows whether they are not here already; whether it is not simply the coarsening of our natures that prevents us from perceiving the atmosphere that we already breathe?[20]

Baudelaire's first book of poems, *Fleurs du mal* (1857), followed Flaubert's *Madame Bovary* into court, the poems presumably offending public morality because of their morbidity. His attitude is reflected in the following passage written after the censure of *Madame Bovary*:

Let us say, if it be permitted to conjecture after the opinions which accompanied the verdict, that if the magistrates had found something truly reproach-

18. Robert Browning, from *"De Gustibus—"* (1885), ll. 14-46.
19. Jacques Barzun, *Berlioz and His Century* (New York, 1956), p. 376.
20. Baudelaire, *The Essence of Laughter and Other Essays, Journals and Letters* ed. Peter Quennell (New York, 1956), from *Fusées*, pp. 174-175.

able in the book, they would nevertheless have amnestied it on behalf of—and in recognition of —the *Beauty* in which it was clothed. This notable concern for Beauty, in men whose minds are only solicited for Justice and Truth, is a most moving sign, compared with the eager covetousness of this society which has without question forsworn all love for the things of the mind, and which, neglecting *its ancient entrails,* has only its own viscera for a cure.[21]

His spiritual despair led him to opium, to excessive drink, and to an end in an asylum for the insane.

The world of painting had a great realist too: Gustave Courbet (French, 1819–1877). A prolific painter of portraits, landscapes, and animal scenes, Courbet thought of himself as a radical as well as a realist and painted a number of canvases of social significance. One was his "Beggar's Alms" (1868), a picture of a frightful beggar handing a coin to a gypsy child. Another was the "Atelier," of which Courbet had to say:

The scene is laid in my studio in Paris. The picture is divided into two parts. I am in the center, painting; on the right all the active participants, that is my friends, the workers, the art colelctors. On the left the others, those whose lives are without significance: the common people, the destitute, the poor, the wealthy, the exploited, the exploiters, those who thrive on death.[22]

The quotation is typical both of Courbet's egotism and of his naiveté. He was a far better painter than a philosopher, and most of his painting far transcended the narrow confines of realism. Daumier, whose work continued into this era, was a greater realist in his superb satires. A new name, impressionism, was used first in the 1860's to describe the work of a group of young painters who had at first been inclined to follow Courbet. The impressionists, like the realists, were theoretically opposed to neo-classicism and romanticism. They painted "what they saw," particularly out of doors. Claude Monet (1846–1926), Edouard Manet (1832–1883), and Edgar Degas (1834–1917) were the first to be so classified. Realistic in that they chose everyday subjects, their work was not "realistic" in its omission of much detail.

In music after mid-century, the problem is not the erosion of romanticism in realism. Rather, romantic music became more nationalistic, such composers as Nicholas A. Rimsky-Korsakov (Russian, 1844–1908) and Richard Wagner (German, 1813–1883) went to folksongs and to folk-

21. Baudelaire, "Madame Bovary (1857)," *L'Art Romantique* (Paris, 1868).
22. Quoted in Roger L. Williams, *Gaslight and Shadow* (New York, 1957), p. 240.

lore for melody and story. And in the case of Wagner and his disciples, music did not escape the mechanization characteristic of much intellectual life after 1848. His use of the *leitmotif* in opera to be the sign of an object or an idea gave the work a mechanical structure; but more significantly, Wagner was convinced that his was the "art of the future." In his hands, the arts could be synthesized—into *Gesamtkunst*—to make art a higher thing than it had been since the Greeks. Thus, in his music dramas, which presumably appealed to all the senses at once, literature, music, philosophy, and religion were molded (or should we say, had evolved) into a superior art form. An age already caught up with ideas of evolution, of materialism, soon made Wagnerism a cult. *Tristan and Isolde* (1859) was the first great *Gesamtkunstwerk,* while the four music dramas comprising the *Ring of the Nibelungen* occupied him with some interruption from 1848 until 1874. A half-century after Wagner's death, it had become common to perform his works in the concert-hall, suggesting that their greatness lay in the music alone.

Around Wagner's Italian counterpart, Giuseppe Verdi (1813–1901), there has been less controversy. With *Rigoletto* (1851) and *Il Trovatore* (1853) and *La Traviata* (1853), he became easily the most popular operatic composer in Europe. In 1871, upon the invitation of the Khedive of Egypt to write a work on an Egyptian subject, Verdi completed *Aida* for production in Cairo. *Aida* was a turning point in Verdi's career and showed the probable influence of Wagner. While the voice continued, as always in Italian opera, to be the center of attention, Verdi greatly increased the orchestra's richness, and this remained characteristic of his later works. The dramatic intensity of Verdi's operas marked him as a first-rate master of the craft.

THE CRIMEAN WAR

Between 1815 and 1915, there was no European war involving all the great powers—what we have come to call a world war. Armed conflicts there were, "expeditions" such as the Algerian venture by France in 1830, or the "small war" for Greek Independence in the 1820's, or the Franco-Prussian war in 1870. But these conflicts were invariably limited, both in the number of participants and in their theaters.

The first of these limited wars in the nineteenth century to involve major powers on both sides was the Crimean War (1854–1856), which grew out of a prior Russo-Turkish squabble. The Near East, in fact, had remained in ferment after the Greek revolution, when Turkey's defeat proved the opportunity for her enemies. Mehemet Ali (*1811–1848*), Khedive of Egypt and a vassal of the Sultan of Turkey, provided the opening difficulties by demanding Syria from Turkey as compensation for services rendered during the Greek revolution. That war having been lost by Turkey-Egypt, the Sultan refused the demand; whereupon the Egyptians occupied Syria in 1832 and began an invasion of Anatolia. The Turks seemed powerless to stop their advance and appealed to Britain for support. Occupied with domestic reform just then, the British did nothing, and it was a real measure of Turkish desperation that the country next turned to Russia. The opportunity to intervene in Turkish affairs was eagerly accepted in St. Petersburg, the defensive treaty of Unkiar Skelessi (1833) being the result. France and Britain were shocked by this diplomatic reversal which threatened to give Russia domination of the eastern Mediterranean.

Egypt, meanwhile, retained Syria, and Mehemet Ali dreamed of complete independence from Turkey and the formation of a great Arabo-Egyptian Empire, a scheme which got French encouragement. To stop this development, the Turks invaded Syria to drive out the Egyptians in 1839, but they were once again beaten. The British then insisted on international intervention, fearful that either France or Russia would profit enormously out of the conflict. Nichols I showed himself conciliatory, for he recognized the opportunity to increase the tension between Britain and France. The upshot was that Britain and Russia forced Mehemet Ali out of Syria, though he was given the hereditary throne of Egypt (1841). As a gesture to Britain, the treaty of Unkiar Skelessi was not renewed. It was soon apparent, however, that the Russians hoped their new understanding with the British would lead to partition of the Turkish Empire, whereas the British merely sought to maintain that empire's territorial integrity to prevent Russian expansion into the eastern Mediterranean.

Ten years later, the Eastern question reopened on a new note. Under pressure form the French Catholics and eager to please them, the new French Emperor approached the Turkish government on the matter of the holy places in Palestine; most of them had fallen under control of Greek Orthodox monks. France, which had the right to protect the Roman Catholic monks in the Holy Land, succeeded in retrieving some of the holy places through Turkish agreement (1852). Russia made a countermove at once, but not only did she demand equality with France in the

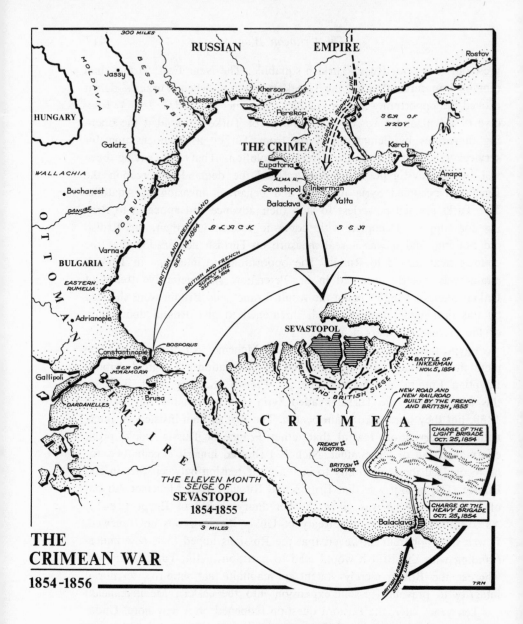

THE CRIMEA

SEVASTOPOL

THE ELEVEN MONTH
SEIGE OF
SEVASTOPOL
1854-1855

BATTLE OF
INKERMAN
NOV. 5, 1854

NEW ROAD AND
NEW RAILROAD
BUILT BY THE FRENCH
AND BRITISH, 1855

CHARGE OF THE
LIGHT BRIGADE.
OCT. 25, 1854

CHARGE OF THE
HEAVY BRIGADE.
OCT. 25, 1854

FRENCH
HDQTRS.

BRITISH
HDQTRS.

CRIMEA

Balaclava

BRITISH & FRENCH
SUPPLY LINE

3 MILES

THE
CRIMEAN WAR
1854-1856

Holy Land, but she also demanded the right to protect Orthodox churches in Constantinople and throughout the Turkish Empire. This extended demand was so great a threat to Ottoman integrity that Britain could not support it. The Turks were thus encouraged to reject the Russian request —leaving the Russians embarrassingly exposed. Nicholas I, however, persisted, sending troops into the Danubian Principalities to intimidate the Turks. The great powers worked for a peaceful solution, but Turkey had concluded that she would have western support in case of a war. She delivered an ultimatum to Russia to evacuate the Principalities and declared war (1853) upon Russian refusal.

The Turks had calculated correctly. Though neither Britain nor France was eager for war, it was impossible to allow Turkey to succumb lest the Near East fall to Russia. Public opinion, especially after 1849, was hostile to the Russian autocracy; when the western governments concluded that they must aid Turkey, their peoples were prepared in spirit. An Anglo-French ultimatum (1854) that Russia evacuate the Danubian Principalities having been ignored, war was declared. Austria's attitude then became critical, for she possessed large forces on the flank of the Principalities. We must recall here that Austria owed Russia a debt of gratitude for services rendered in Hungary in 1849. In all likelihood, Nicholas I expected that debt to be repaid in 1853-1854, either through Austrian support of his demands upon Turkey, or at least with a benevolent neutrality. But politics is not a matter of gratitude but of interest, and the Austrians were no more ready to see Russia dominate the Balkans than they had been in the eighteenth century. To Nicholas' great dismay and anger, Austria delivered an ultimatum (1854) to force Russian evacuation of the Principalities; Russia had to accept this request, considering she was already at war with three powers. Worse, the Austrians made arrangements to occupy the Principalities for the Turks for the duration of the war. The fury in Russia at this "ingratitude" remained a serious diplomatic factor right down to World War I.

The Crimean War has become celebrated for its peculiarities. Neither Britain nor France wanted an expensive war; but Russia could not be subdued without gigantic forces. The ultimate decision was to seize the great naval base of Sevastopol on the Crimean peninsula and hold it as a pawn. Meanwhile, the Allies would endeavor to bring Austria actively into the war. Negotiations for that eventuality went on in Vienna throughout the hostilities, until the western powers and Austria had agreed upon conditions for peace. Since one of the terms meant the demilitarization of the Black Sea region, the Russians could not be induced to accept. In the meantime, the war was conducted in the most inept manner, and it is not the least of the war's peculiarities that the two reputations made in its course were those of an English civilian nurse, Florence Nightingale (1820–1910), and of a colonel in the losing cause, Franz E. I. Todleben (1818–1884).

Miss Nightingale's services as a nurse were made necessary by the almost total want of medical service in the British army. Throughout the campaign, the allied armies were seriously drained by attacks of cholera, and during the Crimean winter they suffered severely from lack of adequate clothing and shelter. In fact, the inadequacies and smallness of the allied forces made it impossible for them to invest Sevastopol completely, allowing the Russians to supply the city throughout the siege. Had Russia's internal system of communication been comparable to anything in the West, the city might have held out indefinitely. But the Crimea was on the periphery of the empire, and there were no railroads in that region. Todleben brilliantly improvised defenses in expectation of relief, but that which came was insufficient. The British army, meanwhile, became so depleted that Britain sought mercenary help from Sardinia-Piedmont. Prime Minister Cavour readily consented to furnish 10,000 men. His little country had no grievance against Russia, but he thirsted for an opportunity to sit at the international peace conference following the war and to air Italy's grievances against Austria at that meeting. His calculation was shrewd—and a supreme example of *Realpolitik*—for neither side in the war was pleased with the nature of Austria's participation. The British Prime Minister, Henry Temple, Viscount Palmerston (1784– 1865), speaking before the House of Commons, remarked, "Austria is with us up to a certain point." He paused, then added with a sneer, "she is with us morally."

Early in 1855, the death of Nicholas I led to general hope that his successor, Alexander II (*1855–1881*), would listen to peace terms, but the conditions arrived at in Vienna still were unacceptable. Then, in the fall, the French took the key position in Sevastopol's defenses, and the city had to be abandoned. Shortly thereafter, Austria notified Russia of her intention to enter the war in the event that Russia continued to refuse peace. This proved to be the necessary threat. Early in 1856, the powers convened in Paris to arrange a peace settlement, and the Congress of Paris proved to be a sounding board for both Napoleon III and Cavour, whose interest lay in revising the Vienna settlement of 1815. Consequently, they raised the issues of Poland and Italy, questions which were successfully tabled by the other powers. In the treaty of Paris, Russia and Turkey accepted the neutralization of the Black Sea, which meant its virtual demilitarization and a blow to Russian expansionist ambitions. Russia also surrendered a part of Bessarabia as well as her claim to protect Christians in the Ottoman Empire.

The Danubian Principalities, finally, were placed under the jurisdiction of the signatory powers, their status to be determined subsequently. Napoleon III, however, increasingly the champion of nation-states in his bid to undermine the Vienna settlement, intended that the Principalities should become a Romanian state. Between 1857 and 1862 this Romanian state was formed, with Colonel Alexander Cuza elected prince. He vigorously promoted liberal reforms, abolishing serfdom and feudal dues, though compensating the great landowners, and he worked to develop the educational system. Cuza soon felt the hatred of all, both of those from whom he had taken away and of those to whom he had not given enough. In 1866, the leading Romanians combined to overthrow him in favor of a German prince, Charles of Hohenzollern-Sigmaringen. The final settlement worked out by the powers left Romania not completely independent, but autonomous within the Ottoman Empire.

RUSSIA: REFORMS OF ALEXANDER II

The loss of the Crimean War had immense import for Russia. Efficiency is one of the few justifications for autocracy, and the war had shown the autocracy to be inefficient. Alexander II was not a reformer by choice, but he was intelligent enough to recognize the immediate necessity of reform. The abolition of serfdom in 1861 was the most striking reform and was long overdue. It is estimated that roughly 40 million people gained their freedom by this decree. Emancipation alone, however, was not enough, and the government took the responsibility for providing the ex-serfs with land. In general, the serfs were allowed to retain the lands they had used while in serfdom, the landowners being compensated for their losses by the state. The new owners, however, were not simply given the lands, but had to repay the state in installments over a period of forty-nine years. It goes without saying that such arrangements produced much dissatisfaction and hardship, though they were an honest attempt to eliminate an inhuman abuse. Generally the land was not given outright to the peasants, but was turned over to the rural communes (the *mirs*) for administration. All peasants living in the *mir* were entitled to an equal amount of land to work, and the *mir* government periodically rotated the lands among the peasants, to give each an equal opportunity at the best lands. This peculiar arrangement was constructed for the financial convenience of the Russian government, it being easier to work out taxes and installment payments with the *mir* authorities than with each individual peasant. The system proved to be harmful to agriculture, the peasants naturally taking little interest in improving lands which they worked only temporarily.

As elsewhere in Europe, the elimination of feudal relationships required new political and legal institutions. The lord's court was a thing of the past, and local government would have to take into account the existence of free landowners who were not aristocrats. Alexander II re-

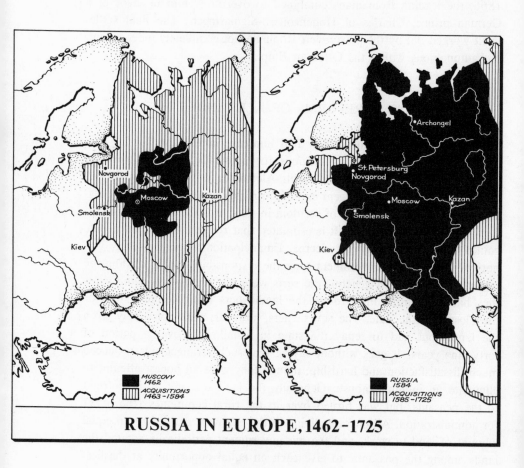

RUSSIA IN EUROPE, 1462-1725

sponded in 1864 by reorganizing local government on both a district and a provincial basis. The property holders in each district elected their own assembly called "zemstvo"; and that Assembly sent delegates to the provincial zemstvo. Granted that the aristocrats still carried the greatest weight in local government, the reform established the principle of self-government by allowing the zemstvos to levy taxes for local requirements. In the same year, the Czar reorganized the judiciary, which had been one of the most inequitable in Europe, as the nature of the reform will suggest. Equality before the law, without regard to class, was established

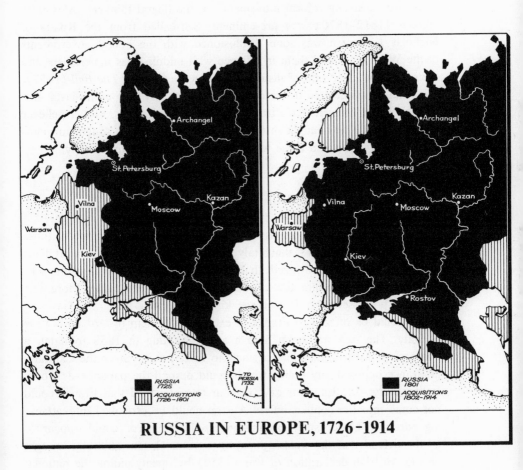

RUSSIA IN EUROPE, 1726-1914

for *the first time;* judges were given tenure secure from political interference; the bar was established; and public jury trials became the rule.

Thanks to the reforms of Alexander II, Russia was soon the scene
of significant social and economic change. The professional and middle
classes began to assume positions of national leadership formerly reserved
solely for the aristocrats. But instead of satisfying the thirst for reform,
Alexander II's reform program stimulated demands for a more thorough-
going democratization of society and for a government based on national
representation. Various methods of achieving these goals were advanced,
but since there was little concensus among the reformers, it was impossible
to provide a strong reform movement. Of the liberal thinkers, Alexander
Herzen (1812–1870) was pre-eminent. Self-exiled from the Russia of
Nicholas I, Herzen was soon disillusioned with the liberal governments
of the West. He found them in alliance with middle-class materialism and
the social abuses of industrialism. In London, he founded *The Bell* (1857),
a journal which greeted the reforms of Alexander II with enthusiasm. But
in their aftermath, Herzen's tragedy came into full focus. Not a believer
in extremes, he was caught in the cross-fire of those who sought to maintain the *status quo* and those who sought vast change immediately.

THE UNIFICATION OF ITALY

Count Cavour, prime minister of Sardinia-Piedmont, was one of those
who realized after 1848 that Italy would not be made by the Italians
alone. He further recognized that Napoleon III's sympathies for self-
determination made him the most likely ally in Italy's cause. Moreover,
Sardinia possessed two French-speaking territories—Nice and Savoy—
which could be offered to France in exchange for help toward unification
of Italy. The two statesmen held a secret meeting in 1858 to hatch a
war against Austria, the chief obstacle to Italian unity. Since the Catholics
in France opposed any policy which could despoil the papacy—as would
Italian unity—the Emperor gave Cavour to understand that France could
not come into the conflict unless Austria could be provoked into attacking Sardinia. Under such circumstances, the Emperor could appear to
be the defender of the weak against aggression. Cavour skillfully brought
on the Austrian declaration of war (1859) by openly aiding the national
movement in other Italian states and refusing to cease when warned to do
so by Austria. Thus, the War for Italian Independence became largely a

Franco-Austrian war. Two inconclusive victories were won by the French, forcing an Austrian evacuation of Lombardy.

Suddenly, the question of German unity was thrust into the Italian war. Prussia mobilized on the French frontier and volunteered to come to the aid of Austria, clearly in an attempt to seize the leadership of the German world from the Austrians. Neither France nor Austria wanted Prussian intervention, and they hastened into armistice without even a prior French consultation of Sardinia. The terms they arranged roused Cavour to fury; Austria would cede Lombardy to France, which, in turn, would cede it to Sardinia. But Venetia, which Napoleon III had also promised to Sardinia, would remain Austrian. These armistice terms became the treaty of Zürich (1859). Coincidental with the war, nationalist uprisings erupted in Tuscany and the Papal States, and their agents begged to be annexed to Sardinia. Napoleon III, embarrassed by Italian rage over Venetia, did not accept Nice and Savoy until it had been arranged to annex Tuscany, Parma, Modena, and Romagna (papal territories) to Sardinia. Plebiscites were held in all six territories, Nice and Savoy voting to join France, the latter four to join Sardinia (1860).

Meanwhile, in the south, Garibaldi and his Thousand Redshirts invaded Sicily (1860), still under the Neapolitan Bourbons. The former Mazzinian had rallied to the Sardinian monarchy, and he now swiftly defeated the Neapolitan Army in a dramatic campaign, forcing its evacuation to the mainland. Garibaldi followed, his advance becoming a triumphal procession. With the final defeat of the Neapolitans, Garibaldi proclaimed himself ruler of Naples, though loyal to Victor Emmanuel of Sardinia. While the Sardinians were delighted, they feared correctly that Garibaldi intended to move into the remaining Papal States and into Venetia. Cavour was horrified at the thought of provoking the French, who had occupied Rome since 1849, and of a renewal of the war against Austria as an invasion of Venetia might provoke. Consequently, Cavour sent troops to Naples, really to hold Garibaldi in check. This force passed through papal territory and, when blocked by the small papal army, smashed it en route. A plebiscite was then held in Naples and Sicily, both territories voting to join Sardinia (1860); and shortly thereafter, two more papal territories voted to join Sardinia: Umbria and the Marches. Early in 1861, Sardinia converted herself into the Kingdom of Italy, with Victor Emanuel as the first king. Only Venetia and Rome herself remained outside the realm. As for Cavour, he survived the proclamation of the kingdom he had done so much to create by only two and a half months.

Above left to right: Czar Alexander II, Napoleon III, Pope Pius
Below: William Gladstone Advising Queen Victoria

The Opening of the Suez Canal at Port Said, November 17, 1869

Right: Louis Pasteur
Below: Charles Darwin

Above: Charles Dickens Reading to His Daughters
Below: *The Woman with the Mirror* by Gustave Courbet

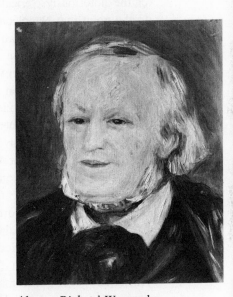

Above: *Richard Wagner* by
Auguste Renoir
Top: Robert Browning
Above left: Gustave Flaubert
Left: Charles Baudelaire

32

THE WANING OF FRENCH PRESTIGE

The French, in the meantime, were beginning to involve themselves in Mexican affairs, in an episode well-known to students of American history. In 1861, the Mexican government of President Benito Juarez suspended payments on debts to European investors, and France, Britain and Spain were all quick to protest. France alone, however, landed troops in 1862, and the reasons for the French intervention have always been much debated. It is true, for instance, that several high personages in the French government stood to profit if the Mexicans could be forced to honor the debts; it is also true that the defaulting Mexican regime was anti-clerical, and that its clerical-monarchial opponents sought the patronage of the notoriously clerical French Empress Eugenie. It is probably more to the point that Napoleon III became convinced by the Mexican clericals that the Mexican population desired a Catholic monarchy and was being denied self-determination as a nation. Moreover, the Emperor had long cherished Saint-Simonian visions of developing the economy of Nicaragua, including the construction of a Central American canal, and Mexico would well serve as the keystone.

It is not clear just when Napoleon III awoke to the true state of Mexican opinion, but certainly not until the invasion of 1862 was well under way. After the capture of Mexico City, the army conducted a rigged plebiscite, and the dutiful votes brought to Mexico an Austrian Archduke, Maximilian, as emperor (1864). He, too, went to Mexico in full confidence of popular support. These events transpired during the American Civil War and were so alarming to Southern politicians in particular that there was serious negotiation to halt the war in order to deal with the French encroachment in the New World. After its victory in 1865, the American government made vigorous protests to the French, but the decision to evacuate all French troops from Mexico did not come until the end of 1866, and then only because of developments in the German world. Napoleon urged Maximilian to depart with the troops, since the cause was hopeless, but Maximilian had greater faith in his cause and refused an escorted flight. His naiveté led to his swift defeat, capture, and execution by the Mexican opposition (1867). The whole episode was a fearful blow to the Imperial French prestige; it was a costly and apparently senseless expedition, which ended in retreat and the death of a liberal and well-intentioned man.

Meanwhile, the French were suffering a second setback in Europe over Polish affairs. Alexander II, as part of his reform movement after the Crimean War and in the hope of rallying the Poles, eliminated many of the abuses and hardships endured by the Poles after their rebellion in 1831. The serfs were freed, as in Russia; native universities were allowed to reopen; and the official persecution of Roman Catholicism was ended. Unfortunately for the Czar's hope to integrate Poland into his empire, there was virtually only one notable person in Poland who favored a close union with Russia: Marquis Alexander Wielopolski (1803–1877). He was given considerable power in 1861 by the Czar, but he was consequently regarded as a traitor by most Polish patriots. The latter were fatally divided among themselves. The great landowners, known as the Whites, were willing to accept the Russian Czar as their king, in the hope of maintaining the social and economic *status quo;* but the price for their support was the boundaries of 1772. Such a price was impossible for Alexander II, partly because Russia did not control all of prepartition Poland, partly because Russian opinion would not have tolerated the surrender of provinces predominately Russian in population. Another group of Polish patriots, the Reds, were largely recruited from the urban professionals and the lesser gentry; they hoped for a liberal republic and were, therefore, hostile to the Whites.

Given this political diversity and the general Polish hatred of Russia, Wielopolski's program was foredoomed. The relaxation granted by Alexander II simply brought demands for greater liberties. Wielopolski, believing in strict law and order, tried to stem the agitation with force, and his action led to an insurrection (early 1863). The revolt spread so quickly that Russian authority was for a time threatened, and over a year was required to extinguish the fires. At that point, Alexander II removed the measures intended to make Poland autonomous, and she reverted to being simply a province within the Russian Empire.

The Polish revolt in 1863, however, inaugurated a series of incidents tremendously influential in international events for the next seven years. Shortly after the outbreak of the revolt, Otto von Bismarck, newly minister-president of Prussia, offered Russia military support in suppressing the Poles (the Alvensleben Convention of 1863). This military support was neither wanted nor required by Russia, but it was a gesture of Prusso-Russian solidarity, which gave Russia the means to resist pro-Polish pressure from the West. The Polish cause was popular in the West, especially because the plight of Poland was one issue on which liberals and clericals could combine, since Poland was Catholic and Russia, Orthodox. The clamor to counter Prussia's gesture to Russia was an embarrassment for the French government in particular. Ever since the Crimean War, Napoleon III had striven to be conciliatory to Russia, his aim being the reconciliation of all the Crimean opponents, as the basis for a durable peace. Both Britain and Austria had been highly suspicious of Napoleon's intentions, anticipating that his goal was a division of the Continent between Russia and France similar to that achieved by the first Napoleon at Tilsit in 1807.

The upshot was that when Napoleon III, forced by French opinion to do something for Poland, proposed that Britain and Austria join France in petitioning the Czar to be lenient and grant further reforms, those two powers joined with France in such a half-hearted way as to encourage the Czar to reject international intervention into Polish affairs. Nothing was done for the Poles, and Russia had cause to be irritated against France alone for raising the issue. Late in 1863, Napoleon III tried to atone for his diplomatic defeat by inviting all the powers, large and small, to Paris, his assumption being that the Vienna settlement was a dead letter and that the peace of Europe required an understanding among all the powers. The beneficiary nations of 1815 were far from enthusiastic, but Britain alone had the courage to reject the invitation. Her position, which was probably tenable, was that until there be an international authority to enforce the decisions of the majority, such congresses could create more problems than they would solve. This rejection was a further diplomatic blow for Napoleon III, but his question raised before parliament that year remains for us today:

> Will the jealous rivalry of the great powers forever obstruct the progress of civilization? Will we always maintain our mutual defiance by exaggerated armaments? . . . Will we forever preserve a state which is neither peace with its security nor war with its chances of fortune?[23]

THE UNIFICATION OF GERMANY

The deterioration of Napoleon III's position in Europe in the 1860's and the gradual isolation of France provided a favorable climate for the rise of Prussia, guided by her brilliant minister-president, Otto von Bis-

23. Quoted in R. C. Binkley, *Realism and Nationalism* (New York, 1935), p. 260.

marck (1815–1898). Much credit for that rise should go to William I (1858–1888), a man not distinguished personally, but able to distinguish ability in others and to recruit them for public office. In 1859, he appointed General Albert von Roon (1803–1879) to head the ministry of war, and Roon's friend, General Helmuth von Moltke (1800–1891), to be chief of the general staff. They were charged with reforming the military establishment. In the same year, the Sardinian success against Austria aroused German national sentiments to an even higher pitch and encouraged Prussia to play a Sardinian role in Germany. William I's military program, however, soon hit a snag in the Prussian Landtag. The Liberals, who became the majority after 1859, balked at the credits necessary to carry out large-scale military reforms, because they saw the army as the bulwark of the autocracy. Underneath this particular question lay the issue of the Prussian constitution, which had been designed to preserve the royal authority behind the façade of representative government. Thus, the Liberals, in blocking the military credits, were striving to enhance the place of representative institutions in Prussian government. The quarrel festered for several years, with the King even contemplating abdication. Instead, he appointed Bismarck to be minister-president, a tough conservative to deal with the Liberal majority. ✓

╈ Bismarck's initial goal was the defeat of Austria, he believed this aim to require an understanding with both Russia and France, as well as the military build-up. Hating parliamentary institutions, he ordered the collection of taxes which the Landtag had refused to vote, and the Prussian population showed little resistance to this illegal collection of money. Without popular support the cause of the parliamentarians was hopeless. Moreover, the quick successes achieved by Bismarck in promoting the unification of Germany rallied nationalist opinion behind him and even won the acclaim of some prominent liberals.

> The agrandizement of Prussia, which is proceeding step by step, scarcely corresponds to our ideals, but it seems to us a lesser evil—indeed, a stroke of fortune—compared with Germany's condition today. In any case, it is within Prussia's power to make a tremendous step forward toward the goal of the unity of the fatherland; and no mortal can say whether or when there will be an opportunity of ending our dismemberment of general mediation.[24]

/ Bismarck's first major step toward German unity had been to secure

24. Heinrich von Treitschke (1865), quoted in *The Quest for a Principle of Authority in Europe 1715-Present*, New York, 1948, p. 222.

Russian friendship out of the Polish crisis of 1863. The following year, he was ready to make capital out of a crisis in Denmark, the issue being the status of the Duchies of Schleswig and Holstein. Since the fifteenth century, the kings of Denmark had simultaneously been the dukes of Schleswig and Holstein, but the duchies had never been incorporated into Denmark. Holstein, largely German in population, was a member of the Germanic Confederation. In the reign of Frederick VII (*1848–1863*), this personal union of Denmark and the duchies seemed doomed since the King was without heir. Denmark's answer was an attempt to annex

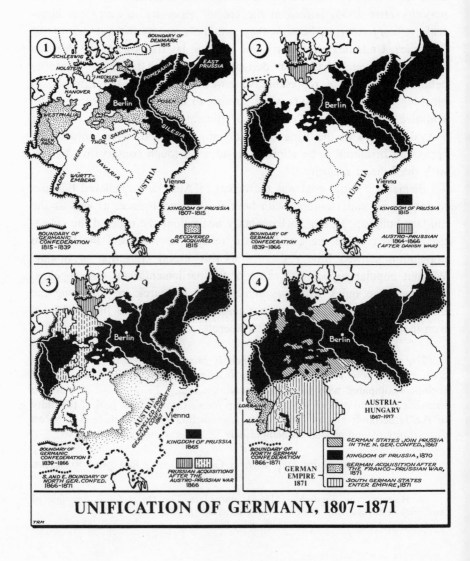

UNIFICATION OF GERMANY, 1807-1871

the duchies, but the duchies preferred their autonomy and received the support of the Germanic Confederation. This quarrel was settled by an international conference in London (1852) which left the Duchies autonomous, united with Denmark only by the common monarch.

In 1863, the throne passed to a collatoral branch of the royal family, and the new king, Christian IX (*1863–1906*), almost immediately violated the 1852 agreement by announcing the annexation of Schleswig, though Holstein was left autonomous. The Germanic Diet then voted to take both the duchies from Denmark, and Confederation troops were sent to occupy

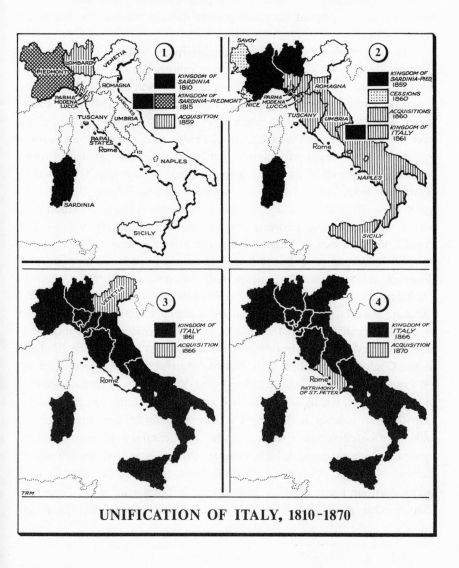

UNIFICATION OF ITALY, 1810-1870

Holstein at the end of 1863. In doing so, the Confederation played perfectly into Bismarck's hands. He could now pose as the defender of the agreement of 1852 and force the Danes to abandon the annexation of Schleswig while seizing the leadership in Germany by elbowing the troops of the Confederation out of Holstein. He offered an alliance to Austria, realizing that Austria would probably not allow him to act alone, and perhaps even sensing that the joint attempt to settle the festering question would provide incidents through which he could discredit Austria and prepare the ground for his ultimate attack upon her. Austria accepted the alliance, an ultimatum was sent to the Danes to abandon Schleswig (1864), and when it was refused, thet two powers quickly crushed the Danes by military force.

The final move in this diplomatic masterpiece was the Convention of Gastein (1865) by which the victorious powers agreed upon a condominium for the two duchies: joint sovereignty in each duchy, with Austria actually administering Holstein and Prussia, Schleswig. This joint sovereignty soon led to irritations, which Bismarck took pains to enhance. His next step was to secure the neutrality of France in the event of an Austro-Prussian conflict, apparently hinting that in exchange for neutrality France would be compensated along the Rhine. Probably Napoleon III hoped to regain territories lost in 1815. He went even farther, helping Bismarck to negotiate a three-month alliance with Italy (early 1866). If within that period war broke out between Prussia and Austria, Italy was to join Prussia, the province of Venetia being the prize promised Italy.

The diplomatic groundwork laid, it remained to provoke the war. This Bismarck accomplished by unexpectedly proposing that the Germanic Confederation be abandoned in favor of a new federal system which would eliminate Austria. Austria retaliated by charging Prussia with a violation of the 1815 settlement and of the Gastein Convention, whereupon Bismarck ordered Prussian troops into Holstein. Most of the German states in the Confederation sided with Austria—fearful of being swallowed up by Prussia—and the Confederation voted to condemn Prussia. Austria, in the meantime, hastily sought French neutrality, agreeing to cede Venetia after the war. Known as the Seven Weeks War, the conflict pitted Austria and the Confederation against Prussia; and contrary to most military opinion, which expected a long struggle, Prussia won a stunningly quick victory. Although Prussia's Italian ally was defeated, the diversion of strong Austrian forces by Italy proved fatal in the north for the Hapsburg Empire. One great battle, at Sadowa, left Vienna open, but Bismarck called a halt. His goal was to eliminate Austria from German affairs. Sadowa would accomplish that, and there was no reason to prolong the war and offer the French an opportunity to intervene. Consequently, Bismarck offered Austria an easy peace, based on the exclusion of Austria from further participation in the German world. By the treaty of Prague (1866), the Germanic Confederation was scrapped; the states north of the Main River were to be organized into the North German Confederation under Prussian presidency. The southern German states were to be free to organize a similar confederation. Prussia annexed several small states (the duchies, Hanover, Nassau, and Hesse-Cassel), bringing to an end the discontiguity of her territories. Italy, though defeated, annexed Venetia. To crown Bismarck's efforts, the Prussian Landtag voted a Bill of Indemnity—really an amnesty for the illegal taxes he had collected for four years. As an embittered socialist, put it, "The oppressors of yesterday are the saviors of today, right has become wrong and wrong right. . . . The stigma of violation of the constitution has been washed from his brow, and in its place the halo of glory rings his laureled head."[25]

The Seven Weeks War had a further significance for Austria: it brought to an end the Bach system of centralization and Germanization of the empire. Defeat in 1859 and 1866 left Austria powerless to resist Hungarian demands for a large measure of self-government. By the *Ausgleich* (equalization) of 1867, the empire became the Dual Monarchy of Austria-Hungary, having two governments, two constitutions, and two parliaments. The Austrian emperor was also the king of Hungary, and the two governments had three important ministries in common: war, foreign affairs, and finance. In the following years, Hungarian influence on the empire's foreign policy proved decisive and helped prevent Austria from re-entering the lists of German affairs. Instead, after 1867, the empire turned more to the southeast.

The swiftness of the Prussian victory in 1866 had been a profound shock to Napoleon III, and the new preponderance of Prussia forced the evacuation of French troops from Mexico. In fact, Napoleon's inability to mediate the Central European controversy, owing to its short duration, was another of the diplomatic defeats he suffered in the 1860's. At the time of the armistice in 1866, the French ambassador discussed compensations for France's neutrality with Bismarck, and it remains a question to this day as to which of them suggested that France get Luxemburg and Belgium. That it was Bismarck is a good bet. France had earlier hoped

25. Wilhelm Liebknecht, quoted in *Ibid.*, p. 223.

for Rhenish territories lost in 1815, but Bismarck rejected this suggestion as incompatible with German national sentiments. Thus, he steered the French to make territorial demands which would arouse the ire of other European powers. In 1867, Napoleon III made an attempt to purchase Luxemburg from its sovereign, the King of Netherlands. Bismarck, who had earlier encouraged the project, engineered its failure behind the scenes by reminding the German press that Luxemburg had been in the Germanic Confederation. The consequent outcry in Germany made the King of the Netherlands retreat from the sale. Napoleon III, who had smiled on the rise of Prussia and was willing to see the unification of Germany, received a bitter blow to his prestige.

The Luxemburg crisis had hardly blown over when there developed in Spain a situation tailor-made for Bismarckian intervention. Isabella II (*1883-1868*) was deposed after a reign characterized by a total want of morality and discretion. Among numerous candidates to replace her was Prince Leopold of Hohenzollern-Sigmaringen, and Bismarck soon saw his candidacy as a means of further provoking France. His desire for war with France arose from his conviction that, whatever the nation-state principles of Napoleon III, the French as a whole would view the formation of an immense Germany as intolerable. Moreover, the anti-Prussian sentiments of the southern German states required that Bismarck magnify the danger from France to frighten them into his arms. Thus, a military defeat of France was the final step in the plan for German unification. In the summer of 1870, Prince Leopold accepted the Spanish crown, Bismarck having pressured William I to urge his nephew to take the throne. When the news got out, the French foreign minister made a violent speech in parliament in which he assumed that Prussia was responsible for the Spanish choice. This made it necessary to approach Prussia, rather than Spain, for the removal of the controversial candidate.

Throughout the crisis, Bismarck feigned ignorance about the candidacy, asserting that it was a Hohenzollern family matter. This forced the French ambassador to visit the King, who was taking the waters at Bad Ems. William I, being disinclined to be pushed into another war by Bismarck, did take the necessary steps to have the Hohenzollern candidacy abandoned. But the French foreign minister was not satisfied with this victory; he insisted further that the King be made to promise that there would never be a renewal of the candidacy. The king understandably shrank from such a declaration, because it would have implied that he had been guilty of wrong-doing in the first place—which had, in fact, not been the case. After this second interview, the King sent a report of it to Bismarck, and the incident would have been closed had Bismarck not edited the dispatch from Ems for publication in a manner which inflamed both German and French opinion. It is useful to compare the original dispatch with Bismarck's version:

M. Benedetti spoke to me on the promenade, in order to demand from me, finally in a very importunate manner, that I should authorize him to telegraph at once that I bound myself for all future time never again to give my consent if the Hohenzollerns should renew their candidature. I refused at last somewhat sternly, as it is neither right nor possible to undertake engagements of this kind for ever and ever. Naturally I told him that I had as yet received no news, and as he was earlier informed about Paris and Madrid than myself, he could clearly see that my government once more had no hand in the matter. His Majesty has since received a letter from the Prince. His Majesty having told Count Benedetti that he was awaiting news from the Prince, has decided, with reference to the above demand, upon the representation of Count Eulenburg and myself, not to receive Count Benedetti again, but only to let him be informed through an aide-de-camp: That his Majesty had now received from the Prince confirmation of the news which Benedetti had already received from Paris, and had nothing further to say to the ambassador. His Majesty leaves it to your Excellency whether Benedetti's fresh demand and its rejection should not be at once communicated both to our ambassador and to the press.[26]

After the report of the Prince of Hohenzollern had been officially communicated to the Imperial French government by Spain, the French Ambassador at Ems made an additional demand of His Majesty, that he should authorize him to telegraph to Paris that His Majesty the King bound himself for all future time never again to give his consent if the Hohenzollerns renew that candidacy.

His Majesty the King thereupon decided not to receive the French envoy again, and informed him through an aide-de-camp on duty that His Majesty had nothing further to say to the Ambassador.

26. A. J. Butler, *Bismarck, The Man and the Statesman* (New York, 1899), Vol. II, Ch. 22.

Bismarck's prediction was correct: the insulting tone of the amended dispatch was "a red rag upon the Gallic bull." An aroused French parliament voted for war without even bothering to read the ambassador's own account of the interview.

The outbreak of war in 1870 found France not only the apparent aggressor, but diplomatically isolated. Hungarian reluctance to re-enter German politics kept the Austrian government from seeking revenge for 1866. Bismarck had earlier secured Russian friendship, and pro-Polish opinion in France was hardly attractive to Russia. To guarantee British neutrality, Bismarck revealed the French negotiations of 1867 for Belgium. As for Italy, the one thing Napoleon III had not yet given her was Rome; and the Italians knew that French troops would now have to be evacuated, so that Rome could be had without involving Italy in war.

The opposing armies in the Franco-Prussian war represented entirely different concepts of military organization and strategy. The French army, the smaller of the two, comprised professionals who had bungled through to victory in the Crimea in 1856 and in Italy in 1859 and who were hostile to technical innovation. They had successfully fought Napoleon III's attempt to inaugurate universal military training (1868) in a system similar to Prussia's. In contrast, the Prussian high command, with virtually no practical experience, had studied modern war as fought by the North in the American Civil War and had learned to use the railroad and the telegraph to speed mobilization and the movement of troops. The weakness of the French leadership was no more clearly shown than through its failure to exploit what technical advantage it did have. Both sides possessed breech-loading rifles, the French chassepot being significantly superior to the Prussian needle gun. Because the French infantryman had had better field training, particularly in the Mexican campaign, his experience and his better rifle should have suggested strategy designed to fight on terrain where infantry could be decisive. Prussia, with breech-loading artillery, was unquestionably superior in that arm, her guns having a faster rate of fire and longer range. Therefore, when we see the two French marshals operating in the field, M. E. P. Maurice de MacMahon in Alsace and Achille Bazaine in Lorraine, with no plan for cooperative action and when we see them after initial defeats, retire into strongly fortified places, where they became hopelessly vulnerable to the Prussian superiority in heavy guns, we may attribute the defeat largely to a failure in leadership. Presumably a professional army ought to have been superior; but professionalism is superior only so long as the professionals are up to date.

Only after Marshal Bazaine shut himself up in Metz did MacMahon go to his aid and was himself forced into the battle of Sedan. Napoleon III was present at Sedan, and when he saw the futility of further slaughter, he surrendered himself and MacMahon's army. Two days later, the Parisian republicans succeeded in overthrowing the Second Empire. A republic was proclaimed and an emergency government of national defense, was organized for the duration of the war. Its principal task was the defense of Paris, which the Prussians soon invested. If the cause was not immediately hopeless, it became so with the unexpected surrender of Bazaine at Metz with an army of nearly 175,000 men— an army which had the means to hold on longer. The surrender of Paris then became a military imperative, but when the Government of National Defense learned the nature of the peace Prussia intended to impose, it refused the terms, for both patriotic and political rasons. Furthermore, the citizenry of Paris became imbued with the notion of its invincibility. One recalled the days of 1792, when the heroic people went out to block the Prussian advance, and the Parisians settled down confidently to await the disintegration of the Prussian army. Meanwhile, the government strove to raise militia south of Paris in the hope of relieving the city, but all efforts were in vain. Early in 1871, with Paris suffering severe food shortages, the Government of National Defense knew the game was up and entered into an armistice with Bismarck.

There could be no peace settlement, however, until a regularly constituted French government could be established. Bismarck, in the meantime, was completing plans for Prussia to swallow up Germany, while the shocked Parisians were considering what to do about the government which had "betrayed" them by signing the armistice. Alexander II, thanks to French incapacity, let it be known, late in 1870, that Russia no longer honored the Black Sea clauses of the Treaty of 1856; and when the Italians were certain of the French defeat, they seized the city of Rome. It was, in sum, a year of extraordinary bad faith and violence. The opportunists and *Realpolitiker* had triumphed, and apparently the old machinery of the European concert was absolute. Brute force, realism, and materialism had become the order of the day, and natural science was increasingly invoked to prove that these qualities are nature's way.

SUGGESTIONS FOR FURTHER READING

Political History of Western Europe

Robert C. Brinkley, *Realism and Nationalism 1852-1871* (London and New York: Harper, 1935), excellent survey with fine biblography.

The New Cambridge Modern History, Vol. X: The Zenith of European Power 1830-1870 (Cambridge University Press, 1960).

Frederick Simpson, *Louis Napoleon and the Recovery of France, 1848-1856* London and New York: Longmans, Green, 3rd ed., 1951), excellent historical literature.

Albert Guerard, *Napoleon III* (Cambridge: Harvard University Press, 1943).

B. K. Martin, *The Triumph of Lord Palmerton* (London: Dial Press, 1924).

A. W. Ward, and G. P. Gooch, *Cambridge History of British Foreign Policy 1783-1919* (Cambridge University Press, 1922-23).

John Morley, *Life of William Ewart Gladstone,* 3 vols. (London and New York: Macmillan, 1903).

E. E. Y. Hales, *Pio Nono, A Study in European Politics and Religion in the Nineteenth Century* (London: Eyre and Spottiswoode, 1954).

Bolton King, *Mazzini* (London, Dutton, 1919).

*Louis L. Snyder, *Basic History of Modern Germany* (Princeton, N.J.: Anvil, 1957), brief survey with readings.

Hans Kohn, *Prophets and Peoples: Studies in Nineteenth Century Nationalism* (New York: Macmillan, 1946).

Koppel S. Pinson, *Modern Germany, Its History and Civilization* (New York: Macmillan, 1954).

G. M. Trevelyan, *Garibaldi and the Thousands* (London and New York: Longmans, Green, 1909).

G. M. Trevelyan, *Garibaldi and the Making of Italy* (London and New York: Longmans, Green, 1911) magnificent narratives.

Lawrence D. Steefel, *The Schleswig-Holstein Question* (Harvard University Press, 1932).

Georges Bonnin, *Bismarck and the Hohenzollern Candidature for the Spanish Throne* (London: Chatto and Windus, 1957), the documents in the German archives.

Michael Howard, *The Franco-Prussian War: The German Invasion of France, 1870-71* (New York: Macmillan, 1961), a first-rate study.

F. Darmstaedter, *Bismarck and the Creation of the Second Reich* (London: Methuen and Co., 1948).

C. G. Robertson, *Bismarck* (New York: Henry Holt, 1919).

Political History of Eastern Europe

Vernon J. Puryear, *England, Russia and the Straits Question, 1844-1856* (University of California Press, 1931), good account of Crimean War.

*Cecil Woodham-Smith, *The Reason Why* (New York: Everyman Paperbacks, 1960), a superb narrative on the Crimean War.

G. T. Robinson, *Rural Russia Under the Old Regime* (London: Macmillan, 1949).

Michael T. Florinsky, *Russia, A History and An Interpretation*, 2 vols. (New York: Macmillan, 1953), often cited as the best history.

Wesley M. Gewehr, *The Rise of Nationalism in the Balkans 1800-1930* (New York: Henry Holt and Co., 1931).

Hugh Seton-Watson, *The Decline of Imperial Russia 1855-1914* (London: Methuen and Co., 1952).

Jerome Blum, *Lord and Peasant from the Ninth to the Nineteenth Century* (Princeton University Press, 1961).

W. E. Mosse, *Alexander II and the Modernization of Russia* (New York: Macmillan, 1959).

Cultural and Intellectual History

*Jacques Barzun, *Darwin, Marx, Wagner* (Garden City: Doubleday-Anchor, 1958), a celebrated, controversial, and stimulating book.

Basil Willey, *Darwin and Butler, Two Versions of Evolution* (London: Chatto and Windus, 1960), a distinguished short work.

*Robert Ames and Philip Siegelman, *The Idea of Evolution* (Minneapolis: Meyers, 1957), readings in evolutionary theory.

*Roger L. Williams, *The World of Napoleon III* (New York: Collier, 1962).

*Alfred North Whitehead, *Science and the Modern World* (New York: Mentor, 1948).

C. J. H. Hayes, *Historical Evolution of Modern Nationalism* (New York: R. R. Smith, 1931).

Edward H. Carr, *Studies in Revolution* (London: Macmillan, 1950), essays on Russian and Utopian socialists.

*Sidney Hook, *Marx and the Marxists* (Princeton, N.J.: Anvil, 1955), contains readings.

D. C. Somervell, *English Thought in the Nineteenth Century* (London: Methuen and Co., 1929).

*Lewis Galantière, ed., *The Goncourt Journals, 1851-1870* (Garden City: Doubleday-Anchor, 1958), an abridgment of a literary classic revealing the artistic currents of mid-century.

* Available in paperbound editions.

❧ 12 ☙

Materialism and Illiberal Nationalism:
1871–1900

THE GERMAN EMPIRE

From the ashes of defeated France the German Empire rose. Both the power of Prussia and German national sentiment had become so great that the southern German states could no longer defend their sovereignty. At the end of 1870, with Paris on the verge of capitulation, the King of Bavaria was induced to invite the King of Prussia to take the imperial title. Early in 1871, the German Empire was proclaimed at the Palace of Versailles, whose mirrors, once reflecting the pomp of Louis XIV, now gave back Teutonic spikes and swords. All that remained was to revise the constitution of the North German Confederation, through which Bismarck had bound the states north of the Main River to Prussia after the defeat of Austria in 1866.

The new imperial constitution created the façade of a federal empire and representative government. Sovereignty was vested in the Bundesrat, the legislative house representing the governments of the member states; but the state delegations had to vote as a unit, and their size was fixed by the constitution. Of the total of sixty-one seats in the Bundesrat, Prussia had seventeen. Bavaria's six was the second largest delegation. Since fourteen negative votes could veto any amendment to the constitution, Prussia possessed the veto power to preserve her dominance. Moreover, because the delegations to the Bundesrat were appointed by the states they represented, the Bundesrat did not reflect popular opinion. In theory, the Reichstag, or lower house, shared the legislative duties with the Bundesrat; in fact, by giving the Bundesrat the power to dissolve the Reichstag, the lower house was kept in check. Thus, it was safe for Bismarck to grant a sop to liberal opinion by permitting the Reichstag to be elected by universal suffrage.

The constitution did not even pretend to provide responsible government. Federal affairs were directed through the chancery, the chancellor being appointed by the emperor and responsible to him. William I, of course, named Bismarck as his first chancellor. Lesser government officials were subordinate to the chancellor. In short, autocratic Prussia swallowed Germany and gave her a Prussian regime. As if to make the point clearer, the German army was given a privileged status, independent of legislature and chancery. Responsible to the emperor directly, the army was an autocracy within an autocracy, an arrangement which the Hohenzollerns of the eighteenth century would have applauded but which was an anachronism in 1871.

DEFEATED FRANCE

The armistice after the surrender of Paris was the occasion for French national elections, necessary because the emergency Government of National Defense was almost exclusively Parisian. Though the military situation was hopeless, the republicans campaigned for a continuation of the struggle and were, in consequence, badly beaten. When the new National Assembly convened at Bordeaux, two-thirds of the seats were held by monarchists: legitimists, Orleanists, and Bonapartists. The varied allegiances of the monarchists, however, prevented the establishment of a monarchy, though the monarchical parties did unite to prevent the establishment of a republic. Adophe Thiers (1797–1877), an Orleanist statesman and long an opponent of Napoleon III's foreign policy, was given the noncommitting title of Chief of the Executive Power. It fell to him to introduce the harsh peace terms announced by the Germans: the loss of Alsace and Lorraine, an indemnity of five billion francs, and an army of occupation in the northeast until that indemnity was paid.

What followed in Paris during March-May, 1871, has always been subject to historical dispute. When the treaty terms became known, Paris rose in angry revolt, denied the authority of the conservative Assembly at

Bordeaux, and turned for leadership to the municipal government of Paris: the Commune of Paris, a committee of ninety. Because Paris was notably more radical than were the provinces, and because many radical leaders —notably Charles Delescluze, Gustave Flourens, and Raoul Rigault— came to associate themselves with the movement, it became common after 1871 to regard this uprising as an attempt to establish a dictatorship of the proletariat in the Marxian sense. Marx, in fact, wrote a pamphlet giving such an interpretation, *The Civil War in France* (1871), the facts of which were tailored to fit the Marxian theory of class conflict. Both radicals and antiradicals saw the Commune in the Marxian light, the misinterpretation greatly affecting French politics for several decades after.

More recent research now suggests that the Commune had two major sources. Paris, stronghold of republicanism, had been shocked by the monarchical successes in the elections and feared a return of monarchy; and when that monarchical National Assembly seemed likely to accept the harsh terms offered by Bismarck, the Parisians, who had endured great hardships during the Prussian siege, felt betrayed by the Assembly. Ever since 1789, the Parisians had grown accustomed to imposing their political will upon the provinces and did not mean, in 1871, to have the political initiative assumed by the "hicks," as one republican called them, especially if that new ascendency were to begin with a shameful treaty. More than anything, the Commune was an outburst of injured patriotism. The movement was soon dominated by radicals, but they represented too many brands of anarchism and socialism to have made a clear-cut program possible. In April, the Bordeaux government having moved to Versailles, Thiers began an armed assault upon Paris. The city put up a desperate resistance but did not have adequate military direction. Reprisals and counterreprisals made the fighting unusually vicious, and the residue of bitterness was enormous. The government imprisoned and deported many hundreds of the Communards once the city had fallen, and amnesties were not granted until 1879 and 1880. In the meantime, as its domestic victory approached, the Versailles government concluded the peace at Frankfurt with Germany. To the horror of the Commune was added the loss of two provinces and a heavy indemnity; it was a peace of unprecedented severity.

The divisions within the National Assembly, which had prevented the establishment of either monarchy or republic, plagued the French until 1875. A near understanding between the legitimist and Orleanist pretenders, which could have restored monarchy, broke down over the legitimist's refusal to rule under the tricolor. This forced Thiers to insist on a republic as the form of government "which divides us least." The disorganized monarchists then allowed Thiers to be given the title of President of the Republic, but they intended to overthrow him as soon as a monarchical constitution could be written. Thiers, in the meantime, set himself to the task of paying off the indemnity to Germany. His government loans were heavily subscribed, enabling him to settle with Germany before the end of 1873 and thus to secure the evacuation of all German troops.

After accomplishing a financial feat generally held to be impossible, Thiers found himself turned out of office by the monarchical majority. In his place, the Assembly elected Marshal M. E. P. Maurice de MacMahon (1808–1893), an avowed royalist, whose task was to hold the republican institutions in check until a monarchy could be restored. Unfortunately for him, public opinion became increasingly republican, in reaction to the bickering of the royalist factions. Early in 1875, when the Assembly began voting on the major constitutional clauses, the republicans had sufficient strength to carry the day. Yet, the republican constitution adopted that year was deeply conservative, not merely because of royalist pressure, but also because the Republicans in the Assembly remembered and feared the radical republicans of the Commune. Significantly, they preferred Versailles to Paris as the seat of government.

The constitution of the Third Republic provided for a bicameral national assembly: The senate was elected by a highly indirect and undemocratic procedure, while the Chamber of Deputies was voted on by direct, universal suffrage. But the Chamber could be dissolved by the president if the senate concurred. The president was not popularly elected, but was chosen by the National Assembly for a seven-year term. His signature was invalid until countersigned by a member of the cabinet, and the ministers were all responsible to the National Assembly. This attempt to weaken executive power was challenged by President MacMahon in 1877, when he dismissed a premier who had the Chamber's confidence. In the subsequent constitutional crisis, MacMahon's premiers could not win votes of parliamentary confidence, which led to his resignation from the presidency in 1879. The republicans had won what was to be the first in a series of assaults upon the constitution.

THE KULTURKAMPF

Bismarck, meanwhile was having a battle of his own, the so-called Kulturkampf, or battle for civilization. We discussed in the previous chapter the growing antagonism between the claims of Church and State which was sharply accentuated by Pius IX's *Syllabus of Errors* in 1864. When the Vatican Council adopted the dogma of papal infallibility (1870), implying that the papacy intended to resist any further encroachment upon spiritual power, it did so in the teeth of excited nationalist sentiments, especially in Germany and Italy. It happened, after 1871, that those groups resisting the centralization and the Prussianizing of the German Empires—Poles, South Germans Alsatians and Lorrainers in particular —were Catholic. Their resistance derived from hostility to Berlin, not to Protestantism. The Poles wanted an independent Poland, Alsace-Lorraine preferred to be a part of France, and the South Germans had enjoyed freer political life before 1871 than they were likely to enjoy under a strongly centralized regime. Bismarck saw that he could strike at this political resistance by deliberately misconstruing the dogma of papal infallibility to mean papal interference into German political affairs. In so doing, he could take measures against the Church in Germany and simultaneously please both liberal and conservative-nationalist opinions. He calculated that pressure on the Church would force the recalcitrant minorities to knuckle under to Berlin.

He began, in 1872, by expelling the Jesuits from Germany. Thereafter, the anticlerical attack centered in Prussia, where the Landtag passed the "May laws" (1873), a series of anti-Catholic measures designed to give the state control of marriage and education and to be a direct challenge to the Pope's view that secular marriage and education are modern errors. The nationalist aspect of the legislation was underscored by a law which prescribed that every official of the Catholic Church must be a German citizen, a graduate of a German university, and authorized by the Prussian government; and that all religious instructions must be given in the German language. Of course, the papacy resisted this assault upon spiritual authority, but to Bismarck's surprise, the German Catholics also fought his program with vigor—defeating his hope to unify Germany further. Worse, the issue attracted support from all the anti-Bismarckian elements in Germany. Having announced that he would not go to Canossa (as had Henry IV in the eleventh century), Bismarck had to wait out the death of Pius IX in order to make a face-saving peace with the papacy. The anticlerical program was relaxed in 1880, and most of the May laws were repealed by 1886.

As Bismarck came to realize the impossibility of making any gains from his anti-Catholic crusade, he came to recognize the Catholics as natural allies against socialism, and socialism to be a greater menace to his aims than Catholicism. In his own words, he had found the "red international" more dangerous than the "black international." German socialism had been divided between Marxist and non-Marxist factions, between those who advocated violent overthrow of the state and those who believed it possible to achieve social advances through the democratically elected Reichstag. In 1875, these two factions merged to form the German Social Democratic party, accepting Marx's materialistic view of history, but advocating parliamentary methods to secure control of the state. Led by August Bebel (1840–1913), the new party made impressive parliamentary gains and began the publication of numerous pamphlets and a party newspaper. Bismarck had a horror of socialists, knowing them to be republicans and suspecting that they were really all anarchists. Their electoral gains, therefore, were regarded as incompatible with the imperial institutions. In 1878, taking advantage of two unsuccessful attempts upon the Emperor's life as the pretext for the law—though the socialists had disavowed the would-be assassins—he pushed through an Anti-Socialist Law:

Organizations which through Social Democratic, Socialist, or Communist activities aim to overthrow the established State or social order are hereby forbidden.

The same ban holds for organizations in which Social Democratic, Socialist, or Communist influence appears to be dedicated to the overthrow of the established State or social order, by breach of the public peace and especially by endangering the harmony of the classes.[1]

Socialist and communist publications were also banned by the same law.

"A GENERATION OF MATERIALISM"

A distinguished historian has called the thirty years folowing 1870 "a generation of materialism." He had in mind both the mechanization of thought—that is, the vogue of Darwinism with its mechanical implications —and the enormous expansion of European industry, with its implications of a better material living for the average man. Science and technology, often indistinguishable in the popular mind, bade fair to solve all hu-

1. Quoted in Louis L. Snyder, *Basic History of Modern Germany,* (Princeton, 1957), p. 131-132.

man dilemmas and enjoyed a prestige unequalled by any other discipline.

As had been true since the beginning of the industrial revolution, coal and iron production were the keys to material advancement. But after 1870, electricity became an increasingly significant source of power. British coal production roughly doubled between 1870 and 1900, but the most striking spurts in coal production occurred in Germany and the United States, both of whom produced only about one-third the British figure in 1870. By 1900, the Germans had drawn nearly abreast of the British in coal, and the Americans had soared past both of them. The iron industries were making commensurate gains in production, but here the most striking innovation was Bessemer's method of producing steel from iron, which made cheap mass-production of steel possible for the first time. By 1856, Sir Henry Bessemer (English, 1813-1898) had found that iron could be converted to steel by blowing air on the liquid iron for a quarter hour. Unlike earlier methods, his was swift and required no fuel. By 1870, the western world was moving from the Iron Age into the Age of Steel.

One could argue that steel shared the stage with electricity. We have already noted that many of the scientists of the first half of the nineteenth century, when investigating light, electricity, and magnetism, considered them related phenomena. It fell to James Clerk Maxwell (English, 1831-1879) to provide mathematical descriptions for the relationship of electricity and magnetism. In so doing, he provided another of those major syntheses so characteristic of mid-century science. His theory of the electromagnetic field (published 1873), not only gave the formulas describing the relationship of light, electricity, and magnetism, but also suggested the existence of electric waves which would be propagated through space with the speed of light. In 1889, Heinrich Hertz (German, 1857-1894) confirmed Maxwell's theory through ingenious experiments by which he measured both the speed of propagation and the wavelength of the waves.

The increasing knowledge of electricity led to its practical application in forms which quickly impressed the public with the utility of science: the telephone, the electric light, electric cars, and wireless telegraphy. In fact, these devices were anticlimactic when compared to the brilliance of the theories and experiments which made the practical application possible.

The Scottish-born Alexander Graham Bell (1847-1922) showed his first telephone in 1876, and two years later the American Thomas A. Edison (1847-1931) invented the incandescent lamp. By 1881, both cars and trams were being powered by electricity in Germany, while the Singer sewing machine—invented earlier—was electrically powered for the first time in 1889. Wireless telegraphy, also based on electromagnetic theory, first became practical in 1896, when Guglielmo Marconi (Italian, 1874–1937) patented his device and organized a company for its commercial exploitation. In the following year he sent a wireless message a distance of eighteen miles, and transatlantic signals were first successful in 1901.

The science of physics entered a new era in the 1890's with the discovery of x-rays (1895) and natural radioactivity (1896). Wilhelm K. Roentgen (German, 1845–1923) accidentally found x-rays when he was investigating the effects of cathode rays with a Hittorf-Crookes tube. Having described the apparatus he was using, Roentgen wrote:

> We soon discover that all bodies are transparent to this agent, though in very different degrees. . . . Paper is very transparent; behind a bound book of about one thousand pages I saw the fluorescent screen light up brightly, the printers' ink offering scarcely a noticeable hinderance. . . . Sheets of hard rubber several centimeters thick still permit the rays to pass through them. (For brevity's sake I shall use the expression "rays"; and to distinguish them from others of this name I shall call them "x-rays.")[2]

The practical application of this discovery in diagnostic medicine was almost immediate, doubly astonishing considering the conservatism of nineteenth-century medicine opinion and the incomplete investigation of the newly found phenomenon. Apart from the obvious benefits to mankind, the discovery of x-rays proved to be the key to other discoveries in the development of modern, or quantum, physics, as distinguished from the classical, or Newtonian, physics. The first came only a few months after Roentgen's announcement, when Antoine Henri Becquerel (French, 1852–1908) announced his discovery of radioactivity. He had been struck by Roentgen's observation that x-rays emanated from the glass walls of the Hittorf-Crookes tube, where they were bombarded by cathode rays, and that the glass had shown fluorescence at those points. It led him to investigate materials known to show fluorescence—or phosphorescence—particularly uranium salts, and he found that the uranium compounds on which he worked gave off a photographic plate. In the search to find radioactivity in other substances, Pierre Curie (French, 1859–1906) and his wife Marie Curie (Polish, 1867–1934) discovered radium in pitch-

2. Quoted in Morris H. Shamos, *Great Experiments in Physics* (New York, 1959), pp. 201-202.

blende. Mme. Curie came to the significant conclusion (1899) that radioactive atoms were actually unstable atoms in the process of disintegration and, hence, were releasing energy.

A third significant contribution to modern physics in the decade of the 1890's was made by Joseph J. Thomson (English, 1856-1940) through his attempt to relate electrical and atomic properties. He held that the study of the passage of electricity through various gases would reveal the relationship he sought to establish. Before his time, the atom was thought to be an indivisible entity. Thomson found particles within atoms which carried negative charges of electricity; he called these particles, corpuscles, but they came to be called electrons. The phenomenon revealed that atoms were composite, not simple, entities.

The world of biology, meanwhile, continued to test the general Darwinian assumptions, though it ought to be made clear that scientists as a group accepted the major premises of Darwin. He had emphasized natural selection as the main source of variation in a species; but recognizing that natural selection could only account for why a given sport (mutation) survived or failed to survive, he added Lamarck's assumption that acquired characteristics are inheritable to account for variation in the first place. August Weismann, (1834-1914), a South German zoologist and a student of heredity in particular, made a distinction between the ordinary bodily, or somatic cells and the reproductive, or germ, cells which transmit a stream of protoplasm from one generation to another. He then pointed out that hereditary characteristics are transferred only by the germ cells; whereas acquired characteristics, being variations in somatic cells, could not be inherited because the somatic cells die with the individual. The loyal Darwinians, especially those in the social sciences, rejected Weismann's findings, but generally by the end of the century scientific opinion held with Weismann and rejected the possibility of inheriting acquired characteristics. This left Darwinism a theory which explained the survival of variations, but not the reasons for variation.

Another man not satisfied with Darwinian theory was the Augustinian monk Gregor Mendel (Austrian, 1822-1884), who began experimenting in his monastery garden in the 1860's by crossbreeding peas. By carefully controlling plant fertilization, he found that he could breed for certain characteristics, and that these characteristics would appear in subsequent generations in proportions that he could predict mathematically. This could only happen, he reasoned, if the germ cells of each parent contained conflicting characteristics—such as shortness and tallness, or lightness or darkness—one characteristic being dominant and the other recessive. In the union of male and female germ cells, the dominant characteristics will appear more frequently than the recessive, and always in a set mathematical proportion. Mendel's findings, published in 1870 in an obscure Austrian journal, were discovered, tested, and publicized in 1900 by a Dutch botanist, Hugo De Vries (1848–1935). Mendelian genetics could account for the appearance of variation in species, while Darwin's natural selection could explain why some variations survived and others did not. Neither man's science, however, tackled the question of the purpose or meaning of evolution. They provided only the descriptions for the mechanisms of evolution.

It is not surprising that the Darwinian era gave rise to the fields of anthropology and eugenics, both concerned with the evolutionary development of man. The physical anthropologists and eugenicists were primarily interested in man's physical and racial evolution, while the cultural anthropologists were more concerned for the evolutionary development of man's religious, social, and political institutions. The discovery of bones belonging to what one scientist called "ante-diluvian man" not only suggested that man had been evolving physically for at least a half-million years, but also presented a direct challenge to those religionists, generally called fundamentalists, who insisted on a literal reading of Scripture. The evidence of man's physical improvement led one anthropologist, Francis Galton (English, 1822–1911), to urge that man take control of his own evolution through programs of birth control and sterilization to prevent the "unfit" from breeding; such programs would presumably hasten the inevitable day when man would evolve into a superman.

The well-known squabble between the evolutionists and the religious fundamentalists not only focused debate on a plane where the facts were a monopoly of one side, but unfortunately also obscured issues of real intellectual merit. Ever since the scientific revolution of the seventeenth century, science had lost its concern for the "whys"—in other words, for the *purposes* of observed phenomena—and dealt only with the "hows." The scientist perhaps did not deny that the "why" was a valid question, but he suggested that it was an insoluble question and, therefore, should be left to metaphysicians and ignored by scientists. Darwin did not deny the existence of God, as many of the fundamentalists assumed he had. In fact, Darwin made no claim to knowing whether or not there is a God, nor was it a question which very much concerned him. In view of this, Darwin's great defender, Thomas Henry Huxley, argued that Darwin ought to be met solely on scientific ground—that religion was not an issue. Huxley's plea was both useless and somewhat naive. Whatever Darwin's intentions, his theories inevitably raised metaphysical issues, in particular the question: what is the purpose of evolution?

We can best illustrate the more sophisticated debates arising from Darwin's proposals by recalling Samuel Butler's (English, 1835–1902) quarrel with them. Butler was a religious man, but not a churchman. Having rejected the Anglican Church, he took up Darwinianism; next, he moved from being a Darwinian to being an anti-Darwinian evolutionist. Which put him in the unenviable position of being an enemy to both the Darwinians and the anti-Darwinian theologians. Butler had arrived at a major premise: that life cannot be explained as mechanistic because of the antithesis of life and mechanism. Lamarck, whose view Butler came to share, sought to explain evolution as an effort of an organism to respond to its environment by developing new habits and organs, a view which suggested will and purpose. Since Darwin's theory permitted no such effort on the part of an organism, Butler concluded that Darwin meant that life is mechanistic: without mind, will, or purpose. Harkening back to such earlier evolutionists as Buffon, Lamarck, and Erasmus Darwin, Butler urged his contemporaries to admit

that animals are modified not because they subsequently survive, but because they have done this or that which has led to their modification, and hence to their surviving.[3]

After Mendel's discoveries biologists had a greater knowledge of the mechanics of inheritance. But the cause of genetic mutation is still unknown, so that the Darwin-Butler controversy remains unsolved.

In the meantime, Herbert Spencer (English, 1820–1903) set himself to a great task on the assumption that the principle of evolution was the fundamental law governing every aspect of life. Between 1860 and 1893, he worked on his *Synthetic Philosophy* in which he sought to deduce laws governing every aspect of life from the principle of evolution. He saw everything developing from a simple, even undifferentiated, state into a highly specialized, individualized, organic state. Optimism for the future of man and nature saturated his thinking:

Progress is not an accident but a necessity. What we call evil and immorality must disappear. It is certain that man must become perfect. . . . Always toward

3. Basil Willey, *Darwin and Butler* (London, 1960), p. 77.

perfection is the mighty movement—towards a complete development and a more unmixed good.[4]

Friedrich Nietzsche (German, 1844–1900) was an evolutionist of the period who rejected the mechanistic optimism of those who shared Spencer's view of the future. It is notable that Nietzsche was a disciple of Schopenhauer, whose pessimism and romantic individualism he shared. Nietzsche turned the tables on those who argued for the inevitable evolution of man to a state of perfection by pointing to the bestial in man's origin and to the immense time it takes for evolutionary changes to be effected. It made no sense to Nietzsche either to sit around and "evolve" toward a state which could not be reached for thousands of years or to believe that our animal ancestry permitted us instincts for the good, the beautiful, and the true. Our true nature, he said, is to strive for power, to strive for greatness, so that an aristocracy of superman shall emerge:

As the smaller surrenders himself to the greater, so the greater must surrender himself to the will to power and stake life upon the issue. It is the mission of the greatest to run risk and danger—to cast dice with death.[5]

This statement amounted to a reassertion of the romantic spirit, and it derived from Nietzsche's horror that man's barbaric instincts, never far from the surface, were apparently resurging in the late nineteenth century. In other words, that the rise of the masses would be fatal to the vitality of the civilization through the substitution of mass culture for individualism. Consequently, he attacked all aspects of the vulgarization of life, including those which seemed to absolve individuals of the responsibility to live greatly and to strive greatly on the grounds that mankind as a whole is evolving inevitably towards greatness. His attack upon the music-drama of Richard Wagner, his erstwhile friend, derived from his growing suspicion that Wagner's music was deliberately pompous, nationalistic, and crude in an effort to reach the mass public; that it was mechanistic rather than artistic. Similarly, Nietzsche recoiled from Darwin in favor of Lamarck, horrified by the passivity of Darwinian evolution. The possibility of greatness must come from strivings:

I teach you the Superman. Man is a thing to be surmounted. What have ye done to surmount him?

4. Quoted in Randall, *Making of the Modern Mind* (Boston, 1926), p. 445.
5. From *Also Sprach Zarathustra* (1883).

All beings hitherto have created something above themselves: will ye be the ebb of this great tide and rather avert to the beast than surmount man?[6]

In sum, one must not run from the horror of reality, as advocated by Schopenhauer; nor compromise with the horror by catering to it, as Nietzsche thought Wagner was doing; but one must struggle unceasingly to surmount it: to become a superman. The violence of Nietzsche's words was taken to mean that he championed brute force, that he thought of the superman as a superior physical specimen who would smash culture as a decadent and odious phenomenon. In fact, he meant quite the opposite. His superman's strength was the vitality and refinement of the truly civilized man, his enemy the vulgarization of European culture.

THE RESURGENCE OF COLONIALISM

Competition for empires had seemed to come to an end early in the nineteenth century. Though France had acquired several new colonies later on (Algeria in 1830 and Indo-China in the 1860's), these acquisitions were made for political expedience and not in the pursuance of a deliberate program of colonial expansion. The revival of colonialism after 1870 was one of the signs that liberalism was a dying creed. To account for the new colonialism, one could start by citing the growth of selfish nationalism after mid-century, which led European governments increasingly to abandon liberal economic policies. The mercantilist had always equated national security with economic self-sufficiency and believed that the state must regulate the economy to achieve this security. Colonies were the traditional answer to the question of how one provided for commodities one's nation did not itself produce; self-sufficiency could presumably be achieved within the framework of an empire, not through free trade. Hence, the reaction after 1870 is referred to as neomercantilism.

The rapid expansion of industry also contributed to colonialism. Profits earned were of such magnitude that capitalists had to seek opportunties for reinvestment beyond Europe. While large amounts of British, German, and French capital found their way into enterprises in North and South America, an overseas colony was often regarded as a safer place to invest one's money; and it had the further attraction of enhancing the national interest and prestige. Yet, it is notable that the economic arguments for

6. *Ibid.,* p. 5.

colonialism were generally rationalizations in support of expansionist policies which were nationalistic at heart. Further rationalizations came from propagandists who feared Europe was in danger of becoming over-populated and who argued that Europeans should feel free to emigrate to places where they could find their traditional customs and products, though in a setting which would give them opportunities lacking at home. Others insisted that any country which failed to push a colonial program was exhibiting a lack of vitality, until many nationalists came to believe that greatness in Europe depended on greatness in Africa, essentially a romantic argument. Biological arguments were soon martialed as further proof of the "inevitability" that the progressive, industrial nations would dominate the "backward" nations, not merely because they are the "fittest," but also because they have a civilizing mission among the backward peoples:

> Take up the White Man's burden—
> Send forth the best ye breed—
> Go bind your sons to exile
> To serve your captives' need;
> To wait in heavy harness
> On fluttered folk and wild—
> Your new-caught, sullen peoples,
> Half-devil and half-child.[7]

Written to remind the Americans of their new responsibilities for Cubans and Filipinos, Rudyard Kipling's (English, 1865–1936) lines expressed an idealistic rationalization common in western Europe by the end of the century.

Neomercantilism had its domestic application, too, in increased governmental interference in the national economic and social life. Continental "big business" sought protection from foreign competition, especially British competition, and the era after 1870 was one of rising tariffs. Economic self-sufficiency was again the justification: the search for national security. In 1879, Bismarck introduced high tariffs on iron, grain, meat, and textiles. Most other manufactures obtained moderate protection, and only industrial raw materials were admitted duty-free. France responded in 1881 by not renewing her low-tariff treaty with Great Britain and raising the duties on most manufactured imports. Russia, meanwhile, began a series of tariff increases which culminated in 1891 with such high duties against foreign

7. Rudyard Kipling, *The White Man's Burden* (1899).

coal, steel, and manufactures as practically to end imports. Austria also sought to protect her industries in the 1880's. Once protectionism became well-rooted on the Continent, agricultural interests were also able to secure protection for themselves. Here again Germany led the way in 1885, followed by France, Italy, Sweden, and Austria.

THE DECLINE OF LIBERALISM

Classical liberalism suffered further after 1870 in that the national states increasingly concerned themselves with social legislation which, though, liberal in spirit, marked a rejection of *laissez faire* theories. The liberal, as earlier in the century, was caught in a philosophical dilemma, believing both in the liberty of the individual from governmental supervision and in the welfare of individuals, which could often be secured only by state intervention. We find him, after 1870, denouncing the new tariffs as a violation of natural economic law, while espousing the causes of state-supported education and public health. Factory legislation bothered him, and he often could justify it only in its contribution to better public health. Ironically, conservatives and socialists generally had to take the lead in promoting factory legislation, often with the backing of clerical groups. In France, for example, the act of 1874 providing for state inspection of factories was voted by a royalist-clerical majority; in Britain, where there was already considerable factory legislation by 1870, the Tories passed measures in 1878, 1891, and 1901 to emphasize and consolidate the previous acts.

During the last quarter of the nineteenth century, British urban workers became increasingly politically conscious. For a time, the growing trade-union movement steered clear of politics, and union members elected to political office generally sat with the Liberals. But the failure of the Liberals to work for social-welfare legislation convinced many of the workers of the desirability of forming a separate political party to work for the interest of labor, a course urgently promoted by English socialists. A Labour Party, finally formed in 1892, only made its appearance in a national election for the first time in 1906. By that time, ironically, the Liberal party was much more dedicated to a program of social reform than it had been earlier.

In Germany, Bismarck was the father of social legislation. Considering factory legislation to be unwarranted interference into employer's affairs, Bismarck preferred social-security laws for the protection of workers. He who had struck at the Social Democratic party came forth in the 1880's with socialistic bills. The accident-insurance law (1885) forced employers to insure their employees against accidents while on the job; a sickness insurance law (1885) forced every employee who made less than 500 dollars a year to insure himself against sickness, one-third of the burden to be paid by his employer; and an old-age-insurance law (1889) required each worker making less than 500 dollars a year to pay into a state fund which would provide him with a pension at the age of seventy, his employer making an equal contribution. The liberals regarded these laws as a dangerous violation of *laissez faire,* and the socialists believed them to be merely a bribe to the workers to enlist their support of the empire. Bismarck confirmed their suspicions when he noted that "as soon as the workingmen see that the government is deeply interested in their welfare, the flocking to [the Socialists] will cease."[8] While Bismarck's social legislation did not prevent German socialism from growing, it did give greater protection to German workers than was available to the workers of any other industrialized nation. Moreover, his "state socialism" impressed other governments. Austria, Italy, and Switzerland quickly adopted both accident and sickness insurance laws; Britain, Belgium, and Denmark imitated all three insurance laws; and several countries—Britain, France, the Netherlands, and Norway in particular—went even further in the 1890's by requiring employers to compensate workers for accidents on the job.

The decline of *laissez faire* and the dilemma of the liberals can further be demonstrated in the career of Joseph Chamberlain (1836–1914), a radical and humane member of the Liberal party in Britain who became mayor of Birmingham in 1873. In his zeal to provide better living conditions, he socialized the municipal gas and water works, providing better supplies of both commodities at less cost, and he initiated programs of slum clearance and public park construction, establishing some model city-owned apartments. The Liberals grumbled at this state interference, while recognizing the benefits conferred. It is notable that Chamberlain ultimately left the Liberal party for the Conservatives. In the meantime, a new Municipal Corporation law in 1882 removed all restrictions against municipal governments' providing local services, opening the way for "gas and water socialism." A similar movement took place in Vienna under

8. From a speech before the Reichstag in 1884 in defense of the bill.

direction of Karl Lueger, head of the Austrian Christian Socialist party and mayor of the city. He not only socialized the gas, water, and tramway services in the 1890's, but also closed off from buildings a band of meadowland and woods around the city. The pioneering of Chamberlain and Lueger was noted and followed elsewhere on the Continent.

We have several times noted that since the seventeenth century, liberal opinion, both religious and secular, had favored creating greater educational opportunities. Educational facilities had gradually expanded, but thanks to the liberal distaste for compulsory education, formal instruction remained largely a monopoly of the upper and middle classes. Illiteracy was common among the masses well past the mid-nineteenth century. Now numerous factors contributed to the spread of education among the masses by 1870. The new industrial wealth was a source for funds in amounts hitherto unknown, and the concentration of the illiterate masses in the industrial cities made mass education more feasible than ever before. Moreover, by 1870, the national governments were readier to insist on a minimum of instruction, though for various reasons. The more democratic governments saw the need to prepare the masses for intelligent participation in public affairs; following the German example, there was general recognition that the technical requirements of an industrial society could only be met through popular instruction; and on the Continent, the trend toward conscript rather than professional armies suggested popular instruction emphasizing the national traditions and physical education. Finally, in the face of the various socialist doctrines promising the emancipation of the masses, the liberal could answer that the only real emancipation came through a liberal education. It is worth noting that none of these new goals reflected the older aims of European education: to produce Christian gentlemen.

The Austro-Hungarian Empire required, beginning in 1868, that all children between six and twelve attend school. Britain, which in 1867 passed her second bill of parliamentary reform, enfranchising the urban masses, followed with the Education Act of 1870. The state provided greatly increased subsidies to the private schools in existence, new provisions were made for establishing greater free-school opportunities, and local authorities were given the power to decide whether or not primary instruction should be compulsory. By 1880, the state made attendance compulsory through age thirteen, the French following this line in 1882. The movement, in fact, was general in western Europe and noticeably nonexistent in eastern Europe, suggesting a close tie between industrialization and literacy. To cite the two extremes, Britain and France had achieved an adult literacy rate of 95 per cent by 1900, while Russia did not surpass 20 per cent.

The national military establishments after 1870 reveal another retreat from traditional liberalism, for the idea of conscription was as abhorrent to the liberal as to the conservative in the earlier nineteenth century. With one major exception, after 1815 the powers had adopted small-scale long-term enlistment armies, as a part of the general reaction against the democratic institutions of French republicanism. The French having adopted mass conscription, it was necessarily abandoned by all but Prussia in favor of professionalism. The Prussians, associating their national resurgence after 1806 with the revolutionary practice of nation-in-arms, were too wedded to the successful innovation to abandon it in 1815. Moreover, their victories in 1866 and 1870, when coupled with the victory of the Union Army in the American Civil War in 1865, suggested the superiority of the mass army; while the swiftness of the two Prussian victories further suggested the need to keep a large military establishment in a state of constant preparation if a nation were to be successfully defended. Finally, rail transportation made the rapid movement of large numbers of troops feasible for the first time. In consequence, the powers abandoned their reliance on professionals alone, in favor of universal military training for short terms, giving each nation a large pool of trained reserves to supplement the regulars in wartime. Between 1868 and 1875, Austria, France, Russia, and Italy all followed the German example, leaving Britain alone to retain the professional army, with her primary strength going into the navy.

Finally, if we turn to the racial theorists of the later nineteenth century and to the increasing persecution of minority groups within the nation-states, we shall find the most convincing evidence that the earlier tenets of liberalism had lost their force—that the new nationalism was illiberal. The word "racial" had long been used loosely to mean national, so that after Darwin, when it became fashionable to discuss species and, in particular, those fittest to survive, it was an easy matter to compare the European "races" as to their "fitness." Let it be noted at once that those who discussed the various European "races" as separate species were in serious biological error though presuming to be scientific. They were, in fact, mistaking cultural or ethnic differences as racial. But whatever their scientific errors, they sought to show that the political and military pre-eminence of the Germans after 1870 proved that the Germanic or Teutonic "race" was the fittest, hence that it was a superior "race."

The modern argument began indirectly with the work of a French aristocrat, Count Joseph Arthur de Gobineau (1816–1882), who published an *Essay on the Inequality of Races* (1854). Gobineau had not the slightest intention of ascribing racial superiority to any nation as a whole. On the contrary, he sought to prove the superiority of the French aristocracy over the masses of the French people on the grounds that the aristocracy represented pure "Aryan" stock and the people an impure mixture of many "races." To use the word Aryan as Gobineau did was to misuse it in the first place. The Indo-European group of languages seems to have stemmed from a single language spoken by a people whom we have called Aryan—and who have long since disappeared. Any nation, therefore, which speaks an Indo-European language, might call itself "Aryan," but only because of its language and not for any racial connotation. In the second place, Gobineau's ideas were misused in the 1880's. He had insisted that the superiority of the French aristocracy derived from its Aryanism, and he defined the Aryan characteristics as northern European in general and Germanic in particular: the purest and the noblest are the tall, blond, longheads. The victory of the Germans in 1870 was thus widely interpreted as the victory of a superior race—and something which Gobineau had predicted. Richard Wagner, who was devoting himself to the construction of a national German art, discovered Gobineau and quickly saw how a purely Germanic art (his own) must be necessarily superior to that of other "races." Such interpretations were not Gobineau's intention, since he thought the German masses to be just as mixed "racially" as the French masses.

By the end of the nineteenth century, the terms Aryan race, Germanic race, Nordic race, Teutonic race, all meant superior race to these theorists, whose chief publicist was Houston Stewart Chamberlain (1855–1926). Born in Britain, Chamberlain became enamored of Wagnerian music and ideology, and moved to Germany, where he married Wagner's daughter. In his book *Foundations of the Nineteenth Century* (1899), Chamberlain emphasized the differences between the Teutonic and Jewish "races." Furthermore, he thought that intellectual and moral qualities are identified with physical qualities: "A mongrel is frequently very clever, but never reliable; morally he is always a weed." And what was true of individuals was also true of "races":

In spite of the broad common foundation, the human races are, in reality, as different from one another in character, qualities, and above all, in the degree of their individual capacities, as greyhound, bull-dog, poodle and Newfoundland dog. Inequality is a state towards which nature inclines in all spheres; nothing extraordinary is produced without "specialisation;" in the case of men, as of animals, it is this specialisation that produces noble races; history and ethnology reveal this secret to the dullest eye. Has not every genuine race its own glorious, incomparable physiognomy?[9]

This may appear to be utter nonsense today, but such theories of race were more easily swallowed in a day when patriots eagerly grasped at any fact which presumed to justify national antagonisms.

After 1871, minorities began to be subjected to discriminatory legislation in the interest of national unity. In Britain, the failure to give the Irish "home rule" was now justified on the grounds that the Irish were Celts—an inferior race—which meant that they were unfit to govern themselves. And the ancient English prejudice against Catholicism was reinforced by identifying the religion with the "backward" Irish.

Bismarck's *Kulturkampf* was another instance of discrimination against minority nationalities. Then, in 1886, the Prussian parliament resolved to "Germanize" the Poles living in Posen and West Prussia. Money was provided to purchase land from the Polish population, to be given to German farmers who would pledge to remain German and to marry Polish women; and Polish was no longer taught in any Prussian school. A similar "Germanization" campaign was directed against Danish culture in Schleswig and against French influences in Alsace and Lorraine.

In the reign of Alexander III (*1881–1894*), a "Russification" program reached its peak. The Poles, it is true, had already lost their autonomy as a result of their two unsuccessful revolts in the nineteenth century, but under Alexander III they reached a national nadir, excluded from public offices even in their own country. The chief figure in this reactionary period was Constantine Pobedonostsev (1827–1907) in his position as Procurator of the Holy Synod, lay head of the Orthodox Church in Russia. An honorable and intelligent man, he had no faith in the honor or intelligence of others; and regarding western society and political institutions as hopelessly corrupt, he saw Russia's salvation in retaining the traditional institutions of the autocracy: "One law, one language, and one religion." Not merely the Poles, but all the national and religious minorities within

9. Chamberlain, *Foundations of the Nineteenth Century* (London, 1912), p. 269.

the empire felt the lash of discriminatory legislation, the culmination of which was Finland's loss of her constitution in 1899.

Antisemitism was a pronounced feature of this Russian program. By a decree in 1882, the Czar denied Jews the right to acquire land, then sharply limited educational opportunities for them, and finally, in 1890, required all Russian Jews to live in the western provinces (the Jewish Pale). Even there they could not own land. This governmental attitude encouraged the Russian population to vent age-old hostility toward the Jews. The frightful pogroms which followed were generally tolerated by the police, and a massive emigration of Russian and Polish Jews to the United States began in 1891. This antisemitism in Russia had its counterparts elsewhere in Europe. It should not be seen as an antireligious movement, but rather as an opposition to Jews on the grounds that they are an alien "race." This was especially true in Germany, where the argument was heard that "the Jews are a nation within the nation, a state within the state, a race in the midst of another race."

France, however, was the scene of the most sensational case of antisemitism, growing out of German espionage in France. French counterintelligence officers had for some time been aware that someone had been supplying the German military attaché in Paris with military information. The evidence ultimately pointed Captain Alfred Dreyfus (1859–1935), because his handwriting seemed similar to that on incriminating documents and because he had access to the particular information being sold. Tried late in 1894 before a court-martial, he was deprived of military rank and sentenced to life imprisonment. During the trial, however, it became evident that the case against Dreyfus had serious weaknesses, but that the Army had been determined to settle the matter quickly, grateful that the traitor was not a "real Frenchman." In fact, Captain Dreyfus had been the first Jewish officer to become a member of the general staff of the army.

Subsequently, a new chief of the counterespionage service, Colonel Georges Picquart (1854–1914), noted that some of the documentary evidence against Dreyfus had been altered after the trial to damage Dreyfus' case even more in the event of a rehearing. Since military information was still reaching the German military attaché, Picquart felt it his duty to inform the chief-of-staff of the likelihood of Dreyfus' innocence and of the probable guilt of a second officer, Colonel Marie Charles Esterhazy (1847–1923), whose handwriting had been matched with that on the incriminating documents. The refusal of the army to reopen the case became the subject of a bitter debate, which rocked the nation to its foundations. In all probability, the initial mistake in arresting Dreyfus had been an honest one; the events that followed, however, suggest that the army chiefs were antisemitic and uninterested in justice. Some of those who defended the army were extreme nationalists, who wanted to prevent any disclosures which might diminish the prestige of the army—especially since the work of recovering Alsace and Lorraine remained. Some were avowed antisemites, imbued with the ideas Edouard Drumont had been publishing since the middle 1880's: that Jews were full of trickery and cowardice and that they could not be trusted because of their international connections. Finally, the army cause drew support from royalist, Bonapartist, and clerical elements—in other words, from those groups which had fought the establishment of a republic in the 1870's. In turn, those who sought a retrial for Dreyfus were less concerned with justice for him than with saving the Third Republic from the right.

The counter-offensive opened in 1898 when Emile Zola (1840–1902) published *"J'Accuse,"* an open letter to the president of France. Accusing the army of deliberately concealing evidence that would have shown Dreyfus to be innocent, Zola added, "What I do is only a revolutionary method of hastening on the explosion of truth and justice." Consequently, the government felt obliged to reopen the case (1899)—only to have a second court-martial again declare Dreyfus guilty. Only after 1900, when the proponents of Dreyfus became politically strong in Paris, was it possible to have justice done; and then it was the highest court in the land which reversed the verdict of 1894. In 1906, Dreyfus was restored to the army, promoted, and decorated.

In view of the outburst of antisemitism across Europe and the general condemnation of Jews as an alien and undesirable "race," a Hungarian Jew named Theodore Herzl (1860–1904) concluded that the only salvation for the Jews was to insist on their separate nationality and to work for the creation of a Jewish national state, preferably in Palestine. He launched his program, called Zionism (1896), and called for an international congress of Zionists in Switzerland the following year. Though a response to antisemitism, Zionism had the effect of heightening antisemitism, as anti-Zionist Jews had predicted, because it seemed to verify the charges made by the nationalistic antisemites.

During the Dreyfus Affair, the papacy gave no aid to those French clericals who were antirepublican, repeatedly warning that the Church was not married to any form of government. Under Leo XIII (*1878–1903*), whose pontificate opened with the general European assumption that the

Church was losing its fight for survival in the modern world, the Church abandoned its alliance with the conservative secular governments dating from 1850. Through a series of encyclicals, the Pope sought to show that Christianity had constructive alternatives to the evils of materialism. Adopting a progressive and scientific outlook, he gave recognition to the significant social and economic changes that had taken place in modern times; but he attacked with equal fervor Marxism and the economic liberalism of *laissez faire*. Rejecting the Marxist attack on the right of the individual to private property, he declared:

Socialists . . . by endeavoring to transfer the possessions of individuals to the community at large, strike at the interests of every wage-earner, since they would deprive him of the liberty of disposing of his wages, and thereby of all hope and possibility of increasing his stock and of bettering his condition in life.

What is of far greater moment, however, is the fact that the remedy they propose is manifestly against justice. For every man has by nature the right to possess property as his own.

Rejecting the notion that class warfare is the natural state of man, Leo XIII also rejected the *laissez-faire* view that labor should be regarded as a commodity destined to find its proper reward in a free market:

Religion teaches the wealthy owner and the employer that their work-people are not to be accounted their bondsmen; that in every man they must respect his dignity and worth as a man and as a Christian; that labor is not a thing to be ashamed of if we lend ear to right reason and to Christian philosophy, but is an honorable calling, enabling a man to sustain his life in a way upright and creditable; and that it is shameful and inhuman to treat men like chattels to make money by, or to look upon them merely as so much muscle or physical power.[10]

THE ARTS

Realism became the dominant artistic creed after 1870. Born of romanticism, of the rejection of classical idealism, the realist went beyond the romanticist in the reaction. Where the romantic made an ideal out of individual portrayal of truth and beauty, permitting free rein to the imagination and the emotions, the realist sought his subject matter from "real life" and eschewed the imaginary. In so doing, he generally pounced upon the more sordid facts of private and social life, and the realistic novels were pessimistic or sardonic in tone as a result. When Gustave Flaubert

10. *Rerum Novarum*, May 15, 1891.

Above: Czar Alexander III and His Family
Left: Chancellor Otto von Bismarck
Below left to right: *Emile Zola* by Edouard Manet,
Friedrich Neitzsche

Above: *Nave, Nave Mohana* by Paul Gauguin
Left: *Self-portrait* by Vincent van Gogh
Below: *Young Girls at the Piano* by Auguste Renoir

Right: *Divan Japonais* by
Henri de Toulouse-Lautrec
Below: *Oranges* by Paul Cézanne

Above: Anton Chekhov and Leo Tolstoy
Below: Oscar Wilde
Bottom: Henrik Ibsen
Below left: Johannes Brahms

wrote *Madame Bovary* (1857), the story of the infidelity of a country doctor's wife, he drew upon an actual instance of infidelity with which he was acquainted. He did not mean to trade on the tawdry, but to expose in the hope of reform. Leo Tolstoy, in one of his later novellas, *The Kreutzer Sonata* (1889), brought the institution of marriage under fire with a story of such bitterness as to suggest his own marital dissatisfaction:

> But when the third and the fourth quarrel followed, I came to believe that they were not mere exceptions but that they would continue to occur. I was horror-struck at the future before me. I was tormented, too, by the horrible idea that I was the only person who had this misfortune, that other couples had no such experiences as I was having with my wife. I had not then found out that this is a common lot—that all men think, just as I did, that it is their exclusive misfortune and so conceal this shameful misfortune not only from others but also from themselves, being unwilling to acknowledge it.[11]

Another Russian, Anton Chekhov (1860–1904), was dedicated to portraying people as honestly and realistically as possible. A physician by training, he did not classify himself in artistic terms, but wrote in an often-quoted letter: "My holy of holies is the human body, health, intelligence, talent, inspiration, love, and absolute freedom—freedom from force and falsehood, no matter how the last two manifest themselves."[12] A masterful writer of stories, he was also a dramatist and journalist.

This passion for realism became extreme in a French group who called themselves naturalists. Where the realists emphasized sociological and psychological realities, the naturalists stood for "scientific" objectivity in their portrayal of reality. They became gatherers of facts and, in some cases, gave their novels a statistical air. The greatest of these writers was Emile Zola (1840–1902). Beginning in 1870, he sketched out a series of twenty novels through which he meant to describe all aspects of life under the fallen imperial regime: *The Natural and Social History of a Family Under the Second Empire*. Zola completed his project in 1893, a triumph of perseverance and organization. But for all the social evils he condemned by exposing their degrading effects upon the national life, the historian must protest against Zola's claim that he wrote objective history. Hating the imperial regime, he focused on the sordid and the appalling. For all its documentation, the series was not a balanced view. Nevertheless, Zola

11. Leo Tolstoy, *The Kreutzer Sonata* (New York, Modern Library Paperback), p. 43.
12. Avraham Yarmolinsky, *The Unknown Chekhov* (New York, 1958), p. 16.

would have agreed with Chekhov and the other realists that "Man will become better when you show him what he is like."

Such was also the view of Thomas Hardy (English, 1840–1928). His novels *The Return of the Native* (1878) and *Tess of the D'Urbervilles* (1891), to mention only two, showed man to be the victim of forces—both natural and social—quite beyond his control. But however pessimistic and bleak his stories, he thought that literature, by exposing "man's inhumanity to man," could work for a more favorable environment for mankind.

Henrik Ibsen (1828–1906), the acknowledged master of the drama, gave an even grimmer view of reality by setting his plays in the dark, cold country of his birth—Norway, whose social conventions he came to abhor. Ibsen was a moralist who found his country so reeking with hypocrisy that he took himself into exile. "I had to escape from the swinishness up there," he wrote from Rome. His *Pillars of Society* (1877) gives us the successful career of a big businessman whose rise to wealth was grounded in a series of lies and double-dealings—in other words, a man who loses himself while becoming a "pillar of society." Two years later, Ibsen presented *The Doll's House,* a play which had grown from his conviction that women are unjustly circumscribed by the conventions of a masculine society. He was, in fact, a champion of individual liberty and saw public opinion in an increasingly democratic age as the greatest threat to freedom:

The majority? What is the majority? The ignorant mass. Intelligence is always in the minority. How many of those who are in the majority do you think are entitled to have any opinion? Most of them are blockheads.[13]

Toward the end of the century, a new kind of "realism" had become established in all the arts. Called symbolism in literature and impressionism in painting and music, their common assumption was that reality is most effectively reproduced by creating the perfect "feeling" rather than by being photographic. It is significant that Edouard Manet (French, 1832–1883), a pioneer in impressionism, had been a student of Spanish baroque painting, that of El Greco in particular. While not copying the Spanish school, the impressionists were similar to them in their concern for the play of light and for the use of distortion. Manet, Claude Monet (1840–1926), and Auguste Renoir (1841–1919) all sought to create the visual impression of the moment—almost as a camera does—though not with

13. Koht, *The Life of Ibsen,* Vol. II, p. 182.

the inclusion of details the camera captures. Hence, they blurred, often distorted canvases to suggest how we really see things at a glance. Another group of extreme impressionists, calling themselves expressionists, argued that the painting should reveal the artist's emotion when he is recording his impression on canvas. The result was great individuality and vivid color, most notable in the work of Vincent Van Gogh (1853–1890) and Paul Gauguin (1848–1903). Paul Cézanne (1839–1906) fell between the two groups: clearly influenced by the impressionists in their emphasis upon "feeling," he also retained a strong sense of composition and deliberate form. Van Gogh, Gauguin, and the well-known painter of posters, Henri de Toulouse-Lautrec (1864–1901), all reveal in their brilliant coloring the enthusiasm in France after mid-century for Japanese woodcuts and art objects.

In literature, the new emphasis on the perfect "feeling" led to a group of writers who doted on pure aesthetics. Theirs was not an art of social criticism, but rather "art for art's sake," an attempt to create beauty for its sake alone. Extreme individualism was the rule, revealing this school, generally called the symbolists, to have been a derivative of romanticism. Walter Pater (English, 1839–1894), as an example, lived in seclusion and preached a high-minded hedonism; that is, that the richest life is the one spent in pursuit of pleasure through beauty:

We are all condemned, as Victor Hugo says: we are all under sentence of death but with a sort of indefinite reprieve, . . . we have an interval, and then our place knows us no more. Some spend this interval in listlessness, some in high passions, the wisest—at least among "the children of this world"—in art and song. For our own chance lies in expanding that interval, in getting as many pulsations as possible into the given time. Great passions may give us this quickened sense of life, ecstasy and sorrow of love, the various forms of enthusiastic activity, disinterested or otherwise, which come naturally to many of us. . . . Of this wisdom, the poetic passion, the desire of beauty, the love of art for art's sake has most; for art comes to you professing frankly to give nothing but the highest quality to your moments as they pass, and simply for those moments' sake.[14]

He was misunderstood by those who, believing that men should live to serve mankind, thought Pater was encouraging self-indulgence.

Oscar Wilde (1856–1900) became the most brilliant and notorious of the British aesthetics, widely known for his eccentricities and effete appearance. The "art for art's sake" movement soon fell victim to cartoons and even an opera, Gilbert and Sullivan's *Patience* (1881), but not even

14. Pater, Conclusion of *Studies in the History of the Renaissance* (1873).

ridicule was sufficient to prevent Wilde's works from achieving popularity. The witty brilliance of his play *The Importance of Being Earnest* (1895) made it an instantaneous success. Shortly thereafter, he was convicted on a charge of sexual immorality and sentenced to two years at hard labor. He emerged a broken man, to write a realistic poem of his prison experience:

> This too I know—and wise it were
> If each could know the same—
> That every prison that men build
> Is built with bricks of shame,
> And bound with bars lest Christ should see
> How men their brothers maim.
>
> The vilest deeds like poison weeds
> Bloom well in prison air;
> It is only what is good in man
> That wastes and withers there.
> Pale Anguish keeps the heavy gate,
> And the warder is Despair.[15]

In France, the most astonishing of those late-nineteenth-century poets who strove to express the totality of their sensations was Arthur Rimbaud (1854–1891). While still an adolescent, he set out to embrace the whole sensory universe—every form of emotion and suffering—which he would transmute into poetry. Two years of such ecstasy and anguish went into his *A Season in Hell* (1873), where he confessed the impossibility of his quest. His verbal fireworks, however, and his obscurity and deep pessimism helped to bring an end to the romantic traditions of poetry and showed the way for the twentieth-century poets.

Music remained romantic for the most part in the latter part of the nineteenth century, Claude Debussy (French, 1862–1918) being the only major innovator; his ideas were related to those of the impressionists and symbolists. Abandoning the traditional tonal scales and chord resolutions, he produced highly individual and sensual effects—vivid orchestral coloring—leaving him closely akin to the expressionist painters of his day. The opera *Pelléas et Mélisande,* first performed in 1902, had a delicacy of construction which contrasted sharply with the massive elegances of the contemporary romantics.

Their distinctiveness was increasingly national rather than harmonic. Subject matter and melodies were locally derived, composers catering

15. Wilde, *The Ballad of Reading Gaol* (1898).

to the national spirit, and national schools of the opera became the rule. Giuseppe Verdi (1813–1901) and Giacomo Puccini (1858–1924) persevered with the native Italian lyric style, the former reaching an astounding mastery and vitality with *Otello* (1887) and *Falstaff* (1892). In Germany, Richard Wagner's successes led to his ideas' being regarded as gospel, and while it is usual to classify him as a romantic, his tendency to reduce the arts to a series of formulas—to make an opera into a giant contraption—suggests the realist rather than the true romanticist. Johannes Brahms (1883–1897) remained the purer romantic; his greatness was recognized with his *German Requiem* (1868). His devotion to absolute music, in the face of Wagner's program music, led the Wagnerites to name Brahms the "anti-Pope." In Anton Dvorák (1841–1904) Bohemia had a great nationalist romantic, while the Russian national school was led by Modeste Moussorgsky (1835–1881) and Peter Ilich Tchaikovsky (1840–1893). Moussorgsky was inspired not only by folk idiom, but also by Russian Church music, as is evident in the opera *Boris Godunov* (1874). Tchaikovsky was perhaps more cosmopolitan than Moussorgsky, but the flavor of Russia is clearly evident in his works— works which were so intensely personal in their emotionalism, so openly sentimental, that they repelled more sophisticated listeners.

INTERNATIONAL RELATIONS, 1870–1900

The Balkans

In tracing the development of international relations after 1870, we must keep in mind several constant factors. The conversion of the old Austrian Empire into the Dual Monarchy (1867) gave the Hungarians immense policy-making power and enabled them to prevent the empire from becoming embroiled in German and Italian affairs, as in the days of Metternich and Schwarzenberg. The Hungarian nationalists preferred to divert the attention of the monarchy toward the Slavic minorities within the empire. Suppression of the national ambitions of their own Slavic minorities also meant that the Dual Monarchy had to hold the line against those independent Slavic nations who sympathized with the plight of the Slavic minorities within the empire. In sum, the Hapsburg Empire, which had long opposed national movements in Europe, came to direct its hostility almost exclusively against the Slavic peoples, paving the way for friendship with the new German Empire.

A second factor was the rise of little Serbia under the leadership of Prince Michael Obrenović (*1860–1868*), an ardent Serbian nationalist. His goal was a political union of all the southern Slavs. Before his assassination in 1868 by the rival Karageorgević faction, which was jealous of his successes, Prince Michael had reached an understanding with the Prince of Montenegro and with the Bulgarian Revolutionary Committee (within the Ottoman Empire) for an eventual union with Serbia. He also signed treaties of alliance with Greece and Romania. His assassination temporarily halted Serbian expansionist ambitions, but they had been noted by the Hungarians in particular. Not wanting to see a larger Serbia nor wanting to annex more Slavic areas into the Hapsburg Empire, the Hungarians had to favor maintaining the *status quo* in the Ottoman Empire.

A third factor grew out of the rapid, and unexpected, recovery of France by 1873. Bismarck's harsh peace not only failed to keep the French prostrate, as he had hoped, but even engendered a fierce determination to recover Alsace-Lorraine and gain revenge. His foreign policy, in consequence, was directed toward keeping France isolated, his reasoning being that France alone would not dare provoke a war against Germany. Since Britain followed an isolationist policy, and since Anglo-French enmity was traditional, Bismarck felt that an understanding with Russia and Austria-Hungary would suffice to isolate France. His main difficulty lay in reconciling Russia to Austria-Hungary. Russian bitterness over Austria's failure to support Russia in the Crimean War merely intensified the long-term rivalry between the two empires to supplant the declining Ottoman Empire in southeastern Europe.

Bismarck's first move in 1873 was to negotiate a mutual assistance pact with Russia, a gesture especially satisfying to Russia because it guaranteed her support in case the western powers should challenge the Russian violation (1870) of the Treaty of Paris (by the remilitarization of the Black Sea region). Bismarck then convinced Russia of the desirability of approaching Austria, and after Russia and Austria had come to an agreement to confer in case the peace were threatened by a third power, Germany adhered to the agreement: the Three Emperor's League (*Dreikaiserbund*) of 1873. Its solidarity was soon tested when an insurrection in the Turkish province of Bosnia (1875) gave an opportunity for international interference into Turkish affairs.

When the *Dreikaiserbund* met in Berlin to consider the crisis, Russia proposed an Austro-Russian occupation of both Bosnia and Herzegovina.

This was vetoed by Germany and Austria, both favoring the maintenance of the *status quo* in the Ottoman Empire. Instead, the three powers supported a note drawn up by the Austro-Hungarian foreign minister, Count Gyula Andrassy (1823–1890), which called for administrative reforms within the Ottoman Empire to meet the grievances of the insurgents. Though the Turks were inclined to bow to this pressure, the insurgents were interested in nothing short of independence from Turkish rule. Great Britain, always interested in maintaining the territorial integrity of the Ottoman Empire as a barrier to Russian expansion, then urged the Turks to resist all assaults upon their sovereignty.

Meanwhile, the crisis became worse as the rebellion spread into the province of Bulgaria in 1876. Here, however, the Turks smashed the insurgents with great ferocity, and their cause seemed lost. Their one hope lay in Russian intervention, and toward that end the Pan-Slavic ideal, first broached by the Czechs in 1848, was invoked. The little Slavic states of Serbia and Montenegro brought the Pan-Slavic issue into focus by declaring war against Turkey (summer of 1876) and entrusting the command of their armies to a Russian general well-known for his Pan-Slavic views. If the Turks should be defeated, a large southern Slav state might be formed, and this eventuality was alarming to Austria-Hungary; that such a state might be a Russian puppet was also feared in Vienna. But the Russians were far from certain that they could control the Balkan nationalities once they had achieved independence. In compliance with the requirements of the *Dreikaiserbund,* the foreign ministers of Austria and Russia met to discuss a common policy and agreed not to allow the formation of a large Balkan state. It happened, however, that the Serbs were quickly defeated by Turkey and appealed to the powers to guarantee their independence.

Toward the end of 1876, consequently, the powers met in Constantinople to take up the Balkan question. They proposed administrative reforms for the Ottoman Balkan provinces, including giving the great powers the right to nominate the provincial governors; and Serbia, despite her defeat, was to remain free and territorially intact. Victorious Turkey rejected the plan early in 1877, but she did procede to negotiate a *status-quo-ante-bellum* peace with Serbia. Russia, in the meantime, did not mean to lose this opportunity to meddle in Ottoman affairs, but notified Austria of her intention to declare war on Turkey. In the Convention of January 15, 1877, the two powers defined their rights and goals in a manner which suggests that neither was concerned for the welfare of

Serbia. The earlier decision not to allow the formation of a large Balkan state was reaffirmed, and in exchange for her neutrality, Austria was to be allowed to occupy Bosnia and Herzegovina at any time. Russia was to be compensated with the Bessarabian territory lost in 1856.

Russia then declared war on Turkey and was promptly joined by the Prince of Romania, who hoped to transform his nation's autonomy into complete independence. The Turks held out brilliantly for a number of months, but they were overwhelmed by the end of 1877 and had to agree to a harsh peace: The treaty of San Stefano (1878). The best that can be said of the treaty, since it violated Russia's prior understanding with Austria, is that the Russian negotiator had no knowledge of his country's obligation to Austria. (The Convention of January 15, 1877, had been kept secret, to avoid outraging Pan-Slavic sentiments.) The major terms of San Stefano angered the Austrians and alarmed the British; among the terms were the creation of a large, independent Bulgaria and autonomy for Bosnia-Herzegovina. Russia had apparently stolen a march on the other interested powers, who now demanded that the treaty be set aside and that a new settlement be negotiated. Bismarck offered Berlin for a meeting of the powers, saying he would preside as an "honest broker." Russia naturally resented this interference, but she had to admit the validity of her opponents' argument that she had acted unilaterally to set aside the Paris settlement of 1856 ending the Crimean War.

The Congress of Berlin (1878) invalidated the treaty of San Stefano and substituted the treaty of Berlin. Bulgaria was greatly whittled down and left autonomous within the Ottoman Empire rather than becoming independent. Romania won her full independence, but ceded her Bessarabian territory to Russia in exchange for the Dobrudja from Turkey; this unequal exchange annoyed the Romanians. As for Bosnia-Herzegovina, the Russians, hoping to prevent Austrian annexation of the provinces, were successful in getting a clause into the treaty which only permitted the Austrians a temporary occupation of Bosnia-Herzegovina if order should need to be restored. Thus, while the treaty of Berlin prevented the creation of a large Balkan state, as both the Russians and Austrians had earlier stated was their common policy, the events of 1878 nevertheless embittered relations between them. Furthermore, both powers revealed their expansionist ambitions in the Balkans: Russia by trying to create a large Bulgaria, which she hoped to dominate, and Austria by her increasing interest in Bosnia-Herzegovina. This suggests, incidentally, a notable change in Austro-Hungarian policy. Formerly there had been a reluctance to annex any more Slaves to the empire; by 1877 the Dual Monarchy considered the annexation of Bosnia-Herzegovina desirable for the defense of the Dalmatian coast against Italy.

Bismarck, who had tried to lead the negotiations in Berlin as a neutral, was caught short by Russian insinuations that he had really sided with Austria. His true intention had been to maintain the peace by maintaining the *status quo*. Russia now hinted that she might seek an alliance with France, leading Bismarck to seek an alliance with Austria-Hungary now that his *Dreikaiserbund* was obviously ineffective. He found Count Andrassy willing to sign a close alliance, providing it was directed solely against Russia and would not commit Austria-Hungary to aid Germany in case of an attack by the revengeful French. Thus, in the Alliance of 1879, the two powers pledged to assist each other in case of an attack from Russia; but they were under no obligation in case of an attack from another country (France or Italy) unless that country be aided by Russia.

Despite the alliance, Bismarck did not abandon his hopes of reconciling Russia and reestablishing the *Dreikaiserbund*. By 1881, the suspicious Russians agreed to renew the ties, thus staving off the possibility of a Franco-Russian accord. As before, the three emperors agreed that there should be no changes in the Ottoman Empire without prior consultation. Austria relaxed her earlier attitude about a large Bulgaria and agreed not to oppose the unification of the Bulgarian provinces, in exchange for which Austria received the right to annex Bosnia-Herzegovina at any time. The tacit undermining of the Berlin settlement is evident.

Italy had been isolated during the 1870's, to her increasing annoyance. Her territorial goal was the Trentino, which Austria flatly refused to give up. The Austrians were also hostile to Italy's moving into the Balkans, into Albania in particular, as Bismarck had on one occasion suggested in the hope that the Italians would direct their attention away from the Trentino. Andrassy, in fact, told the Italians that their proper area of expansion was in North Africa and suggested that they consider Tunis. When no European concessions were made to them at the Congress of Berlin, the Italians did begin to encourage an economic penetration of Tunis. Bismarck, meanwhile, having a personal dislike for Italians, encouraged the French to move into Tunis, hoping perhaps to lessen Franco-German tension. To the great dismay of the Italian government, the French suddenly occupied Tunis (1881), the pretext being an expedition against the Krumirs, who had been guilty of violating the Algerian frontier. The Bey of Tunis soon yielded and signed the treaty of Bardo (1881), giving the French a protectorate over Tunis. Turkish and Italian protests were to no avail because Bismarck backed France. The Tunisian affair, directed by Prime Minister Jules Ferry (1832–1893), marked the beginning of French nationalistic imperialism of the sort which we have already noted as characteristic of the late nineteenth century. And it left the Italians determined to end their diplomatic isolation.

For some years, Bismarck had been so disdainful of Italy that he was indifferent to her requests for an alliance. By the end of 1881, he had modified his views, concluding that it would be better to make Italy an ally than to leave her a free agent in desperate search for an ally. The renewal of the *Dreikaiserbund* that year had failed to stem the rise of Pan-Slavist sentiments in Russia; and it was possible, with Italy's evident interest in North Africa, that she might reach some understanding with France over the partition of North Africa. Thus, Germany and Austria decided to form a Triple Alliance with Italy (1882), the terms of which were consistent with the prior Austro-German alliance. The central powers pledged to come to Italy's aid in case of an attack by France, and Italy was to come to Germany's aid in case of French attack. Only in an instance when any of the signatory powers should be attacked by *two powers* did the alliance oblige all signers of the treaty to go to war. The Austrians deliberately omitted any mention of the responsibility of Italy to come to the aid of Austria in case of a Russian attack, reckoning that Italy would use such an occasion to demand the Trentino. This gave the alliance the further advantage, from Bismarck's view, of being anti-French rather than anti-Russian.

Meanwhile, the small Balkan states of Romania, Bulgaria, and Serbia, all ambitious to expand by annexing territories beyond their frontiers inhabited by their nationals, were keenly aware that they were caught in the cross-fire of Russian and Austro-Hungarian ambitions. Since Russia was already known as the sponsor of a larger Bulgaria, Serbia was led to seek an alliance with Austria. The consequent treaty in 1881 was unpopular in Serbia, because the Serbian government therein promised not to tolerate Pan-Slavist intrigues and to consult the Austrian government before concluding treaties with any other power. That Austria said she would not oppose Serbian expansion to the south (into Macedonia) seemed insufficient compensation for subjecting Serbian interests to Austrian supervision. Two years later Romania, also fearful of a larger

Bulgaria and angry over the loss of Bessarabia, signed a defensive alliance with Austria and Germany (1883).

The Bulgarians, discontented with their autonomous and reduced status, were not long in taking advantage of the terms of the renewed *Dreikaiserbund.* After the Congress of Berlin, Russia had helped the Bulgarians found a constitutional monarchy—another example of the Russian willingness in the nineteenth century to sponsor more liberal government abroad than was enjoyed in Russia. The Bulgarian national assembly, the Sobranje, was elected by universal suffrage, and the monarch was elected by the Sobranje. Rather dutifully, the first Sobranje chose Alexander Battenberg of Hesse-Darmstadt (*1879–1886*), a German prince but also a nephew of Alexander II of Russia, to be Prince of Bulgaria. He proved to be hostile to liberal institutions, and after the assassination of Alexander II in 1881, he abolished the constitution. Since the new Czar, Alexander III (*1881–1894*) was also an autocrat, Russia sanctioned the deed. But Alexander III was a narrow Pan-Slavist and nationalist and resented a German prince's sitting on the Bulgarian throne. The Bulgarian constitutionalists and the Russian-supported Pan-Slavists soon formed a political alliance with the aim of overthrowing Alexander Battenberg. His response was to pose as the champion of Bulgarian nationalism and to expose the danger of Bulgaria's becoming a Russian puppet. To unify the home front and shatter the opposition, he restored the constitution; this action had the added benefit of attracting British support, since the British saw Bulgaria becoming a bulwark against Russian expansion.

To prove his national leadership, Alexander Battenberg plotted the seizure of the Turkish province of Eastern Rumelia, a Bulgar-speaking territory immediately south of Bulgaria which the Bulgarians had been denied in 1878. The seizure was suddenly carried out in the autumn of 1885. Serbia, jealous of any Bulgarian expansion and herself hopeful of expanding southward, declared war on Bulgaria; this war Austria, now regarding Serbia a client, did nothing to prevent. The move backfired, Bulgaria quickly defeating Serbia and forcing Austria to demand an end to the war. Austria not only threatened to enter the war against Bulgaria, but even warned Alexander Battenberg that the Russians planned to occupy his country if he did not make peace. Fearful of losing his crown, Battenberg came to terms with Serbia, which lost nothing. To settle the Bulgarian question, the Sultan of Turkey agreed to nominate Battenberg governor of Eastern Rumelia for a five-year term. The Bulgarians had once again fallen short of unification.

Once again the *Dreikaiserbund* was severely shaken because Austria had neglected to inform her partners before intervening in the Serbo-Bulgarian war. Both Germany and Russia regarded Austria's action to be a breach of the *Dreikaiserbund,* and they protested sufficiently to force Austria again to promise her intention to maintain the *status quo* in the Balkans. Hardly had this Bulgarian crisis cooled down than it reopened with the sensational kidnaping of Alexander Battenberg. The kidnapers were army officers who had been angered by the disappointing results of the Serbian war, but they were aided and abetted by agents of Czar Alexander III. The Prince, after being released, returned to Sofia, where he was advised to abdicate (1886) by the Russian consul. Battenberg's compliance left the throne vacant, and the consequent regency had a difficult time finding a new royal candidate. Those suggested by Russia were discarded at once, but finally Ferdinand of Saxe-Coburg, an officer in the Austrian army, agreed to take the Bulgarian crown (*1887–1918*). The choice angered the Russians further, and they did not recognize him. Therefore all the powers signatory to the treaty of Berlin were led not to recognize Ferdinand either, in the hope of soothing Russian feelings.

Egypt and North Africa

The Egyptian problem also disturbed the peace in the 1880's. Since the opening of the Suez Canal in 1869, the strategic significance of the eastern Mediterranean had heightened; and while the powers had always regarded the region as sensitive, their attention now focused more sharply on Egypt. Here a reforming and ambitious khedive, Ismail (*1863–1879*), had begun to borrow immense sums to finance public works and the establishment of a public-school system. He also sponsored military expeditions southward along the Red Sea coast and up the Nile valley into the Sudan, cutting Ethiopia off from the sea and bringing the Sudan under Egyptian control. By 1875, his debt led him to sell his 176,000 shares in the Suez Canal to the British government, a personal *coup* for Prime Minister Benjamin Disraeli (*1804–1881*), which made the British government the primary stockholder in the canal company. Thereafter, the British took a serious interest in Egyptian stability as the safety of the canal would be jeopardized if the Egyptian government became increasingly chaotic. In 1876, the British organized a financial advisory commission to assist the Khedive, which they invited the French to join. The French, though angry that the British had gained control over the vital (and French) canal company, participated rather than let Britain go it alone.

Egyptian national opinion was soon incensed by this international interference, and the Khedive lent his support to anti-European intrigues and resisted the suggested economies. In 1879, Turkey, which claimed sovereignty over Egypt, was induced by the western powers to depose Ismail, but this only heightened nationalist resentment. Two years later, a portion of the Egyptian Army under Arabi Pasha (1841–1911) rose against outside intervention, forcing the British to land troops to keep order and to protect the new khedive, Tewfik (*1879–1892*). The defeat of the rebels left Egypt virtually a British protectorate, the French having withdrawn from further participation in the venture. In many ways, this occupation of Egypt proved to be an embarrassment for the British. It was an admission of Turkish weakness at the very moment when Britain struggled to maintain the integrity of the Ottoman Empire; it was ordered by Herbert John Gladstone (1809–1898), whose Liberal party was anti-colonialist but who saw no alternative; and it heightened Anglo-French antagonism. Worse, the defeat of the Egyptian army by the British inspired Sudanese nationalists to rise against Egyptian rule. Here Gladstone balked at further expansion and forced an Egyptian evacuation of the Sudan. This left a vacuum in the upper Nile valley, whose water supply was critical for life in lower Egypt and the Suez region. It made no sense to occupy Egypt in the interest of order and then refuse to occupy the Sudan —a fact which the British were soon made to realize.

Meanwhile, in 1887, the entire North African and European power picture became focused on Italy when the Italians sought to reach an understanding with Britain. The initiative, in fact, came from Berlin, where Bismarck had been watching events in the Balkans and in France with increasing alarm. As for the Balkans, he realized that the *Dreikaiserbund* would not long survive Austria's cavalier behavior at the time of the Bulgarian crisis, which had so alienated Russia. And as for France, we noted earlier that the republicans had finally, in the late 1870's, taken over the direction of the Third Republic from the monarchical coalition; but the republicans were as deeply divided in the 1880's as they had shown themselves to be in 1848 and in 1870-1871. Power teetered between the moderate republicans, who were colonialists, and the radical republicans, who were not. Bismarck's encouragement of French colonialism was obviously designed to deflect French energies away from Alsace-Lorraine. It left the moderate republicans open to the charge that they ignored the true French continental interests. In fact, they saw that the revival of French national power lay in abandoning Napoleon III's free trade for a mercantilist, self-sufficient empire. Alsace-Lorraine could come later. In the 1880's, Bismarck correctly feared a coalition of all the opponents of moderate republicanism, having for its upshot a victory for the extreme nationalists. The rise of a popular minister of war, General Georges Boulanger (1837–1891), gave credence to the fear that the Republic would be overthrown in favor of a dictatorship with military ambitions. Boulanger, however, lost his nerve, and his movement collapsed; but at the height of the Bulgarian crisis, it was very much alive.

In sum, Bismarck, seeing the possibility of an alliance between Russia and France, urged the Italians to strengthen the Triple Alliance by seeking an understanding with Britain. It is notable that he did not himself approach the British, because he hoped to avoid any action which would antagonize Russia further. The Anglo-Italian entente of 1887 was welcomed by Britain as a check against possible reprisals arising out of French anger over Egypt. Thus, Italy agreed to support the British position in Egypt if the British would support Italian ambitions on the North African coast. Bismarck, meanwhile, finding that the Russians would not renew the *Dreikaiserbund* in 1887, fell back on a project for a Russo-German treaty as the next best thing. His problem was to negotiate a treaty which would be compatible with his treaty with Austria, which meant that he could not guarantee German neutrality in case of an Austro-Russian war. The result was the three-year Reinsurance Treaty (1887), in which the signatory powers promised to maintain a benevolent neutrality in case either party found itself at war with a third power. This obligation was *not* to apply in the event that Germany attacked France or Russia attacked Austria. The treaty was kept secret at the request of Alexander III, to avoid irritating Pan-Slavist sentiments at home.

The accession of William II in 1888 set off an argument about Bismarck's foreign policy which ultimately led to his dismissal. His Majesty had been much influenced by the military and political views of the German general staff: namely, that Austro-Russian rivalry could not in the long run be rationalized, and that eventually a war for domination of the Balkans and the Straits would develop. As the national interests of Germany were more reconcilable with those of Austria than with those of Russia, the general staff favored an Austro-German "preventive war" against Russia while she was still relatively weak. Bismarck's counter-argument that such a war would give France the opportunity to try to recover Alsace-Lorraine apparently won the Emperor for a time, and preparation to renew the Reinsurance Treaty with Russia was made.

William II, however, was not anxious to share power with the formidable Bismarck, and it was not difficult, in 1890, for the anti-Russian faction to influence the Emperor against his chancellor. When Bismarck offered his resignation, it was accepted, and the immediate result was the failure of the German government to renew the treaty with Russia. Because Bismarck had so long striven to maintain the *status quo* and to preserve the peace, his removal was ominous. Russian alarm was enhanced the same year by the conclusion of the Heligoland treaty (1890) between Germany and Britain. The latter gave Heligoland to Germany in exchange for large German claims in East Africa, and, since the island was considered useless, the exchange was seen as German eagerness for British friendship.

Little remained for Alexander III but to move in the direction of France, however personally distasteful it was for the narrow autocrat to seek support from a democratic republic. A firm alliance was delayed because of the Czar's desire to keep it secret, something impossible for a parliamentary regime like that in France. Clearly, the Russians hoped to avoid antagonizing Germany. But when no overtures were forthcoming from Berlin, Russia agreed to come to terms. The negotiations for the treaty as well as its clauses revealed the reluctance of both powers for the alliance; it was clearly a matter of necessity not choice. Though generally called the Franco-Russian Alliance of 1894, the treaty was actually classified a military convention (which meant that it could be kept secret and that no parliamentary ratification was necessary) and was to remain in force only as long as the Triple Alliance existed. Nevertheless, it did mark the end of French isolation.

During the Franco-Russian negotiations, the Italians and Germans made efforts to tie Britain more closely to the Triple Alliance. The move failed because the British government, working within the cabinet system of government, believed it impossible to commit subsequent governments to policies in advance and hence would sign no treaties of alliance. The Germans suspected this to be a disingenuous argument and rejected the offer of a less binding entente. Thus, just at the time when France and Russia were concluding their agreement, William II realized the advisability of returning to the Bismarckian formula of seeking to reconcile Russia to the central powers. Not only did British isolation alarm Germany, but

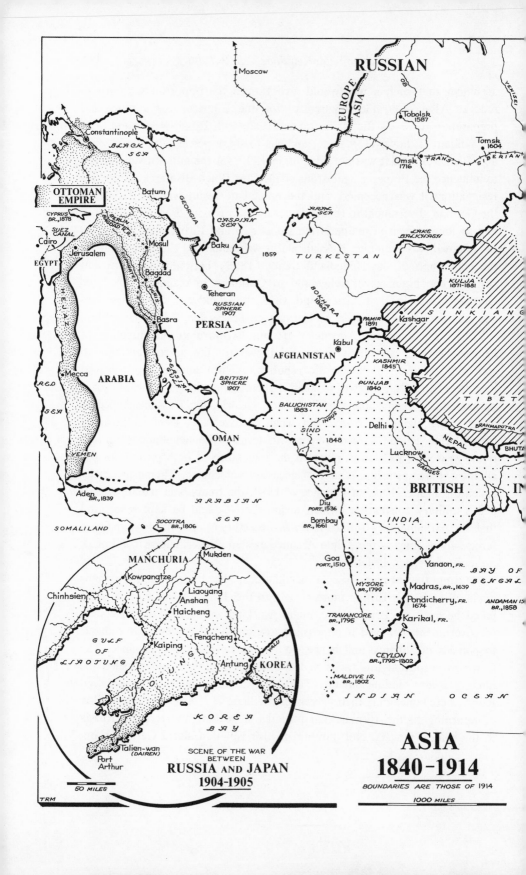

RUSSIAN

• Moscow

OTTOMAN
EMPIRE

Constantinople

BLACK SEA

EUROPE
ASIA

• Tobolsk
1587

• Tomsk
1604

Omsk
1716

TRANS-

SIBERIAN

YENISEI

OB

CYPRUS
BR.,1878

Batum

GEORGIA

CASPIAN SEA

SUEZ
CANAL

*BERLIN
BAGDAD R.R.*

Cairo

Jerusalem

Mosul

Baku

1859

TURKESTAN

*ARAL
SEA*

*LAKE
BALKHASH*

KULJA
1871-1881

EGYPT

EUPHRATES

TIGRIS

Bagdad

Teheran

*RUSSIAN
SPHERE
1907*

PERSIA

*BOKHARA
1868*

PAMIR
1891

• Kashgar

SINKIANG

Basra

HEJAZ

RED SEA

• Mecca

ARABIA

PERSIAN GULF

*BRITISH
SPHERE
1907*

AFGHANISTAN

Kabul

KASHMIR
1845

PUNJAB
1840

BALUCHISTAN
1883

INDUS

TIBET

SIND
1848

• Delhi

BRAHMAPUTRA

NEPAL

BHUTA

OMAN

Lucknow

GANGES

BRITISH

IN

YEMEN

• Aden
BR.,1839

*ARABIAN
SEA*

Diu
PORT.,1536

Bombay
BR.,1661

INDIA

SOMALILAND

SOCOTRA
BR.,1806

Goa
PORT.,1510

Yanaon, FR.

*BAY OF
BENGAL*

MYSORE
BR.,1799

Madras, BR.,1639

Pondicherry, FR.
1674

ANDAMAN IS.
BR.,1858

MANCHURIA

Mukden

TRAVANCORE
BR.,1795

Karikal, FR.

Kowpangtze

Liaoyang

Chinhsien

Anshan

Haicheng

*GULF
OF
LIAOTUNG*

Kaiping

Fengcheng

Antung

KOREA

YALU

CEYLON
BR.,1795-1802

MALDIVE IS.
BR.,1802

INDIAN OCEAN

*KOREA
BAY*

Talien-wan
(DAIREN)

Port
Arthur

SCENE OF THE WAR
BETWEEN
RUSSIA AND JAPAN
1904-1905

ASIA
1840-1914

BOUNDARIES ARE THOSE OF 1914

50 MILES

1000 MILES

TRM

in 1896 the Triple Alliance was humiliated by a monumental defeat inflicted on the Italians when they tried to establish a protectorate over Ethiopia.

The Far East

In his hope to revive Russo-German friendship, William II found it expedient to back Russian interests in the Far East, since suggestions that concessions in the Balkans be made to Russia were opposed by Austria. A Sino-Japanese war (1894–1895) had broken out over rivalry for domination of Korea; the westernizing Japanese quickly won this conflict. In the Treaty of Shimonoseki (1895), China had to recognize the independence of Korea and pay a large indemnity to Japan, as well as to cede Formosa, the Liaotung Peninsula, and the Pescadores to Japan. Britain smiled on Japan's rise as the emergence of a power which could help check the power of Russia. Conversely, Russia was annoyed to see Japan secure a toehold on the Asian continent. Both Japan and Russia were newly industrializing nations. Russia, whose industry was not efficient enough to compete with the West, saw Asia as her natural market and Japanese competition as a serious threat. Moreover—and no less important—Russia's Asian empire had been pushed to the Pacific with an expansionist enthusiasm not unlike our own, and colonization of Siberia would presumably be greatly stimulated by the completion of the Trans-Siberian Railway, begun in 1891. Unfortunately for Russia, the Siberian ports on the Pacific are ice- and fog-bound many months of the year; but in the face of obvious Chinese weakness in the nineteenth century, there was hope of obtaining open harbors in the Manchurian-Korean region. All these plans were threatened by the treaty which gave Japan advantages in Korea and possession of the Liaotung Peninsula.

When Russia asked for international intervention on behalf of China, Germany readily granted her consent, forcing France to do likewise for the security of her new alliance with Russia. Britain refused to have any part of altering the Shimonoseki settlement. The three powers advised Japan to return the Liaotung Peninsula to China and accept an increased indemnity, a demand which the Japanese felt unable to refuse. This revision not only angered Japan, but also left the Chinese vulnerable to demands for concessions from those powers who now posed as the defenders of China. Germany began this "battle for concessions" in 1898 by obtaining a ninety-nine-year lease on Kiaochow Bay and the right to develop the economic resources of the Shantung Peninsula. The obvious economic advantage for Germany ought not to obscure us to her greater interest, which was to lead Russia into greater Asiatic involvement. Russia had already negotiated an agreement with China (1896) which permitted the Russians to build the Trans-Siberian railway across Manchuria—the most direct route from Lake Baikal to the port of Vladivostok. Now, following Germany's lead, Russia asked for a twenty-five-year lease on the southern tip of the Liaotung Peninsula, including the warm-water ports of Talien-wan and Port Arthur, with the right to connect them by rail to the main Trans-Siberian line. Britain and France then asked and received equality in territorial concessions. Little wonder, however, that Japan in particular was incensed by this Russian encroachment upon Manchuria.

The cooperation of Russia, Germany, and France in the Far East, by crossing the lines of the established alliance, threatened to destroy the balance of power on the European Continent and make British isolation dangerous. In another sector, too—in South Africa—the British were subject to European hostility which revealed isolation to be not "splendid," as the British had been calling it, but downright uncomfortable. The long-festering quarrel between the British and the Boers, dating from 1815 when Britain acquired the Cape Colony from Holland, brought Britain to the brink of war with the Boer republics in the 1890's. World opinion in general held with the Boers, but the Germans went beyond the other nations in manifesting pro-Boer sentiments, to the great fury of the British.

INTERNATIONAL TENSION
AT THE TURN OF THE CENTURY

In retrospect, the German attempt to bully the British in the 1890's seems shockingly short-sighted. Given the serious grievances separating Britain from Russia and France in that era, it would seem that the Germans ought to have been less insistent on a firm alliance. Instead, they persisted in tactics which so alarmed Britain that, after the turn of the century, she was to be forced to seek an understanding with the French and the Russians. In 1896, on the twenty-fifth anniversary of the founding of the German Empire, William II made a speech in which he implied that he had abandoned Bismarck's policy of maintaining the *status quo* in favor of an aggressive "pan-German" program:

The German Empire has become a world empire. Everywhere at the most distant points on the globe dwell thousands of our fellow countrymen. German

merchandise, German science, German energy sail the oceans. The value of
our sea trade amounts to thousands of millions. It is your duty to aid me in
creating firm links between this greater Germany and our fatherland.[16]

Implementation of this policy came the following year, with the appointment of Admiral Alfred von Tirpitz (1849–1930) to be head of the
German navy. Von Tirpitz was an Anglophobe who shared the Emperor's
hope that the two continental alliances could be merged to challenge
Britain's international position. It would not be sufficient to have the
largest army in Europe; Germany must develop her navy, too. The naval-
building program established by von Tirpitz in 1897 was a sufficient threat
to British security to lead Foreign Secretary Joseph Chamberlain to hint,
in 1898, that Britain was ready to enter the Triple Alliance. At that point,
however, Russo-German cooperation in the Far East had developed to a
point where the Germans felt easier in Europe and, therefore, saw no
reason to jeopardize that cooperation by tying themselves to Britain. Thus
vanished the last best hope of an Anglo-German treaty.

German complacence was no doubt encouraged by a simultaneous
Anglo-French squabble in Africa. French nationalists burned to revenge
the loss of Egypt as a traditional sphere of influence and, in the 1890's,
they began an expansion of French power across Africa from west to east,
in the hope of jeopardizing the British position in Egypt. Based on the
French West African colonies of Senegal and Dahomey, this effort was
designed to extend French control eastward to the Ethiopian frontier; such
occupation would not only prevent the expansion of the British Empire
from north to south, but would also give France control of the headwaters
of the Nile. This fact will explain, incidentally, Britain's willingness to let
friendly Italy seize Ethiopia in the 1890's as a barrier to French expansion
—and the enthusiasm of the French for Ethiopian independence. When
Italy was defeated by the Ethiopians (1896), the British government
reluctantly concluded that the Sudan must be reoccupied and "Egyptian"
control resumed, as the French scheme was only too clear.

Shortly before, a small French party under Captain J. B. Marchand
(1863–1934) set out from West Africa for the upper reaches of the White
Nile. Marchand reached the river only after incredible hardships, finally
settling at Fashoda (1898), where he constructed fortifications and settled
down to await instructions from Paris. The British Sudanese expedition,

16. Luigi Albertini, *The Origins of the War of 1914,* Oxford University Press,
1952, Vol. I, pp. 95-96.

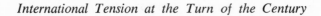

meanwhile, commanded by General Horatio Herbert Kitchener (1850–1916), had to fight its way up the Nile valley. Kitchener finally crushed the Sudanese Dervishes at Omdurman (early in 1898), but when he reached Fashoda, Marchand was already entrenched. Marchand, however, had only a handful of men, compared to Kitchener's three battalions. The outcome was left to the home governments, and in the end, the French decided to back down. In case of war, the French had to recognize that Kitchener would obviously win over Marchand; that the British navy was too strong for the French; that the Franco-Russian alliance would not be binding on Russia in such a situation; and perhaps most significant of all, that the home front was seriously divided by the Dreyfus Affair.

The African settlement (1899), by which France agreed to evacuate the Nile watershed, west of which the British gave the French a free hand, reached by the two powers had long-term significance. French public opinion was tremendously embittered by these results, but the French foreign minister, Théophile Delcassé (1852–1923), insisted that the incident demonstrated the need for France to reach an understanding with Britain lest the greater grievance—Alsace-Lorraine—be forgotten. Italy, viewing this agreement as a possible threat to her hopes for African gains, undertook secret discussions with the French which led to a mutual recognition (1900) of Italy's "interest" in Tripoli and France's in Morocco. Thus did the Nile provide the seeds for an Anglo-French reapproachment and for the undermining of the Triple Alliance.

Similar results came from the First Hague Conference (1899), which met following a proposal of Czar Nicholas II (*1894–1917*) that the arms race be checked by international agreement. Though on the surface this was a humanitarian proposal, Russian sincerity in the matter was rightly questioned in light of Russia's aggressive policy in the Far East. Disarmament, however, was an issue with considerable popular support in Britain and the United States, and none of the major powers felt it politic to ignore the Russian invitation, despite their general opinion that such a conference could not remove the real issue threatening the peace. Historians have since shown that the Russian proposal stemmed from Russian fear that her economy would not sustain the competition engendered by the arms race. The German military budget, for instance, had nearly trebled since the Congress of Berlin. No doubt a limitation on armaments honestly arrived at would have relieved some of the tensions in Europe, not to speak of the wasteful expenditure; but with Russian sincerity in the matter questionable, no one wanted to make the first move. When the conference met at the Hague, Russia proposed that all armies be kept at present levels for five years. It fell to the German delegation to veto the proposal. It was agreed to forbid the use of dumdum bullets and gas for a period of five years.

The British then proposed that the powers establish a permanent court for compulsory international arbitration; France warmly supported this suggestion as a blessing for humanity. Moreover, the French begged the Germans to accept the proposal for a court, in the hope of salvaging the Czar's conference. This French action created a favorable impression in St. Petersburg, but it did not prevent William II from rejecting the idea of compulsory arbitration. A permanent court was established at the Hague, but it was not given the teeth of compulsory arbitration. But the conference did reveal the community of Anglo-French interests and their more liberal views of international relations, just as the conference put the Germans in a poor light. In the aftermath, the French and Russians tightened their alliance by prolonging the military convention indefinitely.

The total effect of the Hague Conference was discouraging. However important the international court proved to be, the people of that day saw only the failure to halt the arms race. Thus the twentieth century was born under an inauspicious star.

POSTSCRIPT

In the two preceding chapters, we have examined the creation of a new European society, a "mass" society when compared to the society which existed before 1848. Accelerated industrialization produced a mass economy; the gradual democratization of political life led to increasing mass influence on politics; and the rapid spread of popular education contributed to the creation of a mass culture. In a short span of time, Europe ceased to be primarily agricultural. The swiftness of the transformation to an industrial society destroyed fundamental traditions of behavior and belief and left individuals increasingly specialized and less self-sufficient—though with the promise of higher standards of living.

In the same period, notably after 1870, the nation-states began to organize and exploit their populations as never before. All these tendencies did not evoke a uniform response. The average man may have counted himself better off in the world and talked confidently of progress, but the cultural critics—from Ruskin to Nietzsche—warned that if the judgment and the taste of the masses should become the standard, European civilization would enter a barbarian age. Moreover, even if living standards were rising, individual liberties presented another problem. Was the individual rapidly becoming submerged in the mass so that his emancipation was actually an illusion? A study of the twentieth century amounts to a consideration of these warnings and questions.

SUGGESTIONS FOR FURTHER READING

⋙⋘

The Age of Materialism

Carlton J. H. Hayes, *A Generation of Materialism 1871-1900* (London and New York: Harper, 1941), a distinguished work with good bibliography.

Basil Willey, *Darwin and Butler, Two Versions of Evolution* (London: Chatto and Windus, 1960), very useful essays.

Anthony Trollope, *The Way We Live Now* (London: Oxford University Press 1957), a revealing period piece originally published in installments from 1874-75.

J. H. Randall, *The Making of the Modern Mind* (Boston: Houghton Mifflin, 1926).

The New Cambridge Modern History, Vol. XI, Material Progress and World-Wide Problems, 1870-1898 (Cambridge University Press, 1962), stimulating essays rather than a survey.

*Morris H. Shamos, ed., *Great Experiments in Physics* (New York: Holt-Dryden, 1959), an imaginative approach to understanding modern physics.

*Alfred North Whitehead, *Science and the Modern World* (New York: Mentor, 1948).

Alfred Vagts, *A History of Militarism* (New York: Norton, 1937).

F. A. Lange, *The History of Materialism and Criticism of Its Present Importance* (New York: Harcourt, Brace, 3rd ed., 1925).

*Jacques Barzun, *Darwin, Marx, Wagner* (Garden City: Doubleday-Anchor, 1958).

C. S. Coon, *The Races of Europe* (New York: Macmillan, 1939).

Ruth Benedict, *Race: Science and Politics* (New York: Modern Age Books, (1940).

Guy Chapman, *The Dreyfus Case, A Reassessment* (New York: Reynal, 1955), a balanced, stimulating treatment.

H. Feis, *Europe, The World's Banker, 1870-1914* (Yale University Press, 1950).

R. N. Carew Hunt, *The Theory and Practice of Communism* (New York: Macmillan, 1951).

F. Borkenau, *Socialism, National or International* (London: G. Routledge and Sons, 1942).

George Dangerfield, *The Strange Death of Liberal England* (New York: Random, 1935).

P. W. Massing, *Rehearsal for Destruction: A Study of Political Anti-Semitism in Imperial Germany* (New York: Harper, 1949).

National and International History

G. P. Gooch, *History of Modern Europe, 1878-1919* (London: Cassell and Co., 1923), largely diplomatic history.

R. H. Fife, *The German Empire Between Two Wars* (New York: Macmillan, 1916), an examination of the rival liberal and conservative forces.

Gustave Stolper, *German Economy, 1870-1940* (New York: Reynal, 1940).

R. C. K. Ensor, *England, 1870-1914* (Oxford University Press, 1936).

D. W. Brogan, *France Under the Republic, 1870-1939* (London and New York: Harper, 1940), a superb survey.

Jean T. Joughin, *The Paris Commune in French Politics, 1871-1880*, 2 vols. (The Johns Hopkins Press, 1955), detailed and authoritative.

Karl Marx, *The Civil War in France* (with an introduction by Frederick Engels written in 1891) (New York: International Publishers, 1937), originally an address to the International given on May 30, 1871, the basis for the Marxian Tradition about the Commune.

John Plamenatz, *The Revolutionary Movement in France, 1815-1871* (New York: Longmans, Green, 1952), good brief survey leading to the Commune.

Melvin Kranzberg, *The Siege of Paris* (Cornell University Press, 1950), valuable as an analysis of Parisian conditions which contributed to the Commune.

William L. Langer, *European Alliances and Alignments, 1871-1890* (New York: Alfred A. Knopf, 1931) and *The Diplomacy of Imperialism 1890-1902*, 2 vols. (New York: Alfred A. Knopf, 1935), near classics.

B. H. Sumner, *Russia and the Balkans, 1870-1880* (Oxford: The Clarendon Press, 1937).

R. W. Seton-Watson, *Disraeli, Gladstone and The Eastern Question* (London: Macmillan, 1935).

P. T. Moon, *Imperialism and World Politics* (New York: Macmillan, 1936).

The Cambridge History of the British Empire (Cambridge University Press, 1929-   ).

André Lobanov-Rostovsky, *Russia and Asia* (Ann Arbor: Wahr, 2nd ed., 1951).

H. I. Priestley, *France Overseas, A Study of Modern Imperialism* (New York: Appleton-Century, 1938).

Mary E. Townsend, *The Rise and Fall of Germany's Colonial Empire, 1884-1918* (New York: Macmillan, 1930).

E. L. Woodward, *Great Britain and the German Navy* (New York: Oxford University Press, 1935).

Koppel S. Pinson, *Modern Germany* (New York: Macmillan, 1954).

René Albrecht-Carrié, *Italy from Napoleon to Mussolini* (Columbia University Press, 1950).

Arthur J. May, *The Hapsburg Monarchy 1867-1914* (Harvard University Press, 1951).

William L. Langer, *The Franco-Russian Alliance 1890-1894* (Harvard University Press, 1929).

Charles Jelavich, *Tsarist Russia and Balkan Nationalism, Russian Influence in the Internal Affairs of Bulgaria and Serbia, 1879-1886* (University of California Press, 1958).

*Available in paperbound editions.

❧ 13 ❧

The Collapse of the Peace
1900–1923

THE TURN OF THE CENTURY

In the remaining chapters, the reader will notice, we have in large measure abandoned our usual technique of examining as many aspects as possible of a period in the attempt to reach a comprehensive judgment about it. In dealing with the twentieth century, the historian's usual advantage of hindsight is limited, while the possibility that personal bias will affect his views increases. Lacking the proper distance from the mass of material available, his task of selecting the most significant developments of his own era becomes the more difficult. And even when the choice has been made, he cannot do more than touch on the highlights of a period remarkable for the rapidity and complexity of political, economic, scientific, and intellectual changes. Thus, when it comes to contemporary history, both the historian and the student of history must confine themselves to provisional judgments—even where the evidence seems reasonably complete. One historian has recently classed these provisional judgments as "journalism," adding that the vaster syntheses must be reserved for the historians of the future.[1]

That the crises which confronted European civilization at the turn of the century have not yet been resolved is evident. Moreover, it would

1. G. de Bertier de Sauvigny, "The Riddle of Post-War France," *Antioch Review,* Vol. XX (Summer, 1960), p. 240.

seem that the most pervasive influence on the civilization of Europe in the first half of the twentieth century was that which stemmed from the two great world wars. In the concluding chapters, then, the emphasis is on the international developments which culminated in these conflicts and on their effect upon the civilization.

Looking backward, historians have found it convenient to label epochs. Generalizations at best, the labels do suggest the character of an age. We hear the medieval period called the Age of Belief or the Age of Faith; the Renaissance and early modern periods, with their far-flung explorations new faiths, and new sciences, their delight in life, called The Age of Adventure. It is customary to refer to the seventeenth century as the Age of Genius and to the eighteenth as the Age of Reason or the Enlightenment. When we come to the nineteenth century, the picture seems suddenly less clear. It is sometimes called the Age of Ideology, the very name suggesting the actual fact: that the self-evident truths of previous eras had been brought into question. Alfred North Whitehead (1861–1947) has noted that, in comparison to the thought of previous centuries, the thought of the nineteenth seems perplexed and muddled. What, then, are we to think of the twentieth?

It may be useful, by way of introduction to the twentieth century, to note a number of labels recently suggested for our era. One author refers to it as the Era of Violence; another prefers the Age of Anxiety, and this, along with the Age of Analysis, might lead us to think of the Age of Freud. Others argue that the twentieth century belongs as much to Einstein as to Freud: in other words, the Age of Relativity, a notion which appeals especially to the cultural relativists who have cast aside absolute values as outmoded. A professor of philosophy, writing at mid-century, remarks that we live in an "age of unprecedented cultural crisis and confusion, where there is little courage and little sanity," which would suggest either the Age of Uncertainty, the Age of Obscurity, or the Age of Fear. What is the common denominator of all this? Fear would seem a pervading characteristic, but it does not adequately express the loss of nerve, the dehumanization, and the vulgarization of culture that some of the aforementioned terms imply. But whatever the word, the climate of opinion is strikingly pessimistic.

The twentieth century has not been, of course, without its hopeful aspects. Those years immediately before 1914, as far as the average man was concerned, gave promise of immense progress—social, political, and scientific—and if one were unaware of the underlying cultural currents, as was likely to be true of the average man, the comfort and complacency of those years was justifiable. Even after the shock of the "Great War," the victory of the liberal powers, when coupled with the creation of the League of Nations, held the promise of a better international order, at least in the 1920's. For some, the political experiments of the 1920's and 1930's in Russia, Italy, and Germany aroused hope and enthusiasm in the expectation that "efficient" totalitarian regimes would produce social and material progress. By mid-century, however, most of the factors contributing to optimism proved to be cruelly disappointing: who could be complacent in the wake of two world wars? Who could feel confident in the unlimited progress of science when faced with possible atomic destruction? Who, after the performance of the League of Nations in the 1930's, could feel absolutely confident in the success of international organizations? And who, as the viciousness of the various totalitarian regimes became apparent, could hold them the hope of mankind?

But even before 1914—at the opening of the century—the intellectual leaders were aware that their world was in deep trouble. For one thing, the liberal and democratic advances of the previous century seemed threatened by brutal nationalism and militarism. When all is said about the defeat of liberalism after 1848, it remains to note that many liberal and democratic advances were made during the nineteenth century. The Russian serfs had been emancipated and Russia had been launched in the direction of a modern state by Alexander II; the French Third Republic, for all its instability and crises, represented the victory of democracy; the two Reform Bills in Britain, the rise of the trade-union movement, and the broadening of educational opportunity, all contributed to the democratization of British society; and even in Imperial Germany, Bismarck's paternalism contributed to the welfare of the workers. Many autocratic regimes survived in 1900, but the realistic liberal of that date could see that a great deal had been accomplished since 1815, just as he could see it all threatened by the deepening of hostile nationalism.

A second anxiety for the intellectuals rose out of the emancipation of the masses. This liberation, which they had championed, might end in the vulgarization of European culture. While at the turn of the century the average man and the average politician were caught up in the enthusiasm of the inevitability of progress, many intellectuals felt increasingly threatened by violence and vulgarity, and they were further benumbed by their inability to see any purpose in the universe—inducing what we might call a spiritual crisis—which contributed to demoralization. Add to this the

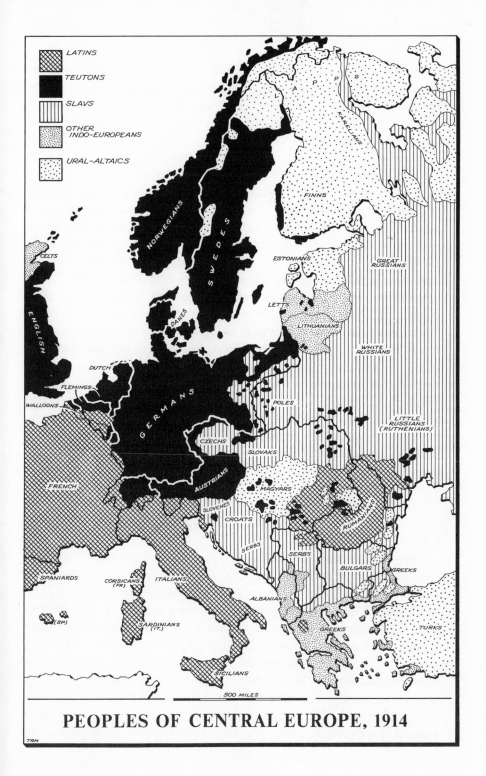

PEOPLES OF CENTRAL EUROPE, 1914

increasing complexity of the total culture in the twentieth century, and one has constructed a scene in which confusion reigns and chaos threatens. Meanwhile, non-European countries were beginning to modernize, to "westernize," and their emergence at once affected the balance of power in Europe and increased the demands of colonial peoples for self-government.

For a century following the defeat of Napoleon, the major powers solved their problems at the conference table or, when this method failed, through wars. But the latter were limited in scope and time. To put it another way, the diplomacy of the nineteenth century, even when unable to avert war, was able to contain conflict, to make war an instrument for a limited political objective. In 1914, diplomacy not only failed to prevent war, but also failed to prevent it from becoming a total engagement. Europe thus entered an age of conflict of unprecedented proportions, bringing colossal ruin. The destruction of lives and capital was only a part of the story. As a result of World War I, long-established regimes were brought down, notably the autocracies of Russia, Austria-Hungary, and Germany; but any jubilation over the victory of the democratic West was cut short by the emergence of new, modernized autocracies. Total war had spawned the total state. In 1917, "making the world safe for democracy" was an American watchword. By 1939, the chances of doing so seemed increasingly faint. Then came the second great bloodletting. By the time it ended, the balance of power on the Continent had passed to the peripheral nations—the United States and the Soviet Union.

THE FAR EAST CRISIS

The inroads made upon Chinese sovereignty at the end of the nineteenth century produced an anti-foreign explosion known as the Boxer Rebellion (1900). Led by an organization called the Society of Harmonious Fists, Chinese militia attacked the concessions held by foreigners, the Chinese government then identifying itself with the movement. Most of the foreigners took refuge at the British legation in Peking, where they were besieged. Chinese troops also attacked the Russian railway system under construction in Manchuria. This action led the Russians to send troops into Manchuria, which was virtually occupied by the end of 1900, as well as to contribute a large contingent to the international force which relieved the British legation. The Russian occupation of Manchuria set off a critical policy squabble in St. Petersburg, where opponents of the occupation, led by Count Sergei Witte (1849–1915), recognized that the brash move would give Japan opportunity to demand Korea as a compensation. Witte seemed to win out over the Russian expansionists as Sino-Russian negotiations for the evacuation of Manchuria began in 1901. The Japanese did consider for a time seeking an arrangement with Russia as an opportunity to get Korea, but in the end they pursued an alliance with Britain to gain the diplomatic strength to force Russia out of Manchuria.

Britain, in the meantime, had had reason to doubt the wisdom of her "splendid isolation." Germany, by supporting Russia in the Far East, Austria in Europe, and France in Africa, seemed bent on establishing a continental bloc, while the new German naval program seemed designed to challenge Britain both in European waters and all over the world. A Japanese alliance would serve to check Russia in the Far East and allow the British to concentrate their naval strength in the West. The Anglo-Japanese Treaty of 1902, a five-year alliance, guaranteed the independence of China and Korea but recognized Japan's interest in Korea. In the event of war, the signatory powers were bound to keep a benevolent neutrality and to enter the war only if a third party intervened. This alliance did spur the procrastinating Russians to conclude an agreement with China for the Russian evacuation of Manchuria.

Unfortunately for Russia, her realistic foreign-policy architects soon lost control of Far Eastern policy to a group of adventurers who had political and commercial aspirations in Manchuria and Korea and who got the ear of the rather unperceptive Nicholas II. The promised evacuation of Manchuria was thus obstructed in 1903, bringing on a surprise attack by Japan (early in 1904). There followed a series of engagements in which Russian disadvantages were compounded by Russian errors. Japan had the advantage of preparation and surprise. Destroyers from the fleet of Admiral Count Heihachiro Togo (1847–1934), using Russian signal lights, made a sneak torpedo attack upon Russian naval units in Port Arthur. The damage was sufficient to give Japan decisive control of the sea and allow her to land large forces on the Asian continent. Korea was occupied, Port Arthur was besieged, and the Russian forces in Manchuria were obliged to move northward. Reinforcement of the Russians was incredibly difficult, since the Trans-Siberian Railroad had not been completed, leaving them no alternative but to conduct holding actions until reinforcement would permit an offensive. Public criticism of this inaction led the government

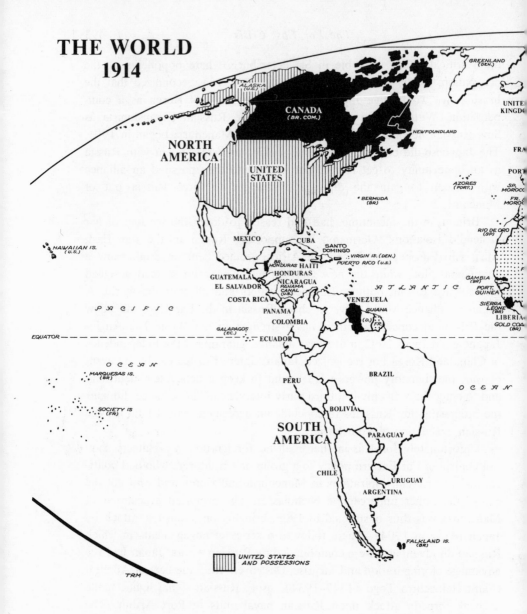

THE WORLD
1914

UNITED STATES
AND POSSESSIONS

to send the Baltic fleet to relieve Port Arthur (late in 1904). Few naval operations have been so poorly conceived and wretchedly executed. The fleet arrived in the Pacific hardly fit for battle; and, in the meantime, its objective had been lost by the inexplicable surrender of the commander at Port Arthur (1905) whose supplies would have enabled him to hold out three months longer. This forced the Russian fleet to make for Vladivostok, but it was intercepted and destroyed in the Straits of Tsushima by Admiral Togo.

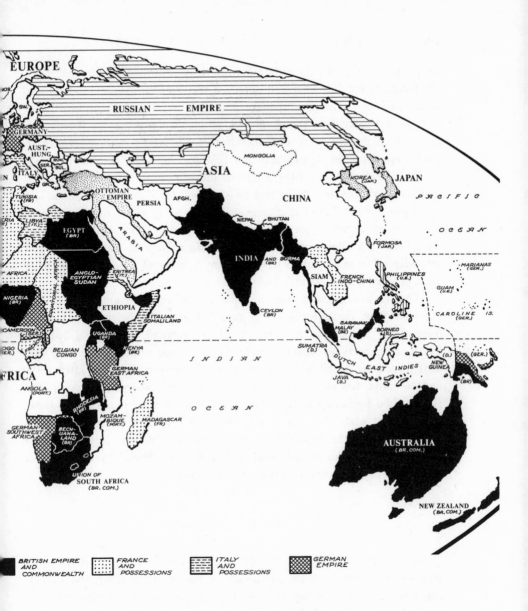

In the meantime, the surrender of Port Arthur enabled the Japanese to turn their full strength against the Russian field army in Manchuria. General Iwao Oyama (1842–1916), though appreciably outnumbered, inflicted a major defeat upon the Russians at Mukden. These disasters were the opportunity for a radical uprising against the autocracy (1905), of which we shall say more later; and because of widespread indignation over the conduct of the war, the Russian government dared not pursue the hostilities. This proved to be the last of the major mistakes; it became apparent later that Russia withdrew from the war at the very moment when her forces in the Far East had achieved the strength to make a Japanese defeat probable. The pro-Japanese American president, Theodore Roosevelt, offered to mediate the conflict. A relatively soft peace for Russia was arranged at the treaty of Portsmouth (1905), which outraged Japanese public opinion; but it also revealed that the Japanese statesmen recognized the necessity of calling a halt to the war. Both sides agreed not to intervene in Chinese affairs and to stay out of Manchuria. Russia lost her bases on the Liaotung Peninsula, these being given over to Japan, and allowed Japan a free hand in Korea. Finally, the southern half of the island of Sakhalin was ceded by Russia to Japan. The Russians felt themselves fortunate not to have lost any portion of Siberia nor to have been charged an indemnity.

The Russo-Japanese war had important repercussions. As in the Crimean War, the autocracy was revealed to be inefficient and became increasingly vulnerable to internal attack. Abroad, the defeat led the European powers to underestimate Russia's true military strength, just as it forced the Russians to reform their military establishment after 1905 and to move toward parliamentary government. No one, including the British, had foreseen the Japanese attack upon Russia, much less a Japanese victory when the war came. Thus, all the European powers were caught short by the implications of the Japanese victory, just as colored and colonial peoples in Asia and Africa were impressed by this oriental triumph over an occidental power of first rank.

NORTH AFRICA

North Africa proved to be the second focal point of international tensions after 1900. In the aftermath of the Fashoda affair, the French came to see the necessity of reaching an accord with Britain and the possibility of shaking Italy's loyalty to the Triple Alliance by making her a partner in an African settlement. After 1900, when France and Italy secretly agreed to recognize their interest in Morocco and Tripoli respectively, Theophile Delcassé (1852–1923), the French minister of foreign affairs, secured Italy's promise to remain neutral in case the French found themselves "directly provoked" to declare war. This gave the Italians the latitude to decide who was the real aggressor and, thus, the opportunity to shirk the obligation to aid Germany. The ambiguity of

Italy's position by 1902 left her mistrusted by all. In the case of Britain, Delcassé based his search for a rapprochement on the 1899 Anglo-French agreement over the Nile and on Anglo-French cooperation in the establishment of the Hague Tribunal. In 1903, he honored the latter with the Anglo-French Treaty of Arbitration, by which the two nations pledged to refer all their disputes to the international court. Meanwhile, the Anglo-French diplomats reviewed and compromised on various long-standing disputes in an effort to reach a friendly understanding. Most important of these was the decision to recognize their respective interests in Egypt and Morocco. The *Entente Cordiale* (1904), therefore, though not an alliance, removed the major grievances and made close cooperation possible.

Technically a part of the Ottoman Empire, Morocco had been virtually independent under a Sultan at Fez during the nineteenth century. Continual uprisings and conflict amongst the ethnic groups in Morocco (Berbers, Negroes, Arabs, and Jews) led thirteen powers (including the United States) to sign the Convention of Madrid (1880) with the Sultan; it provided for the protection of foreigners entering Morocco. The Sultan's authority, however, continued to decay, and when several German nationals became embroiled with the Sultan's government (1904), Germany could obtain no satisfaction from Morocco. Knowing of the simultaneous Anglo-French discussions, the German government hesitated to intrude into Moroccan affairs, for fear of driving the two powers into an even closer agreement. On the other hand, it soon became known that France wished to establish a special status for herself in Morocco, leaving Germany several difficult options: to defend the independence of Morocco in order to promote her own world policy and to contain France; or to take a soft line on Morocco in order to please France and enhance the possibility of a continental bloc against Britain.

Prince Bernhard von Bülow (1849–1929), chancellor from 1900 to 1909, believing that the Anglo-French entente was probably a secret alliance, favored a strong line against France. Bülow's hand was strengthened by Delcassé's failure to communicate the Anglo-French accord on Morocco to Berlin, a courtesy to which Germany, as cosignatory of the 1880 convention, felt entitled. If Germany did nothing, her prestige might suffer. Delcassé's omission allowed Bülow to proceed as if there had been no change, and he persuaded the Emperor to visit Tangier and to pronounce for Moroccan independence. The French were considerably taken aback, since they had already suggested to the Sultan a program of reforms which would have led to the "Tunisification" of Morocco. Consequently,

French prestige was also at stake. When the Sultan, at Bülow's instigation, then proposed a conference of the powers signatory to the treaty of 1880, the French government felt it had no alternative but to accept the invitation, and Delcassé paid the penalty for his blunder by being dropped from the cabinet.

William II, however, had preferred his pet policy of building a continental bloc against Britain, and he had backed Bülow's Moroccan policy reluctantly. In fact, he pursuaded an independent course incompatible with that of the Chancellor. In the summer of 1905, little more than three months after the visit to Tangier, the yachts of William II and Nicholas II met in the Baltic. The two monarchs, who called each other Nicky and Willy, reviewed recent events, Willy especially playing on the theme of the Russian humiliation in the Far East. He found the Czar irritated by British support of Japan and by the failure of the French to support Russian sea power in the Pacific. Seeing the possibility of a Russo-German alliance, and unhindered by the presence of foreign ministers, Willy tells us that

My heart beats so loudly that I can hear it: I pull myself together and say, casually, "Should you like to sign it? It would be a very nice souvenir of our interview." He scanned the paper again, and then he said: "Yes, I will." I opened the ink-well and gave him the pen, and he wrote with a firm hand "Nicolas," then he handed the pen to me and I signed. When I arose he clasped me into his arms deeply moved and said: "I thank God and I thank you; it will be of the most beneficial consequences for my country and yours; you are Russia's only real friend in the whole world."[2]

Both men were soon disabused of their enthusiasm when their respective governments had to abandon this hasty treaty as incompatible with prior commitments.

The international conference on Morocco met at Algeciras (Spain) early in 1906. If the calling of the conference was a German diplomatic victory, the results of the conference were not: all the powers except Austria supported France. Moroccan economic and political independence was reaffirmed, but France was given control of the police along the Algerian frontier, and France and Spain together were to control the police elsewhere in Morocco. British support of France at the conference was the first demonstration of the new Anglo-French solidarity, but Britain's concern went beyond creating a good impression. Given the German naval

2. Quoted from Sidney B. Fay, *The Origins of the World War,* 2nd ed. (New York, 1930), Vol. I, pp. 174-175.

program, the British suspected that Germany's solicitude for Moroccan independence was a bid for an Atlantic base on Moroccan soil.

In 1905, the British and French began a series of "conversations" directed toward the cooperation of their military and naval forces. The events of that year left both powers uneasy; France was alarmed by Russia's apparent weakness, and Britain was doubtful about Germany's intentions in Morocco. These "conversations" between the British and French military and naval staffs, however, have been rightly criticized, because—in the absence of an alliance between the two nations—they were not binding. Neither party was clear as to the extent of his obligation and as to the intention of the other party. Furthermore, because no alliance existed, the governments concerned did not reveal the "conversations" to their parliaments until 1914, by which date the question of who was committed to what was hopelessly ambiguous.

Naturally enough, the French, with their alliance with Russia and their entente with Britain, hoped to commit the British more clearly by encouraging an Anglo-Russian rapprochement. The Russo-Japanese War proved to be helpful in producing that rapprochement. The destruction of Russian naval power removed a major factor alarming to Britain; while the wartime criticism of the Russian government for its handling of the war made political reforms necessary and brought to power individuals sympathetic to the British rather than to the German system of government. In 1906, Alexander Izvolski (1856–1919), a Russian diplomat who had favored an understanding with Britain as the key factor in reestablishing Russia's position in Europe after the war with Japan, became foreign minister. Negotiations for an entente were opened that year and the entire gamut of Anglo-Russian frictions was reviewed, especially those along the inner frontiers of Asia. Through a series of compromises, the two powers achieved their entente in 1907; but again it must be emphasized than an entente is not an alliance—merely an understanding.

THE BALKANS

The Balkans continued to be a troubled spot, as they had been in the nineteenth century. After the turn of the century, attention focused on Serbia, where, for twenty years, many nationalists had been protesting that the treaty with Austria jeopardized the independence of Serbia. The Obrenović dynasty took the view, however, that the Austrophile policy had

saved Serbia from Bulgaria in 1885 and had prevented the rise of a large
Bulgaria. Alexander Obrenović (*1889–1903*), King of Serbia, incurred further unpopularity by denouncing the liberal constitution adopted by his
father, which brought the patriotic and constitutional parties into alliance.
In 1903, the King and Queen, and some twenty courtiers, were murdered
in an uprising of army officers, who then called on Prince Peter Kara-
georgivić to take the throne and rule as a constitutional monarch (Peter
I, *1903–1921*). The most nationalist of Serbian parties, the Radicals, led
by Nicholas Pasić (*1845–1926*), then came to a dominant position and
expressed their anti-Austrian prejudice.

The subsequent deterioration of Austro-Serbian relations forced the
Austro-Hungarian government to face the probability that Serbia would
become expansionist in the hope of annexing all areas where Serbs lived.
In this light, the Anglo-Russian entente of 1907 seemed the more serious
to Austria, since she presumed that Britain probably had given her consent
to revising the regulation of the Straits in favor of Russia. (Since the
Crimean War, the Straits had been closed to warships by international
agreement.) The British, still the defenders of Ottoman integrity, had not
given Russia any such green light, but it was understandable that Austria
should have anticipated it. Rather than be faced with a series of unpleasant
accomplished facts, the Austrians decided to take the initiative. A sudden
revolution in the Ottoman Empire (1908), the so-called Young Turk
Revolution, provided an opportunity for the seizure of Turkish territory.
The Russian and Austrian foreign ministers, Alexander Izvolski (1856–
1919) and Count Alois von Aehrenthal (1854–1912), met at Buchlau
(Moravia) to discuss their mutual ambitions. Their Buchlau bargain, as
it has been called, permitted Austria to annex (rather than merely occupy)
Bosnia-Herzegovina, while the Russians got Austrian support for opening
the Straits to the free passage of Russian warships.

There followed an international crisis of such proportions that war
seemed likely for a time, and its origin lay in the imprecise diplomacy at
Buchlau. Izvolski, rightly assuming that his agreement with Aehrenthal
would have to be sanctioned by all the powers signatory to the treaty of
Berlin, set out to secure their permission. Whereas Aehrenthal, making no
such assumption, simply announced the Austrian annexation of Bosnia-
Herzegovina. The first angry reaction came from Serbia, which had her
own eye on the provinces. Then, to his chagrin, Izvolski discovered that
Britain and France would support the opening of the Straits only if they
were to be opened for *all* warships, not merely those of Russia. The out-
maneuvred Izvolski then protested that he had not approved the Austrian

annexation, a protest so transparent that even the German government, which had been initially furious that Austria had taken such a major step without prior consultation with her ally, saw no other course than to back Austria in the crisis. Von Bülow successfully advocated giving Austria a "blank check" in dealing with Serbia, thus establishing an unfortunate impression that Germany would back any Austrian move; but Bülow felt it important to support the Triple Alliance. Austria then silenced Izvolski by threatening to publish the minutes of the Buchlau meeting, while the Turks undermined the Serbian position by accepting from Austria an indemnity for the annexed province. The incident drove the Russians and the Serbs into a common camp, revealed Austria's dubious diplomatic methods, and put Germany in a bad light for supporting an action she had initially disapproved.

ON THE BRINK

Beginning with the Moroccan affair in 1905, Europe endured a rash of crises, any one of which might well have brought war. After the Bosnian crisis of 1908, Morocco was again the scene of trouble. Anti-foreign riots in Morocco finally induced the French to occupy Fez (1911), though this time they gave Germany prior warning, since the action was an alteration of the Algeciras agreement. The Germans were willing to give France a free hand in Morocco in exchange for colonial concessions elsewhere in Africa for Germany. This the French were ready to do, but negotiations foundered when the Germans refused to state their price and the French refused to make an offer. To spur the French, a German gunboat (the *Panther*) called at Agadir on the Moroccan coast. Its presence aroused the British, partly because it appeared that France was being bullied and partly because it revived the fear that Germany was out to secure a naval base on the Moroccan coast. After some months, a Franco-German convention was signed (1911), by which the Germans accepted much less than they had hoped for, thus avoiding war. France was given a free hand in Morocco while turning over to Germany bits of the French Congo and some adjacent territory.

With a French protectorate over Morocco probable, the Italians concluded that the time was ripe to seize Tripoli. Her Triple Alliance partners had earlier encouraged the venture, in the hope of deflecting Italian attention from the Trentino; Britain and France had also recognized Tripoli to be a sphere for Italian penetration; and in 1909, Italy reached a secret agreement with Russia in which the signatories recognized each other's special interests in Tripoli and the Straits respectively. Yet, with all this encouragement, no great power wanted to see Italy make her move in 1911, because any assault upon the Ottoman Empire could set off new troubles in the Balkans. The Italians proceeded, nevertheless, by sending the Turks an ultimatum to the effect that Turkey had been resisting Italian commercial penetration of Tripoli; and when the ultimatum was rejected, the Italians announced the province's annexation. Seizing the territory was another matter; the Italians found it stubbornly defended by Enver Bey (*1881-1922*), and they were unable to make headway. Frantic to prevent Tripoli from becoming another Ethiopia, the Italians occupied Rhodes and the Dodecanese Islands (1912), in an attempt to force Turkey to terms. The Turkish decision to yield, however, came less from Italian pressure than from Turkish need to face an expected onslaught from the Balkan powers. By the Treaty of Lausanne (1912), Italy received Tripoli. The Turks were to recover the Dodecanese Islands upon their evacuation of Tripoli.

After his humiliation in 1908, Izvolski had urged the formation of a Balkan alliance to block any further Austrian expansion southward, but the Serbo-Bulgarian rivalry prevented any final understanding. With Turkey distracted by her war with Italy (1912), the opportunity to seize Turkish territory in the Balkans proved to be an overpowering temptation. Serbia and Bulgaria signed an alliance whose ostensible purpose was to prevent any great power (Austria) from expanding in the Balkans; but a secret clause, which was made known to Russia, pledged coordinated military action in the event of disorders in Turkey. The two powers planned to take territorial compensation in Macedonia and Albania. When the premier of France, Raymond Poincaré (1860-1934), was shown the treaty some months later, he protested against its warlike intentions; but the new Russian foreign minister, S. D. Sazonov (1861-1927), was confident that Russia could control the Balkan alliance and employ it solely for defense against Austria. In the meantime, Bulgaria and Greece signed an alliance (1912) which was definitely directed against Turkey. Sazonov, suddenly awaking to the realization that he could not control Balkan nationalism, fell in with Poincaré's proposal that all the great powers join in warning the Balkan states not to disturb the peace. This warning was indeed given late in 1912, but it came too late—on the very day that Montenegro declared war on Turkey. The Bulgarians, Greeks, and Serbs quickly joined the fight, and the Turks were easily defeated.

Making peace was far less easy because the victorious powers' interests were at once in conflict. Moreover, the Albanians unexpectedly declared their independence from Turkey in order to forestall annexation by Serbia; this move cut Serbia off from her intended war gain. Greece and Bulgaria expected to partition Macedonia as their share of the spoils, but Serbia now insisted on a portion of Macedonia in lieu of Albania; this demand was rejected by Bulgaria. Britain interfered at this point by inviting the great powers to meet in London to settle the Balkan disputes. The powers imposed a peace settlement, the treaty of London (1913), by which Turkey abandoned her European territory beyond the Enos-Midia line. Serbia, in the meantime, pursued her Macedonian quest, to which end she bought Greek support. Then, taking advantage of a border incident involving Serbian and Bulgarian troops, Serbia and Greece declared war on Bulgaria (1913); the action constituted the Second Balkan War. Immediately, Turkey and Romania joined the war against Bulgaria, who was consequently defeated within a month. The London settlement was then altered by the treaty of Bucharest (1913) and the treaty of Constantinople (1913) at the expense of Bulgaria. Turkey regained European territory to the line of the Maritza River; Romania got another part of Dobrudja; and the Greeks and Serbs divided most of Macedonia between them. The most significant result of the two wars was the enlargement of Serbia to nearly double her former size and the consequent whetting of her nationalistic appetite.

In fact, Serbia declined to evacuate Albania during the months when the conference in London was trying to agree on the frontiers for the new state. All the powers warned Serbia that she must evacuate, but Austria sent an eight-day ultimatum to Serbia to evacuate or face war, which forced the Serbs to back down. Romania's position was also equivocal. Though an adherent to the Triple Alliance, her decision to join Serbia against Bulgaria in 1913 was contrary to Austrian pleasure. Romanian national sentiment, moreover increasingly noted the presence in Transylvania of a Romanian population, nearly three million people ruled by Hungarians. Although the ruling house of Romania was a branch of the Hohenzollern family and pro-German, King Carol I (*1881–1914*) privately admitted to his allies the impossibility of joining Austria-Hungary in a war. Austria's response was to favor building a Turkish-Bulgarian bloc to offset Serbia-Romania-Greece, but Germany shrank from offending King Carol and Constantine I of Greece (*1913–1917*), the brother-in-law of William II.

Germany did, however, have an interest in Ottoman integrity, and we must review the rising German concern with Turkish affairs as background for the last diplomatic crisis before the war itself. As we noted earlier, the growth of German industry, German technology, and military prestige after 1870 was phenomenal. The Ottoman Empire, in contrast, was living on borrowed time, owing to the refusal of her sultans to modernize the country, and it is generally believed that the empire would have long since been partitioned had not the conflicting interests of the great powers prevented this action. Toward the end of the nineteenth century, the British, traditional upholders of Turkey, had begun to recognize the hopelessness of the reform movement there and, therefore, to anticipate the impending collapse. Simultaneously, the Germans, seeking new outlets for their capital, began to invest in Turkey while William II was trumpeting his "world policy." By 1900, German activity in Turkish business enterprise and railway building clearly surpassed that of any other nationality. Until recently, historians often held that the deepening of Anglo-German hostility in those years was to a large extent attributable to Germany's displacement of Britain in the Ottoman Empire; but studies of the commercial value of the Ottoman Empire to Britain and Germany suggest that economic grievances were a poor second to the political implications of German expansion. Not only did Germany send military missions to train the Turkish army, but concessions won by German railway companies by 1899 opened the way for rail connections between Berlin and the Persian Gulf via Constantinople and Baghdad. The Russians saw this course of events with alarm, not because they feared German economic competition in Turkey, but because they saw German power moving to stiffen Turkish resistance to Russian ambitions. After the turn of the century, this German axis seemed designed to cut off Russia from her western friends, and the British began to fear for their position in Egypt.

In this light, the appointment (1913) of a German general, Otto Liman von Sanders (1855–1929), to command the Turkish troops at Constantinople aroused a storm from the entente powers. Though he came at Turkish request and with a mission of forty-two officers to train the Turkish army, the Russians immediately envisioned the Straits in German hands. The incident illustrates the separation of civil and military authority in Germany, which we earlier noted, as well as its dangers. Apparently the arrangement with Turkey had been worked out by the German military without consultation with the foreign office. Theobald von Bethmann-Hollweg (1856–1921), chancellor since 1909, recognized the legitimacy of

Anglo-Franco-Russian protests and had to assume the responsibility for smoothing out the dangerous situation created by the military. Not the least of Bethmann's troubles came from the Turks, who were disinclined to give way to Russian pressure. Ultimately a compromise was achieved: von Sanders was promoted a grade in the German army; by the terms of his contract with Turkey, this action forced the Turks to promote him to the rank of field marshal in the Turkish army. As a consequence, he could no longer command a corps (at Constantinople), and he became instead inspector general of the Turkish army.

THE ASSASSINATION AT SARAJEVO

The von Sanders affair proved to be the last major diplomatic crisis before the actual war crisis in 1914, which grew out of the assassination of the Archduke Franz Ferdinand (1863–1914) heir to the throne of Austria-Hungary. Franz Ferdinand, while an autocrat at heart, knew perfectly well that unless the empire were reformed to accommodate the minority nationalities, its days were numbered. While his actual plans for reform are not known, he did leave a draft of the manifesto he intended to publish at the time of his accession to the throne:

> Since all people under Our scepter shall have equal rights in regard to participation in the common affairs of the Monarchy, this equality of rights demands that to every race be guaranteed its national development within the frame of the common interests of the Monarchy, and that to all races, ranks, and classes the preservation of their just interests be made possible through just laws of suffrage—wherever this has not yet been carried through.[3]

Before 1914, however, it was merely suspected that the Archduke had major plans for reforms, and he was thus feared equally by the conservatives within the empire and by the nationalists in Serbia and Romania. The betting was that his first step would be to convert the Dual Monarchy into a Triple Monarchy, the third unit being a Croatian state to include the southern Slavs in the empire. Since such a development would have served to integrate Bosnia-Herzegovina into the empire, the Serbs were especially apprehensive that their immediate ambitions might be blocked.

There existed in Serbia three nationalistic organizations. The Radical party, headed by Prime Minister Nikola Pašić (1845?–1926), had been

3. *Ibid.,* Vol. II, p. 23.

anti-Austrian since its origin in 1881 and had come to power after the overthrow of the Obrenović dynasty in 1903. Its goal was to strengthen Serbia to a point where she could become the Prussia or the Sardinia-Piedmont of the Balkans. Secondly, after Austria's annexation of Bosnia-Herzegovina in 1908, the Serbian foreign minister founded an "unofficial" patriotic society called the National Defense Association (*'Narodna Odbrana'*) dedicated to giving military training to volunteers, in anticipation of an eventual clash with Austria. The consequent difficulty in distinguishing between an official and unofficial Serbian action or attitude became even more perplexing with the establishment of a secret society called the Black Hand (1911). Its membership came largely from the army, including officers who had engineered the coup in 1903; and its leader, Colonel Dragutin Dimitrijević (1876–1917), was a member of the Serbian general staff. The Black Hand regarded the *Narodna Odbrana* as insufficiently aggressive.

In March, 1914, an announcement was made of the Archduke Franz Ferdinand's intended visit to the summer maneuvers in Bosnia. The occasion was a logical opportunity for the heir to the throne to make himself known to the people of the newly annexed province, because he had long taken an interest in military affairs. In fact, the Archduke hoped that the army could become an important unifying element for the empire by instituting German as the language of command while requiring that officers commanding non-German regiments also speak the language of their regiments. The Bosnian maneuvers were quite routine and involved defensive tactics to be used in case of invasion from the Adriatic coast. In other words, neither the maneuvers nor the visit to the Bosnian capital, Sarajevo, were contrived to irritate Serbia. The visit did, however, provide an opportunity for Serb extremists to make trouble, and an assassination plot was hatched in Belgrade—the assassins leaving for Sarajevo three weeks before the scheduled visit.

Since "war guilt" became a major issue after 1914, and given the closeness of official and unofficial agencies in Serbia, a legitimate question later arose as to how much the Serbian government knew of the plot and what kind of warning it passed on to Austria. The evidence today suggests that Prime Minister Pašić had wind of the plot but found it impolitic to send the information directly to the Austrian foreign office. It was, for instance, unwise to admit that anti-Austrian plotting went on within Serbia, and Pašić did not want to arouse the ire of the superpatriots in Serbia by exposing them. Finally, Austro-Serbian relations had been so strained for a decade that it had become difficult for the two powers to communicate through the usual diplomatic channels. These factors led the Serbian government to pass on to a secondary minister in the Austrian cabinet its information about possible trouble for the Archduke, in the expectation that he would pass it on. Thus, a warning existed, but in a form which proved ineffective and which gave Austria grounds to claim that she had not been properly warned. The further question arises of whether or not she wanted to be warned. Balkan nationalism, particularly that of Serbia and Romania, may have reached such a point that vigorous retaliation had become necessary, to prevent the empire from coming apart along its national seams.

Six assassins were placed along the Archduke's route to Sarajevo on that fateful June 28, 1914; these men had received training from the *Narodna Odbrana*. The fatal shots were fired by Gavrilo Princip, a Bosnian student of Serb extraction who belonged to a group of young hotheads advocating violence as the only method likely to achieve unification of the southern Slavs. International opinion was shocked by the event and sympathetic toward Austrian claims for satisfaction. Count Leopold von Berchtold (1863–1942), who had replaced Aehrenthal in 1912, first consulted Germany, to be sure of her support. Her first response was not as favorable as Berchtold had hoped; he had come to believe that an immediate war against Serbia was necessary for the empire's survival:

> Zimmerman [German under-secretary of state for foreign affairs] assured me [the Austrian ambassador to Germany] that he would consider decisive action on the part of Austria, with whom the whole civilized world today was in sympathy, quite comprehensible, but still he would recommend the greatest caution, and advise that no humiliating demands be made upon Serbia.[4]

Berchtold then drew up a letter to William II, to be signed by Francis Joseph, with the intent to show Germany that the assassination was simply part of a Serbian program to achieve the unification of the southern Slavs; that if Austria did not deal promptly with Serbia, the Hapsburg dynasty and its territories (and thus the Triple Alliance) would be in grave danger. This letter achieved the desired effect; William II informed Vienna that he would back Austria's settlement with Serbia. On the other hand, in giving Austria what has been called a "blank check," Germany assumed that the crisis would be successfully localized. At least, William II believed that even Russia would see the necessity of punishing Serbia in defense of the

4. *Ibid.*, Vol. II, p. 199.

monarchical principle, and if Russia did not come to the aid of Serbia, Austria could settle the issue alone. Berchtold, on the other hand, believed he had received unconditional German backing, but the manner in which he proceeded suggests that he recognized that the German foreign office was more lukewarm than William II in encouraging Austria.

The Austrian ultimatum to Serbia, which allowed only forty-eight hours for an answer, was delivered by the Austrian minister in Belgrade late in the afternoon on July 23, a Thursday. Berchtold did not notify the German foreign office of the clauses in the ultimatum until the evening of July 22, by which time the text had already been transmitted to the Austrian representatives abroad—including the one in Belgrade. And there is no question that the ultimatum was drawn up in a form to make it unacceptable, since acceptance would have jeopardized Serbian sovereignty. Hence, Berchtold saw to it that there was no opportunity for German interference at the critical moment. On the grounds that the "Royal Serbian Government . . . has permitted the criminal machinations of various societies and associations directed against the Monarchy, and has tolerated unrestrained language on the part of the press," Austria demanded that all patriotic societies engaged in anti-Austrian activity be suppressed, that Serbian schools be ordered to cease anti-Austrian teaching, and that officials accused by Austria of fomenting trouble be dismissed. Of greater import was the demand that Austrian agents be allowed to work with Serbian officials within the Serbian borders on the investigation of the assassination. The Serbian response was conciliatory, but it necessarily rejected that portion of the ultimatum which would have allowed Austrian officials the right to pry into Serbian affairs. Knowing that this rejection meant war, Serbia ordered mobilization even before sending her answer to the Austrian ambassador; and he immediately left Belgrade upon its receipt. The expected Austrian declaration of war upon Serbia came on July 28.

WAR

Hopes that the conflict would be localized were quickly dashed.[5] The Russian government, intensely sensitive about Austro-German gains in

5. A Partial List of the Declarations of War
1914

July 28 Austria on Serbia
Aug. 1 Germany on Russia
Aug. 3 Germany on France

the Balkans and the Ottoman Empire, ordered general mobilization. Then, on second thought, it tried to mobilize only against Austria, in the hope of neutralizing Germany, finally returning again to general mobilization because of the technical difficulties of a limited mobilization. This led Germany to send Russia a twelve-hour ultimatum demanding an end to mobilization, while Austria decreed her general mobilization. A German inquiry to Paris as to French intentions brought an indefinite response, following which both countries decreed mobilization—within five minutes of each other. And when the Germans received no answer to their ultimatum, they declared war on Russia (August 1) and upon France (August 3).

In the meantime, Germany asked Belgium for permission to send troops across her territory, as was required by the German plan of attack on France. Belgian refusal brought on a German invasion, in what was not merely unprovoked aggression but a violation of the treaty (1839) guaranteeing Belgian neutrality. The British government found itself in anguish. Unlike the continental powers, Britain was not bound by any alliance, though she was signatory to the Treaty of 1839. Fur-

Aug. 4	Germany on Belgium	Aug. 4	Britain on Germany
Aug. 6	Austria on Russia	Aug. 6	Serbia on Germany
		Aug. 12	France on Austria
			Britain on Austria
		Aug. 23	Japan on Germany
		Aug. 25	Japan on Austria
Aug. 28	Austria on Belgium		
		Nov. 2	Russia on Turkey
			Serbia on Turkey
		Nov. 5	Britain on Turkey
			France on Turkey
		1915	
		May 23	Italy on Austria
		Aug. 21	Italy on Turkey
Oct. 14	Bulgaria on Serbia	Oct. 15	Britain on Bulgaria
		Oct. 16	France on Bulgaria
		Oct. 19	Russia on Bulgaria
		1916	
		Aug. 27	Romania on Austria
Aug. 28	Germany on Romania	Aug. 28	Italy on Germany
Sept. 1	Bulgaria on Romania		
		1917	
		Apr. 6	United States on Germany
		June 27	Greece on Austria, Bulgaria, Germany, and Turkey
		Aug. 14	China and Germany-Austria
		Dec. 7	United States on Austria

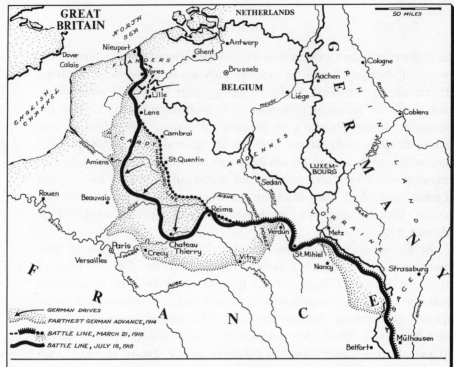

1914 TO JULY 18, 1918
WORLD WAR I – WESTERN FRONT
JULY 18, 1918 TO THE ARMISTICE

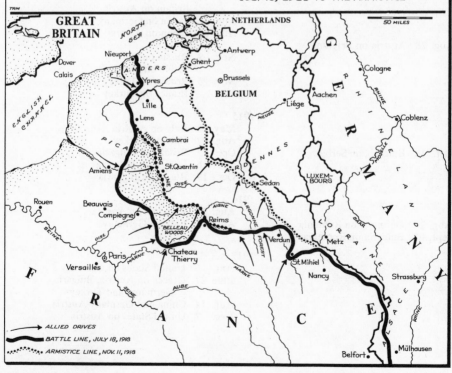

thermore, having engaged in military and naval discussions with the French, the British had encouraged the French to expect support in case of war and to deploy their forces accordingly. Sir Edward Grey (1862–1933), foreign minister from 1905 to 1916, had not informed the whole cabinet of the discussions until 1912, and Parliament did not learn of them until the crisis of 1914. Thus, the whole nation was in a quandary, and, as late as August 1, the government was unable to assure France and Russia of support, just as it could give the Germans no assurance of British neutrality. On August 3, however, Grey pulled the issues into focus in a brilliant parliamentary speech in which he showed both Britain's moral obligation to France and the catastrophe to Britain of a French defeat. If the balance of power on the Continent were shattered by a country with an aggressive world policy like Germany's, the security of Britain and her empire would vanish. The news of the invasion of Belgium the following day brought the remaining waverers into line, but there is not much doubt that Britain would of necessity have entered the war, even without the invasion of Belgium.

That invasion, which the Germans admitted to be a violation of international law, was a military requirement. Ever since the signing of the Franco-Russian alliance, the Central Powers had had to face the probability of a two-front war in case a conflict should break out. To await an attack from two sides would be sheer madness, especially in view of Italy's doubtful loyalty to the Triple Alliance. Moreover, the military canons of that day were based on the swift Prussian victories of 1866 and 1870, rather than upon the lessons of the American Civil War. Therefore, instead of a war of deadlock and attrition, most European strategists saw victory quickly achieved through vigorous offensives. The improvement in communications after 1870 only confirmed their faith in the technical feasibility of swift movement. By 1905, a German plan of attack had been prepared under the direction of General Count Alfred von Schlieffen (1833–1913), head of the general staff from 1892 to 1905. Modified somewhat in 1912, the Schlieffen plan further assumed a slow Russian mobilization, which would make it possible to hold the Russians in check with inferior forces while the main German army defeated the French. (The Germans had no high opinion of Austrian ability to contain Russia, and if Italy should prove to be hostile, major Austrian strength would have to be diverted to the Italian frontier. That the Germans thought they could capture Paris and the northern industrial regions of France within six weeks suggests that they also had a low opinion of the French army and its probable British ally.) Rapid victory in the West would then allow the transfer of the bulk of the German army to the East.

Von Schlieffen knew that the best French troops would be concentrated for an invasion in the region of Alsace-Lorraine. His assumption was, however, that if Germany moved in great strength through Belgium and into a region less well defended by the French, the French would be forced to abandon their invasion of Alsace-Lorraine and withdraw to the defense of Paris and the northwest. The most critical factor was time, and that went against the Germans from the start. Though in retreat, the Belgians managed to delay the German advance nearly two weeks, giving the British opportunity to cross the Channel and get into the line on the French left. Then the major German sweep into France began. Using the Metz-Thionville region as a pivot point, the German right wing began a clockwise wheeling movement which was designed to outflank the Anglo-French troops and force them eastward into the fire of the German left wing, which was to wait on the defensive in Alsace-Lorraine.

For several weeks the German advance was spectacular, forcing the allied line back until the French reached the valley of the Marne east of Paris. General Joseph Joffre (1852–1931), commanding the French, massed his reserves, in preparation for a counterattack. His opportunity came early in September, when the Germans, by wheeling eastward, exposed their right flank to attack by the French reserves. General Helmuth von Moltke (1848–1916) saw the danger, but not until he had already dispatched several corps to the Russian front, so confident was he of victory. Moreover, his headquarters was finding difficulty in maintaining communications with the fast-moving forces in the field. Moltke's attempts to modify the advance to meet the threat on the flank were thus unsuccessful, and gaps developed in the German line which Joffre exploited at the first Battle of the Marne. The result was a general German retreat to the north bank of the Aisne River, where the forces entrenched. Each side began a series of unsuccessful flanking movements on the west; this action had the effect of extending the battle lines westward until they reached the sea in Belgium. A stalemate was achieved by the spring of 1915, neither side able to crack the other's lines, which extended from the North Sea to Switzerland. This check destroyed the Schlieffen timetable and condemned the Germans to a two-front war.

The Russians, in fact, moved prematurely into East Prussia in the hope of diverting pressure from the French. Disorganized and unready for battle, the Russians were beaten near Tannenberg. Hardly a decisive battle like that on the Marne, Tannenberg did serve to boost German morale. Of greater import, Tannenberg misled the Germans into thinking that victory on the eastern front would be easy, and they abandoned the strategy of first knocking out the Anglo-French.

The Austrians, in the meantime, were in difficulties almost from the start. Half the strength earmarked for their invasion of Serbia had to be diverted to contain the unexpectedly early Russian advance. Consequently, the Austrian drives into Serbia were beaten back, until, by the end of 1914, they were temporarily abandoned. On the Russian front, the Austrians initially fared better; but in trying to send help northward to the Germans, the Austrians were caught in the flank and badly whipped. The Austrian chief of staff, General Franz Conrad von Hötzendorf (1852–1925), had to order a general retreat to avoid envelopment, and the defeat seemed to take the fight out of his forces from then on.

The threat of an Austrian debacle forced the Germans to send support and to consider the evacuation of territory occupied in Poland after Tannenberg. But because the Russians had not been ready for war in 1914 (their military reforms projected after the 1905 defeat were not scheduled for completion until 1917), they were forced to halt their offensives in the late fall of 1914. Moreover, since the Russians did not encode their wireless messages, the Germans were informed of serious Russian shortages in material and of the necessity to halt the offensives. Since the Germans could have spared few troops from the western front in 1914, it is tempting to speculate that, had the Russians possessed adequate supplies of rifles, ammunition, and equipment, they might have knocked Austria-Hungary out of the war in a few months and made the German position in Poland and East Prussia untenable. As it was, the eastern front was stabilized by the end of the year much like the western front. What is more, an entirely different kind of war than anyone had anticipated was developing, and one for which the prevailing vogue of the swift offensive could provide no successful tactics. The long lines on both the eastern and western fronts presented no vulnerable flanks to be turned, and the entrenched defenders soon proved the superiority of defensive firepower over offensive tactics. Not that the generals learned the lesson quickly; a survey of the campaigns after 1914 reveals the appalling fact that faith in the offensive led them to organize attack after attack at great human cost, without any appreciable decision being attained.

The entrenched defenders gained their superiority from the use of barbed wire as a defense against the sudden surprise attack; from machine guns, which were murderous against advancing infantry; and from an elaborate system of dugouts, which greatly reduced the effect of artillery fire.

Two civilians, both of them cabinet ministers, were the first to recognize the military stalemate in 1914 and the inadequacy of current strategy and tactics to end it: Winston Churchill (1874–) and David Lloyd-George (1863–1945). Churchill, First Lord of the Admiralty since 1911, saw the necessity of by-passing the western front by opening a new front elsewhere, and he sponsored the development of new weapons and tactics designed to eliminate the superiority of defensive firepower. The entry of Turkey into the war (October, 1914) on the side of Germany suggested a new theater of war to Churchill. Russia, just then showing that she could not sustain her offensive, for lack of supplies and equipment, now had to face Turkish pressure in the Caucasus region. Churchill's response to the entire crisis was to propose that the British navy blast its way through the Straits, force Turkey out of the war, and thus open a supply line to the Russians as well as open a new military front in the Balkans to take pressure off the Russians. In time, that new front would serve to link the eastern and western fronts. The British army, having already lost half its men on the western front, could spare no men, and the admirals opposed risking ships in confined, mine-laden waters against the fixed batteries of the Dardanelles. Yet, by the end of 1914, the cabinet gave Churchill permission to organize the naval assault upon the Dardanelles; and when it was agreed that the shores of the Dardanelles also ought to be taken (early in 1915), a mixed expedition of marines, regular army troops, Australians, New Zealanders, and French colonials was assembled.

These bold plans soon provided a classic example of a brilliant stroke's being reduced to humiliating fiasco, the consequences of which were enormous. The initial Anglo-French naval bombardments at the mouth of the Dardanelles were postponed by bad weather and gave the Turks valuable time to prepare. They were thus able to repulse the naval assault and inflict serious losses. Allied landings on the Gallipoli peninsula followed, but were not in sufficient force. Reinforcements were poured into the tiny area held, but they were always more than matched by Turkish reinforcements. By the end of 1915, there was nothing to do but evacuate, and the Allies had nothing to show for their 200,000 casualties. In the meantime, the Austro-Germans sought to take advantage of Russian exhaustion in early 1915—and to take action before the Allies might open the Dardanelles—by opening an assault (April, 1915). The Russian command was guilty of almost inexcusable laxity in the face of a German build-up and had no adequate reserves to meet a German breakthrough. A mixed Austro-German force cracked the Russian line, forcing the Russians to begin a general retreat to avoid envelopment. By fall they had abandoned Poland, Lithuania, and Courland, not to speak of the loss of nearly a million men. The final disaster for the Allies in 1915 came in Serbia, which was invaded in the fall after the halt of the Austro-German campaign in Poland. Earlier, the Serbs had bravely checked the Austrians. Now they had to face not merely Austrian and German forces, but those of Bulgaria as well. (The Russian defeat had encouraged Bulgaria to side with the Central Powers and Turkey.) The Serbs underwent terrible hardships in their retreat toward Albania and were eliminated as a fighting force by the end of 1915. The one bright spot for the Allies that year was the entrance of Italy on their side. Both sides had bidden for Italian support, and since the price seemed to be the Trentino and the Trieste area, which the Austrians refused to give up, the Central Powers had expected Italy to join the western allies in time. The secret Treaty of London (1915) conceded not only these territories to Italy, but the Cisalpine Tirol, the Dalmatian coast, and the Dodecanese islands as well. Austria, having committed much of her strength to the Russian front in 1915, was in danger on the south, but the Italian drives of 1915 did not achieve spectacular or decisive results.

Meanwhile, the deadlock in the West produced nothing but casualties and helped to turn Western attention to naval tactics to break the deadlock. Britain's blockade of the Central Powers was concentrated on the Channel and the North Sea; but since the United States insisted on the right of Americans to trade with neutrals, American goods reached Dutch and Scandinavian ports, a great part of them ultimately reaching Germany. Both the British and French governments increasingly checked this trade by more rigorous interpretations of what constituted contraband, and the North Sea was declared to be a military zone late in 1914. Faced with a shrinking flow of supplies, the Germans decided to risk a naval raid into the North Sea early in 1915. Admiral Ritter von Hipper's squadron was caught by Admiral David Beatty (1871–1936) off the Dogger Bank and taught the lesson of British naval superiority. This led the Germans to employ their last naval ace: their submarines. They issued a notice that they were blockading the British Isles and the

Channel and that all enemy ships coming into this war zone would be destroyed without warning. The effectiveness of submarines, after all, depended upon surprise attack, and if they surfaced to give warning, they were easily outrun and extremely vulnerable to the fire of armed merchantmen. And since Britain had urged her merchantmen to fly either neutral flags or no flags at all when in British waters, the Germans warned neutrals to stay out of British waters, since mistakes could easily be made. There might be no difference legally between Allied seizures of neutral merchandise as contraband and the German sinking of neutral ships, but world opinion reacted differently to the two procedures. Both could be called theft, but the sneak attacks cost many lives. The first neutral vessel sunk in 1915 was Norwegian; and when the Cunard liner *Lusitania* was torpedoed in May with a loss of 1,198 lives, including 139 Americans, the horror of the German blockade outraged American opinion and brought the United States close to war. Not until fall, however, was the German ambassador in Washington able to convince his government of the serious import of American opinion, whereupon William II gave assurances that there would be no more attacks upon passenger ships and neutral vessels without warning.

By 1916 the supreme commanders in the West, Joffre and Erich von Falkenhayn (1861–1922), were preparing vast efforts to break the stalemate, both convinced that the war could ultimately be decided in northern France. In the view of the Central Powers, the Russian front had been pushed so far eastward that the difficulties in maintaining communications suggested a concentration on France and Italy. It happened that Falkenhayn was ready to strike before the Anglo-French offensive was put in motion. Rather than attack all along the front, Falkenhayn decided to concentrate great strength against a point of spectacular value which the French considered impregnable. A victory here would give the Germans a great psychological advantage as well as a breakthrough. He selected the fortified city of Verdun, because it lay in a salient, with German forces on three sides. The opening bombardment was scheduled to open early in February, but bad weather forced a postponement of eight days and gave the French time to bring up reinforcements to meet the evident German concentration. The Battle of Verdun lasted into July, and the narrow confinement of the French meant that they were subjected to a frightful artillery pounding. As the Germans grew fearful of a collapse of their effort, they had recourse to poisonous gas. The French were ready for that, too, since gas had been used for the first time the previous year against the British. When the fighting ceased after four months of battle, the Germans counted 336,000 casualties, the French, 362,000. For this price, the Germans had advanced their lines around Verdun between 2000 and 4000 yards. No commander could justify such slaughter, and Falkenhayn was soon replaced by Generals Paul von Hindenburg (1847–1934) and Erich Ludendorff (1865–1937), who had won laurels on the Russian front. Hindenburg began construction of a defensive line which would soon permit a German withdrawal in order to shorten the front from 111 miles to 85 miles.

To keep the Germans off balance after Verdun, the British launched attacks along the Somme River. In the fall of 1916, they employed the new weapon which Churchill had sponsored before his dismissal from the Admiralty (following Gallipoli). Convinced that infantry alone could not overcome the barbed wire and machine guns, Churchill wanted a vehicle which could smash through the wire, protect its occupants from enemy fire, and bridge enemy trenches. The "tank" was the answer, so called because its development was hidden from the enemy with the pretense that the British navy was constructing new water storage tanks. The army had initially been uninterested in the tank, leaving the problem to the navy; and when tanks were first used in the Somme, only thirty-six were sent into action—and those were not properly followed by infantry. This circumstance led the Germans to minimize the effectiveness of tanks, but the British Commander, Sir Douglas Haig (1861–1928), saw their future and ordered a thousand more. Toward the end of 1916, the Hindenburg line was ready for occupancy, and the German retreat into it amounted to a withdrawal of between fifteen and thirty miles. Casualties along the Somme front were in excess of 600,000 for each side.

Elsewhere, in 1916, the Austrians had massed in the Trentino for an invasion of Italy, which the Italians had been expecting and were reinforced to meet. Timed to coincide with the German assault on Verdun, the Austrian drive was disappointing and finally had to be abandoned to meet a Russian attack in the east. All the participants had planned major offensives in 1916, but the Russians were not well organized or supplied for their effort. The first Russian commander ready to move, General Aleksei Brusilov (1835–1926), attacked the Austrians in June, his left flank adjacent to Romania. The swift collapse of the Austrian front revealed the serious demoralization of the Austrian army. Had the remainder of the Russian forces been ready to take advantage of the collapse, the whole eastern front might have crumbled as German counterattacks to aid Austria proved ineffective. Brusilov's drive halted only when he became starved for ammunition, leaving Russia to experience her anguish a second time: she was again denied victory for lack of supplies.

Brusilov's momentary success did encourage Romania to enter the war against Austria-Hungary, since the Russian victory seemed certain to lead to the partition of the Hapsburg Empire. While Romania had strong positions in the Transylvanian Alps, her situation became critical with Brusilov's failure. German, Austrian, Bulgarian, and Turkish troops converged on Romania, which was conquered in a few months. The Romanians had vainly hoped for some support from the Salonika front, an Allied army based on Greece. In 1915, when the Gallipoli campaign had been going badly and there was reason to suspect that Bulgaria would enter the war to participate in the destruction of Serbia, the Prime Minister of Greece, Elutherios Venizelos (1864–1936), offered to collaborate with the Anglo-French. He reasoned that Greek national interests would not be served by Bulgarian and Turkish victories, but he was handicapped by the pro-German attitude of Constantine I (*1913–1917*), who forced Venizelos's resignation. Late in the fall, the western allies shifted some of their troops from Gallipoli to Salonika, but this force accomplished nothing significant to aid Serbia because of uncertainty about Greek intentions. This ineffectiveness was repeated in 1916, when continual wrangling within the Salonika command prevented any aggressive moves against Bulgaria, which permitted her to concentrate her efforts against Romania.

The longer the stalemate in the West persisted, the more the German admirals were critical of the government's unwillingness to risk battle with the British in the North Sea. They argued also about the necessity of breaking the British naval blockade, which was affecting the morale of the home front, where food was in increasingly short supply, and they further advocated a return to unrestricted submarine warfare. The appointment of Admiral Reinhard Scheer (1863–1928) to command the High Seas Fleet in 1916 promised a more aggressive policy. His strategy was to begin sorties into the North Sea in the hope of engaging advance units of the British fleet and departing before major British support could reach the battle. As the Germans had some advantage ship for ship (their navy was of more recent construction), the strategy had merit; it was the only way to eliminate the British superiority in numbers, which was roughly eight to five. On the third such sortie, Scheer lured a British advance guard under Admiral Beatty into action off Jutland with the main German fleet and might well have destroyed Beatty's command had not the British grand fleet under Admiral John Jellicoe (1859–1935) suddenly appeared out of the mist. The Germans were able to escape into the night by dint of superb maneuvering and marksmanship and because the confusion of the battle made Jellicoe exceedingly cautious and unwilling to press his advantage. Because the Germans inflicted greater damage than they received, they claimed a victory; but they left the British in control of the North Sea and never again repeated the challenge. Had Jellicoe been less cautious, his casualties would have soared; but he had the strength to destroy the German fleet and failed to do so. It may be reckoned a serious error, which had momentous results. The retirement of the German fleet into the Baltic, where the British dared not follow, meant that Britain could not close in on the submarine bases nor open a supply line to Russia. Beginning in 1917, the Germans renewed unrestricted submarine warfare against almost all shipping in European waters as their only naval alternative, facing the fact that the Allied ability to buy munitions in the United States would spell doom for Germany unless she were able to prevent the supplies from reaching Europe. The United States immediately broke relations with Germany.

In a few weeks, British shipping losses rose tremendously, reaching a peak in April, 1917, when a quarter of the ships leaving British ports never returned. Lloyd-George then forced the naval authorities to adopt a convoy system, and there was a tremendous increase in shipbuilding and repairing. The entrance of the United States into the war that month was almost welcomed by the Germans as likely to divert supplies into the American effort, which could not become effective in Europe for some months. When the various reasons traditionally given to account for American intervention are examined, many of them must be discarded. While subject to Allied propaganda, the United States was not the victim of it. When Germany began sinking neutral ships and murdering noncombatants, she stood condemned in the United States. Britain was in desperate straits, and for all the traditional American suspicion of the British, it was nothing compared to the country's abhorrence of the possible victory of the German system with its avowed policy of world domination. Even economic interests in Britain and France as major customers became insignificant when compared to the frightful political implications of a German victory. President Woodrow Wilson himself contributed to obscuring the issues by viewing the conflict as a defense of international law and the freedom of the seas, thus turning American participation into a moral crusade to make the world safe for democracy. A useful device to whip up popular enthusiasm for the war, it had the effect of blinding many Americans to their political and economic interests in the war. Furthermore, when the world seemed not notably safer for democracy soon after 1918, many Americans concluded that they had been bilked by powers less righteous than themselves and advocated a withdrawal from further participation in continental affairs.

Excluding American intervention in 1917, the year was one of serious Allied reverses. General R. G. Nivelle (1856–1924), who had convinced the French government that he could crack the Hindenburg Line with shock assaults, was given command in place of Joffre. By then, most French generals had grown doubtful of the success of such tactics, and they were not wrong. His spring offensive gained a small salient, but at astounding cost of life, leading to considerable indiscipline in the infantry. Nivelle was then replaced by General Henri Philippe Pétain (1856–1951), while the British stepped up pressure on the Germans in the Arras area to give the French time to recover.

An Italian drive was timed to coincide with Nivelle's offensive, and a painfully slow advance inched the Italians forward all summer. Then, in October, the Austrians, reinforced with German units, counterattacked at Caporetto, in a region thought unsuitable for major action by the Italians. This surprise was augmented with the use of gas in the initial bombardment, which caught the Italians without proper gas masks. In the consequent panic, the Italians had to withdraw behind the Piave River. The German divisions were then gradually withdrawn from the Italian front for use along the Hindenburg Line, while the British and French had to rush troops—ultimately eleven divisions—into Italy to keep the Italians in the war.

By far the most disastrous military collapse occurred in Russia. Gigantic efforts had come to nothing, and the casualty figures were the highest of all the participants in the war. The backwardness of the national economy and the failure of the British to break through a supply line put a strain on Russia under which the imperial regime cracked. After the abdication of the Czar in March of 1917, a provisional government tried to rebuild the armies in the face of the advancing Germans while the country plunged deeper and deeper into revolution. A midsummer counteroffensive (the Kerensky offensive) against the Germans was a pathetic gesture with a hopelessly inadequate army—and one fatally undermined by

Communist agents; and when the Communists, pledged to peace at any price, seized control of the provisional government in November, the Russian war effort ended. The empire had begun to dissolve even earlier, in the wake of military defeat. Germany had recognized an independent Poland (March, 1917), which the Russian provisional government and Britain both recognized. In November, the secession of minorities to found independent states became a torrent; the Ukrainians, the Estonians, the Finns, the Bessarabians, and the Latvians followed in that order. On March 3, 1918, Russia signed the treaty of Brest-Litovsk with the Central Powers, agreeing to abandon the territories of the above-mentioned minorities, as well as Lithuania and Transcaucasia. German troops were ordered into the Ukraine and Finland to clear out the Russian Communists, the Germans hoping that the Ukraine would provide great quantities of food to offset the effects of the British blockade.

Despite these serious reverses to the Allied side during 1917, there were signs which justified Allied optimism. First, the British had been able to stir up an Arab insurrection against the Ottoman Empire (late in 1916) under the direction of Hussein, the Grand Sherif of Mecca, who called himself the King of the Arabs. Direct British military support in Mesopotamia and in Palestine provided a long succession of Anglo-Arabic victories. Secondly, Britain was evidently winning her fight against the submarines by the end of 1917. She was building at a faster rate than the Germans were destroying, and her antisubmarine tactics were inflicting serious losses on the German submarine fleet. A third indication of things to come was revealed in the battle of Cambrai late in the year. Haig used tanks in mass formation for the first time and did so with no preliminary bombardment. A spectacular breakthrough occurred, with sections of the Hindenburg Line succumbing. Most of the gains were wiped out, since the British had not anticipated the success and were unready to exploit it. Finally, only a few months later, fresh troops in large numbers would be crossing the Atlantic, more than offsetting the loss of Russia.

Unquestionably, the Germans saw the urgency of a quick decision in the West. At a time when the Allies had had to send eleven divisions to Italy, the Germans were transferring large numbers from the Russian to the western front. By March, 1918, when their last great blow fell upon the Allies, the Germans had built a force of 194 divisions. Pétain had 100 divisions, but many of them were not up to strength, and Haig had 51 divisions. Only the Americans could provide the reserves which were obviously needed. Allied weakness served to breed bickering between the British and French as to how their reduced strength should be employed, and after the German offensive began in March, Haig appealed for a combined command and volunteered to serve under Ferdinand Foch (1851–1929), who appeared to be more aggressive than Pétain.

By skillful use of his reserves, Foch managed to contain the German blows for several months, but in May an assault by forty-one German divisions against sixteen Allied divisions in the Chemin des Dames region achieved a breakthrough. The advance carried to the Marne River east of Chateau-Thierry, but produced a dangerous salient, since the Allies contained the wings. At that point, American forces were first introduced into the French line. Understandably, the Germans tried to widen their sector, but French artillery broke up all German efforts. Moreover, French intelligence began to provide unusually accurate information of German intentions. Thus, on July 15, the French were able to open heavy counter-battery fire on the Germans precisely thirty minutes before a scheduled German attack. This fight, which developed into the three-week second Battle of the Marne, broke the back of the German offensive and wiped out the Chemin des Dames salient. German casualties were notably higher than those of the Allies.

The initiative now went to the Allies, who began small-scale assaults upon isolated German salients; but the Germans recognized the likelihood of a major drive by Foch at any time. A German crown council met at Spa on August 14, in the presence of the Austrian Emperor, and decided to open negotiations for peace through the King of Spain and the Queen of the Netherlands. The expected Allied drive began on September 26, and after hard fighting, the Germans began giving ground. Then came news from the Salonika front, where the Allies, now with active Greek support, began pushing the Bulgarians back. On September 29, with the Central Powers withdrawing their troops for service elsewhere, Bulgaria asked for an armistice. General Ludendorff at once informed his government that the end had come, that it would be well to seek an armistice while the German army was reasonably intact. In response, William II reconstituted his government, naming the liberal Prince Max of Baden (1867–1929) as chancellor and decreeing the beginning of true parliamentary government. This belated enthusiasm for democracy was ostensibly aimed at uniting the country for a great defensive effort, but on the same day the German and Austrian governments appealed to President Wilson for an armistice, using the Fourteen Points as a basis for a peace settlement; such action suggests that this new democracy had an ulterior motive.

Wilson's Fourteen Points had first been voiced in an address to Congress (January 8, 1918) as an outline of American policy:

1. Open covenants openly arrived at.
2. Absolute freedom of navigation alike in peace and war, except as the seas might be closed by international action to enforce international covenants.
3. The removal, for far as possible, of all economic barriers.
4. Adequate guaranties that armaments would be reduced to the lowest point consistent with domestic safety.
5. An impartial adjustment of all colonial claims on the principle that the interests of the population must have equal weight with the claims of the government.
6. The evacuation of Russian territory and the free determination of her own political and national policy.
7. Evacuation and restoration of Belgium.
8. Evacuation and restoration of French territory and righting of the wrong done to France in the matter of Alsace-Lorraine.
9. Readjustment of the frontiers of Italy along clearly recognizable lines of nationality.
10. Opportunity for autonomous development for the peoples of Austria-Hungary.
11. Evacuation and restoration of Romanian, Serbian, and Montenegrin territory, together with access to the sea for Serbia.
12. The Turkish parts of the Ottoman Empire to be given a secure sovereignty, but the other nationalities to be given an opportunity for autonomous development, and the Dardanelles to be permanently opened to the ships of all nations under international guaranties.
13. An independent Poland, to include territories indisputably Polish, with free and secure access to the sea.
14. A general association of nations to be formed to afford mutual guaranties of political independence and territorial integrity to great and small states alike.

Prince Max's government was surprised to learn that Wilson now demanded, in addition to acceptance of the Fourteen Points, cessation of submarine warfare and evacuation of all occupied territory as precedents of an armistice. Just when the German government reconciled itself to the necessity of accepting these terms, Ludendorff recovered his nerve and denounced the terms. It became necessary to require his resignation.

On the Italian front, meanwhile, the Austrians had had bad luck in their attempt to coordinate their 1918 drive with that of the Germans and were seriously handicapped by wholesale desertions, especially on the part of minority nationalities within the army. Foch had vainly urged the Italians to counterattack at the time he was setting the Allied offensive in motion, but only in October, when the game had already been played on the western front, did General Armando Díaz (1861–1928) cross the Piave with the aid of his French and British divisions. The consequent victory at Vittorio Veneto was won at the expense of the demoralized Austrians and led to an armistice on November 4. This news reached Berlin just as a mutiny erupted in the German fleet at Kiel, the crews refusing to go on raiding sorties. The mutiny spread to other port cities and finally led to rioting in favor of peace. Prince Max finally prevailed upon the Emperor to abdicate, and on the same day, November 9, the Socialist leader Philipp Scheidemann (1865–1939) proclaimed the fall of the empire and the establishment of a republic.

The armistice commission had been received by Foch the previous day and was entirely civilian; Hindenburg hoped to place the onus of the defeat on others than the general staff, though it had been Ludendorff and he who had first insisted on a quick armistice. The terms were harsh, but there was no alternative to accepting them: Evacuation of Alsace-Lorraine and the Rhineland; troops to be withdrawn from occupied areas; the treaties of Brest-Litovsk and Bucharest (with Romania) abrogated; vast quantities of arms and submarines to be transferred to the Allies; the fleet to be disarmed and interned; and a large number of locomotives, trucks, and railway freight cars to be surrendered, to aid the immediate recovery of France and Belgium, whose industrial areas had been systematically razed by the retreating Germans in 1918. Hostilities ceased on November 11, 1918, ending the most appalling bloodletting Europe had ever known.

WORLD WAR LOSSES

	Dead	Wounded	Prisoner
Great Britain	947,000	2,122,000	192,000
France	1,385,000	3,044,000	446,000
Russia	1,700,000	4,950,000	2,500,000
Italy	460,000	947,000	530,000
United States	115,000	206,000	4,500
Germany	1,808,000	4,247,000	618,000
Austria-Hungary	1,200,000	3,620,000	2,200,000
Turkey	325,000	400,000	No figures

THE RUSSIAN REVOLUTION

Before summarizing the postwar settlement, we must return to the Russian Revolution. In reviewing the rise of the revolutionary movement, one is struck by evidence that even well-meaning attempts by the imperial government to reform produced an inordinate amount of dissatisfaction. The emancipation of the serfs, for example, and the subsequent redistribution of land left an immense residue of grievances on the part of those who felt they had been despoiled and on the part of those who felt that they ought not to have been required to pay for lands received, not to speak of those who were dissatisfied with what they received. Peasant rioting was widespread in the 1860's, often receiving encouragement from liberals and radicals who organized themselves into the Land and Liberty Society (1862). On the whole, the peasants did not trust these intellectuals who supported them, driving many of the latter to the conclusion that there was no hope of a revolution based on the rural population. Nevertheless, the intellectuals' dissatisfaction with the land reforms kept them on the peasants' side and made them ungrateful for Alexander II's other progressive reforms of local government, the judicial system, and education. As the hope for a peasant revolution faded, radical opinion increasingly favored terrorism, culminating with the formation of the Will of the People (1879), a society openly dedicated to the assassination of the Czar.

The organization achieved its mission in 1881, only to find that the assassination did not set off general revolt. Instead, Alexander III launched a program of vigorous repression which cost many lives and postponed the development of more liberal government. This was the more critical, because it came during the beginning of industrialization with its usual abuses, creating a further dimension of grievances to which a repressive government was indifferent. Furthermore, industrialization brought with it more socialist movements like those in the West, and these competed with the earlier anarchist and terrorist organizations. The first Russian Marxist party was organized in 1883 by Georgi V. Plekhanov (1857–1918), then an exile in Switzerland. Not until 1898, however, was the party organized within Russia with a direct appeal to industrial workers —the Russian Social Democratic party—under the leadership of Julius Martov (1873–1923) and Vladimir Ulianov, known as Lenin (1870–

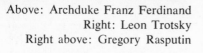

Above: Archduke Franz Ferdinand
Right: Leon Trotsky
Right above: Gregory Rasputin

Above: Lenin (Vladimir Ulianov)
Left, left to right: Vittorio Orlando (Italy), David
Lloyd-George (Great Britain), Georges Clemenceau
(France), Woodrow Wilson (United States),
at the Paris Peace Conference, 1919 Below: Nicholas II,
the Last Czar, and His Family

1924). Governmental repression was swift, forcing the leaders to promote the party from exile.

A second socialist party appeared in 1901, the Socialist Revolutionaries organized by Victor Chernov (1876-1952). More in keeping with traditional radicalism, the SR's worked among the peasants and saw the struggle strictly in national terms, whereas the Marxist SD's favored international organization; class warfare, as the Marxists saw it, knew no national distinctions. The SD's, however, were soon divided among themselves, the split appearing at a party congress in London in 1903. One faction, led by Lenin, wanted to restrict party membership to a few, highly disciplined professional revolutionaries who would direct the masses; the other faction, led by Martov and supported by Leon Trotsky (1877-1940), preferred a party open to all supporters, as was the case with the German Social Democratic party. This dispute mirrored a deeper division; the uncompromising revolutionaries of the Lenin persuasion were opposed by those who preferred nonviolent, parliamentary, evolutionary means. By a narrow margin, the Lenin factions gained control of the congress of 1903; henceforth, the word Bolsheviks (majority) was used to describe Lenin's group, while Mensheviks (minority) referred to the Martov-Trotsky faction. The SD party maintained its outer unity, but the inner split was never healed and actually deepened.

It should not be thought, however, that all the opponents of the autocracy found their way into one of the two socialist parties. Men whom we should call liberals in the nineteenth-century sense, who sought representative government, began to organize after the turn of the century. These liberals were often men who had participated in the district and provincial zemstvos and who felt it was high time to crown the reforms of Alexander II with the creation of a national parliament. They were joined by many professional men with the organization of the Union of Liberation (1903) by Professors Paul Miliukov (1859-1943) and Peter Struve. Instead of bending with the storm, the government became increasingly intransigent; and it happened that those ministers who favored closer cooperation with the liberals—and were therefore dropped from the government—were also the ones who opposed the aggressive foreign policy in the Far East. Nicholas II (*1894-1917*) showed little political sagacity and was kind to a point of weakness. He was simply incapable of fathoming the growing opposition and easily fell victim to conservative advice. Thus, in response to a message from the Zemstvo of Tver (1895) on the subject of national representation, he could write of the "senseless dreams as to the participation of the Zemstvo in the general direction of the internal affairs of the State"; and he gave notice of his adherence to the principle of autocracy.

Liberal and socialist agitation produced strikes and rioting which continued to get worse, despite the repressive efforts of the minister of the interior, Viatscheslov Plehve (1846–1904). The outbreak of the Russo-Japanese War early in 1904 served to moderate opposition to the government as patriotism naturally increased; but when military disasters were compounded by naval fiascos, criticism revived. In St. Petersburg on January 9, 1905, a Sunday, a great crowd of striking workers, with their families, marched to the Winter Palace to petition the Czar to grant a constituent assembly, to transfer the land to the people, and to establish an eight-hour day. Troops, ordered to break up the demonstration, did so at the cost of hundreds of lives, whereupon the outraged public protested violently, and disorders and assassinations grew in number. As we noted earlier, the government became sufficiently alarmed to make an untimely peace with the Japanese.

Because this revolution in 1905 grew spontaneously from the Bloody Sunday incident, it caught the radical leaders unprepared to exploit the opportunity. Not until October was Trotsky able to organize a Workers' Council (Soviet) in St. Petersburg, and this body served as the real governing agency of the city for nearly fifty days. Both factions of the SD party took part in the soviet, as did the SR's, but Lenin arrived in Russia too late to seize the initiative from Trotsky. The Bolsheviks also led an uprising in Moscow which produced a week of bloody fighting. By the end of 1905, the government was able to bring back sufficient forces from the Far East to restore its authority, and the savage reprisals were reminiscent of the Paris Commune.

In the meantime, Nicholas II had been forced to recognize the necessity of modifying the autocracy. On the advice of Count Witte, the Czar issued his Manifesto of October 17, which promised the election of a national assembly—the Duma—on a broad franchise and further stated that all legislation in the future would require consent of the Duma. The October Manifesto rallied the liberals to the government and helped break the back of the revolution. The new constitution presented by Witte in 1906 was a great disappointment and revealed the insincerity of the Czar's promise to inaugurate true parliamentary government. Popular representation in the Duma was sharply restricted by a complex system of indirect election designed to insure the election of the wealthy, and the Duma was denied any check upon the budget, foreign affairs, and the armed forces. Moreover, an upper house, the Council of State, half-appointed by the crown, was created to provide a check upon the Duma. The arrangement smacked all too much of Bismarck's constitution for the German Empire, as the liberals were quick to see.

The socialist parties took no part in the elections for the 1906 Duma and remained dedicated to the overthrow of the monarchy, leaving the field to the liberals, who had just reorganized themselves in the Constitutional Democratic Party (known as Cadets), with Miliukov still their leader. Looking back on the first Duma, nothing reveals the bankruptcy of the imperial regime more than its total failure to produce a legislative program to meet an undeniable national crisis. The government had grudgingly granted the election of a Duma, and it expected the deputies to be satisfied with the form rather than the substance of a parliamentary regime. In the absence of any governmental program, the Cadets provided one, proving simultaneously that the monarchy required the services of the liberals if the monarchy were to survive. Not that the government saw the light: a quarrel quickly developed when the Cadets proposed a land-reform measure which would have compelled landowners to sell large tracts to peasants at moderate rates. The Cadets saw no other way to rally the peasantry to the government and to destroy the SR party, but the Czar dissolved the Duma rather than permit the legislation.

Meanwhile, in 1906, the Czar had appointed a new minister of the interior, Peter Stolypin (1863–1911), whose chief recommendation for office was that he had not lost control of the province of which he was governor in 1905. He became prime minister at the time of the dissolution of the Duma, and he announced the summoning of a second Duma for 1907. In the meantime, he devoted himself to a ruthless suppression of all opposition which followed in the wake of the dissolution, often declaring martial law in particular regions to deal more quickly with his opponents. He did not, however, obtain a more docile Duma in 1907. The Cadets did lose strength, but much of it went to the socialist parties, who had decided to participate in the second election. It was an opportunistic move, since the socialists' aim was to show (by the use of obstructionist tactics) that the Duma could not effectively deal with critical national problems and to discredit further the Cadets, who were still the majority party. On the extreme right, the Cadets were under fire from reactionaries who hoped not merely for dissolution, but for abolition, of the Duma. Stolypin tried to solve the deadlock by excluding the SD deputies on the grounds that they were attempting to subvert the army; and when other members demanded proof of the charge, Stolypin replied with a decree of dissolution.

The government then drastically revised the election law, with the result that the subsequent Dumas were conservative and did not represent popular opinion. For a time, the government even fell victim to the illusion that it had vanquished the revolutionaries, because many of them went abroad after the second Duma. But nothing was done to satisfy peasant demands for lands belonging to the nobility and industrial conditions failed to improve measurably, showing that governmental optimism reflected a sad inability to gauge public sentiments and a childish faith in the possibilities of unending repression. Aside from the government's embarrassment over the obvious influence of the notorious Gregory Rasputin (1871–1916) upon the imperial family, all *seemed* well by 1914 as far as the regime's stability was concerned. Rasputin's ascendance at court, on the other hand, suggests that the regime had succumbed to the most disreputable and irresponsible interests and could provide no vigorous or enlightened leadership. A debauched Siberian peasant parading as a holy man and a healer, Rasputin had been presented at court by people who knew the Empress' predilection for anyone who might protect the life of the Czarevitch—a hemophiliac. Repeated demonstrations of an ability to stop the Czarevitch's bleeding won Rasputin a position with the imperial family which enabled him to dictate many appointments in the state and church. Whether he was inspired by reactionary elements at court has remained a question, but certainly his appointments favored reactionaries.

The coming of war in 1914, as in 1904, rallied the public behind the regime, and the morale of the army seemed excellent. But as we know already, nothing went right for the Russians from the start. The reorganization and equipping of the army, begun after 1905, was not scheduled for completion before 1917, and Russia's industrial plant was not capable of supplying deficiencies at a satisfactory rate. Her field and staff commanders were untried and poorly trained, and, in one notable case in 1914, showed an unwillingness to coordinate the movements of armies, presumed to be cooperating, because of intense personal antagonism. This latter instance led to the disaster at Tannenberg and the loss of men and guns which were hardly replacable. By 1915, infantry reserves were being committed unarmed to battle, forced to remain under fire until they could pick up the weapons of the dead and wounded. The wonder is that under such demoralizing conditions the army remained intact during the necessary retreat of 1915.

News of the disaster reached the capital, though the ministers tried to keep the Duma uninformed of the true situation at the front. The evident incompetence in high places condemned the reactionaries in power and revived the reform movement in the Duma. By mid-1915, two-thirds of that body joined the progressive bloc led by the Cadet Miliukov, and their attacks upon the minister of war finally forced the Czar to replace him. On the other hand, the Czar decided to go to the front to take command himself, a task for which he had no preparation. He ignored the Duma's plea that he remain in St. Petersburg as head of the government and really turned over his powers to the Empress—in effect, to Rasputin. In this situation, the Duma found it impossible to promote the candidacy of reputable officials. Given the desperate efforts of the troops during 1916 against Austria only to suffer failure for lack of munitions, it is small wonder that the progressives in the Duma were stirred to high anger at those around the throne. Miliukov put it squarely before the Duma: "Is this stupidity or is it treason?" Two members of the highest nobility took matters into their own hands by assassinating Rasputin late in 1916, but the deed came much too late to save the regime.

The outbreak of revolution in March, 1917, was not led by the radical parties but seems to have been a spontaneous outburst of public outrage at governmental incompetence, which had produced nothing but defeat, food shortages, and inflation. Strikes of protest in St. Petersburg brought great mobs into the streets, and the government soon found its troops unreliable. Only after the government had lost control of the major cities did the radicals organize a soviet in the capital; and in the meantime the Duma had sent word to Nicholas II that his abdication was necessary, suggesting that he appoint a regency. The Czar gave way with his usual softness, but he was unable to persuade his brother to accept the throne, in view of the obvious hostility of the people to the monarchy. To fill his void, the leaders of the Duma felt the need to form a government; otherwise the more radical soviet might well assume power. On March 16, 1917, a provisional government took office under the Prime Ministry of Prince George E. Lvov (1861–1925), a Cadet. Professor Miliukov became foreign minister, A. I. Guchkov the minister of war, while a member of the SR party, Alexander Kerensky (1881–   ), became minister of justice. Kerensky was also a member of the soviet, and while he served as a useful link between the provisional government and the soviet, he joined the government as an individual rather than as a member of the SR.

The provisional government was seriously handicapped from the outset by the presence of the soviet, the former being more conservative than the latter; each was distrustful of the other. Moreover, the first order promulgated by the soviet, directing the troops to obey the provisional government only insofar as its orders did not conflict with those of the soviet, was not only a direct threat to the provisional government, but also an assumption of sovereignty by the soviet. As the soviet proceded to organize soldiers' councils (soviets) in all army units, the provisional government soon recognized that it was dependent upon the soviet for military support. For the moment the military problem was not serious, since the Soviet was dominated by Mensheviks and SR's who favored continuation of the war just as the provisional government did; but when it came to the old question of distribution of land to the peasants, both governments recognized the probability of conflict.

This initial harmony over foreign policy was short-lived. Miliukov, in assuring his western allies that Russia intended to stand by them, let it be known that Russia expected to obtain the Straits and Constantinople. This demand produced an outcry from the socialists in the soviet who, while favoring a defensive war, followed the line that wars are imperialistic and that all peoples should demand that their governments abandon annexationist policies.

The chief pillar of reaction in the world, the "Gendarme of Europe," [the Czar] is no more. May the earth turn to heavy granite on his grave! Long live freedom! Long live the international solidarity of the proletariat, and its struggle for final victory! . . .

Conscious of its revolutionary power, the Russian democracy announced that it will, by every means, resist the policy of conquest of its ruling classes, and it calls upon the people of Europe for concerted, decisive action in favor of peace. We are appealing to our brother-proletarians of the Austro-German coalition, and first of all, to the German proletariat. . . .[6]

Lenin, who was still in Switzerland at the fall of Nicholas II, held the view that wars are manufactured for the benefit of capitalists, and that those socialists who had been patriotically backing the war in their own countries were traitors to the proletariat. He meant to return to Russia and lead the Bolsheviks in an attempt to seize control of the soviet in St. Peters-

6. Appeal of the Petrograd Soviet, March 27, 1917, quoted in J. S. Curtiss, *The Russian Revolutions of 1917* (Princeton, 1957), pp. 119-120.

burg, whereupon it would be possible to bring the war to an end while establishing a dictatorship of the proletariat. No Allied country, understandably, would permit Lenin to cross its territory; but the German government made it possible for Lenin to reach Denmark across German territory, in the hope that he would succeed in his desire to remove Russia from the war. He crossed Scandinavia and reached St. Petersburg in mid-April, but his antiwar program at first failed to stir even the Bolsheviks. He immediately embarked on a campaign of speeches to sell his program, and it was not difficult to convince the war-weary, land-hungry masses that it was time for peace and time to give all the land to the peasants. His growing popularity forced the Bolsheviks to fall in line and laid the ground for a direct challenge to the provisional government. Popular demonstrations for peace became so threatening that General Laurent G. Kornilov (1870–1918), commander of the troops in St. Petersburg, proposed to crush them; but the soviet prevented the soldiers from leaving their barracks. Miliukov and Guchkov saw the hopelessness of their positions and resigned from the government, whereupon the entire provisional government was reconstituted.

This revised regime, while still Cadet-led, had six socialist ministers, including Kerensky as minister of war. On July 1, the last Russian offensive of the war was launched and had some success in Galicia; but the army was far too impoverished and demoralized to sustain a drive. Austro-German counterattacks turned the offensive into an appalling rout. Meanwhile, the troops in the capital, apparently fearful of being sent to the front, set off demonstrations demanding that the soviet replace the provisional government. Without much doubt, the soviet could have assumed power, but the socialist leaders held back, reluctant to sanction the overthrow of the provisional government by force. In the aftermath, considering that even Lenin had failed to take advantage of the opportunity to seize power, the charge was made that he was a German agent. The charge, though probably not correct, was believable, considering German efforts to put Lenin into Russia, and he found it necessary to go into hiding in Finland to avoid being arrested for treason.

These events gave the provisional government a lease on life, and had that government possessed an ounce of political acumen, it would have moved to satisfy the evident popular demand for peace and land redistribution. Instead, the government held to its earlier view that the war must be continued in search of victory and that major internal adjustments must await the election of a constituent assembly in November.

This attitude prevented the provisional government from winning the support of the masses, who turned more and more to Bolshevik leadership; and it provided the extreme right with an opportunity to muster strength for a reactionary coup. Worse, the weakness and passivity of the government encouraged two national minorities to assert their independence: the Finns and the Ukrainians. The government's uneasy position was revealed by Prince Lvov's resignation on July 21, and though the consequent reshuffling of ministers made the government more socialist than before, it seemed even less inclined to take those drastic steps necessary to win national support. In short, the provisional government reached a paralysis not unlike that which afflicted the imperial regime before its downfall.

At the end of July, Kerensky, who had become the chief figure in the government, appointed General Kornilov to be head of the army. There was good reason to suppose this dashing martinet to be the only commander who might be able to restore discipline and turn what had become an armed rabble into a fighting force. Yet, his known conservatism rightly raised a question as to his loyalty to a socialist government; and when he proposed to deal with the soviet as if it were composed of pro-German traitors while Kerensky was still hoping for harmony and unity, Kornilov lost all faith in Kerensky. The General then involved himself in a plot to seize power in the process of crushing the soviet in St. Petersburg, and an attempt was made to bring Kerensky into the camp of the conspirators. He wavered and ended by ordering Kornilov's resignation and by warning the soviet of its danger. His equivocation wrecked his remaining prestige and left the field to the two extremes; and those who wanted to save the Revolution had no alternative but to throw themselves into the defense of the capital, under eventual Bolshevik leadership. Kornilov's advance in September was obstructed by the railway workers under soviet direction; they managed thoroughly to confuse all troop movements by rail, and the attempted coup collapsed without any fighting.

The provisional government's authority waned with Kerensky's prestige, and in the fall of 1917 the peasantry had begun the seizure of landed estates. At the same time, the Bolsheviks came to dominate the soviets in St. Petersburg and Moscow. Lenin insisted that the time had come to overthrow the provisional government, but most of the Bolsheviks were as reluctant as they had been in July; and Lenin's task was to persuade his own party that a tiny minority, if backed by the masses, could establish a government. It is revealing of Kerensky that, expecting an attack by the Bolsheviks, he took no effective measures to meet it. His final days of office in November were full of confused orders and counterorders, and he saw his troops—under the influence of soviet propaganda—refuse to fire on the forces sent by Lenin and Trotsky to seize the government and the command of the army. He had to flee in disguise and found refuge in France.

While it is true that the program of the victorious Bolsheviks had never been clearly spelled out, Lenin did mean to take immediate steps to insure his support by the mass of the peasantry—which was the bulk of the population. He let it be known, therefore, that there would be an immediate end to the war and that the property rights of the nobility would be destroyed. His pronouncements were not limited to the national scene; he also suggested that the revolution in Russia would prove to be merely the prelude to an international revolution. His first speech before the St. Petersburg Soviet (November 7) ended with the cry: "Long live the world socialist revolution!" The following day the soviet government proposed to establish a three-month armistice and to renounce all the gains Russia had been promised by her allies. A second decree pronounced the immediate end of private landholding without compensation to landowners, the lands to be turned over to soviets of peasants' deputies for distribution to the peasants. They were not to own it, but merely to work it; but the decree did establish individual rather than collective farming.

For some weeks, the exact nature of the soviet government was in doubt. Would it be a coalition of the socialist parties or an all-Bolshevik cabinet? In the end it was largely Bolshevik but included the ex-Menshevik Trotsky and three of the more radical SR's. Beginning in December, 1917, the revolutionary decrees of the new government became a steady flow. All banks were nationalized that month, followed by a ban on all dividends and securities. On February 10, 1918, the government repudiated all debts, including foreign debts, contracted by the imperial regime; this ruling hit the French especially hard, since they had been the primary lenders to Russia. While Lenin intended to nationalize the industries too, he wanted to postpone this in order to keep industry functioning. Nevertheless, industrial workers were allowed to form soviets for the purpose of supervising the managerial personnel; since this dual control only produced confusion, however, the government assumed the power to nationalize wherever necessary. To deal with deliberate political opposition as well as with the everyday disorders of a society made chaotic by war and revolution, the government appointed the All-Russian Extraordinary Commission (Cheka), an agency which did not shrink from using terror to shut off opposition and illegal activity; very informal people's courts were used by the regime to obtain speedy convictions without benefit of traditional law.

The provisional government, before its overthrow, had promised the calling of a constituent assembly, and elections had been set for November 25, 1917. Lenin feared to hold elections, believing that the peasantry would probably vote for its traditional party, the SR, leaving the Bolsheviks a minority. His ultimate decision to proceed with the elections was made in the knowledge that he had the military power to dissolve the assembly if it became obstructive. The outcome was as Lenin had predicted, the SR's gaining the majority; but the Bolshevik minority was far better organized, and its strength lay in the industrial centers and in its control of the army. This fact enabled Lenin to intimidate the majority from the outset. If the constituent assembly were not willing to promote the general program outlined by the Bolsheviks, the assembly would have to go. At the assembly's first meeting, the SR's gave evidence of intending to seize control, which led Lenin to disallow a second session. No longer was there any doubt that a dictatorship by the Bolsheviks had been established. Nor was there any doubt that violence would be regarded a legitimate weapon by that dictatorship:

Comrades! Every time I speak on this subject of proletarian government someone . . . shouts "Dictator." Yet [there was a time] . . . when everybody was in favor of the dictatorship of the proletariat. . . . You cannot expect . . . that socialism will be delivered on a silver platter. . . . Not a single question pertaining to the class struggle has ever been settled except by violence. Violence when it is committed by the toiling and exploited masses is the kind of violence of which we approve.[7]

THE POSTWAR SETTLEMENT

We may now turn to the postwar settlements beginning in 1919, having already noted the earlier Treaty of Brest-Litovsk. The Peace Conference opened in Paris early in 1919 under the presidency of Georges Clemenceau (1841–1929), the premier of France; aged, cynical, and probably the ablest diplomat at the conference, he sought the permanent

7. Lenin's speech of January 24, 1918, quoted in *Ibid.*, p. 183.

weakening of Germany as a measure of French security. David Lloyd-George (1863–1945), the Liberal prime minister since 1916, represented Britain and found himself in an equivocal position; he favored a moderate peace with Germany but knew that the British public expected a vengeful peace. Public opinion had been especially inflamed late in the war when the retreating Germans systematically destroyed property in Belgium and France. The Italian representatives, Premier Vittorio Emanuele Orlando (1860–1952) and Foreign Minister Baron Sidney Sonnino (1847–1921), were chiefly concerned to see that the secret treaties which had brought Italy into the war were honored. The idealistic American President Wilson was a sharp contrast; by far the most popular man in Europe because of the generosity of his views, his authority had been undermined when the Democrats lost the congressional elections of 1918; and his idealism equipped him poorly to be a diplomat, because compromise was inconceivable to him. Twenty-eight other states were represented, many having become belligerents late in the war simply to obtain a seat at the conference; and many national groups wishing to become states sent representatives. The Russians, already engaged in civil war, were unrepresented, as were the defeated powers and the neutrals; these absences contributed to the notion that peace was to be imposed by the victors rather than negotiated.

On the whole, the great decisions were made by Clemenceau, Wilson, and Lloyd-George, and if one dared to name a focal point for the mass of complexities with which they dealt, it would be the problem of squaring the Fourteen Points with the realities of European politics. First, Wilson had composed the Fourteen Points without a profound knowledge of European problems and before the Germans had revealed themselves at Brest-Litovsk. Secondly, the Germans were soon to raise the protest that they had surrendered on the promise that the Fourteen Points would be the basis for the peace. It is true that they had offered to surrender on that basis; but by that time their treatment of Russia and Romania revealed that they did not truly adhere to the Wilsonian principles. This led even Wilson to insist that the German surrender must be unconditional, which it was; aside from the actual armistice terms, none of the defeated powers knew what the final terms would be. Since great publicity had been given to the Fourteen Points, it was an easy matter, when the harsh peace settlement became known, for the defeated powers to cry that they had been betrayed. Excluding them from the negotiations in Paris simply lent weight to the charge.

The harsh peace settlement had not been easily achieved by the Allies. A mass of compromises, it did seek to guarantee that Germany would not revive as a military state. The treaty of Versailles (1919) required Germany to return Alsace-Lorraine to France and to cede two small frontier areas around Eupen and Malmédy to Belgium. A plebiscite was to be held in Schleswig to determine how much of the province should be returned to Denmark. On the east, since the Allies were committed to re-establishing Poland, they required Germany to surrender the old Polish provinces of Posen and West Prussia, where the population was still largely Polish. This created a difficult problem by separating East Prussia from Germany proper and by isolating the German city of Danzig within Polish territory. Germany was, therefore, given the right of free transit across the "Polish Corridor," while Danzig was made a small free state under the supervision of the League of Nations. On the southeast, a plebiscite was to be held in Upper Silesia to see, on a national basis, what portion should be given to the new state of Czechoslovakia.

The ultimate status of the Saar Basin, adjacent to Lorraine, was left in doubt. France was given ownership of the coal mines in the Saar for fifteen years to compensate her for the deliberate destruction of property by the Germans in 1918, but the area was to be administered by the League of Nations. After fifteen years, the League was to conduct a plebiscite in the region to determine whether it should be annexed by France or restored to Germany. France further obtained a demilitarization of the Rhineland—that is, Germany was forbidden to fortify her territory on the left bank of the Rhine as well as on a band of territory on the right bank to a depth of thirty miles. The German armed forces were sharply limited by the treaty: 100,000 men and 4000 officers in the army on long-term enlistment; no air force; a small navy without submarines, a personnel no larger than 15,000.

The treaty also contained a "war-guilt" clause: "Germany accepts the responsibility of herself and her allies for causing all the loss and damage to which the Allied and Associated Powers and their nationals have been subjected as a consequence of the war imposed upon them by the aggression of Germany and her allies." Therefore, Germany was to pay reparations for damage done to civilian property and population, a sum which was not determined by the treaty, but which would be calculated by an Allied Reparation Committee by May 1, 1921. Germany was to make a token payment of five billion dollars in the meantime. By signing the treaty, Germany pledged to pay an unknown amount, at a time when her territorial losses reduced her ability to pay. Aside from the total loss of her colonial empire, which was given to the League of Nations for disposal, Germany lost only one-eighth of her country; but that eighth contained 65 per cent of her iron ore and 45 per cent of her coal. Further pressure was put on Germany by making the Covenant of the League of Nations the first section of the treaty of Versailles. A violation of the harsh treaty could put Germany at odds with all the members of the League. On the other hand, as Wilson saw it, the existence of the League would make possible the removal of the injustices in the treaty; and however harsh the treaty seemed in retrospect, the evidence is that the one which the Central Powers would have dictated would have been harsher.

It remained to draw up treaties for the other defeated powers, all of whom had surrendered unconditionally. An attempt was made to recognize the rights of self-government for nationalities in the establishing of new frontiers; as a result, the Austro-Hungarian Empire was virtually dismembered. The fact that this empire had had an economic unity, which was to be destroyed by the new frontiers, led a member of the British peace delegation, John Maynard Keynes (1883–1946), to argue that the entire 1919 settlement was being made without any consideration of economic realities. Since Keynes also anticipated that Germany would be charged an unrealistic figure for reparations, he began a major assault upon the peace settlement; this criticism was soon copied by all those whose interest it was to show the settlement to be unjust. Probably Keynes was right to protest against the indifference to economic realities, but his book, *The Economic Consequences of the Peace* (1919), had the unfortunate result of obscuring both the just aspects of the peace and the reasons for German liability.

The Hapsburg monarchy did not survive the war, and separate treaties were arranged for Austria and for Hungary, St. Germain-en-Laye (1919) with the former, and Trianon (1920) with Hungary. Austria was reduced to roughly 25 per cent of her former share of the Dual Monarchy in both population and territory. Bohemia, Moravia, and most of Austrian Silesia went to the new state of Czechoslovakia; Galicia was ceded to restored Poland; and the Teschen district was ultimately divided between Poland and Czechoslovakia. To Italy, the Austrians ceded the Trentino, Trieste, Istria, and a few islands off Dalmatia. The South Tirol was also given to Italy, despite its predominantly German population, because the Italians insisted that they must control the Brenner Pass region for defensive purposes. Bosnia, Herzegovina, and the Dalmatian coast joined Serbia in the new state of Yugoslavia. Finally, Bukovina was given to Romania. The

Austrian army was to be limited to 30,000, and the treaty forbade union with Germany (*Anschluss*), which some Austrians had intimated would be the salvation of Austria in the face of these territorial losses. *Anschluss,* however, would have strengthened Germany and constituted a threat to Czechoslovakia, which accounts for the Allied disapproval. In the treaty of Trianon, Hungary ceded Transylvania and about two-thirds of the Banat to Romania. The remainder of the Banat went to Yugoslavia, as did Croatia-Slavonia. Slovakia and Ruthenia were given Czechoslovakia, while a small territory called Burgenland was ceded to the Republic of Austria. While the Allies had insisted that Austria form a republican government, they permitted the Hungarians to retain the forms of monarchical government but forbade the restoration of the Hapsburgs. The extraordinary political chaos in Hungary was the reason for the concession. Her army was limited to 35,000 men. She emerged from the war reduced to about 40 per cent of her former population.

Bulgaria astonished the Allies by trying to avoid any responsibility for the war, blaming Ferdinand I, who had abdicated immediately before the armistice, and thereby insisting that Bulgaria should be given territories "properly" hers on ethnic grounds. The treaty of Neuilly (1919), however, obliged Bulgaria to give Western Thrace to Greece, thus cutting Bulgaria off from the Aegean Sea; and she ceded four small but strategically valuable border districts to Yugoslavia. The treaty of Sèvres (1920) was the last work of the Paris peacemakers and the first to be undermined. Signed by the Sultan's representatives for Turkey, the treaty outraged Turkish nationalist opinion and contributed to the overthrow of the monarchy. In consequence, the treaty was never executed, but was replaced in 1923. The treaty of Sèvres did acknowledge an actual fact, however: Turkey had lost her claims in North Africa, in Arabia, Palestine, Mesopotamia, and Syria; and the future of this lost empire was to be determined by the League of Nations.

The victorious Allies were soon given a slap which seriously compromised the peace settlement from the outset: The Senate of the United States failed to ratify the treaty of Versailles, necessitating a separate peace with Germany. No doubt the reasons for this rejection of Wilson's treaty were many, and, of course, since ratification of a treaty requires a two-thirds majority, the rejection was actually the work of a minority. Yet, it cannot be ignored that in the face of considerable popular enthusiasm for the League of Nations, the country returned a Republican congress in 1918 and elected a Republican president in 1920, thus greatly enhancing the probability that the treaty would fail. It has been noted that the United States demobilized rapidly after 1918, and the public showed itself more eager for "normalcy" than for any other cause or condition. Perhaps this was an expression of American immaturity when it came to international politics; but more likely it was an expression of deep suspicion that Wilson had gone to Europe and fallen into a den of wolves. Security from further betrayal at the hands of America's friends suggested to the nation a withdrawal from further participation in world affairs. Had the war been more realistically approached in 1917—or before—the United States would have been spared much of the subsequent disenchantment. As it was, the Messiah came home to witness his work disavowed, and the useless crusade he undertook to rally public support suggests that he had not learned the necessity of politics from the initial failure. In any event, he did not live long enough to see his goal of "perpetual peace" fade farther into the future.

THE SOCIAL IMPACT OF THE WAR

Population losses during World War I were of such magnitude as to affect drastically the social fabric of all the belligerent countries. Russia suffered the most casualties in sheer numbers, but the nation suffering the greatest casualties in proportion to its total population was France. All the countries involved, however, found themselves with a serious deficit of men after 1918; in Britain, for example, the discrepancy approached the figure of 1100 women for every 1000 men. Moreover, the European birth rate, already declining before 1914, dropped sharply during the war, forecasting a manpower shortage for years to come. Such an imbalance, quite apart from its economic and military consequences, had a long-term impact upon the morale of the European peoples. The fact that while their men were at the front, women had been mobilized as never before for work on farms and in factories accounts for their greater emancipation after 1918. Britain rewarded her women over thirty with the vote in 1918.

Indeed, the total mobilization of all the national resources, to which the belligerent powers had been driven during the war years, had a lasting effect upon European economic and social thinking. It became reasonable to suggest that governments direct equal efforts toward peacetime mobilization of the national resources, so that the benefits of industrialization could be more quickly and generally realized. It seemed inconsistent to assume that the state had the right to draft a man only during times when he was likely to be killed. Such thinking merged with the postwar hopes that the national states would provide security against any further wars, so that one might describe the climate of opinion as "welfare-minded." Whereas the liberal of the nineteenth century dwelt upon those things which the government ought not do, postwar liberalism defined new realms for government controls. This movement was not suddenly born in 1918, of course, but was the culmination of tendencies toward mercantilism which we have already seen to be characteristic of Europe after 1871.

THE AFTERMATH: REFLECTIONS ON VIOLENCE

The loss of life and the vast waste of capital during World War I was only the beginning of the catastrophe. It is not an exaggeration to insist that Europe, along with much of the rest of the world, has never since enjoyed real peace. Granted that the world war was not solely responsible for the militant climate after 1918, it did serve to break up the old order of nineteenth-century Europe and to bring into primacy the forces of nationalism and socialism, which, as we earlier noted, had been gravitating toward violence for several decades before the war. In 1908, a French engineer named Georges Sorel (1847–1922) published his *Reflections on Violence,* which suggested a curious blend of Marxian dialectical materialism and class struggle with Nietzschen ideas of the will to power. Out of this synthesis, Sorel saw the labor union as the logical organization to promote the proletarian revolution, making the general strike the ultimate weapon in class warfare; this political creed has been called syndicalism. In the next chapter, we shall see that many of the postwar dictatorial states, whether leftist or rightist, were led by men who accepted violence as the solution to social and international problems. This is not so surprising when we discover that, whether they ended as leftists or rightists, they generally began political life on the extreme left and were imbued with a common body of ideas, which we may loosely call "Sorelian." Thus we can understand the reasoning of a distinguished Spanish philosopher who wrote:

When the reconstruction of the origins of our epoch is undertaken, it will be observed that the first notes of its special harmony were sounded in those groups of French syndicalists and realists of about 1900, inventors of the method and the name of "direct action." Man has always had recourse to violence; sometimes this recourse was a mere crime, and does not interest us here. But at other times violence was the means resorted to by him who had previously exhausted all others in defence of the rights of justice which he thought he possessed. It may be regrettable that human nature tends on occasion to this form of violence, but it is undeniable that it implies the greatest tribute to reason and justice. For this form of violence is none other than reason exasperated. . . . Civilization is nothing else than the attempt to reduce force to being the *ultima ratio* [final reason]. We are now beginning to realise this with startling clearness, because "direct action" consists in inverting the order and proclaiming violence as *prima ratio,* or strictly as *unica ratio.* . . . It is the Magna Charta of barbarism.[8]

8. Jose Ortega y Gasset, *The Revolt of the Masses* (New York, 1932), pp. 81-82.

SUGGESTIONS FOR FURTHER READING

᠈᠈᠖

The Coming of the First World War, and the War Itself

Sidney B. Fay, *The Origins of the World War* (New York: Macmillan, 2nd edition, two volumes in one, 1930), an immensely valuable and moderate work.

Bernadotte E. Schmitt, "July, 1914: Thirty Years After," *Journal of Modern History,* XVI (1944), 169-204.

The New Cambridge Modern History, Vol. XII: The Era of Violence, 1898-1945 (Cambridge University Press, 1960), many good essays rather than a survey.

G. P. Gooch and H. W. V. Temperley, eds., *British Documents of the Origins of the War, 1898-1914* (London: British Foreign Office, 1926).

Edward M. Earle, *Turkey, The Great Powers and the Baghdad Railway* (New York: Macmillan, 1923).

E. L. Woodward, *Great Britain and the German Navy* (New York: Oxford University Press, 1935).

Luigi Albertini, *The Origins of the War of 1914,* 3 vols. (London: Oxford University Press, 1952-57).

Chung-Fu Chang, *The Anglo-Japanese Alliance* (The Johns Hopkins Press, 1931).

A. J. Marder, *The Anatomy of British Sea Power: A History of British Naval Policy in the Pre-Dreadnought Era, 1880-1905* (New York: Alfred A. Knopf, 1940) and *From the Dreadnought to Scapa Flow: The Royal Navy in the Fisher Era, 1904-1919* (London and New York: Oxford University Press, 1961).

Gordon A. Craig, *From Bismarck to Adenauer: Aspects of German Statecraft* (The Johns Hopkins Press, 1958).

R. H. Lutz, *The Fall of the German Empire, 1914-1918,* 2 vols. (Stanford University Press, 1932).

G. Ritter, *The Schlieffen Plan* (New York, Praeger, 1958).

D. W. Brogan, *France Under the Republic: 1870-1939* (New York: Harper, 1940).

R. H. Soltau, *French Parties and Politics, 1871-1921* (London and New York: Oxford University Press, 1930).

William C. Askew, *Europe and Italy's Acquisition of Libya, 1911-1912* (Duke University Press, 1942).

Hugh Seton-Watson, *The Decline of Imperial Russia, 1855-1914* (London: Methuen and Co., 1952).

Oscar Jászi, *The Dissolution of the Hapsburg Monarchy* (University of Chicago Press, 1929).

A. F. Pribram, *Austrian Foreign Policy, 1908-1918* (London: G. Allen and Unwin, 1923).

Oswald H. Wedel, *Austro-German Diplomatic Relations, 1908-1914* (Stanford University Press, 1932).

Ernest E. Ramsaur, *The Young Turks: Prelude to the Revolution of 1908* (Princeton University Press, 1957).

W. S. Vucinich, *Serbia Between East and West: The Events of 1903-1908* (Stanford University Press, 1954).

B. H. Liddell Hart, *A History of the World War, 1914-1918* (Boston: Little, Brown, 1935).

Sir James E. Edmonds, *A Short History of World War I* (London and New York: Oxford University Press, 1951).

Harry B. Rudin, *Armistice, 1918* (Yale University Press, 1944).

Sir Frederick B. Maurice, *The Armistice of 1918* (London and New York: Oxford University Press, 1943).

The Russian Revolution

William H. Chamberlin, *The Russian Revolution, 1917-1921,* 2 vols. (New York: Macmillan, 1952).

Edward H. Carr, *A History of Soviet Russia: The Bolshevik Revolution 1917-1923,* 3 vols. (New York: Macmillan, 1951-53).

Hugh Seton-Watson, *The Pattern of Communist Revolution: A Historical Analysis* (London: Methuen and Co., 1953).

Alexander F. Kerensky, *The Prelude to Bolshevism* (New York: Dodd, Mead, 1919) and *The Catastrophe* (New York: D. Appleton, 1927).

Robert D. Warth, *The Allies and the Russian Revolution from the Fall of the Monarchy to the Peace of Brest-Litovsk* (Duke University Press, 1954).

Richard Pipes, *The Formation of the Soviet Union: Communism and Nationalism, 1917-1923* (Harvard University Press, 1954).

John S. Reshetar, *The Ukrainian Revolution, 1917-1928* (Princeton University Press, 1952).

Leon Trotsky, *The History of the Russian Revolution*, 3 vols. (New York: Simon and Schuster, 1932).

Clarence J. Smith, *Finland and the Russian Revolution, 1917-1922* (University of Georgia Press, 1958).

John S. Curtiss, *The Russian Revolutions of 1917* (Princeton University Press, 1957).

The Peace Settlements

Harold W. V. Temperley, ed., *A History of the Peace Conference of Paris*, 6 vols. (London: H. Frowde, and Hodder and Stoughton, 1920-24).

P. Birdsall, *Versailles Twenty Years After* (New York: Reynal and Hitchcock, 1941).

John M. Keynes, *The Economic Consequences of the Peace* (New York: Harcourt, Brace and Howe, 1920).

Thomas A. Bailey, *Wilson and the Peacemakers*, 2 vols. (New York: Macmillan, 1947).

S. P. Tillman, *Anglo-American Relations at the Paris Peace Conference of 1919* (Princeton University Press, 1961).

L. A. Yates, *United States and French Security, 1917-1921: A Study in American Diplomatic History* (New York: Twayne Publishers, 1957).

Louis Fischer, *The Soviets in World Affairs, 1917-1929: A History of Relations Between the Soviet Union and the Rest of the World*, 2 vols. (Princeton University Press, 1951).

Stanley W. Page, *The Formation of the Baltic States* (Harvard University Press, 1959).

Titus Komarnicki, *Rebirth of the Polish Republic: A Study in the Diplomatic History of Europe, 1914-1920* (London: W. Heinemann, 1957).

⚹ 14 ⚹

The Decline of Europe
1923–1945

THE MORAL CLIMATE AFTER VERSAILLES

If, in 1919, one looked at the general results of the world war, one might well have concluded that the world had indeed been made safer for democracy. The bastions of liberal government—Britain, France, and the United States had emerged victorious while the four major autocracies—Germany, Austria-Hungary, Russia, and Turkey—had crumbled. As for the prospects of "perpetual peace," a League of Nations had been born, providing an agency for the settlement of international disputes and a sounding board for international opinion. Yet, when Marshal Foch remarked that year, "This is not Peace. It is an Armistice for twenty years," he was much closer to the truth than were the postwar optimists. General war, in fact, broke out exactly twenty years later. Moreover, in 1939, the war was broader in scope than in 1914—more truly a world war. No single factor can be cited to explain the failure of the peace settlement, but it may not be amiss to list a number of factors, which, together, contributed to the instability of the European order:

1. The failure of the victorious Allies to cooperate in promoting the peace, most critically exemplified by the refusal of the United States to participate in the League of Nations.

2. The fantastic costs of the war, an unheard-of destruction of life and capital, left a multifaceted problem of recovery, not the least of which was a recovery of morale. The very magnitude of the catastrophe called for the utmost in international cooperation to plan economic and financial recovery; but instead, selfish national interests were allowed to take precedence.

3. This suggests the immense residue of hatred after 1918. Nationalism did not become less virulent than before the war, but seemed intensified. The harshness of the peace inflamed the defeated peoples, while the newly independent nationalities seemed bent on revenge against former oppressors; and however attentive the peacemakers had been to the formation of nation-states, it was quite impossible to construct them without including national minorities, who almost invariably proved to be troublesome.

4. The League of Nations was improperly constituted. Without power to enforce its decisions, the League soon found itself ignored and insulted by bullies the world over.

5. The success of the Bolsheviks in establishing their dictatorship in Russia, when coupled with their call for revolution elsewhere, threatened all established regimes and all those who believed in the right to hold private property. Given the other factors hampering a quick European recovery, the threat of communism loomed even larger.

Taken together, these factors constituted fear, weakness, lack of vision, opportunism, and materialism expressed by selfishness and hatred—hardly a suitable climate for the growth of a durable peace. It would be a gross oversimplification, however, to ascribe the climate solely to the demoralization spawned by devastating war. European civilization had been approaching a cultural crisis decades before 1914; the war laid bare the sickness, a sickness which culminated in the phenomenon of Nazi Germany. There every great tradition of European civilization was to be ridiculed or perverted, to be replaced by a barbarism comprising violence, irrationality, power for its own sake, anti-intellectualism, and racism. In essence, the Third Reich was to evince a total disdain for God and man.

THE NEAR EAST

It is possible to go beyond Marshal Foch and insist that, not only was there no peace after 1919, but that even the armistice was too consistently violated to be called a true armistice. Conflicts were limited in scope, and some of them took nonmilitary forms—what we have come to call in our time "cold war"—but the general climate was militant. Let us look first at the circumstances in the Near East which upset the treaty of Sèvres with Turkey. During the war, it had been understood between Russia, Britain, and France that Russia would get Constantinople and the Straits upon the defeat of Turkey, that Palestine would be internationalized, and that Britain and France would have spheres of influence in Mesopotamia and Syria respectively, as well as in the independent Arab state that would emerge from the war. By 1919, the Bolsheviks had abandoned all claims to Turkish territory, and a strong national movement led by Mustapha Kemal Pasha (1880–1938) was determined to prevent the partition of the country by the western Allies. This led the Allies to occupy Constantinople to protect the Sultan and to allow the Greeks to occupy Smyrna and the Italians to occupy southwestern Anatolia; after which the treaty of Sèvres was signed with Sultan Mohammed VI (1918–1922). As noted in the previous chapter, all non-Turkish territories were abandoned by the Sultan; Greece was to administer Smyrna for five years, after which a plebiscite would be held to determine the district's future; Italy was to keep Rhodes and the Dodecanese; Armenia was to become independent; but Constantinople and its hinterland were to remain Turkish, though the Straits were to be internationalized and demilitarized.

In 1920, a nationalist regime led by Kemal was established at Angora (later Ankara) and immediately disavowed the Sèvres settlement. This led the Greeks to advance from Smyrna toward Angora. The new regime promised a liberal republic for Turkey, and it was only too evident that it would have popular support. Thus, Italy, France, and Russia decided to negotiate with Kemal, leaving the Greeks—who had British backing—dangerously exposed. In 1922, Kemal began a counteroffensive against them which ended in the destruction of Smyrna and the evacuation of the Greeks. A British threat to defend the internationalization of the Straits brought Kemal to terms, but he was given Adrianople and a portion of eastern Thrace at the expense of Greece in exchange for accepting the neutralization of the Straits. Kemal then proclaimed the overthrow of the Sultanate, and a new peace conference undertook the revision of the treaty of Sèvres to embody the above changes won by fighting and negotiation; by the treaty of Lausanne (1923), Italy did retain the Dodecanese islands, and the non-Turkish parts of the Empire were lost, but Kemal had made a come-back at the expense of Greece, and he negotiated a compulsory exchange of populations with Greece in order to expel Greek residents of

Turkey. Greeks had, of course, lived in Anatolia since ancient times. The transfer of populations, directed by the League of Nations, uprooted roughly one million Greeks, sending them to tiny Greece; while the Turks retrieved about 100,000 of their nationals still living in Greece. This exchange had grievous results for Greece, which could hardly absorb such an influx of population. The crisis incidentally found the British and the French on opposite sides and marked the beginning of their postwar antagonism.

FIUME

Given the limited value of Italian military efforts during the war, it might be thought that her postwar territorial acquisitions were generous. But the Italians had expected even more, the city of Fiume and the Dalmatian coast in particular. Dalmatia, on national grounds, had been given to Yugoslavia, and the Italians had walked out of the Paris conference when it became evident that Wilson rejected their claim to Fiume. Late in 1919, the poet Gabriele D'Annunzio (1863-1938) flew a small force of Italian war veterans to Fiume, which they seized for Italy. Since Yugoslavia claimed the city, it was left for Italy and Yugoslavia to settle by negotiation. Their treaty of Rapallo (1920) made Fiume an independent city-state, and D'Annunzio and his cape-and-dagger-wearing band were expelled. Italian opinion remained outraged and led Mussolini, after his rise to power, to curry favor by renegotiating Fiume's status with Yugoslavia. In 1924, Yugoslavia gave in and allowed Italy to annex most of the city, leaving several outlying areas of the port for Yugoslav use.

RUSSIA AFTER BREST-LITOVSK

Far greater violence was the case in Russia, where the Bolshevik ascendance was soon challenged, especially after the signing of the treaty of Brest-Litovsk (1918) at a time when the war was still being fought by Russia's former allies. Lenin might argue that Russia had no power to resist the harsh settlement dictated by the Central Powers, but any treaty which cost Russia about 1,300,000 square miles and over sixty million people was bound to shock patriotic opinion. When this was followed later in the year with a treaty by which the soviet government agreed to pay Germany six billion marks in reparations, many Russians, like the western Allies, believed that Lenin was turning Russia into a German puppet state and permitting Germany to turn her full military power into those last offensives of 1918. The Russian nationalists realized with horror that if France and Britain were to fall, there would be nothing to prevent the entire Soviet Union from being annexed to the German Empire. Thus, the developing civil war in Russia was not merely an ideological opposition to Bolshevism, but a patriotic outburst as well. On the other hand, Lenin found backing for his peace settlement from those who wanted an end to the war at any price. Their support gave the Bolsheviks the opportunity to build the Red army, which Trotsky undertook as commissar for war.

The Great Civil War (1918–1920)[1] was actually a series of struggles between the Bolsheviks (who had newly moved the capital from St. Petersburg to Moscow) and various opposition groups; and the inability of those various factions to coordinate their efforts proved fatal to their cause. Perhaps it was too much to expect that monarchists, liberals, Social Revolutionaries, and Mensheviks could form a common front. They were somewhat compromised, too, by the appearance in Russia of foreign troops— especially British, French, and American—who hoped to prevent arms from falling to the Germans and who were hostile to the revolutionary regime. Naturally, this intervention favored those parties in Russia which opposed peace with Germany, and the Bolsheviks portrayed it as an improper foreign interference into Russian affairs. A third factor hampering the opposition, commonly called the White movement, was its ambiguous attitude toward the newly independent states (Poland, Finland, Lithuania, Latvia, and Estonia) carved out of the Russian Empire, not to speak of the fact that neither Reds nor Whites were sympathetic to demands for autonomy by such peoples as the Cossacks and the Ukrainians.

This conflict of interests can be illustrated by what happened in the Ukraine, where an independence movement had been recognized early in 1918 by Germany and Austria. The Bolsheviks soon unseated the Ukrainian regime in Kiev, but they were forced to abandon the province by the treaty of Brest-Litovsk. After the collapse of Germany in the West, White forces under General Denikin overran the Ukraine and received support from a French mission which landed at Odessa. (It may be noted that the French, of all the Allies, were most embittered by the Bolshevik defection during the war and persisted in regarding the Reds as German agents.) Meanwhile, the Poles saw this confusion in the Ukraine as an opportunity

1. In its course the Czar and his family were shot (July 16, 1918), by Red guards. Red, the traditional radical color, now meant Bolshevik.

to amend the Paris peace settlement, from which they had emerged dissatisfied. Poland's eastern frontier had been a controversy even in the nineteenth century, when Poland was a Russian province. From among the conflicting claims, the peacemakers in Paris had selected the "Curzon Line" (named after Lord Curzon, a British diplomat) as Poland's eastern frontier, depriving the Poles of Vilna (incorporated into Lithuania) and of a slice of White Russia (Belorussia) and the Ukraine. When the Bolsheviks determined to drive General Denikin and his Whites out of the Ukraine (1919), the Whites sought alliance with the Poles but could reach no satisfactory arrangement, being unwilling to cede any substantial amount of territory to the Poles. Consequently, the Poles did not intervene and allowed the Bolsheviks to drive General Denikin out of the Ukraine by the end of 1919. Several months later, they demanded that the Soviet government grant them the frontiers of 1772—that is, those of prepartition Poland—and when these negotiations failed, the Poles both began an invasion of the Ukraine and seized the city of Vilna.

While the Poles succeeded in taking the Ukraine, the Red army in a counteroffensive swept them out and all the way back to Warsaw. There the Poles were stiffened with the aid of a French military mission and were able to drive the Reds out of Poland. By the treaty of Riga (1921), the Poles made some gains on the eastern frontier at the expense of Russia, but Vilna, in the meantime, had been ceded by Russia to Lithuania; this act the Poles refused to accept. Since Vilna was an ancient center of Polish culture, the Poles demanded that a plebiscite be held in the city under the auspices of the great powers. In the plebiscite of 1922, the city voted to go with Poland, whereupon the Polish-Lithuanian frontier was revised at the expense of Lithuania. Diplomatic relations between the two countries were not restored until 1938, so infuriated had the Lithuanians become over the issue.

As for the Russian civil war, the isolated centers of resistance in the Ukraine, in Siberia, and in the Caucasus succumbed by the end of 1920. In the Far East, the Soviet government had to deal with the Japanese, who had taken advantage of the Revolution to land troops at Vladivostok late in 1917. This led the United States, Britain, and France to land contingents as well, principally to contain Japan, but also to provide help for an army of Czechs which was moving toward Vladivostok in the hope of being transported to Europe. Taken prisoner earlier on the Austrian front by the Russians, these Czechs had formed a legion after the collapse of the Russian regime (1917) in the expectation of helping in the fight against the Central

Powers, out of which would emerge an independent Czech state. The Allies in Siberia, as elsewhere, were anti-Bolshevik, and they only evacuated when it became evident that the Bolsheviks were winning the Civil War. Japan did not remove her troops, however, until 1922. By that date, Lenin was well under way with his program of national recovery.

THE LEAGUE OF NATIONS

These samples of postwar conflict, while perhaps the most violent to be found in Europe, were symptomatic of the militant climate everywhere in Europe. Woodrow Wilson had argued that the League of Nations would become an instrument to remove the injustices from the postwar treaties and to impose a durable peace; it was evident that the League's work was tailored and ready, only awaiting the completion of the organization. The Covenant of the League formed the first part of each of the postwar treaties and became effective in January, 1920, when the treaty of Versailles was ratified. The League was an association of sovereign states, at first to include the thirty-two nations who had broken relations with Germany and thirteen neutrals who would be invited to join. Additional members could be elected by a two-thirds vote of the member nations. An assembly, a council, and a secretariat comprised the League's machinery, each member nation being allowed three delegates (but only one vote) in the Assembly; thus all states were put on an equal footing. In the Council, however, five of the nine seats were given permanently to the great powers—Britain, France, the United States, Italy, and Japan. The four nonpermanent seats were to be filled by election from the Assembly, presumably to represent the smaller states. Most decisions by both Council and Assembly required a unanimous vote. Geneva, in neutral Switzerland, was chosen for the headquarters of the Secretariat. As for policing League decisions, everything depended upon the willingness of the member states to honor their obligations to the League. A nation could resign from the League by giving two years' notice of its intention. As we noted earlier, the League was given the responsibility of guiding the development of former German colonies and parts of the former Turkish Empire. These territories were to be mandated to "advanced nations" by the League, and their development toward self-government was to be annually reviewed by the League. Otherwise, the chief League functions involved the reduction of armaments and the investigation of all disputes in order to promote inter-

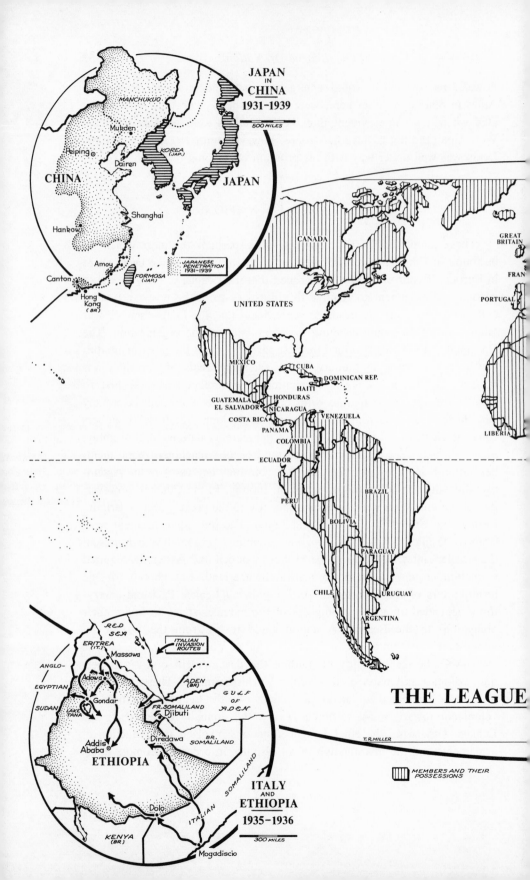

JAPAN
IN
CHINA
1931-1939

500 MILES

MANCHUKUO

Mukden

Peiping

KOREA
(JAP.)

Dairen

CHINA

JAPAN

Shanghai

Hankow

Amoy

JAPANESE
PENETRATION
1931-1939

Canton

FORMOSA
(JAP.)

Hong
Kong
(BR)

CANADA

GREAT
BRITAIN

FRAN

PORTUGAL

UNITED STATES

MEXICO

CUBA

DOMINICAN REP.

HAITI

GUATEMALA
EL SALVADOR

HONDURAS

NICARAGUA

VENEZUELA

LIBERIA

COSTA RICA

PANAMA

COLOMBIA

ECUADOR

BRAZIL

PERU

BOLIVIA

PARAGUAY

CHILE

URUGUAY

ARGENTINA

RED
SEA

ERITREA
(IT.)

Massawa

ITALIAN
INVASION
ROUTES

ANGLO-
EGYPTIAN

Adowa

ADEN
(BR)

GULF
OF
ADEN

SUDAN

Gondar

FR. SOMALILAND
Djibuti

LAKE
TANA

Addis
Ababa

Diredawa

BR.
SOMALILAND

ETHIOPIA

THE LEAGUE

T.R.MILLER

Dolo

ITALIAN
SOMALILAND

ITALY
AND
ETHIOPIA
1935-1936

300 MILES

KENYA
(BR)

MEMBERS AND THEIR
POSSESSIONS

Mogadiscio

RHINELAND REOCCUPIED

MARCH, **1936**

|———| 100 MILES

NETHERLANDS

• Essen

Cologne

BELGIUM

GERMANY

Sedan •

LUX.

Verdun •

Metz

• Karlsruhe

Paris
⊙

FRANCE

Toul •

Strasbourg

RHINE

WEST
WALL

MAGINOT
LINE

Besançon •

SWITZ.

SWEDEN
FINLAND

ESTONIA
LATVIA
LITHUANIA
GERMANY
CZECHOSLOVAKIA
POLAND
AUSTRIA
HUNGARY
RUMANIA
BULGARIA

DEN.

SOVIET UNION

YUGO.

ITALY

TURKEY

GREECE

SYRIA
(FR. MAND.)

IRAQ
(BR. MAND.)

IRAN

AFGH.

CHINA

JAPAN

EGYPT

SAUDI
ARABIA

PALESTINE &
TRANS-JORDAN
(BR. MAND.)

MARIANAS IS.,
MARSHALL IS., &
CAROLINE IS.
(JAP. MAND.)

(BR.)
CAMEROONS
(FR. MAND.)

ETHIOPIA

TANGANYIKA
(BR. MAND.)

AUST.
MAND.

W. AFRICA
OF S.A. MAND.

UNION OF
SOUTH AFRICA

AUSTRALIA

NEW
ZEALAND

OF NATIONS

NON-MEMBERS

LEAGUE
MANDATES

FRANCE

Zaragoza •

Barcelona

PORTUGAL

Toledo •

⊙ Madrid

• Teruel

SPAIN

MAJORCA

Cordoba •

• Granada

OCCUPIED
BY FRANCO
MARCH, 1937

**SPANISH
CIVIL WAR**

1936–1939

SP.
MOROCCO

Ceuta •

ALGERIA
(FR)

|———| 150 MILES

FR.
MOROCCO

national peace. The Secretariat was also to pursue international cooperation for humanitarian projects, such as the suppression of slavery and
forced labor, and ending the traffic in women, children, and drugs.

One notes at once that the League was designed with an assumption
of American participation. The British Parliament had accepted the Covenant of the League unanimously on that assumption and was then rudely
awakened to several of the implications of the American retreat. While
the Covenant did not provide the League with an armed force to back up
its decisions, it did contain a provision obliging all member states to break
trade and financial relations with any nation which went to war. It had
taken courage for a trading nation such as Britain to pledge support of
such a provision, and when the British came to realize that the United
States would not be bound by such a commitment, the question was raised
as to whether economic sanctions against an aggressive power could succeed. In the case of France, the American withdrawal was shocking for
other reasons. France had wanted the Rhine as her northeastern frontier,
but she had been persuaded by Wilson and Lloyd-George to abandon the
claim in exchange for treaties guaranteeing French security. When the
United States then refused to ratify such a treaty, the French felt betrayed;
this sentiment was heightened when the British allowed their treaty with
France to lapse. The collapse of allied wartime unity had the effect of
hardening the French attitude toward Germany, since German recovery
seemed increasingly menacing to a France deprived of allies.

ECONOMIC CRISIS: WAR DEBTS AND REPARATION

The spirit which had founded the League of Nations found little reflection in the economic policies of most European countries after the war.
Instead, one finds conflict and revenge. In some cases, we find nations
enacting discriminatory economic measures, such as high protective tariffs
as an expression of hostility. This was especially evident in Central Europe,
where the large free-trade area of the Dual Monarchy dissolved into small
sovereign states, each with separate currencies and tariffs. An even more
serious problem derived from the fantastic costs of the war, which had
forced all belligerents into heavy taxation and borrowing. France, for
instance, doubled her tax income during the war years, while Britain
tripled hers, and both governments had been obliged to liquidate sizable
foreign assets in payment for badly needed supplies. Interallied borrowing

was also necessary, the wealthier nations assisting the weaker. By the end of the war, the United States was a creditor for roughly seven billion dollars, Britain for about the same, and France for two and a quarter billion dollars. Repayment of such debts could only take place after the various national economies had made the adjustment to peacetime production, and this was usually hindered by the political dislocations and unrest during the first years of the peace. In the meantime, governments borrowed more money to quicken economic recovery, so that by 1922, the United States had become a net creditor for ten billion dollars and France a creditor for three and a half billion dollars, while the British had slipped to four and a half billion dollars. Both Britain and France felt that debts incurred during the war should be written off to the war effort, especially since there was no hope of collecting what had been lent to Russia and that only postarmistice debts should be honored. Both powers granted major concessions, therefore, to their debtors, only to find themselves in difficulties because in America the Harding administration held firm on collecting the entire debt. As President Coolidge later phrased it, "They hired the money, didn't they?" This American attitude left the European Allies no alternative but to press for German payment of reparations, even when there was considerable doubt about the wisdom of having demanded reparations in the first place.

In 1921, the Reparations Commission submitted to Germany a total bill of thirty-three billion dollars, a staggering sum for a country which had at that point an unfavorable balance of trade. The installments were to be spread over thirty years. Considerable German private capital was immediately invested abroad to avoid the high taxation which was obviously coming, a factor hindering the transition to a peacetime economy. Worse, an inflationary spiral was spawned when the government began to print paper money to meet its expenses and when the Germans began to purchase foreign currencies to meet the first installment. Both practices lowered the value of the German mark on the international market. Before the end of the year, Germany notified the Reparations Commission that she could not meet the 1922 payment and asked for a two-and-a-half-year moratorium. Allied reaction was mixed, the British being inclined to give Germany time to recover, the French and Belgians, in greater need of immediate economic relief, being unwilling to grant the moratorium. At the beginning of 1923, when Germany was found to be in default by the Reparations Commission, Franco-Belgian troops occupied the Ruhr to force payments. The apparent split in the Allied ranks encouraged the

German government to sponsor passive resistance in the Ruhr; this action gave the final impetus to the German inflation rocket. Before the end of the year, the mark had fallen to a rate of 4,200 billion marks to the dollar —meaning that it was worthless. Germany was as bankrupt as were Franco-British relations.

Perhaps the French would have been less militant in 1923 had the Germans not drifted toward the Soviet Union during the previous year. The two countries signed a treaty of friendship at Rapallo (1922) which, by threatening the existence of the new state of Poland, sharply alarmed France. Had she known of the secret clauses in the Rapallo agreement, her alarm would have been greater, because they provided for the training of German troops in Russia. The instructions of German Chancellor Joseph Wirth (1879–   ) to his new ambassador to Russia shed considerable light on German intentions: "Poland must be disposed of. My policy is set towards this goal. . . . It is . . . with my agreement that many things, too, have happened relative to the eastern frontier which are known only to a few besides myself. On this point I am in complete agreement with the military."[2]

Meanwhile, a new reparations commission was appointed under the leadership of the American Charles G. Dawes; this group reduced the annual payments required of Germany to a point thought consistent with her power to pay and recommended that certain taxes be earmarked for reparations funds. The Dawes plan did not, however, reduce the total burden, but did grant a moratorium on payments until 1926. It also recommended a 200-million-dollar loan to encourage German recovery. In 1929, a new reparations committee under another American, Owen D. Young, provided new loans to Germany and reduced the annuities by extending the period of the debt to 1988. These arrangements were completed just in time to be doomed by the world economic crisis.

The debate continues as to how much Germany really did pay in reparations. Except for those reparations demanded immediately after the armistice, it is doubtful that Germany paid in reparations as much as she gained from foreign loans. She had been able to force her creditors to help finance her recovery in the hope of recovering their money, and in the end they got nothing. The residue of bitterness, however, was enormous. Interallied confidence had vanished, and, what was more important, by 1923, the Germans experienced a psychological and moral collapse in response to economic ruin. Hatred, fear, and hysteria overcame them

2. Quoted in *The New Cambridge Modern History,* Vol. XII, pp. 469-470.

—especially the property owners—to the point where, ten years later, they were ready to hail the most irrational of modern regimes.

THE SUCCESSION STATES

So far, we have chronicled an unsavory story. One might well ask whether there were no positive results from the World War; at least, whether there were not honest attempts to nail down the peace and establish more democratic governments. In fact, there were many honest attempts, and to review them is to revive the heartbreaking drama of good intentions engaged with insuperable forces of degradation and ruin. The "succession states"—those which emerged from the disintegration of the autocratic empires—had their individual problems; but they all suffered economically from the plethora of new frontiers, and all were rendered politically unstable by aggravated nationalism, which kept both foreign and domestic relations in a stew. Moreover, those who wished to make European society more democratic were continually fought by those whose sole wish was to destroy the postwar settlement and to recover lost ground and power.

Take the new Republic of Austria. Her loss of territory and population left her in the peculiar position of a state in which nearly half the remaining population lived in Vienna and its environs. She had become a head without a body. Her political parties soon revealed internal divisions so sharp that the practice of "loyal opposition," so crucial to the development of genuine party government, seemed improbable. The Social Democrats, an anticlerical party, drew strength from Vienna, including the Jewish community; the Christian Socialists, a Catholic party, was strong in rural areas. Finally, the Nationalist party was a pan-German organization which agitated for *Anschluss* (union) with Germany. The Christian Socialists, who were the most middle-of-the-road, were the majority party, but they found themselves opposed on many occasions by a coalition of the two extremes. Englebert Dollfus (1892–1934), who became the chancellor in 1932, tried to end party strife by ending parliamentary government and establishing a dictatorship of the Christian Socialists. In 1934, he was assassinated during an unsuccessful attempt by the Nationalists to seize power and deliver Austria to Germany.

The Hungarian experiment with democratic institutions was even less impressive. Count Michael Károlyi (1875–   ) organized a government

EUROPE
AFTER WORLD WAR I
1925

500 MILES

ARCTIC

ICELAND
(DEN.)

FAROE IS.
(DEN.)

NORWAY

Oslo

SWEDEN

Stockho

NORTH

SCAPA
FLOW

SEA

DENMARK

1914

19

Edinburgh

GERMANY

SCHLESWIG

Danzig

IRISH
FREE
STATE

GREAT
BRITAIN

HELIGOLAND

Dublin

Hamburg

NETH.

Bremen

London

Berlin

BELG.

RUHR

Cologne

Dresden

EUPEN

Weimar

ATLANTIC

Compiegne

LUX.

Prague

Versailles

Paris

RHINE

SAAR

CZECHOS

ALSACE-
LORRAINE

Munich

FRANCE

Vienna

OCEAN

SWITZ.

AUSTRIA

Budap

Geneva

Locarno

H

Bordeaux

Fiume

Bilbao

Florence

Zara
(IT.)

YU

PORTUGAL

Marseilles

Lisbon

Madrid

Barcelona

CORSICA
(FR)

ITALY

SPAIN

Rome

Seville

SARDINIA
(IT.)

Tangier

GIBRALTAR
(BR.)

SP.
MOROCCO

MEDIT

SICILY

Algiers

FRENCH
MOROCCO

FRENCH
ALGERIA

FRENCH
TUNISIA

MALTA
(BR.)

TRM

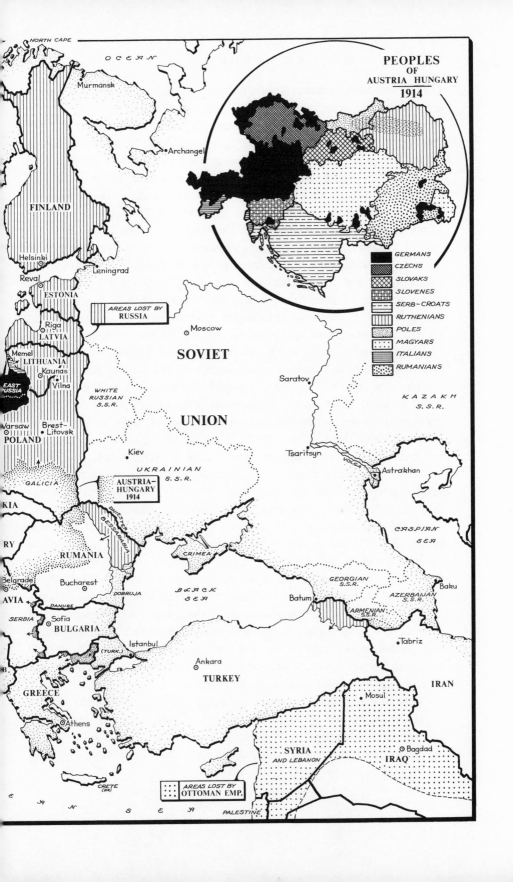

PEOPLES
OF
AUSTRIA HUNGARY
1914

GERMANS
CZECHS
SLOVAKS
SLOVENES
SERB–CROATS
RUTHENIANS
POLES
MAGYARS
ITALIANS
RUMANIANS

NORTH CAPE

OCEAN

Murmansk

Archangel

FINLAND

Helsinki

Reval

Leningrad

ESTONIA

Riga

LATVIA

Memel

LITHUANIA

Kaunas

EAST
PRUSSIA

Vilna

Warsaw

Brest-
Litovsk

POLAND

Moscow

SOVIET

UNION

WHITE
RUSSIAN
S.S.R.

Saratov

KAZAKH
S.S.R.

AREAS LOST BY
RUSSIA

Kiev

UKRAINIAN
S.S.R.

Tsaritsyn

VOLGA

Astrakhan

GALICIA

AUSTRIA–
HUNGARY
1914

KIA

DNIESTER

BESSARABIA

CRIMEA

CASPIAN
SEA

RY

RUMANIA

Belgrade

Bucharest

DOBRUJA

BLACK
SEA

GEORGIAN
S.S.R.

Batum

AZERBAIJAN
S.S.R.

Baku

AVIA

SERBIA

DANUBE

Sofia

BULGARIA

ARMENIAN
S.S.R.

Tabriz

Istanbul

(TURK.)

Ankara

TURKEY

Mosul

IRAN

GREECE

Athens

SYRIA
AND LEBANON

Bagdad

IRAQ

CRETE
(GR.)

AREAS LOST BY
OTTOMAN EMP.

PALESTINE

E   GA   N   S   E   GA

(1918) and made democratic pronouncements and expressions of concern for the subject nationalities, in the hope that Hungary would not be deprived of them by the peace settlement. When it became clear in 1919 that she would lose her Romanians, Croats, and Slovaks, Károlyi resigned. Power fell to a soviet government established in Budapest by Béla Kun (1885–1937), who announced the beginning of a dictatorship of the proletariat. He organized a Red army and tried to curry favor with the Hungarians by attempting to retrieve Slovakia and Transylvania by force. Romania fought back, scattered the Red army, and soon occupied Budapest. The soviet collapsed and was replaced by a regime of conservative aristocrats late in 1919, the Romanians then withdrawing. By 1920, the conservatives had re-established the monarchy (permitted by the treaty of Trianon) and named Admiral Nicholas Horthy (1868–1957) as regent. The interests of the great landowners were catered to exclusively, and the government crushed demands for reform, all the while preserving a certain popularity, owing to the widespread belief that this regime would gain revenge for the humiliation of 1918 and restore the Hapsburgs.

The new state of Yugoslavia grouped together the Southern Slavs but failed to mold them into a harmonious, democratic nation. Nearly 50 per cent of the population was Serbian and the royal house was the former house of Serbia, leading most Serbs to believe that Yugoslavia was really a "greater Serbia" and ought to be a highly centralized state dominated by Serbs. This irritated the Croats and Slovenes, who, while minorities, rightly considered themselves as more advanced culturally and economically than the Serbs. They preferred, therefore, a decentralized state in which the various groups enjoyed considerable "home rule." The constitution of 1921 was a victory for Serbian principles, but the outraged Croats continually agitated in Parliament for autonomy until the Croatian leader was murdered on the floor of Parliament (1928). Alexander I (*1921–1934*) then dissolved Parliament and established a royal dictatorship, driving the Croatian movement underground. The experience of Yugoslavia's three Balkan neighbors—Greece, Romania, and Bulgaria—with parliamentary government was similar to Yugoslavia's. None had parliamentary traditions, none understood orderly party government, and all ended in the 1930's with royal dictatorships.

In restored Poland, democratic aspirations were similarly disappointed, because a multitude of disruptive factors deprived her of the leisure and security to nurture parliamentary government. Factionalism, deriving partly from the traditional split between the conservative magnates and the liberal bourgeoisie, and partly from Poland's uneasy geographical position between Germany and Russia, made a concensus nearly impossible. It took three years to produce the democratic constitution of 1922, during which time the anti-Russian Marshal Josef Pilsudski (1867–1935) was chief of state. Modeled on the French constitution, the document provided for weak executive power and a dominant parliament, a provision which proved to be fatal in a country seriously divided. In 1926, Pilsudski overthrew the cabinet, revised the constitution, and from then on, while not assuming the presidency himself, was virtual dictator of Poland, with army backing.

The best hope of democracy among the small states was Czechoslovakia. She was beset, like other succession states, with minority problems, having Germans, Hungarians, and Ukrainians (Reuthenians) within her borders. Even the Czechs and the Slovaks came from different ethnic backgrounds (the former being more culturally advanced and more anticlerical), a situation which made the Slovaks agitate for autonomy. Yet Czechoslovakia had two distinct advantages denied her neighbors: her natural resources, agriculture, and industry permitted her a sound economic system; and in the distinguished scholar, Thomas Masaryk (1850–1937), Czechoslovakia found a president of the first rank who provided an inspiring example of democratic leadership which enabled the young nation to pursue its ideal of free government. Difficulties there were, but not until outside interests began to exploit the national divisions within Czechoslovakia did her experiment in democracy begin to crack.

The rapid drift toward dictatorship in a number of the larger countries of Europe not only revealed a similar failure of parliamentary regimes, but was usually accompanied by the development of an ideological underpinning to justify the jettisoning of democratic institutions. If one may risk a generalization about the unique courses followed by Germany, Italy, and France in the 1920's and 1930's, one finds that parliamentary government was undermined by the fearful economic dislocations of the postwar period. It made little difference whether a country was on the winning or the losing side in the war; where recovery was slow and the propertied classes felt the pinch, their faith in the effectiveness of parliamentary processes flagged. And when one adds, as a backdrop, the success of the Bolsheviks in Russia, whose propaganda appealed to all people caught in the hard time of recovery, it is not hard to understand why so many middle-class people came to believe that a rightist dictatorship was the only barrier to communism. Fear and frustration prevented rational argument as to whether Marxism was either a valid explanation of history or provided the most desirable system of production and distribution of goods. Instead, Marxism was to be met with force: violence against violence. The upshot was the establishment of totalitarian regimes which represented the perversion of the main streams of European civilization. Individual rights vanished, and justice became synonymous with the right of the state; intellectual freedom gave way to thought-control programs administered by ministers of propaganda. In fact, the totalitarian states of the left and the right were so similar in methods and values that the traditional differences between extreme left and extreme right were eliminated by the 1930's; and he who held to the liberal virtues of our civilization could no more accept the one than the other.

FASCIST ITALY: THE CORPORATE STATE

Italy was the first major country with parliamentary institutions to turn her back on them. Disappointed by her part in the war and in the peace settlement, Italy was also the scene of slow economic recovery and considerable poverty. The upper classes feared the spread of Bolshevism and fell upon the Fascist movement as their salvation. The Fascist party was founded in 1919 by Benito Mussolini (1883–1945), who had broken away from the Italian Marxist movement because of factional conflict. Initially, then, the Fascist movement embodied the socialist, republican, and anticlerical sentiments of its founder, as well as being vehemently nationalistic. When Mussolini became convinced that the road to power lay in making himself the darling of the right rather than in trying to assume the leadership of the Marxian party, he dropped those aspects of party philosophy offensive to the propertied classes, the Church, and the monarchy. Retaining its strong nationalist tenor, the Fascist party now represented itself as anticommunist and the champion of order. Mussolini was, in short, what we earlier called a "Sorelian."

When Mussolini was named prime minister in 1922, he ordered the writing of a philosophical work to give Fascism its ideological basis. The half-baked result—a mixture of Sorel, the usual misconstruction of Nietzsche, and the racist theories of the later nineteenth century—offers proof that the Fascists were not long on intellectual dignity. The single greatest contribution to Fascist philosophy was drawn from the works of Vilfredo Pareto (1848–1923), an Italian economist and sociologist greatly influenced by his friend Sorel. Pareto believed human behavior to be irrational and inexplicable in scientific terms and man's instinct to be to employ brute force rather than logic. Accordingly, he held, if one is to have order in the state, it must be imposed by authority, because order cannot derive from rational control by individuals themselves. Thus, Pareto advocated that political power be limited to those who had the biological rather than the intellectual talents for ruling, to that "elite" who never hesitates to use violence. He even glorified force by insisting that slaughter was merely the outward sign that the elite was in the process of obtaining what it rightly owns.

A quick review of Mussolini's state will suggest its militant nationalism and anti-intellectualism. His foreign policy was aggressive from the start and provided the first test of how the League of Nations would deal with aggression by a major power. In 1923, an international commission was investigating a border dispute between Albania and Greece when its Italian member was murdered. Presuming the assassin to have been Greek, Mussolini ordered the bombardment and occupation of Corfu. He then demanded a large indemnity from Greece as a price for evacuation. The League responded to a Greek appeal and was on the verge of getting the dispute referred to the World Court, when the great western powers suddenly ordered the Greeks to pay Italy the indemnity. The following year, the Fiume question was settled in favor of Italy, Yugoslavia being in no position to risk a showdown with Mussolini. For all the blustering about the revival of Rome, Mussolini's quarrels suggest that he was doubtful that his Italians were the Romans of old. He picked on the weak, selecting Ethiopia and Republican Spain in the 1930's and France in 1940, after she had been previously defeated by Germany. One recalls old Bismarck's words to the effect that Italy would follow a "jackal policy."

On the home front, Mussolini moved swiftly to achieve dictatorial power. He simultaneously attacked Italian economic problems and political opposition. Rigorous governmental economies made tax reductions possible, but the income tax was raised. Strikes and lockouts were strictly forbidden in order to stimulate production; this measure became a permanent feature of what Mussolini called the corporate state. Public works were projected in order to reduce unemployment. As for political opposition, socialists and communists were purged from governmental offices, and in 1923, Mussolini got parliament to pass an electoral law giving the political party with a plurality of votes two-thirds of the seats in parliament. The elections of 1924, with twenty opposition parties to split the vote, provided the Fascists with their two-thirds majority. From there on in, Mussolini used terror more freely, along with strict censorship of the press, to silence opposition. The parliamentary farce was climaxed in 1928, when candidates for office were all approved before election by the Fascist party.

While we classify Mussolini's corporate state as an obvious dictatorship of the right, its basic ideas grew out of nineteenth-century syndicalism, originally part of the labor-union movement. Fascist Italy did not permit associations of employers and employees to exist independently, but within each industry recognized one syndicate to which both employers and employees belonged. All disputes had to be settled within that syndicate, and no strikes were allowed. Officials who directed the syndicates were Fascist party members. Syndicates were organized for all professions as well as trades. The system may have eliminated much strife, but it also subjected the entire economic life of the country to the will of the state, which was to say the Fascist party. Economic recovery and material progress were evident under Mussolini, but at the price of political and personal liberty.

THE THIRD REICH

If Germany seemed to follow Italy into fascism, the fact was that the German situation was considerably more complex than the Italian and much more difficult of analysis. Though a defeated power and one with the worst economic dislocation after the war, Germany showed greater faith in democratic institutions during the 1920's than did Italy. Opposition to the German (Weimar) Republic there was, from the Communist party on the left (the Spartacist uprising was crushed in 1919); and from the ultraconservative Nationalist party which wanted a restoration of the monarchy (the *Kapp Putsch* in 1920), and the National Socialist party of Adolf Hitler (1889–1945) on the right. Yet, the Republic found support in a coalition of socialists, Catholic centrists, and Social Democrats, which, as late as 1928, outpolled the combined opposition nearly three to one. What makes it difficult to fathom the true commitment to the republic, however, is our inability to gauge the strength of the myth that the republic had sold Germany down the river by accepting the Treaty of Versailles (the so-called stab in the back) or to a second myth to the effect that Germany had surrendered in 1918 on the basis of the Fourteen Points and had then been betrayed by the victors. When one sees how quickly, after 1928, a popular drift developed toward the National Socialists, the party which built its platform on an acceptance of these myths, it makes one wonder whether the initial loyalty to the republic was genuine or an expedient.

There is less question about what launched that drift: namely, the general economic crisis which began in the United States with the stock market crash of 1929. While not the only cause of the crash, the primary cause was a vast overexpansion of credit. Public interest in the stock market greatly increased in the 1920's and much of the buying of stocks, by both great and small investors, was on margin; that is, the investor put up perhaps a fourth of the purchase price for stocks, the broker advancing the rest by borrowing from banks. It has been estimated that 90 per cent of the market transactions in that decade were not permanent investments but gambling ventures. By 1929, speculation had forced prices (and profits) to a point where they had no real relation to wages. When the market finally broke, a panic of selling ensued; and the resulting collapse had international repercussions owing to the interdependence of national economies in the modern world—especially acute in the light of war debts and reparations.

The hardships soon endured by German business and labor were reflected at once in the rising strength of the extremist political parties. Chancellor Heinrich Brüning (1885–   ), a Centrist who took office in 1930, called for new elections in order to appeal to the Germans to rally to those parties devoted to the republic, but the results were shocking. Communist membership in the Reichstag rose from 54 to 77 seats, while the National Socialists rocketed from 12 to 107 seats. As in Italy, the more moderate parties failed to stand together when challenged by the extremes. Brüning therefore had recourse to Article 48 of the constitution under which, in national emergency, the president could suspend constitutional rights. The result was rule by decree in the event that a parliamentary majority could not be obtained, and this uneasy governance continued until 1932. That year, President Paul von Hindenburg (1847–1934) took offense at Brüning's proposal to divide large estates in East Prussia, dismissed him, and appointed the ultraconservative Nationalist Franz von Papen (1879–   ) as chancellor. Evidently the old aristocrats thought they could govern with the support of the National Socialists, since social distinction more than party principle divided the two groups; but the National Socialists (Nazis) merely used the coalition as a step toward power. By 1932, the Nazis were a much larger party than the Nationalists and had raised a party police—the storm troopers—to bully the opposition. The last months of 1932 saw a maneuvering for power by the rightist parties which ended early in 1933 with Hindenburg agreeing to appoint Hitler to the chancery.

Since Hitler's parliamentary strength at that point consisted of 196 of the 584 seats, non-Nazi conservatives had to be included in the cabinet. He prepared for new elections by launching a frenzied attack upon communists, even firing the Reichstag building in order to accuse the communists of it; but the Nazis still won only 44 per cent of the vote in March, 1933. Coalition with the National party, however, raised Hitler's parliamentary strength to 52 per cent of the seats, and he had himself voted dictatorial powers under the Law to Combat the Misery of People and Reich; now he could rule by decree. The symbols of the republic were at once replaced with the symbols of the Nazi party, including the national flag, and the new regime called itself the "Third Reich." A ministry of propaganda and enlightenment was created to insure popular enthusiasm. Under the direction of Joseph Goebbels (1897-1945), it hammered away on the old themes of republican duplicity and the "betrayal" at Versailles, also adding such new issues as the superiority of the German race and nation and the danger which the presence of Jews presumably constituted.

The extermination of opposition was vicious. Hermann Goering (1893–1946), one of the three Nazis in Hitler's first cabinet, ordered the police to shoot communists on sight. In June of 1933, Hitler's troopers carried out a purge of nearly 1000 rightists, to prevent the formation of a coalition against him from that quarter. And the campaign to purify Germany by harassing Jews began with a civil-service law (April, 1933) dismissing "non-Aryans" from official, military, and professional posts. "Non-Aryan" included anyone with one Jewish grandparent and Aryans who married non-Aryans. Mobs were incited to attack Jews and their property, and Jewish professionals were excluded from public life. As a group, they were deprived of citizenship in 1935, and many were put in concentration camps. All this was by way of implementing the Nazi race theory, which provided the "intellectual" justification for the regime; the racists of the late nineteenth century had found their champion.

For the Nazis, race was the prime determinant in society. It fell to Alfred Rosenberg (1893-1946) as editor of the principal Nazi newspaper, to expound Nazi racial theory: the notion that pure Aryans (by which was meant Nordic people) are inherently superior and are born to rule over Slavs, Latins, Jews, and Negroes, and that Jews particularly contaminate a society. Those who objected to this unscientific theorizing, or who found the Nazi rituals based on racial theory absurd, were counted as heretics and were liable to confinement in concentration camps. The entire German culture was entrusted to Goebbels. In the hands of the censor and the propagandist, the purpose of all learning and art was the support and glorification of the state; while the educational system was geared to prepare the young for service to the state. The end, in other words, was the dehumanization of the German people to a point where they would wish for nothing more than total subservience to the state.

SOVIET RUSSIA

Soviet Russia differed from Germany and Italy in that Russian democracy was a sham from the outset. Though the Constitution of 1918 provided representative government, the system of voting was highly complex, indirect, and discriminatory against the rural population; and many groups of people were disenfranchised for their association with the fallen regime. The All-Union Congress, which was the national parliament, was rendered ineffective by its vast size, since it encompassed about 2000 delegates; and in its meetings once every two years, it did little more than ratify the work of the cabinet—the Council of People's Commissars. Finally, the Communist party was the only legal party in Russia, and no one could belong who did not submit absolutely to party discipline. The party had a tribunal, the Cheka, before which it tried opponents before executing them. That the party and the state were identical was seen in 1922, when the Cheka was abolished and its duties taken over by the OGPU, a department of the state police. It was proved again after Lenin's death in 1924, when a short struggle for power between Trotsky and Joseph Stalin (1879–1953) ended in the latter's victory. Trotsky had been a long-time associate of Lenin and the organizer of victory in the civil war, but Stalin, the secretary-general of the party, gained ascendancy.

In 1936, Stalin granted a new constitution, which was heralded as a great advance in democracy and personal liberty. It provided for a bicameral parliament, one house representing the many nationalities within the Soviet Union, the other directly elected by the people. But single-party government remained. Not only was that party's position maintained by terror, but between 1935 and 1937 Stalin carried out a systematic purge of the party hierarchy which broke the back of possible resistance to his .

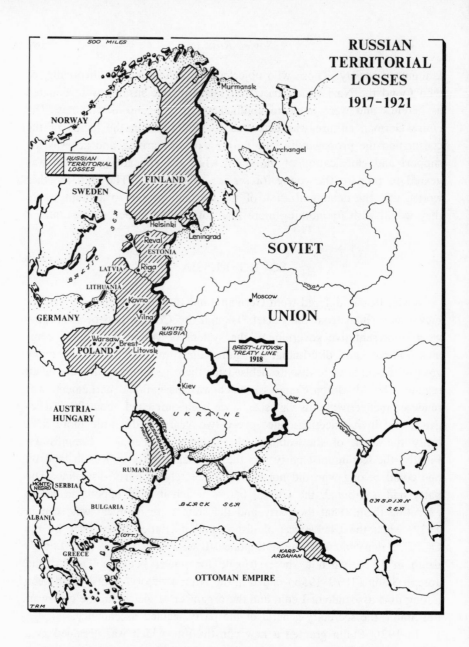

RUSSIAN
TERRITORIAL
LOSSES
1917–1921

500 MILES

RUSSIAN
TERRITORIAL
LOSSES

NORWAY

Murmansk

Archangel

SWEDEN

FINLAND

DVINA

Helsinki

SOVIET

Reval

Leningrad

ESTONIA

LATVIA

Riga

LITHUANIA

Kovno

Moscow

VOLGA

GERMANY

Vilna

UNION

WHITE
RUSSIA

Warsaw

Brest-
Litovsk

BREST–LITOVSK
TREATY LINE
1918

POLAND

Kiev

DON

AUSTRIA-
HUNGARY

UKRAINE

VOLGA

DNIESTER
BESSARABIA

RUMANIA

CASPIAN
SEA

MONTE-
NEGRO

SERBIA

BLACK SEA

BULGARIA

ALBANIA

(OTT.)

KARS-
ARDAHAN

GREECE

OTTOMAN EMPIRE

TRM

dictatorship. The nationalization of the economy, begun in 1918, gained
new momentum in 1928 with the First Five Year Plan (nothing less than
a government-supervised transition of Russia from an agrarian to an
industrial country) and with the program to collectivize agriculture. Because of greater governmental control over the economy in Russia than

in Germany or Italy—and probably because Russia earned enormous enmity for her separate peace in 1918 and her subsequent call for international revolution—it became usual in the West to prefer the fascist dictatorships to that of Stalin. In this attitude lay a great danger for European and American civilization, since all three regimes were a denial of those human and spiritual values which had made western life worth living. To prefer any one of these regimes was to prove, to use Ruskin's words, that one did not know when to die.

SPAIN

The development of fascism in Spain in the 1930's, while preluding the failure of parliamentary government as elsewhere in Europe, was less surprising because it was a variant of an already existing political tradition in Spain. Spanish national unity came out of a late-medieval crusade against the Moors, the memory of which kept many Spaniards traditionally loyal to the monarchy, the Church, and the army. In the nineteenth century, when the army no longer could justify its claim on a major slice of the national budget, and when the Spanish Church was so conservative that it was occasionally chided by Rome, the position of the monarchy was automatically weakened. Liberal, socialist, anarchist, and syndicalist currents found considerable adherence among those who wished to bring Spain into the ranks of the modern, progressive countries, while the deepening chasm between left and right was complicated by Basque and Catalan demands for national independence. The humiliating defeat in the Spanish-American War of 1898 was a blow from which the traditional triumvirate governing Spain never recovered, and the antimonarchical forces were finally able to win an election in 1931, causing Alphonso XIII (*1886–1931*) to abdicate.

Overthrowing the monarchy was the one issue on which the victorious republicans could agree: The Constituent Convention contained delegates of nine different republican parties, and of the 470 delegates elected, only fourteen had had previous parliamentary experience. Not once in the short history of the republic did the government enjoy the backing of a parliamentary majority in the hands of one party, and it was the opinion of the last president of the republic, Manuel Azaña (*1936–1939*), that the conflicts between the parties supporting the republic were chiefly responsible for the defeat of the republic in the Spanish Civil War. Anticlerical legislation, expected from the republicans, was too swift and far-reaching for a country with a long clerical tradition, and it offered a rallying point for antirepublicans. The Jesuits were expelled, clerical control of marriage and education was sharply reduced, and all ecclesiastical property was confiscated by the state. The army, too, was affected, being greatly reduced in size and finding many of its useless officers retired on full pay.

When the old forces of Spain sought to make a comeback, they did not back a restoration of the monarchy but drew on the experiences of fascist governments such as the Italian. Though the Communist party received only 2.5 per cent of the parliamentary seats in the election of 1936, the Spanish fascist movement (called the Falange) justified its opposition to the republic on the grounds that the republic was communist-ridden. No doubt the communists made difficulties for the republic, since their party was one of the republican group, but the Falangist charges were window-dressing which masked the fundamental conflict between the new order and the old order in Spain. The revolt began in 1936, led by the military units in Morocco, and the rebels were quickly able to seize control in the south, west, and northwest of Spain, since only about 500 officers remained loyal to the government. General Francisco Franco (1892–   ) was soon chosen by the rebels' generals as their chief (*caudillo*), and a provisional government was established at Burgos. Aid and advice reached the rebels promptly from Italy and Germany, while the Soviet Union contributed to the cause of the republic. The decision of the western democracies to adhere to a policy of nonintervention was a bitter blow to the republicans. The decision was largely based on a pathetic hope that their lead would induce the fascist powers to discontinue support of Franco and upon their fear that general intervention would bring on another world war. Antagonism toward the Soviet Union, too, made Britain and France reluctant to join forces with it; and given the fact that the republic was supported by a coalition of parties, ranging from liberals to communists, the temptation to excuse western nonintervention as a reluctance to back any government which had the support of communists was too great to be resisted. In fact, the republic was continually hampered by radical uprisings in the rear, and the more moderate elements in power would have been greatly strengthened by western aid and approval.

The wonder is that the Spanish army, substantially aided by Italy and Germany, required three years to overthrow the republic. Madrid was not taken until 1939, at which point the communists were making a last, and unsuccessful, bid to capture control of the republican government. What the civil war cost Spain in lives can only be estimated; the figure is probably over one million, a third of whom died in purges after the capture of Republican strongholds. A half-million people escaped to France, which had to construct camps for them in lieu of proper housing. The Franco government, while posing as an interim regime preparing the way for a restoration of the Bourbons, established a corporate state modeled on Mussolini's Italy. Not the least of the results of the civil war, however, was the widening of the rift between the Soviet Union and the West; and whatever the arguments to be made for and against intervention in Spain, western neutrality was interpreted in the fascist capitals as indicative of weakness and decadence.

THE CRISIS OF THE 1930's

The western attitude toward Spain was repeated in numerous crises during the decade of the 1930's. It stemmed in part from a genuine concern for peace, from a recognition that the wounds of World War I were far from healed; but it also reflected the deep divisions in the western world after 1919 and the disillusionment with "peace." There was not even agreement as to the treatment of defeated Germany, the British and Americans being inclined to suffer from bad consciences about the harsh settlement in 1919 and tending to overlook its violation. Furthermore, a great body of opinion in the West was so imbued with a fear of international communism that any regime avowedly anticommunist was, if not enthusiastically embraced, at least tacitly tolerated. Finally, the collapse of democratic governments on all sides led many people in the western democracies to question the vitality and future of democracy. This last reaction reached its apex in France.

French Disunity

The deterioration of the French political situation in the 1930's was the more remarkable considering the astonishingly successful economic recovery of France during the previous decade, not to speak of Premier Raymond Poincaré's (1860–1934) administrative and tax reforms (1926) which produced confidence and stability. France was, in fact, the last major European country affected seriously by the stock market crash of 1929; but, as in the case of Germany, that collapse ultimately produced economic dislocation and widespread hardship. Leftist parties, promising varying degrees of remedies, won control of parliament in 1932, but they could not form stable coalition governments, given their differences on the extent of nationalization of industries and enterprises. The result was a governmental near-paralysis—a rapid succession of "caretaker" cabinets—which reduced popular confidence in democratic procedures and encouraged the revival of those political elements which, since 1870, had been unfriendly to the republic. Moreover, the weak stand made by these "caretaker" governments against the rising menace of Hitler and Mussolini convinced the rightist groups that the future lay in fascist-style government. The leftist parties finally formed a coalition known as the Popular Front (1936), under the Socialist Leon Blum (1872–1950), for the purpose of saving the republic from the drift to the right. But the political wounds were grave and kept the French deeply divided and disillusioned.

Depression in Britain

British economic recovery after the war was never as complete as that of the French. Where the French had had to rebuild much of their industry, the British tried to compete in the world market using an industrial establishment that was seriously outmoded and inefficient compared to that of France, Germany, the United States, and Japan; and British shipyards stood idle as an unforeseen result of the confiscation of the German merchant fleet. Low wages and unemployment became the rule and contributed to the rapid rise of the Labour party, which formed its first government (with Liberal party support) in 1923.

Continued depression brought on the General Strike of 1926, which began in the coal industry. Thanks to the ineptitude of the leaders in government, labor, and industry, the strike not only spread unnecessarily, but the genuine grievances of the workers were lost sight of by the middle class, which saw the strike as revolutionary—an attempt to use direct action in place of the usual parliamentary methods. After the failure of the strike, the Labour party sought to recruit more members from the middle class, in time reducing class tensions and cutting a wide swath through Liberal party membership.

As the national crisis deepened in response to the stock market crash of 1929, the British parties tended to close ranks and cooperate in defense of the British system and way of life, and while unemployment remained high in the 1930's, suggestions that the parliamentary monarchy be overthrown were very few and came largely from extremists. On the other hand, it was natural that the government and the public shrank from the expenses of rearmament, despite the obvious aggressive designs of a Hitler.

Left to right: Francisco Franco, Benito Mussolini, Joseph Stalin

Below: Adolf Hitler

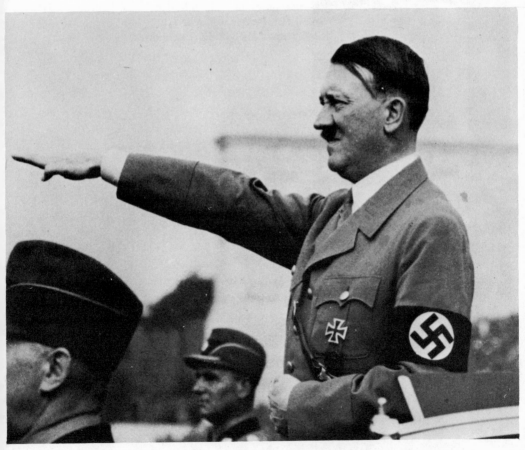

Above left to right: Winston Churchill (Great Britain), Franklin Roosevelt (United States), Joseph Stalin (U.S.S.R.) at Yalta, February 1945
Left: Neville Chamberlain
Below: Dwight D. Eisenhower

Manchukuo

Given these conditions, acts of aggression unsettling to the peace and destructive of the League of Nations went weakly challenged in the decade of the 1930's and left the fascist dictatorships stronger than ever. Japan was the first major aggressor (1931) when she used a minor incident in Manchuria as a pretext for attacking China. It was only too evident that Japan was pursuing her old expansionist policy on the continent, and the Chinese appealed to the League. Japan ignored the League's request for a negotiated settlement, overran Manchuria, and set up a puppet state called Manchukuo. When the League formally condemned Japan (1933) after an investigation of the incident, Japan gave notice of her intention to withdraw from the League. Moreover, she invaded North China and controlled three Chinese provinces by the end of 1935. Neither the League nor the United States took any punitive action.

Ethiopia

Weakness of this sort invited new aggression. The Italians, who possessed Eritrea and part of Somaliland, and who had had an eye on Ethiopia since the 1890's, made their move in 1935, following a border incident along the Somali-Ethiopian frontier. The League tried to move quickly to halt Mussolini's invasion, the Assembly voting to impose economic sanctions against Italy but excluding coal and oil from the goods to be withheld. This ambiguous action probably was a result of Anglo-French reluctance to push Mussolini too hard at a time when Hitler had denounced the disarmament clauses of the Versailles settlement. Mussolini was thus able to take advantage of the fact that the Anglo-French were eager to prevent an Italo-German tie, and he pressed his offensive successfully in 1936. The final indignity came when, after the League lifted the sanctions against Italy, she resigned from the organization (1937). Collective security had been shattered, and the prestige of the western democracies fell sharply. By then, too, the Spanish Civil War was adding a further dimension to their embarrassment.

The Rhineland

Hitler, meanwhile, implemented his denunciation of the disarmament clauses in the Treaty of Versailles by sending troops into the Rhineland (1936), in the greatest and most significant gamble of his career. Prompt Anglo-French action would certainly have ended in a German defeat, which could have seriously injured Hitler in Germany; but he reckoned correctly that there would be no concerted and immediate retaliation. All of the Allied bickering since 1919, added to the western tendency to buy peace at any price, came home to its fatal roost in 1936. A strong French government might alone have dealt with Hitler, since British support was not forthcoming; but the cabinet of Premier Sarraut was really a caretaker government, which hesitated to act and ended by doing nothing. Aside from a further suggestion of western inertia, allowing the Germans to remilitarize the Rhineland greatly enhanced the probability that any future war would again be fought on French soil.

Anschluss

Hitler's next move was toward *Anschluss* with Austria, a union expressly forbidden at Versailles. His own book, *Mein Kampf* (*My Struggle*), had revealed his desire to unify all Germans into a Greater Germany and a particular desire to annex Austria, his native country. However eager many Austrians had earlier been for *Anschluss,* the idea had considerably less appeal after 1933. The Christian Socialist leaders increasingly followed a pro-Italian policy, knowing that Italy might well fear to have Germany as a direct neighbor, since such a boundary would complicate the Tyrolian issue; but the chances of Mussolini's defending Austrian integrity faded as he became involved in Ethiopia and Spain and required German assistance against western pressure. In 1938, after an unsuccessful attempt by the Austrian National Socialists (Nazis) to seize power, Hitler forced the Austrian Chancellor Kurt von Schuschnigg (1897-   ) to give a Nazi the ministry of the interior, with its control of the police. Schuschnigg then tried to foil Hitler by announcing a plebiscite in Austria on the question of independence, but the Nazis stirred up such trouble that he gave way and turned over the government to Arthur Seyss-Inquart (1892-1946), the chief Austrian Nazi. *Anschluss* followed at once, and the western powers did nothing, falling back on the reasoning that they had no right to interfere with the wishes of Germans to be united. Hitler responded by holding a plebiscite in Austria; 99 per cent of the cowed population dutifully accepted the union.

The Sudetenland

This success encouraged Hitler to turn his attention to Czechoslovakia, where a minority population of three million Germans, living in the Sudetenland, were encouraged to hope for *Anschluss* with Germany. Czechoslovakia, unlike Austria, had strong defenses and alliances with France and the Soviet Union; an open annexation would therefore likely be resisted. When British Prime Minister Neville Chamberlain (1869–1940) was asked if Britain would join France in resisting German demands upon Czechoslovakia, he took the position that such collective action would simply produce war; that if war were to be prevented, one must negotiate in good faith with Hitler as each crisis arose. When the leader of the German Nazi party in Czechoslovakia, Konrad Henlein (1898–1945) understood that Chamberlain was refusing to guarantee support of France, he demanded that the Czechs give the Sudeten Germans complete autonomy. Prague resisted the demand and mobilized the Czech army to face the threat of a German invasion. Henlein then asked for outright *Anschluss* with Germany.

The Czechs were in an agony of indecision. Their treaty with Russia did not obligate Russia to fight for Czechoslovakia unless France did, and French help was uncertain as long as no commitment was forthcoming from Chamberlain. President Eduard Beneš (1884–1948) tried to bargain with Hitler by offering some territory to Germany; thereupon Poland and Hungary also immediately demanded territory from the Czechs. (And the Poles, uneasy about Hitler's future ambitions, sought to appease him by refusing Russia permission to send troops across Polish soil to aid the Czechs.) Worse, Hitler demanded more than the Czechs offered, so that the Czechs understood Hitler to intend their destruction. It appeared that they would resist, with or without assistance, and Hitler sought to neutralize the West by insisting that his demand upon the Czechs would be his last territorial claim in Europe. On September 29, 1938, an infamous day on the conscience of western democracy, Hitler met with Chamberlain, Mussolini, and Premier Daladier (1884–   ) of France at Munich; the Czech representatives were not admitted. To save the peace, the western leaders agreed to stand with the fascist dictators, and the Czechs were asked to surrender 25 per cent of their territory and a third of their population. They had no choice but to comply. The Slovakian demand for autonomy was also granted. Chamberlain had won his "peace in our time," and six months later Germany occupied Bohemia and Moravia without resistance. Chamberlain could no longer have any illusions that Hitler's word could be trusted.

Whatever the western distrust of Russia, her exclusion from the Munich conference was neither Britain's nor France's idea, but Hitler's. He wanted the two united fascist powers pitted against the British and French without Russian support, and Chamberlain had agreed in order to obtain the conference. Russia interpreted these events as a western attempt to turn Germany eastward and, therefore, sought a way to appease Hitler in order to deflect him westward. That opportunity lay in Poland, which not only had a German minority, but also had the German-speaking Free City of Danzig as an enclave. It must be noted, however, that behind western softness toward Hitler was the hard reality of military unpreparedness. Rearmament had been slow in the face of rising German and Italian power, thanks to wishful thinking that war could be avoided; and what money was spent often went into conventional weapons and elaborate fortifications, such as the French Maginot Line. Air arms were especially neglected, and western statesmen knew they were exposing their cities to bombardment in case of war in 1938. The balance of power had shifted against the western democracies, and they had no knowledge of how long it would take, in case of war, for the Dominions,[3] the United States, and the Soviet Union to come to their aid.

The Nazi-Soviet Pact

The full horror of the Munich agreement was not long in coming. Suspecting that Hitler would turn next on Poland, Britain and France both gave her guarantees of support. After Munich, Hitler had reason to suppose the guarantees would not be honored, but he sought an understanding with Russia to clear the way. Premier Stalin was now willing to enter into a partition treaty with Germany, dividing Poland between them, hoping thus to involve Germany in a lengthy war with the West and to give Russia breathing time for military preparation. When the German-Soviet Pact of August 23, 1939, was announced, its implications were at once clear in London and Paris. Chamberlain tried to warn Hitler that Britain really would stand by Poland, but Hitler had prepared his way militarily and diplomatically and felt sure of victory. On September 1, he began his attack upon Poland without a declaration of war. Britain and France retaliated on September 3.

We have a clear conscience, we have done all that any country could do to establish peace, but a situation in which no word given by Germany's ruler could

---

3. After World War I, the self-governing Dominions achieved a new relationship with Britain: the British Commonwealth of Nations, a constitutional status defined in the Statute of Westminster (1931): "They [Britain and the Dominions] are equal in status, in no way subordinate one to another in any aspect of their domestic or external affairs, though united by a common allegiance to the Crown, and freely associated as members of the British Commonwealth of Nations." The law left the Dominions virtually independent.

be trusted, and no people or country could feel themselves safe, had become intolerable. . . . For it is evil things we shall be fighting against, brute force, bad faith, injustice, oppression, and persecution. But against them I am certain that right will prevail.[4]

WAR

Though Hitler and Mussolini had earlier in 1939 converted their long-time cooperation into a formal alliance (the "Pact of Steel") Mussolini did not live up to his obligation immediately but followed the same "wait-and-see" policy which the Italians had followed in 1914. Meanwhile, the German might fell on Poland, whose forces were not only badly outnumbered and outgunned but also could not match the mobility of the Germans. The tactics of blitzkrieg (lightning war) were employed by the Germans, beginning with the use of aircraft, especially dive bombers, as artillery, to break up enemy formations and destroy communications. Swiftly moving armored divisions could then take advantage of enemy confusion to range far behind the enemy lines and develop encircling movements which could cut the enemy into hopelessly isolated pockets. Air attacks against the civilian population were calculated to increase confusion and demoralization. The tactics were so effective that Poland capitulated after twenty-seven days, and the campaign would have been notably shorter had not Warsaw held out heroically. Russia occupied her share of Poland, as well as the three Baltic states; Hitler allowed this occupation in order to insure Russian neutrality while he turned on the West.

Russia also proposed an exchange of territory with Finland in order to improve the defenses of Leningrad, but the Finns rejected this proposal. Determined to do everything possible against the probable day of German invasion, Russia attacked Finland (November, 1939). The Finns defended themselves magnificently in their hopeless cause, and though the Russians made a poor showing, Finland had to make the required territorial concessions in March, 1940. Because the western front had been inactive, Britain and France had been preparing an expedition to aid the Finns, but their surrender came too soon for the Allied help to get under way. Hitler, in fact, used the incident to his own advantage, occupying Denmark and Norway in April, on the pretext that the Allies would use the Scandinavian route to attack his ally, Russia. This last calamity forced

4. From Neville Chamberlain's radio speech to the British people.

WORLD WAR II
EUROPEAN THEATER
1939-1942

AXIS STATES AND
ANNEXED AREAS

AXIS
ALLIES

AXIS-
OCCUPIED

BOUNDARIES ARE THOSE
OF JULY 1, 1944

500 MILES

ICELAND
Reykjavik

ARCTIC

Narvik

NORWAY
Trondheim
Oslo

SWEDEN
Stockholm

EIRE
Dublin

UNITED
KINGDOM
Edinburgh

Coventry

London

NORTH

SEA

DENMARK
Copenhagen

BALT

Hamburg
Bremen
Berlin
Danz

Essen
Cologne
GREATER
GE

EUPEN
SUDETEN-
LAND
SILESI

NETH.
Rotterdam

BELG.
LUX.

Sedan

BOHEMIA
MORAVIA

Brest

ATLANTIC

Paris
Compiegne

LORRAINE
Strassburg
ALSACE

Munich

Vienna
AUSTRIA

St.Nazaire

LOIRE
Tours

(OCCUPIED)

FRANCE
VICHY FR.
TO NOV.1942

SWITZ.

Milan

Venice

CROATIA
Y

OCEAN

Bordeaux

Vichy

ADRIATIC

Bilbao

Marseilles
Toulon

Florence

ITALY

SEA

PORTUGAL

Lisbon

Madrid
SPAIN

Barcelona

CORSICA
(VICHY)

Rome

Foggia

Naples
Taranto

GIBRALTAR
(BR)
SP.
MOROCCO

MEDITERRANEAN

SARDINIA

SICILY

Casablanca
MOROCCO
(VICHY)

Oran

Algiers

ALGERIA
(VICHY)

Tunis
TUNISIA
(VICHY)

SEA

MALTA (BR)

CZECHOSLOVAKIA
AND
THE MUNICH TREATY
1938

BOHEMIA–MORAVIA
GER. PROTECT., MAR. 15, 1939

SLOVAKIA
GER. PROTECT., MAR. 16, 1939

SUDETENLAND
TO GERMANY, 1938

150 MILES

DECEMBER, 1941
FARTHEST AXIS
PENETRATION
NOVEMBER, 1942

WORLD WAR II
EUROPEAN THEATER
1942-1945

500 MILES

AXIS STATES AND
ANNEXED AREAS

AXIS
ALLIES

BOUNDARIES ARE
THOSE OF JULY 1, 1944

Reykjavik
ICELAND

Narv

NORWAY
Trondheim

SWEDE

Oslo

Stockho

NORTH

Edinburgh

UNITED
KINGDOM

DENMARK
Copenhagen

SEA

EIRE
Dublin

Hamburg

ATLANTIC

Plymouth   London

NETH.

BATTLE
LINE
JAN.,1945

Berlin

GREATER

Essen
RUHR
Cologne

Po

NORMANDY
INVASION
JUNE 6, 1944

BELG.

Torgau

GERMANY

Bre

OCEAN

Brest

SURRENDER
AT REIMS
MAY,7,1945

Paris   Reims

Prague

BOHEMIA

St.Nazaire

MORAVIA

FRANCE

Munich   Vienna

AUSTRIA

Vichy

SWITZ.

Bordeaux

Mar-
seilles
Toulon

Milan

Trieste

Zagram

PORTUGAL

Madrid

CRO

Lisbon

SPAIN

Barcelona

BATTLE LINE
SEPT., 1944-
APRIL, 1945

ALLIED
LANDINGS
AUG.,1944

ITALY

Rome

CORSICA

BATTLE
LINE
SPR., 1944

Naples
Salerno

SARDINIA
(IT.)

MEDITERRANEAN

GIBRALTAR
(BR)

ALLIED
INVASION OF
SICILY & ITALY
JULY-SEPT.,1943

SICILY

MOROCCO

Oran   Algiers

Tunis

Casablanca

ALLIED
LANDINGS
IN
N. AFRICA
NOV. 8, 1942

MOROCCO
(VICHY)

ALGERIA
(VICHY)

AXIS
SURRENDER
IN TUNISIA,
MAY 13, 1943

TUNISIA
(VICHY)

MALTA
(BR)

ITALIAN
SURRENDE
AT MALTA
SEPT. 29, 19

SURRENDE
IN BERLIN
MAY 8, 1945

150 MILES

WITHDRAWAL OF THE
**WESTERN
ALLIES**
*SUMMER AND FALL
1945*

Chamberlain from office, and Winston Churchill (1874–   ) took the prime ministry.

That very day, Hitler broke the calm in the West with an invasion of the Netherlands and Belgium (May 10, 1940). Once again the tactics of blitzkrieg were employed to produce total paralysis and demoralization. Parachutists and fifth columnists (subversives) seized points controlling vital communications, cities were bombed, and civilians fleeing along roads were strafed from the air. The Dutch surrendered after five days. Meanwhile, British and French units moved northward to the assistance of the Belgians, exposing almost at once the hiatuses in Allied military preparation. The French had poured millions into the Maginot Line, a defensive line of undeniable strength extending along the northeastern frontier from Switzerland to Belgium. It had not been extended to the sea for fear of weakening Belgium's determination to resist German attack, and it was therefore necessary to help the Belgians hold firm in order to defend the northern French frontier. The trouble was that this tactic left the military policy of a great power at the mercy of a weak power, and when King Leopold capitulated on May 28, France and Britain paid the penalty for faulty strategy. Their forces in Belgium were suddenly isolated by the Belgian surrender, and a German breakthrough at Sedan—bypassing the Maginot line—cut their retreat to the main French army. Thereupon began the desperate and heroic attempt to evacuate the trapped forces through the port of Dunkirk. Under constant ground and air attack, the French fought a successful rearguard action that enabled the bulk of the British forces to escape: nearly 340,000 men. The audacity of the operation raised British morale tremendously, almost masking for a moment the appalling defeat which had been suffered. The French commander, General Maxime Weygand (1867–   ), notified his government that the losses of the Allies and the outflanking of the Maginot Line had made the defense of France impossible, and his recommendation that an armistice be sought plunged the French cabinet into a turmoil of indecision.

On June 10, Mussolini launched thirty-two divisions against the six which France had left to guard the Italian frontier. The Italians made some headway, but nothing commensurate with the odds they enjoyed. In the north, however, the French defensive was soon paralyzed by the destruction of communications, and when Marshal Henri Pétain (1856–1951) assumed the prime ministry on June 16, it was with the intention of making peace with Germany. The armistice was signed on June 22, Germany occupying all of northern France and the Atlantic coastal zone, the southern part of the country to remain unoccupied. The French navy was to be disarmed and held in port, but the British were rightly fearful that its units would fall into German hands. Because a combined Franco-German fleet would have the power to gain control of the Channel, the British had no alternative but to ask the French admirals either to join the British or to sail to neutral ports. Some units of the French fleet complied, though more in response to General Charles de Gaulle (1890–), who had flown to London to organize a Free French movement, but much of the navy remained loyal to the new French regime, which established its capital at Vichy. At Oran, however, the British attacked and disabled a French squadron whose commander refused the British invitation.

As for Britain, the fall of France left her alone against the Continent, almost as she had been in 1807, and much of her military equipment had been sacrificed at Dunkirk in favor of her men. Hitler expected that the British would now see the wisdom of surrender, especially since he was eager to turn eastward to expand his continental empire at the expense of Russia—a tactic he thought the British ought to favor. Britain, however, no longer had illusions about the possibility of peace with a German-dominated Continent, and outgunned as she was, she still had naval control of the Channel as a barrier to German invasion. This advantage the Germans sought to destroy with air power. If they could eliminate the Royal Air Force, the British fleet would not dare operate in the narrow confines of the Channel. The air attacks upon Britain began in July, 1940, and here Hitler received his first setback and what appears in retrospect to have been a decisive defeat. British aircraft, though outnumbered, proved substantially superior to the German and were assisted in seeking their targets by a new device called radar. German air losses over the Channel and over Britain were so high that by September it was decided to postpone plans for an invasion of Britain. Nevertheless, the German bombing cost Britain heavily by disrupting production, and submarines were sinking her merchant ships at an alarming rate. At that point in 1940, President Franklin Roosevelt heading a United States still deeply isolationist, took the initiative in getting help to the British, convinced as he was that a British defeat would be a catastrophe for America. He traded fifty overage destroyers, which could be used for convoy duty, for long leases on British bases in the Caribbean and the Atlantic; and in early 1941, the Lend-Lease Act gave the American president the right to provide American help to any nation whose defense was vital to American security. Not only did this action provide Britain with an increasing stream of supplies, but it also stimulated American industry to begin retooling for wartime production.

In the meantime, the Italians launched an offensive from Libya, with the intention of driving the British out of Egypt and the Near East. Toward the end of 1940, the British had built up sufficient strength for a counter-attack, which drove the Italians headlong back into Libya; whereupon the British turned southward towards Mussolini's East African empire and won it after a five-month campaign. The British navy further damaged Italy, first when an aircraft carrier sent her planes against the base at Taranto (November, 1940), sinking three Italian battleships, and secondly off Cape Matapan early the following year, when the British inflicted serious damage on the Italian fleet without loss to themselves. The final humiliation for Mussolini during the fall of 1940 was his campaign to take Greece, which ended in miserable failure. German troops were soon sent into Italy to bolster Mussolini against popular criticism and, in early 1941, into Libya to stiffen the Italians. To bail out the Italians in Greece, Hitler forced Romania, Hungary, and Slovakia to join the war against Greece and Britain, and Bulgaria also participated, to serve as a base for a German invasion of Greece. Yugoslavia attempted to resist pressure from Germany and Italy but was overrun (early in 1941), leaving the road clear for the renewed assault on Greece. The British had only a token force to send to the Greeks, and their position was quickly impossible as the Germans swept into the country. An evacuation of the British to Crete was brilliantly met by the Germans, who attacked Crete with parachutists and troops flown in by towed gliders. Aside from the Italian fiascos, the war was going badly for Britain.

Yet, she had not been knocked out, and her ability to begin serious bombing of Germany in 1941, when added to the increasing support from the United States, might well have suggested an all-out assault on Britain. Instead, Hitler chose to invade the Soviet Union (June 22, 1941), thus choosing the two-front war which the Germans of 1914 had worked so hard to avoid. No doubt a clash between Germany and the Soviet Union would ultimately have come, not merely because of their rival ambitions in the Balkans and the Baltic region, but also because Hitler intended that Russia should provide the economic foundation for the New Order in Europe under German aegis. Hitler's decision to attack Russia was based on the twin assumptions that he need expect no invasion from the Atlantic and that the Russians could be knocked out during the summer. He would then be in a position to deal at leisure with the British, having brought

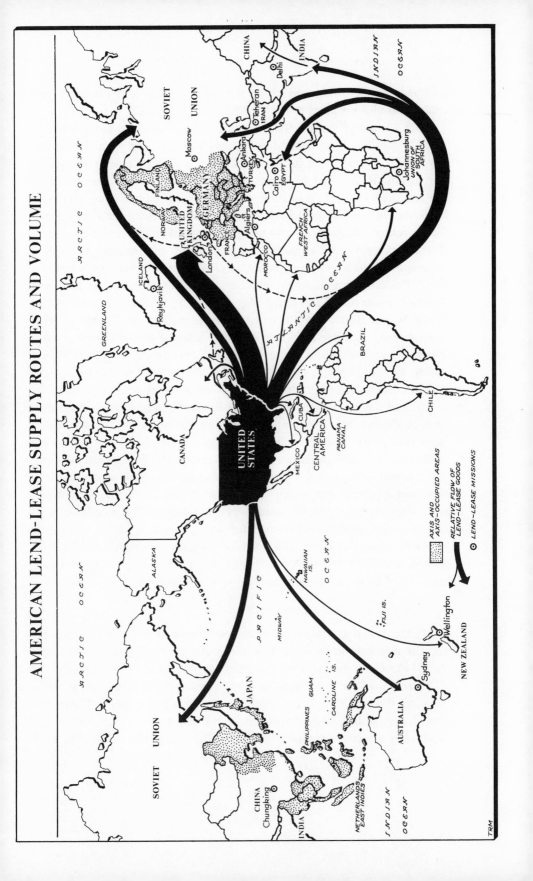

AMERICAN LEND-LEASE SUPPLY ROUTES AND VOLUME

the great food-growing regions of the Soviet Union into his orbit, and could return his attention to the Mediterranean in the fall.

The Germans invaded Russia in three major sectors: toward Leningrad, toward Smolensk and Moscow, and—with a Ukrainian offensive— toward Kiev. They were further assisted by a Finnish resumption of the war against Russia and by Romanian and Slovak troops. Russia did as she had done in 1812, retreating swiftly to avoid the encircling tactics of blitzkrieg, refusing to be brought to bay, and scorching the earth as her forces retired. Both sides had roughly 160 divisions in the field, and Russia's strategy was to pull the enemy far into the interior, to increase his communication problems immensely. At such a point, the inferiority of the Russian divisions would be offset, while help from Britain and from America under the Lend-Lease Act could bolster the Russians. As in World War I, supply lines to Russia were precarious, and much of what ultimately reached her from the West was shipped through Iran, a risky, laborious, and inefficient route. The Germans moved deep into Russia during the summer and fall of 1941, but the defense in depth kept the Russian forces intact despite a retreat of as much as 600 miles on some fronts; and the main cities remained in Russian hands. Hitler's announcement in October that the campaign was virtually at an end was more of a hope than a fact; since Napoleon's time, no one relished being committed in Russia as winter came on. In fact, German confidence that the campaign would be ended in a few months meant that the German divisions were not equipped for winter campaigning, and the areas of scorched earth they occupied offered scant hope for foragers. The Russians, however, better equipped and trained for winter warfare, began a counter-offensive which regained land west of Moscow. German suffering was intense, but when the winter campaign was over, the Germans still held much territory in the Ukraine and in western Russia.

The United States Enters the War

In the meantime, the scope of the war became global with the Japanese surprise attack upon the American fleet based at Pearl Harbor (December 7, 1941), which knocked out 8 battleships, 3 cruisers, 3 destroyers, and 177 aircraft. It had been clear for some years that Japan had great ambitions on the Asian continent, and her aggressiveness against China had contributed both to the destruction of the peace after 1919 and to the weakening of the League of Nations. By 1936, Japan drew close to Germany, a recognition of their common interests; and though they did not sign a formal military alliance, there was little reason to doubt that they would cooperate against Russia and the West. Italy adhered to the Berlin-Tokyo axis in 1937. This understanding collapsed (August, 1939), when Japan was shocked by the news of the conclusion of the Russo-German Pact, but in 1940, Japan joined Germany and Italy in the Tripartite Pact, suggesting that Hitler had reassured the Japanese that he ultimately meant to invade Russia. This alliance pledged the signatories to come to each other's aid in case of war with a country not yet a belligerent, which meant Russia and the United States.

Nothing effective, meanwhile, had been done to halt Japanese aggression against China, even though that aggression was in direct violation of international agreements to which the Japanese were signatory. In 1922–1923 the Nine-Power Treaty had been signed in Washington, guaranteeing the territorial integrity of China and reiterating the older "Open Door" policy. Furthermore, though that conference had sought to restrict the growth of naval power, there was increasing evidence by the 1930's that the Japanese were secretly building naval units in defiance of the international regulations. The seizure of Manchuria (1931) brought forth nothing more effective than condemnation and must have encouraged the Japanese to believe that the Nine-Power Treaty was a dead letter. In 1937, they resumed their aggressive policies, apparently determined to conquer China before she became sufficiently unified and strengthened to be able to resist successfully, and obviously taking advantage of western preoccupation with the rise of Germany and Italy. After the outbreak of war in Europe, America began taking steps to help the western democracies; American industries were therefore beginning to be retooled for war. In 1940, the unprecedented step of adopting peacetime universal military training was taken in the U.S., while naval appropriations for that year were literally earmarked for a "two-ocean" navy. Since the Japanese had long seen their own plans in global terms, requiring the cooperation of Germany and Italy, it was only logical that they should see the gradual development of an American commitment to Britain and Russia as aimed also at Japan in the long run. Since the mobilized power of the United States would array a formidable force against the fascist powers, the Japanese realized the need to strike at the United States before that mobilization could be completed.

Six months before the attack upon Pearl Harbor, the Japanese extorted

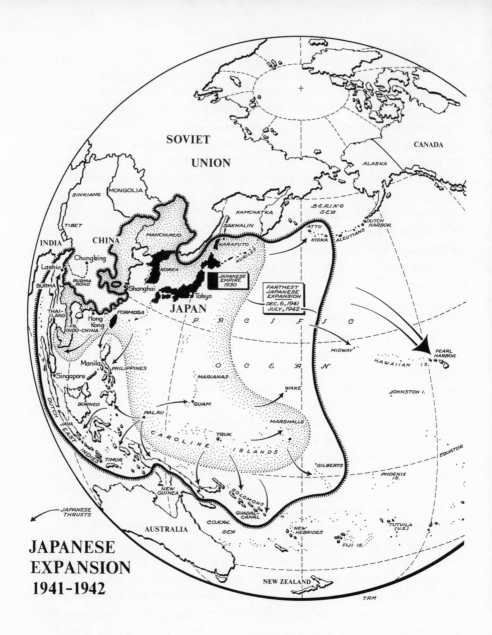

JAPANESE
EXPANSION
1941-1942

military control of Indo-China from the Vichy French, thus gaining bases
for assaults upon the Philippines, Hong Kong, and Malaya. These were
attacked the same day on which the Japanese hit Hawaii, Guam, and
Midway Island. On December 8, the United States declared war on Japan,
and three days later, Germany and Italy honored their Tripartite Pact by
declaring war on the United States. The subsequent Japanese victories
were swift and impressive in their scope. (The loss in prestige by the old

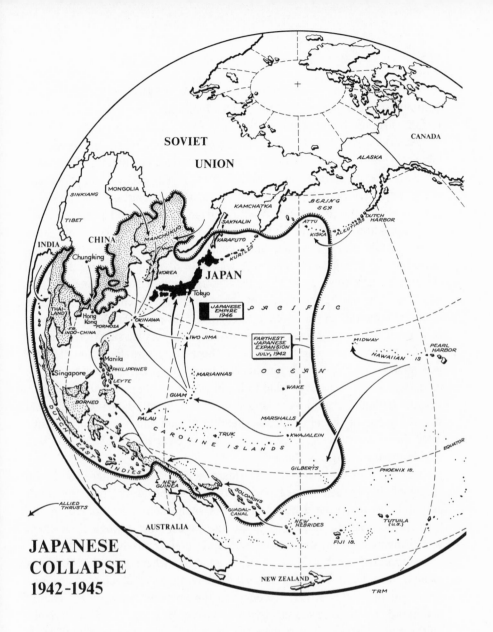

CANADA

ALASKA

SINKIANG

MONGOLIA

KAMCHATKA

BERING SEA

DUTCH HARBOR

TIBET

SAKHALIN

ATTU

KISKA

ALEUTIANS

CHINA

MANCHUKUO

KARAFUTO

INDIA

Chungking

KURILES

KOREA

JAPAN

Tokyo

JAPANESE EMPIRE 1946

P A C I F I C

THAILAND

Hong Kong

OKINAWA

FORMOSA

FR. INDO-CHINA

IWO JIMA

FARTHEST JAPANESE EXPANSION JULY, 1942

MIDWAY

PEARL HARBOR

HAWAIIAN IS.

Manila

Singapore

PHILIPPINES

LEYTE

MARIANNAS

GUAM

O C E A N

WAKE

BORNEO

PALAU I.

CAROLINE ISLANDS

TRUK

KWAJALEIN

MARSHALLS

EQUATOR

DUTCH EAST INDIES

GILBERTS

PHOENIX IS.

NEW GUINEA

SOLOMONS

GUADAL-CANAL

NEW HEBRIDES

FIJI IS.

TUTUILA (U.S.)

ALLIED THRUSTS

AUSTRALIA

**JAPANESE
COLLAPSE
1942-1945**

NEW ZEALAND

TRM

colonial powers contributed to the early independence of their southeastern Asian colonies in the postwar period.) Early in 1942, the British
at Hong Kong and Singapore were overrun, Thailand signed a hasty
alliance with Japan, and the Dutch surrendered the Netherlands East
Indies at Batavia in March. At the same time, the Japanese occupied
Burma, thus posing a serious threat to the Chinese still resisting Japan,
because the "Burma Road" was the chief western supply line to the slowly

retreating armies of General Chiang Kai-shek (1886–   ), head of the Nationalist Government in China. The Philippine Islands were the next to fall, surrendering in April, 1942.

Australia was in imminent danger of invasion when the American General Douglas MacArthur (1880–   ) was given command of all Allied forces in the southern Pacific (March, 1942). The recovery of American sea power after the serious blows dealt it at Pearl Harbor was, however, chiefly responsible for saving Australia from invasion and preserving her communications with the United States. No such recovery would have been possible had we waited until Pearl Harbor to start our rebuilding program. As it was, an Allied fleet was able to repulse a large Japanese invasion force (May 7, 1942) in the waters between New Guinea and the Solomon Islands, in the Battle of the Coral Sea. A month later, when another Japanese naval force approached Midway Island, it, too, was beaten off with heavy losses. Thus, the Japanese naval superiority in the Pacific achieved at Pearl Harbor was short-lived, and the United States was able to send significant numbers of troops to Australia and New Zealand. The Allies were even able to begin a counteroffensive late that year, when American marines were landed in the Solomon Islands. Guadalcanal was the scene of the most terrible fighting in that campaign, but the ultimate American success early in 1943 was a clear sign that the tide was beginning to turn against Japan.

On the Russian front, the Germans renewed their offensive in the spring of 1942, their strategy being to cut off the north from the south and thus to deny the Russian army its main petroleum source in the Caspian Sea region, as well as to cut the supply line through Iran which was bringing the Russians munitions and food from the United States. Sevastopol fell after a siege of eight months, whereupon the Germans turned their main attention toward Stalingrad, a vital communications center on the Volga River. Recognizing the absolute necessity of holding Stalingrad, the Russians launched an offensive designed to relieve pressure on the city's garrison. The maneuver succeeded in driving a wedge through the front in a manner to isolate the German force attacking Stalingrad from the main German army. As the winter came on, the Russians surrounded the Germans at Stalingrad, finally forcing their surrender early in 1943. This defeat cost Germany twenty-two divisions, but the blow to German morale was even more costly, and the momentum of the invasion was now lost. The Russians pressed their advantage during the remaining winter months, regaining much territory in the Ukraine and raising the siege of Leningrad.

In North Africa, meanwhile, the British need to dispatch troops to aid the Greeks (1941) had robbed them of their victory over the Italians in Libya. Aided by German troops, the Italians were able to expell the British from Libya, but their drive was halted at the Egyptian frontier. Later in the year, when the Germans had to send troops to the Russian front, the British were able to penetrate Libya for a second time. By 1942, the Axis offensives became a German—rather than an Italian— responsibility under General Erwin Rommel (1891–1944), a specialist in desert warfare. In May of that year, he began a far more serious invasion of Egypt than the Italians had launched in 1940; it swept to within seventy miles of Alexandria, the British finally containing his drive at El Alamein. Four months later, a British counterattack directed by General Sir Bernard Law Montgomery (1887–   ) sent the Germans reeling back into Libya. At that point, the Mediterranean theater took on a new dimension, with Anglo-American landings in Algeria and Morocco (November 8, 1942), in a move designed to end the stalemate in Egypt and to secure new bases for an ultimate Allied invasion of the Continent. Not the least of the preinvasion problems was the question of how to deal with the Vichy French officials in North Africa. The Allies hoped to avoid a fight, yet they did not wish to risk revealing their plans to anyone who might be in a position to pass them on to Berlin. And these French officials were in a tight spot: officially responsible for the defense of North Africa and uneasy about German reprisals in France should they violate the armistice, they were silently hoping for a German defeat. Except at Casablanca, much of the resistance to the Allied landings was token. Hitler responded by taking over the remainder of France and by sending troops through Italy for embarkation to Tunisia. The remaining units of the French fleet at Toulon were scuttled by their crews to prevent their capture by Germany. It required only six months from the initial landings to catch and defeat the Axis forces in North Africa, caught as they were between the two Allied armies. In May, 1943, the entire coast was in Allied hands, and Italy lay open to invasion.

Early in 1943, President Roosevelt and Prime Minister Churchill met for ten days in Casablanca to plan the invasion of Europe, and they announced that nothing short of "unconditional surrender" of the enemy would be acceptable. Shortly thereafter, General Dwight D. Eisenhower

(American, 1890–   ) was named Allied commander-in-chief in the American theater. The Italo-German surrender in North Africa, when coupled with Japanese reverses in Asia and the German debacle at Stalingrad, made it clear that the tide had turned against the Axis powers—who were given little respite. Though Germany was able to muster a spring offensive in Russia in 1943, it lacked the punch for success and was handicapped by losses in North Africa. Moreover, Russian production, greatly supplemented by lend-lease supplies, gave the Russians superiority in material. By July, they had contained the German thrusts and had begun to roll back the Germans along a broad front. German industrial production, in contrast, was suffering heavily from increasing Allied air bombardment, and the earlier failure to reduce Britain was proving ruinous. While the British preferred low-level night bombing, the Americans were in favor of high-level daylight raids, which permitted constant assault upon Germany; this attack provided a psychological factor and helped to reduce German production through continuous alerts. Once the Allies had North Africa, "shuttle bombing" was possible. Bombers leaving Britain for targets in Germany, especially those in eastern Germany, could fly to bases in North Africa rather than return to Britain, greatly reducing Allied casualties over Germany. As Germany lost air control of the Continent, she necessarily turned to manufacturing fighters rather than bombers, but she tried to keep up the bombardment of Britain with robot missiles launched from the Channel coast.

The Allied decision to invade Italy rather than western Europe in the summer of 1943 has remained controversial. Western eagerness to divert German strength from the Russian front probably dictated the choice, because it was calculated that the Italian front would be considerably softer than the Channel coast and its invasion would require less preparation. As it turned out, the Italian campaign proved more costly than had been anticipated and was subsequently criticized as strategically ill advised. There seems little doubt, however, that the choice enabled the Allies to maintain pressure on the Axis, whereas an assault upon the Channel coast could not have been mounted until months later; and it tied down German divisions badly needed on the Russian front. The Allied invasion of Sicily began on July 10. Within two weeks, its success was so obvious that the Fascist Grand Council overthrew Mussolini in favor of Marshal Pietro Badoglio (1871–1956). Italy technically remained in the war with her ally, but Bagdolio soon secretly sought peace with the Allies. On September 3, the day after American and British troops had crossed the Straits of Messina into southern Italy, Badoglio achieved an armistice on the basis of unconditional surrender. A few days later, Mussolini was rescued by his German friends and established a separate government in the north, another Nazi puppet regime. Aside from this swift defeat of Italy, the campaign proved laborious and costly. The Germans sent in heavy reinforcements and took full advantage of the rugged terrain in their desperate attempt to plug this breach in what they had called "Fortress Europe." A rugged winter also hampered Allied operations, and all these factors postponed the capture of Rome until June 4, 1944.

D-Day

Two days later all attention shifted to the Normandy coast, where the western Allies, under General Eisenhower, began their major assault upon "Fortress Europe"—D-Day (June 6, 1944). To accomplish a successful landing against such a heavily defended coast, the Allies had to mass an overwhelming air cover, a massive fleet to provide artillery against shore batteries, and a stock-pile of enormous quantities of supplies in anticipation of serious initial losses. No doubt, too, the amphibious experience gained in North Africa, Sicily, Italy, and against the Japanese in the Far East was an essential preparatory feature. Perhaps the most novel feature of the Normandy invasion was the creation of artificial ports for the landing of troops and supplies, done by sinking lines of ships and concrete caissons. Not until three weeks after the initial landings did the Allies capture a major port—Cherbourg—suggesting the vital importance of the artificial harbors during the first days of the campaign. Meanwhile, heavy bombing of German communication lines hindered the gathering of German strength, though strong German armored counterattacks had to be contained around Caen. Only when American armor broke through at St. Lo, southward into Brittany and then eastward toward the Seine, were the Germans obliged to fall back, leaving the Allies firmly established on the Continent. On August 15, the Germans had to face a new invasion along the Mediterranean coast between Nice and Marseilles, a Franco-American army which moved northward along the Rhone Valley. Both Paris and Brussels were liberated in the late summer, but the initial penetration of German territory was contained by the stubbornly manned defenses. The Allied forces then paused to regroup for the final assault.

In December, 1944, the German commander, General Karl von Rundstedt (1875–1953), made a supreme effort to break the Allied lines, selecting points along the Belgian-Luxemburg sector known to be thinly held by American troops. For a number of days, the Germans drove a deep wedge into the Allied front, but they could not muster the strength for flanking movements. Instead, in this Battle of the Bulge, the Germans themselves were assaulted on the flanks, and their counteroffensive broke down. In light of similar disasters in Russia, the game seemed nearly up for Germany by the end of 1944. On the eastern front, after the failure of the German summer offensive in 1943, the Russians had been steadily pushing westward. In early 1944, they reached Estonia and Poland; by the end of that spring, the Ukraine had been liberated, enabling Russia to turn her attention to an invasion of the Balkans. With the Allied invasion of France, Germany had few men to spare for her eastern front; in view of this development, Romania and Bulgaria abandoned Germany. The Russians were now enabled to move swiftly into Yugoslavia, where the retreating Germans were seriously hampered by guerrillas. Toward the end of 1944, the Russians advanced upon Budapest, which was bitterly defended for several months, while in the north the Russians swept the Germans from the Baltic states. Thus, as in the West, Germany lay open to invasion early in 1945; such an invasion was made necessary by German determination to continue the fighting.

As the end was in sight, however, Churchill, Roosevelt, and Stalin met at Yalta in the Crimea (February 7-12, 1945) to discuss plans for defeated Germany. They included provisions for occupying Germany, the country to be divided into four zones to be confided to Britain, France, the United States, and the Soviet Union, with a joint control commission to be seated at Berlin. It was also agreed that a conference should be held in San Francisco on April 25, 1945, to draft a charter for a permanent international organization: the United Nations. Finally, the three powers pledged themselves to aid the recovery of those nations which they had liberated from German control, an agreement which has been controversial ever since. Because that particular decision recognized the Soviet right to reorganize eastern Europe, Churchill and Roosevelt were soon accused of "selling out" to Stalin at Yalta. In fact, they had no alternative but to give Russia her due, unless, of course, they were prepared to drive the Russians from eastern Europe by force. Russia had contributed greatly to the defeat of Germany, and no peace settlement would be possible which ignored Russian interests. If one wants to engage in faultfinding for Russia's powerful position in 1945, it would be necessary to recall those years during which the western powers, including the United States, failed to take the steps which would have prevented Hitler's rise to power; and failed, once he had come to power, to stand firm against his violations of the Versailles settlement. No one knows whether the western world, without the aid of the Soviet Union, could have defeated Hitler; but since the assistance of the Soviet Union was accepted, and accepted gladly, there was no making peace without a consideration of her goals, however little Churchill and Roosevelt may have liked the price which had to be paid. Probably the final verdict will be that American isolation in the 1920's and 1930's made possible the Soviet domination of eastern Europe by 1945.

By February of that year, the Russians had swept through Poland and were approaching Berlin from the east, while the Russian forces in Hungary were invading Austria and cutting off the Axis forces still fighting in Italy from those in Germany. In the West, British, French, and American troops crossed the German frontier and quickly destroyed the defensive system on the left bank of the Rhine. Anglo-American forces also routed the Germans in the Po Valley in Italy, where Mussolini, trying to escape to Switzerland, was caught and shot by anti-Fascists guerrillas. The German forces in Italy surrendered on April 29, there being no hope of escape northward, and it was known that at that moment Berlin was coming under attack by Russian units. Moreover, American and Russian forces had joined on the Elbe River several days before, suggesting that further resistence was futile. On May 1, the Berlin radio admitted the death of Hitler and announced that Admiral Karl Doenitz (1891–   ) had become chancellor. A week later, but only after proposing that the West join Germany against the Soviet Union, the Germans surrendered to General Eisenhower at Reims—and did so unconditionally. Doenitz's government was soon replaced by the Allied Control Commission in Berlin, and the previously delineated occupation zones were assumed by the American, Soviet, British, and French military authorities.

The End of the War in the Pacific

No doubt the Germans would have been defeated more quickly had the western Allies not had the problem of halting the Japanese advance in the Far East. American commitments in particular had been strained by global responsibilities; and while a decision had been made to concentrate on first ending the European conflict, the need to contain Japan diverted American strength and sentenced the nation to peripheral campaigns in 1943—North Africa and Italy—rather than permitting a direct assault upon France. The Russians fretted about American unwillingness to make a more major contribution in Europe at once, while conversely, there were American generals who believed that the primary efforts should be directed against Japan; but certainly United States strategy began to pay off in 1943 as the Russians held firm, the Axis was defeated in the Mediterranean, and the Japanese were stopped and forced to assume the defensive.

After the American victory in the Solomon Islands (early in 1943), Allied pressure was increased on the Japanese garrison on New Guinea. Later that year, the Gilbert Islands and Tarawa were assaulted by the Americans, who crushed the Japanese after a few days of fierce fighting and denied them their easternmost bases, which had been used for air attacks against American sea communications with Australia. The Marshall Islands to the north were next to taste American invasion (February, 1944), following which, the neighboring islands of Kwajalein and Eniwetok were taken. This victory denied the Japanese their bases nearest the Hawaiian Islands. The American and Australian attack then turned westward in two main lines, but both pointing for the Philippine Islands. One drive carried along the north coast of New Guinea and included a successful attack upon the Admiralty Islands. The second drive moved into the Mariana Islands, recaptured Guam, and swept up some of the Japanese bases in the Carolines. In October, 1944, General MacArthur's forces were poised for the reconquest of the Philippines. Japan herself was also beginning to experience the war directly as massive bombing began in the summer of that year.

This "island-hopping" campaign proved to be the major theater in the Far East. In the early days of the war, the Japanese had driven into Burma and threatened an invasion of India, but their supply lines were overextended and vulnerable. But the Japanese had accomplished their main mission—cutting off China from her principal supply route through Burma. To reopen that route, the Southeast Asia Command was established (1943) under Admiral Lord Louis Mountbatten (British 1900–   ), whose troops included a British army, British and Indian guerrillas, and Chinese and American forces. Though they fought in near-impossible terrain and climate and had to be supplied largely by air, they eventually drove the Japanese from Burma. It is probable that they saved India from ultimate invasion, but like the Italian campaign in Europe, the Burma theater was peripheral to the arena of decisive action. Early in 1945, the Burma Road to China was reopened, but by that date much of the Allied assistance to China was airlifted.

MacArthur's campaign to retake the Philippines began with a massive assault upon the island of Leyte (October 19, 1944). The Japanese fleet made its last major effort of the war by trying to interrupt the invasion. Though considerably outnumbered and outgunned by that date, the Japanese came perilously close to success when they managed to decoy one American squadron away from the scene of the main Japanese attack. The remaining American naval units fought a desperate and successful battle to save the Leyte beachhead (Second Battle of the Philippine Sea), permitting the invasion to continue. Preparations were also under way for attacks upon Iwo Jima, 750 miles from Yokohama, and upon Okinawa, which was less than 400 miles from Japan. Both islands were defended stubbornly, the Japanese being perfectly aware that their loss would mean air attacks upon Japan of far greater intensity than had been previously known, but the former fell by mid-March of 1945 and Okinawa was lost in June. There followed the heaviest air offensive of World War II, launched by both land-based and carrier-based planes and supported by the American navy, which dared to shell the Japanese coastal cities. Though deprived of all allies by the summer of 1945, the Japanese continued to resist, and estimates were that the Allied attack upon the home islands would prove costly.

The decision to drop an atomic bomb on Japan has remained controversial ever since, for both political and moral reasons. While the bomb's destructiveness was fully realized, an invasion of Japan with conventional weapons would have cost not only thousands of Japanese lives but those of the attackers as well. The Soviet Union, which had promised to join the Allies against Japan after the defeat of Germany, had made no move to do so, and the evidence was that Stalin would maintain a benevolent neutrality as long as possible to allow Russia to recover in the West. Thus, to bring the war to an end as cheaply and quickly as possible by showing the Japanese the futility of further resistance, two atomic bombs were dropped: the first one on Hiroshima (August 6, 1945) and the second three days later on the naval base at Nagasaki. The first bomb brought the Russians into the war at once, fearful of being denied a part in the Far Eastern settlement. On August 14, 1945, the Japanese agreed to sign an unconditional surrender; the formal ceremony took place only on September 2, on board the battleship *Missouri* in Tokyo Bay.

The awful war had come to an end, but mankind had come to face the fearful prospects of an atomic age, which possessed not only a weapon with enormous destructive power, but also one whose side effects—radiation—seemed likely to alter man's genetic structure and to produce incalculable mutations in future generations. This particular factor accounts for the wave of horrified reaction in the wake of the bomb. In Asia, it was generally believed that the United States would never have used such a weapon against a European nation, and the fact that we did not have the weapon in time to use it against Germany carried little weight in arguments to the contrary. In a world where colored peoples were everywhere on the rise, the atomic bombing of Japan was taken as a significant sign of western disdain for the lives of non-Caucasians.

The formal surrender terms left the United States in occupation of Japan and her island possessions in the Pacific, but the Japanese civil administration was permitted to continue its duties. Only the general staff and military organizations were abolished. China regained control over Inner Mongolia and Manchuria, but she had to share the control of Port Arthur and of Manchurian railroads with Russia. As Stalin put it, Russia had gained revenge for her losses in the war of 1904–1905. Outer Mongolia was recognized as a sphere of Russian influence, and Russia regained the southern half of Sakhalin. The Chinese recovered Formosa and the Pescadores, the total terms revealing that Japan had lost more than the war—she had lost everything accumulated in a half-century. And Russia's gains in the Far East, while seemingly disproportionate to her seven day's war against Japan, were another measure of the price the West needed to pay at Yalta for Russian assistance against Germany. Had the United States and Britain known at the time of Yalta that an atomic bomb would be ready in time to give Japan a knockout blow, they would not have bargained for Russian help against Japan. But no one could have foreseen such contingencies with any certainty, so that, however regrettable it was to make concessions to Russia in Eastern Europe and Outer Mongolia, Allied dependence upon her support required them. Nor did the United States foresee how frightening American possession of an atomic weapon would be for her Soviet ally. It awakened her deepest distrust and made her increasingly determined to retain a protective screen of satellite states. In short, the groundwork had been laid for the uneasy peace after 1945.

SUGGESTIONS FOR FURTHER READING

❧❦

The Post-Versailles Era

The New Cambridge Modern History, Vol. XII, The Era of Violence, 1898-1945 (Cambridge University Press, 1960), note especially the chapters on the League of Nations, on Economic Interdependence, and the British Commonwealth.

Robert Ergang, *Europe in Our Time: 1914 to the Present* (Boston: D. C. Heath, 1953), a standard text with a political emphasis.

George F. Kennan, *Soviet-American Relations, 1917-1920,* 2 vols. (Princeton University Press, 1956-58).

Edward H. Carr, *A History of Soviet Russia,* 6 vols. (New York: Macmillan, 1950-60).

Donald W. Treadgold, *Twentieth Century Russia* (Chicago University Press, 1959).

Max Beloff, *The Foreign Policy of Soviet Russia, 1929-1941,* 2 vols. (London and New York: Oxford University Press, 1947-49).

John M. Hazard, *The Soviet System of Government* (Chicago University Press, 1957).

F. P. Walters, *A History of the League of Nations* (London and New York: Oxford University Press, 1960).

Alfred Cobban, *Dictatorship: Its History and Theory* (New York: Charles Scribner's Sons, 1939).

W. M. Jordan, *Great Britain, France, and the German Problem, 1918-1939* (New York: Oxford University Press, 1943).

Charles L. Mowat, *Britain Between the Wars* (Chicago University Press, 1955)

David Thomson, *Democracy in France: The Third Republic* (London and New York: Oxford University Press, 1946).

Alexander Werth, *The Twilight of France, 1934-1940* (New York: Harper, 1942).

John C. Cairns, "Along the Road Back to France 1940," *American Historical Review,* LXIV (April, 1959), pp. 583-603.

Dante Germino, *The Italian Fascist Party in Power: A Study in Totalitarian Rule* (University of Minnesota Press, 1959).

Robert L. Wolff, *The Balkans in Our Time* (Harvard University Press, 1956).

Hugh Seton-Watson, *Eastern Europe Between the Wars, 1918-1941* (Cambridge University Press, 1946).

Charles A. Gulick, *Austria from Hapsburg to Hitler,* 2 vols. (University of California Press, 1948).

Robert Kerner, ed., *Czechoslovakia* (University of California Press, 1945) and *Yugoslavia* (University of California Press, 1949).

C. A. Macartney, *A History of Hungary, 1929-1945,* 2 vols. (New York: Praeger, 1957).

Bernadotte E. Schmitt, ed., *Poland* (University of California Press, 1945).

John K. Galbraith, *The Great Crash, 1929* (Boston: Houghton, Mifflin, 1955).

H. V. Hodson, *Slump and Recovery, 1929-1937: A Survey of World Economic Affairs* (London and New York: Oxford University Press, 1938).

Robert T. Clark, *The Fall of the German Republic: A Political History* (London: G. Allen and Unwin, 1935).

Clinton L. Rossiter, *Constitutional Dictatorship: Crisis Government in the Modern Democracies* (Princeton University Press, 1948).

J. W. Wheeler-Bennett, *Wooden Titan: Hindenburg in Twenty Years of German History, 1914-1934* (New York: W. Morrow and Co., 1936).

W. Ebenstein, *The Nazi State* (New York: Farrar and Rinehart, 1943).

J. F. Meenan, *The Italian Corporative System* (Cork, Ire.: University Press, 1944).

The Coming of the Second World War

Charles A. Micaud, *The French Right and Nazi Germany, 1933-1939* (Duke University Press, 1943).

R. W. Seton-Watson, *Britain and the Dictators: A Survey of Post-War British Policy* (New York: Macmillan, 1938).

Norman J. Padelford, *International Law and Diplomacy in the Spanish Civil Strife* (New York: Macmillan, 1939).

E. Wiskemann, *The Rome-Berlin Axis: A History of the Relations Between Hitler and Mussolini* (New York: Oxford University Press, 1949).

Edward H. Carr, *The Twenty Years' Crisis, 1919-1939* (London: Macmillan, 1946).

A. H. Furnia, *The Diplomacy of Appeasement: Anglo-French Relations and the Prelude to World War II, 1931-1938* (Washington, D. C.: University Press, 1960).

Francis C. Jones, *Japan's New Order in East Asia: Its Rise and Fall, 1937-1945* (London and New York: Oxford University Press, 1954).

Hugh Thomas, *The Spanish Civil War* (New York: Harper and Bros., 1960), as close to definitive as anything yet published.

L. B. Namier, *Europe in Decay: Study in Disintegration, 1936-1940* (London: Macmillan, 1950).

John W. Wheeler-Bennett, *Munich: Prologue to Tragedy* (New York: Duell, Sloan and Pearce, 1948).

B. H. Klein, *Germany's Economic Preparations for War* (Harvard University Press, 1959).

Konrad Heiden, *Der Fuehrer: Hitler's Rise to Power* (Boston: Houghton Mifflin, 1944).

Herbert Feis, *The Road to Pearl Harbor: The Coming of the War Between the United States and Japan* (Princeton University Press: 1950).

The Second World War

Sir Winston S. Churchill, *The Second World War,* 6 vols. (Boston: Houghton Mifflin, 1948-1953), a brilliant tour de force.

John F. C. Fuller, *The Second World War, 1939-1945: A Strategical and Tactical History* (New York: Duell, Sloan and Pearce, 1949), by a well-known military authority.

Louis L. Snyder, *The War: A Concise History, 1939-1945* (New York: J. Messner, 1960).

Samuel E. Morison, *History of the United States Naval Operations in World War II,* 15 vols. (Boston: Little, Brown, 1947-1960), a monumental work of great distinction.

Gerhard L. Weinberg, *Germany and the Soviet Union, 1939-1941* (Leyden: E. J. Brill, 1954).

Herbert Feis, *Churchill, Roosevelt, Stalin: The War They Waged and the Peace They Sought* (Princeton University Press, 1957) and *Between War and Peace: The Potsdam Conference* (Princeton University Press, 1960).

John L. Snell and others, *The Meaning of Yalta, Big Three Diplomacy and the New Balance of Power* (Louisiana State University Press, 1956).

Herbert Feis, *Japan Subdued: The Atomic Bomb and the End of the War in the Pacific* (Princeton University Press, 1961).

❧ 15 ❧

Epilogue:
The Culture of the Twentieth Century

From our view, limited as it is by contemporaneity, the twentieth century seems fraught with contradictions. We have lived in political and social crisis ever since 1914 and now possess the power to destroy much of civilized life; our arts reveal not merely our cultural crisis, but also our spiritual sickness; while our sciences enjoy an almost unparalleled vitality and prestige. Especially can this be said of physics, where two revolutionary ideas undermined classical physics and led us into the atomic age.

THE SCIENCES

Starting in 1905, Albert Einstein (German, 1879–1955) began to publish a criticism of Newtonian mechanics; his position we have somewhat misnamed the theory of relativity. Classical physics held time to be an absolute, so that the past, present, and future were perfectly clear and unmistakable terms. Moreover, space was seen as an absolute, within which all phenomena were seen in three dimensions. Such a mechanics was applicable to this world alone, but Einstein sought new laws of mechanics which would be absolutely applicable in all coordinate systems and not merely to earth. He suggested, therefore, that motion is always relative to the motion and position of the observer, and that the only constant factor to be related to motion is the speed of light. To put it another way, he saw that the interval between the past and the future has a finite extension in time which depends on the distance in space between an event and its observer. Space and time, therefore, attain an absolute character only when they are fused (space-time) and become part of a four-dimensional continuum. The argument has been called the theory of relativity for evident reasons, but it appears that Einstein's theory was a new "absolutism" and can be regarded as the culmination of classical physics.

The postulation of quanta was the second revolutionary theory, and though its importance was not immediately recognized, quantum theory completely unsettled classical physics. We must recall that the Newtonians saw the universe as a precise mechanism whose motions and evolution could be predicted with considerable exactness. This was possible because the Newtonians, as noted above, saw space and time as fixed, and therefore each phsyical event could be localized. Furthermore, all dynamic quantities, such as energy and motion, were regarded as derived quantities, requiring the aid of velocity. The difficulties began in the late nineteenth century, when classical physics seemed unable to account for certain phenomena, the emission and absorption of radiation in particular.

This problem was recognized when it was noticed that a "black body" (a body which absorbs all the radiation falling on it) gave off a continuous spectrum rather than discrete spectral lines, and the shape of its spectral curve could not be accurately deduced either by using Newtonian mechanics, electromagnetic theory, or thermodynamics. Clearly a new physical mechanism had to be found, and it fell to Max Planck (German, 1858–1947) to propose the solution—the quantum theory—which launched physics on an entirely new course. His answer was that energy is emitted and absorbed only in whole quanta—that is, whole units of energy. In classical physics, the energy of an oscillator depended solely on its frequency and amplitude; but Planck assumed that, while all frequencies are possible, an oscillator may possess only discrete amounts of energy. As he put it, "matter can emit radiant energy only in finite quantities proportional to the frequency."[1] Yet, he found it difficult to accept the notion that natural processes could be discontinuous. Subsequent investigation by others, however, has confirmed the theory, and

1. Louis de Broglie, *The Revolution in Physics* (New York, Noonday Press, 1953), p. 106.

while it has revolutionized physics, it has not yet had the same impact upon other disciplines as, for example, Newton's or Darwin's ideas.

In astronomy, however, scientists in the twentieth century are optimistic that we are on the verge of collecting new data on a problem which will clearly have enormous and immediate philosophical implications: the problem of the origin of the universe. Optical telescopes in use today give us information about the universe up to distances of two billion light years and reveal the existence of several million galaxies, further suggesting a high degree of uniformity in the structure of the universe. Under construction, however, are radiotelescopes which will presumably push back the universal frontier several billion light years. The expectation is that the new information will enable us to formulate new physical laws about the past and the future, as well as settle the age-old argument about how the universe came to be.

Currently there are four major hypotheses, the first three of which are evolutionary models of creation: (1) that the universe started from a given point at a given time and expanded continuously, and will continue to expand infinitely; (2) that the universe, at the beginning of time, had a definite radius, and then began to expand infinitely; (3) that the universe began at a given point, expanded to a certain maximum, and then collapsed to a point again, this evolution repeating itself infinitely; (4) that though the stars and the galaxies may evolve, they do so within the framework of a fixed universe. Thus the universe would look pretty much the same despite the passage of time.

If the radiotelescopes, by taking us back billions of years in time, show that the universe was more compact than it is now, then one of the evolutionary hypotheses would be correct; but if the number of galaxies was the same then as now, the steady-state theory would presumably be correct. The latter would be especially baffling, since it would raise a question as to whether there had ever been "a beginning." None of the data available today gives a definite advantage to any cosmology, and we broach the problem here partly because it is one of the great questions of twentieth-century science and partly because it reveals the traditional optimism of modern science that it is on the verge of some definitive answer. Yet the history of experimental science shows that new discoveries, while adding to our knowledge, generally reveal deeper mysteries for our solution; and one contemporary astrophysicist, the Englishman Alfred C. B. Lovell, frankly avows that metaphysics will have to provide explanations which science, by definition, cannot.

THE ACCELERATION OF LIFE

Acceleration has been one of the most characteristic qualities of post-1914 life. It is especially to be seen in the speed with which new sciences feed each other and with which they are applied technologically. Only fifteen years, for example, elapsed between the splitting of the atom and the production of an atomic bomb. Compare that to the application of Watt's engine to locomotion, which took four times as long. Such speed hampers the development of an integrated civilization; hence, while adding immeasurably to improving conditions of material existence, the dynamism of science has been contributing to the cultural crisis already gathering in the nineteenth century.

War may not be the only mother of invention, but Europe's preoccupation with military matters since 1914 no doubt stimulated the development of scientific and technological enterprise. In contrast, the impact of the continuing threat of total war upon those whose lives are devoted to the quest for beauty or for the meaning and purpose of life was almost wholly negative. Philosophical systems and artistic creeds, with some exceptions, have revealed a perplexity, a loss of purpose, a state of shock. Given some other aspects of acceleration in contemporary life—the speed of various modes of transportation and communications especially—the dilemmas of the universe are piled upon us with increasing swiftness. We fail to notice, when it comes to such everyday matters as communication by telephone or travel by air, that the lives of Europeans one hundred years ago had a tempo more comparable to life in Periclean Athens than to that of our own day. The pace of life, the pace of change, was relatively slow, and men were not required to adjust to a swiftly changing environment, where old traditions are shattered and new ones have little time to congeal.

Those who wish to retain a grip on reality today and in the future, despite the fantastic piling up of information in all disciplines, will have to resist the apparent drift toward specialization which has been spawned by the increasing complexity of our culture. This specialization has been all the worse, as the novelist-physicist Sir Charles P. Snow (1905–   ) has shown,[2] because it has tended to divide our intellectual and practical lives into two polar groups—what he calls the literary and scientific groups.

2. Sir Charles P. Snow, *The Two Cultures and the Scientific Revolution* (Cambridge University Press, 1961).

Above: *Guernica* by Pablo Picasso
Left: Sigmund Freud
Below: Albert Einstein

Above: Arnold J. Toynbee
Left: Igor Stravinsky

Between them there is incomprehension, distrust, and downright hostility. Part of the misunderstanding derived from the industrial revolution and the subsequent debate over whether it had been a triumph or a disaster for European civilization. The literati, who had had no part in the technical advances, hated the industrial revolution for its presumed brutalization of the working classes and its emphasis on material gain. In many respects, the "humanists" remained relatively indifferent to man's social condition in their primary preoccupation with man's tragic destiny as an individual. The scientists were seen as annoyingly optimistic, since they saw the possibility of improving the social condition of man. Sir Charles is right to insist that these are not incompatible perceptions of man's lot, though they are usually seen as such. And he argues that the only solution to the growing schism is a rigorous general education, without which western culture will disintegrate.

Indeed, most historians today are concerned about the signs of cultural decay around us; this concern has driven us to study the nature of civilization itself more than was customary in the past. In 1918, the German Oswald Spengler (1880–1936) published his *The Decline of the West,* which was soon translated into English and widely read in Europe and America. A prophet of doom, he drew a parallel between European civilization in the twentieth century and that of the ancient world in its last stages, seeing the rise and fall of civilizations as rigorously mechanistic and beyond our ability to control through reason. This organic approach to history has also been used by Arnold J. Toynbee (1889–   ) in his twelve-volume *Study of History,* but with results considerably less pessimistic than Spengler's. Despite the controversial nature of Toynbee's views in historical circles, it is notable that he remains the outstanding historian of our time in the public mind, reflecting, as he does, the temper of our time. The public, in short, demands that the historian pronounce on the state of our civilizational health.

Some historians, it is true, resist the tendency to look at history on the grand scale and emphasize the uniqueness of every historical event. They warn against grand historical patterns as being figments of our need to see meaning and unity in the past. Some would go so far as to question, in view of the disparate elements within western society, whether we can really even properly speak of something unified called "European civilization." Unquestionably, it is important to recognize where there is disunity or disagreement within an apparent unity, and it may even be that a civilization is not the story of continuous development as much as it is the story of distinct societies which are linked together. What links them are basic ideas and traditions, and where one finds those basic ingredients, he may assume the existence of a common civilization. It is generally agreed that European civilization was the merger of the Roman and Christian traditions; and if—to go back to the questions being asked of historians today—one wishes to know the state of our civilization, one must inquire about the current commitment to the ideals of the traditions that formed it.

TRADITION AND THE ARTS

Conventional art forms were increasingly abandoned after 1914 as a reflection of, or a reaction to, the destruction of time-honored traditions and truths. The discord and lack of melody in music, the disappearance of subject matter in the plastic arts, and the absence of rhyme in verse, all reflected the increasing discord between man and an environment which was expanding in complexity.

> We are the hollow men
> We are the stuffed men
> Leaning together
> Headpiece filled with straw. Alas!
> Our dried voices, when
> We whisper together
> Are quiet and meaningless
> As wind in dry grass
> Or rats' feet over broken glass
> In our dry cellar
>
> . . .
>
> Those who have crossed
> With direct eyes, to death's other Kingdom
> Remember us—if at all—not as lost
> Violent souls, but only
> As the hollow men
> The stuffed men.
>
> . . .
>
> *This is the way the world ends*
> *This is the way the world ends*
> *This is the way the world ends*
> *Not with a bang but a whimper.*[3]

3. T. S. Eliot, fragment from "The Hollow Men," *Collected Poems 1909-1962,* Harcourt, Brace and World, Inc.

The emphasis in the arts was upon abstraction, suggesting that the natural world was to be avoided in life itself, not merely in artistic representation. It is undeniable that abstract representation has revealed new aesthetic truths; it is equally important to recognize the cultural crisis which these experimental forms reveal.

No naturalistic representation was intended in either cubism or surrealism, the dominant schools in the plastic arts during the 1920's and 1930's. The surrealist movement, led by Salvador Dali (Spanish, 1904–   ), was influenced by Freudian psychology. The principal idea was to explore the subconscious through the use of free association. Cubism had the greater impact upon contemporary art. Here deliberate distortions were obtained by using either abstract or geometric linear arangements, methods most brilliantly employed by the Spaniard Pablo Picasso (1881–   ) and his French contemporary, Henri Matisse (1869–1954).

The rejection of ancient and refined traditions was also evident in music. Arnold Schönberg (Austrian, 1874–1951), for instance, insisted that there is no real difference between concord and discord, and that man must learn to perceive tonalities which are present. Thus it followed that all possible tonal combinations ought to be accepted as chords. Schönberg's music has sometimes been called *Augenmusik* (eye music), because its intricacies can be more easily seen on the page than heard by the ear. The Russian Igor Stravinsky (1882–   ) and the Hungarian Béla Bartók (1881–1945) moved in a different direction from Schönberg. Dissonance was evident in their music, too, but they made much use of primitive sounds and rhythms, and, in the case of Bartók, of folk music.

In the literary world, André Gide (French, 1869–1951) was one of the giants, exerting tremendous influence upon other writers in the decades between the two world wars. While the novel was his usual medium, it is better to think of him as a moralist investigating the deep conflict between social values and individual sensuality, a conflict of which he was a tragic victim and for which his *Journal* covering the years 1889–1949 is the best source.

Among German novelists of the period, Thomas Mann (1875–1955) stands out. *Buddenbrooks* (1901) seemed to be a portrait of the decline of middle-class, capitalist society, but this was intended to symbolize the decay of the traditional values of old Europe.

Beyond the tendency to portray the conflict in, or the decay of, society, writers increasingly built their novels by drawing on inward experience. The Irish James Joyce (1882–1941) was so inspired in writing *Ulysses*

(1922) and the *Portrait of an Artist as a Young Man* (1917). The most astonishing practitioner of inward analysis, however, was Marcel Proust (French, 1871–1922), whose literary achievement may well be the most impressive in the first half of our century. Though the lengthy work is generally published in a number of volumes, Proust's *A la Recherche du temps perdu* (Remembrance of Things Past) was intended to be one long novel. Appearing in sections between 1913 and 1927, the novel has been variously described as the revelation of a decaying society and as a pessimistic analysis of love. While this is true, the real subject of Proust's novel is the unreality of the external world where life goes by and time is lost. He discovered through sensation-memory, not merely the materials for his novel, but a device for recapturing time—of making time stand still, as if in eternity. The past then becomes the present, but only within the mind of the individual.

SOCIAL AND ECONOMIC THOUGHT

In the recent past, the social sciences in general reflect a growing recognition of the complexity of both the individual and society. This means that we are less ready than were the eighteenth and nineteenth centuries to approach man and his society with a faith in the universe as a self-regulating mechanism, with its various components discoverable through the use of human reason. (Beyond that, it has been increasingly questioned whether laws of nature are even applicable to man in society.) Individuals are seen to behave irrationally, hence in an unpredictable fashion; economic "laws," such as the price-regulating mechanism of supply and demand, seem somewhat less reliable than laws should be; different cultures are seen to respond variously in their development of social controls; and irritating creatures called historians now insist on the uniqueness of events, making it embarrassingly difficult to generalize.

Thus, the pattern of the social sciences after World War I was similar to that of the sciences: a trend away from a rigid, mechanistic view of reality, toward a more organic or relativist view. To this perceived complexity of reality one must add the complexities wrought by improved communications and by the rapidly increasing world population—which have made universal and immediate many matters which earlier ages could meet with the luxury of time and isolation. For all the wonders and benefits of burgeoning science and technology, they open new worlds of problems and, if anything, deepen the mysteries of the universe yet to be plumbed. Small wonder, then, that men, since 1914, have increasingly seen the need to take a hand in the management of human affairs.

In the economic realm, for instance, *laissez faire* has come to imply a studied indifference to reality. Beginning in the 1920's, John Maynard Keynes (British, 1883–1946) set out to revolutionize "the way the world thinks about economic problems." Assuming that economic life is not self-regulating and that the price mechanism is especially unresponsive to the needs of the highly complex modern society, Keynes urged the planned governmental management of critical economic life. Devices such as the regulation of interest rates, of production ceilings, of subsidies, and of government spending, and the raising or lowering of taxes to encourage or restrict investment—all so familiar to us in the western world today— are the results of the Keynesian revolution. Since the alternative to the Keynesian revolution in the twentieth century has been total economic planning by the state, as in Nazi Germany, Fascist Italy, or the Communist states, it is fair to support Keynes' own contention that his purpose was to preserve liberal capitalism by the use of limited controls to prevent the ruinous "boom and bust" cycles of *laissez faire* capitalism.

NATIONALISM OVERSEAS

The scientific and technical culture which has been grafted to the main shoots of European civilization in the past century and a half, contributing notably to the material well-being of the western peoples, was associated with the rise of the powerful nation-states of the West. As a result, peoples living in other parts of the world came to equate progress with national independence. By the mid-twentieth century, the decline of the old colonial empires and the urgency to industrialize the newly independent nations had become the most revolutionary factor in global politics and economics.

This wholesale "westernization" has not been an unmitigated good, in part because the culture being borrowed was already in deep trouble on its home ground. Nationalism, for example, had come to a point of virulence in Europe, where statesmen recognized the absolute need to secure international organization for European salvation. Exported, nationalism is breeding nationalism and provides an artificial façade behind which are hidden grave problems perhaps insoluble for the new nation-states.

Arab nationalism is a good case in point, for by diagnosing all Arabic problems as foreign-inflicted, Arab nationalists tend to ignore the inadequate economic resources and the anachronistic social structure within Islam, which are the real reasons for Arabic weakness in the modern world. Independence, moreover, has sometimes been given to people whose political, social, or economic realities do not permit the integration of a viable nation-state, developments which should bring to mind at once the experience of the succession states of Central Europe after 1919. Another matter is the tendency of the newly independent states to insist on equality with all other states in world affairs, demands which in no way correspond to their national strengths. Freedom has, of course, made some things better. In India, as one example, only a native government could tackle the age-old problem of caste; the British had necessarily backed away from the religious issue. But the over-all picture is not bright. As a distinguished historian recently put it, the world is faced with new states with "inadequate economic resources, with erratic frontiers, with dissident minorities, with delusions of grandeur and, what is worse, of goodness."[4]

The most paradoxical aspect of the new nation-states arising out of the decaying empires in Africa and Asia is that they turn more easily to the Soviet Union than to the United States for guidance—in other words, to international communism, which is antithetical to their own national movements. The Soviet Union takes great advantage of her ability to pose as a recent rebel against an imperial regime, while the United States rarely exploits her similar origin nor makes it clear that she, too, has been the champion of the right of nationalities to self-determination. A more subtle and critical matter, however, is the Soviet argument that ideology follows economic development—in other words, that ideas merely justify private and national interest. Free men have usually argued to the contrary: that institutions ought to be formed according to ideals. While it is understandable that national leaders intent upon rapid economic growth will see merit in the Soviet argument, the fate of freedom throughout the world is put in jeopardy; and largely because Europe and America failed to demonstrate the greatness of their Roman and Christian traditions. If there is no longer any faith in them, should we expect them to be adopted by others?

4. Denis W. Brogan, "The End of Empire," *Saturday Evening Post* (Nov. 29, 1958), p. 98.

A SUMMING UP

Historians of the future will surely see the generations after 1918 as unusually plagued with dilemmas of the first magnitude, and they will likely be struck by the defeatism and the pessimism with which the most sensitive elements of western society greeted these troubles. The world has never been without its troubles, but response to them has differed greatly. On occasion, men have understood the imminence of disaster, yet have known the necessity of going out to meet the danger unflinchingly, even against overwhelming odds; and there are times when men have seemed unequal to the odds against them and turn inward in their despair. Self-doubt, which soon becomes self-analysis, demobilizes the human machinery for great deeds; and if we assume that the individual is a microcosm of his society, we may assume that widespread self-doubt reflects anxiety for the future of one's civilization, that life itself has lost its meaning and purpose. When that point is reached, the individual lives only for the death of himself and his society.

The study of the unconscious in the twentieth century has made us aware of the nonrational and instinctive impulses which underlie human nature. Sigmund Freud (Austrian, 1856–1939), the most brilliantly suggestive of the modern students of psychology, defined his new science of psychoanalysis as the "discovery of the unconscious in mental life." Psychoanalysis was really based on the theory of repression—that is, that society necessarily represses the individual, and the individual represses himself. As a result, the individual is really disowning some of his ideas and desires, forcing them into his unconscious, where the conscious will no longer be aware of them. But banishing them to the unconscious does not render them impotent. Dreams, neurotic symptoms, and certain errors (Freudian slips) reveal not only the presence of unconscious ideas and desires, but also their nature. All are forms of what Freud called "wish fulfillment." His further assumption is that we are all neurotic, and that civilization itself, being the initial represser, is the source of neuroses. Since the conscious and the unconscious will necessarily be in conflict, Freudian therapy was designed to force the unconscious into consciousness. Most of our repressed desires presumably are those of childhood, especially sexual desires, repressed because they are classified as abnormal or perverse by society. This suggests, of course, that "normal" adult sexuality is a cultural, rather than a biological, phenomenon; and while

Freud's therapy is designed to free us of neuroses, one wonders about the future of civilization if neuroses must all wither away.

We are, none the less, in the age of psychology, as many novels of the last few decades reveal. The modern novelist is not generally concerned with great problems—that is, universal issues—but dotes on individuals whose lives run the gamut of human frailties and frustrations. The "hero" is always *alone,* and we are asked to pity him, warped creature that he is, and enter into the halls of hopelessness wherein he dwells. There is no tragedy here, for there is no greatness: merely his sad problem, which the novelist "analyses." The rest of the universe, if it appears at all, is incidental scenery. This concern for the individual out of social context represents the contemporary loss of feeling for history, for tradition. The past seems worthless; the present has no meaning; and the future, if ever contemplated, promises insupportable horrors. If the novel implies any virtue at all, it will fall into the tiny bailiwick of self-gratification, likely as not sexual. Nothing great is seen in the world. "What a piece of work is man," wrote Shakespeare. "How noble in reason, how infinite in faculties! In form and moving, how express and admirable! In action how like an angel! In apprehension how like a god!" And so, in three short centuries, from being a bit less than the angels man has come to think of himself as being only a few evolutionary hops ahead of Pavlov's dogs. The equation is clear: since animals see no order in the world, they see no meaning or purpose to life.

The contemporary loss of feeling for history is also linked to the rapid acceleration of human life in our century:

[The] material and spiritual changes in the conditions of human existence have occurred since 1900 at a tremendous rate and with a speed that accelerates geometrically. We can no longer speak accurately of "the slow change of time." As I see it, mankind is faced with nothing short of the loss of its memory, and this memory is history.[5]

When an individual loses his memory, his primary loss is the sense of who he is and where he is going. Loss of civilizational memory amounts to the same thing—but on a grand scale.

If one were to judge the vitality of the art of any era by its volume, then we would have to admit that the art of the twentieth century commands respect. Novels appear by the bushel, verse pops out at us from

5. Carl Bridenbaugh, "The Great Mutation," *American Historical Review,* Vol. LXVIII, No. 2 (Jan., 1963), p. 326.

every magazine and newspaper, music has become an impressive industry employing millions, and any child not taught to sketch, model, or render something on the piano is judged to have been deprived. The word "therapeutic" is heard throughout the land to explain this use of time: each one of us must be able to "express himself," the saying goes, suggesting that the arts are seen as self-administered emotional purges. One might not object to such common views, were they not a reflection of attitudes expressed by serious artists and critics. Contemporary poetry, painting, and music wallow in an obscurantism which, while it parades itself as the latest subtlety, represents a conscious refusal to reach out for those hearts and minds which turn to the arts for their power to invoke beauty and truth.

No one should quarrel with the artistic experimenter who seeks new richness and freshness, the better to give us pleasurable insights; but we have desperate reason to shout "Fraud!" at that which is novelty for novelty's sake and at that which would astound by confounding us. Too much has been made of incidents of masterpieces' going unrecognized as such by contemporaries. Much great art has been quicky recognized, and largely because the artists give form to the deepest aspirations of their age. But not in the twentieth century! Our arts must be taught before they can be enjoyed, and their obscurities must be defended by professional critics. Such *aloneness* is sickness: alienation.

This brings to mind the philosophy of existentialism, whose roots are deep in the nineteenth century but which really flourished in Europe only after the holocaust of the world wars. Never an easily defined movement because of its many branches (there are, for instance, both Christian and atheist existentialists), several basic assumptions were made by all existential enthusiasts. They generally denied man's ability to know reality through the use of reason, suggesting an anti-intellectualism; and they did not see truth or reality in anything but subjective, highly personal, terms. Existence alone, in other words, is reality and is regarded as a fearful, agonizing plight. Men are seen as cast into an alien and hostile world, with death as the final absurdity. Each man is inevitably alone, both in his knowledge and in his values. This is not merely a recognition, which we all have, that some things can be known only to us alone, but a pessimistic assertion that there are no eternal truths and that human life has no meaning or purpose beyond what we ourselves invent in our search for security. Thus, existentialism is a philosophy of aloneness which does not admit that man has a place in the rationale of nature.

Perhaps we have arrived, in the twentieth century, at one of those points in the history of all civilizations when stocktaking is overdue. Values must be reassessed and their origins re-examined, especially to ascertain the relation of modern science to man's values. It means tackling again the age-old dilemma of man's nature and the implications of his being a social animal no longer in the state of nature, since from that contradiction are born the key paradoxes which baffle our judgments and benumb our wills. We are in search, in short, of meaning and purpose to give our lives direction, that we may fulfill our natures and not be doomed to pointless existence.

There is no escaping certain paradoxes of which only the thinking animal can be aware. We recognize that there is much about life which is admirable and lovable, just as the cruelty of life strikes us at every turn. We tend to think of life as such a wonderful and sacred thing that we deny ourselves the right to destroy it; yet even a casual glance at nature reveals it to be a state of war where life lives on life. Men are perplexed by the question of whether they have the right to take another's life in defense of their own, and they cannot properly turn to nature for the answer because there is no right or wrong in nature. What is the answer if we ask whether nature is kind to a toad by feeding him a bug, or cruel to a bug by feeding him to a toad? Neither can we turn to natural science for answers about values. As the noted physiologist Sir Charles Sherrington (1861–1952) insisted, it is the business of natural science to distinguish the true from the false, but not what is right from what is evil. In other words, scientific man is different from moral man, not because their judgments are at odds, but because they supplement each other in the whole man. Similarly, nature and society are different realms, and their rules must not be confused.

Paradise was lost, we are told, when the apple of knowledge was eaten and man first became aware of good and evil. Expelled from Eden, or nonmoral nature, man has suffered ever since for his ability to do evil. In times of trouble, he has yearned to return to the supposed comfort and perfection of nature; and you will note how many cultural manifestations of our century amount to a desire to escape society—civilization—to evade the responsibility of living in the imperfect world. Not only is man's lot otherwise, but thinking men have generally been in revolt against nature, not only seeing nature as a state of war, but also recognizing the higher life possible only in society. Life in society, however, implies certain responsibilities against which "the generation of aloneness" is sinning. Only in nature is the individual properly concerned for his own survival alone. Society requires individuals who not only sense the suffering and pain of others, but who also make that external suffering their own. Transcendence of the self is the highest plane of life, and its possibility belongs uniquely to man. Its actuality makes us able to distinguish a man from a pig. But if our values continue to erode toward aloneness, then we shall surely perish from the earth.

SUGGESTIONS FOR FURTHER READING

Twentieth Century Civilization

H. Stuart Hughes, *Consciousness and Society: The Reorientation of European Social Thought, 1890-1930* (New York: Alfred A. Knopf, 1958).

Max Beloff, *Europe and the Europeans: An International Discussion* (London: Chatto and Windus, 1957).

Raymond Williams, *Culture and Society, 1780-1950* (Columbia University Press, 1958).

Cassou, Pevsner, and Langui, *Gateway to the Twentieth Century: Art and Culture in a Changing World* (New York: McGraw Hill, 1961).

Sidney Hook, *Marx and the Marxists: The Ambiguous Legacy* (Princeton University Press, 1955).

Herbert Read, *Art and Society* (New York: Macmillan, 1937).

M. Colum, *From These Roots: The Ideas That Have Made Modern Literature* (Columbia University Press, 1944).

A. N. Wilder, *Theology and Modern Literature* (Harvard University Press, 1958).

Sir Charles P. Snow, *The Two Cultures and the Scientific Revolution* (Cambridge University Press, 1961).

Theodore H. White, *Fire in the Ashes: Europe in Mid-Century* (New York: Sloane, 1953).

Hajo Holborn, *The Political Collapse of Europe* (New York: Alfred A. Knopf, 1951).

Sir William C. Dampier, *A History of Science* (New York: Macmillan, 4th ed., 1949).

Ernst Zimmer, *Revolution in Physics* (New York: Harcourt, Brace, 1936).

*Louis de Broglie, *The Revolution in Physics* (New York: Noonday, 1953).

*Morris H. Shamos, *Great Experiments in Physics* (New York: Holt, Dryden, 1959).

*Edwin Schrödinger, *What Is Life* (New York: Anchor, 1956).

Carleton S. Coon, *The Origin of Races* (New York: Alfred A. Knopf, 1962).

Theodosius Dobzhansky, *Mankind Evolving* (Yale University Press, 1962).

*Clement V. Durell, *Readable Relativity* (New York: Harper Torchbook, 1960).

*Ortega y Gasset, *The Dehumanization of Art and Other Writings on Art and Culture* (Garden City: Doubleday-Anchor, 1956).

*Sigmund Freud, *A General Selection from the Works of* (Garden City: Doubleday-Anchor, 1952).

*C. G. Jung, *Psyche and Symbol: A Selection from the Writings of* (Garden City: Doubleday-Anchor, 1958).

*Will Herberg, ed., *Four Existentialist Theologians* (Garden City: Doubleday-Anchor, 1958).

* Available in paperbound editions.

Genealogical Tables

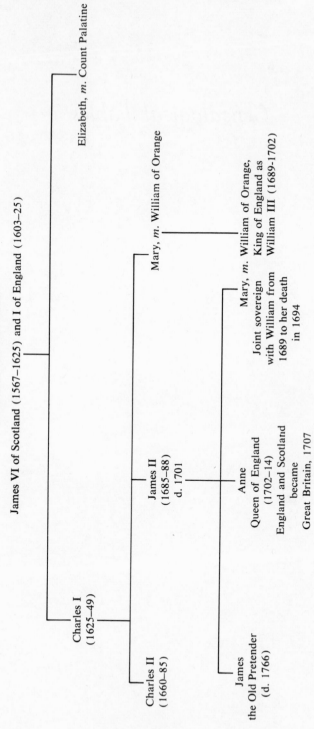

HOUSE OF STUART

James VI of Scotland (1567–1625) and I of England (1603–25)

Elizabeth, *m.* Count Palatine

Charles I (1625–49)

Charles II (1660–85)

James II (1685–88) d. 1701

Mary, *m.* William of Orange

James the Old Pretender (d. 1766)

Anne Queen of England (1702–14) England and Scotland became Great Britain, 1707

Mary, *m.* William of Orange, King of England as William III (1689-1702)

Joint sovereign with William from 1689 to her death in 1694

HOUSE OF HANOVER

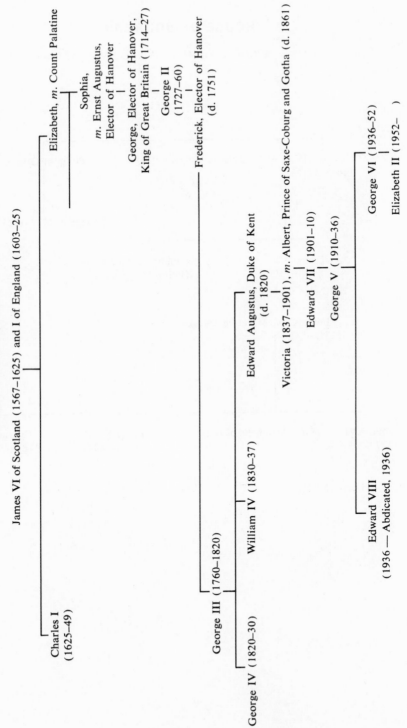

James VI of Scotland (1567–1625) and I of England (1603–25)

Charles I (1625–49)

Elizabeth, *m.* Count Palatine

Sophia, *m.* Ernst Augustus, Elector of Hanover

George, Elector of Hanover, King of Great Britain (1714–27)

George II (1727–60)

Frederick, Elector of Hanover (d. 1751)

George III (1760–1820)

George IV (1820–30)

William IV (1830–37)

Edward Augustus, Duke of Kent (d. 1820)

Victoria (1837–1901), *m.* Albert, Prince of Saxe-Coburg and Gotha (d. 1861)

Edward VII (1901–10)

George V (1910–36)

Edward VIII (1936 — Abdicated, 1936)

George VI (1936–52)

Elizabeth II (1952–)

HOUSE OF BOURBON

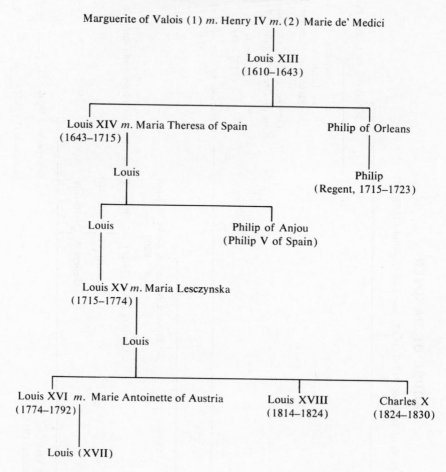

Marguerite of Valois (1) *m.* Henry IV *m.* (2) Marie de' Medici

Louis XIII
(1610–1643)

Louis XIV *m.* Maria Theresa of Spain
(1643–1715)

Philip of Orleans

Louis

Philip
(Regent, 1715–1723)

Louis

Philip of Anjou
(Philip V of Spain)

Louis XV *m.* Maria Lesczynska
(1715–1774)

Louis

Louis XVI *m.* Marie Antoinette of Austria
(1774–1792)

Louis XVIII
(1814–1824)

Charles X
(1824–1830)

Louis (XVII)

HOUSE OF ORLEANS

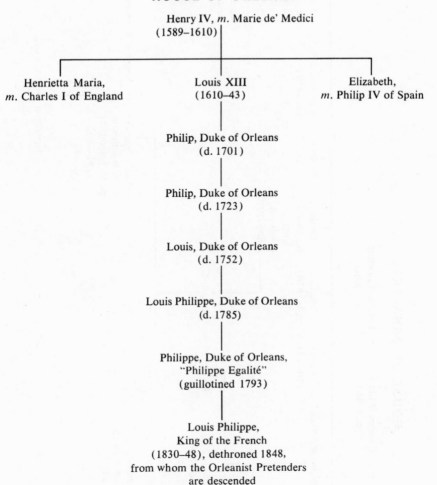

Henry IV, *m*. Marie de' Medici
(1589–1610)

Henrietta Maria,
m. Charles I of England

Louis XIII
(1610–43)

Elizabeth,
m. Philip IV of Spain

Philip, Duke of Orleans
(d. 1701)

Philip, Duke of Orleans
(d. 1723)

Louis, Duke of Orleans
(d. 1752)

Louis Philippe, Duke of Orleans
(d. 1785)

Philippe, Duke of Orleans,
"Philippe Egalité"
(guillotined 1793)

Louis Philippe,
King of the French
(1830–48), dethroned 1848,
from whom the Orleanist Pretenders
are descended

HOUSE OF BONAPARTE

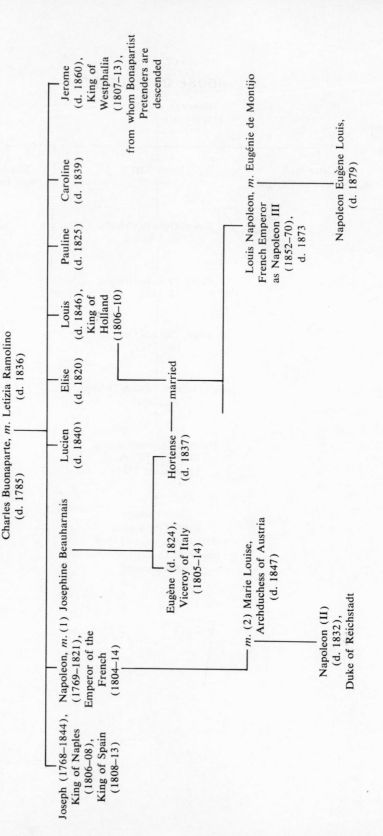

HOUSE OF ROMANOV

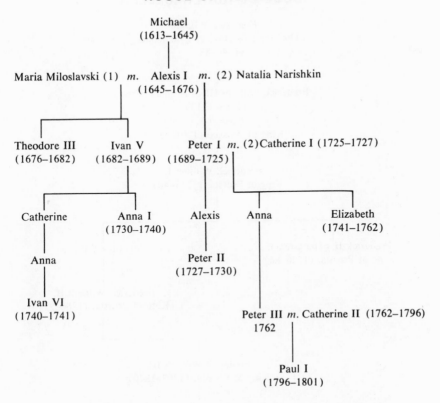

Michael
(1613–1645)

Maria Miloslavski (1) *m.* Alexis I *m.* (2) Natalia Narishkin
(1645–1676)

Theodore III   Ivan V   Peter I *m.* (2)Catherine I (1725–1727)
(1676–1682)   (1682–1689)   (1689–1725)

Catherine   Anna I   Alexis   Anna   Elizabeth
               (1730–1740)   (1741–1762)

Anna   Peter II
                             (1727–1730)

Ivan VI
(1740–1741)
                                         Peter III *m.* Catherine II (1762–1796)
                                         1762

                                         Paul I
                                         (1796–1801)

HOUSE OF HOHENZOLLERN

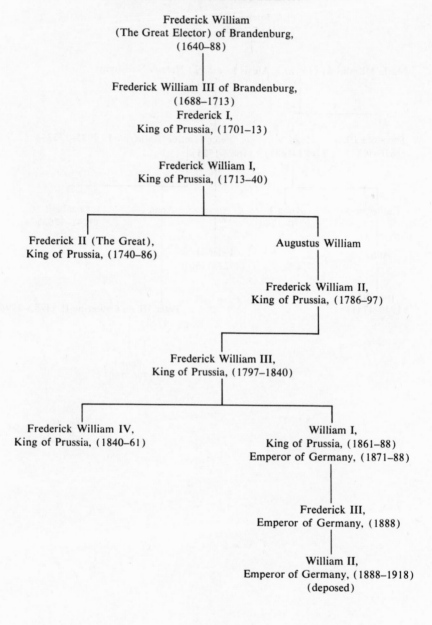

Frederick William
(The Great Elector) of Brandenburg,
(1640–88)

Frederick William III of Brandenburg,
(1688–1713)
Frederick I,
King of Prussia, (1701–13)

Frederick William I,
King of Prussia, (1713–40)

Frederick II (The Great),
King of Prussia, (1740–86)

Augustus William

Frederick William II,
King of Prussia, (1786–97)

Frederick William III,
King of Prussia, (1797–1840)

Frederick William IV,
King of Prussia, (1840–61)

William I,
King of Prussia, (1861–88)
Emperor of Germany, (1871–88)

Frederick III,
Emperor of Germany, (1888)

William II,
Emperor of Germany, (1888–1918)
(deposed)

THE AUSTRIAN HAPSBURGS

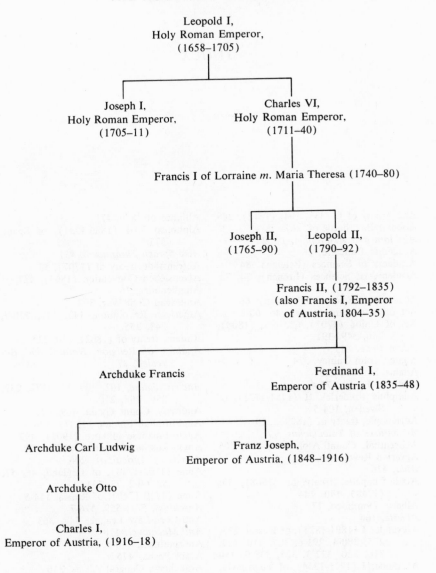

Leopold I,
Holy Roman Emperor,
(1658–1705)

Joseph I,
Holy Roman Emperor,
(1705–11)

Charles VI,
Holy Roman Emperor,
(1711–40)

Francis I of Lorraine *m.* Maria Theresa (1740–80)

Joseph II,
(1765–90)

Leopold II,
(1790–92)

Francis II, (1792–1835)
(also Francis I, Emperor
of Austria, 1804–35)

Archduke Francis

Ferdinand I,
Emperor of Austria (1835–48)

Archduke Carl Ludwig

Franz Joseph,
Emperor of Austria, (1848–1916)

Archduke Otto

Charles I,
Emperor of Austria, (1916–18)

Index

SOURCES OF ILLUSTRATIONS

Key to Credits

B   The Bettmann Archive
C   Caisse Nationale des
    Monuments Historiques

L   The Louvre
S   Sovfoto
W   Wide World Photos

PLATE 1.   Left: British Information Services/National Portrait Gallery, London; right: French Cultural Services; below: B.
PLATE 2.   Right: C.
PLATE 3.   Below: Art Reference Bureau, Bildarchiv Foto Marburg.
PLATE 4.   Above: The British Travel Association; right: Art Reference Bureau, Bildarchiv Foto Marburg.
PLATE 5.   Right: C; below: L.
PLATE 6.   Left: L; below: L.
PLATE 7.   Above: Italian State Tourist Office; right: L.
PLATE 8.   Left: L; below, left: From the Photo Archives of the Austrian National Library in Vienna; below, right: Art Reference Bureau, Inc.
PLATE 9.   Below: British Information Services/The National Portrait Gallery, London; bottom: Charles Phelps Cushing; right, top: B; right, center: British Information Services; right, bottom: Art Reference Bureau, Inc.

PLATE 10.   Right: C; below: German Information Center.

PLATE 11.   Above, left: L; above, right: C; right: C.

PLATE 12.   Above: Bibliotheque Nationale, Paris; top: Bibliotheque Nationale, Paris.

PLATE 13.   Left: L; above: B; below: Bibliotheque Nationale, Paris.

PLATE 14.   Below: B; bottom: Stockholm Museum; above: Art Reference Bureau; top: L.

PLATE 15.   Above: From the Photo Archives of the Austrian National Library in Vienna; right: The Metropolitan Museum of Art, Gift of J. Pierpont Morgan, 1908; below: C.

PLATE 16.   Above: Austrian Information Service; right, top to bottom: C, Vienna Kunsthistorisches Museum, German Information Center.

PLATE 17.   Left: B; right: B; bottom: B.

PLATE 18.   Above: B; left: B; below, left to right: B, B, B.

PLATE 19.   Left, top to bottom: B, B, British Information Service; above: The Metropolitan Museum of Art, Gift of H. O. Havemeyer, 1888, French Cultural Services.

PLATE 20.   Above: Musee Carnavalet, Paris; below, left to right: Musee Carnavalet, Paris, Musee Carnavalet, Paris.

PLATE 21.   Above: C; right: C.

PLATE 22.   Left: The Metropolitan Museum of Art, Rogers Fund, 1926; above left: Musee Carnavalet, Paris; above right: German Information Center; below: B.

PLATE 23.   Above: L; below, left to right: Austrian Information Service, Musee de Versailles, L.

PLATE 24.   Right: B; below: L.

PLATE 25.   Above, left to right: Charles Phelps Cushing, B, French Embassy Press and Information Division; bottom, L.

PLATE 26.   Above: L; right: L; below: B.

PLATE 27.   Left: C; above: B; above: B; right: S.

PLATE 28.   Above: C; right: Charles Phelps Cushing; below: Art Reference Bureau, Inc./National Portrait Gallery, London.

PLATE 29.   Above, left to right: Charles Phelps Cushing, Palais de Compregne, B; below: B.

PLATE 30.   Above: B; right: French Cultural Services; below: Art Reference Bureau, Inc./National Portrait Gallery, London.

PLATE 31.   Above: B; below: The Metropolitan Museum of Art, Bequest of Mrs. H. O. Havemeyer, 1929, The H. O. Havemeyer Collection.

PLATE 32.   Above: Musee de l'Opera, Paris; top: B; above, left: French Embassy Press and Information Division; left: French Cultural Services.

PLATE 33.   Above: B; left: Charles Phelps Cushing; below, left to right: L, German Information Center.

PLATE 34.   Above: Musee de Lyon; left: L; below: L.

PLATE 35.   Right: Collection, The Museum of Modern Art, New York, Mrs. John D. Rockefeller, Jr., Purchase Fund; below: Collection, The Museum of Modern Art, New York, Lillie P. Bliss Collection.

PLATE 36.   Above: S; below: B; bottom: B; below, left: B.

PLATE 37.   Above: Courtesy of the Photo Archives of the Austrian National Library; right: Charles Phelps Cushing; right, above: B.

PLATE 38.   Above: S; left: W; below: Charles Phelps Cushing.

PLATE 39.   Above, left to right: W, W, S; below: W.

PLATE 40.   Above: W; left: W; below: W.

PLATE 41.   Above: On extended loan to The Museum of Modern Art, New York, from the artist, M. Picasso; left: Austrian Information Service.

PLATE 42.   Left: S.

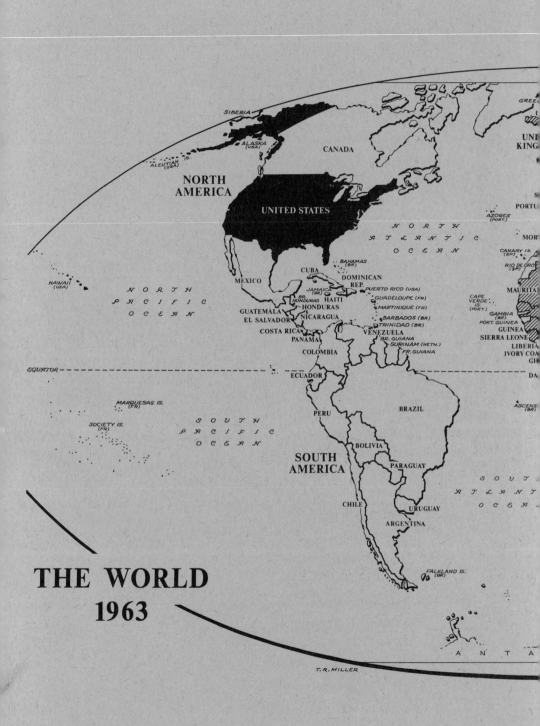

THE WORLD
1963

T. R. MILLER